D1595651

School Bullying

Bullying is a socially and culturally complex phenomenon that until now has largely been understood in the context of the individual. This book challenges the dominance of this approach, examining the processes of extreme exclusion that are enacted in bullying – whether at school, through face-to-face meetings or virtual encounters – in the context of group dynamics. Contributors draw upon qualitative empirical studies, mixed methods and statistics to analyse the elements that allow bullying to emerge – the processes that produce exclusion and contempt, and the relations between children, teachers and parents. Introducing a new definition of bullying, the book goes on to discuss directions for future research and action, including more informed intervention strategies and re-thinking methods of prevention. Exploring bullying in the light of the latest research from a wide variety of disciplines, this book paves the way for a new paradigm through which to understand the field.

ROBIN MAY SCHOTT is a philosopher and senior researcher at the Danish Institute for International Studies and formerly professor in the research project eXbus at the Department of Education (DPU), Aarhus University.

DORTE MARIE SØNDERGAARD is a professor of social psychology in the Department of Education (DPU), Aarhus University. She is the director of the research project eXbus and of the research programme for Diversity, Culture and Change.

School Bullying

New Theories in Context

Edited by

Robin May Schott
Dorte Marie Søndergaard

CAMBRIDGE
UNIVERSITY PRESS

CAMBRIDGE
UNIVERSITY PRESS

University Printing House, Cambridge CB2 8BS, United Kingdom

Published in the United States of America by Cambridge University Press, New York

Cambridge University Press is part of the University of Cambridge.

It furthers the University's mission by disseminating knowledge in the pursuit of
education, learning, and research at the highest international levels of excellence.

www.cambridge.org
Information on this title: www.cambridge.org/9781107027763

First published 2014

Printed in the United Kingdom by Clays, St Ives plc

A catalogue record for this publication is available from the British Library

ISBN 978-1-107-02776-3 Hardback

Contents

Figures

Tables

Contributors

AMY BARNES is a senior research officer for the Child Health Promotion Research Centre at Edith Cowan University in Perth, Australia. She received a Bachelor of Arts with first class Honours in Psychology from the University of Western Australia, and a Masters of Public Health in Health Promotion from Curtin University of Technology. Her research interests include the social and psychological bases of health behaviour amongst children and young people, including the prevention of bullying behaviour and aggression in primary and secondary Australian schools.

DONNA CROSS is the foundation professor of Child and Adolescent Health in the School of Exercise and Health Sciences and the founding director of the Child Health Promotion Research Centre at Edith Cowan University in Perth, Australia. She conducts applied multi-disciplinary school and family-based research addressing children's and adolescents' health and well-being, including mental-health promotion, injury control and drug-use prevention. She has published widely on a variety of children's health issues, particularly in the areas of bullying- and cyberbullying-intervention research and related methodologies.

BRONWYN DAVIES is a professorial fellow at the University of Melbourne, Australia. She works as an independent scholar and is well known for her work on gender, literacy and pedagogy, and for her critique of neoliberalism. Her most recent books are *Deleuze and Collaborative Writing: An Immanent Plane of Composition* (with Wyatt, Gale and Gannon) and *Place Pedagogy Change* (with Somerville, Power, Gannon and de Carteret). More details can be found on her website, bronwyndavies.com.au.

CONSTANCE ELLWOOD is an honorary research fellow in the School of Languages and Linguistics at the University of Melbourne, Australia. She is a specialist in writing for academic publications.

HANNE HAAVIND is a professor of psychology at the University of Oslo, Norway. Her research interests are directed at personal trajectories and social pathways of development, with a particular focus on the meanings that become attached to gender and age-related transitions. She has been involved in several studies about interpersonal relationships between men and women, and the interconnectedness of female and male parenting and social changes in how parents tend to and care about their children. Across a range of substantive themes, she has a particular interest in interpretative methods in psychology, and also works part-time as a psychotherapist.

HELLE RABØL HANSEN is an assistant professor at the Department of Education, Aarhus University, Denmark. She received her Masters in Law from the University of Copenhagen, Denmark, in 1998. She has worked as a government official at the Danish National Council for Children, with a focus on the rights of children and intervention strategies against bullying. Her Ph.D. dissertation was entitled 'Teacher life and pupil bullying', and she has written several books about school bullying aimed at practitioners. Her academic work is based on a combination of legal and educational psychology issues, and she is an active lecturer.

NINA HEIN holds a Ph.D. in social psychology and is currently an adjunct professor at the Department of Education, Aarhus University, Denmark, where she is part of the eXbus research team. With theoretical perspectives primarily within a post-structural, cultural psychological and discursive analytical field, her current research is focused on parental positions, parents' perspectives and possible agency concerning bullying amongst their children at school.

INGE HENNINGSEN is a senior researcher with the eXbus project at the Department of Education, Aarhus University, Denmark. She was educated in statistics and held a professorship in statistics at the University of Copenhagen. Her present research interests centre on the application of mixed methods in bullying research and on gender studies with special regard to equality at universities and within higher education.

JETTE KOFOED is an associate professor at the Department of Education, Aarhus University, Denmark. Her research interests cover processes of inclusion and exclusion amongst children and youth in educational settings. Her research has three main foci: the subjective becoming in technologically mediated processes of inclusion and exclusion; virtuality and social categories (gender, race, nationality and sexuality); and affectivity. She has published widely within these fields.

CARSTEN BAGGE LAUSTSEN is an associate professor of political sociology at the Department of Political Science, Aarhus University, Denmark. His research interests are social theory, politics and popular culture, terrorism and the politics of security, religion in international affairs and sexualised violence as a weapon of war. His books include *The Culture of Exception: Sociology Facing the Camp* (with Bülent Diken), *Sociology Through the Projector* (with Bülent Diken) and *The Subject of Politics: Slavoj Žižek's Political Philosophy* (with Henrik Jøker Bjerre).

CHARLOTTE MATHIASSEN is an associate professor of psychology at the Department of Education, Aarhus University, Denmark. Her research interests are twofold: bullying with a special focus on adults' recollections of bullying during childhood; and the meaning of these childhood experiences throughout life. Another central interest is prison research and research in prisoners' life-projects both during imprisonment and release; a gendered perspective is also applied in exploring the conditions of incarcerated men and women. She conducts qualitative empirical research, interviews and participatory observations and draws upon socio-cultural and social–psychological theories in her work.

ELIZABETH J. MEYER is an assistant professor at the School of Education at California Polytechnic State University, San Luis Obispo (Cal Poly-SLO) in the United States. She is the author of *Gender, Bullying, and Harassment: Strategies to End Sexism and Homophobia in Schools* and *Gender and Sexual Diversity in Schools*. She is a former high school teacher and completed her Master of Arts at the University of Colorado, Boulder, and her Ph.D. at McGill University in Montreal, Quebec, Canada. She blogs for *Psychology Today*.

ROBIN MAY SCHOTT is a philosopher and senior researcher at the Danish Institute for International Studies in the section for Peace, Risk and Violence. She was previously employed as a professor at the Department of Education Aarhus University, on the eXbus research project. She is editor and co-author of *Birth, Death, and Femininity; Philosophies of Embodiment* (2010), editor of *Feminist Philosophy and the Problem of Evil* (2007), and has published numerous other books and articles. In addition to her work on school bullying, her research has focused on the concept of evil and issues of conflict, war and gender.

DORTE MARIE SØNDERGAARD is a professor of social psychology at the Department of Education, Aarhus University, and the director of the eXbus research project. She has conducted research in social and subjective becomings amongst young adults and children for many years and published extensively on exclusion and marginalisation in relation to the enactments of sex/gender – including gender and power in academia, and gender and leadership in private organisations – and currently focuses on children and school bullying. Her work is based on qualitative data and her theoretical engagement includes analytics across cultural psychology, post-structuralism, agential realism and new materialism.

EVA SILBERSCHMIDT VIALA is an associate professor of social psychology at the Department of Education, Aarhus University, Denmark. Her recent work is placed within family studies and human development, exploring practices and challenges linked to everyday family life. Her research interests include issues related to gender and gender equality, parenting and the collaboration between home and school. She is currently part of the eXbus research team.

Acknowledgements

We would like to thank the *TrygFonden* (TrygFoundation) in Denmark for supporting the basic research on school bullying carried out by the project 'Exploring Bullying in Schools' (eXbus) at the Department of Education (DPU), Aarhus University, Denmark. Several of the contributors to this volume participated in eXbus during the period 2007–12.

We would also like to thank Hans Reitzel Publishers for permission to publish articles that originally appeared in Danish in *Mobning: Sociale Processer på Afveje* (2009) and *Mobning Gentænkt* (2012).

We thank Taylor & Francis (www.tandfonline.com) for permission to reprint here in expanded form Søndergaard, D. M. (2012). 'Bullying and Social Exclusion Anxiety in Schools' in the *British Journal of Sociology of Education* 33(3): 355–72; and for permission to reprint Ellwood, C. and B. Davies (2010). 'Violence and the Moral Order in Contemporary Schooling: A Discursive Analysis' in *Qualitative Research in Psychology* 7(2): 85–98.

We thank our colleagues – both near and far – for ongoing discussions, commentaries and engagement with this research.

And finally, we thank Amy Clotworthy for her superb professionalism and efficiency. Her editorial work in the final preparation of this manuscript has been, quite literally, invaluable.

Note on the chapters

Most of the authors who have contributed chapters to this anthology live and work in the Nordic countries (primarily Denmark and Norway), and others are from Australia, Canada and the United States. This geographical breadth means that the contributors have conducted their empirical research in a variety of countries and, as such, there are both similarities and differences amongst national school systems. To avoid confusing readers – who may come from yet other systems in other countries – the co-editors have decided to standardise certain terminology. This is not to suggest that these school systems are interchangeable or equivalent in any way, but rather, to simplify the text without distracting from the main content and analytical presentation of the chapters.

> **Grade** – the different classes where lessons are taught are universally called 'grades' (i.e. fourth grade), and this is meant to be equivalent to Year 4, 4th class, etc. in other international school systems. In Denmark, for example, students attend the same school from *0 klasse* until *9. klasse* (some until *10. klasse*). After that, they may choose to attend upper secondary school (*gymnasium*) or enrol in some other kind of youth education (*ungdomsuddannelse*).
>
> Where possible, the authors have specified children's ages instead of the level of their class/grade/year, and we hope these distinctions are clear.
>
> **Primary school** – this refers to the school attended by younger children (generally between the ages of 6 and 12); there is no use of 'elementary school' or similar. Kindergartens, nursery schools and preschools are referred to as such, and typically refer to formalised, preparatory classes with children under the age of 5 or 6.
>
> **Principal** – this refers to the senior administrator of a primary or secondary school (equivalent to headmaster, head teacher or rector); he/she is the director of the school and holds responsibility for budgets, staff, cooperation with the state/municipality,

parents and pedagogical staff. He/she is also responsible for students' well-being, the curriculum, hiring/supervising teachers and other school staff, etc.

Secondary school – this refers to the school attended by older children (generally between the ages of 12 and 18) before they might attend university; the term comprises both lower and upper secondary school. There is no use of 'middle school', 'high school', 'college' or similar.

Student – preferred by the authors to 'pupil', the term 'student' refers to any child enrolled in a primary or secondary school; a distinction is made only for older students who are attending university.

Teacher – this term is used universally to designate a specially educated adult who leads children in their regular classroom lessons and activities (equivalent to a form tutor, professor, etc.).

In addition, the identities of all the informants referred to in this anthology have been made anonymous. Their names have also been anglicised, except in cases where there is a specific reason; for example, for a name to retain its ethnic character.

1   Introduction: new approaches to school bullying

Robin May Schott and Dorte Marie Søndergaard

As we write this Introduction, it is shortly after Stefani Germanotta –
better known as Lady Gaga, one of contemporary pop music's icons –
visited Harvard University in Cambridge, Massachusetts, to launch her
Born This Way Foundation (http://bornthiswayfoundation.org). At the
appearance, she was interviewed by talk-show host and media personality
Oprah Winfrey and spoke openly about the cruelty her peers demonstrated towards her as a teenager, including an episode where she was thrown
into a dustbin. 'I was called really horrible, profane names very loudly in
front of huge crowds of people, and my schoolwork suffered at one point.
I didn't want to go to class. And I was a straight-A student, so there was a
certain point in my high-school years where I just couldn't even focus on
class because I was so embarrassed all the time. I was so ashamed of who
I was'.[1] Lady Gaga said she planned to tour the United States on her 'Born
Brave Bus' to 'talk about love, acceptance, kindness'; she told the audience that she doesn't have the answer for how to stop bullying, but
students should do 'simple acts of kindness' to foster acceptance, tolerance and individuality.[2]

Lady Gaga's appearance at Harvard shows that the problem of bullying is
one that touches a nerve in the public – amongst her pre-teen and teenaged
fans as well as families, educators and researchers. It also highlighted the
importance of research in this area. During the panel discussion at Harvard,
she repeatedly said, 'We don't have the answer'.[3] But many researchers
believe that they do have the answer – both about how to understand

---

[1] Nicholas D. Kristof, 'Born to Not Get Bullied', *The New York Times*, 29 February 2012;
http://www.nytimes.com/2012/03/01/opinion/kristof-born-to-not-get-bullied.html?_r=1;
last accessed 5 March 2012.
[2] Denise Lavoie, Associated Press, 'Lady Gaga at Harvard, launches youth foundation', 29
February 2012; http://www.macon.com/2012/02/29/v-print/1925297/oprah-others-to-
attend-lady-gaga.html; last accessed 5 March 2012.
[3] Emily Bazelon, 'Lady Gaga launches her Born This Way Foundation at Harvard'; Slate.com,
2 March 2012, http://www.slate.com/articles/news_and_politics/bulle/2012/03/lady_gaga_
launches_her_born_this_way_foundation_at_harvard_.html; last accessed 5 March 2012.

bullying and what to do about it. In this anthology, we argue that answers to both questions are more complicated than even researchers often assume.

This book is intended to be an intervention into current research debates about bullying. Much of the published research is still dominated by the model of school bullying that was first developed by Norwegian researcher Dan Olweus; this model explains school bullying in terms of individual personality traits. In this model, the personality traits of bullies include being aggressive and impulsive, having a positive attitude towards violence, a need to dominate and little empathy with their victims; he also describes the personality traits of victims as passive, submissive, anxious, insecure and weak (Olweus 1993a: 32–4; see Schott, Chapter 2, page 21 for a critical discussion). Here, we refer to this approach as *paradigm one*. Despite the predominance of this approach, the past decade of research on bullying has seen contributions from social psychologists and sociologists who have begun to focus on bullying as a social dynamic. This anthology contributes to the shift away from *paradigm one* and towards this new focus on social dynamics; for the purpose of simplicity, we refer to this approach as *paradigm two*.

Emphasising that there needs to be more knowledge about bullying, as Lady Gaga did at the Harvard University event, obviously does not solve the problem of what kind of knowledge is needed. Is knowledge about bullying really a matter of learning about bullies and victims in terms that describe their pre-existing personality traits? Or is it instead a matter of having knowledge about children's social environments, as in recent social–ecological approaches (Espelage and Swearer 2004)? Perhaps the knowledge needs to be even more analytically sensitive to the constitutive processes of bullying practices that exist amongst children, and include not only their social environments but also the cultural, technological, psychological and material forces involved in the enactment of bullying. And the answer to the *ontological* question about what bullying is has implications for the *epistemological* question of what concepts are necessary to gain knowledge about it (Eriksson et al. 2002). If bullying practices were determined only by individual personality traits, then the relevant explanations would be based on these personality traits. For example, researchers who adopt *paradigm one* ask: what kind of family system or environment creates aggressive children? And what kind of power do individuals possess by virtue of their personality traits? But if bullying is understood as having been created by the dynamics of social relationships and as an effect of intra-activity[4] amongst a range of different forces and

---

[4] See the discussion of the term 'intra-action' – in contrast to the more usual 'interaction' – later in this chapter in reference to Karen Barad's work.

processes, then quite different concepts of power become necessary to understand the problem. Individual characteristics and preconditions should be understood as intra-acting with a range of other forces and processes, and not viewed as the only – or even the primary – cause of bullying. The nature of these epistemological commitments has implications for the type of methods that are used to acquire knowledge about bullying.

Most of the research that begins with *paradigm one*'s understanding of bullying is based on quantitative data, and it endeavours to identify causes, predict occurrences and develop evidence-based intervention programmes. Both researchers and practitioners measure data that can be individualised, and they are often blind to other constituting and enacting forces. However, the chapters in this book describe alternative methods that are based on both qualitative and quantitative studies; the ambition here is to uncover the complex processes by which bullying is enacted as well as its complex effects. Our analyses investigate the different and often shifting positionings – i.e. how individuals assume various positions – within group interactions. And in focusing on a wide range of relationships that are relevant to bullying, we challenge both the dyad of perpetrator–victim and the triad of perpetrator–victim–bystander. Instead, group relations and dynamics become the focus.

In this Introduction, we first outline the need for a transition from *paradigm one* to *paradigm two* in the research on school bullying; next, we provide a brief overview of the theoretical concepts that are the background and inspiration for applying theories of power and intra-action to the arena of school bullying; and finally, we offer the reader – who may be either a researcher, student, parent, educator or practitioner – a road-map for navigating through this anthology.

Background of *paradigm one*

Focusing on the social dynamics within the knowledge about bullying has many dimensions. It includes acknowledging that the concept of bullying itself has a social history, as pointed out by Swedish sociologist Ola Agavall (2008). This shift in the research highlights the role of the social in the ontology, epistemology and methods that have developed in relation to research on bullying – in contrast to the primarily individualised approach of *paradigm one*. And this new focus has implications for practical interventions, as Dorte Marie Søndergaard discusses (see Chapter 15, page 389).

Research into school bullying is a relatively recent field of inquiry (see Schott, Chapter 2, page 21). To understand the development of this field, it is enlightening to examine its origins and trace the genealogy of its central concepts, particularly how they developed over time. Agevall wrote an eye-opening report on the social history of the concept of bullying (Agevall 2008), which we draw upon in the following pages. Peter-Paul Heinemann originally introduced the term 'mobbing'[5] in Sweden in 1969. Heinemann was a physician and also the adoptive father of a black boy who was excluded and harassed at school. Heinemann first introduced this term in a small Swedish journal after being inspired by Konrad Lorenz's work on the mob behaviour of animals. And he explicitly linked the word to the system of apartheid, writing, 'I am the father of a seven-year-old Negro boy. . . During his lifetime, I have been convinced that the mechanisms of apartheid are alive and well in our country. I share this experience with all parents whose children strongly deviate from their peers'.[6] In this way, Heinemann borrowed a term from ethology (the science of animal behaviour) and connected it with everyday, human examples of harassment and exclusion. Using Lorenz's language helped to naturalise the phenomenon of bullying and situate it as a subset of aggression, thereby giving it scientific legitimacy (ibid.: 13–14). For Heinemann, 'mobbing' was equivalent to an all-against-one situation and later, in contributions by laypersons, it became synonymous with group violence.

As both adoptions of foreign-born children and migration in Sweden reached new peaks in the 1960s, the issue of racism began to emerge. Heinemann's description of racism was taken up by Swedish local and national media, and in this process, 'mobbing' became linked to perceptions of the leading social problems of the day, including the belief that large schools have adverse effects on youths and that alienation is inherent in metropolitan life.[7] The term 'mobbing' entered the public domain with discussions between an array of participants – from non-governmental organisations, journalists, the media, politicians responsible for migration issues and education professionals; thus, the term has multiple authors. In the process, the concept of 'mobbing' became entwined with several other recognised social problems, which allowed it to gain credibility in what

[5] The word 'mobbing' (in Swedish, 'mobbning') was used in these early Swedish debates and was borrowed by other languages. In discussing the early development of the concept in this Introduction, we acknowledge its early usage by enclosing 'mobbing' in quotation marks. But 'bullying' has now become the standard term in English; thus, we use that word later in the Introduction and throughout the anthology.
[6] *Dagens Nyheter*, 13 November 1969; cited in Agevall 2008.
[7] Subsequent research into school bullying has shown no definitive connection between school size or population density with regard to either the frequency or intensity of bullying occurrences.

Agevall refers to as a process of 'issue-symbiosis' (ibid.: 26). Through this process of conceptual contagion, 'mobbing' absorbed other current issues, such as debates about the role of discipline and democracy in schools. Furthermore, different organisations – e.g. parent organisations or associations representing the disabled or immigrants – emphasised those parts of the concept that were relevant to their members, feeding these examples back into public debates in the media, literature, theatre and so on (ibid.: 19–26).[8]

Meanwhile, the publication in 1973 of Dan Olweus's book, *Hack-kycklingar och översittare: forskning om skolmobbning* (*Whipping Boys and Bullying: Research on School Bullying*) constituted a watershed moment in the meaning of the term 'bullying'. Olweus had conducted the most ambitious, large-scale quantitative study of the phenomenon to date. His doctoral dissertation about the psychology of aggression was pub-lished in 1969, and it was an attempt to 'predict overt aggression in an interpersonal situation on the basis of aggressive responses to a specially constructed projective test' (Olweus 1969). When the problem of 'mob-bing' gained traction amongst the public in Sweden and emerged in the debates, he was already equipped with a psychological theory and method to study aggression.

His model of the mechanisms that inform aggressive behaviour relied heavily on the notion of stable personality traits – i.e. habitual aggressive and aggressive inhibitory tendencies. In his view, these tendencies func-tion as dispositions to respond to certain stimulus situations with rela-tively consistent reactions. If 'mobbing' was an issue of aggression, he could easily take the trait approach to aggression used in his previous research and transfer it to this new field. In this way, he extracted the view of aggression from Lorenz's study of animal behaviour and reformulated it into a model of individual aggression based on personality traits (Agevall 2008: 28–30, 34). As social scientists often do when confronted with an unknown entity, Olweus proceeded to apply the knowledge he already had about his field and transplant it to a new area via methods, theories and concrete procedures (ibid.: 48).

A consequence of Olweus's theoretical framework for the concept of psychological aggression, however, is that the idea of 'mobbing' as *group* violence – as Heinemann had originally conceived it – almost disappears from view. Olweus acknowledges that all-against-one situations do occur, but he views these as a tiny fraction of 'mobbing' behaviour; instead, he focuses primarily on single-perpetrator 'mobbing' (ibid.: 36–7). Anatol

---

[8] Agevall refers to this phenomenon as 'institutional bootstrapping' (2008: 23).

Pikas objected to this focus on the single perpetrator in formulating his own definition of 'mobbing', which in other respects echoes Olweus. For Pikas, 'mobbing' 'refers to repeated negative activities (physical and mental assaults and/or exclusions from the group) directed against a single individual by two or more interacting individuals' (Pikas 1975). Olweus later formulated another definition of 'mobbing', which has become the standard in the literature and research on bullying: 'mobbing' is when 'one or more individuals are subjected to negative actions, on several occasions and over an extended period of time, by one or more individuals' (Olweus 1986 cited in Agevall 2008: 34).

This short exegesis of the conceptual genealogy of 'mobbing' – or what is now definitively referred to as 'bullying' in English – explains why the field has usually been dominated by researchers from certain traditions within psychology and education who have focused in particular on the individual as an entity, as opposed to social psychologists, researchers in education focusing on social dynamics or sociologists for whom aggression tends to be poorly suited as a theoretical category (ibid.: 28). There are many more parts to the story about how the concept of bullying has developed and been applied, including its use in relation to adults and work-life (see Leymann 1986[9]) – which we do not explore in this anthology – and the interaction between scientific studies and the law. But we include this discussion about the concept of bullying in relation to the sociology of knowledge to highlight that the individualised approach to bullying in *paradigm one* is situated within the social dynamics of knowledge production.

It is also crucial to emphasise that debates about the ontology, epistemology and methods used to study bullying are far from mere academic exercises – they have explicit and potentially disturbing consequences for schools' intervention programmes. This is evident from the report published in 2009 by David P. Farrington and Maria M. Ttofi for Campbell Systematic Reviews, entitled 'School-based programs to reduce bullying and victimization'.[10] In the report's concluding discussion about policy implications, the authors call for 'a system of accrediting effective anti-bullying programs'. They also note that such an accrediting system should 'ensure that programs contain elements that have been proved to be effective in high-quality evaluations' (Farrington and Ttofi 2009: 70). In arguing for a standardised national, and even international accreditation

---

[9] Heinz Leymann has numerous publications on the topic of workplace bullying, including Leymann and Zapf (1996).

[10] We refer to this report as the Campbell Collaboration.

approach, one must have a very robust level of knowledge about how to understand school bullying; specifically, the extent to which it is measurable and, if so, the means as well as the interventions that are considered 'appropriate' on the basis of this knowledge. But as Søndergaard argues here (see page 389) and in a commentary to the Campbell Collaboration co-authored with Inge Henningsen and Helle Rabøl Hansen (2010), this entire approach calls for discussion. Although the Campbell Collaboration reviewed 622 articles and reports that address anti-bullying programmes, they excluded 578 of the programmes for not meeting all four criteria in their research design: (1) randomised experiments; (2) experimental-control comparisons with before-and-after measures of bullying; (3) other experimental-control comparisons; and (4) quasi-experimental age-cohort designs. In other words, only 44 studies met the Campbell Collaboration's meta-analytic standards, which raises a question about the knowledge that may be *lost* when studies are limited to evidenced-based concepts of measurement. Such an evidenced-based approach may be appropriate for measuring a phenomenon that remains the same across different contexts or groups – as bullying is assumed to be in *paradigm one* – and this is the oldest and most established approach in the field.[11] But an evidenced-based approach may be poorly suited to understanding social complexities and complicated interactions, which *paradigm two* researchers argue are central in bullying dynamics. Instead, a combination of qualitative and quantitative approaches – such as the method Donna Cross and Amy Barnes present in their assessment of intervention programmes – seems more productive. Amongst the 578 programmes that were not included in the Campbell report, valuable knowledge about potential intervention strategies may have been lost – knowledge that might be better suited to engage with the theoretical and conceptual framework that *paradigm two* develops in relation to the complexities and shifting nature of bullying. Thus, as Søndergaard argues (see page 389), with the predominance of evidence-based approaches, we must also ask: what knowledge is prevented from being generated?

---

[11] All of the references named in the Campbell Collaboration are researchers working with the individualised approach of *paradigm one*, and they view bullying as an encounter between a strong child and a weak child. The report's section on definition, however, mentions researchers like Roland and Salmivalli, who recognise bullying as a phenomenon that also involves social dynamics. See Henningsen, Hansen and Søndergaard (2010): 'Hvad måler Campbell Collaboration? En kritisk kommentar til rapporten ('What does the Campbell Collaboration measure? A critical commentary of the report): *School-based programs to reduce bullying and victimization*'; www.exbus.dk; last accessed 5 March 2012.

The social turn in *paradigm two*

Despite the continued dominance of *paradigm one*, several researchers as well as practitioners at non-governmental organisations over the past decade have begun to view bullying as a socially and culturally complex phenomenon, warning that an individualised approach can contribute to the exclusion of individual children within their local school contexts. A growing number of scholars are focusing on bullying as a group phenomenon that is generated within social environments where children interact with each other, such as the school class. Some studies describe the relation between the individualised perspective on bullying and social perspectives on bullying as first- and second-order perspectives (Slee and Mohyla 2007), where second-order perspectives recognise that bullying involves a multitude of participants and cannot merely be understood in terms of the perpetrator–victim dyad or the perpetrator–victim–bystander triad. For example, researchers have pointed out that there are several participant positions (e.g. Salmivalli et al. 2004); that some children are both bullies and victims (Cook et al. 2010); and that the construct *bullying* must be contextualised in a situation (Beran 2006). Others have utilised a socio-ecological lens, which includes a focus on family, home environment, school climate, community factors, peer status and peer influence (Espelage and Swearer 2004). Much of this literature emphasises the need for whole-school and multi-contextual approaches. But there remains a tendency to concentrate on specific problems associated with individual children and to emphasise the development of empathy and social skills rather than focusing on patterns of interaction between children. Furthermore, as noted in one recent report, the more intense bullying is perceived to be, the more individualistic the intervention tends to become (Kousholt and Fisker, unpublished manuscript).

The language of first- and second-order perspectives might allow us to draw the conclusion that researchers should combine the two paradigms by adding social interactions and dynamics to the individualised approach. In a discussion about epistemology, Barbara Thayer-Bacon raises this problematic in reference to the children's version of a tale from India called 'The blind men and the elephant': 'There were six men from Industan/to learning much inclined/who went to see the elephant/though each of them was blind/so that by observation/each might satisfy his mind' (Quigley 1959 cited in Thayer-Bacon 1996). Depending on which part of the animal they touched, the blind men variously described it as a rope, tree, fan, snake, wall or spear. Thayer-Bacon uses this imagery to argue that different perspectives can contribute to an interactive, cooperative and more comprehensive definition of knowledge.[12] But this suggestion about the partiality of epistemological perspectives does *not* imply an add-on approach. Rather, as evidenced by the chapters in this anthology, analysing the social dimensions of bullying calls for theories and methods that challenge the first-order approach of *paradigm one* (see Schott, page 21).

For example, whilst *paradigm one* invokes the concept of power to refer to powerful individuals, some contemporary researchers – including several authors in this volume – draw upon the work of Michel Foucault to develop a quite different understanding of power within the context of bullying. Foucault argued that power is not a static category but is 'exercised from innumerable points, in the interplay of non-egalitarian and mobile relations' (Foucault 1978: 270). This approach implies that power differences in bullying situations are themselves 'the effects of social relations' (Horton 2011: 270). Researchers inspired by Foucault's theories tend to ask how individuals are positioned in relation to the dominant social and moral orders; for example, in relation to ethnicity, gender, sexuality or other 'social vectors of inequality' (Whitehead 2002 cited in Horton 2011: 270; see also Ellwood and Davies, page 81 and Meyer, page 209). Bullying, they argue, may be an attempt by some children to act as 'over-zealous guardians of the normative moral order' (Bansel et al. 2009; Davies 2011).

New theories in context

School Bullying: New Theories in Context brings together the work of scholars who utilise ontological, epistemological and methodological approaches that move beyond *paradigm one*, contributing to the shift in research on school bullying that we call *paradigm two*. Several of the authors have participated in a five-year research project based in Denmark called 'Exploring Bullying in Schools' (eXbus) and others have been collaborative partners. Many are based in the Nordic countries, and others are from Australia and the United States; their collective experiences with conducting empirical research in these countries highlights both the similarities and differences amongst national school systems. Most importantly, the authors share an analytical ambition to understand bullying as a complex phenomenon that is enacted or constituted through the interactive/intra-active entanglements that exist between a variety of open-ended, social, discursive, material and subjective forces.

---

[12] See also Thornberg (2011) for more about this elephant image.

Instead of approaching bullying as a phenomenon that can be explained and defined in terms of one factor (e.g. aggression), the authors in this anthology focus on a range of different forces that are central in bullying: teachers (Hansen), school principals and parents (Hein), classroom culture with its particular experiences and histories (Hansen, Henningsen and Kofoed) and the virtual experiences of children – both in terms of their electronically mediated communications and the media products with and through which they play and interact (Kofoed; Søndergaard). Other chapters focus on social factors in relation to gender, sexuality, race and class (Meyer) and the role of normativity in understanding bullying more generally (Ellwood and Davies; Laustsen). These chapters by no means exhaust the range of intra-acting forces at work within school bullying, and further investigation would be welcome in order to address, amongst other subjects, the economic and political structures of school systems. In the chapters produced through the eXbus project (Hansen; Hein; Hansen, Henningsen and Kofoed; Kofoed; Mathiassen; Schott; Søndergaard; Viala), the authors have addressed this analytical ambition through a conceptualisation of multiple intra-acting forces and an analysis of different and often shifting positions within group interactions. Thus, the group relations found within bullying dynamics move into focus.

With the subtitle 'New Theories in Context', we are calling attention to the importance of the theoretical approaches that are either implicit or explicit in current research on bullying. And we seek to open up the field of school bullying – which has been heavily dominated by researchers from certain theoretical traditions within psychology that focus on the individual as a demarcated entity – to theoretical approaches developed and applied within the humanities (e.g. history, literature and philosophy) and the social sciences (e.g. anthropology, law, psychology/social psychology and sociology). Foucault's work, for example, has been making a substantial impact on these disciplines for more than three decades, but bringing his theoretical perspectives into research on school bullying is a new endeavour. By challenging and expanding the theoretical resources for research on bullying, we are contributing to our ambition of opening up the field of research to a dialogue among many different disciplines in order to enhance knowledge about bullying.

The analytical goal of this anthology is inspired by a range of thinkers who analyse complex processes of subjective and social becoming, including several who are loosely labelled 'poststructuralist', such as Foucault, Gilles Deleuze, Félix Guattari, Julia Kristeva and Judith Butler. Both Foucault's and Butler's analyses of the processes of becoming with regard to the subject and the social provide an important basis for many of the perspectives brought forward in this volume. The social,

historical and cultural constructions of subjectivity and relational practices – as well as the abjections by which subjects and social groups are
formed – have inspired several of the chapters, and the authors seek to
reveal complex patterns of relating amongst children in school classes
that are saturated by marginalisation and bullying practices. Foucault's
conceptualisation of the *dispositif*, for example, comprises the basic
analytical premise of Carsten Bagge Laustsen's analysis of approaches
to bullying (see page 97).

New materialist thinking, such as that which has been developed by
Karen Barad (2003, 2007), takes some of the insights from
Foucault and Butler and propels them further in the direction of post-
humanism to analyse matter–discourse as an active agent in processes
related to the enactment of phenomena – including the becoming of
the social. Although, as a physicist and philosopher, Barad offers quite
an abstract conceptual framework, her approach to the processes of
material–discursive enactments establishes important premises for the
recurring basic assumptions that the eXbus team have developed about
bullying being enacted by multiple intra-acting forces and about their
entangled agencies (see Søndergaard, page 47, for an explication of
this idea). Barad emphasises that phenomena are always the effects
of open-ended dynamics and intra-active processes. She introduces
the term 'intra-action' (as opposed to the more usual 'interaction') to
signify the mutual constitution of entangled agencies. In Barad's
thinking, matter and discourse both have agency, and both are agential
in their mutually entangled processes of enactment (Barad 2007: 33).
Consequently, there are no separate, individual material–discursive agencies that precede their interaction (Barad 2003: 815). Rather, 'the notion
of intra-action recognizes that distinct agencies do not precede, but
rather emerge through, their intra-action. It is important to note that the
"distinct" agencies are only distinct in a relational, not an absolute, sense,
that is, *agencies are only distinct in relation to their mutual entanglement; they
don't exist as individual elements*' (Barad 2007: 33; emphasis in original). Her
incorporation of many material–discursive forces – which includes forces
that are typically called 'social', 'cultural', 'physical' and 'biological' – offers
inspiration for our analyses of complexities in the research material, including interviews and observations. This focus on the intra-active processes of
material–discursive enactment also echoes some of the ambitions evident in
Deleuze's conceptualisation of the rhizome: this concept enables an analysis
of the extensive and entangled network of processes that make it possible to
grasp how aspects of the social–discursive–temporal–technological are
entangled with each other in processes of becoming; e.g. in cyberbullying
(see Kofoed, page 159).

The cultural–historical tradition in psychology – including the work of theorists such as Jerome Bruner, Jaan Valsiner, Klaus Holzkamp and Ole Dreier – also provides background to some of the chapters in this anthology (Hansen; Haavind; Mathiassen). Thinkers in this tradition have analysed human practices in terms of an 'inner' and dialectic relationship between the social and the individual as well as narrative structures and processes of subjective becoming, as opposed to many other psychological approaches that overlook the role of activity, societal practices, cultural mediation and often also the intertwining of past, present and future.

Contemporary researchers like Sarah Ahmed and Brian Massumi, who explore the sociality and circulation of emotions and affects, have also brought attention to how emotions shape both individual and collective bodies, and how the intensity of affects works and translates into a diversity of specific emotions. This research has inspired the analysis of cyberbullying included here (Kofoed).

Many of the chapters in this anthology are based on qualitative research and data, such as interviews, observations, school essays, drawings, school-policy documents, online/virtual ethnography and various other forms of fieldwork. As the authors specify, each chapter is built upon its own set of data, and readers are referred to other publications that include the authors' unique data and research. The theoretical and analytical perspectives already mentioned here were involved in the authors' analyses of these various datasets, and enabled them to provide insights into the complex processes of becoming that exist between the actors involved in bullying practices. Theoretical approaches based on deconstruction, discourse analysis and narrative analysis as well as mixed methods have been utilised to analyse the data. This anthology makes a particular contribution in highlighting the importance of qualitative research in the field of school bullying. However, the authors also acknowledge the importance of insights obtained through quantitative studies, such as survey material, and through mixed methods (see Hansen, Henningsen and Kofoed, page 267, and Cross and Barnes, page 405).

Road-map to this anthology

This book does not offer a new model of or a new programme for anti-bullying intervention – although Søndergaard does propose certain analytical attentions and key foci that could be used to guide intervention and/or prevention strategies (see page 389), and Donna Cross and Amy Barnes point out new directions for intervention programmes, emphasising that interventions should have a flexible and adjustable character (see page 405). Instead, the chapters offer new ways to think about bullying in order to expand and deepen current research and intervention strategies. Although debates about how to understand bullying as a phenomenon are deeply entwined with debates about how to respond to occurrences of it, we are aware that the readers of this book may have a range of different interests – from researchers and students to educators, administrators, teachers, parents, psychologists, counsellors and politicians responsible for educational policies. We present here a brief roadmap to help orient the reader who embarks on the journey through this volume.

Part I of the book, 'Definitions and theories', includes chapters that focus on how to think about bullying, or – to use Søndergaard's phrase – how to develop the new thinking technologies that are required. Since concepts construct the framework for how we know and what we know – and thus, also what we do not know and what we do not do – they deserve critical attention. This part may be of special interest to researchers and students. The first two chapters by Schott and Søndergaard explore the complex questions related to the central definition of bullying, such as: do we need a definition of bullying? What are the standard approaches in the field? (See Schott, page 21.) And how can we develop a definition of bullying that is sensitive to its complexity whilst highlighting bullying as a social and relational phenomenon in which practices of exclusion are integral to practices of group inclusion? In these chapters, the authors utilise concepts from their specific research disciplines: for example, as a philosopher, Schott draws upon the concepts of 'otherness' and 'abjection' to define bullying; as a social psychologist, Søndergaard also discusses 'abjection' whilst introducing the concepts of 'social exclusion anxiety' and the 'production of contempt and dignity' to understand bullying processes.

The chapters by Constance Ellwood and Bronwyn Davies (see page 81) and Laustsen (see page 97) develop the implications of Foucault's theories in the understanding of bullying. Ellwood and Davies explore how the figure of the bully may be active in the construction and maintenance of norms within a school – instead of being moral deviants, bullies may be acting as guardians of the moral order (Davies 2011: 283). Analysing the practices that normalise violence in schools, the authors call for school communities to develop non-violent ethical practices, as opposed to practices that pathologise and punish individuals who are labelled as bullies. Laustsen draws upon the notion of the *dispositif*, or apparatus, in Foucault's later work to interpret bullying. He argues that, to understand bullying in its concreteness, it is necessary to understand the complex social reality from which it arises. To do so, we need a 'pre-theory' of bullying that will allow us to know which questions to ask in orientating ourselves towards this phenomenon. He discusses models of sovereignty, discipline and terror to examine the elements involved in bullying, including the students themselves, teachers' responses, the classroom environment, frameworks of knowledge and intervention programmes.

Moving from a focus on theoretical debates about how to orient ourselves towards the phenomenon of bullying, Part II of the book, 'Youth experiences', highlights the perspectives of youths. As such, these chapters may be of special interest to educators, parents, psychologists and counsellors. Jette Kofoed (see page 159) continues the theoretical thread of inquiry, using Deleuze's concept of the rhizome to understand the circulation of emotions within 'bitch-fights' and encrypted messages on social-networking websites like Arto and Facebook. She highlights how the positions of bully, victim and bystander can be much more complex and fluid than they might appear, leaving adults fairly powerless in their attempts to interpret messages involved in cyberbullying. She also introduces the concept of 'non-simultaneity' to characterise the temporal displacement between message and emotion. Hanne Haavind (see page 129) explores the links between peer bullying and the norms and practices of establishing friendships, specifically in relation to when young people's negotiations about friendships intensify as part of their identity projects. Based on interviews with schoolchildren in Norway, her analysis explores the transformation from being a child to becoming a youth, and how social rules about making friends sometimes cause children to destructively turn against each other in bullying practices. By analysing John Ajvide Lindqvist's vampire novel, *Let the Right One In*, Schott examines the relationship between bullying and violence as described in this contemporary work of gothic fiction (see page 185). She explores the subjective experience of being bullied by focusing on the role of social death, friendship and hate within bullying practices.

Part III, 'School talk', takes the school framework, its policies and culture as an optic to study bullying. As such, this would be of particular interest to researchers as well as teachers, counsellors and administrators. Elizabeth J. Meyer (see page 209) provides a post-structuralist and feminist critique of the research on bullying and harassment in secondary schools. She argues that bullying and harassment are intimately linked, but few scholars or educators have actually addressed the connection between these issues. Bullying research has generally overlooked gendered, sexual, homophobic and transphobic forms of bullying and harassment. Meyer argues for the need to understand how educational professionals are being trained, in order for them to become advocates for social justice at their schools and to address gender and sexual diversity in inclusive and age-appropriate ways. Helle Rabøl Hansen (see page 241) provides a close analysis of some of the typical anti-bullying policies at schools in Denmark, with a critical eye towards certain legal aspects. She argues that anti-bullying interventions and policies that focus on punishment are rooted in the individualised approach to bullying in *paradigm one*, which clearly delineates victims and aggressors. Not only do such policies risk criminalising children, but teachers quickly start to see sanctions as a solution to quite different challenges in the classroom, such as noise, disruption and unruliness, which may have little to do with bullying. The chapter by Helle Rabøl Hansen, Inge Henningsen and Jette Kofoed (see page 267) relies on quantitative methods commonly used by *paradigm one* researchers, but combines them with a sensitivity towards the role of the social group in bullying. Their analysis of individual children's responses shows that the culture within a classroom and not children's self-image or their relationships with parents, as is often assumed, is the most significant factor for determining the level of bullying at a school. Moreover, the authors find an important correlation between children's experiences with bullying and their feelings of fear and anxiety.

In Part IV, 'Adult perspectives', the authors highlight the importance of various adult positions in relation to school bullying, and this part could be especially interesting to parents, school administrators and psychologists. Nina Hein (see page 301) highlights the mutual sense of frustration and powerlessness that both parents and school principals tend to experience in their attempts to label – or resist labelling – certain children as bullies or victims. And using shared empirical data, both Charlotte Mathiassen and Eva Silberschmidt Viala focus on adults' retrospective accounts of their own bullying experiences in order to investigate the dynamics of the traces left by bullying in adulthood (see Mathiassen, page 331) and the complex role of family and social contexts, and how they impact a child's position as included or excluded in classroom dynamics (see Viala, page 361).

The final part, 'Moving forward', is addressed in particular to practitioners in the field. Søndergaard (see page 389) critically assesses some of the standard intervention approaches currently in use. She argues for flexible strategies as opposed to standardised techniques, and presents a series of questions that are designed to function as a kind of 'litmus test' for practitioners as they develop anti-bullying approaches; e.g. does the intervention strategy produce dignity for the various actors involved? Does the strategy produce new forms of contempt? Is the strategy attentive to the variety of exclusion practices and varying form of bullying? Søndergaard does not attempt to recommend specific strategies and methods of intervention, but rather, to pinpoint the key foci and analytical attentions brought forward by the thinking technologies developed throughout the anthology – the goal here is to enhance reflections about bullying practices and improve the quality of intervention strategies as they are developed and/ or adopted in local contexts.

The final chapter, by Cross and Barnes, relies on data from their research into the implementation of intervention programmes in Australia. Although these authors come from an experimental research tradition, they, too, caution against the implementation of overly standardised approaches that have no regard for situated analyses of the concrete contexts in which the interventions are meant to take place. Their chapter, based on their study of whole-school indicators to reduce bullying in Australia, emphasises the need for flexible approaches to intervention programmes, in contrast to the typical one-size-fits-all view employed in most programmes.

On a final note

This anthology aims to shift the research on school bullying away from the individualising approach of *paradigm one* with its focus on static personality traits and towards an understanding of bullying in terms of the complex relational dynamics and negotiations that occur within social groups and which include a variety of intra-acting forces. When encountering this new wave of research, it may be tempting to rethink the definition of bullying, as Schott and Søndergaard both discuss (see pages 21 and 47, respectively). There are arguments both for and against developing new definitions of bullying. On the one hand, a definition can be a useful tool to help both researchers and practitioners keep sight of the shift from *paradigm one* to *paradigm two* in bullying research. On the other hand, any definition will be inadequate, and constructing rigid frameworks risks closing down the field of research instead of keeping it open to new, vibrant and compelling input from researchers – both those in the field of bullying and in related disciplines.

Although we share a healthy amount of scepticism with regard to the role of definitions, we also share a degree of pragmatism about their usefulness as strategies for intervention. In this spirit, we close our Introduction with a definition of bullying for *paradigm two*; we ask the reader to keep this suggestion in mind during the journey through the anthology, and to use it as a point of departure for further development of and further research within the field of bullying:

Bullying is an intensification of the processes of marginalisation that occur in the context of dynamics of inclusion/exclusion, which shape groups. Bullying happens when physical, social or symbolic exclusion becomes extreme, regardless of

whether such exclusion is experienced and/or intended. One of the central mechanisms of bullying is social exclusion anxiety, which may be alleviated by the
production of contempt. This contempt for someone or something may be
expressed by behaviour that, for example, humiliates, trivialises or makes a person
feel invisible, involves harm to person or property, abuses social-media profiles or
disseminates humiliating messages via technological communication. Although
some members of the social group may experience these marginalising processes
as positive, robbing an individual(s) of the social recognition that is necessary for
dignity can be a form of psychic torture for those who are targeted.

Part I

Definitions and theories

The social concept of bullying: philosophical
reflections on definitions

Robin May Schott

> We offer exemplars illustrating how a society lives in its youth.
> (Daiute et al. 2006: 10)

Introduction

In her book on youth conflict and development, American psychologist
Colette Daiute observes that a society lives in its youth. The problems that
youths face are not peripheral to society, but mirror central problems of
social life in important ways. This approach may seem obvious in cases of
extreme conflict, such as when societies are in the midst of civil war or
seeking to rebuild themselves after conflict, or when they are torn apart by
intense social, racial or ethnic violence. But it may be the case more
generally as well. Understanding the problems youths face is central to
understanding the societies in which they live.

School bullying can also tell us something about how a society lives in
its youth. In an international context, many instances of bullying need to
be understood in relation to broad social problems like racial discrimination, sexual harassment and homophobia (Meyer 2007a). But here,
I focus on how school bullying needs to be understood in terms of the
basic challenges of living in a community with others. I seek to contribute
to understanding school bullying as a social phenomenon rather than as a
relation between individual bullies and victims. This approach reflects
recent research that focuses on the social dynamics of bullying (Eriksson
et al. 2002) in contrast to the individualistic approach that has dominated
the field. Shifting the analytical lens to the group does not devalue the
meaning of bullying for individuals who are involved in its processes,
which in some cases creates meaning that lasts into adult life. But
this analytical shift focuses on how group processes produce social recognition from being included in a group, as well as pain and humiliation
from being excluded. As a researcher and a parent, I have struggled to
understand why – even after removing the child(ren) directly responsible
for incidents of serious bullying – the negative dynamics within a class

remain unchanged and why different children take on new roles in the dynamics of bullying. An individualistic approach to bullying is inadequate to grasp this pattern.

Background on bullying research

Bullying in Denmark, as in other countries, is a widespread and serious problem. In a 2008 study of sixth-grade students[1] (12-to-13 years of age) conducted by the National Council for Children, 32 per cent of the children surveyed said that they had been bullied, while 20 per cent responded that they had engaged in bullying (Pedersen 2008). Some acts of bullying and some school responses may be in violation of the 1989 Human Rights Convention on the Rights of the Child. Article 16 of the Convention ensures children the right to protection against unlawful attacks on their honour or reputation; article 19 ensures children the right of protection from physical or mental violence, injury or abuse; and article 28 stipulates that school discipline must be consistent with a child's human dignity. When the collaborative research project eXbus began its work, we issued an open invitation on our website for adults to post their stories of childhood bullying anonymously. Phrases that appeared in these stories include 'psychic terror', 'total isolation', 'depression', 'thoughts of suicide', 'evil', 'powerlessness', 'humiliation' and others (www.exbus.dk, Galleriet).

In Scandinavia, research on this subject began in the early 1970s with the publication of work by Peter-Paul Heinemann (1972) and Dan Olweus (1973). Further public concern about school bullying in Norway was sparked in 1982 by the suicides of three boys between the ages of 10 and 14. Newspaper reports on the suicides stated that they were likely to have been caused by severe bullying (Olweus 1993a: 1–2). Similarly, public shock in Japan was generated in 1986 when a 13-year-old schoolboy committed suicide in Tokyo. His classmates had treated him as if he were dead and had even staged a mock funeral for him in their classroom (Morita et al. 1999 in Smith et al. 1999: 311).

The words '*mobning*'/'*mobbning*' in the Scandinavian languages and 'bullying' in English each have their own genealogy. When Heinemann introduced the term '*mobbning*' in Swedish, he was referring to group violence against a deviant individual, which occurs and stops suddenly (Smith et al. 2002: 1119). Heinemann borrowed the term from Konrad Lorenz, an Austrian zoologist and Nobel Prize winner, whose 1966 book, *On Aggression*, was popular reading. The Swedish translator of Lorenz's book used the term

---

[1] This corresponds to seventh grade/year in American or British schools.

mobbning to refer to a collective attack by a group of animals on an animal of another species, usually a natural enemy of the group (Olweus in Smith et al. 1999: 8–10). In this translation of Lorenz's book, *mobbning* was also used to characterise the action of a school class or group of soldiers who ganged up on a deviant individual. This initial use of the term to focus on a collective group resonated with the English word 'mob', which refers to a loosely organised group that is accidentally formed and relatively short-lived. Despite this linguistic emphasis on the group, Olweus quickly sought to shift the meaning of *mobbning* to the role of individuals. He argued that a focus on the group obscures the role of individuals, puts the blame on the victim, who may be assumed to provoke the 'normal' majority, and treats the group as a temporary constellation. Olweus's work has shaped the prevailing view that bullying is systematic, repetitive harassment of an individual(s) by one or more individuals.

In English, current usage draws upon terms such as 'bullying', 'bully/victim problems' and 'victimisation', and there is no reference to a mob or group. The history of the word 'bully' also traces a shift from an earlier positive connotation to its current negative meaning. 'Bully' has its etymological roots in the Middle Dutch word *boele*, which means 'sweetheart', 'fine fellow' or 'blusterer' (in Smith et al. 2002: 1120). In both the Scandinavian and English cases, the history of the word moves from its more positive meanings (e.g. normal group behaviour or individual well-meaning behaviour) to more negative meanings. This linguistic shift corresponds to a moral shift as well. Whereas earlier attitudes held that 'children will be children', today there is a widespread moral disapprobation of bullying. On the one hand, we can applaud this moral shift for bringing public and political attention to issues of prevention and intervention. On the other hand, we must be wary that this moral shift may also represent a moralising approach to bullying, which could undercut researchers' ability to analyse its fundamental dynamics.

Attending to language opens up the more general question of whether it is possible to define bullying cross-culturally. Is there a common phenomenon of bullying that is expressed differently in various languages, or is the experience of bullying culturally and linguistically coded? Here, I give a few examples of variations across language. In Japanese, the counterpart for bullying is the term *ijime*, which is loosely translated to mean treating someone badly, teasing, being cruel or annoying. The Japanese term emphasises social manipulation and refers to mental or physical suffering within a group-interaction process (ibid.: 1121). In Italian, the terms *prepotenza* and *violenza* are used to signify bullying and imply violent, physical actions. In French, the phrase *faits de violence* is used and *malmenances* has also been suggested (ibid.: 129–309). There is no comparable Spanish term, however, and some Spanish researchers suggest that this semantic absence reveals a deficiency in social understanding (Smith et al. 1999: 161). Even within one language, like English, there are several national and cultural variations related to the connotations of bullying. For example, in Scotland, there is a strong oral tradition that discourages victims from telling: 'Tell-tale tit, your mammy cannae knit...' (ibid.: 94). This oral tradition gives a very different meaning to bullying than its American usage, which associates bullying with harassment and, as such, refers to actions that are punishable by law (e.g. sexual harassment).

Some problems of definition

As the resident philosopher of the eXbus research group, it fell on my shoulders to reflect on definitions of bullying. In my view, it is neither desirable nor possible to develop a definition of bullying that is universally valid or final. Research in this field takes place in specific national, cultural and linguistic environments – all of which contribute components to the more general understanding of bullying. Although it is impossible to develop a universally valid definition, we can learn a great deal from the way researchers have defined bullying: what these definitions take for granted and what they overlook (Eriksson et al. 2002: 19). We can learn about the family of concepts to which these definitions belong. We can learn what kind of dualisms these definitions call forth. In this way, studying definitions is useful in developing a critical lens to view the research in this field. Critical insights also point to alternative paths for understanding bullying. Before I turn to the specific definitions of bullying, I present some of the problems with definitions that one faces along the way.

Firstly, there is the question: what is a definition? Researchers into bullying typically assume that the purpose of a definition is to place a specific phenomenon into a subset under a general category or concept. For example, Olweus considers bullying to be a subset of the more general category of aggression. By this, he means that bullying is always a form of aggression, but that there are also forms of aggression that are not bullying (Smith et al. 1999: 13). With this approach, what is true of the general category (i.e. aggression) is also true of the subset (i.e. bullying). If we assume, as Olweus does, that aggression is intentional and harmful behaviour, then it follows that bullying is also intentional and harmful.

But this basic approach to definitions may be misguided. It may be more useful to think of a definition not in terms of placing a specific phenomenon under a general category, but instead in terms of interpreting a phenomenon as a complex constellation of elements. With the subset approach to definitions, the assumptions made about the general category become definitive for the specific phenomenon. For example, if bullying is a subset of aggressive behaviour, then bullies are aggressors. But this approach precludes the possibility that individuals may sometimes be bullies and sometimes victims. Understanding large-scale atrocities brings forth the notion of the 'grey zone', which refers to a physical and moral space where individuals are both victims and perpetrators.[2] In bullying, there may also be a grey zone where children contribute to the harmful patterns of behaviour from which they also suffer. This example illustrates that the assumption that a definition of bullying must be placed as a subset within a general category limits being able to understand the complex subjective experiences involved.

Secondly, there is the question: what is the process of developing a definition? Philosophers in critical theory and in science studies point to the social history of knowledge. Knowledge is a result of processes of struggle over legitimacy and justification. Uncovering this social history involves asking: what institutions and paradigms have the power to name or define? Which perspectives are included or excluded in the process of defining knowledge? What are the ongoing effects of dominant paradigms? In the research on bullying, the dominant paradigm draws upon methods of research from individual psychology and education. With the growing number of social psychologists and sociologists contributing to research on bullying, this paradigm is now being challenged (Eriksson et al. 2002: 14). But in practice, the dominance of the individual-psychology paradigm has resulted in a highly homogeneous research field. Researchers have typically adopted a definition of bullying as a form of individual aggression and applied this definition to their own national and cultural contexts, and the homogeneity of the research reinforces the legitimacy of this definition. The strategy of developing a definition that is considered context-independent is well known within philosophy and the philosophy of science. This strategy assumes that a researcher can formulate universal principles that are subsequently applied in practice; it could be called a top-down approach to knowledge (Schott 2003: 107–10). By contrast, a bottom-up approach emphasises that knowledge always emerges from the social life of participants. This approach acknowledges that there is a concrete descriptive dimension of knowledge, and also that knowledge is open-ended, changing and revisable rather than fixed and unchanging. A bottom-up approach to

---

[2] Primo Levi, an Austrian-born Jew who wrote about his experiences at Auschwitz, used the term 'grey zone' to describe the Kapos in the death camps, prisoners who were given power over other prisoners in exchange for food or privileges from the Nazis (Card 1999: 7–8).

knowledge calls attention to how the users of concepts are also producers of these concepts. In the context of bullying, a bottom-up approach seeks to reflect on how students and teachers define bullying based on their own experiences, and how one best involves them in the process of debate (Lee 2006: 64–8). If a definition is context-dependent, produced by its users and revisable, then it is likely that the definition will be flexible enough to cover a range of meanings and be open enough to incorporate new meanings along the way.

Thirdly, there is the question: which perspectives are articulated in definitions? If definitions are the result of conflicts and debates, then there is a risk that some perspectives are recognised as legitimate while others are dismissed. In the field of bullying, this means that we may ask whether there are systematic differences in the perspectives of teachers, parents and students, and to what extent a research definition acknowledges these differences. Many researchers do acknowledge such differences: for example, some suggest that teachers have a broader concept of bullying than students, since they focus on bullying as a form of both physical and psychological power (ibid.: 64–5). Other researchers suggest that students have a more inclusive idea of bullying than teachers, since they view bullying as a systematic abuse of power; hence, their understanding is closer to the researchers' approach (Naylor et al. 2006: 554–5). From a practical point of view, the observation that students have a more inclusive definition of bullying than teachers may be linked to the observation that teachers do not see many of the incidents of bullying that children see. From a theoretical point of view, this observation suggests that the researcher may be well-advised to 'adopt the perspective of the child rather than that of the adult' (Lee 2006: 71). Such an approach does not mean that researchers should simply mirror the perspective of a child; rather, they should seek to understand the complexities of the world that produces these perspectives (Hastrup 1992: 73).

With these clusters of problems with regard to definitions in mind, I now turn to some of the leading definitions of bullying. My discussion does not pretend to be inclusive. A quick online search for 'bullying' in English during February 2009 produced over two million hits, with 300,000 articles listed as research articles. A search in Danish produced over 58,000 articles on bullying, with over 10,000 listed as research articles. Such a massive output attests to the growing importance of this subject. My goal is not to give a comprehensive overview, but to reflect on three paradigms that emerge when one attempts to become oriented in the field. I do not use the term 'paradigm' in the strict sense often found within the natural sciences, where it refers to the prevailing method of experimentation and interpretation. But I am suggesting that the social scientists who have studied bullying have reached widespread agreement on certain definitions that map out the field. My goal is to focus on the general assumptions and implications of these definitions, rather than on the details and modifications made by individual authors.

Paradigms of bullying definitions

Here, I examine three definitions of bullying: (1) bullying as a form of individual aggression; (2) bullying as a form of social violence; and (3) bullying as a form of dysfunctional group dynamics. These definitions map out the leading conceptual approaches to defining bullying. Although my interest is more in the pattern of the definition and less in the contribution of any particular author, Dan Olweus holds an exceptional position. Olweus's approach has dominated this field of research since the 1970s, and he gave his own name to the intervention programmes he designed. A review of the literature from 2002 indicates that three out of five articles in the field are influenced by his work (Eriksson et al. 2002: 51). The primary differences between the three definitions I examine here relate to the ontological question: what is the nature of bullying (ibid.: 98)? Answers to this question have implications for the epistemological question: how does one recognise bullying? In other respects, however, there is a good deal of overlap between these three definitions.

The first definition of bullying as a form of individual aggression was formulated by Olweus, and it continues to hold a dominant position in the field. Olweus summarises his definition as follows: 'A student is being bullied or victimized when he or she is exposed, repeatedly and over time, to negative actions on the part of one or more other students' (Smith et al. 1999: 10ff.) Olweus stresses that these negative actions are intentional forms of 'harm-doing' and that bullying is a subset of aggressive behaviour. Violence, which he defines as using one's own body or an object to inflict injury on another individual, is also a subset of aggressive behaviour. Some bullying is carried out by physical means, so there is an overlap between these two subsets. However, much bullying is not carried out by physical means but is instead verbal, involves the use of offensive gestures or social exclusion. Olweus also stresses that bullying is done repeatedly and over time, as opposed to occasional or insignificant acts of aggression in order to emphasise its systematic character. And he underscores that bullying happens in relationships of asymmetric power. Differences in power may be real or perceived, they may refer to differences in physical or mental capacities, or they may refer to differences in number (e.g. several students ganging up on one victim). Since bullying often occurs without any provocation, Olweus considers it to be a form of abuse. In his view, the positions of 'bully' and 'victim' are stable over time (Olweus 1993a: 27); some individuals are bullies for a long period of time – even years – while others are victims for a long period of time. Olweus describes bullies as aggressive individuals who are impulsive, have a need to dominate, have a positive attitude towards violence and have little empathy for their victims. His view is echoed by other researchers who have characterised bullies as powerful, sadistic, dysfunctional, anti-social or proto-criminal (Farrington 1993). Olweus explains this aggressive-reaction pattern as a consequence of poor child-rearing, particularly on the part of the 'primary caretaker (usually the mother)' (Olweus 1993a: 32–9). When the primary caretaker lacks warmth and involvement or has been permissive and tolerant, then she will rear an aggressive child with a tendency to become a bully. Just as Olweus focuses on the personality characteristics of bullies, he also highlights the typical personality traits of victims. Victims are passive, submissive, anxious, insecure and weak, largely because they have overprotective mothers (ibid.). He notes that bullying can also be a group phenomenon. When neutral observers witness the actions of a bully, their own ability to resist aggressive tendencies is weakened (ibid.: 43–4).

In claiming that bullying is an expression of individual aggression, Olweus makes a number of problematic assumptions. His strategy assumes that something outside of the classroom is the root of problems that occur inside the classroom (Eriksson et al. 2002: 39). Therefore, by virtue of their home environments, some individuals are natural bullies and others are natural victims. This focus on individual personalities expresses Olweus's explicit interest in analysing bullying ('*mobbning*' in Swedish) in terms of the individual, in contrast to the etymological origin of the word. In doing so, he stipulates personality types with a stable set of characteristics instead of exploring how individuals may also be transformed by the situations in which they find themselves. Thus, Olweus views bullying quintessentially as a relation between two fixed personality types – bully and victim – and he overlooks the experience of children who sometimes act like the bully and other times are bullied. Recent research indicates that the positions of 'bully' and 'victim' are much more fluid than Olweus's theory allows. In fact, qualitative interviews conducted by several researchers in the eXbus group indicate how quickly these positions can shift because individuals are constantly aware of the precariousness of their roles within a group and feel a need to assert their value to it. Jette Kofoed's and Dorte Marie Søndergaard's chapters (see pages 159 and 47, respectively) both discuss such a fluidity of positions. Further, this approach implies that the personal qualities of an individual are less significant to bullying than the complex dynamics within a class. Although Olweus acknowledges that groups may also play a role in bullying, he understands 'the group' as being made up of a leader – an aggressive individual – and his/her followers, whose defences become weakened so that they model the aggressor's behaviour. This understanding of group relations overlooks the many processes by which groups define themselves, including deciding who is included and excluded.

Another problem with Olweus's focus on personal aggression is his claim that bullying expresses the intention to harm another person. Intentionality is a notoriously difficult problem, as attested to by other philosophical writing on the subject. How does one know an individual's intentions? Does an individual know his/her intentions best? Does 'intentional harm' refer only to harming for its own sake, as with sadism? Or does it also include harm that is instrumental in achieving some other goal, such as higher status in the group? If harm is only instrumental, then does an individual intend to achieve status rather than inflict harm? How does an observer know the intentions of another person? Does the observer elicit self-reports or does she/he observe the effect(s) on the victim(s)? And do all individuals who inflict harm have a common intention? These theoretical questions indicate the problem with anchoring a definition of bullying in terms of individual intentions. Invoking intention in such a definition may be, at best, a postulate of the researcher.

Olweus's concept of power is also derived from his individualistic approach. He is concerned with the power of one individual to dominate or subdue another (Olweus 1993a: 35) rather than how power functions in an institutional context, which is the focus of social theories of power.[3] But to understand power with regard to the institution of the school raises a broad range of questions. As Nina Hein asks (see page 301): do parents experience themselves as empowered or powerless in relation to the school? Do teachers have 'usable' or 'unusable' power (Terry 1998: 258)? What kind of power is exerted within the school by social norms; for example, norms about sexuality (Meyer 2007a; Phoenix et al. 2003: 179)? What kind of power is exerted by governmental directives that stipulate the content of the curriculum, the amount of time used for different tasks and the nature of testing? In other words, a child is not

---

[3] With the phrase 'social theory of power', I refer to a very broad range of work from the nineteenth century to the present day that develops a theoretical understanding of concepts of power, the social, the political and identity in contrast to strictly empirical studies of institutional relations. A few of the major figures in this field include Karl Marx, post-Marxist philosophers in France (as varied as Lucien Goldmann, Jean-Paul Sartre, Louis Althusser, Pierre Bourdieu and post-structuralist theorists such as Michel Foucault and Gilles Deleuze), in Hungary (e.g. Georg Lukács), in Germany (including several generations of critical theorists from the Frankfurt School) and in the United Kingdom (e.g. E. P. Thompsen and Terry Eagleton) as well as contemporary theorists writing about race and gender.

just either dominant or submissive, but is involved in a range of power relations, many of which may be relevant to a situation of bullying.

Olweus's definition has long been the dominant paradigm for understanding and responding to school bullying. Researchers in many different countries often rely on his definition when asking teachers or students about the frequency of bullying and their roles in it. The widespread influence of Olweus's work makes it especially important to address it critically. Recalling some of the problems with definitions, one could ask: which perspectives are reflected in his definition? And whose position is treated as worthy of respect? On first glance, Olweus seems to construct a definition of bullying that is based on the victim's point of view. He locates the cause of bullying within the aggressor, even though he does note that some victims are 'provocative' and may have both anxious and aggressive reaction patterns (Olweus 1993a: 32–4). But he also describes victims as anxious, insecure, withdrawn, suffering from low self-esteem, feeling stupid, ashamed or unattractive and apt to cry (for younger children). This description hardly exudes respect for the victim. His description of bullies as anti-social aggressors is also negative. However, he notes that 'typical' bullies do not suffer from anxiety or insecurity, and they have physical (or non-physical) strength; as such, bullies appear to have some qualities that are widely valued in Western societies. Olweus's description of parents is also negative: in his view, bullying is ultimately explained by poor parenting, particularly parents who love too little, who allow too much freedom, who use physical punishment and/or who give way to violent emotional outbursts (ibid.: 39–40). In this analysis, it is particularly the mother as primary caregiver who is under attack. But Olweus also views teachers as doing 'relatively little to stop bullying at school' (ibid.: 20), although he sees their role as decisive in preventing bullying and 'redirecting such behaviors into more socially acceptable channels' (ibid.: 46). It seems the position most deserving of respect in his theory is that of the researcher, who can design a programme of intervention to stop what poor parents and inadequate teachers have been unable to do.

Moreover, Olweus's focus on the dualism of aggressor/victim as the key to understanding bullying overlooks how children may move in and out of these positions. In linking bullying to a family of concepts, such as pathology, criminal behaviour and anti-social behaviour, he suggests that bullying is abnormal and occurs when socially integrative practices fail. But this pathologisation of bullying is disturbing, given that Olweus also cites the incidence of bullying to be consistently 5-to-10 per cent of the students questioned (ibid.: 17). Instead of assuming – along with Olweus – that nearly 10 per cent of children are trapped in pathological relations, it may be more useful to look at bullying as a phenomenon experienced by ordinary children in specific group contexts.

In contrast to the first paradigm that defines bullying in terms of individual aggression, the second paradigm defines bullying in terms of social violence. My focus here is not on the work of an individual researcher, as with the first paradigm wherein the influence of Olweus is so extensive. Instead, I try to map a position that is held by both policy-makers and researchers in several different countries where bullying is debated. My source material is taken from several contributors to the anthology *The Nature of School Bullying: A Cross-National Perspective*, co-edited by Peter K. Smith.[4]

The approach to bullying as a form of social violence is expressed, for example, in the policy plan issued in 1996 by the Dutch Ministry of Education:

It should be realized that lack of safety in schools cannot be viewed in isolation from the social environment of the school. [...] The violence that manifests itself in schools has its origins mainly outside them. It reflects a general problem for which society as a whole is responsible. (cited in Smith et al. 1999: 217)

In a similar vein, prominent British criminologist David Farrington writes, 'School bullying is to some extent a microcosm of offending in the community' (Farrington 1993: 394). As with the paradigm of individual aggression discussed above, researchers and policymakers who focus on violence as the source of bullying tend to look outside the classroom for an explanation of the problems inside the classroom. When researchers do view bullying in terms of individuals' use of violence, they are apt to invoke the theory of aggression implicit in the first paradigm. Despite this overlap between the two paradigms, this second approach also looks to social causes of violence, including socio-economic factors and the media. For example, in France, bullying is understood as *'faits de violence'* or acts of violence, defined by the French Penal Code (Smith et al. 1999: 129–31), which includes offences against persons and/or property and offences committed by a school through a misuse of power. In a French context, this view of bullying as a social problem may be influenced by factors such as increased unemployment, increased

[4] This book was inspired by a cross-national study on bullying conducted by the Japanese Ministry of Education, Science, Sports and Culture, which was coordinated by Yohji Morita. Peter K. Smith edited the English-language version of a similar Japanese book, *School Bullying Around the World: Challenges and Interventions*, edited by Morita (Smith et al. 1999: 3–4). Although Smith is a leading figure in this field of research, I do not focus on his specific contributions here. He follows Olweus's definition of bullying and studies developmental factors, amongst other things, in children's concepts of bullying.

social and racial segregation, increased 'social distance' between teachers and children from working-class families and the media's attention to violent crime (ibid.: 134–5). In defining bullying through the judicial concept of violence, French responses to bullying have focused on legalities; for example, by stressing the need to improve cooperation between schools, the police and the legal system.

In Germany, a country that has experienced major social changes since its reunification in 1990, researchers also understand bullying primarily as a social problem linked to youth crime and youth violence against foreigners (ibid.: 228). Some researchers argue for the need to differentiate bullying from other forms of violence, such as vandalism and inflicting serious physical injuries, since bullying is 'relatively frequent and long-lasting aggressiveness within relationships characterized by an imbalance of power' (ibid.: 242). A conceptual strategy can be traced here, wherein the paradigm of individual aggression is invoked to differentiate between physical violence and repetitive, relational aggression. But this strategy fails, since both phenomena could be explained by either individual or social factors.

In Poland, researchers interpret bullying as a form of social brutality – a brutality that is also evident in the rapid rise of juvenile crime, in the behaviour of fans at football matches and in clashes at political demonstrations. This increased brutality is explained by the political and social transformation that Poland has been undergoing since 1989; this includes the 'system-transforming process' with its subsequent poverty and economic inequalities, the opening of borders and a related increase in organised crime. One Polish researcher describes severe bullying in schools as 'the second or the "hidden" curriculum typical of totalitarian. . .organizations':

Examples include having one's head put in a toilet bowl and being forced to eat the larvae of worms from rotting fruit. [. . .] Students who spontaneously and readily think up and use torture against their school mates will develop a durable tendency to bully after a few cases and will often feel beyond any punishment. (ibid.: 270)

This author connects bullying to the terror inflicted by senior soldiers on new military recruits in the 1980s when soldiers were routinely blackmailed, beaten and forced to perform humiliating services. In comparing school bullying to torture, the author implies that bullying is also an exercise of arbitrary power through practices of humiliation.

Developing countries in Latin America, Asia and Africa also connect bullying and school violence to their region's economic, cultural and political conditions, including poverty, unemployment, malnutrition, social marginalisation, congested classes and, in some cases, ethnic violence and post-civil war conditions. In this context, researchers tend not to draw a clear distinction between violence and bullying. In countries that are preoccupied by the consequences of war, political repression and underdevelopment, researchers are less interested in the distinction between 'aggressors' and 'victims' than with 'the victimization of individuals by the system and politics' (ibid.: 370–4).

As a final example of interpreting bullying in terms of the violence in society, I mention the United States (US). In Austin, Texas, an anti-bullying project was developed by an agency that works with sexual- and domestic-violence prevention and intervention. This agency considers bullying to be related to sexual harassment and dating violence; in its view, all of these phenomena are 'aggressive acts that are intended to hurt or control another person, are often repeated over time, and occur in the context of a relationship in which the bully/harasser/abuser has more physical or social power than the target/victim' (Smith, Pepler and Rigby 2004: 211–12). The authors rely on Olweus's work to define bullying in terms of aggressive acts by an individual, but they also link it to widespread problems of sexual violence in families, the workplace and social life. With this approach, bullying is an expression of power that ultimately resides in an individual because of his/her access to social authority (e.g. gender or bureaucratic authority).

These examples of cross-national perspectives indicate that many researchers see bullying as a reflection of the violence in society at large, and they do not focus on individual aggression rooted in the family. However, emphasising that the roots of bullying are found in social violence does not preclude a discussion about individual aggression. For example, some researchers suggest that social upheaval produces families that breed aggressive behaviour. Based on these examples, it appears that societies marked by social upheaval or transformation – such as system changes, immigration or increased social inequalities – write their national narratives into an understanding of bullying. When politicians and researchers believe that their society is in violent upheaval, then social violence provides a framework for interpreting bullying. Although this may be an obvious strategy to utilise when societies are in crisis, it is also important to recognise how researchers may carry basic social categories into their analyses of bullying under ordinary circumstances. In this way, crises narratives are useful in order to shed light on processes of interpreting ordinary social relations. However, a weakness of the social-violence approach is that attentiveness to the social relations outside of school is linked to a relative inattentiveness to the nature of the social groups within the school.

In the paradigm of social violence, public institutions and language play an important role in defining bullying. This is true in France where the penal code governing violence provides a framework for understanding bullying; in the US, where laws regarding sexual and domestic violence affect the approach to school bullying; and also in a post-communist society like Poland, where the country's history of military power and torture is echoed in the understanding of bullying. In this sense, some researchers are more aware of their own relationship to public institutions than those who strictly adopt the paradigm of individual aggression wherein bullying is attributed to individual characteristics isolated from other social processes. When Polish researcher Andrzej Janowski compares extreme bullying to torture, he implies that bullying and torture deserve the same moral abhorrence. However, he distinguishes the attitude of the authorities in these two cases: whereas the Polish senior military officers 'welcomed' violent acts to terrorise new recruits (Janowski in Smith 1999: 270), school authorities do not approve of such behaviour – rather, they are either blind to it or helpless to cope with it. In condemning bullying as being similar to torture, Janowski focuses on the harm and humiliation to which the victim is subjected. And it seems to be more generally the case that the paradigm of social violence is attuned to the victim's position. This attentiveness may be enhanced, as noted by UNESCO researcher Toshio Ohsako, by the sensibility that all members of a society are victimised by the violence that is endemic in their political and social systems.

The paradigm of social violence places bullying into a family of concepts that includes violence, totalitarianism, crisis and social and political upheaval – an alliance that emphasises the severity of some acts of bullying. The description of certain acts of bullying as 'torture' may be well-founded, as suggested in literature about torture. Torture may be both physical and psychological. With psychological torture, severe pain and suffering can be inflicted by non-physical methods that may appear insignificant when considered individually (e.g. verbal abuse, petty humiliations, intimidations, verbal threats). But the repetition and accumulation of such acts create a system that wears a person down, disrupting his/her personality and eventually breaking him/her; as such, it counts as psychic torture (Reyes 2007: 612). But in placing bullying in the context of crisis, the social-violence approach also implies that violence is contrasted with peaceful relations, and crisis conditions are contrasted with normality. In this respect, the social-violence paradigm, like the individual-aggression paradigm, also situates bullying as a deviation from ordinary interactions.

The third approach that I examine here defines bullying in terms of oppressive or dysfunctional group dynamics. As opposed to the preceding two paradigms, this approach considers the dynamics within a class to be the source of problems inside the classroom. One young Swedish researcher suggests that bullying is a form of group-think, invoking Irving Janus's theory in which the social influence of a group leads to behaviour by it that is more exaggerated and destructive than the behaviour of any individual member would otherwise be. In a group, individuals gain a form of anonymity, assume the norms of the group and achieve a sense of belonging (Heintz 2004: 10). By striving to maintain a sense of in-group identity, an illusion of invulnerability is created along with a strong belief in the rightness of one's own moral position, which leads to forming stereotypes about other groups (ibid.: 53–5). In a group context, great pressure to conform contributes to self-censorship, so that the group only absorbs information that is self-fulfilling about its stereotypes and rationalisations. In this approach, destructive group-think is an expression of dysfunctional group dynamics; in a school context, this can be manifested as bullying.

Finnish researcher Christina Salmivalli and her colleagues have focused on the internal group dynamics of bullying as well. In their analysis of the social interactions within a group, they highlight six 'participant roles' in a bullying situation. In addition to (1) victims 'who are systematically attacked by others' and (2) bullies 'who have an active, initiative-taking...role', there are (3) assistants of bullies who 'eagerly join in', (4) reinforcers of bullies who 'offer positive feedback...by laughing, by encouraging gestures, or just by gathering around as an audience', (5) outsiders who withdraw 'without taking sides with anyone' and (6) defenders who 'may comfort the victim, or actively try to make others stop bullying' (Smith, Pepler and Rigby 2004: 252). This focus on the different roles within the dynamics of bullying has contributed to analyses about the role of bystanders which have emerged in studies of large-scale atrocities (Staub 1989, 2003). Salmivalli's research develops the insight that bystanders enable harm-doing, either by actively encouraging the harm (i.e. acting as assistants and reinforcers) or by passively allowing it through their failure to intervene (i.e. acting as outsiders). It is also important to recognise the flexibility of these positions; this means that, for example, an active bystander can become an active bully or can withdraw, while an outsider can become either a reinforcer or a defender.

Japanese researchers have also been particularly attentive to bullying as a group phenomenon. In 1985, Yohji Morita proposed the following definition of bullying:

A type of aggressive behaviour by which someone who holds a dominant position in a group-interaction process, by intentional or collective acts, causes mental and/or physical suffering to another inside a group. (cited in Smith et al. 1999: 320)

This approach overlaps with the first paradigm by stressing aggressive behaviour and intentionality. But in contrast to the first paradigm, Morita emphasises that group interaction is key to the suffering that is inflicted, and he recognises that a target of bullying is inside the group rather than outside. This approach is in alignment with recent research that considers bullying to be a process of social inclusion and exclusion. And it opens the door to understanding the ways in which social exclusion is a significant mechanism for defining processes of social inclusion.[5]

Australian researchers have also highlighted group processes. Ken Rigby and Phillip Slee, prominent researchers in the field, propose the following definition: 'Bullying is oppression directed by more powerful persons or by a group of persons against individuals who cannot adequately defend themselves' (ibid.: 324). And bullying is 'the systematic abuse of power in interpersonal relationships' (Rigby 2008: 22). This approach includes elements of each of the three paradigms I have discussed here. By emphasising words such as 'power' and 'oppression' and invoking the term 'unjust', the authors take concepts typically applied to societal interaction and use them as a lens to view in-group dynamics. In doing so, they adopt normative judgements about social violence as a frame of reference for understanding bullying. But they also draw upon a theory of anti-social behaviour rooted in individual aggression. It is important to recognise, as they do, that an analytical focus on the group as well as on the individual are not exclusive approaches but are, instead, complementary in understanding the complex processes of bullying. Thus, a coupling of both social and individual dynamics is appealing to new researchers in the field. Rigby points to the ways that individual behaviour is context-dependent and not independent, as well as to how a child's role as bully is fluid and not fixed; for example, a child may bully at one school but not another (ibid.: 29). But he also describes bullying as intentional harm-doing (in the case of 'malignant bullying') that creates pleasure for the perpetrator, and he explains its genesis from dysfunctional families (Smith et al. 1999: 332) to which he adds genetic factors and early child-care. Thus, he imports many of Olweus's problematic assumptions into his analysis. And in seeing power as an expression of individuals' social or manipulative skills (Rigby 2008: 23), he misses the opportunity to explore how power within a group shapes individuals' opportunities to act.

---

[5] There is substantial literature in social psychology about the complex processes of inclusion/exclusion, which I do not review here. Some key insights from this literature are that people seek belonging and inclusion, but this then requires boundaries and exclusion (Abrams et al. 2005). Researchers focus on individuals' strategies of negotiation as a way of 'making sense of social conditions that are not of their own making' (Benjamin et al. 2003), and researchers often pair a focus on inclusion/exclusion with the individual-aggression paradigm (Totten and Quigley 2003).

This third paradigm, which focuses on dysfunctional groups and intra-group oppression, is imbued with normative terms such as right/wrong, good/evil and just/unjust (ibid.: 25, 180). By implication, these authors suggest that groups without bullying are functional groups with 'just' social and moral relationships. Although they highlight the role of group interaction, they do not provide an analysis of why some individuals become oppressors within these groups. That is, their explanation of *why* bullying occurs ultimately reverts back to the first paradigm, and they invoke a child's upbringing or biology to explain what they label 'anti-social behaviour' (ibid.: 51, 55). These researchers are incensed with abhorrence for severe bullying and filled with righteous anger about the suffering of the victims. But there is danger in a theoretical approach that only treats the position of the victim as being worthy of respect. Such an approach cannot provide an analysis of how ordinary group dynamics create situations in which ordinary children also may assume positions as either bullies and/or active bystanders.

I have focused on three patterns of response to the question: what is bullying? In all of these approaches, researchers assume that there is a general concept under which bullying can be subsumed: individual aggression, social violence or dysfunctional groups. These responses have powerfully influenced how the meaning of bullying has been con-structed (Smith et al. 2002: 1131). However, there are researchers who challenge several of these assumptions. Some of them do not believe that there can only be one universally acceptable definition, preferring instead to examine a range of behaviour that causes distress (Arora 1996 in Monks and Smith 2006: 819). Others emphasise that bullying refers to a broad range of negative actions, and is best understood as a continuum (Lee 2006: 73). And there are yet other researchers – whose lead I follow – who stress the need to open up the understanding of bullying as a complex reality (Eriksson et al. 2002: 103).

Bullying as a social concept

As already noted, the homogeneity of the research on bullying is partially explained by the dominant use of individual psychology to examine this subject. However, when researchers from fields like social psychology, sociology, anthropology, minority studies and philosophy begin to study bullying, they initiate new approaches to understanding it. I study bullying as a philosopher, analysing it in terms of theories of conflict, otherness and abjection that have been developed by thinkers working in continental philosophy, critical theory, poststructuralist theory, race theory, post-Holocaust studies and feminist theory.[6] With this background – and on the basis of an ongoing dialogue with the eXbus researchers conducting empirical research – I present four hypotheses about social processes. My goal is to see how these reflections may foster new perspectives on bullying. In philosophical language, one might consider these hypotheses to be loosely part of social ontology, in that they address the fundamental question: what is a society (Searle 2003: 1)? A response to this question is thereby useful for answering the more specific question: what is a social group within a class? Like the paradigm of social violence, I claim that concepts developed to understand large-scale social processes are useful for understanding small-scale group processes within the class. But I also underscore the role of group dynamics, which is highlighted by the paradigm of dysfunctional groups. In contrast to the latter, however, I focus my attention on processes within ordinary groups. My four hypotheses about social processes follow.

- **Hypothesis 1:** Power inheres in a social system and is distributed in such a way that some individuals have access to more material or symbolic power than others. All individuals have access to power – not primarily because of their personalities, but because of the distribution of roles, functions or identities within a social system. Since all individuals are dominated by power in the social system, they are also at risk for and vulnerable to losing the privileges with which they identify.
- **Hypothesis 2:** Conflict is an inherent dimension of social relations. Hence, society needs to manage conflict rather than attempting to eradicate it entirely in the hope of achieving stable, harmonious relations. Conflicts within society are not an expression of pre-existing, natural antagonisms between individuals or groups. Rather, opposing identities are generated from within a social group.
- **Hypothesis 3:** A society is defined in terms of whom it both includes and excludes. Exclusion is necessary to establish the borders of society (e.g. national, geographical, cultural, political, economic, linguistic). Such borders are not rigid, but are constantly under pressure to be re-negotiated. Individuals or groups who are excluded become viewed as 'the other' by the society that excludes them. In principle, the concept of 'the other' is not harmful to those who are excluded, since they also belong to a society that is defined by whom it includes/excludes. But if

---

[6] This is not the place for a discussion about the theoretical background for these insights. But some of the thinkers who have inspired this approach include Giorgio Agamben, Benedict Anderson, Hannah Arendt, Simone de Beauvoir, Seyla Benhabib, Pierre Bourdieu, Jacques Derrida, Mary Douglas, Terry Eagleton, Michel Foucault, G. F. Hegel, Julia Kristeva, Luce Irigaray, Herbert Marcuse and Patricia Williams.

individuals or groups become excluded from all *possible* societies, then they lose the social meaning in their lives (e.g. recognition, rights, privileges, etc.). Individuals or groups who move across borders disturb the system for organising inside/outside; thus, they are viewed as potentially dangerous.

- **Hypothesis 4:** Interpersonal relations are mediated by social institutions and symbolic representations, such as language and values.

As a thought experiment, I propose that these insights about social ontology, which have been developed in relation to large-scale groups, may apply to small-scale groups as well. With this background, I formulate the following provisional definition of bullying:

Bullying occurs in relation to formal institutions, such as the school, where individuals cannot easily leave the group. The ongoing process of constituting informal groups through the mechanisms of inclusion and exclusion provides a social context for bullying. Changes in position are dangerous to group order, becoming a source of fear and anxiety since all members of the group risk being excluded. Bullying occurs when groups respond to this anxiety by projecting the threat to group order onto particular individuals; these individuals become systematically excluded as the 'other'. Although these processes may appear to be functional to the group, they deprive individuals who are bullied of the social recognition necessary for human dignity. In this way, being bullied may be experienced as a form of psychic torture.

This definition theoretically addresses the questions: where does bullying take place? (in formal institutions); what is it? (the systematic exclusion of the 'other'); who is involved? (all members of the group); how does it take place? (through mechanisms of inclusion/exclusion); why does it take place? (to secure group order); and when does it take place? (when anxiety in the group becomes mobilised). This proposal is closely related to Dorte Marie Søndergaard's reflections (see page 47) about the role of social fear, social anxiety and abjection in understanding the processes of bullying. Søndergaard gives a close analysis of the subjective processes involved when the fear of social exclusion triggers a form of panic that produces contempt and disgust towards a figure(s) in the group. In doing so, she also analyses the movement that occurs between the dynamics of both non-bullying and bullying situations.

My provisional definition includes many elements that are widely accepted in current research, including the importance of the social space at school as well as the recent emphasis on inclusion and exclusion. As with Morita's approach, this definition acknowledges that the outsider in the process of exclusion is not absolutely outside, but is a constitutive element of the group. It differs from the first paradigm by focusing on group processes rather than individual characteristics, intentions or power; it differs from the second paradigm by focusing on processes within the class; and it differs from the third paradigm by viewing bullying as a social process that occurs within normal groups, as opposed to dysfunctional groups.

Since I recognise the severity of harm that can result from bullying, one might wonder whether it makes a difference to insist that such groups are not dysfunctional or pathological. In my view, this assumption is necessary in order to keep the analytic lens on the dynamics within a class. Without this assumption, one is forced to ask: why are some groups dysfunctional? To this question, researchers have most often resorted to the first paradigm and answered the question by referring to aggressive individuals within the group. I think it is advisable to disqualify the question: *why* are some children bullies and some children victims? In my view, one gets no further by posing this question than from asking: why are women treated as the 'other' in society (Schott in Card 2003: 240)? Like Simone de Beauvoir in her book *The Second Sex* (1949/1974), I answer the question of 'why' with 'how'. One can understand *how* group processes operate and how some individuals *become* bullies, victims and/or bystanders. Individuals who are excluded from the group – who are positioned as the 'other' – are attributed with characteristics that define them as outsiders to the group.

One of the contributions made by the eXbus research group to discussions about inclusion/exclusion is the insight that exclusion does not produce an absolute outside to the group, but more accurately, produces a borderline position.[7] Children who are bullied still belong to the formal group because they are members of the class. But they also belong to the informal group, in the sense that the social relations are charged with the emotional dynamics of negotiating positions in relation to the group. The notion of abjection, taken from the work of anthropologist Mary Douglas and psychoanalyst and linguist Julia Kristeva, is useful in understanding borderline positions.[8] Both of these writers develop the idea that human groups – and indeed, individual subjects – require order, systems or lawfulness to give meaning to the world. At the same time, order is fragile and easily disrupted, and this disruption requires a social response. Douglas

[7] Jette Kofoed has worked extensively with processes of inclusion/exclusion, including in her Ph.D. thesis (2004). Helle Rabøl Hansen uses the phrase '*inkluderet eksklusion*' (included exclusion) to emphasise that an individual is both excluded and included in the group at the same time. She also uses the notion of 'longing for belonging' as a psychological impetus to understand both bullying and the anguish it causes (2011a).

[8] As mentioned, Dorte Marie Søndergaard introduces the importance of the concept of abjection in her analysis of bullying. In this discussion, she refers to Judith Butler's work, while I refer to Kristeva and Douglas.

uses the term 'pollution' to refer to disorder, to matter out of place (1966: 2). Kristeva introduces the term 'abjection' to refer to what is disgusting and degrading. She describes 'the abject' as that which is opposed to the 'I'; it is 'what disturbs identity, system, order. ... The in-between, the ambiguous, the composite' (1982: 2–4).[9] The notion of abjection in the context of bullying points to the need for group borders as well as the fragility of these borders, with the latter provoking intense feelings of disgust. Since every group creates an outside to make its internal order possible, then every individual is at risk of being set outside or placed on the border.[10]

From this perspective, the social dynamics of inclusion and exclusion are central to groups and cannot be eliminated, although they may simultaneously create feelings of anxiety in group members, as Søndergaard analyses. Shifts in position both inside and outside of the group occur relatively frequently, so these positions are not rigid. But when the positions do become rigid – when certain individuals become fixed as the 'other' and lose the potential to become part of the group – then they also lose the social meaning that is bound to recognition.[11] When this occurs systematically and over time, this experience can be compared to psychic torture.[12]

My provisional definition of bullying is informed by the four hypotheses about social relations that I discussed above. Firstly, since power inheres in social relations and is shifting and precarious for any given individual, it is often more useful to look at individuals' vulnerability to becoming powerless, rather than to examine who has power at any given moment in time. In a bullying context, this approach shifts the focus away from the perception of power in the prevailing definitions of bullying. Olweus, and

---

[9] Elsewhere, I draw upon the notion of abjection in my analysis of war rape (Schott 2003: 110).

[10] Popular films about school dynamics, such as the American film *Mean Girls* (2004), illustrate this threat. The dynamic is also useful for understanding the role of sacrifice in societies, including the role of the scapegoat. I develop this analysis further in my article 'Sexual violence, sacrifice, and narratives of political origins' (2010).

[11] In her analysis of anti-Semitism in Germany during the Second World War, Hannah Arendt points to how Jews became excluded from the concept of humanity. In one sense, this implies that Jews were excluded from being citizens of a country and thereby lost the right to belong to it. In another sense, this implies that they lost the sense of humanity in their own persons. The problems with being fixed in the position of 'the Other' are explored by de Beauvoir in *The Second Sex* (1949/1974). As she notes, otherness is inherent both in human consciousness and in society. Otherness is not problematic as such – rather, it is the lack of reciprocity, whereby some groups retain the position of Subject and other groups are only defined as the Other and never as subjects, that is problematic.

[12] Primo Levi, a survivor of Auschwitz, uses the term 'shame' to describe the feeling of being chained to an impossible self (1989/2008: 52–67). Giorgio Agamben elaborates, saying that in shame, the self 'becomes witness to its own disorder, its own oblivion as a subject' (Agamben 1999b: 106).

those influenced by him, define bullying as taking place amidst asymmetric power relations, and he considers this asymmetry fundamental to express the relationship between individuals who are naturally either dominant or weak. The compelling aspect in this alternative approach is not just asymmetry, but also symmetry. Despite their unequal positions in a group, all members risk losing their positions in the social order. And the need to fight for their positions within the group is one of the driving dynamics of bullying.

Secondly, this approach calls attention to how the opposing identities of individuals in conflict may be less an expression of pre-existing characteristics and more the way that characteristics are produced through the process of conflict. In the context of bullying, this approach allows one to understand how both standard 'bully' and 'victim' characteristics are themselves produced by processes in which some children become aligned with insider, outsider and borderline positions. Such an approach, in my view, treats the individuals involved with greater respect than in the standard approach, and it keeps the focus on the process of transformation for all individuals involved in a bullying situation.

Thirdly, this approach highlights a fundamental tension within group dynamics by which processes of inclusion and exclusion are both necessary and dangerous. This insight leads one to realise that bullying is an old phenomenon, although its particular strategies and techniques may be new. At the same time, one can acknowledge the severity of bullying and the emotional intensity involved in negotiating group relations.

Fourthly, this approach draws upon the insight that the values and language that mediate social relations do not have truth-value as such, but are decisive for constituting individuals' understanding of their social realities. In a bullying context, this perspective reminds us that the values by which children are bullied are rooted in a system of oppositions, so that children who have temporarily 'secured' an insider position define themselves in contrast to those who are excluded. Having the wrong cut of jeans is then not merely a different style or an indifferent acquisition, but becomes proof that a child just does not fit into the class group.[13]

At this point, it is useful to refer to my critical questions about definitions. What is taken for granted by focusing on processes of inclusion/ exclusion, and what is overlooked? This approach assumes that one must examine the dynamics within the class for an explanation of the problems inside the classroom; therefore, the concept of the group is placed as central to understanding bullying. One might object that this approach

---

[13] This example is taken from Søndergaard's chapter (see page 47).

overlooks the role of individual personalities, since every interaction takes place between specific individuals. The role of personality differences in human interactions is undeniable, but personality differences cannot provide an analytical anchor for a theory of bullying, because every individual both acts within a group and is affected by group interactions. Hence, I believe it is a serious misjudgement to base interventions against bullying primarily on responses to individual persons.

The definition of bullying with regard to inclusion/exclusion is explicitly linked to a family of concepts related to the social group, including concepts of power, conflict and the 'other'. Although these concepts are anchored in the role of the social group, they address the impact on individuals through notions of risk and vulnerability. This approach moves away from the dualisms of aggressive/passive and pathological/normal that are implicit in an individualist approach to bullying. And it also moves away from the dualisms of functional/dysfunctional and oppressor/oppressed that characterise some group-based understandings. By focusing on processes of inclusion/exclusion, this approach avoids the tendency to naturalise a position as being either inside or outside the group and maintains attention on how positions can shift. When children are identified with an outsider position over a long period of time, it should be understood in terms of the processes by which group positions have become rigid and not as an expression of their personal qualities (Kofoed 2004).

It is with some reservation that I sketched out my thoughts here about an alternative definition of bullying. In my view, it is essential to involve those affected by bullying in the debates about how to understand it. But as part of these debates, researchers' new definitions can shake up habitual ways of thinking so that it is possible to let go of familiarities that have become truisms. This critical role is especially important in light of the prevalent tendency amongst researchers and educators to focus on a child's personality characteristics in order to change the roles and responsibilities in a bullying situation. One advantage of this proposed alternative is that it heeds the wisdom to respect the child's perspective. In this approach, children are neither demonised nor viewed as provocative victims. Instead, the children involved are viewed as individuals who are struggling to negotiate the social dynamics of their daily lives, which can be either a vital source of recognition or a deathly form of isolation. And rather than focusing on individuals' intentions as a way to explain the dynamics of bullying, this approach also respects the complexity of factors that complicate individuals' intentionality. Here, we should remember Michel Foucault's comment: 'People know what they do; they frequently know why they do what they do; but what they don't know is what what they do does' (cited in Dreyfus and Rabinow 1982: 187).

How a society lives in its youth

By way of conclusion, I want to stress that I am proposing a definition of bullying as a thought exercise that I consider compelling, and it is not meant to be a definition that claims any scientific grounding or legitimacy. However, I do call into question many of the prevailing definitions of bullying that profess to be scientifically valid. I have tried to present the difficulties posed by differences in language as well as national and cultural contexts in constructing a shared definition of bullying. I have questioned the method of applying a pre-formulated definition to a wide variety of actors as a strategy to gain a broad and complex understanding of the phenomenon of bullying. And I have challenged many of the assumptions made by the standard definitions that bear the imprint of Olweus's approach. But we can learn a great deal from reflections on definitions; amongst other things, definitions can teach us about ourselves.

I began this chapter with Colette Daiute's words that a society lives in its youth (Daiute et al. 2006). There are myriad ways in which the obstacles that children and youths face may express some of the core challenges within their societies. And foremost amongst these is how to live in a community with others. Bullying is a process that demonstrates such challenges of living in a group. I have proposed an approach to bullying that places it centrally within the core dynamics of ordinary group interactions. I have also suggested that, within the broad spectrum of processes by which groups constitute themselves, positions may emerge wherein individuals are assigned absolute otherness or treated as abject. In comparing bullying to psychic torture, I mean that the latter can be a useful lens through which to view the harms of bullying; these include humiliation and isolation and, in extreme cases, can contribute to the breakdown of an individual's sense of self. I am not suggesting that bullying is structurally similar to torture, since torture typically involves intended and/or authorised harm-doing, and I do not believe that these concepts are useful for understanding the central harms of bullying. However, a comparison between torture and bullying suggests that understanding extreme harms can be useful in capturing the destructive dimensions of ordinary harms like bullying.[14] And in bullying, being absolutely excluded

---

[14] I discuss the relationship between extreme and ordinary harms in Schott 2009a. The notion of abjection, which both Søndergaard and I apply here to the context of bullying, is also important in understanding torture. See Carsten Bagge Laustsen's discussion of torture (Laustsen 2007 and Diken and Laustsen 2005b).

from the group deprives an individual of the sense of meaning in life that is vital to social existence.[15]

Noting that extreme suffering can result from ordinary group interactions does not diminish our interest in reducing these harms. Nor does it blur the borders between bullying and group violence. Violence – whether motivated by racist, homophobic, sexist or sadistic impulses – involves a transgression of an individual's rights, and it should be morally and legally condemned.[16] But the approach I propose here enables us to view bullying, even in forms that lead to extreme isolation, as a process that involves ordinary children – not pathological, anti-social deviants – who interact together in ordinary – not dysfunctional – groups. As such, this approach enables us to grasp how bullying takes place and why it is such a common occurrence.

Nordic societies in particular put a great deal of emphasis on the social group or community. Smith and Morita have suggested that one reason why research on bullying has emerged from Scandinavian countries (especially Sweden, Norway and Finland) may be because of the 'generally high standard of living, peaceful nature, and concern for human rights and liberties' (in Smith et al. 1999: 2). They imply that the high standards of welfare states have made researchers quick to spot those who are left behind. But one could also play devil's advocate and ask whether there are specific aspects of Nordic culture that contribute to bullying. In Denmark, for example, children are typically together in the same class for up to ten years. One wonders: do schools need to strengthen the group in order to make sure that no one falls outside? Or do they need to weaken the group?

I would like to invite us to think about the second possibility. If groups are inherently based on dynamics of inclusion and exclusion, then it is impossible to strengthen the group so that no one falls outside. In fact, it could be argued that the stronger a group's identity, the more hard-and-fast the position of outsider would be as well. Since bullying takes place in the institutional environment of the school, where there are formal groups within which informal groups are configured, it may be important to strengthen the proliferation of informal group ties. In other words, if children have more opportunities to develop relationships across class and age groups, and on the basis of a wide range of interests and talents (e.g. in sports, music, writing, painting, theatre productions, technology,

[15] Claudia Card uses the notion of 'social death' to refer to the loss of relationships that create community, which is one of the central harms of genocide (Schott 2007: 71).
[16] Mikael Håfström's film *Evil* (2003), based on the Swedish novel *Ondskan* by Jan Guillous (1981), depicts acts of extreme violence rather than bullying.

etc.), then a wider social spectrum would be available to them. In such a context, a child's position inside or outside any informal group within the class may be less likely to become an all-or-nothing condition of his/her social self. Hence, the role of cultural and recreational activities both during and after school hours must be taken seriously as a way to address the problem of bullying. This approach is in accordance with David Galloway and Erling Roland's view that a direct anti-bullying strategy is not necessarily effective in the long term (Smith, Pepler and Rigby 2004: 38). Encouraging the formation of more small, informal groups at school could and should go hand-in-hand with an individual being able to identify with a large group on a more abstract level, such as the level of the school. When a large group is comprised of a multitude of heterogeneous small groups that each has the opportunity to speak and be heard, then the risk of group polarisation[17] is diminished. As noted by legal scholar Cass Sunstein, the more a heterogeneous society can expose its members to differing views, the more it avoids structures of self-insulation and the greater the possibility that 'heterogeneity, far from being a source of social fragmentation, will operate as a creative force...' (2000: 74, 119).

There is no way to avoid the vulnerability and risk of pain that life presents to us, either as children or adults. At best, we can try to be well-equipped to face the challenges we will encounter in our daily lives. Thus, the further education becomes oriented towards complex processes of understanding, the better equipped education will be to support children as they navigate the complexities they encounter, helping them to avoid the hazards of simple categorical us/them forms of moral thought. In this way, education can help children understand their own roles in bullying processes and realise how the children themselves may move in a grey zone wherein they contribute to the very processes that create harm. In this respect as well, specific anti-bullying strategies may be less important than the overall quality of the pedagogy and school environment. With the renewed worldwide interest in the work of Karl Marx, one might do well to recall his statement that, to change circumstances, it is essential to educate the educator himself [sic!] (Marx 1845). Researchers, educators and parents need to have a complex understanding of the processes of social life in order to avoid moralising attitudes about bullying that lock children into fixed and demeaning roles. Developing such complex understandings will help adults to help youths along the path towards a dignified future.

---

[17] With polarisation, groups have a tendency to adopt more extreme positions than those that were evident in the previous views of individual members.

3   Social exclusion anxiety: bullying and the forces that contribute to bullying amongst children at school

*Dorte Marie Søndergaard**

A dream

When I interviewed Sarah, a 12-year-old student, she told me about a recurring dream she had that always made her shake herself awake. Sarah was an enthusiastic player of the computer game *The Sims*, and her dream was set in a Sims scenario. *The Sims* is especially popular with girls: it offers a virtual world where each player creates characters, then designs and furnishes their houses, directs their moods, desires and relationships with each other, and organises the events and stories that are played out.

In her dream, Sarah was playing *The Sims* and simultaneously living as a Sims character within the game. She stood on top of a building, watching herself and her schoolmates run around its perimeter. They were trying to escape from something dangerous of a nature they did not know. It was black, and its presence could be sensed somewhere nearby, but she could not see whether it was a person or something else. The children fled in panic, and Sarah saw those at the back of the group disappear. She managed to keep ahead of the danger, but only by running as fast as she could and pushing others aside. At one point, she happened to knock over her best friend, cracking her friend's skull, but Sarah was unable to stop and help her. She continued to run while, at the same time, she was standing on top of the building, watching herself run with all of the others, who were also trampling her friend lying on the ground.

Then she would shake herself awake.

During one of my interviews with Sarah, I remarked that the atmosphere she had described in her classroom was reminiscent of the atmosphere in her dream. She replied, 'Yes, that's what it's like in my class – you

* This chapter was published as a shorter article in the *British Journal of Sociology in Education* 2012, and in Danish in Kofoed and Søndergaard (2009). Thanks to Bronwyn Davies for helping with its first translation from Danish to English.

47

never know when you're going to have to deal with something, but you have to be ready for it.'

Obviously, the events in Sarah's dream did not actually take place in her classroom, but the dream's images and moods illustrate Sarah's experience with *social exclusion anxiety* and *social panic*. The dream centred on 'something' intangible that threatens 'us' (i.e. the children in the class), making 'us' panic and act destructively towards each other. 'We' can't understand what this 'something' is, but 'we' react to it. Because of this threat, 'we' unwillingly do things that end up hurting 'us'. This thing affects 'our' social relations, which we are a part of and upon which 'we' depend, just as Sarah was dependent on both her friendship with another girl in the class and on the class as a whole.

An interesting element of the dream is the diffuse nature of the threat. It is 'something black', but the children in the dream cannot make out what it is. They cannot even determine whether it is a person, a monster, a force or something entirely different. It is simply 'something' that is 'black' and dangerous. Some children disappear, but it is impossible to see how it happens – perhaps they are captured or consumed or dissolved, or maybe they are absorbed into the black thing. They just disappear. There is a menace of destruction, the separation of those who remain and panic from those who disappear or are about to disappear.

The focus of the chapter and its empirical basis

The purpose of this chapter is to introduce a *thinking technology*[1] that will foster a deeper understanding of some of the more complicated social processes that emerge in the day-to-day functioning of a school classroom, with a particular focus on the interactions that culminate in bullying. The concepts I work with are *the need for belonging, social exclusion anxiety* and *the production of contempt and dignity* by both children and adults. I develop a new definition of bullying, drawing upon Judith Butler's (1999) concept of 'abjection' as well as Karen Barad's concept of 'intra-acting forces' (2007). My definition in this chapter contributed to the shorter definition of bullying in the Introduction (see pages 16–17), but it is more fully developed here in relation to the types of mechanisms and processes involved. Barad's term 'intra-action' helps draw attention to the mutually transformative effects of the many entangling forces that are involved in the enactment of bullying

---

[1] I use the term 'thinking technology' (Haraway 1992) here to signify something different from theory. As I elaborate on later in this chapter, a thinking technology is more fluid because it is shaped by and shapes the field of study it sets out to examine.

practices, and the chapter ends with a description of a few of these forces and how they may entangle.

To develop an alternative thinking technology, I draw upon observations of schoolchildren and interviews with them about bullying and social life. The research in this study was produced as part of a comprehensive five-year study of bullying.[2] Data is still being gathered, but at the time of writing, it has included interviews with approximately one hundred students between the ages of 8 and 14, and interviews with parents, teachers and school principals, together with interviews with educators from fifty recreation centres. In addition, observations were made of the children during class, at recess and at the recreation centres where they play video games. These interviews and observations (Chase 1995; Gubrium et al. 2003; Haavind 2005; Søndergaard 2002) have enabled analyses of subjectification processes (Davies 2000; Søndergaard 2005a), analyses of patterns in how children and adults act and relate to each other within schools and analyses of the enactment of bullying practices among children.[3] I conducted interviews and made observations with the help of two research assistants, K. Høgsbro and D. D. Christoffersen. Sarah was one of my respondents, and I use her story as an analytic point of departure for the theoretical and conceptual development in this chapter.

The predominant trends in bullying research have been inspired by Dan Olweus (1973, 1993), who argues that bullying is a consequence of individual aggression conducted with the intention to harm. Bullying is still widely conceptualised in terms of individual or family pathology (for a critical discussion, see Bansel et al. 2009; Galloway and Roland 2004; Meyer 2007a; the Introduction, page 1, and Schott, Chapter 2, page 21). Bullying positions are most often considered to be stable over time and are ascribed to the particular personalities of the bullies as well as the victims. Of course, there are alternative conceptions of bullying (see the Introduction, page 1, and in particular Schott, Chapter 2, page 21, for a review and analysis), but the Olweusian formulation of bullying tends to be dominant in both scholarly research on bullying as well as in intervention programmes and research (Farrington and Ttofi 2009). Still, in recent years, an increasing number of researchers have called for sociological and social–psychological analyses of the phenomenon (see, for example, Bansel et al. 2009; Eriksson et al. 2002; Meyer 2007a). This chapter contributes one such social–psychological perspective on the issue.

---

[2] The study is part of the research project 'Exploring Bullying in Schools' (eXbus), which was financed from 2007 to 2012 by the Tryg Foundation in Denmark.
[3] Analyses based on this data have also been published in Søndergaard (2008, 2009, 2011 and 2013) as well as Højgaard et al. (2012).

Sarah's class negotiates norms for acceptance and inclusion

I have chosen to focus first on Sarah's class because it was characterised by an extremely high level of social exclusion anxiety plus continual mutual evaluations between the children. Sarah's class cannot be considered to be a 'typical' class in any generalisable sense, but it is useful to bring in as a case because the dynamics I want to explore were obvious. Later, I focus on other cases to draw out the analysis.

The children in Sarah's class designated narrow paths of 'appropriate' and 'inappropriate'[4] to each other. It took only a split-second for them to read each other's behaviour, interests and artefacts (i.e. clothes, bags, mobile phones, etc.), and they negotiated norms of appropriateness through petty arguing, mutual appraisal and the appraisal of others. Such evaluations and judgements are typical and occur in all school classes, but their nature varies greatly from one social setting to another. Schoolchildren use a variety of means to evaluate each other: they talk about other children in the same class or in other classes at school; they discuss media representations of other children and young people in the virtual profiles on social-networking websites; or they discuss representations in music videos, the performances of different bands and singers, and performers in television series, films, talent shows and reality shows. This variety of images and discourses provides numerous opportunities to negotiate appropriate and inappropriate appearances, behaviours, movements and equipment,[5] and these negotiations blend into parallel negotiations with parents, siblings and other participants in the children's social arenas.

In Sarah's class, as in many of the other school classes in our project, topics such as which clothes someone would choose were central to evaluations of appropriate or inappropriate appearance. Thus, when an interviewer asked why Jessica had left the class and changed schools, it seemed to be quite natural and sufficient for one of the girls to answer: 'Well, she really didn't fit in with our class. You should have seen her pants! I don't think she could have been happy in our class. She wore those pants with wide bottoms!'

---

[4] The conceptualisation of 'appropriate' and 'inappropriate' as used by Haraway (1992) is close to Butler's concept of the 'culturally intelligible' and 'cultural recognition' (1999) as developed and applied in, for instance, Søndergaard (1996, 2002).

[5] For analyses of negotiations of appropriateness, see Cawood Højgaard (2007); Davies (2000); Gulbrandsen (2003); Haavind (2003); Juelskjær (2009); Kofoed (2008a); Kofoed and Staunæs (2007); Petersen (2009); Skjær Ulvik (2005); Staunæs (2009); Søndergaard (2002, 2005a, 2008); and Thorne (1993).

Exhibiting artefacts – such as wearing trousers with the 'right' leg width – functions as a sign of respect for the community to which one belongs or wishes to be a part. In addition to other elements that I discuss later, exhibiting artefacts affirms the tastes, values and priorities through which community members confirm their reciprocal allegiance to each other. Discussions about the correct brand of hair-wax for boys, the correct and incorrect ways to be funny or wearing 'sad' t-shirts from the supermarket are thus far from arbitrary and indifferent. They constitute positioning tools within the social–emotional landscape in which the children manoeuvre, where inclusion and marginalisation forge pathways and movements that evoke both hope and fear.[6]

In this context, parents who reject the significance of, for instance, a new pair of trousers at a particular time, of a particular brand and with a particular leg width can, in their children's eyes, mark the parents as 'just not getting it'. The children see their parents as neither understanding nor able to respect that it may be a matter of social life or death if this material artefact is withheld from them. The trousers are a tool with which to hail their group, their community, and which they see as a necessity for social survival. In this situation, matter communicates in very direct ways.

Socio-economic class is a relevant factor in this equation. In many school contexts, it takes substantial financial resources to maintain children's access to the artefacts, activities, experiences and hairstyles that can enable or optimise their inclusion in the group. In alignment with Bourdieu's concept of 'cultural capital' (1979), inclusion also requires the ability and readiness to familiarise oneself with the current norms of appropriateness as they materialise via the concept of taste. However, access to the 'correct' artefacts does not in itself guarantee inclusion: the social manoeuvring within a group of children may (to a greater or lesser extent) follow a pattern in which the meaning of a particular artefact changes radically once it becomes adopted by 'inappropriate' individuals. In other words, the opportunity to signal appropriateness by wearing the right kind of trousers may be missed by the child who, for the moment, is positioned as marginalised. If the situation is particularly precarious, the excluded child may risk that the meaning of a specific style of trousers will change as soon as he/she is seen wearing them at school. The conditions for appropriateness within the group in which the child is striving to be included may be swiftly reconfigured according to the patterns of inclusion/exclusion, even though they were initially legitimated based on the taste for a certain style of trousers, or a particular ringtone or type of mobile phone.

[6] See Davies and Harré (1990) for more on the concept of 'positioning'.

Thus, the children in Sarah's class assess, condemn and despise whilst they simultaneously admire and imitate. Sarah herself suffers as a result of this practice and also actively participates in it. She is burdened by the production of contempt that is mutually circulating, but she is also invested in maintaining it as a participant in the process.

In the same class, two pairs of girls were sharply opposed to each other – the best friends Emily and Chloe on one side, and the best friends Olivia and Sophie on the other. Emily protected herself and her relationship with Chloe by maintaining distance from and expressing contempt for Olivia and Sophie. The appraisal of Olivia and Sophie was mostly linked to how both girls – but especially Olivia – related to others in the class. Olivia, according to the appraisal, spent too much time with the boys and her edges were too sharp, even in her relationship with Sophie, whom the other children considered far too submissive and subordinate to Olivia.

When a new girl, Lily, joined the class after moving from another school because of bullying, the children closely studied her and her social manoeuvring. For a few weeks, all the girls held their breath as they watched how Lily approached the groupings. But one day, Olivia said something about someone wearing 'a sad jacket', and Lily looked hurt. This was a signal to Emily and Chloe, who brought the new girl into their circle. They ate lunch with her and hung out together during breaks. Lily had demonstrated potential for marking a distance to Olivia and her 'subordinates', as they called Sophie and a few others; before long, Lily joined in the explicit assessments of Olivia as 'insanely irritating' and 'just so different from us'. Lily's place was assured for a while. The period of renegotiating the girls' groupings was nerve-wracking until everyone fell into place. These negotiations impacted several other girls, including Sarah.

From 'girl nonsense' to the need for a new thinking technology

Sarah, Emily, Olivia and the others were active in the production of these manoeuvrings. Generally, when such manoeuvres become visible to adults, they are often dismissed as 'girl nonsense' – rendering the events at once intangible (as part of the mystique of girlhood), inexorable (because nothing can be done about gender, which is thought to be driven by the primordial force of biology itself) and consequently difficult to approach if change is desired (Davies 2000; Gulbrandsen 2003; Haavind 2003).

However, if the problems cannot be classified under the heading 'girl nonsense', the next move is often an attempt to explain the phenomenon as provoked by the presence of particularly scheming personalities. A process is thus initiated to identify the scheming aggressors on one side and, on the other, the vulnerable victims or those children who are treated especially unfairly by their peers. The progression of this identification process depends significantly on the voices involved – children's, parents', teachers' – and on which events or moments are chosen as the basis for gauging 'the truth' of the situation. Was it the day when Emma sent a hateful Arto[7] message (which can be produced as evidence) or was it the day when Grace came home crying because her jacket had been torn to pieces (which can also be produced as evidence)? Or was it that particular incident in the first grade that no-one can remember exactly but which is always raised as the point in time when the evil originated (and here, it's difficult to produce evidence)? Or perhaps the time when Jack was sent home from summer camp (and where the evidence produced in connection with blame for Megan's ruined shoes never found legitimacy amongst those implicated)? When the power of definition has been adjusted to final positions and the culprits have been singled out and identified, the recourse may be behaviour-regulating forms of intervention. And the adults want to talk about consequences and punishments, make agreements to change behaviour, etc.

This is the typical course of events. However, there may be ways to understand the destructive social–emotional interactions other than with the generic label of 'girl nonsense' or individualising investigations and problematisation. An alternative to the individualising and behaviour-regulating approach might take its point of departure via a new type of inquiry that moves away from the usual questions: Who's to blame? Who started it? What's wrong with Emily and Olivia? Who is the victim and who is the aggressor? Instead, we might ask: Why does Emily see it as unquestionably necessary to maintain contempt for Olivia and vice versa? What makes it imperative for the children to conduct this type of social–emotional manoeuvring? What kinds of hope on the one hand and perceived threats on the other feed into the movements within the social space – not only of these two girls, but on the part of all the other children in the class? This is where the concept of social exclusion anxiety can be introduced as one of the key concepts of an alternative thinking technology that might be more productive in trying to understand the intra-activity of bullying.[8]

---

[7] During the period of this study, the Danish social website Arto was the most popular with children; it contained many of the same features as Facebook.

[8] The mechanisms and affects that are nurtured by social exclusion anxiety all need concrete empirical investigation, regardless of whether they take the form of demonisation, idealisation, revenge, helplessness, specific fear, misunderstandings, envy, over-involvement, distortion of personal narratives, etc.

Social exclusion anxiety

In this context, 'social exclusion anxiety' should not be confused with 'social phobia', a clinical psychological concept that focuses on the individual and refers to a psychological phobic state. Because social phobia is sometimes called social anxiety, it is necessary to carefully demarcate the way in which I develop this term. 'Social exclusion anxiety' builds on a social–psychological concept of human beings as existentially dependent on social embeddedness (Søndergaard 1996, 2000, 2005b).[9] The assumption that people need this kind of community belonging is highlighted in order to focus on the anxiety that arises when social embeddedness becomes jeopardised and a person's hope and longing to be part of a community is threatened.

In existential psychology, the concept of 'angst', which is sometimes translated as 'anxiety', is taken from the work of Søren Kierkegaard, amongst others; it is applied to an individual's existential angst as it relates to basic questions about mortality and loneliness. In Danish, 'social exclusion angst' (*social eksklusionsangst*) can be used without necessarily referring to an individualising connotation; however, in English, the term 'anxiety' more adequately conveys the thinking technology that I develop here. There are certainly similarities between the existentialists' term 'angst' and my 'social exclusion anxiety'. Both point to a basic human affect and/or emotion, but the existentialists' term focuses on an individual's experience, whereas my concept underlines the angst/anxiety that is a feature of the necessary social dimensions of human existence. The focus is not on biological death, but rather, social death. Further, social exclusion anxiety is potentially an affect that circulates amongst members of a group, and it is generated through the intra-action of many forces: social, cultural, discursive, material (Barad 2007). In this sense, affect and/or emotion are removed from a merely individual realm and reconfigured as fundamentally social.

Social exclusion anxiety emerges in relation to communities of belonging. It is a fear that smoulders beneath the surface when people

---

[9] The assumption that the human individual is fundamentally a social and cultural being is found in a number of theoretical traditions: activity theory, cultural psychology, social anthropology, socio-cultural theory, critical psychology and post-structuralist thinking, amongst others. Although the weight of and the tendency to emphasise the universal aspect of this assumption is different in each of the conceptualisations, the idea is basically the same: human beings are dependent on/man is made through social/cultural embeddedness; alternatively, human creation happens through discourse, subjectification, etc. See also Eriksson et al. (2002) for a suggestion about how this kind of thinking could be relevant to the analysis of bullying.

interact. When people expect or are expected to become part of groups or communities – whether within the formal environments of educational institutions, workplaces or in certain family contexts, or through more informal processes related to leisure-time activities, friendship groups or different types of familial arrangements – then there is a possibility that someone's belonging may be questioned. Individuals may feel pressure and insecurity about whether they legitimately belong to this particular group or whether they risk being excluded and marginalised.

The risk of being judged unworthy to belong to the group – or of a small, local group being judged unworthy to belong to the greater community – is possible in every social context. It is not the only possibility: the hope of inclusion and the anticipated joy and pride at being included are also present. But the possibility of being judged unworthy is part of the equation. And with this possibility, an anxiety follows – social exclusion anxiety. It depends on many things whether the anxiety is mitigated by and absorbed into the eagerness to be included, or whether the curiosity about and openness to the possibilities of belonging flare into an unmistakable anxiety that has its potentiality near the actualisation of exclusion and unworthiness; in other words, the anxiety itself may eventually feed the processes of exclusion and lead to a loss of dignity.

At this point in the argument, however, if we draw a simplified map of some of the emotions that guide the children in being able to manage the tension between inclusion in and exclusion from the group, then the emotions about exclusion and meaninglessness are about feeling unknown, not-seen, socially threatened and deprived of worthiness. On the other side, the emotions connected to inclusion are about feeling accepted, seen, acknowledged and included, and consequently experiencing worthiness and meaningfulness. There are undoubtedly numerous emotional nuances in and around these two positions, but in this outline of the thinking technology, a simplified account will suffice.

In this sense, feelings of meaningfulness and worthiness become evaluative emotions connected to acknowledgement and legitimacy within the group.[10] This explains the priorities of Ryan, another boy from Sarah's school. Ryan perceived being accepted by the gang of boys who hung out down by the railway station and participating in their shady activities to be meaningful and worthwhile – certainly more so than his lessons at school and especially with Joanne, the teacher who constantly criticised him. Joanne's contempt for Ryan did not have to compete for

---

[10] This is not to say that dignity and meaningfulness cannot constitute emotions linked to evaluation in other aspects of life. Here, their evaluative power is emphasised in relation to social participation.

long with the gang's mutual production of worthiness before Ryan started to experience meaningfulness with the boys at the railway station rather than the context of school. I return to Ryan later in the chapter.

As already suggested, there are a number of ancillary concepts to the thinking technology wherein social exclusion anxiety is an anchoring concept. Several of these suggest the need to develop an analytical approach to examine the tension between deprivations as well as constructions of dignity. The concepts of 'contempt production' and 'dignity production' – and the transition between them – constitute an important part of the bullying dynamic being explored. By extension, it is important to understand the kinds of dignity and worthiness that various children and adults strive to build, and the kinds of deprivations of dignity they try to avoid. This applies both to an individual like Ryan who plays truant and to a teacher like Joanne who criticises him. It is important to realise that the 'dignity projects' of related individuals may collide, and a deprivation of dignity severely harms both children and adults. Finally, it is worth mentioning that pride about successful dignity projects may produce a generosity to include others; however, this success and pride may also be blind to the potential inclusion wishes of others who are (for the moment) positioned as 'unworthy'.

The negotiation of terms for inclusion, which may be connected to projects of dignity and worthiness, are often hidden in seemingly unrelated discussions about taste in clothes, hairstyles, music, films, hobbies, etc., as well as in the constant mutual appraisals that occur with or without the participation of the parties being assessed. When children describe the activities commonly referred to as 'talking behind somebody's back' and 'backstabbing' as something humiliating and threatening, it should be noted that these activities are not merely cases where someone hurts someone else to maintain the social order.

'Backstabbing' can be the result of many types of tensions within a group, and the hidden social–emotional manoeuvrings of backstabbing may accommodate potential effects, such as the unworthiness of certain others and positioning these others as illegitimate and irrelevant to the community. However, an even more threatening experience is when the 'backstabbing' simultaneously contains a negotiation of the conditions for inclusion, twisting the norms of appropriateness that have informed and orientated the targets of the 'backstabbing' up until that point. The norms may be changed and thus cancel out previous norms, leaving the one who was 'backstabbed' without an opportunity to reorient themselves, let alone to influence the potential direction of change. To ignore these manoeuvrings, as adults often advise children to do, is at best a neutralising show of strength by the offended party. At worst, trying to ignore these manoeuvrings can result in disorientation and confusion about the rules at play within the group.

It is important to realise that backstabbing *need not* consciously contain these aspects. In the accounts given by the children, backstabbing was practised by both centrally positioned and marginalised actors. Backstabbing may be used as a form of retribution with the intent to produce a 'better balance' by 'hurting back'. But 'talking about' someone can also be used as part of the work to construct a coherent narrative about the group as well as the positions and actions of individuals. In this case, backstabbing is a kind of side-effect associated with the central purpose, which uses narrative means to make sense of what is going on around 'us' in 'our' class.

Social panic and the production of contempt: on the road to bullying

As mentioned earlier, the feeling of worthiness is closely linked to feeling accepted as a part of something – to being included in a community. And the concept is closely connected to the existential need for social embeddedness – the necessity of belonging. But then, how can we understand the mechanisms that are set in motion when the production of dignity within a school class goes wrong? As I said before, this question cannot be answered in any generalised and abstract way, since the mechanisms that are activated – and the questions about how this happens and what effects they have on children and adults – must always be investigated empirically and locally.

But nevertheless, with the thinking technology that I develop here, I allow myself to point out a few of the mechanisms that seem to recur across the empirical data recorded in the eXbus project. For example, it appears as though the production of contempt for and judgement of someone or something in the community may provide temporary relief from the social exclusion anxiety that characterises the climate of many school classes – and the production of contempt is interesting to understand a bit more closely in relation to the type of processes that many would recognise as bullying.

The central mechanism seems to work this way: if a group of individuals agree that some individuals, activities or things are repulsive, creepy and/ or disgusting whilst others are 'seriously cool', then it becomes possible to experience a sense of community and consensus in the shared assessment that 'we' and 'our' interests are not creepy and disgusting. It is not what 'we' use, have and are that is despicable; it is not our mobile phones, clothes, hobbies or tastes that get a thumbs-down. Perhaps this strategy will provide 'us' with security for a while. Perhaps 'we' can be strong enough in 'our' shared contempt to ensure that the hunt for something to despise will not target us and what we represent. Perhaps we can anticipate setting the terms for what can be targeted, thereby guaranteeing our own safety and long-term social belonging.

Quite unreflectively, this is how the social–emotional reasoning seems to coalesce as part of the social–emotional manoeuvrings that occur in groups saturated with social insecurity. Still, the alleviation of anxiety that results from contempt production seems to last only temporarily. In fact, the production of contempt, which should relieve social exclusion anxiety, may exacerbate it. And an escalation of social exclusion anxiety requires more alleviation and prompts further efforts within the group to gain control.

In this context, the concept of 'social panic' does become relevant. If anxiety is merely latent, then there remains a possibility to empathise with the relatively despised persons – or at least a willingness to understand some of their experiences and interpretations of themselves, others and the situation itself. When a despised student weeps, those who are temporarily socially secure may feel compassion or merely dispassionate indifference. As Lauren said when she was asked whether she ever considered befriending Conor, who apparently cried every day: 'You can't help lonely boys.' She understood perfectly well that he was suffering as a result of being the object of the other boys' constant rejection, but she didn't connect her ability to feel sorry for Conor with the possibility to change the situation by including him in her own social group or simply giving him acknowledgement from her own position as a socially secure girl.

However, a shift seems to take place from this state of relative understanding to a situation where the dignity-producing empathy closes down. At this intersection, contempt strengthens and dehumanisation increases to a degree conducive to the actions we recognise as bullying. As this movement occurs, we see that social exclusion anxiety turns into social panic, followed by an intensified production of contempt. The anxiety builds and seeks assuagement, the contempt production seeks a target – and one day, the group turns its focus to that child who has been *so* annoying in *just* that way for *so* long: 'Did you all see what he was doing? Did you see it? You know he said this and did that?' and 'Now that's enough...now he just has to be stopped.' Thus, the situation can deteriorate. It may also happen without words, as a choreography of actions and movements within a group that perceives an opportunity to reduce the discomfort of their anxiety through producing contempt, directing their loathing and taking destructive control.

This is not the only way that bullying practices emerge, nor is it the only route to attacks and possible violence. Another route might be via anxiety-alleviating strategies that identify a target who represents something desirable, yet contemptible – as, for example, when third-grade boys look up to those in the fourth grade who are bigger, capable of much more and apparently secure in their social embeddedness, which invites respect. But then the younger boys notice an older boy who does not have a central place in the attractive fourth-grade culture; this boy may become a target of attack. The boy who lacks the status attached to the positioning of 'big boy' – with the visible production of worthiness that follows – must be destroyed; or more precisely, the position of unworthiness itself must be destroyed, and this means the child who holds that positioning.

Another route may occur via anxiety-alleviating strategies that seek out a target within their own group: someone who, to a pronounced degree, actualises the vulnerability and exposure that the group members share and fear most. This vulnerability must be destroyed; or more precisely, the position of vulnerability must be destroyed, and this means the child who holds that positioning. This place also holds the germ of an escalating process because the more vulnerable a child becomes due to being destroyed, the more destruction is required to alleviate the discomfort that comes from the actualisation of such vulnerability. And if the child temporarily steadies him/herself, it may become necessary to test whether he/she is stable enough. Andrew described a child in another class, saying with surprise, 'It's as if he *has to* cry every day. Even though he looks happy one day and doesn't do anything to them, they still go at him and don't stop until he cries.' In this sense, there are many possibilities for empirical nuances and additional analytical specifications.

In such situations, certain children may be picked on and attacked in ways that are so obvious that adults are bound to react. As with many other classes, Sarah's experienced a number of physical assaults that were brought on by social panic. In direct response to these events, the school administrators, teachers, and other adults sometimes used the term 'bullying' – they described and understood these particular events as 'bullying'. But they did not use the word 'bullying' during other, lengthy periods that were characterised by varying levels of indirect aggression and contempt production meant to ostracise and exclude someone in the school class. Such processes were largely invisible to the adults, and when they were noticed, they tended to be placed in the aforementioned category of 'girl nonsense' or dismissed with essentialising comments like 'Boys will be boys' or 'Boys fight and do things to enforce their hierarchies.'

However, children often actively try to keep many of these relational praxes and events hidden from adults; as many of the children related to us, these situations often became much worse when adults got involved. They explained that the grown-ups had no idea what was going on. Besides, they told us, a child who speaks to the adults risks being called a 'tattletale' by the others: exposing these processes to the inquiring gaze – and possible involvement – of adults is not received kindly. And, according to the children, once adults get involved, the situation often becomes uncontrollable; it is hard to know what definitions and categorisations the adults will come up with, who they will determine to be the victim(s) and aggressor(s), and who they will decide to punish. But there are even more complications: the children told us that if the adults disagree with each other, then there will be weeping or furious mothers and irascible or humiliated fathers, and all sorts of other issues that must be managed while a child is trying to manoeuvre through his/her own collective and individual problems. Reading across these accounts in the empirical data, the processes seem to include doubling and reflecting movements, which make the children's and adults' interpretations and conflicts appear to intertwine, distort and muddle each other. This is where children often feel like a situation is becoming even more unmanageable.

Varying positions and varying recognitions

Both direct and indirect forms of aggression result from social exclusion anxiety. However, adults are primarily inclined to notice direct aggression. When it is also possible to identify a relatively passive and helpless victim, we tend to see a situation that adults recognise as 'bullying'. But if the victim reacts and actively strikes back, either physically or verbally, then the term 'bullying' seems to lose its relevance to the adult observers (Søndergaard 2008).

Therefore, it appeared reasonable for Thomas's mother to urge her humiliated and outraged son to remain completely passive and silent when a gang of boys who had been harassing him for two years sent text messages calling him 'a fucking pansy' and saying they were just 'waiting to cut off his balls'. Thomas's mother advised him to refrain from responding to them, insisting that he simply go to school and be friendly to everyone. In her attempts to activate the bullying category to elicit help from the school, Thomas's mother realised that if this strategy were to succeed, then Thomas had to act within precise parameters: he must refrain from responding and reacting. However, Thomas's parents did not agree on this issue. One day, when the boys were goading Thomas in his father's presence, his father yelled at them; and in doing so, he de-legitimated Thomas's chances of being recognised as a 'victim of bullying'. The school authorities reacted by saying there was 'fault on both sides'. Thomas was not acknowledged as a victim of bullying and 'unfortunately, the school cannot help'. Thomas eventually changed schools.

In other words, the direct aggression towards a victim who remains passive is most likely to be noticed by adults because it is more accessible to their way of thinking. Indirect relational aggression can be far more difficult for adults to comprehend and, although it is by no means less destructive, it requires far more comprehensive evidence to be presented if the child or his/her parents wish to use the term 'bullying' to elicit a reaction from the school (see Hein, page 301). There can be both direct and indirect relational aggression in a school class, which runs parallel to both the stable and changeable positionings of children within it.

This was the case with 12-year-old Alex's school class. For over two years, Alex had continually been the target. Fatty Alex, Clumpy Alex, Creepy Alex: these were some of the names he was called during the worst of it. But Alex was one of the children who was not recognised as a victim of exclusion because, amongst other things, he reacted with anger when he felt humiliated by the others.

The teachers certainly recognised that there were problems, and they resolved to take an active stance, but with the thinking technologies available to them, they determined that Alex himself was the root of the problem. To them, he became a child whose behaviour needed to be regulated with 'consistency and punishment'. Sometimes he was referred to as 'a difficult child with special needs'. Thus, for a certain period, Alex was assigned a fixed position as the one excluded from the group. Over time, names like 'Fatty Alex' functioned as the focus of the children's production of contempt, which both alleviated and sustained the social exclusion anxiety within the class.

The adults' reaction to Alex supported his classmates' production of contempt. By attributing personal responsibility to Alex for the clashes, the adults involved in these judgements contributed to the ongoing dissolution of his dignity. Furthermore, they managed to convince Alex's mother to adopt their definition of the problem. As a result, Alex was rather alone in the world during his first years at school.

When we met Alex, however, he had managed to extract himself from the position he was assigned by the class, and he talked about this situation as something that gave him an enormous sense of relief. Yet he still felt very pressured by the adults not regarding his position as conducive to the production of dignity. In his experience, if there were problems within the classroom, the teacher would always glance in his direction. And in the interview with Alex's teacher, it came out that she considered him to be a child who created problems and, at the same time, a boy who angled for adult contact in a clingy way. From the adult perspective, the teacher experienced Alex's attempts to produce dignity as unpleasant and inappropriate relational ambitions.

However, Alex's positioning was not the only exclusionary practice within this class. The classroom had become the scene of seemingly sudden attacks on children whom neither teachers nor parents would have guessed were at risk. The adults were shocked. The term 'bullying' was used, and the adults reacted by punishing the children who were considered to be the most active in the confrontations. However, the children who had contributed to the intensification of contempt leading up to the physical attacks – but who were not actually present when these acts of aggression occurred – remained invisible actors in the bullying scenario, and they were not included in the adults' condemnation and punitive reactions.

But Alex's class is also an example of a school class that perpetually sets the stage for anxiety, which reverberates throughout the group and generates a continual hunt for something or someone to despise. The level of noise is high. The jokes that the group finds funniest are sharply personal and ridiculing. There is a constant stream of contemptuous appraisal via text messages and the available online social-networking websites. The children struggle against each other in their attempts to gain control through reciprocal definitions of and conditions for humiliation. And the positions change: there are variations in who is assigned the position of being excluded and who is chosen as the primary target of contempt and humiliation. Very few in the class can feel certain that they will not be involved – at some point and for an unknown amount of time, they could be struck by the production of contempt that they themselves are invested in reproducing.

Defining bullying: a conceptual–technological challenge

If positioning practices vary so widely, then how and when is it possible to speak of bullying? There are several factors that the definition must accommodate. Firstly, there are *fixed positions* – regardless of whether they refer to a division into the expected and unambiguous positions of 'aggressor' and 'victim' or, as in the example with Alex, a child is positioned as a recognisable victim since he loses his temper and strikes back. Secondly, there are situations that include *sudden attacks*, which can perhaps happen once or several times; and thirdly, there are *variable practices of inclusion and exclusion*, where it becomes almost impossible to firmly assign the labels 'aggressor' and 'victim'.[11] Considering these factors, does the concept of 'bullying' become both too narrow and too broad to apply? And if the concept is so difficult, then how can we address a problem that few would deny exists?

Scholars have outlined the difficulties associated with the current definitions of bullying and in producing a workable definition of bullying as an actual phenomenon (Bansel et al. 2009; Ellwood and Davies 2010; Meyer 2007a; Shariff 2008). Nevertheless, and despite these definitional difficulties, I suggest some possible paths to follow in developing a clearer definition of bullying. These proposals have been inspired by my reflections about social exclusion anxiety as the anchor for a new thinking technology within this field.

A research praxis that uniquely isolates and fixes meaning has both advantages and disadvantages, especially when applied to the phenomenon of bullying. Given its operational transparency and applicability, this kind of definition has obvious advantages, because it determines which aspects of the phenomenon (e.g. relational asymmetry, repetition, particular character traits, a specific intention, etc.) must be present for it to be recognised as 'bullying'. From there, the researcher, teacher or parent can simply follow the manual: once the problem and different individuals' roles are identified, then one is prompted to move on to the next section in the manual about sanctions.

However, the obvious drawback of this definitional praxis is its blindness to the forms of exclusion, contempt production and relational destruction that the definition does not recognise or reveal with similar ease. This definition does not help us see relational nuances and complexities. Individuals identified as victims are understood simply as victims, and individuals identified as aggressors merely as aggressors – but these characterisations may be far from the whole story about the becoming of them and their relationship. It is even more troubling that such a fixed definition may inhibit an understanding of the situation that would allow these individuals and their respective groups to move on. Furthermore, those who struggle in the blurred positions of 'aggressive victims' or 'excluded aggressors' – as well as those who simply struggle to survive

---

[11] See also Kofoed, Chapter 7, page 159, for more about the attention given to displaced positionings in bullying as an alternative to focusing only on fixed positions with regard to the bully, the bullied and the bystanders. Additionally, for many years, Christina Salmivalli and her colleagues have incorporated more roles into their thinking on bullying, yet this ambition tends to remain (as indicated by the choice of the concept 'role') linked to a definition of a fixed yet expanded number of categories; see e.g., Salmivalli et al. (1996).

socially in a context characterised by intense fighting for social inclusion – tend to fall outside the boundaries of focus that the definition delineates. These individuals will quickly be perceived as irrelevant shadows in the field of the problem, or perhaps identified as mere bystanders: 'actors' who might be roused to fight on the side of the victim in this landscape that contains fixed definitions of victims and aggressors. In other words, such a fixed-definition praxis creates a risk that we – adults, children and researchers – may gain a conceptual tool that impedes the development of analyses and understandings of everyday life that are nuanced and sensitive.

In the empirical material produced by the research team in our eXbus project (see note 2 above), we find another complication related to fixed definitions. When the phenomenon of bullying is subject to a fixed definition, it seems to gain a self-validating force. For example, the definition might be used reciprocally as ammunition amongst children as well as adults, and it may activate a completely new evasive praxis or escalate the conflicts ('She called me a bully, and she'll have to pay for that' or 'If you call my son a bully, there's nothing more to discuss. I'll go straight to the principal and tell him that. . .'). With a very rigid definition of bullying, the parties involved may resort to using the definition to serve their own tactical means and as a tool to confirm their positionings. When this happens, the definition does not allow them to gain insights into the children's actual social–emotional experiences and the possible effects of the participants' manoeuvres on them. It also does not allow insights into how this process both produces and excludes other relational possibilities. We have also seen cases where school administrators tend to use the rigid definition of bullying to improve the reputation of their schools: anything that doesn't correspond to the very narrow definition of it cannot be acknowledged as 'bullying', which thereby helps to reduce the number of such cases and improve the statistics on the school's website.

One area of research interest is clearly prompted by these considerations; specifically, the investigation of how such a definitional praxis delineates the premises of thinking technologies and appropriate forms of intervention. Who utilises the concept, how do they use it and what are the effects of its usage on certain children, adults and social problems? Following Carol Lee Bacchi (1999, 2009), one might ask how the problems (i.e. acts of bullying) are represented in the relevant conceptualisation, and with what consequences? Who is singled out as a problem? Bacchi advises us to question which assumptions underlie the representation, which praxes are made possible by this representation and with what effects. Then, given this representation, what is left unproblematised? And finally, what would the reactions look like if a different representation had been developed and applied?

Research into the constituting effects of definitional praxes in connection to bullying is very important. However, if we want to improve our understanding of how the phenomenon is perceived, experienced and retold by children – including their accounts of the bullying and exclusion practices as well as all the struggles, contempt and anxiety about being left out – then we must consider aspects of the problem other than the (re)constituting movements of the bullying concept.

To do this, I draw upon Karen Barad's conception of phenomena as real effects of previous and present 'onto–epistemological processes' (2007). Barad emphasises a need to dissolve the divide between ontology and epistemology. This dissolution is aided by her concept of 'intra-activity' amongst discursive and material enactments. According to Barad, the real effects must be understood as the effects of intra-active forces[12] that constantly blend and weave together; the forces' real effects maintain ongoing processes of reconstitution. In this formulation, there is no claim that discourse constitutes either materiality or the subject, nor that materiality constitutes the subject or discourse. Instead, the assertion is that all of these elements – and more – must be understood in their reciprocal entanglements and enactments (Højgaard and Søndergaard 2011; Søndergaard 2013b). 'The world' is always infiltrated by and implicated in 'understandings' of 'the world'. For the same reason, in any intra-action between 'the world' and 'understanding', determinism in either direction is cancelled out.

As researchers, we can conceive of our scholarly contributions as thinking technologies that are developed in close intra-action with the material–discursive empirical material. Our contributions also enter into intra-action and, over time, they become enacting forces in the machinery from which the empirical material has been derived. Our conceptual models and definitions of phenomena like bullying evolve through an analytical praxis, which itself intra-acts with a number of mutually infiltrated phenomena: empirical data and their representations of practices and local discourses about everyday life; popular psychological discourses about the types of practices seen in the empirical material; subjectification processes amongst the adults and children involved (Davies 2000; Søndergaard 2002, 2005a); and finally, scientifically produced and analytically generated thinking technologies

---

[12] Barad speaks of 'intra-activity' instead of 'interactivity' to emphasise that intra-action enacts new phenomena; it is not simply movements between discrete phenomena that remain intact (2007). She goes on to discuss material–discursive intra-actions, hyphenating materiality and discourse in order to argue that these elements can never be understood apart from each other: they will always be intra-active in any phenomenon (see also Søndergaard 2013b).

developed to grasp the phenomena. In this entanglement of intra-active forces, there is no point from which anyone can proclaim that they are the ultimate and elevated witness to truth (Haraway 1992). With this approach, the validity of research is found in its value as a productive thinking technology related to the understanding of processes and complexities – and these should be estimated and evaluated by the participants: researchers, subjects, practitioners, etc.

Emily, Olivia, Alex, Thomas's mother, teachers, school administrators, politicians and we as researchers can all agree that there are problems between some children. And because the conceptual models have thus far not been able to provide a satisfactory understanding of these problems, a new kind of research is needed. The work done by researchers involves using scientific tools, generating data, investigating and analysing, and developing new thinking technologies. By offering these technologies to other participants in the field, we may see how they work in relation to the problem. These are onto-epistemological movements with real effects (Barad 2007).

A definition of bullying: following the lines of abjection and the production of contempt

It is against this background that we should understand the work needed to develop a new thinking technology in connection to the phenomenon of bullying – such as it is designated by the children and parents in our empirical data, and such as the technology can be generated when these statements are being combined in intra-action with the theory and analytics. The conceptual work here becomes an analytical effort to formulate a definition that is directed towards establishing a locally and empirically informed analytical view of the phenomenon – a view that keeps its focus on processes and movements, and expands in relation to developing an understanding of the many interacting and intra-acting perspectives. I present this definitional clarification by pulling together some of the most important points already mentioned here to form the basis of the thinking technology.

Earlier in the chapter, the emphasis on social exclusion anxiety as a risk connected to the human need for social embeddedness – along with a number of related concepts regarding the production of dignity and contempt – provided the foundation to suggest such a thinking technology. I also referred to social panic as a marker in the transition to more acute rejection praxes. As long as social exclusion anxiety is kept in abeyance, there is still a chance to include those who are relatively despised and understand how they experience the situation, themselves and other people. I argued that, from that point, the situation may shift to a phase in which empathy – which facilitates the production of dignity – evaporates, and contempt and dehumanisation increase. This change accompanies the movement from social exclusion anxiety to social panic. As I pointed out, this movement can be driven by a production of contempt that is expressed verbally and/or through a wordless choreography amongst a group of children experiencing social exclusion anxiety. This then paves the way for the kind of actions that are often understood as 'bullying'. But the marginalisation and exclusion practices that hover on the brink of bullying undoubtedly require further qualification based on questions like: How should the boundaries of a phenomenon like bullying be understood? When exactly can the term 'bullying' be applied? When are children 'only' teasing and having 'fun'? (See Søndergaard 2011).

The relationship between a practice like teasing and bullying simultaneously marks a continuum and a difference: they are the same kind of thing, but also different. Teasing, policing (Frosh et al. 2002) and certain kinds of harassment and conflict can be seen as strategies to maintain and reproduce the social order by involving someone in the group while, at the same time, ensuring conformity to its norms. The children adjust and negotiate the conditions for inclusion, and this process operates along with the possibility of exclusion. However, when bullying practices emerge, several changes occur: as already described, the dignity-producing form of empathy becomes closed off to the target of bullying; the production of contempt increases and becomes focused on the loathed person or thing, either temporarily or for long periods of time; and the empathy that might have been activated instead transitions into an understanding of what will be most painful and humiliating. In this connection, the concept of 'abjection' can help us delineate the special character of bullying: namely, that the target of bullying is someone under pressure to assume an abject position.

The concept of abjection can be traced far back in the history of theory, but my inspiration for using the term in this context derives from the work of Judith Butler who, in turn, was inspired by Julia Kristeva's definition of the abject.[13] Butler writes: 'The "abject" designates that which has been expelled from the body, discharged as excrement, literally rendered

---

[13] Schott (2009b) traces the concept from Kristeva back to Mary Douglas's analysis of impurity in *Purity and Danger* (1966). Douglas discusses social processes, so it is Kristeva who draws inspiration from Lacan in applying the concept with individualising significance. Butler also traces her ideas to Douglas (Butler 1999: 166–9). See also Bülent Diken and Carsten Bagge Laustsen for an application of the abject to analyse attacks of war (2005a).

'Other'. This appears as an expulsion of alien elements, but the alien is effectively established through this expulsion. The construction of the 'not-me' as the abject establishes the boundaries of the body which are also the first contours of the subject' (Butler 1999: 169).

In developing a thinking technology for bullying, the strength of the abjection concept is its focus on the disgust and desire for a radical rejection, maybe even obliteration, of the Other; this pervades most bullying practices. Practices of abjection have a particular character that is experienced differently from practices of teasing or policing. Someone can be teased or policed into their 'appropriate' place in the community, but that is not necessarily the intention with the target of bullying. The kinds of affects and emotions involved in the act of bullying include nausea, fear, disgust and the wish to eliminate what the despised person represents – that is, to remove what the person is reminiscent of, to remove the kind of positioning and identity that the person actualises. Bullying involves an attempt to rid oneself or the group of whoever or whatever may, more or less arbitrarily, have attracted the group's attention in its search for an object to despise and thereby alleviate the discomfort of anxiety. These features are central to our new thinking technology for bullying.

When the concept of abjection is applied in relation to the understanding of bullying, it becomes important to grasp the loathing and, while doing so, capture this disgust as a function closely related to the fundamental need for social belonging. When this need is threatened, it can awaken the processes of abjection and the emotions and affects that facilitate them. In this sense, my emphasis is on understanding that abjection is bound to processes related to social participation and embeddedness. But its use in relation to bullying as a phenomenon is linked to a further understanding of the potential anxiety that exists in the embeddedness being threatened. Symbolism and emotions connected to the concept of 'abject' are thus linked to actual social processes.

Therefore, abjection is not taken to be an individual matter but a social one; it has to do with performing and forming the social context upon which one is dependent. Viewed this way, the target of bullying functions as – or is under pressure to function as – the outer side that can contribute to the cohesion of the inner side/social group under the exposed circumstances. The child who is abjected performs this function by being positioned as a target of contempt, hatred or other degrading assessments that work to confirm that, at any rate, 'we' are inside and accepted. 'We' need this kind of affirmation because our insecurity, social anxiety and the constant threats of exclusion and contempt whirl around and between us, creating panic and the desire to control the processes of exclusion. For these reasons, participating in abjectification can be experienced as an alleviation of social exclusion anxiety.

From this position, the target of bullying is not available to receive dignity-producing empathy, respect and understanding, and also loses access to negotiations about the conditions for participation (Søndergaard 2008). The position of being bullied shifts the target from one reality to another in a movement from one interpretative frame to another, and from one set of normative options of evaluation to another (Haavind 2003). This process drifts towards what Judith Butler calls 'derealisation' (2004). Aversion and contempt work to legitimate this derealisation: 'She's just *so* clammy'; 'Do you realise *how* irritating he is?'; 'It's his own bloody fault, he hit Jacob yesterday, and anyway he stinks.' 'Clammy', 'irritating', 'stinks' now become the only aspect that defines him or her.

However, one more thing is necessary to make the concept of abjection productive in relation to the empirical material: the concept must be specified in a movement that detaches it from individual persons and attaches it to *figures* – in other words, to view 'contempt' as something with the potential to grip different members of a community that is being ravaged by social exclusion anxiety and expose them to abjectification (for the concept of *a figure*, see Søndergaard 1996/2000, 2002). This conceptual movement renders it possible to capture the quality of the aversion and the desire to exclude whilst maintaining an analytical view of the multiplicity of ways in which aversion and the desire to exclude can operate. For example, the situation with Alex – with or without his resistance to the exclusion to which he is exposed, and together with the sudden attacks and the fluctuating and variable positionings – could be grasped analytically without a definition of bullying dazzling our eyes to the relational destructiveness that is central to the phenomenon. As mentioned, bullying positions are not necessarily stable, although they can be. The bullying figure can invade the positioning of a particular child over a lengthy period of time, or it can be mobile and attach itself to different children at different times. Regardless, the figure brings the same kind of contempt production into the social group. The concept of the abject also helps us maintain our analytical focus in relation to this point.

The origin of bullying in the intra-action of many forces

We now know that social exclusion anxiety fuels bullying through a set of mechanisms that are bound to the desire for alleviation and a wish to allow oneself and one's group to control the conditions for inclusion/exclusion. But what makes social exclusion anxiety escalate? The final section of this chapter asks: What contributes to the escalation of social exclusion anxiety, insecurity and intolerance? What fans the flames of abjectification, creating an aversion to and ostracism of something or someone in a school class? What nurtures social exclusion anxiety so that it tips over into social panic and feeds the urge to abjectify?

The uncomfortable answer to these questions is that it can be many things. Further, it is not just one but many of these things that interfere and intra-act with and transform each other in ways that may reinforce, distort or perhaps displace social exclusion anxiety. To qualify an understanding of these processes requires an analytical perspective that includes a sharpened awareness of the elements – the forces – that contribute to the bullying apparatus.[14] When looking more closely at the forces involved, it is tempting to consider them as separate from each other, but it is important to remember that the forces continuously intra-act with each other (Barad 2007). The forces are mutually constitutive, and they intra-act and transform each other in their continuous encounters.

Some of the central forces that intra-act in the enactment of children's community-building include, for example: teachers and the understandings and praxes built into their positionings; parents' understandings and the praxes built into their positionings; children's past experiences both in and outside of school; the history of the class and the relational praxes; communications technology, media use and interactive media products; the material conditions of school life – to mention just some. Further research will undoubtedly make our analytical gaze sensitive to more forces. Next, I open up the understanding of a few of these forces as examples of what is involved in the process.

Teachers

The realisation of teachers' positionings intra-acts in a number of ways (see Hansen, Chapter 10, page 241, and 2011a). In this context, I consider only two aspects that seem to contribute to the

[14] Barad reworks the concept of 'apparatus' by reading physicist Niels Bohr diffractively with Donna Haraway (apparatuses of bodily production) and Michel Foucault (*dispositif*). Barad says apparatuses signify 'a dynamic set of open-ended practices [as these are] iteratively refined and reconfigured' (2007: 167). She further defines the concept as such: 'Apparatuses are material-discursive practices – [...] intra-actions through which matter is iteratively and differentially articulated, reconfiguring the material-discursive field of possibilities and impossibilities in the ongoing dynamics of intra-activity that is agency. Apparatuses are not bounded objects of structures; they are open-ended practices' (ibid.: 170). The apparatus designates the varying intra-activities – and their resulting reconfigurings of the world – through an ongoing and always temporary boundary-making, which simultaneously establishes demarcations of these enacting processes (ibid.: 145ff). Apparatuses have no intrinsic boundaries; they always intra-act with other apparatuses of enactment (Søndergaard 2013b).

overall intra-action with the other forces involved: specifically, teacher stability and authority strategies.

Reading across the eXbus empirical material, teachers appear to have great significance – both as individuals who teach school subjects and as stable adults who support the class's attainment of norms, providing models for appropriate relational praxes. Such praxes are constructed over long periods of relating between the children; during these periods, they may experience social processes that succeed or fail, make evaluations of each other along with the teachers, and develop understandings and perceptions that they can use in similar situations to test, react, assess, etc. This lengthy and complex process is closely intertwined with the students' progress in their academic learning, and it requires support from and dialogue with committed adults. Being deprived of regular *qualified* adult dialogue and guidance seems to feed social exclusion anxiety and thus fuel the processes that position the children against each other with destructive results.

For example, a situation wherein a school class has experienced the following type of process: the children have a good beginning with a stable pre-school teacher, but they get a new teacher when they enter first grade. The first-grade teacher takes maternity leave after three-quarters of the year; the substitute teacher only stays for six months; there is a rotation of substitute teachers until the main teacher returns after a lengthy maternity leave. In the middle of third grade, the main teacher takes sick leave; the class now has more substitute teachers while the principal awaits the return of the main teacher; six months later, she reports that she will not return because she has a new job. The class gets a new teacher; he stays with the class for one-and-a-half years then takes paternity leave; the class has more substitute teachers. The new main teacher leaves the school after his paternity leave, and the class gets a new teacher – this is just about at the point where it is no longer attractive to enter the class as a new teacher, so the principal has a hard time finding someone to take over. The solution is to hire a newly educated teacher, who is 25 years old and fresh out of teacher training college. The new teacher stays for a year. . .etc. In varying configurations, this is the course of events experienced by many school classes when the focus is on continuity and teacher positioning.[15]

---

[15] In Denmark, many children have the same main teacher (*klasselærer*) for the first three or four years after preschool, then they have a new main teacher from fourth/fifth grade (3./4. *klasse*) until eighth (7. *klasse*) and then another teacher from ninth grade (8. *klasse*) to tenth (9. *klasse*).

It tends to contribute to the children's anxiety if they are largely left to create their own cultural and relational norms, especially if they have to develop these norms in an atmosphere full of signals from the teachers and other adults that the children interpret as indifference. In our interviews, the children said that they consider it a signal when there are several teacher changes during a school year or prolonged teacher absences with many substitute teachers: 'The grown-ups don't really care about "us"; they come and go, and aren't particularly serious about anything they say or do.' In such an atmosphere, projects that are designed to establish continuity and to promote cohesive academic and social processes may lose credibility and meaning in the children's eyes; they experience this instability as a deprivation of dignity. The rotation of substitute teachers may or may not attempt to maintain academic and social continuity, but it probably does not matter; as some of the children said, 'Why should we take them seriously? They'll only be here for a short time' and 'They don't know us anyway.' Thus, being at school may become boring and meaningless.

If the adults in charge believe that simply informing a substitute teacher about what the children are supposed to be doing in class is a professional way to handle this situation, then they are operating under a separation of the academic and the social that seems to have no meaning for the students. Social, emotional and learning processes are intertwined for the children, and what they find meaningful is stable support from adults to form collective and individual experiences as well as productive praxes within and through these intertwined processes.

However, there is no unambiguous causality in these processes. The children might manage to activate some kind of dignity production and build a cohesive community despite an absence of continuous, stable adult relationships – or they might not. It all depends on which other forces are involved in the enactment of their communal life. The children's history, the class's history, the parents' contributions, the other norms the children are offered and the storylines and imaginary positionings[16] provided to the children by media products, for example, are all active in these intra-actions. Decisions made by school administrators also transmit signals and effects: it is significant which norms the leadership practices and supports, and which strategies of authority, intervention practices and types of problem analysis they may impede or advance in relation to the children, classes and parents. All of these elements are also constituent forces in the apparatus.

[16] For more on storylines, see Davies (2000) and Søndergaard (2002).

The authority strategies used by the teachers are also significant constituent forces: if they contain elements that contribute to contempt production, then social exclusion anxiety will be exacerbated. Authority strategies that deny dignity by activating teasing, ridicule and humiliation may bolster contempt-producing praxes that already exist amongst the children and may sometimes incite them: 'Elliott is a loser, and the teachers don't like him either!' Furthermore, in order to function this way, the teachers' authority strategies do not always need to be directed towards the same students as the children's production of contempt. The power lies in the norm established by the practice – the norm for what is acceptable in *this* class; that norm can exacerbate social exclusion anxiety.

But the extent to which such authority strategies contribute to the enactment of an increased level of anxiety depends on the other enacting forces with which they intra-act. For example, there may be other forces that work to neutralise or decrease the anxiety. A given class might be particularly fortunate to have a stable substitute teacher who, against all odds, gains the trust of the children and, for limited periods, is permitted a genuine position as a social–emotional–academic sparring partner. Or there may be forces amongst the parents which work to produce community in the class, stabilise it and provide relational models in ways that are conducive to the production of dignity. Or perhaps the students have developed strategies to curb and contain the power of their teacher's authority strategy: they might say to each other, 'Yes, yes, the teacher is just grumpy; we shouldn't take any notice of him'; or else they discover disarming manoeuvres that confirm that this case is an anomaly that should not establish the norm for their relational praxes: they might turn to humour by saying, 'That teacher is the school's very own Darth Vader!'[17] and then continue building other relational praxes, secure in the knowledge that the Jedis always win in the end.

Parents' contributions intra-act with teachers' contributions intra-act with personal and collective histories intra-act with...

There is a risk that the effects of such forces will be destructively amplified, but whether this happens and the extent to which it does is dependent on

---

[17] For the uninitiated, Darth Vader is the personification of evil in the film series *Star Wars*. The Jedi Knights are in contact with the Force, which is the power of good and harmony in the universe. Children often use figures and stories like this – as well as those from other television series and movies – to clarify and support their own individual and communal orientation praxes.

several other forces. If contempt-producing practices are also wide-spread amongst the parents of the class – being aimed at each other, the children, the teachers – then those forces may intra-act in the development of praxes and the formation of norms to which the teachers' contempt-producing authority strategies contribute; this entire complex can inter-act with and give support to the relational praxes that the children are using or developing. This whole process may exacerbate social exclusion anxiety, which in turn creates further contempt production. This can then ignite the parents' anxiety, leading them to seek protection for their own children by means of tentative contempt-producing practices directed at certain other children and/or parents or teachers, etc.

The production of contempt can also move along other routes. If the parents themselves cultivate authority strategies towards their own children – strategies that may build upon contempt production, mockery, humiliation, cynical competition, etc., or if the parents' priorities work to deprive their children of dignity – then these forces can intra-act with and support the escalation of social exclusion anxiety within a group of children. An example of this situation from the empirical material is linked to an intra-acting personal and class history: when Ryan's father prioritised his sexual–romantic desires over seeing and spending time with his children – he left the family and moved in with his 18-years-younger girlfriend across the country – Ryan read this as a signal about his value. When his mother had to give up their house for a two-room flat where she slept on the sofa whilst Ryan and his little sister shared a $15m^2$ bedroom, this sent signals to the two children in the family about what they were worth to whom. The signals materialised in people laughing at their father because of his girlfriend's age; in the difficulty of inviting friends to a home that was suddenly small and overcrowded; and in the difficulty of doing homework in a bedroom shared with a younger sister who was also trying to maintain relationships with her friends. These signals were also sent through a suddenly reduced financial situation that cut off access to artefacts and leisure-time activities that previously functioned to optimise the children's inclusion in their respective school communities. For the children, their social embeddedness, continuity and security in a particular way of life had suddenly deteriorated.

In this situation, a deprivation of dignity is occurring that may follow certain channels to become entangled with other kinds of intra-acting forces that lurk within Ryan's class; for example, the teacher's position. Ryan abandons doing his homework and cannot find the energy to gain acceptance and respect from the new teacher, Joanne; he turns his attention in a totally different direction, getting together with the gang of boys who hang out at the railway station. Within the gang, Ryan is able to pull himself up due to the mutual production of dignity that prevails; that strategy makes sense to him. And it includes norms about being tough and sharing the view that grown-ups are just unreliable idiots. Ryan actually gains self-worth through the dignity projects that these boys offer him, and he brings new forces into the class that intra-act with everything already going on between the children and amongst the children and their teacher Joanne.

One day, Joanne scornfully derides Ryan for not doing his homework, calling him 'lazy' and 'unreliable'. Ryan loses his temper and retorts with the kind of discourse that gives him dignity within the gang: he calls her a 'bloody whore'. Joanne hauls Ryan up to the office, where the principal corroborates her view that 'we don't need boys like Ryan in this school'. Then the whole situation turns around on itself, contributing to the escalation of social exclusion anxiety in the class. Ryan's eventual expulsion from school is just another cog in the machine that spins social exclusion anxiety in the wrong direction. And the teacher's rhetoric about 'having helped Ryan to find a kind of school that's better suited to a boy like him' is no help at all. The children have witnessed a process that culminated in exclusion: they did not witness any help being given, either to Ryan or to the class.

Ryan's story is an example of how the teachers' enactments of dignity/ contempt become entangled with the parents' enactment of dignity/ contempt, as well as how an individual's history intra-acts with contributions from the teachers and parents; together they form processes that interweave with the history of the class. But an individual's personal history and the collective history will also intra-act and become entangled with other forces in other configurations. The experiences that the children generate with regard to loyalty and disloyalty, as well as the reciprocal production of dignity and shame, constitute a social–emotional experiential history. That history will intra-act with the actual events taking place in the life of the class – (re)actualising it and thereby generating conditions for the interpretation of these events. This is yet another force that becomes entangled with the personal stories that comprise the interpretation of events.

For instance, a history that contains the experience 'we have already bullied' can become a collective memory that is difficult to reinterpret in any dignity-producing way. Therefore, it can become a type of enacting force that creates problems in the machinery. Certain children in the class may have learnt from bitter experience that once someone is positioned as a stable target for the production of contempt, then there is no chance that one's emotional reactions will be listened to and respected. Talking about the experience of being humiliated will not end the humiliation: in fact, if a child's account is accompanied by an emotional reaction – e.g. if he/she cries, gets angry or asks for understanding – then the child risks increased humiliation. Children have seen it, contributed to it, experienced it. To stand there as a victim of bullying is like standing in quicksand, and children know that it is difficult and sometimes impossible to get out again. This type of collective experience seems to be constantly frightening, and it may continue to inflame social exclusion anxiety: it happened to 'us' once, so it could happen again.

Communication technology and media products

The intra-active forces also include material–technological means of communication and the concomitant circulation of social–emotional manoeuvrings that are enabled by text-messaging, instant-message chats and profiles on social-networking websites like Instagram and Facebook (see Kofoed, Chapter 7, page 159; Shariff 2008).

These forms of communication technology also function as intra-acting forces in the apparatus that enacts relational praxes and sometimes bullying amongst children. Mutual appraisals by the children can be quickly disseminated to a wide audience via these technologies. And, perhaps because of the lack of a direct response, the children sometimes have a tendency to 'speak' very clearly and 'loudly' when using these forms of communication, with everything from 'I love you, you're my best friend, I can't live without you' to 'You're a filthy whore, die – now!' The information circulated by the children on the social-networking sites may contain anything from details about love affairs offered by one of those involved to detailed accounts of the 'day's mood' (Arto[18]). In the same way, the visual presentation is often emphatic: photo galleries on Arto, Facebook, Instagram, etc., offer self-presentations where the children may assume various kinds of clichés (e.g. gender, class, posturing like famous pop icons, etc.) in their efforts to increase visibility and popularity or just to play with potential identities. It is as if the message somehow becomes intensified through the use of these forms of communication; and, of course, these intensified messages and relational praxes contribute their particular effects and possibilities of intra-action to the other enacting forces at work in the apparatus of a school class (Kofoed and Ringrose 2012).

Experiences from other contexts are also constituent elements that entangle and contribute to the machinery and, amongst these, the experiences that children have in virtual spaces provide material for

---

[18] Arto is a Danish social-networking website that dominated the market amongst school-children until Facebook came along. The 'day's mood' feature mentioned here was a central part of Arto's design.

intra-action. The children cultivate experiences, physical and relational skills and narrative structures as they play online shooting games or fantasy games, for instance; they joke around and play with and transform in conjunction with the various virtual and non-virtual options and praxes they encounter. Training in physical manoeuvring generates intra-acting forces (e.g. online shooting and strategy games: a sniper's tactics and precautions; the violence of a soldier with an automatic weapon; the speed and deftness of a pilot flying above enemy tanks). Likewise, the virtual options for training in relational praxes become forces at work in the machinery, just as the models for orientating and constructing the particular types of narratives woven by participants in virtual games become entangled in the enactments. All of these things also become incorporated into the intra-activity within their community (Højgaard, Juelskjær and Søndergaard 2012; Søndergaard 2013a and b).

A recreation centre's computer room filled with boys playing the first-person shooter game *Counter Strike* may be completely saturated with the production of contempt.[19] The boys cultivate and play with the characterisation of contempt that is being acquired by or interpreted as part of the virtual battle on the computer screen. Phrases like 'Get that faggot, pig' and 'Smash the motherfucker, nerd' fly across the room between participants. The battle provides a framework for playing with contempt, and for cultivating, but also ridiculing contempt strategies and violence. And the way the boys enter and enjoy the game simultaneously involves lots of joy and mutual affirmation amongst some of the players; sometimes, however, there is marginalisation amongst others (ibid.). The way this training and playing may contribute to the classroom culture in which the boys also participate is by no means unequivocal: it depends on the contributions from and intra-action with the other enacting forces, and which orientation praxes they may invoke from experiences across all the real–virtual spaces they inhabit. There are no simple causal connections here, only entangling movements and intra-actions: the children choose from their online resources, using and transforming them based on the experiences, social–emotional and relational praxes by which they live in other contexts, including school. Media products are developed at the intersection between many other types of forces, but market forces, demand and the producers' own fascination and career praxes play a significant part. Thus, the media products and experiences from virtual contexts are intra-active at many levels; both in other types of apparatuses and together with the other forces that constitute the children's social–relational praxes.

---

[19] This example is based on observations from my data generated in the eXbus project.

Conclusion: understanding bullying as social processes gone awry

The idea of *many forces* is central to the definition of bullying that I propose in this chapter. There are many different forces that work to increase, reduce and/or prevent the production of anxiety. In order to understand the ways in which these forces operate, it is necessary to be acutely attuned to both their multiplicity and their intra-action, and thus to the ways in which they support, impede and transform each other.

Social exclusion anxiety constitutes another central point in my proposed understanding of bullying, which has been developed based on an empirical investigation that incorporates analyses of interviews with and observations of schoolchildren. A brief recapitulation: the concept of social exclusion anxiety is grounded in a social–psychological understanding of the individual as existentially dependent on *social embeddedness*. Anxiety is seen as a condition that can intensify and emerge when social embeddedness is threatened. The children seek to alleviate the tension and discomfort of social exclusion anxiety and, in this context, they may see the *production of contempt* as a way to achieve potential relief. In this situation, the communal *dignity production* may be reserved for some children, whilst contempt production increases as a force that can be directed in different ways. Its aim may be diffuse and reciprocal within a group of children – or affect the interaction between both children and adults – and thereby it manifests as a heightened sense of insecurity and a general readiness for reciprocal condemnation and exclusion. This may be exhibited through sudden attacks on individual children or groups of children. The contempt may also be concentrated in lengthier, focused attacks on particular children or groups of children. Thus, in addition to *varying positionings*, more *stabilised positionings* may be seen in a school context where bullying occurs.

A situation in which anxiety spills over into *social panic* may thus prompt sudden attacks in addition to more long-lasting, focused attacks and abjectifying movements. The aversion found at the heart of *abjection* marks a condition in which the empathy that accompanies dignity production becomes closed off, and destructive control – along with manoeuvrings to exclude – may take over as a reaction directed towards particular children. However, this does not mean that all empathy is closed off in the process. Dignity-producing empathy may even become amplified and improved within a group that is engaged in excluding a particular child or group of children. But empathic capacity may also be used to serve the abjectification instead of functioning as a dignity-producing element; in this way, it may be utilised to increase the effects of aversion towards the child(ren) being attacked and excluded. In such a situation, empathic capacity is employed to discover what in particular would most hurt and humiliate the current target of contempt.

The concept of the abject is used here to establish a sense of the boundaries of *the phenomenon of bullying*. With this concept, we may begin to comprehend aversion and dehumanisation as processes that, although seemingly contra-intuitive at first, are nevertheless invested in a desire to create social order – but these processes have gone decidedly awry. In bullying practices, attempts to use harassment or teasing to put certain group members 'in their place' and to negotiate the conditions for inclusion break down in a certain sense. For instance, by seeking relief through the production of contempt the attempt to produce social order slides into even more destructive social movements.

If one follows this thinking, then as a first step, a professionalisation of praxis should be about developing the analytic gaze and adjusting it to examine complex problems in local, empirical contexts. Thus, it is not so much the technical tricks that are envisaged in this context; instead, it is about gaining insights into the mechanisms and processes in this highly complex machinery (for reflections on praxes, see Cross and Barnes, Chapter 16, page 405, and Søndergaard, Chapter 3, page 47). Furthermore, it is not certain whether the most effective way to use the gaze for mechanisms and processes is always to act as super-detectives and reveal the 'truth' about what actually happened. Because 'actually' and 'processes' tend to move, depending on when one asks, who one asks and through which subsequent events the original event is interpreted and reported. The past comes into being; it is actualised in the present in numerous ways, depending on how it is 'invited' in and made relevant as a sounding board, as experience, as confirmation of an interpretation or in parallel, contrast or in comparison to events in the present. But on the other hand, pastness is also not passive. Pastness offers its phenomena with greater or lesser force via the intersection that lies between what was there and how the antecedent has thus been made accessible as currently invitable into our lives as lived now. In this sense, the past and the present cannot be definitively separated (Juelskær 2009; Mathiassen, Chapter 13, page 331; Søndergaard 2005a).

Due to this complexity, it might be more effective to turn our analytical gaze to the question of how to move forward by reforming the institutional apparatus of which children (and parents, teachers, school administrators, politicians) are a part, and in such a way that it begins to promote dignity and embeddedness instead of breaking down these processes, which damages trust amongst children and between children and adults. In other words, it might sometimes be more effective to keep the focus on progressive ways to reduce social exclusion anxiety, bringing it to a level where it becomes productive rather than destructive. When more severe affronts occur, however, one should certainly not underestimate the significance of processes that make dignity-producing positionings and re-inclusion possible for the excluded (Søndergaard 2008). This type of process can imply an assignment of responsibility, but for the manoeuvring to succeed within the group as a whole, more extensive strategies must be developed.

4   Violence and the moral order in contemporary schooling: a discursive analysis*

Constance Ellwood and Bronwyn Davies

Violence in schools has been the subject of a great deal of empirical research since the early 1970s. This research has informed the development of intervention strategies that do not appear to make a lasting difference, as David Galloway and Erling Roland demonstrated in their meta-analysis of bullying programmes: 'The general picture has been one of considerable difficulty in maintaining the impact of anti-bullying programmes' (Galloway and Roland 2004: 37, 49). In the face of this intransigence, one particular study set out to re-think approaches to violence in schools (Davies et al. 2007). We invited teachers to collaborate with us as co-researchers in order to develop a new understanding of school violence. The teachers, however, found the daily task of handling violence in schools so pressing that they felt the idea of asking questions – rather than just dealing with the depressing, ever-present violence – was a luxury they could not afford. Finding new answers was up to us researchers, they said. It was a serious challenge.

One of the major strengths of qualitative research is its capacity to re-theorise a particular field through an examination of the discursive constructions that underpin a particular body of research. Such work enables us to ask whether there is some type of limitation or inherent problem in the conceptual configuration of the field, and to ask how else the problem might be understood. In this chapter, we continue the discursive work begun by Alexa Hepburn (1997a, b, 2000) in order to further open new ways of thinking about – and acting in relation to – school violence. We examine discourses of bullying and violence that appear in both the empirical research literature and in the talk of teachers and students who have been involved in implementing the findings of that research in their schools.

In order to engage in this work, the first author conducted a pilot study in which she recorded and transcribed teachers' and students' talk about

* An earlier version of this chapter was published in 2010 in *Qualitative Research in Psychology*: 7(2) 85–98.

bullying in order to create an archive of talk about bullying. We chose schools that had an active programme for dealing with bullying – one secondary school and one primary school. Our purpose was to make available for discursive analysis the habitual and repetitive discursive constructions being used by students and by teachers who were attempting to bring about change, by drawing upon programmes that had been informed by the empirical research. Twenty-four interviews were conducted with fourteen teachers and nine students about the programmes operating in their schools. The primary school used a restorative-justice approach, which brings bullies and their targets together in a dialogue that is designed to open up an understanding of consequences and effects (see www.realjustice.org). Through workshops and posters around the school, the secondary-school programme offered students a series of strategies: three strategies for the targets of bullying (to stand up for themselves against the bullying; to report the incident(s); and to document it in writing) and one strategy for bystanders (to support the target in these three strategies). With these programmes, both schools sought to increase staff and student awareness of a school ethos in which bullying is considered inappropriate behaviour.

The analytic work we engage in here, drawing upon our archive, should not be read through the same empirical lens that was employed in the studies it is setting out to critique. Empirical findings are 'derived from or relating to experiment and observation rather than theory' (Collins English Dictionary). In such research, claims of truth rest on following narrowly specified experimental methods. In contrast, the focus of discursive research is on the interpretive work that is involved in formulating and asking research questions, in generating data and in articulating new, emergent forms of understanding. Our task is not to establish whether or not the programmes that the interviewees in our current project discussed are working – or even how they are working – but, rather, to examine the discursive constructions of bullying in these contexts. We ask how 'bullies' are being discursively constituted at these sites and with what effects.

We draw upon the work of Michel Foucault, who was interested in the way discourse functions to constitute subjects – including the researcher. He describes his own research/writing as an experiment with the purpose of opening up new ways of thinking: 'I write in order to change myself and in order not to think the same thing as before' (Foucault 2000a: 240). Discourse analysis, as Foucault defines it, does not adopt a form of linguistic analysis (i.e. the study of discourse as a set of linguistic facts linked together by syntactic rules). He treats discourse 'as games, strategic games of action and reaction, question and answer, domination and evasion, as well as struggle. On one level, discourse is an ordered set of polemical and strategic facts, while on another level it is the set of linguistic facts which express these polemics and strategies' (Foucault 2000c: 2). This study of 'discourse as a strategic and polemical game' is linked to the study of the formation of an individual subject through particular forms of knowledge. He is interested in a 'subject that constitutes itself within history and is constantly established and re-established by history. It is towards that radical critique of the human subject by history', he suggests, 'that we should direct our efforts. . . . In my view, what we should do is show the historical construction of a subject through a discourse understood as consisting of a set of strategies which are part of social practices' (ibid.).

Thus, our focus here is on the way the real world is produced through the mobilisation of statements (*enoncés*) or things said about violence in schools, which might be thought of as 'events of certain kinds which are at once tied to historical contexts and capable of repetition' (Olssen 2006: 9). In this analysis, we take discourse to be 'not merely spoken words, but a notion of signification which concerns not merely how it is that certain signifiers come to mean what they mean, but how certain discursive forms articulate objects and subjects in their intelligibility' (Butler 1995: 138). We are interested in how particular versions of the world are made to seem evident, and naturally the way things are. Such analytic work:

. . .does not consist in saying that things aren't good the way they are. It consists in seeing on what type of assumptions, of familiar notions, of established, unexamined ways of thinking the accepted practices are based. [. . .It shows] that things are not as obvious as people believe, making it so that what is taken for granted is no longer taken for granted. To do criticism is to make harder those acts which are now too easy. (Foucault 2000b: 456–7)

In this chapter, we show that a psycho-social model of the bully is now taken for granted, and we aim to make it harder to interpret bullying in that way: as the transparent actions of a single individual who can be identified as standing outside the normal order of things.

Definitions of bullying

In this first section, we examine teachers' difficulties in applying the definitions of bullying that have emerged in the research literature. These definitions generally include an intention to do harm, repetition of the behaviour and an imbalance of power. In this definition, bullies are (pathological) people who engage in 'a specific type of aggression in which (1) the behaviour is intended to harm or disturb, (2) the behaviour occurs repeatedly over time, and (3) there is an imbalance of power, with a more powerful person or group attacking a less powerful one' (Nansel et al. 2001: 2094). The 'deliberate' negative action of the bully is contrasted with the randomness of an 'odd' fight or quarrel; 'a bit of a tiff': 'Students sometimes bully weaker students at school by deliberately and repeatedly hurting or upsetting them in some way; for example, by hitting or pushing them around, teasing them, or leaving them out of things on purpose. But it is not bullying when two young children of about the same strength have the odd fight or quarrel' (Slee 1995a: 62).

These definitions work to distinguish not just the bullying behaviour from other modes of normalised violence, but also to distinguish the character of the bully from other students. However, in examining our archive of teachers' talk, it becomes evident that intentions are difficult, if not impossible, to ascertain. Indeed, intentions are most often opaque – not only to the subject who acts, but also to those who attempt to read the intentions of others. Intentions may be made apparently transparent, as we demonstrate later, through the device of 'reading' or, more precisely, discursively constituting students' characters. The fact that teachers often attribute negative intentions incorrectly is confirmed by students, who comment on their experiences of being caught – often unfairly – in an unbreakable circuit of 'recognition' (Osler 2006). Although 'intention to do harm' is usually present in definitions used by both researchers and teachers, it is rarely highlighted in student definitions (see Guerin and Hennessy 2002; Naylor, Cowie and del Rey 2001).

The reading of students' negative intentions can be revised – and the students re-constituted – when the teacher is able to attribute a conscience to them. In the teachers' talk, the identification of a conscience becomes evidence of a non-pathological (that is, non-bullying) individual. For example, two girls around the age of 9 had participated in an act of violence that their teacher was at a loss to understand:

There was a session two weeks ago on a Friday where they actually physically I guess you'd call it abused a child, a Sudanese child. [. . .] They thought this Sudanese boy was playing 'kiss and catch' with the girls. . .and they didn't like that, so one of them went and held his head against the wall and the other child just went and slammed it three times so the child then had a missing tooth and the parents had to be called in and they've never gone physical but, this was their first time.

At first, the teacher described the girls' behaviour as bullying: 'just a very cruel and very worrying form of, you know, of bullying'. However, during the follow-up strategy, when she went through the 'restorative questions' from the Real Justice programme, the girls demonstrated what could be called remorse, indicating the presence of a conscience. The teacher then said:

They've actually become quite upset, we haven't yelled at them but when the other child has been talking about how it makes them feel, they actually get tears in their eyes so they do get quite emotional, you know they do get quite upset because they know how much they've hurt. You know, and with the incident of the banging against the – you know, the banging of the head against the wall, and parents were brought in, the children were actually quite upset because they know that they had done something wrong.

In the teacher's reading of them via this questioning, the girls are recon-stituted as capable of empathy. They 'know how much they've hurt' and are 'upset because they know they had done something wrong'. The girls are no longer constituted (or constitutable) as bullies since their apparent demonstration of a conscience absolves them of negative intentionality.

But one's conscience may not be as readily open for inspection as liberal humanist models of the subject have led us to believe. For example, one primary-school student explained that when he engages in violent acts, he is opaque to himself:

When you're having a fight, you're actually different to who you are like because I don't know – when I'm having a fight, I don't know what I'm thinking and I just like attack and that's not right but I think like good kids can like you know can attack and they don't know they're angry.

This student's talk constitutes him as someone with a conscience. Even though he admits to violence, he separates the good person from the one who temporarily does not know himself.

Like negative intentions and lack of conscience, the misuse and abuse of power is often included in definitions of bullying (Indiana Department of Education 2003; Nebraska School Safety Centre 2007; Rigby 2007; Victoria Department of Education 2007; Wikipedia contributors 2007). The play of power and power differentials are present in almost all inter-actions, but what distinguishes the bully is the misuse or abuse of whatever power they have. Like negative intentions, however, misuse of power differentials is not always easy to assess. Although it may be clear that a group has more physical power than an individual – and a bigger individ-ual usually has more physical power than a slighter one – what constitutes an *abuse* or *misuse* of power may often be difficult to pinpoint (Victoria Department of Education 2007).

The practical difficulty of distinguishing 'misuse' versus 'use of power' leads to the inclusion of 'repetition' in the definition: if the harmful use of power is repeated, it can supposedly enable an observer to distinguish bullying from everyday conflict. Repetition was emphasised by the teachers and students as a key factor in recognising bullying:

Bullying is something that happens, and it continues happening over and over. (secondary-school student)
   We've had three or four girls here making complaints about that – now their initial thing would be 'Well, I'm being bullied' but it's a one-off kind of situation so it's not really. (secondary-school staff member)

But this does not solve the problem of recognition. The participants still have to decide what it is that has to be repeated, how to establish that it has or has not been repeated, and how they can predict whether or not it will be repeated. An investigation of these questions opens up the emptiness of the term 'repetition'. What, for example, would the teacher be looking for as a repeated act in the case of the two girls breaking the Sudanese boy's tooth? Racism? Invigilation of 'correct' social relations on the playground? Or simply banging heads against walls hard enough to break teeth?

Limitations of the psycho-social discourse in making sense of bullying

The unexamined way of thinking that is made to seem obvious in the empirical research literature is that school violence is a problem created by individuals for other individuals. It is assumed that it is psycho-social in origin, and that the problem lies with those students who exhibit troublesome behaviours because of their home backgrounds and/or who are deficient in social skills. The argument that is assembled for preventing school violence is also psycho-social: violence must be stopped because of its impact on individuals; it has a negative physical, emotional and cognitive effect on individual recipients, including poor physical health and unhappiness at school. It is considered to cause low self-esteem, absenteeism, anxiety, depression and poor psycho-social adjustment, each of which contributes a negative impact on an individual's development and learning (Callaghan and Joseph 1995; Nansel et al. 2001; Nolin, Davies and Chandler 1996; Olweus 1978; Osler 2006; Rigby 2007; Slee 1994a, b, 1995b; Slee and Rigby 1993a, b; Sourander et al. 2000).

As documented in the literature, the extent of bullying is consistently high. In Australia, for example, Phillip Slee (1994b) found that one-third (33 per cent) of children between the ages of 8 and 12 felt unsafe because of bullying. Ken Rigby's large-scale survey of 25,000 children between the ages of 9 and 17 found that 14 per cent were bullied at least once a week (Rigby 1997). In a separate study, Slee and Rigby (1993a) found that 10 per cent of boys and 6 percent of girls between 7 and 13 years of age were subjected to peer-group bullying at least once a week, and that 8 per cent of these cases involved episodes that went on for six months or longer. In 1995, studies in New Zealand found that half to three-quarters of children were bullied in any one year, with 10 per cent being bullied weekly (Youth Education Service NZ Police 2007).

The pathologisation of bullying and its extent alerts us to a line of fault in the bullying discourse. What could it mean for such a high percentage of any population to be pathological (that is, diseased)? Galloway and Roland (2004) ask whether the rates are higher in geographical areas where poverty and disadvantage might lead one to predict an increase in anti-social or pathological behaviour patterns. But they found no correlation between the areas where the schools were located and the rates of bullying. Further, in a three-year study, Mortimore et al. (1988) showed that, whilst teachers might identify 30 per cent of their students as having problem behaviour, only 3 per cent of those students – that is, less than 1 per cent overall – were identified as being problematic during all three years. In other words, problem behaviour was not a consistent feature of the individuals themselves, but of individuals-in-relation within particular contexts.

The interventions that have been developed to reduce bullying (for example, Berne 1999; Bonds and Stocker 2000; Elliott 2001; Limber and Small 2003; Noble 2005; Rigby 1997, 2001, 2002a, b; Sullivan 2000) are generally based on the psycho-social model. Both bullies and their targets are understood as being deficient in social and personal skills as well as in need of explicit instruction about the collective ethos of the school. However, Galloway and Roland (2004) suggest that the problems of bullying lie more broadly in what they call the 'school climate', or what we refer to here as the 'contemporary ethos' or 'moral order' of schools.

Introducing an alternative to the psycho-social model

Theodor Adorno argues that moral questions emerge in the context of social relations 'when moral norms of behaviour have ceased to be self-evident' (Adorno 2001: 16). Our analysis suggests an interesting reversal of this dynamic. It may be that the norms of behaviour are being adopted and imposed too avidly by some students in the everyday life at schools. Citing Adorno, Judith Butler suggests that 'the collective ethos is invariably a conservative one, which postulates a false unity that attempts to suppress the difficulty and discontinuity existing within any contemporary ethos' (Butler 2005: 4). Indeed, she suggests that the collective ethos 'can impose its claim to commonality only through violent means' (ibid.). We postulate that violence amongst students may, at least in part, be connected to the accomplishment of this collective ethos, suggesting the need for a fresh examination of the ways in which identities are accomplished in the context of contemporary schooling. The second author's previous ethnographic research of pre-school and primary-school playgrounds suggests that the figure of the bully may be more active in the construction and maintenance of the norms of schools than indicated by the empirical literature on bullying (Davies 1982, 1989/2003, 1996, 2004; Davies and Hunt 1994).

In her ethnographic studies, the second author has shown that it is vital to students' survival to know how the social order works, and this involves knowing how one's identity can be made to make sense in terms of that social order. The students thus actively participate in establishing and maintaining that order. In her studies of pre-school children and gender, for example, she found that the children were engaged in 'category-maintenance work', which often involved aggressive and punitive behaviour towards those who disrupted the already established binary categories, such as male and female or strong and weak. Stephen Frosh et al. have also observed punitive responses to overly feminised behaviour in boys and of overly masculine behaviour in girls (Frosh, Phoenix and Pattman 2002: 70). The aggressive defence of the known order enables students to take up their own identities in predictable ways within that order. Thus, they are engaged in discursive, constitutive work, reiterating, in this case, gendered conditions of possibility and taking them up in their own lives. They work on themselves and their own borders in creating themselves as recognisably and successfully male or female.

The processes of subjectification developed in those studies – as well as in the work of both Foucault and Butler – suggest that 'what I can "be," quite literally, is constrained in advance by a regime of truth that decides what will and will not be a recognisable form of being' (Butler 2005: 22). The regimes of truth through which the gender order and, more broadly, the moral order are established cannot be bypassed in the ongoing constitution of individual subjects:

[T]here is no 'I' that can fully stand apart from the social conditions of its emergence, no 'I' that is not implicated in a set of conditioning moral norms, which, being norms, have a social character that exceeds a purely personal or idiosyncratic meaning. [...] When the 'I' seeks to give an account of itself, it can start with itself, but it will find that this self is already implicated in a social temporality that exceeds its own capacities for narration; indeed when the 'I' seeks to give an account of itself, an account that must include the conditions of its own emergence, it must, as a matter of necessity, become a social theorist. [... since] the 'I' has no story of its own that is not also a story of a relation – or set of relations – to a set of norms. (ibid.: 7–8)

Current strategies for dealing with violence (Davies 1996; Ellwood 2007) require students to make an account of themselves as having an understanding of the consequences of their social actions. As we examine in this chapter, however, making an account of oneself is not a simple task. Far from being a straightforward representation of an observably real self with transparent motives and intentions, the account is a relational accomplishment; a positioning of oneself within the moral order and, simultaneously, the reiteration and maintenance of that order (Davies 2008).

School violence as normative and normalised

The archive of teacher and student talk generated in the pilot study revealed a major problem in distinguishing between conflict (seen as 'normal' violence) and bullying (seen as pathological). In the teachers' talk in the secondary school, we observed a reiterated question that they asked in response to each incident that came to their attention: is it normal, schooling-as-usual, or are there pathological individuals at work who must be stopped?

I honestly didn't know if it was just two schoolgirls having a bit of a tiff or if it was a sustained bullying. Knowing what both girls are like, I really wasn't sure what to do. (secondary-school teacher)

Trying to, really trying to discern whether it is really actually bullying or whether it's just conflict and whether it's just sort of some kind of in-fighting. And so I guess, and, again, that's a very fine line and um it's hard enough for me always to know, to think well was that incident bullying or was it conflict? (secondary-school teacher)

The teachers' talk-as-usual shows a complex tension between reading violence as normal and the task of identifying bullies. This was despite the fact that the anti-bullying programme was meant to undo the practice of turning a blind eye to violent incidents amongst students:

The goal of the programme I think was to um. . .first of all make students aware of what bullying was . . . make . . . staff aware that these things happen and even the very subtle things that happen that staff often dismiss as 'Oh, it's just a one-off' . . . a lot of the teachers used to say things like um 'Oh, look you know, that's just life. You'll just have to be a bit tough you know. Get over it' or 'It'll pass, don't worry. You know just ignore them', which seems to be a favourite adult advice to kids who are feeling unhappy and intimidated by other kids. (secondary-school executive staff member)

The official strategy in this secondary school concertedly widened the definition of what would count as bullying (and would therefore be deemed unacceptable). It worked to de-normalise the everyday violence that teachers had previously accepted. We suggest here, however, that the failure to question the psycho–social model of bullying that pathologises individuals and families who are caught up in bullying creates problems, both in relation to identifying what counts as bullying and in formulating an appropriate response. Overwhelmed by the number of complaints from parents about bullying once the programme had been established, the same executive staff member quoted above found herself pathologising the complaining parents and appealing to the definition of bullying as repetitive:

I think that word [bullying], because of the media, has been overused and every time a kid has conflict now, it's bullying. . . . I hear it from parents all the time, 'They're always being bullied', 'They're being bullied' and they're talking about a one-off incident you know. And you know conflict's part of life. . . . I guess bullying is about the kind of information that you are given and how prepared people are to make complaints. And often I find the parents who are prepared to complain about it are you know. . .over-protective, um there aren't. I don't believe that they are all genuine cases, I think they come in with the mindset of the victim as well.

In effect, this staff member succeeded in re-establishing violence as unavoidable in the normal everyday life of the school in order to manage the flow of complaints from parents.

Students also invoked a normalising discourse, suggesting that some violence is necessary for survival. For example, in the case of one of the primary-school boys, what was constituted as bullying by teachers was sometimes necessary as self-defence:

Well, I don't like fighting, like I want to get along with someone, but sometimes when I'm annoyed or someone annoys me, I sometimes get really annoyed that I have to hit. I don't like doing that, I like just to play handball, get along with everyone but sometimes you've got to use your – like your defence. . . . You know what I mean?

For a student in the secondary school, verbal bullying was something that could not be stopped since 'bitching' is 'human nature': 'Everyone bitches because you have to let it out sometimes and some people just let it out more.' Another secondary-school student saw survival benefits in having verbal bullying skills:

Sometimes you want to be witty and intelligent and snappy when someone bullies you, you just want to have the right thing to say back to them. So wanting to be, I suppose, smarter or wittier than the other person, or wanting to be bigger which you think means having a better call.

However, the students in the primary school objected to their teachers' resumption of 'normal' forms of violence control, even after the latter had learnt alternative strategies. When asked how the programme in the primary school was functioning, the students described a decrease in commitment from the teachers, who were still 'yelling' at the students instead of utilising the programme strategies:

They [the teachers] are just back to their normal routine where they ask them [the students] what happened and then they yell at everyone.

She [the teacher] just yells. [. . .She] comes to us and tells us off and goes 'If I was [the principal], I'd put you on a week of detention' and I said to her 'Miss, you don't even know the real reason why we're here' so she never went through any of the restorative practice questions, she just told us off and sent us to [the principal].

My teacher like when I get in trouble sometimes, she doesn't let me explain, she just 'Da, da, da, da' [imitates teacher yelling] and I go 'Okay, I'm trying to explain.' 'Aah aah' [imitates teacher screaming] like there she goes again. I try and explain to her what happened but she won't listen.

These primary-school students constitute the teachers' shouting and yelling as inappropriate because it pre-empts the possibility that they have learnt to anticipate and desire, which is to talk through what has happened. Another said:

When someone's been hurt or when someone's hurt someone else, they get to talk about it to someone and they don't just get yelled at or something because they've done it, they get to talk about it. . .first.

And another student related this problem directly to unequal power structures:

Because I think it's not the way to talk to others and like we're speaking now, we're low [both researcher and student were sitting on low, child-sized chairs] and we're sorting something out and um I think it's better like this because it works well. And if teachers scream at us, we don't like it and like sometimes we can scream back and we get in more trouble and I just don't like screaming, I like staying quiet.

It seems that there is something about the moral order of the school that makes the new relationality difficult to sustain. We suggest that this is intricately connected to the twin strategies of pathologising bullies and normalising everyday violence.

Violence as a means of maintaining the collective ethos: pathologising bullies

In this section, we configure those who engage in normative violence as 'classic bullies', readily recognised by their depictions in classic semi-autobiographical novels such as *Tom Brown's School Days* (Hughes 1857) and *Cat's Eye* (Atwood 1988). What we suggest is that the definition of bullies as 'pathological' diverts attention away from the classic bully. The classic bully is a powerful figure on the playground: someone who is admired and feared, and who functions to maintain social and moral order through aggressive behaviour towards those who fail to meet certain norms – either the moral ethos of the school or something else that is (randomly) being defined as correct 'in group' behaviour within the peer group (see Søndergaard, Chapter 3, page 47). The normalising of everyday violence – and the individualising and pathologising of bullies that we found in teachers' talk – works to exclude the figure of the 'classic bully' from being considered as part of the problem. The figure of the classic bully may be read as the champion of – or even an expert in – the collective ethos. Far from being disliked, marginal and socially unskilled, the classic bully may be popular, due to his/her knowledge of how the dominant social order works, and powerful in his/her insistence that others conform to it. Knowing how school culture works may allow one to gain friends, admiration and social power (Sutton, Smith and Swettenham 1999).

In stark contrast – and for the purposes of this argument – the 'sad bully' is someone who lacks the skills and characteristics of the properly socialised student-citizen. It is the sad bully who stands outside of the common ethos and the relational networks of recognition and care. The sad bully may be amongst that 1 per cent identified by Mortimore et al. (1988), whose lives have been such that they have not had appropriate opportunities to develop a conscience or the reflexive skills for analysing what will and will not count as acceptable, ethical behaviour. Whereas the acts of the 'classic bully' may go unremarked, the 'sad bully' is likely be caught in an unbreakable re-citation: one is recognised as engaging in bullying behaviour because one has already been recognised as one who is likely to engage in bullying behaviour.

In studying our archive, we found that teachers were not aware of the constitutive nature of these acts of recognition. Instead, they naturalised bullying, locating it in the character of particular individuals. For example, several secondary-school teachers said:

Because the other girl, I feel, is one that we need to watch and she probably will turn into a bit of a school bitch I think. Call a spade a spade.
These two boys, I wouldn't be surprised if they turned around and started you know antagonising and bullying other people.
Most of these kids are not hardcore toughies, they are just silly kids.
There are some kids that are just nasty, right, but they are really a minority.

The subject positions of 'hardcore toughies', 'just nasty' kids or 'the ones we need to watch' are waiting for individual subjects to occupy them – to be known through them, to be constituted by them.

Acts of violence that are engaged in by those not occupying these positions or that are being taken up within these positions, in contrast, are not read as bullying, but rather, as part of the everyday, inevitable violence in schools. Students may be observed behaving in homophobic, racist or sexist ways or in ways that harm others – like the two girls with the Sudanese boy – yet their behaviour may not be addressed through the strategies for dealing with bullying. Instead, the violent behaviour may be read as innocent, natural or as a one-time mistake. Violence may also be read as an inevitable repetition or reflection of the violence happening in the world outside the school (Taylor 2008), or it may just be seen as 'normal conflict', as 'boys being boys' or as the inevitable tensions generated by social and cultural differences:

I think that students of that age group, of [secondary] school, you know, there's always going to be bullying. There are always going to be issues, there's always going to be secular groups of the tough kids, the dags, the this and that, and that will always be there and, in some schools or some situations, there's going to be more friction than in others. (secondary-school teacher)

Relationality and ethical responsibility

In the discursive space we are trying to open up here, the question becomes: what sort of moral order is being constructed within contemporary schools? Is it a moral order in which the individualistic 'I' takes precedence, ignoring its embeddedness in relation to others? Or can it be something other than this, where each participant sees him/herself in relation to others and is open to differences in these others (Davies and Gannon 2009)?

If we were to envisage a pedagogical space in which bullying was no longer the regular occurrence that the empirical literature in our archive shows it to be, then the school programmes that currently focus on the pathologised bully would change into programmes in which schools take responsibility for developing relational practices that recognise and honour the other – with all their differences. Someone's 'difference' would not be seen as an error to be tolerated at best and obliterated at worst, but an expansion and extension of each-in-relation-to-the-other. Such relations cannot depend on an imposed moral order based on a set of rules, but instead need an ethical practice that requires all participants to reflect in each specific moment:

For an action to be 'moral,' it must not be reducible to an act or a series of acts conforming to a rule, a law or a value. Of course all moral action involves a relationship with the reality in which it is carried out, and a relationship with the self. The latter is not simply 'self-awareness' but self-formation as an ethical subject. (Foucault 1985: 28)

Butler (2005) argues that self-formation as an ethical subject requires that, in relation to the other, each of us must work to create the conditions of existence that enable recognition and survival of both self and other. This recognition does not require the other to become 'the same', shaped by the same rules and interpretive practices, but it begins with the recognition of one's own opacity and vulnerability. Gilles Deleuze (1980) makes a similar point when he argues that we move towards ethics and away from morality. Whereas morality involves judgement of the other, he states that ethics rests on an openness to the other and the possibility of becoming different oneself, of coming to know and to be different in that openness:

> Morality is the system of judgment. Of double judgment, you judge yourself and you are judged. Those who have the taste for morality are those who have the taste for judgment. [. . .] In an ethics it is completely different, you do not judge. [. . .] Somebody says or does something, you do not relate it to values. You ask yourself how is that possible? How is this possible in an internal way? In other words, you relate the thing or the statement to the mode of existence that it implies, that it envelops in itself. How must it be in order to say that? Which manner of Being does this imply? You seek the enveloped modes of existence, and not the transcendent values. It is the operation of immanence. (ibid.: np)

In this Deleuzian sense, ethical practice is openness to the other; openness that does not judge but is responsive and responsible. Katerina Zabrodska et al. (2011) 'propose an ethics that requires each one of us, singly and collectively, to see the multiple ways we are caught up in the production of bullying [where] agency is not simply or solely located in individual subjects, but in events, and in institutional discourses and practices that are collectively maintained'. Further, the ethical practice they advocate gives each person:

> . . .responsibility for being mindful of what is made to matter, and for singly and collectively engaging in rigorous critique of discourses and practices that cause harm to self and to others. [. . .It] requires us to recognize the potential to do harm, so it also undoes the inevitability of the normalization of bullying. (ibid.)

Conclusion

We began with an approach to discourse analysis that understands the individual as a 'subject that constitutes itself within history and is constantly established and re-established by history', and discourse as being that which constructs that subject through 'a set of strategies which are part of social practices' (Foucault 2000c). In this analysis, we were interested 'not merely

[in] spoken words, but [in] a notion of signification which concerns not merely how it is that certain signifiers come to mean what they mean, but how certain discursive forms articulate objects and subjects in their intelligibility' (Butler 1995: 138). We asked how bullying and bullies are constituted in the research as well as in the interventions that have been developed from that research. We argued that the bullying discourse has itself become part of the problem. Our analysis suggests an urgent need to re-think the definitions of bullies and bullying. Part of the problem may be the school ethos, especially as it is championed and manipulated by powerful figures in the classroom and/or playground, including both teachers and students who assume the task of imposing 'moral norms of behaviour' (Adorno 2001: 16). It may be possible for members of school communities to establish non-violent ethical practices – not by imposing an ethos that locates and punishes individual bullies, but rather, by developing practices that encourage and facilitate being open to differences as well as promoting the value of differences. Such practices entail a reflexive awareness of self and the other – of both their similarities and differences – and this implies an ongoing responsibility of self-in-relation-to-other and self-in-relation-to-self. New research in schools is needed to test this proposition.

5 *Dispositifs* of bullying*

Carsten Bagge Laustsen

Introduction: who thinks in the abstract. . .about bullying?

In one of his texts, German philosopher Georg Wilhelm Friedrich Hegel (1808/1991) asks what it means to think abstractly. Most people would almost immediately say that philosophers think in the abstract. The next suggestion would probably be theologians, followed by scientists in general. When we leave the concrete appearance of this world and the air starts to become rarefied, then we are thinking in the abstract. Philosophers study pure thoughts, shunning any kind of disruptive and intrusive reality. Theologians think about an ethereal world that we cannot know: about God and the divine. And scientists sit in their ivory towers, which have a magnificent view, but the implication is that everything is observed from a distance.

However, it is the other way around for Hegel. It is precisely those who, time and again, pick on philosophy for being abstract and nonspecific who are exactly that. Contrary to what most people may think – even many philosophers – (good) philosophy is about concrete thinking. How is that? In the aforementioned text, Hegel gives an example (ibid.: 68ff): think about a murderer! Normally, laypeople, vicars and judges would regard the alleged murderer with condemnation and contempt if the crime appears to be nasty, or with tolerance and maybe even sympathy if the accused is good-looking, vulnerable and contrite. The focus on a person's physical appearance and on the murder as an isolated act is an example of thinking in the abstract. In contrast, (good) philosophy is concrete thinking because it does not focus on what happened as an isolated act or on the individual as a loner. Concrete thinking pursues the history of the murderer (what kind of troubles did he/she experience

* I would like to thank Dorte Marie Søndergaard, Robin May Schott, Helle Rabøl Hansen and an anonymous referee for many good and useful comments; also Lone Winther and Amy Clotworthy for help with the translation.

in the past?), it relates to the act as being conditioned and circumstantial (where, how and under what circumstances can a murder make any sense?) and, finally, it relates to everything as embedded in social processes; i.e. as conditioned by the way individuals relate to each other. A holistic explanation – such as the one we have just outlined – is concrete, whereas an isolated explanation or perhaps just a single observation, feeling or taste is an abstraction.

If we must think concretely and practise specificity with regards to bullying, then we cannot stop with a diagnosis of the victim or the bully. The point of departure should not be 'abstract' questions, such as: 'Who is he?'; 'Does he have a diagnosis?'; 'Is he aggressive?'; or, if the focus is on the victim, 'Is he particularly vulnerable?'; and 'What is bullying?' A repeated, violent act is a suggestion or in continuation of classic power theory, an act where one individual forces another against his will. And finally, 'How can bullying be avoided?' For example, can it be done by removing the victim or bully? No. Instead of these abstract questions and answers, we must understand bullying as something that has a history, that is tied to an environment marked by fear and conflict, that is practised in a concrete physical setting, that is perhaps facilitated by technological artefacts and that takes place in a complex interaction between teachers, parents and students in different positions as bully, victim, bystanders, third parties – or perhaps in several positions at once. To be more precise: it is acceptable to ask who is being bullied, what bullying is and how it can be combated. The problem with that approach is simply whether those questions will lead to abstract thinking where the social determinants and concrete social context of bullying are ignored.

A concrete view of bullying has an eye towards its social circumstances. The eye looks towards the bigger picture and, for that reason, the view must be complex. Consequently, a concrete view must direct its attention towards the specific circumstances of bullying, which does not necessarily mean focusing on what appears to be given as such. Just like the vicar, the judge or the layperson in Hegel's example, we might only see the immediate act – Joan bullied Ann – but we do not see how this act may be situated in an environment characterised by a fear of social exclusion, by a desire to be a part of a group (see Hansen, Chapter 10, page 241), by frequent teacher changes and/or by a dissenting, weak group of teachers. If bullying is our object of study, then it is an object we must construct. We need thinking – or what Dorte Marie Søndergaard and Jette Kofoed (2009) have called thinking technologies[1] – to identify bullying as the complex

---

[1] Dorte Marie Søndergaard and Jette Kofoed define 'thinking technologies' as tools that, firstly, contribute to forming a description of a given phenomenon, and secondly, that

and social phenomenon that it is. If we choose to consider bullying as acts that are isolated, exclusive and/or individually driven, then we will end up thinking in the abstract.

How do we promote theoretical distance to facilitate empirical proximity – or, in Hegel's terms, concrete thinking? It may be advantageous here to stress the similarities between the idea of thinking technologies and the ideal type that forms a methodological basis for Max Weber's work. For Weber, the ideal type was not just an average consideration with numerous observations as its point of departure. It was not a generalisation in the positivistic sense of the word. Rather, the ideal type was a reflection on the possible connections between factors, elements, forms and effects, which would facilitate questions about their empirical bearing and interrelations. The ideal type enables a view of the whole, but the fact that Weber always worked with several ideal types (e.g. different forms of authority) simultaneously makes his analyses sensitive with regard to empirical diversity.

The ideal type is tied to an observation of a number of complex, interconnected phenomena. As such, it does not come out of the blue. At the same time, however, some aspects must be 'purified' to elicit a clear picture of their interrelation. For example, when Weber analysed Protestant ethics (Weber 1905/1991), he did not find it in a pure form amongst its adherents. They were not necessarily – and in fact, were seldom – completely aware that they were complying with a type of cohesive doctrine. Consequently, Weber was interested in Benjamin Franklin's work when he, as a kind of grammarian, articulated Protestant ethics in a coherent, complete and reflective manner.

In relation to bullying, we are facing a similar set of problems. Often, the individual actors do not consider how bullying occurs as a complex phenomenon. But if the level of bullying should decline, it is necessary to focus on its complex determinants and settings. In all likelihood, it will not be as cohesive as claimed by the ideal types that I am suggesting in this chapter. But it will have some kind of form, and the ideal types allow us to highlight exactly that. Thinking technologies help us pose the right questions, and consider the right determinants and their interrelations; then, on that basis, we may enable effective and strategic interventions. In other words, we are looking for a sort of pre-theory of bullying – something that is less ambitious than casual theory and more ambitious than grounded theory.

create the conditions for this description. Further, it is characteristic that thinking technologies are not merely academic inventions, but also that they become a part of the reality they describe (Kofoed and Søndergaard 2009: 8).

My thematisation of bullying as a complex social phenomenon is inspired by Michel Foucault's *dispositif* analysis.[2] In brief, a '*dispositif*' is an apparatus or, when formulated in more general terms, an order that affects and thus situates certain propensities in a given material.[3] The analysis of *dispositifs* is a kind of power analysis, focusing on why and how certain ways of thinking and acting become possible and likely; i.e. how they are predisposed. At the same time, however, focusing on proclivities and predispositions implies that a reduction of power to the level where one individual exerts force over another no longer makes sense; or at least, it is seen as reductive. A *dispositif* predisposes certain outcomes of action but does not determine them.

This chapter is divided into five parts. It starts with an introduction of *dispositif* analysis and argues for its applicability as a pre-theory of bullying. The next three parts each present a 'bullying *dispositif*': the *dispositif of sovereignty*, which thinks about bullying as an action that is both theoretical and binary within the bully–victim relationship;[4] the *dispositif of discipline*, which thinks about bullying as being connected to probabilities and risks, and thus as something everyone may potentially practise and to which anyone may be subjected; and finally, the *dispositif of terror*,[5] which thinks about bullying less as being systematically practised and more as being connected to an environment characterised by the fear of social exclusion. The chapter ends with a short discussion about the advantages of a dispositif-inspired analytical view.

[2] There are several examples of Foucault-inspired analyses of bullying available, which typically take their points of departure in Foucault's work on discipline and punishment (see, for example, Jacobson 2010). Others use Foucault's discourse analysis and his combined thoughts about knowledge, power and subjectivity as their basis (see, for example, Ellwood and Davies 2010). I have not found any studies on bullying inspired by his analysis of *dispositifs*.

[3] In my review of *dispositif* analysis, I am greatly indebted to Sverre Raffnsøe and Marius Gudmand-Høyer for their excellent mapping of it as an analytical strategy (Raffnsøe and Gudmand-Høyer 2005).

[4] Let me make a few brief comments to address a possible objection: when I argue that sovereignty predisposes bullying in an action–theoretical and individualistic perspective, isn't this in conflict with an understanding of dispositif analysis as a concrete form of thinking in Hegel's sense; that is, a thinking that understands bullying in its complex social context? The answer is no. As sociology has tirelessly emphasised – from Durkheim to Althusser – the notion of an individual is a social construction. We are taught to be individuals. It is not our nature, but rather, a role or position, one could say, into which we are born. A focus on bullying as something individuals do also has its background in a wide range of social relations: a specific knowledge regime, certain practices, the organisation of schools, etc.

[5] In everyday politics, the terror concept is highly politicised, not least of all because of its strong normative charge. The use of the terror concept in this chapter, however, is analytical; it is used descriptively in relation to a particular form of stochastic and fear-producing demonstrations of power.

What is a *dispositif?*

The concept of *dispositif* only begins to emerge in Foucault's later works. Despite this marginal placement, it is a term through which he retrospectively rationalises his entire work. He sees it as an investigation of a number of different *dispositifs*, their historicity and interconnections. In general, the French word '*dispositif*' is translated as 'apparatus', which suggests an affinity with Louis Althusser's thinking (Althusser 1971: 121–73).[6] To Althusser, the state apparatuses (most importantly, the repressive and the ideological) are complex institutions that do not determine, but rather, 'overdetermine' a given material. It is precisely these two elements that are also central to Foucault's thinking about the dispositif: it is a complex, cohesive whole that influences rather than determines the material it affects. Raffensøe and Gudmand-Høyer define the *dispositif* as such:

> In Foucault, the dispositif also refers to an apparatus that consists of numerous parts arranged in a certain way in relation to one another so that they work together to determine the field of action that the apparatus is processing. A dispositif denotes an arrangement that determines its own environment through the introduction of certain dispositions in it. (2005: 154; author's translation)

In continuation of Foucault's typical interest in the relationship between knowledge, power and subjectivity, we may benefit from focusing on four central aspects that are seen in every *dispositif*: first, it is a complex social whole (or what Foucault elsewhere calls an apparatus); second, it seeks to influence or, in the words of Raffensøe and Gudmand-Høyer, process a given material; third, it contains and draws upon a certain form of knowledge; and finally, it contains an implicit normativity. All in all, the *dispositif* may be seen as a social technology. The classic history of technology is an itemisation of different ways to process given materials – for example, technologies may transform raw materials into saleable products. Similarly, *dispositifs* process a material – but in this case, it is human beings and their relations. In other words, dispositifs affect and create the social in a continuous process (ibid.). So let us examine each of these four aspects (referred to as 1 to 4 below) as they relate to an analysis of the *dispositifs* of bullying.

---

[6] Naturally, there are also differences between Foucault's and Althusser's thinking with regard to the apparatus. Foucault is primarily interested in its various modes of functioning (i.e. sovereignty, discipline, control) while Althusser – in an extension of the Marxist foundations of his theory – is more interested in its function in relation to the reproduction of a given form of control.

1: In an interview, Foucault mentions that the *dispositif* (the apparatus) typically consists of a number of heterogeneous elements: 'discourse, institutions, architectonical forms, regulative decisions, laws, administrative measures, scientific statements, philosophical, moral, or philanthropic propositions – in short, the said as much as the unsaid' (Foucault 1980: 194–6). We could probably add to the list, but the important element must be that it cannot be excluded beforehand that something will be in a *dispositif*. Thus, the *dispositif* analysis is given – due to an interest in the complex character and context of demonstrations of power – to what might be relevant to the likelihood of one particular outcome.

If the above is related to the problematic of bullying, then from the perspective of *dispositif* analysis, we must pay attention to how the following elements may form a cohesive whole: discourses (the thematicisation of bullying in public debates, films, school books, etc.); institutions (primarily the school as an institution standardised by numerous informal and formal rules, but also other institutions, such as sports clubs, before- and after-school care, media and public authorities); the physical organisation of the school (temperature, division of classes, placement of desks, noise levels, etc.); and regulative statements, such as action plans for bullying and the legislative decision that such plans must be instituted and assign subject positions (as teacher, student, victim, bully or bystander, and the interrelation between these roles and positions). In the identification of various bullying *dispositifs*, I draw attention to everything that interacts and pulls in the same direction, and that thus 'clicks together'. One cannot claim *a priori* that something is not relevant, so we must study a *dispositif* thoroughly to determine the elements of which it is comprised.

2: The second element is strategic. The *dispositif* instals certain tendencies in a material, and the material is then influenced in a certain direction. As mentioned earlier, it is not about a causal understanding of 'x determines y'. Something being influenced means there is a propensity for a certain outcome. But the intricate power struggles are performed by a number of different actors who interact with their surroundings in a complex way and, as such, we may see that only certain outcomes and connections are probable. With regard to the strategic dimension, Foucault writes:

The nature of an apparatus [read: *dispositif*] is essentially strategic, which means that we are talking about a certain manipulation of power relations, of rational and concrete interventions in power relations, and that is either to develop them in a particular direction, block them, stabilise them or utilise them. (ibid.)

Thus, a *dispositif* affects a complex force field by trying to influence it in a certain way.

If we examine the actor level, it seems obvious that the relationship between students is affected by a number of power relations. From this point of departure, bullying is a strategically founded attempt to revalue the bully and devalue the victim. It is also an attempt to reconfigure the relations between different individuals in the class and the groups to which they belong. In addition, bullying affects relations to family, teachers, parents, etc. If we take a broader perspective, it is obvious that physical surroundings and technological artefacts – for example, mobile phones – may be strategically used in the aforementioned power positioning. Finally, if we turn this perspective around and examine the attempts to combat bullying, these interventions must also be understood as strategic attempts to influence certain students, the formation of groups, the artefacts that the actors have at their disposal and the environments they inhabit.

3: The third element of the dispositif is connected to certain forms of knowledge, which implies several things. The spirit of the times dictates that some things are important and others are less important. In other words, what appears to be a problem will always be given discursively, and since the *dispositifs* are answers to these problems, they will – for that reason alone – be intimately connected with a knowledge horizon. But the *dispositifs* themselves are also borne by knowledge. In part, they thematicise the complex field where they set norms that regulate, and they also hold knowledge intrinsic to the *dispositifs* about how their various components should be organised. One can see intervention programmes as examples of such *dispositif*-intrinsic knowledge. Finally, on one hand, there is the explicit scientific knowledge at our disposal and, on the other, there is the knowledge that is embedded in practice. The three forms of knowledge – the knowledge within social discourse and problematicisation; the knowledge the *dispositif* draws directly upon in its operations; and social knowledge in the form of general scientific knowledge and lay knowledge – are, of course, mutually dependent and mutually constituted.

Bullying has reached the political agenda and is now thematicised as a far more serious problem than before. The distinction between the form of bullying that requires intervention and what is considered 'natural' teasing has been displaced. Bullying appears to be unambiguously negative and something that should and can be eliminated. It is no longer about 'teaching children not to hit each other' and otherwise strengthening them to play the social game, but rather, about changing the game and its rules. A number of operative definitions of bullying are at work, and these correspond to a range of ideas for useful tools to combat bullying. For example, Dan Olweus's research (1973, 2000) about bullying has dominated the academic discussion, and this has resulted in part in numerous 'normal-scientific' research projects (in Thomas Kuhn's sense) and informed several concrete interventions. This scientific knowledge is often combined with practical knowledge and lay knowledge, since teachers and the school leadership will implement the various initiatives, drawing upon what they think is 'obvious' and 'the obvious thing to do'. As we see later, ordering a student to stand outside the door, for example, is fixed to a certain form of knowledge: it is an action that conceives bullying as being tied to individuals and as a phenomenon that can be combated with disciplinary sanctions.

4: The fourth element, which is implicated by the previous three to some extent, is that the *dispositif* contains its own normativity. This is seen in three ways. Firstly, it makes some outcomes more likely than others, and a normativity already lies therein: something must be stimulated, and something must be fought or made unlikely because it is unwanted. *Dispositifs* are designed to tackle complex and precarious social problems and tasks, and thus they take their point of departure from the premise that something is not as it should be. Therefore, and secondly, the *dispositif* often contains an explicit thematicisation of what is given high/low value, respectively. The law, for example, contains such a notion about the forbidden. Thirdly, the *dispositif* can operate with concepts that are themselves normative, and thus it contains within itself information about what should be done and not done.

The relevance of these normative aspects in relation to an investigation of bullying seems obvious. Intervention efforts against bullying are specifically intended to solve a precarious social problem, and they do this by attempting to make some actions more probable and others less likely; e.g. those that qualify as bullying. It is also obvious that the *dispositifs* explicitly thematicise the outcome of actions as either wanted or unwanted. But more than that: to a greater or lesser degree, they also contain a notion of what a good and healthy sociality entails and, on the other hand, which conditions stimulate bullying. Finally, we can note that the very idea of bullying is a normatively laden concept that intends to create a 'drama' about actions that are thematicised within this framework. There is something particularly serious about bullying behaviour that should generate very specific efforts. The concept intends to mobilise and provoke both a response and a change.

In Foucault's lecture at Collège de France in 1978 (entitled 'Sécurité, territoire, population'; 2007), he demarcated three *dispositifs* i.e. specific ways to connect the three aforementioned elements.[7] *Dispositifs* are

---

[7] Foucault reads *dispositif* modalities through the confrontation with historically given material. Thus, for him, there are principally no finite number of *dispositifs*. Foucault often gives the *dispositifs* new names when he confronts a new substance, which is why it may be argued

historically given, but they have a tendency to resemble one of the three *dispositifs* or a combination thereof. One could say that the three *dispositifs* are particularly cohesive ideal types: 'law', 'discipline' and 'security'. The 'law' is a prescriptive social technology that establishes a binary distinction between the legal and illegal. With this, it is made clear which types of behaviour are unwanted and not tolerated. In contrast, discipline is not about exclusion and ostracism, but about preventing unwanted behaviour. Thus, the rationale is preventive. Finally, the security *dispositif* remedially relates to unexpected events.

I have been inspired by Foucault's trichotomy, and I adapt it to a study of bullying in this chapter. Furthermore, I substantiate the description of the three *dispositifs* on the basis of Foucault's other works, and this approach may capture aspects of the bullying problematic other than the time-specific aspect (i.e. the focus on effectuated actions, the prevention of unwanted actions and the repair of damaging actions). Foucault describes the two aforementioned dispositifs in *Discipline and Punish: The Birth of the Prison* (1977), and I have chosen to adopt his terminology here. Instead of 'the law', he describes 'sovereignty' as a *dispositif* that relates to certain unwanted actions or movements. In both cases (law and sovereignty), we are referring to a *dispositif* that functions by excluding single individuals who fall outside of the norm. He calls the preventive *dispositif* 'discipline', and I adhere to that terminology. I name the third and final *dispositif* 'terror' – this focuses on a stochastic, unsystematic and sudden demonstration of power that instills a feeling of fear.[8]

I follow the same systematic in discussing all three *dispositifs*. On the basis of Foucault's thinking, I develop them as ideal types and, subsequently, I relate them to the study of bullying. In the representation of

that there are other *dispositifs* than the three I mention here in this chapter. When I chose to focus on the three *dispositifs* that Foucault mentioned in his lecture from 1978, it is because, firstly, they are the three that were found in my empirical material, which is not a denial that there are other applicable definitions, and new ones may still be added. Secondly, there is a quality that we are talking about three relatively sharply demarcated *dispositifs*. My use of the *dispositif* analysis is more structuralist than historically given; i.e. the idea about a pre-theory and ideal types, which is why I have emphasised the presentation of three distinctly different prisms, rather than a large number of partially overlapping *dispositifs*. In my view, the three *dispositifs* are to be understood as basic forms, and I do not discuss in this chapter how these can be modified, coexist with each other, be in conflict or otherwise changed into or become part of hybrid forms.

[8] To varying degrees, the names of the three *dispositifs* characterise either bullying or the intervention that is set against it. 'Sovereignty' can be said to describe both parts; 'discipline' (and control) focuses exclusively on the sanctions (interventions); while 'terror' focuses exclusively on the type of bullying. Of course, I have endeavoured to find a balance here between applying concepts that retain the reference to Foucault's work and applying concepts that provide the best associations in relation to the context of bullying. Finally, I have also attempted to maintain the conceptualisations used in my previous work (e.g. Diken and Laustsen 2005a: 57–75).

the *dispositifs* of bullying, I put emphasis on the same five elements, although the stress is weighted differently in the three *dispositifs*. Firstly, (A) I identify the actors in bullying; i.e. the view of those who bully and those who are bullied on one side, and the view of the teacher and the rest of the class on the other. Secondly, (B) I focus on how bullying is thought to be avoided, curtailed or handled. Thirdly, (C) I look closely at the thinking within the class environment and culture, the significance of the surroundings and the use of technological artefacts. Fourthly, (D) I shed light on the widest possible social frameworks: on discourse, on social development and on the scientific knowledge about bullying. Fifthly and finally, (E) I give some examples of intervention programmes that present themselves after being unfolded in the three *dispositifs*.

The dispositif *of sovereignty*

In mapping the *dispositifs* of sovereignty and discipline, I am inspired by Foucault's *Discipline and Punish* (1977). The primary task of this work is to identify the contours of a *dispositif* of discipline. It can be read from a historical perspective and understood as an analysis of how the *dispositif* of discipline develops, particularly the way it is expressed in modern penitentiaries. However, we may also understand the work as an identification of the logic of discipline. Foucault discusses Jeremy Bentham's suggestion for a panopticon.[9] Obviously, this is relevant in a book about the history of penitentiaries, but Foucault's main point is that Bentham developed and thought through a universal principle to maximise utility – a principle that says a lot about what discipline is. The principle could be applied in prisons where the asymmetrical visibility holds the prisoners at bay, but it could also be applied in hospitals, where the man in the central tower would no longer be a prison guard but a doctor who

---

[9] In brief, the panopticon is an architectural idea that supports the production of the greatest possible utility. Bentham's and Foucault's main example of the panopticon is a prison that consists of a guard tower centrally located within a ring of cells. All of the cells can be observed from the tower in the middle, while the prisoners in the cells can only see the shadow of the guard in the tower. The manipulation of lighting conditions means that the prisoners cannot see when they are being monitored (or not) and, therefore, they will potentially feel watched constantly. And instead of monitoring all of the prisoners at once for his entire shift, the prison guard can simply be present in the tower. In fact, he does not even need to do that – a mere silhouette can be sufficient to instill in the prisoners a feeling of being watched. A contemporary example of the panopticon might be a language lab where the students do not know that the teacher only occasionally listens to every student (and the effect is that each student feels listened to the whole time). This example also illustrates that we are dealing with a principle that is not necessarily bound to an asymmetry in visibility and observation. The asymmetry can be created through any medium; for example, sound.

listens to patients' moans through the copper tubes from the tower to the cells/the wards; that way, he could attend to the largest possible number of patients with the fewest possible resources. Foucault contrasts the *dispositif* of discipline to an earlier *dispositif* of sovereignty that had been pushed into the background with the expansion of discipline. I am interested in an understanding that attempts to ignore discipline from its historical genesis and, in that way, unfolds it as a kind of ideal type that can be rediscovered within a range of different fields (the prison, health care, education, etc.). Foucault writes:

> If it is true that the leper gave rise to rituals of exclusion, which to a certain extent provided the model for and general form of the great Confinement, then the plague gave rise to disciplinary projects. Rather than the massive, binary division between one set of people and another, it called for multiple separations, individualizing distributions, an organisation in depth of surveillance and control, an intensification and a ramification of power. The leper was caught up in a practice of rejection, of exile-enclosure; he was left to his doom in a mass among which it was useless to differentiate; those sick of the plague were caught up in a meticulous tactical partitioning in which individual differentiations were the constricting effects of a power that multiplied, articulated and subdivided itself; the great confinement on the one hand; the correct training on the other. The leper and his separation; the plague and its segmentations. The first is marked; the second analysed and distributed. ... Underlying disciplinary projects, the image of the plague stands for all forms of confusion and disorder; just as the image of the leper, cut off from all human contact, underlies projects of exclusion. (1977: 198–9)

It makes sense here to begin with the last sentence. Foucault is not interested in the difference in actions directed towards people with leprosy or plague as such. The key is that these two ways of relating to disease give him the opportunity to examine two very different *dispositifs*. If we follow this idea, the task is to think about the two dispositifs as pure forms; i.e. to clear away all particularities and then rediscover the same *dispositif* in relation to bullying. So first, I address the *dispositif* of sovereignty – as Foucault characterises it in connection with the treatment of lepers – followed by the *dispositif* of discipline in the next section.

In Foucault's example, the Sovereign is the one who can exclude an individual from a given community, and the leper is sent out of town and forbidden to enter again. The focus here is on the deviant – both the one with the ability to cast out/exclude individuals (the Sovereign) and also the one who is being excluded (the leper). The other individuals – the majority – are unmarked identities who do not exert power and are not subjected to it. One is either a leper or not a leper – a binary logic rules, as mentioned by Foucault in the quotation above. And when obvious signs of leprosy are found, one is spurred into action. It is mainly about deciphering essences – and keep in mind that it varies from a standard that is only vaguely defined. The deviation is defined – normality is not. Or better, it is only indirectly defined: as not being infected by leprosy.

The individual repressed by a demonstration of power is not just someone from whom we are different and who is no longer part of an 'us'. The exclusion is an 'inclusive exclusion', to use a term from Italian post-Foucauldian scholar Giorgio Agamben (1998). The repressed is kept in a relationship to the repressor precisely because 'the victim' is still affected by this status. Thus, Agamben prefers the term 'abandonment' (ibid.: 104–11). Sovereignty is having the power to banish another individual. During the Middle Ages, anyone could kill a banished individual without consequences. Therefore, the banished most often lived in forests where the Sovereign was no longer in control. However, the Sovereign is the one who has the power to banish someone – it is this ability that allows a sovereign to be a Sovereign. The Sovereign may deny individuals status as rightful subjects, and hence they are neither beholden to nor protected by the law (ibid.: 71ff). After this brief introduction to Foucault's interpretation of sovereignty, let us examine how this *dispositif* unfolds itself in a bullying context, which I do in relation to the five aforementioned parameters.

(A) As we have seen, the *dispositif* of sovereignty is associated with the exception. There is no difference whether the issue is sovereignty (as given by the ability to banish unwanted individuals) or the law as an instance that may be brought into play in connection with the transgression (the forbidden). With regard to bullying, the *dispositif* of sovereignty is connected to it as a deviation from a predetermined norm (from the 'normal', as poorly defined as it is). Bullying is unnatural and unwanted; therefore, it can and should be eliminated. In that connection, the focus is partially on the bully and partially on the victim. As with the leper, there are some clearly identifiable characteristics and actions that make it possible to identify the bully and the bullied, respectively. For example, the bully may be aggressive by nature, have a psychiatric diagnosis or be otherwise deviant. The urge to bully is a 'sick' characteristic. And the one who is bullied can be similarly identified: he may have a weak ego, lack social competences, have certain physical characteristics that make him 'stick out' (e.g. obesity) or perhaps be slightly gifted, etc. The bully sees the bullied as a 'leper' and believes he has 'the right' to expel him from the community.

As its point of departure, bullying is considered in binary terms – a bully (or a group of bullies) has power over the bullied (or a group of those who are bullied). The bully forces the bullied to do something that he does not want to do or that somehow restricts him. The other students in the class are considered bystanders who do not affect the relationship. When bullying is thematicised in connection to the *dispositif* of sovereignty, the bystanders are not given much, if any, attention. Furthermore, bullying is seen as a relation between students or, in rare cases, a relation between a teacher and one or more students where they take the positions of bully and bullied, respectively.

(B) The teacher is often thought to be the one who intervenes with sovereignty in the bullying relation. This can happen by punishing the bully or by protecting the bullied (see Hansen 2009). In both cases, these two individuals or groups are given particularly exceptional treatment. For example, the teacher can punish the one who has bullied by presenting his actions to the other students as deviant, ordering him out of the classroom, ordering him to see the principal, assigning him a new seat in the classroom (e.g. directly in front of the teacher with his back to the rest of the students and thus unable to disturb the lessons) or moving him to another class during school hours (ibid.). In the same way, extraordinary efforts may be applied to the bullied. The teacher may talk to his parents, send the bullied to the school psychologist, put him in another class or perhaps even assist him in changing schools and getting a fresh start. Given that it is a matter of essences, it is also only bullying that is focused on as a repeatable and therefore predictable phenomenon – both in terms of aggressors and victims. An aggressive nature will instill a tendency towards bullying within the potential attacker whilst, for example, a lack of social skills will make certain individuals obvious targets for bullying.

(C) The third element in my five-part classification of bullying's *dispositifs* concerns the class environment and culture, the significance of the surroundings and the use of technological artefacts. The interesting thing here is that this third level is not included in the *dispositif* of sovereignty. Considering that bullying is seen as an action exercised by one particular person against another, the social dynamics of the class become secondary: bullying has its foundation in the character of individuals and not in the dynamics of the class. Similarly, certain materials are considered to be nothing more than 'tools' and 'surroundings'. Although objects can be used to attack somebody – one can bully someone on the internet or by using a mobile phone – it is more important to understand the individuals who use the objects and technologies, and not what these artefacts may render possible in their own right.

This way of thinking about bullying still dominates (see Schott, Chapter 2, page 21), and it should not come as a surprise: we have a learned tendency to think in the 'abstract' – to ignore the social connections that form the basis for identities and actions, and which are perhaps not directly revealed through them. The present era is still characterised by a high degree of individualism and, not surprisingly, this is also reflected in relation to how bullying unfolds and is thought about. We have a tendency to think about power as something exercised in a relationship between two individuals where one harms the other. And we have a tendency to think essentially: when one party is stronger than the other, it is about the stronger one's nature and resources. The strong (or aggressive) one dominates the weak. When we act against bullying, we often do it as a reaction to unacceptable actions against which we feel we must intervene. The response is usually punishment or exclusion of the bully and protection of the one who was subjected to assault. This *dispositif* is strong because it is bound together with our immediate patterns of behaviour, which are not necessarily conscious. This bullying *dispositif* also seems obvious to us since it is thought about in relation to 'the law'; i.e. to the way we normally relate to strong, unwanted behaviour. But all of these notions and reactions also have a 'scientific superstructure', which brings us to the *dispositif*'s fourth element.

(D) As mentioned in the introduction, the most widespread paradigms within bullying research – and, for decades, the most influential on anti-bullying actions – are inspired by the work of Swede Dan Olweus (1973, 2000). On the one hand, Olweus's work may be seen as the basis for the development of the *dispositif* we have associated here with sovereignty; on the other, it may be seen as a rationalisation of the same *dispositif*. Olweus was influenced by Konrad Lorenz's work on aggression in his book of the same title (1966), but Lorenz's focus on the group was narrowed to a focus on individuals. These individuals fall primarily into one of two groups – they are either aggressors or victims (one cannot be both at the same time). Third-party and hybrid subject positions are not given much attention. Bullying is identified as an aggression; i.e. an intentional action performed by one individual against another. According to Olweus, when people end up as one or the other – the one bullying or the one being bullied – it is due to their character and nature. And because bullying has this starting point, it will also appear as repeated acts. In other words, violence that is not repeated cannot be identified as bullying in Olweus's perspective.

The bully is typically aggressive and impulsive, he lacks the ability to feel empathy, he is dominating and sees violence as a legitimate tool. These characteristics may also be explained on the basis of, amongst other things, the bully's family relationships. Bullies have grown up in uncaring and indifferent families who have not succeeded in giving their children the love and attention they need. And the parents have failed to build a framework for their children's behaviour towards other children (see Schott, Chapter 2, page 21). The other party, the bullied, is seen as a weak individual: they are passive, insecure, anxious, submissive, etc. These characteristics may again be explained by their upbringing – they have been dominated by over-protective mothers and thus lack skills in the game of social positioning. Both aggressor and victim thus fall outside of what is considered 'normal'. This has produced a range of research projects that, first of all, try to map these deviant personality traits; and second, recommend strategies to prevent them from forming. It is about the development of a *dispositif* that relates to deviant actions in a regulating way. These actions are identified as being associated with specific actors and, by extension, the development of a preventive strategy that effectively addresses the social background factors that foster those characteristics.

(E) Finally, if we focus on intervention programmes, we can identify several of these traits as integral elements of a *dispositif* of sovereignty. Let me give two examples, both of which are mentioned in a Swedish survey of anti-bullying efforts (Skolverket 2011). The first is the so-called '*farstametode*' (the Fasta Method): when bullying occurs, this intervention programme recommends establishing an anti-bullying team that consists of resource people; e.g. a teacher and a school psychologist. This team first works to define and map the situation and what happened. If the assessment is that there is bullying, they conduct a series of conversations with the bullying victim in order to help him. Over the next two weeks, they keep a close eye on the victim to prevent repeated acts of bullying. If it continues for one-to-two weeks, then they hold conversations with the bully to stop the bullying; if that does not happen, then they can transfer the bully to another class or school.

The second example of an intervention programme that follows the *dispositif* of sovereignty is, not surprisingly, the Olweus programme. When bullying occurs, the relevant teachers intervene and have separate conversations with the victim and aggressor, along with their parents. The programme is built around a series of progressively stricter sanctions: in the first conversation, the school's rules and the prohibition against bullying are emphasised. After this, other measures may be used; for example, a 'timeout' where the student spends three-to-eight minutes in solitude with a teacher. It is also important to mention that the teacher is supposed to keep a logbook, so that violations of the school rules can be recorded and recalled later, if necessary.[10]

---

[10] The Olweus programme also includes a number of elements that, in an extension of the chosen terminology, I would call disciplinary. For example, organising a theme day about

The dispositif *of discipline*

Discipline and Punish, however, is not primarily about the *dispositif* of sovereignty. This *dispositif* is mentioned to emphasise the contrast to a new order: the order of discipline. We met the leper earlier through the *dispositif* of sovereignty, but now the plague is being combated through a disciplinary *dispositif*, and the differences to sovereignty could hardly be greater. Whereas sovereignty relates to abnormal cases – those who deviate – with the disciplinary *dispositif* of discipline, every person is subject to the management of the plague. Each day, everyone must report to the 'plague constable' to have their health status checked; thus, everybody is affected by the plague. They all have a risk of becoming infected and, in fact, may unknowingly already be carrying the infection. Whereas the excluded and the included made up two amorphous masses in the *dispositif* of sovereignty, the ones subjected to power in the *dispositif* of discipline appear as individuals. Power relates to the individual with regard to examining their degree of morbidity. It is essential to note that power is exercised over *everyone* and not only single individuals who fall outside of a norm, as is the case in the *dispositif* of sovereignty.

On the face of it, one could think of the prison as an institution that embodies the principle of sovereignty. It is designed for the few, whilst the many law-abiding citizens are left alone. But according to Foucault, nothing could be more wrong. If we follow Bentham's reflections about the panopticon, to which Foucault also refers, it is central that the citizens are constantly aware of the possibility of punishment. The law is internalised and comes to function as a sort of super-ego. It is only for the individual in whom this functioning has failed that the prison becomes a reality. Thus, discipline aims to be a preventive measure. The internalisation of punishment as a moral code should ensure that a violation of the law never happens. And if something criminal does occur, discipline should ensure that it does not happen again. The leper was banished to a remote place to rot in peace – a type of societal trash heap – whilst the central concept in the *dispositif* of discipline is that one relates to the individual in a procedural and gradual manner. Over time, this will change along a scale. It is not about including or excluding, but about increasing or reducing; e.g. to continuously reduce the risk of disease and improve the health status of the individual.

bullying and talking together in groups about the same topic. In contrast to the programme's other elements, these are about techniques that should strengthen the students' super-egos, thereby making bullying less likely. It also refers to efforts that are directed towards all students and not just the person who bullies and the one who is a victim of bullying.

Here, we may distinguish between two forms of discipline, and the question is whether there really are two separate *dispositifs*. Because discipline is based on an inside/outside logic, physical discipline may be seen as an independent *dispositif* (e.g. the demonstrations of power to which the prison inmates are subjected) that differs from a more mobile and gradual exercise of discipline (e.g. what the citizens in the village experience – they can freely walk around because discipline is internalised as a super-ego). The second form of discipline is called 'control' by Foucault in some places. Control is a form of flexible and fluid discipline; the idea of discipline fully realised, one might say. Foucault writes:

While ... the disciplinary establishments increase, their mechanisms have a certain tendency to become 'de-institutionalised' – to emerge from the closed fortresses in which they once functioned and to circulate in a 'free' state; the massive, compact disciplines are broken down into flexible methods of control. ... Sometimes, the closed apparatuses add to their internal and specific function a role of external surveillance, developing around themselves a whole margin of lateral controls. (1977: 211)

Foucault is conceptualising two logics of power here: first, the closed institution placed 'at the edge of society turned against its negative functions' (classic discipline); and second, a *dispositif* that strengthens the demonstration of power 'by making it more superficial, faster, and more efficient' (control/de-territorialised discipline) (ibid.: 209). It is this second logic that Deleuze (1995) rediscovers later in a post-disciplinary 'control society', where a new social topology renders superfluous the geographic and institutional delimitations of discipline. Power is no longer an 'anti-nomadic technique' meant to stabilise the fleeting – power itself has become fleeting (Foucault 1977: 215, 218).

In the control society, a person no longer moves from one enclosure to another (family, school, military barracks, prison, etc.); rather, one is increasingly subject to free, fluid, nomadic forms of control (Deleuze 1995: 178). Inclusion and exclusion take place through continuous and mobile forms of surveillance; for example, electronic tagging, risk assessment and the border-crossing regulation of deviant streams of individuals and objects. Whereas discipline is immobilising, the post-panoptic form of power aims to regulate mobile individuals. Without demanding normalisation, the focus is directed towards preventive risk management. I raised the question earlier whether discipline and control were two separate *dispositifs*. From this point, I choose to treat them as one because I believe it makes the most sense to see control as a sophisticated form of discipline – i.e. a modus where discipline is transformed into self-discipline.

(A) I now draw an outline of how the *dispositif* of discipline may be seen when it is outlined in a bullying context. First, we must examine how the actors in bullying are perceived. If we begin with aggressors and victims, the main point is that everyone can take both roles, but rarely at the same time. Everyone can end up in the bully role if their super-ego – along with the self-censuring and self-regulating abilities it facilitates – is weak. Bullying is a type of virus that can infect everybody. However, it is not totally random. One can develop a range of risk profiles. The more and stronger the risk factors are, the greater the likelihood of ending up in the bully role. A focus on risks is matched by a gradual focus on behaviour. In the optic of sovereignty, one works with an either/or approach – either something is bullying or it is not – but in the optic of discipline, one sees bullying along a scale. The line between teasing and bullying (and bullying and violence) is thus given by differences in degrees. Gradualism is also applied with regard to which actors are relevant and to the level of social anxiety experienced in the class. There is the potential to see everyone, and thus not only 'aggressor' and 'victim'. In the *dispositif* of discipline (and control), attention is also directed towards a third party or, more precisely, the 'bystanders'. Bystanders are involved by not intervening or by expressing disapproval or acceptance.

In relation to the *dispositif* of sovereignty, the teacher takes an excluding stance towards the bully, but the central point in the *dispositif* of discipline is that the teacher does not merely try to punish the aggressor, but also tries to change him. Socialisation (or better, re-socialisation) is more significant than punishment. Thus, it is not exactly about essences (e.g. an inherent aggressiveness), but rather, about character, which can be influenced and actively formed. The teacher must be present as an educator in all possible contexts: not just during classes, but also during free periods, in the schoolyard and ultimately outside of school grounds. The teacher may not participate in birthday parties and does not facilitate play-dates, but the information from these contexts is relevant in being able to intervene when there are movements in an individual's 'bullying scale' or in another's exposure to bullying. Incidentally, the view of bullying as an ongoing risk has led to an extension of the bullying problematic into adult life. For example, bullying at the workplace is intensively studied.[11] When one focuses on essences or early socialisation within the family in the

---

[11]   In an extension of Foucault's and Deleuze's reflections about control and the breakdown of discipline's boundaries, one could point to a phenomenon like 'lifelong learning'. School matrices increasingly seem to be spread over an individual's entire life. We are like 'children' throughout our whole lives. And with this 'infantilisation', it is easy to see how the bullying problematic can also be relevant in adulthood.

dispositif of sovereignty, socialisation becomes a problem; when it is considered in terms of the *dispositif* of discipline (and control), it becomes a lifelong challenge. Bullying does not disappear in the upper grades at school or in adult life. It simply changes its expression.

(B) Anti-bullying interventions are directed not primarily towards actions, but towards risk factors. By extension, it is not primarily about punishing bullying, but about preventing bullying behaviour before it is actualised. Teachers can direct their attention to who plays with whom during breaks, rotate seating assignments in class so that everybody sits next to each other at some point, etc. In this perspective, further sanctions and punishment become the last option. Instead, one must educate – getting each student to understand why bullying is wrong, and making the students apply this knowledge to their interactions with each other. The focus now is not primarily on growing up and family relationships – as with Olweus, for example – but rather, on behaviour at school. The role of the teacher changes as well. In the *dispositif* of sovereignty, power asymmetries were considered hierarchical, and now the desire is to make them less so. The student should not refrain from bullying because he will otherwise be sent to the principal's office, but rather, because he understands that what he did was wrong and hurtful after having a conversation with his teacher. Excluding behaviour on the part of the teacher contributes to socialising children into a culture where someone can put himself in the sovereign position and others are reduced to being his minions. This should be avoided.

(C) Just like in Bentham's and Foucault's analyses of the panopticon, physical surroundings are considered to be something that can support the promotion of specific roles or subject positions, one could say. Typical interventions are intended to increase and enhance the efficacy of surveillance if bullying seems to be a problem; the hope is that, over time, the student will internalise the surveillance as self-control. Furthermore, it is not just certain individuals who are under surveillance, but everyone. I have already mentioned the organisation of the classroom and different seating arrangements as ways to prevent the roles and positions of the students from stagnating. The central point in relation to the *dispositif*-analytical approach is that surroundings are understood exactly as that – an outer framework within which sociality may unfold itself. In the *dispositif*'s meaning, the framework may be manipulated with a view to creating certain forms of subjectivity; i.e. a form of art in social-engineering. But the relation is seldom thought about the other way – as a question about how subjects use material artefacts and interact with their physical frameworks. Objects are considered to be tools: things may be thrown, windows may break, hate-mails may be sent, etc. To Foucault, the panopticon was an apparatus that should instill certain proclivities into its inmates (patients, detainees, etc.). The schoolroom can be seen as a parallel.

(D) As an example of scientific knowledge that can readily be associated with the *dispositif* of discipline, we can mention some of the work conducted by the eXbus team (see, for example, Søndergaard 2009). This has been characterised by an intention to move the focus away from dysfunctional individuals and towards the class and its dynamics. It is about analysing social processes that have gone awry. Thus, the gradualistic focus is clear. Anyone can potentially end up in the role of bully if the circumstances are right – or perhaps more precisely, if they are formulated wrongly. All students are now the objects of scientific interest because, on the one hand, everyone may become a bully and, on the other hand, everyone feels a need to be heard and to belong. Aggression and social exclusion anxiety thus become character traits that are potentially found within everyone, and which can be activated whenever social processes move in a negative spiral. In this perspective, the teacher becomes an agent who can reverse the negative spirals and, in a more preventive perspective, the person who can ensure that students acquire the necessary social competences. Teachers must support their students in developing sensible practices for relating to others. In general, discussions with adults are very necessary to counteract social exclusion anxiety.

(E) As examples of intervention programmes that can be combined with the *dispositif* of discipline, I can again mention two – and again, these were mapped and discussed in a Swedish investigation of bullying interventions (Skolverket 2011). The programme '*Stegvis*' (step by step) aims to prevent aggression, which is done by implementing socio-emotional training in students' classes. The purpose of this training is to strengthen students' empathy skills and their ability to control their impulses and inclinations. Self-control must be increased. The training also emphasises problem-solving. This can take place, for example, by discussing a number of hypothetical situations during class lessons – perhaps something illustrated on a poster that the teacher shows to all the children.

Another intervention programme is SET, which like '*Stegvis*', is about socio-emotional training (hence the acronym). Whereas skills in problem-solving are said to be the most crucial in '*Stegvis*', emotional training is primary to a higher degree in SET. And where '*Stegvis*' directly thematicises bullying – e.g. the class lessons – the point in SET is that the emotional training becomes built in as an integral element in a range of school subjects. Both social and emotional skills are fostered, and thus the thematicisation is not necessarily in an explicit bullying context.

The dispositif *of terror*

Up to this point, I have described two *dispositifs*: the *dispositif* of sovereignty and the *dispositif* of discipline. Sovereignty was related to exceptional individuals and actions; interventions were considered to be the exclusion of the bully and protection of the bullying target; and the environment was marked by a distinction between an inside and an outside where both spheres were unregulated but the transition between them was standardised by the Sovereign's interventions. Power consisted solely of moving an individual from the 'inside' to an 'outside'. In contrast, discipline related to everyone, although still on an individual level; proclivities and risks rather than actions were central; and intervention efforts consisted of surveillance and monitoring to harness certain tendencies before they were actualised. The environment was thought of as a manipulable outer framework, and material artefacts were considered tools.

The *dispositif* of terror implies a shift in all these dimensions. Instead of individuals, the group and its dynamics, terror is in focus. Terror is like a fire that jumps and spreads from person to person. Obviously, anti-bullying interventions in the *dispositif* of terror also aim to combat bullying, but they do this primarily by trying to strengthen the community to prevent bullying behaviour. And if terror (bullying) does strike, the interventions are primarily about re-establishing the social bonds within the class and minimising the feeling of fear. Finally, the surroundings and artefacts are seen as things with which actively to interact. They are actants in a complex game, and thus must be seen as more than simply unchangeable, material and pre-social frameworks around given conflicts. The point of departure for the *dispositif* of terror – or security, if we use Foucault's concept – is that one cannot completely avoid something going wrong. Therefore, it's about taking the sting out of the bite; i.e. minimising the consequences of the unwanted actions as much as possible.

What is terror? One might immediately say that it is indeed a sovereign action. The actions of exclusion, which can be thought of in relation to the *dispositif* of sovereignty (and the law), are actions that allow themselves to be explained on the basis of an excess. With this, expectations are very high for who is bullying and who is being bullied. But the *dispositif* of terror is devoid of this predictability. Terror strikes like lightning from a clear sky. The victim of an act of terror can be anybody. And this is exactly the point – terror always hits the innocent. But terror also strikes twice. First, it strikes the immediate victim and then it hits everyone else in the second round. The medium of terror is not an attack or assault in and of itself, but rather, the fear – or better, anxiety – that is caused by the wrongdoing within a given community. Terror strikes everybody by fostering a feeling of anxiety and insecurity.

René Girard's discussion about the scapegoat is useful here (1979, 1986). The central point for Girard is that anyone can function as a scapegoat. Therefore, one can never be absolutely sure. Does one belong to a given group or is one about to be pushed out of it? Pinpointing a scapegoat is a way to project the internal tension of a group onto an innocent victim. The fact that the words 'mob' and '*mobbning*' (which means 'bullying' in Danish) are etymologically connected is interesting (Schott 2009b: 227–8). A 'mob' is an uncontrollable and marauding group that becomes incensed in the hunt for a common enemy. But the emphasis is not that the group gathers together and has certain objectives (e.g. a common enemy) that prompt a particular kind of behaviour. The point is rather that the group becomes constituted in the hunt for the scapegoat. Without the outburst of energy that the chase enables, the group would fall apart. Thus, a 'mob' is an unstable entity. This is a totally different and more superficial way of thinking about sociality than is found in, for example, the *dispositif* of discipline.

It may be relevant here to distinguish between fear and anxiety. If we follow Danish philosopher Søren Kierkegaard's famous distinction, then 'fear' is the fear of something given whilst 'anxiety' is the fear of an existential 'nothing'. Fear has an object; anxiety does not. What is thematicised as social exclusion anxiety in the *dispositif* of discipline should – with Kierkegaard's distinction – be understood as a feeling of fear. It is a discomfort that is provoked by a person imagining that certain exclusionary acts are directed towards himself. As such, social exclusion anxiety is bound to an understanding of bullying as a phenomenon that is identified by its repetition. In contrast, bullying as terror is about acts and events that strike unpredictably: friends today – enemies tomorrow. Anxiety is the feeling of never being certain – not even amongst those that one considers to be his 'in group'.

Foucault has not written much about 'terror'; however, he has written quite a lot about the attempts to avoid it. The point of departure here is what Foucault calls a *dispositif* of security. The basis for such a *dispositif* is that something can and will go wrong, and thus one must try to be prepared. The *dispositif* of security does not relate directly to accidents, but in trying to reduce their frequency and practise a community's regenerative power should an accident occur. Foucault's works on public health/hygiene and social policy seem relevant here. These do not focus on single, exceptional individuals as in the *dispositif* of sovereignty, nor do they focus on everybody as individuals like as the *dispositif* of discipline. In contrast, the central focus of the *dispositif* of security is the group, social processes and the significance of the surroundings. On the surface, this formulation could be reminiscent of the description of the *dispositif* of discipline, but the crucial difference here is that the idea of positive and negative spirals – that is, the gradualist understanding of the scales of bullying – has been abandoned, and thus also the predictability that such thinking about spirals provides. Bullying can happen, even when we least expect it.

In the text, *The Birth of Social Medicine* (2001), Foucault tracks the *dispositif* that I am calling terror here. State medicine, urban medicine and industrial medicine are all disciplines that are produced by an orientation towards the population as such. The focus of state medicine is the general health condition of the population, and how its health may be improved through lifestyle changes. Urban medicine is about creating urban environments that reduce morbidity rates. And the purpose of industrial medicine is to prevent workers' accidents and other forms of illness or injury connected to specific job functions. Foucault vividly writes about how, for example, urban medicine recommended that fish markets should not be constructed on top of cemeteries. Also, in France during the mid-seventeenth century, there were orders that cemeteries should be moved out of the city (ibid.: 18).

Obviously, it is no coincidence that I have chosen texts from Foucault's work that concern themselves with morbidity and health. Many of the points from *Discipline and Punish* are repurposed in this text on social medicine. The leper, the plague-stricken and the lifestyle-sick individual are all objects in the demonstration of power, but to different types of power. I claim that three distinct *dispositifs* stand apart from the rest. Foucault saw them as forms of problematisation – they articulated specific problems, and they tried to process them in specific and unique ways. Let us now try to re-examine the *dispositif* of terror – or the *dispositif* of security, to use Foucault's terminology – in relation to bullying and anti-bullying interventions.

(A) What does it mean that bullying is understood as terror and the fight against it as an issue of 'security'? As with the other two *dispositifs*, it means that bullying is considered a strategic standardisation – or better, distribution – of a power relation between two individuals or groups. However, power is only immediately relational – as mentioned earlier, the central point is that anyone can be hit by terror. It is precisely its unpredictability that makes it frightening and gives rise to intense emotional reactions. In one text, Dorte Marie Søndergaard refers to 'Sarah's' experience with bullying, which clearly illustrates the feeling that bullying is a terror that can hit innocent individuals: 'Well, that's how it is in the class. You never know when something will strike you. You can't predict it, you just have to be ready for it to happen' (quoted in Søndergaard 2009: 22). In the *dispositif* of terror, bullying is to be understood as a violent action that strikes 'randomly' and thus, it creates a feeling of anxiety amongst many more individuals than just the person towards whom the bullying is immediately directed.

In the first instance, bullying behaviour is not explained in reference to specific individuals (as in the other two *dispositifs*), but rather, to the climate and social conventions within a particular class. The point is that certain climates and environments produce aggressors and victims. One can remove individuals from the class, but if nothing is done about the social conventions, then new individuals will fall into the same roles of aggressors and victims. Furthermore, it is important that the roles are changeable and unstable. Someone who is the victim one day can be bullied the next. And individuals can fall into both roles; they can simultaneously be bullied and bully others. Thus, an unambiguous categorisation of different types of actors and their 'level of bullying' is not possible.

But the explanation of bullying with regard to the class environment is problematic. One can do something to minimise bullying, but the art of social-engineering will never quite get it to come to life. A cliché is that if you build a wall ten metres high, the terrorist will build a ladder eleven metres high. Something similar applies in relation to bullying when seen from the perspective of terror. The point is that bullying inevitably happens and that, at a maximum, interventions merely change its forms. If one takes the position that bullying can be completely eliminated through intervention efforts, then one has taken an unsuccessful approach. Interventions will always be based on an understanding of bullying as a repetitive act and, therefore, they will systematically mistake bullying as terror because it has that stochastic viewpoint as a fundamental principle.

Bullying in and of itself can no longer be seen as one individual's attack on another. The anxiety about being bullied and excluded attaches itself to everyone who in their background has a fundamental need to belong. As in 'the real terror', a third party is always involved as an audience that either is hit or participates indirectly. Firstly, bullying affects the environment of the class – conflicts and tensions increase and, with them, a feeling of exclusion anxiety. Secondly, to bully or to be bullied affects the relationship to other individuals in the class. For example, bullying behaviour may be seen as a type of behaviour through which one strives to obtain a particular position in class. Furthermore, bullying can at times be a way to avoid being bullied. Similarly, someone who is being bullied can quickly be seen by other individuals as an easy and obvious target. As Girard describes and as I have outlined above, the hunt for a common enemy, a scapegoat, can relax the relations between group members. We can agree about someone who, for example, walks around in ugly 'supermarket clothes', uses the wrong brand of hair wax, is religious or in some other way is totally wrong. The central point is that anyone can become a scapegoat. What people are being bullied for is quite arbitrary – the right clothes one day can be completely wrong the next.

(B) From the terror point of view, bullying is seen as an extreme mechanism of positioning that unfolds within a class where normal positioning tools and conflict-resolution strategies are not working. Again, bullying as such cannot be completely combated. But one can attempt to influence the environment of the class and give the students some tools with which to handle social relations and conflicts, with the purpose of making the class more robust. Anti-bullying strategy typically includes these two elements: to work with the climate and environment of the class and, on that basis, to make bullying behaviour less likely; and to give the students tools to solve conflicts. One example of a concrete technique used to reach both goals is role-playing, where the student puts himself in the place of both the bully and the victim, and thus learns to analyse the social processes that can escalate into bullying. Whereas the teacher in the *dispositif* of discipline was an authority who intervened with sovereignty in the children's reality by punishing bullying students, the teacher is now more of a facilitator who supports the children's own resources and regenerative capacities.

(C) The third element of the *dispositif* is the surroundings and individuals' relation to them. In the *dispositif* of sovereignty, we saw that very little significance was attached to them; and in the *dispositif* of discipline, they were seen as an outer framework that could be designed to foster certain social forms. In the *dispositif* of terror, the view of surroundings and technological artefacts is different. If we draw upon actor-network theory, they should be understood as actants. Surroundings and material artefacts are not just frames around social processes, but elements that, through their interaction with others, constitute the social in different ways. One example is the use of mobile phones and the internet in connection with bullying. The possibility for anonymity and displacement in time – i.e. that the one who bullies and the one who is being bullied are not necessarily present in the same room at the same time – creates new forms of bullying and new subject positions (see Kofoed 2009).

The view of the material and the social as intertwined also means that the optimism found in the *dispositif* of discipline with regard to designing 'bullying-limited' environments is not found in the *dispositif* of terror. Here, it is crucial that neither pure sociality nor pure materialism exists. Just like a terrorist who re-purposes a technology meant to serve the well-being of humans (e.g. an aeroplane) into a weapon, the person who bullies can use the resources meant to prevent bullying to damage another individual. The mobile phone or the internet, for example, can be a medium through which bullying is done, but at the same time, it may also enable vulnerable children to build communities that do not have the physical classroom as a frame. The social-networking site Facebook, for example, can facilitate friendships, but it can also be used to make fun of someone.

(D) We have now arrived at the knowledge dimension of the *dispositif* of terror. Of course, one can immediately find studies and insights that inform this *dispositif*, especially the relevant intervention efforts. But they are scattered. It is interesting to reflect on why this is the case, and I suggest two explanations. The first relates to the repetition of bullying. Bullying as terror breaks with the idea of repetition and, along with it, as a common premise in the *dispositifs* of sovereignty and discipline. How can one create scientific knowledge about a phenomenon that is not repeated? One cannot very well. But of course, it is also incorrect that there is something identified as repeated: terror is characterised by sudden, violent acts that create anxiety. So one can have a theory about this and it can be located (e.g. as inspired by Girard), but what cannot be theorised about is who is struck by bullying. The art of social-engineering, which is the basis for the intervention programmes in the first two *dispositifs*, is certainly not found in this third *dispositif*. Some students are inclined towards bullying behaviour and, as such, terror may be said to be a third *dispositif*, but it predisposes bullying as a 'random', 'sudden' and 'stochastic' phenomenon. Bullying as terror will often not be identified as bullying at all. It is 'found' and not really noticed, and here we also have an explanation for why this *dispositif* is scientifically reflected on less often than the other two.

The second explanation is simultaneously diagnostic. Are the three *dispositifs*' modalities time-bound and accrued? Is what I have called 'bullying as terror' a form of bullying that has only gained ground over the past few decades? And could this be an explanation for why scientific knowledge is lagging behind? There could be a real-historical and a cognitive dimension here. The real-historical aspect is obvious because sociality has become more fleeting – Zygmunt Bauman (2000), for example, talks about a fluid modernity. If our sociality is characterised by jumps, ruptures, ambivalence and hybridity, then it makes sense that bullying would be as well. The stability of social relationships that are at the heart of Olweus's view of bullying may perhaps no longer exist.

(E) There are few intervention programmes that 'think' in an extension of the *dispositif* of terror. But some have elements that point in this direction. One example is '*Skolmedling*' (school mediation), in which the basic idea is to train children in conflict mediation and resolution. This has two purposes: firstly, to concretely help the children resolve their conflicts themselves and prevent them from escalating into bullying behaviour; and secondly, to create a peaceful environment that reduces the frequency of bullying behaviour. Whereas the second goal points back to the disciplinary perspective and the idea of social processes gone awry, the point of departure for the first goal is that conflicts happen and thus, it is important to have a contingency plan that can repair the damage and prevent anxiety from spreading to others.

A second example of an intervention programme that has long understood bullying through the optic of terror was developed around the American television series *Friends*, which is described as a model of companionship. The essence of the programme is that classes each appoint two students who will serve as buddies and role models for those who are bullied. Again, we see that the key is not so much to prevent bullying from occurring, but rather, to mitigate the effects of bullying when it does happen.

Conclusion

The *dispositif* analysis provides an orientation tool to those who relate to bullying as a problem. On the one hand, the analysis maintains a specific and delimited way to approach bullying. The three *dispositifs* all contribute a distinct view of bullying. However, the perspective is broader than a mere definition. The *dispositif* analysis makes it possible to analyse and relate to how a plurality of elements works together. On the other hand, this pre-theory gives us a way to view different possible *dispositifs* of bullying and, on this basis, allows us to understand bullying as a complicated and therefore complex problem. Søndergaard writes the following about the pros and cons of using definitions, and here I claim that the *dispositif* analysis opens up a perspective when the outlined dilemma is exceeded:

An unequivocal, fixating and identifying practice with regard to defining bullying contains both pros and cons. Obviously, it is an advantage that the operationability of such a type of definition makes it immediately applicable in practice. When the definition has decided which aspects of the phenomena should be present (e.g., asymmetry in relations, the aspect of repetition, particular personality traits, a specific intentional direction and similar), then one can proceed according to the recipe, problems and roles can be decided relatively efficiently and one may proceed to the next section in the manual about sanctions and intervention. . . . The disadvantage is evidently that the defining practice makes one blind to the exclusion, production of contempt and relational destructiveness that is not immediately comprised by the definition; one becomes blind to the relational nuances and complexity. The identified victims are unequivocally understood as victims, and the identified aggressors are unequivocally seen as aggressors – and perhaps this is not the whole story about them or the story that will best bring them and their group further. ... In other words, the fixating definition practice easily risks delivering a tool that inhibits sensitive decoding and analyses of concretely lived lives. (2009: 39–40)

By understanding bullying in the *dispositif* of sovereignty in the same way – as a definition – the analyst or the practitioner becomes blind to the aspects that are captured by the other *dispositifs*. The solution to this problem is to understand the *dispositif* analysis as a tool that enables, or at least facilitates, a shift in perspective. Logically, these can be divided into four types.

Firstly, the *dispositif* analysis allows one to rediscover the same logic – or proclivity, one could say – in a new artefact, actor or social context. If certain behaviour is analysed in relation to the *dispositif* of sovereignty, then the teacher who orders students to stand outside the classroom, or in some other way punishes them, may understand that the behaviour is repeating the hierarchical distinction that is established in the relationship between bully and victim (Sylvester 2011). The perspective may be transferred from one artefact to another or from one relation to another, and the same logic would be found. The knowledge that is thus made possible can help the relevant parties break away from rigid structures and vicious spirals. By using *dispositif* analysis, we can see how things that seem to stand in direct opposition (e.g. bullying and intervention programmes) might actually follow the same path and contribute to reproducing the same constellation.

Secondly, the perspective can be fixed on the same object even whilst the analytical prism is replaced. Thus, it becomes possible to see something in a completely different way. For example, one cannot claim that bullying must be explained on the basis of social-background variables and, at the same time, to see bullying as a form of terror related to dysfunctional group dynamics. But if one just 'takes his time', it is possible to observe different aspects of the same object and thus contribute to greater knowledge about it. The more perspectives one can master, the more one can see. Bullying is not a unique phenomenon; thus, the teacher's task is not merely to determine whether bullying is taking place (which, of course, depends on how bullying is understood), but also to realise how it becomes bullying in the first place. An understanding of what bullying is and how the phenomenon plays out in a complex game between a wide range of elements is a prerequisite for effective intervention. Thus, Peter K. Smith and Sonia Sharp (1994: 9) call for a 'more

detailed taxonomy over different forms of bullying or victim behaviour ...
which are likely to have implications for help and intervention directed
towards individual students or specific families'. I have attempted to
contribute to the development of such a taxonomy, but in contrast to
Smith and Sharp, I not only focus on different types of bullying (and
different types of victims, aggressors, families, teachers' roles, etc.), but
also on a range of complex, interconnected determinants and relations.
The emergence of sociality only becomes visible through a particular
view – or better, different emergent properties become visible through
different views.

Thirdly, the *dispositif* analysis provides an opportunity to relate itself
analytically and interventionally in relation to differences and conflicts
between *dispositifs*. Intervention programmes, for example, can contain
elements that draw upon different *dispositifs* and thus be in conflict with
each other. This can potentially reduce their efficacy. If wished, the
dispositif analysis can ensure that the efforts being proposed are designed
in such a way that they pull in the desired direction. But one could
also imagine a situation where many different types of bullying exist and
are woven together in a complex game. Here, the *dispositif* analysis can
help to separate things and optimise the single elements in efforts to
combat bullying. If we take the descriptions of the different bullying
intervention programmes, it is obvious that they are often not as transparent and reflected as the *dispositifs* I have presented here. But they could
be improved by being so.

Let me insert a comment here on my use of both Weber's thinking
about ideal types and Foucault's about *dispositifs*. Foucault thinks genealogically and emits the *dispositifs* laboriously through empirical, historical
work. Accordingly, his texts contain quite a large amount of *dispositifs* that
overlap to a certain degree. In contrast, I have constructed *dispositifs* as
pure forms or ideal types, which will naturally only be found in a modified
form in the concrete analyses. It is just talk about a pre-theory. One
argument here could be that there is a helicopter perspective that detaches
itself from practice. No practice is so rigorous as the three *dispositifs*
suggest. No, as the *dispositifs* are laid out here, they are just grammatics
and models but, as such, they create a possible approach to a practice that
is richer and actually more concrete than an observation that gets close to,
for example, an aggressor or a victim, and therefore does not see the
actions' larger and more complex context. Again, my argument is that
dispositif analysis actually helps us to think concretely, as it was initially
defined in the extension of Hegel's philosophical markings.

The *dispositifs* can be applied as thinking technologies – as prisms
through which we meet reality. But they can also be understood more

'realistically'. We find *dispositifs* out there in 'reality'. Some classes may function in relation to the *dispositif* of sovereignty whilst others function in relation to the *dispositif* of terror. My fourth and final point is that it is also possible to think that a displacement has happened, making a formerly dominating *dispositif* (sovereignty) no longer as dominating. It requires an independent investigation to explore it, but on the basis of this work, I cannot otherwise pose the questions.

I ended the section on bullying as terror by raising a question about whether bullying today is practised on the premises of a fluid modernity. If it is, then something new has been at play, which therefore must be thought about. Scientific advances and evidence-based knowledge rest on the premise that the phenomenon, as it were, is kept constant. The only thing that changes is our knowledge about the phenomenon – it becomes larger still. But if the phenomenon itself changes, the scientific practice should not only be about accumulating knowledge about it, but also about facilitating a possible shift in perspective. Two points were central to Foucault in connection to the study of *dispositifs*: firstly, to examine them genealogically; i.e. to understand them as being in constant motion and genesis. And secondly – and by extension – to see these *dispositifs* as the answer to precarious social problems; i.e. as solution and management models. It could also be said that if social difficulties change character, if bullying takes new forms, then the *dispositifs* will also change character or new ones will emerge. The advantage of cultivating the *dispositifs* as I have done is that this manoeuvre allows us to observe what is new as something new.

It is obvious that social reality is complex and ambiguous. Therefore, navigating through it requires one to establish points of orientation again and again and to attempt to find a way. This necessitates concrete thinking: a type of thinking that approaches the social as a complex whole, but at the same time – and with respect to the circumstances and particulars – leaves it to the practitioner to orient themselves and act in the given context. Thus, I have presented nothing more or less than a pre-theory of bullying.

Part II

Youth experiences

'Who does he think he is?': making new friends and leaving others behind – on the path from childhood to youth

Hanne Haavind

Introduction: affiliations and animosities amongst children

As they become older, children make new friends. Some experience being abandoned whilst others turn their backs on old friends and focus on new ones. Friendships between children become especially apparent in activities at and around school. The formation of friendships between children happens continuously alongside the school's educational objectives, and during children's day-to-day movements to, from, around and within the school. Making friends plays a key role in every child's school life – regardless of whether or not they achieve high educational goals (Rubin, Bukowski and Laursen 2009). Each child enters the social landscape that unfolds within the school in their own distinct way, as this landscape contains both restricted and closed communities as well as some social circles that are relatively open to many participants. The school and the class are usually large enough so that friendships between children can be built from some kind of personal preference and reciprocity. In this way, the communities also end up having a double meaning. Whilst some children are welcomed and acknowledged, there may be others who experience feeling rejected or excluded. As children mark affiliations with their new friends, they may also create animosities in the same social landscape. The experience of being abandoned or excluded is felt more clearly amongst those who remain standing on the outside, rather than those who more naturally belong to and protect the boundaries of the social circle in question (Asher et al. 1990; Sandstrom and Zakriski 2004).

The adults who are a part of children's surroundings often advocate an ideal that everyone should be together with everyone else. It is a sign that the students are thriving at school if no-one feels rejected, even though everyone understands that this is actually impossible to accomplish. Friendships are based on choice and a sense of belonging. It is not always easy for the children themselves – or for the adults around them – to understand who prefers whom and who dislikes whom. It is based on experience and often linked to intense feelings of wanting to be together or not be together.

The objective of this chapter is to link the formation of friendships to how bullying arises amongst children. These two phenomena are not only opposites, but also precondition each other (Mishna, Wiener and Pepler 2008). Because friendships are so important, rejection is an inherent risk. Exclusion is painful for anyone who experiences it, and most children know that it could happen to them at some point (Søndergaard 2009). The renegotiation of friendships between children happens throughout their school years, but it particularly intensifies when they are on the verge of transitioning from childhood into adolescence. I learnt this after conducting a study with several colleagues where we followed a number of children from the time they were 12 until they turned 14 years of age – with repeated interviews specifically about friendship and animosity.[1] At this age, they are in the process of discovering what kind of youths they are going to develop into, and it also becomes important for them to determine the type of companionship they have in order to accomplish that transition. Existing friendships are put to the test for nearly everyone. It is crucial to look around and pay attention. Thus, what our interview-subjects had to say provided insights into how friendship and bullying are linked; specifically, through the form of reorientation required during this age transition, and with the accompanying expectations for what they may encounter and what they may fear.

For this purpose, I draw upon a series of interviews with children who were invited to talk about the small and large events of their daily lives – such as where they were, what they were doing and who they were with – but they were not directly asked whether they had been subjected to bullying, or whether they themselves had bullied anyone. In terms of events from school and their neighbourhoods, most of what they discussed had to do with friendships, but also animosities. Since all the children attended the same school, we learnt about the same friend-ships – or animosities – in terms of how they were viewed and experi-enced from different positions in the social landscape. Through five or six interviews with the same children over a two-year period, we learnt a great deal about how they themselves and others changed friends, and also how they viewed and explained such changes regarding who could and wanted to be friends with whom. In this way, incidents that might

---

[1] The study was conducted in Norway by a research group led by the author and Liv Mette Gulbrandsen (Gulbrandsen 2002, 2003, 2006; Haavind 2003, 2006, 2007a; Hauge 2009; Hauge and Haavind 2011).

usually be referred to as bullying were discussed, but without the interview subjects necessarily labelling them as such.

Most studies of bullying amongst children and youths start with a
definition and provide examples of what falls into that definition. This
has not been my objective. I believe it is an advantage that the interviews
refer to a series of events that clearly include incidents beyond just bullying. Following Dorte Marie Søndergaard (2011), I consider bullying
to be an amplified and distorted version of the exclusion mechanisms
that can be a part of how children relate to each other. Like Søndergaard,
I view bullying to be a practice that emerges from everything the social
community encompasses – which can also be found in these interviews –
in the sense that these communities spring forth through a combination of
selection and inclusion, boundaries and exclusion. At the same time,
amplified forms of social exclusion also involve a change in the nature
of the process itself. This happens when these types of exclusion take on an
extreme form and turn into humiliation or even annihilation in a social
sense (Søndergaard 2009; see also Hansen 2005 and Schott 2009b).
I assumed that the children – and later, youths – whom we interviewed
also had some awareness about these kinds of social processes, and that they
were familiar with how things could go wrong. Beyond being able to talk
about incidents of bullying, the knowledge that it could happen was present
in everything they said about the social life of which they were a part.

The children oriented themselves broadly in the social landscape, and
described not only the social circles to which they belonged and the ones
they wanted to join, but also the circles of which they did *not* want to be
a part. From successive interviews in particular, we gained a broader
understanding of how making new friends was also about leaving others
behind or even being left behind (Faircloth and Hamm 2011; Parker and
Seal 1996). Throughout this section, I introduce a number of examples.
I begin with a change in friendships that seemed to happen in a straightforward and unproblematic manner, and end with a form of rejection that
came dangerously close to annihilation.

In the first interview, 12-year-old Martin told us that he mostly
hung out with Ken because he was his best friend and had been for a
long time – actually, since kindergarten. Still, Martin also joined other
boys in different playful activities:

Yes, but not like. . . all the time, in a way. I am on good terms with all the boys in my
class, you know. But I am not together with them like, every day.

For Martin, this was a safe and wholly unproblematic arrangement. He
thought of Ken as funny, cool and nice. They lived next door to each
other, and walked to and from school together. Eventually, though,

Martin discovered that he was about to change his opinion about his best friend's jokes and pranks. He quite simply thought that Ken was fooling around too much. Martin started to become interested in girls, and he began to confide in two other boys about his crushes. As a group, they related more intensely to a social cluster of girls who were initiating, arranging and following romantic relationships between the boys and girls. Martin realised that Ken did not care about that sort of thing, and it seemed like his best friend was simply not interested in having a girlfriend. He did not even pay attention to what Martin was up against in his efforts to establish his life as a teenager. Martin felt that Ken was being a bit childish, and when they started secondary school they were not quite as close. Martin hung out with some of the other boys more often, and he did not see Ken regularly anymore. In the transition from childhood to youth, they did not keep the same rhythm or follow the same path. As Martin described the situation in a series of interviews, this was an account of how he himself was changing and redirecting himself. The account had a natural feel to it, and it did not trigger any negative feelings towards Ken.

If Ken reacted with disappointment and felt hurt, it was not apparent from what Martin said. If they had continued to hang out regularly, certain conflicting preferences might have arisen between them anyway. Drifting apart is a type of indirect conflict resolution. It is precisely because friendly companionship can diminish in ways that do not assume the form of bullying that it becomes natural to ask how the maintenance of friendships – and the transition from old to new ones – can lead to bullying. When the question was raised here, it was also because we actually did not know if this transition happened in such a painless manner for Ken. When he just 'fools around and messes about' and generally carried on in his childish way, it could also be a form of self-protection: as long as he does not participate in the same social space as Martin and his new friends, Ken may reduce the likelihood that he will be rejected or excluded from it.

Growing older: with a little help from my friends

When children and youths are asked why certain kids seem to fit together, they usually point to a combination of categorical and personal character-istics. They find themselves being one of the girls or one of the boys (Gulbrandsen 1998). But the fact that they are of the same gender is so self-evident that it often goes unmentioned. In the same way, the fact that friends are preferably the same age is also obvious (Frønes 1998, 1999). It can be nice and rewarding to have a friend who is a little bit older. Yet sticking with younger friends could give the impression that one cannot make changes that are consistent with his/her own age group. Though not impossible, the fact is that friendships across age and gender happen infrequently between children; this indicates that the condition of likeness leads to reciprocity. It is the cultural content linked to categories such as age and gender that can then offer children important markers in the construction of their matching identities. They get to know themselves through others, and they change themselves along with others. It is important for them to figure out to which kinds of girls and boys they want to belong.

This means that a sense of belonging and identity are two sides of the same coin, and that the formation of friendships between children is an important part of their own exploration and testing of who they are and who they could be (Bagwell and Schmidt 2011; Dunn 2004). Still, that does not mean that everything is based on personal preferences when certain children find each other. In addition to gender and age, which everyone naturally utilises as relevant markers, other categories of identity are at play between children. They explore what kind of girl – or what kind of boy – they want to be with the help of other categories that can be relevant for the youths when they attempt to identify themselves to each other. In the actual school district in Oslo, Norway, the meanings that become attached to gender and age are all clearly modified by ethnic categories of where a child has come from and where they are heading. Ethnic affiliations are significant markers of cultural origin, and they may or may not create doubts and battles about where a child is heading. Consequently, none of these social categories have entirely fixed meanings. But for most, gender affiliation is enduring, even though personal expressions of gender may change.

Coming of age during the transition that children experience between the ages of 12 and 14 takes place specifically through the transformation of one's gendered expressions. This means that, for girls, it is important to act as each other's face-to-face reference group. Along with other girls, they can refer to, evaluate and support each other. Ethnic affiliation plays a big role in the formation of these types of reference groups, and thereby also for a child's perception of choices and opportunities. One thing is that the evaluation criteria for how to become a young girl in a positive way may be different between the young, white girls of the majority and the young, coloured girls from immigrant families. Such criteria are conflicting and somewhat incompatible, yet they are still at play within the same social landscape. This is also to some degree true for the establishment of interrelationships between boys (Gulbrandsen 2003; Haavind 2003; Hauge 2009).

Growing up and getting older is not something a 12-year-old can choose to do, let alone stop. The fact that this is a social transition means that everyone is evaluated according to how they transform meanings related to age by referring to shifts and variations in meanings related to gender and ethnicity. When approaching adolescence, a young person's body is undergoing changes that call attention to the gender divide and create an awareness of heterosexual attractions. Yet a child cannot merely let this happen and then wait and see. Whether they want to or not, every single child becomes challenged to determine how they will move out of their childhood and into their youth (Gulbrandsen 2006; Hauge 2009; Hauge and Haavind 2011). There is a rich offering of developmental domains for youth within culture; that is, activities that they can actually engage in, developing skills and modes of expression that they as teenagers can claim as their own. They are held accountable for their choices – not just towards friends and others at school, but also towards the families with whom they live and on whom they depend. This combination is more demanding for girls and boys from immigrant families than for those who come from native Norwegian families with permanent residency. Not all developmental domains are equally accessible to everyone, but everyone tries to find something that will help make them who they are and who they can be (Haavind 2007a).

Again, this is why personal communities based on gender and age – and also based on ethnicity, as I discuss later – are so important. Younger children can certainly learn from older ones and follow in their footsteps, and older children can attend to and follow up on the younger ones. Yet above all, it is homogeneous age groups of the same gender that develop sufficient interest in investing time and energy into developmental domains and, in this way, demonstrating that they are growing older (Gulbrandsen 2006; Haavind 2003). Although similarity in age provides a sense of solidarity, it also creates competition and rivalry. No-one is exempt from the responsibility involved in managing the meanings that can be triggered by and linked to one's gender. In this age transition, being a girl amongst other girls – as opposed to being a boy amongst other boys – is also a condition for establishing 'the opposite sex' as a category, and in a new way that comes from increasing in age (Gulbrandsen 2006). This has to do with the introduction of heterosexual romance. Not necessarily an introduction to any sort of sexual practice, but a type of interest in someone of 'the opposite sex' as potentially attractive. It is undoubtedly possible for some children to transgress prevailing notions of what constitutes gender affiliation, but such transgressions require some form of justification. Since such justifications may not always be accepted, this involves a risk of being isolated and excluded.

In our interviews, the children transitioning into youth had a lot to say about how they developed several modes of expression to indicate who fits together and who does not. It was natural to examine the interview data more closely to see whether such modes of expression in certain contexts could assume the character of bullying, and whether the modes of expression that are prominent in instances of bullying could also be said to have commonality with less negative forms of children's inclusion and exclusion of each other.

The material I studied and analysed was produced from personal interviews with thirty-two youths from one primary school in Oslo. In this school, about half of the students lived in families with parents who had immigrated to Norway from various countries in northern and eastern Africa, Asia and the Middle East, along with Eastern Europe. The other half were native Norwegians and constituted a kind of majority, and Norwegian was definitely the predominant language.[2] When we met them, they were all 12 years of age and in seventh grade, which is the last year of primary school in Norway. We were able to follow them through to secondary school because they agreed to continue being interviewed during their first year at the new school, where they also were part of new classes.[3] There, they attended school with a mix of children they knew from their previous school as well as new children from other primary schools. When our interviews concluded after nearly two years, most of them had turned 14 years of age – no longer children, but defined by themselves and others as 'teenagers'. In total, we met all the children at their school five or six times during this transition period, and we spoke to them for between one and two hours each time.

The interviews confirmed that it is fairly common to switch friends specifically to affirm that one is in the process of getting older. This pertains to both boys and girls, and the youths themselves and the adults around them both expected this to happen. The point of forming new friendships is not primarily about consolidating a shared history, but also for the youths to determine new possibilities for the future. Friends do

[2] Several researchers have analysed the material, either in part or entirety, and with different objectives. I have thereby been able to make use of other analyses and have got to know the different children through this work. See also Gulbrandsen (2006) and Hauge (2009).

[3] In Norway, there is a clearer distinction between primary and secondary school than in many other countries. Most children switch schools and, just as in this case, children from one or several primary schools become combined into new classes. In this way, the transition from child to youth is institutionally marked. In Norway, primary schools are called Children's Schools and secondary schools are known as Youth Schools. The children may have expectations about what kinds of 'new' young people they are going to meet. This also reinforces the experience that all friendships are being put to the test.

not merely share activities here and now, because the selection of these activities is an expression of shared notions and fantasies about who they can become (Dunn 2004). Thus, it was important for them to be attentive to all kinds of new criteria for marking who belonged with whom. The events about which the youths spoke derived their drama from negotiations regarding the other children with whom they did or did not belong. For boys as well as girls, this tends to be a game that includes selection, affirmation and rejection.

Why do you wear those floral-print trousers?

Sometimes, 13-year-old Norah[4] felt like the other boys and girls in her class looked down on her. She said that she did not have any Norwegian friends – at least not anymore. She tried to find out what it means that she is 'one of the foreigners' here at this school. The children from families with Norwegian parents possess a taken-for-granted hegemony and do not need to label themselves 'Norwegian'. In this way, they are unmarked; it is the others who are marked as 'foreigners'. Thus, the implicit question posed to the foreign girls is: 'What are you like?' It was difficult for Norah to present herself because she faced the challenge of defining who she is and who she might be in a way that was not entirely pleasant for her (Haavind 2006).

The Norwegian girls did not address Norah out of interest, but rather, as though there was something wrong with her. She told us about Eva and Margaret, who approached her and asked, 'Why do you wear those floral-print trousers?' The attention made her feel insecure. She had not considered the idea that she might stick out before they asked, and she also did not realise that an explanation was needed. She linked this episode to another where the same two girls asked, 'Why are you always humming that melody?' Norah did not know how to answer, but she stopped wearing the floral-print pants, and she avoided humming to herself when others could hear it. This was not because she expected any of the Norwegian girls to become her friend if she adapted to their style. She cannot be like them, cannot hang out where they do or do the things in which they are interested. Her family expected her to come right home after school, where she can do homework and enjoy the company of her younger and older sisters. The activities and modes of expression

---

[4] Just like Martin and Ken, Norah is a pseudonym, but one that leads to double associations – Nora without an 'h' is a well-known Norwegian name from Henrik Ibsen's classic play *A Doll's House*, while the silent 'h' at the end hints at an association with countries located in northern Africa and the Middle East (Haavind 2006).

that were interesting to budding teenaged girls like Eva and Margaret were not accessible to her. Norah knew that she was in the process of remaining childish in their eyes, so she stayed away from them. Yet they might still observe her, and it could always be possible that two or more of the 'popular' girls – as Norah referred to them – would question some of the things that characterised a girl like her. If so, she would be unable to account for herself.

For the most part, this situation was not about face-to-face comments made between two children. Norah can avoid this kind of interaction by staying away from the places where the 'popular kids' hang out during recess. Still, when they are in each other's purview, certain insinuations emerge that may single out an individual girl in front of several others, so that all of the others can see her. The gaze of the majority has incisive force when it is perceived via suggestion. Norah noticed that the other girls were tough on 'us foreigners' because, in her view, they always thought that 'we are like, the lame girls whilst they are the cool girls…we don't have the right back-packs or nice clothes whilst they exclusively wear fashionable clothes and all that.' In Norah's experience, the girls' sudden outbursts of 'Look at her!' were usually directed towards her two girlfriends rather than her. In particular, Norah was let off the hook more easily than Hafid. One time, when they were preparing to take a class picture, Hafid wore her hair down. Some of the popular girls were standing behind them, and Norah could hear one girl say to someone who was standing farther ahead: 'Look at her, she's done herself up – and look – she looks like a bush.' This was not said more than once. Yet both Norah and Hafid knew that, from then on among themselves, the girls were probably going to call Hafid 'bush'. Hafid cried when they all returned to their classroom, and Norah and another girlfriend who also belonged to the 'foreigners' tried to comfort her by saying, 'You don't have to worry about them.' Still, Norah could see that Hafid was not happy.

This is a social pattern: one child takes the initiative to address one or several others by making an announcement. This announcement is directed towards everyone who is present, but appeals especially to those who are a part of the same social circle. Questions are raised about something that everyone can see is a trait of a certain child who is also present. This child is singled out in a way that makes them visible as an object for others' often unspoken, yet nonetheless concurring, critical evaluation. The girl who is labelled in this way with 'that hair' (or something else) would automatically feel some increased uncertainty and most likely approach a state of fear and helplessness. From several other interviews, we learnt that the fear of additional ridicule made it difficult to engage in struggles about how one's 'hair' should be. Instead, a girl who is singled out with such a question typically prefers to withdraw in a way that constrains her further participation. Even if the girl who is singled out changes her hairstyle, trousers or whatever, she would still not be of any interest to those who possess the social hegemony. She remains on the outside whilst the camaraderie is strengthened between those who belong to the trendsetting group.

Norah repeatedly talked about episodes that illustrated how she was kept in a constant state of uncertainty and worry. This uncertainty did not just stem from the fact that the popular girls did not see her as one of them. She tried as hard as she could not to let that bother her. But she felt a constant burden and source of despair because the emotional climate between her, Hafid and their other friend was also affected by the three of them feeling insecure and fearful about being excluded – even by each other. They sought out each other's company in the shadow of the popular girls, and it was as if that shadow haunted them. They were singled out one at a time and not together as a group, so instead of being unified, they were divided in their insecurity. Norah herself did not entirely understand what was so awful about her or Hafid. Nothing she said indicated that she wanted to mark herself as a more visible representative of another culture. She said that she could not imagine herself wearing a headscarf or other clothing that would distinguish her from native Norwegians, or presenting any other links to her parents' country of origin. What she really wanted was for things to be another way immediately. Yet neither she nor her two girlfriends could know in advance what the popular girls were going to notice or comment on, and in what way it would single out one of the three as different. As a result, their loyalty to each other – which they desperately needed – started to become unsteady (Haavind 2006).

If it is merely the question 'why' that creates worry and shame, it would not be reasonable to call events like this incidences of bullying. Yet there is something about the social pattern that is similar to descriptions by others who analyse bullying as a social process gone awry: the child being singled out has to deal with the fact that empathy is being withdrawn and replaced by further contempt (Søndergaard 2009). Norah could not begin to answer back without making herself stick out even more. Every attempt would reinforce the others' disparagement. She could not say, 'Floral-print pants are my cultural tradition' because that was not the case. Moreover, Norah did not perceive herself as a foreigner, but rather, as a permanent Norwegian resident with parents from another country. Her hopes and dreams of belonging are connected to the place where she attends school; her parents' native country is just a place she visits. She was careful not to reveal that she wore those floral-print pants because her mother and older sister bought them for her; the two of them had searched around in several stores because they wanted her to have something really nice. If she made this known, she would only prove to the girls at school that she was childish because she was not allowed to choose her own clothes. The floral-print trousers became her downfall, and she knew it. She could imagine that native Norwegians and immigrants could perhaps be friends in other places, 'but not here at this school, I don't think'. It was not Norah who wanted to activate an ethnic distinction, but she was subjected to it in an implicit manner.

Every child narrates from a shared social landscape

Presumably, Norah herself did not perceive the girls' somewhat sarcastic but seemingly innocent questions as bullying. Still, they were not empathetic or approachable, and she stopped wearing the floral-print trousers to school. It is possible that Norah thought her friend Hafid was bullied, especially because it happened again and again. At any rate, the reality was that she could not stop the girls from tormenting Hafid when it was happening, but she could try to comfort her afterwards. Again, it is important to remember that we did not explicitly ask the girls and boys whether they had been bullied or if they had bullied anyone. Instead, I am trying to put the phenomenon of bullying into a context that makes it possible to understand the intensity of personal preferences, and what is at stake in children's inclusion and exclusion of each other. Thus, I am building upon the children's understanding of what happened in the social landscape where a larger group of children were present. The children – and later, youths – willingly discussed what they did and with whom they hung out. The children were good observers, and whatever happened to the others also pertained to them. In the system of who did and did not hang out together, a picture of the social circles emerged. Some stood out, and some overlapped; some were quite open whilst others seemed more closed off. And several of the children who attended school every day were almost entirely alone during those two years. We did not just learn about each individual child, but about what took place in the broader social landscape at that particular time. When we returned after several months, they were even more direct in emphasising what had happened since the last time we met and how it mattered to them.

It was also important for us to be able to put several of the accounts together. The children personally made their own experiences, so to speak, but they also learnt something important about themselves and who they could or wanted to be through observing other girls and boys. We interviewed thirty-two children, which was half of all the students in seventh grade and approximately one-third of the children in eighth grade, where the total number of children was higher. We invited them to participate because, through a period of participant observation, we wanted to select children from different social circles and those who were involved in different types of activities. For the most part, they spoke about the same events but from different positions. What they did and did not talk about also referred to precisely how they positioned themselves within this landscape of children during their two years at school.

If we examine what Ken said about himself in light of what Martin said, it becomes part of a complete picture. Ken was really preoccupied with messing around and making others laugh. Further, he plainly stated that he was simply not interested in girls, even though Martin was. He liked to sneakily rent and watch movies with 16- and even 18-year-old age restrictions. Yet he found that Martin would not really make an effort to participate. Eventually, Ken started to frequently call attention to another boy along with Martin, saying that he had two best friends. In secondary school, he discovered that he and Martin were actually very different on a personal level. In the end, Martin disappeared from Ken's activities. So the two sets of accounts complement each other. If Ken felt rejected by Martin, he did not let on; he did not express disappointment, but allowed events to happen as they happened. Insofar as Martin had a place in Ken's account, it was in alignment with Martin's; namely, that he was someone who was friendly with all the boys.

Yet, as previously mentioned, many of the other children's accounts were characterised by an entire spectrum of intense feelings when new friendships formed and old friendships ended. Norah suffered from being kept on the outside, and she made her complaints known to the interviewer. Also, because she observed Hafid, she knew that things could actually be worse than they were. Hafid, however, did not say much – if anything at all – about her tormenters to the person who interviewed her. And to Eva, Margaret and their girlfriends, both of these 'foreign' girls were so insignificant that they were hardly mentioned, except in passing.

From our interviews, we learnt that many children dreamed of having access to – and participating in – social circles to which they knew they were unable to belong. In comparing many accounts, I am piecing together an understanding of how the entire system of regulation and criteria for 'who is a friend to whom' becomes intensified at this particular age; thereby, I hope that we may also gain a better understanding of how this intensity can turn into bullying. Through selected examples in the next section, I draw the reader's attention towards several events in which the youths' various forms of selection, affirmation and rejection developed in and around social circles of girls and also boys.

The events that are given as examples here, along with their participants, underscore processes that are key to the youths' fear of not managing to become older in a way that could be acknowledged and attract social support. Even though every child and youth was aware that the opposite of bullying is respect for the individual and a positive interest in the differences between oneself and others, it was not always possible to generate this kind of interest in each other. The significance that is linked to being a girl or a boy – or in being labelled as a 'foreigner' or 'unlabelled Norwegian' – during the transition from childhood to youth seems to be just an individual matter formed by personal preferences. Each one has to create a subjective stance that will be recognised and perceived as viable by some others. The young ones have to express themselves in ways that resonate with some other young people. Even though there are many ways to grow older, personal vulnerability and social risk are also linked to the steps that are taken during this process (Kofoed 2004; Palmen et al. 2011; Staunæs 2004).

Could I make someone else my best friend?

During seventh grade, friendships were renegotiated and new constellations appeared. This mutability was further reinforced in eighth grade with new classes that included students who had attended another primary school. If we compare all of the children's accounts, we see that personal preferences – in terms of who can be whose friend, and the experience of fitting in better with some children than with others – follow a set of ideas about how to proceed in order to become older. Amongst the girls, it was those who were 'popular' who solidified their position. 'Popular' was not a term they used themselves. It was the others who did not quite belong who referred to them this way. This was a social circle of girls who engaged in hetero-feminine practices: who can fall in love with whom, and for what reasons? They spent their time on clothes and make-up, but mostly they talked to each other about what they were doing and what they are going to do (Gulbrandsen 2006; Hauge 2009). Everyone who did not belong to this social circle still knew who these girls were. Ellen spoke with sorrow and pain about how she lost her best friend, Gwen. She said that it just happened – Gwen stopped speaking to her, even though they had been best friends since first grade. Now, Gwen always went over to the new girls. Ellen quickly gave up; she did not attempt to follow. Instead, she looked around. She was able to identify other girls who had been abandoned in the same way she was. She empowered herself by choosing to get close to Rachel. That ended up being a stroke of good luck, and in time they appeared to be exactly as they were – the best of friends. They exchanged mutual affirmation and enthusiasm. In this way, everyone else knew that these two girls always hung out together. It became impossible to point out one without the other also being there, having the same stuff and doing the same things.

Ellen felt secure about her new friend because Rachel had been abandoned as well. Together, they felt safe at school. One day, along with the other students in their class, I watched them as they entered the computer room. There are no permanent seats there, and several of the other students were quicker than Ellen and Rachel to snatch up two-person desks. Still, Ellen turned to her friend, who ended up at the other end of the room, and smilingly yelled: 'We can still wave to each other!'

From this example, I suggest that friendship serves as protection. Other research has demonstrated that there is a statistical correlation between having good friendships and not being subjected to bullying (Bollmer et al. 2006; Hodges et al. 1999). I am emphasising the social dynamic, which implies that two children who are closely tied together yet keep to themselves are not as easily subjected to bullying by the majority. Bullying tends to befall those who desire to broaden their affiliations and seek out new groups. That cruel demonstration – in the form of a message that says there is no sympathy to be found right now – can strike one or more children who try and assert themselves as a classmate and friend. But two friends who interact primarily with each other are promptly ignored by everyone else, and they may remain content to exist for each other. What makes bullying successful is not simply the fact that certain actions and remarks cause injury and hurt. The main objective of bullying is not to inflict pain, but rather, to achieve a social effect; namely, that the social space is void of empathy for the child(ren) who are being singled out (Søndergaard 2008, 2009). When Ellen and her girlfriend did not get to sit next to each other in the computer room, they waved excitedly to each other from opposite sides of the room. In this way, they demonstrated to everyone present that the empathy they had for each other could not be eradicated.

Life-mode interviews as a source of insight

I observed Ellen and Rachel stand up and smilingly wave to each other over the heads of everyone else. Yet it was only though my interviews with Ellen that I was able to understand the significance of this incident in how she secured both companionship and protection for herself in her efforts towards becoming a youth. If we are going to study bullying and/or the social patterns that may precede bullying, then it is not sufficient to be merely an observer. Bullying usually takes place when adults are not present, or it occurs in ways that adults would not automatically perceive as bullying. As a researcher, I was also dependent on the children's accounts. In this study, we used the life-mode interview method as a source of insight (Haavind 1987).

This interview format invites children to be both an observer and participant in their own everyday lives. They are asked to talk about what is happening with regard to specific events that they can localise in time and space. At the same time, it is desirable to have a subjectively engaged participant who can talk about what a specific event means to that child in particular. In the interview, the narrator and the participant occupy different positions whilst, through the narrator's privileged access to the participant's experiences, they simultaneously offer interpretations and emotional colouring about what took place. In the narrative format, the narrator and participant are fused together, and an event derives its significance not just from what goes on in the moment, but also from the ways in which those involved draw upon experiences from the past and bring expectations into the future (Bruner 1990).

The life-mode interview format is suited to this objective (Haavind 1987). According to how this interview is set up, the interviewer does not introduce thematic questions. Instead, the conversation is directed towards how events are part of the interview-subject's everyday life. The conversation outlines a day from morning until night, with specific references to the previous day, which should still be fresh in the subject's memory when starting to recount it. As the youths gradually moved from event to event and from place to place in their narratives, they were asked about what happened and who participated. Each event was expanded on with questions about whether things usually happened in this way, or whether there was something in particular that caused things to turn out the way they did during the previous day (Andenæs 1991; Gulbrandsen 1998; Haavind 2011). This allowed an opportunity to link events across time and place. In this way, the life-mode interview was not limited to yesterday's events, but functioned as a gateway to what the youths themselves considered significant in their own lives (Haavind 2011; Gulbrandsen 2008). It was possible to compare and expand on events within the pattern created by the weekdays or the year, and it was possible to extract events from the youths' own personal stories.

We explained to the entire group of children that we wanted to know how they transitioned from being 12-year-olds to being 14. Moreover, since neither they nor we could know in advance how that was going to happen, we wanted to speak to them several times. We stressed to each individual child that we wanted to learn as much as possible about what they did on a daily basis, where they went and who they spent time with, both at home with their families, at school and in other places. In order to make it easier for them to speak freely, we offered a promise of confidentiality and trust. Because they knew that we were also interviewing other children from the same class, they needed to know that everything they said would stay between them and the interviewer, and would not be shared with any other children or adults at school.

Although the content of each life-mode interview can be characterised by the interview-subject's involvement in their own lives, the interviewers adhered to the present day as a common thread. They could constantly turn back to 'And what happened then?' and 'What was that like for you?' The first two interviews with each child were conducted during the autumn they were in seventh grade. On average, it took approximately three-to-four hours to cover events according to their daily patterns from morning until night, but these events could also vary during the week. In the four or five follow-up interviews, this conversational format was well-rehearsed, and the interviewer and interview-subject could go more directly into what had happened since the last interview and what was happening at present. In these follow-up conversations, the interviewer also took the opportunity to introduce some topics that had arisen in everyone's interviews, and which appeared to be significant for becoming a teenager in this social landscape.

The interviewers followed up on what had changed, and what the youths themselves were trying to accomplish with their lives. We could juxtapose and compare different types of events according to how they were narrated by youths occupying different participant positions. This is the analytical approach I have used in this chapter. I examined many events and the various ways they were recounted by many different people, but I selected the one set that illustrates and documents the different ways to renegotiate and change both friendships and community. The principal question is quite simply what happens, when it happens, as it happens; namely, with regard to the idea that children and youths renegotiate access to social circles and affirmations in the form of friendships. Yet in order to examine bullying as a social opportunity more closely, there is also reason retrospectively to ask the following question when re-reading the interviews: what happens when the majority of children within a social circle – who both spend time together and influence a social landscape – single out and turn against one of their own in a way that enables them to turn off emotional understanding and thereby exclude that child? It could be that one child initiated the labelling that was then enacted by a majority. Yet its continuation presupposes that more children participate. The others' fear of becoming victims themselves can lead to an absence of protest (Søndergaard 2009). There is a perception that the child who is singled out is to blame, which removes one's own internal empathy at a decisive moment.

She has been so irritating lately

The members of the social circle of girls whom the others perceive as 'popular' are aware that they are leading the way. They are the ones who take the initiative in crossing the boundary of what is considered childish, trying out new things and having a promising future in their existence as youths and young women. If they themselves claimed to be popular, they could end up casting doubt on whether this was true. In their own estimation, they are just enjoying each other's company – particularly because they share a taste for authenticity and feel like they are able to be themselves with each other.

This perception of community amongst those who have gone the furthest in proving themselves to be youths provides a sense of security and a feeling of doing the right thing whilst, simultaneously, the reciprocal relationship between the girls can be characterised by both powerful demands for loyalty and a fear of conflict. Since they are not only searching for safety in the moment but also in certain imaginings about their futures, questions about who belongs and who is left behind constantly emerge between them. Norah experienced that, as a 'foreigner', she was excluded. Whilst ethnic contrasts clearly played a role in the formation of social circles in the class, such markers were not used in an entirely systematic manner. For example, Vendela and Dawny were included amongst the popular girls, even though they are from Croatian and Somali families, respectively. Yet both participated in the kinds of activities that are understood as a matter of course for Norwegian teenage girls: going to the youth club, visiting each other's homes, using and experimenting with clothing and make-up – all whilst talking about their own social affairs.

What they created is a running system for an exchange of aspirations and dreams, and also the exchange of support and acknowledgement on their way to becoming young girls. The fact that the system is fluid means that it is not quite enough to do the right thing and make sure to follow up on what the others are doing. Twelve-year-old Diana stated with some satisfaction that she was the one with the most designer clothes and that she was allowed to watch the 'right' series on TV. There was no doubt that she wanted to fit in amongst the most popular girls, and the others talked about her as if she did. Still, too much of the 'right' thing can quickly be regarded as wrong in the eyes of some of the others. At one point, Gwen questioned Diana's enthusiasm for participating in conversations with the boys about who had a crush on whom. She thought Diana had been irritating lately, and she told the other girls that her feelings about Diana were persistent. At first, she thought they did not bother her that much, but after a while she noticed that it was not that simple.

The situation was as follows: Paul sent a message through one of the other girls in the group that he had a crush on Gwen, and she agreed to be together with him. Several weeks passed, and then Gwen sent a message back through one of the other girls that she wanted to break up. Not long afterwards, Diana sent word to Paul about her crush on him, and Paul agreed to be together with her. Before doing so, Diana had checked with Gwen to be certain it was OK; Gwen said it did not bother her because she no longer had a crush on Paul, and she was undeniably the one who broke it off. Still, she later discovered that this was not entirely true; Gwen noticed that she did feel hurt, and it ruined her relationship with Diana. Gwen then experienced Diana's enthusiasm for and interest in the boys as irritating and tiresome. She was not sure what she could do about it, and she shared her irritation and doubt with the other girls.

Gwen's feelings mattered to the other girls and when Gwen disclosed her feelings to them, she knew what was going to happen: Diana would get left out of their social circle. Whatever feelings Diana may have had, the other girls were not going to take them into consideration. In their minds, it was Diana who did not realise how one should treat a friend. When the girls decided to be sympathetic to Gwen's feelings, they made themselves unfeeling towards Diana.

Simply put, this joint creation of indifference towards certain others' reactions and positions makes exclusion and rejection possible (Crick and Ladd 1993; Faircloth and Hamm 2011). Yet, as this example illustrates, the exclusion of Diana did not happen to strike out at her per se, but instead because the other girls in the group gathered together and sympathised with Gwen's feelings. This type of indifference towards one child is created when sensitivity towards another becomes relatively dominant and more important to the group.

I am a tomboy

The events that led to the exclusion of Diana occurred without any open conflicts between her and the other girls. The reality of Diana no longer hanging out with the 'popular' girls happened in an almost unnoticeable way. Yet Diana herself offered a different explanation than Gwen. Diana did not stress the fact that the girls turned against her. There was nothing to indicate that she knew she misjudged Gwen's feelings, and Gwen did not say this to her in any direct way. In Diana's narrative, she realised that she wanted something else and, therefore, it was she who pulled away from the group.

By leaving the social circle of popular girls of her own accord, Diana referred to the idea that she had discovered something about herself: she had a clearer sense of how she had always been and how she was going to be. She was a tomboy and not interested in girly things. In her view, she was not able to figure this out until she had personally experienced what the other girls were doing. But she was the kind of girl who likes to get her fingernails dirty, so it was better for her to hang out with the boys, who were usually real and straightforward. She knew now that she really wanted to become a mechanic, so she would train for this work and readjust her education plans. The boys confided in her and, when she gave one of them a hug, it was simply a friendly gesture and an expression of understanding.

In this case, Gwen's and Diana's narratives appear to be inconsistent. Yet no prolonged conflict arose between them because, as they both explained, they found themselves on completely different paths. And because this change did not develop into accusations of Diana being a 'whore' or any other type of negative sanctioning, it is possible to imagine that it was because she beat them to the punch and sought out other social circles on her own.

During our interviews, we viewed all the children as a part of the social landscape, even when this landscape changed dramatically over the course of two years. When the children spoke to us, they went into detail about their own participation in the social circles in which they were directly involved, but they also turned their gaze towards the broader landscape at school. They were aware of what was happening there, even activities in which they themselves were not involved but that were significant to youth culture: who kissed whom, who got drunk at a party, who tried hash. These events were sent out as messages across the different social circles. Violations of the norms for decent behaviour amongst children point to the challenges that young people experience. Such violations were interpreted as dangerous, and thus also had the potential to be perceived as courageous. There seemed to be an immediate link between misconduct according to adult standards and either exclusion or bullying amongst the young people (Haavind 2003). The youths shared certain information about the different ways to grow older, even ways that might not be possible for them. This was because everyone had access to the global youth culture represented in the media and popular music as well as through designer clothes and other material possessions. This cannot just be picked up and copied, like Diana once believed. Each child must make it their own. They must develop their own preferences when confronting this globally accessible and virtually represented youth world. Through this world, they can also find new friends and allies. For Diana, the word 'tomboy' was redemptive. She got herself a cap and wore it backwards.

Intensity and development

Some friendships change peacefully and almost unnoticeably, like between Martin and Ken. Many, like Ellen, contain intense feelings that are linked to being excluded and abandoned, even though from the outside it may appear to happen without any drama or open conflicts. Ellen controlled her intense feelings by using them to find a new friend and affirm her relationship with Rachel. Seemingly innocent questions from the popular girls confirmed to Norah that she would never be allowed into their social circles, and those who kept her at a distance were unaware of her insecurity and despair. They were also unaware of the intense feelings of suspicion and disappointment that shifted between Norah and her two friends whilst they were operating in the shadow of the popular girls' hegemony. Gwen and her girlfriends allowed their irritation and resentment towards Diana to grow in a way that strengthened their own community. There is reason to examine more closely how these intense feelings arise, and also how they are controlled and used towards an objective that can be different from what provoked them (Parkhurst and Asher 1992). Again, a prerequisite for understanding is how this combination of intensity and control can be gathered and then used to steer the course of action before it goes too far.

The answer lies in the relationship between children's personal development and their social participation. The research refers to the statistical correlation between friendship and social competency (Ladd 2005); thus, the question becomes whether those who are well-developed have an easier time making good friends, or whether good friendships contribute towards development. My intention is not to regard friendship and development as a linear correlation between two variables, but rather, as an internal relationship where one is included in the other. When seen as two sides of the same issue, social participation through friendship would become an important tool for getting older as well as an expression of having done so (Haavind 2005). What happens in the moment derives its emotional charge from what it might mean for the participants involved and who they can become.

There is a fierce intensity in both children's commitment to becoming older and their dependence on others to do so. Transforming oneself according to age is not something that just happens; it must be done. A child cannot continue to stay the way they already are, but must find out who they can become. The effort of each child has to be directed as well as open-ended (Haavind 2000, 2007b), and to find the answer, each child depends on someone who is potentially the same.

When this happens almost exclusively in same-sex groups, it is not because children and youths have been separated from the opposite sex at school. Such notions are only held by some of the immigrant parents. Rather, gender homogeneity is a device created by the children themselves to replace the world of childhood and establish themselves in the world of youth. In this world, one has to dress in gendered outfits – both in the literal and symbolic sense. Playing with gendered expressions of self is both the joy and the ordeal. Some young boys who want to distance themselves from other boys may call them 'fags', and some young girls may call each other 'whores' – here, the intention is familiar to children of both sexes. Such epithets can be used to keep gender in place. Negative statements about gender are not claims that someone is actually a homosexual or a prostitute; rather, they are used to appeal to feelings of community or rejection. But it is precisely in the transition from ages 12 to 14 that the youths draw upon and invent new suggestions of what gender can mean (Hauge and Haavind 2011). Insults used to create ethnic distinctions also occur, but are more tentatively expressed. Still, as Norah stated, 'foreigners' were tacitly told to stay with their 'own' kind.

If one views bullying as something that can emerge from children's efforts to develop as well as their dependence on each other to have the courage to move forward into unknown social terrain, then deciding when something qualifies as bullying is also affected by this. The defining elements do not become a set of criteria, but are instead a special social–psychological dynamic. Amongst the researchers in the Danish project eXbus, this is called 'the many forces', and such forces include anxiety about being socially excluded along with the potential for experiencing the social space as void of empathy (Søndergaard 2009). The various roles that exist within the drama of bullying are more fluid when the children involved have irreconcilable and conflicting developmental efforts. The bystanders, who seem to do very little either way, still play a central role because they can be dragged into what may be achieved by bullying. When the bystanders are passively dragged to the side of those who are bullying in order to protect themselves, then those who are subjected to bullying obviously become more alone. The conditions for bullying exist in the idea that social exclusion is an act of necessity. If bullying is seen as a form of rejection and exclusion that spins out of control, then it is not clear that the children who bully are the ones who have lost control. As I explain, their behaviour can be very purposeful and, when that is the case, it is the victim instead who loses control of the course of events and their own actions.

The bystanders become hangers-on when they, through their passive presence, bear witness to and thereby substantiate the exclusion.

Everything they do – or, more precisely, do not do – leads to the event becoming some sort of one-time lesson for the excluded child. It is thus possible to pose another question about bullying: what makes a child who has experienced being neglected and rejected withdraw whilst another child does not give up but attempts to become re-established in the community?

Some of the children we have discussed thus far – Ken, Norah, Ellen and Diana – experienced doubt about their own belonging in entirely different ways: they were kept on the outside, left behind or pushed out. And they immediately gave up. Or, at least that is how it appeared because they pointed their interests in other directions. They did not come back, but instead turned towards other opportunities to establish community. Some of them certainly experienced their communities as existing in the shadow of the popular group.

With regard to finding one's place

Sharif arrived from another school to start seventh grade. His family is Palestinian, but he has lived in Norway his entire life. He could see how large segments of the social landscape at the school unfolded and made space for a 12-year-old boy: the easy way for a new boy to gain social access was to play football. All the 'straight' boys met on the field during recess. Occasionally, some of the girls also tagged along. Sharif became just like one of the others when he participated in the football matches. But otherwise, he stood out because he always went straight home after school. There, he played with his younger sisters. The other boys were too old for that kind of thing. However, since he did not hang out with them outside of school, there was no-one to tell him that. By secondary school, the boys stopped playing football in this open kind of way. Only those who systematically pursue it and train with the football club continue playing (Hauge and Haavind 2011), but that was not something Sharif was interested in doing. New patterns of friendship and reciprocity formed between the other boys; Sharif was not included in that, either. He said his best friend was Chen, a boy from a Chinese family. Both were marked as foreigners, and Chen also had to go directly home after school. In this sense, there was a fit between them.

Everything Sharif talked about indicated that he was becoming rather lonely in the social landscape at school. Still, I would argue that no-one would ever think about bullying him. This had to do with how he found and accepted his position in the social landscape. Most of the other students knew almost nothing about him, and they hardly noticed him. For both Sharif and Chen, school was primarily a place for academic aspirations. Sharif's parents focused on school as a place for his scholastic accomplishments, and he knew that. In this respect, he was protected rather than singled out by his differences. As the children – and later, the youths – talked about what they themselves and others were involved in, no-one said that they spent any time or energy in creating contempt for Sharif. It seemed like it was unnecessary for the ruling majority to drive out someone who was already on the outside, and bullying seemed to be reserved for those who could not find their place. And for that to happen, there has to be something at stake.

He acts tough, so we had to teach him a lesson!

Peter was interviewed again at the very end of seventh grade. With the interviewer, he went over who he did and did not like in the class. Some of the other boys were really important to him whilst he hardly knew who some of the girls were. He said the following about Ali:

Peter: He really doesn't have very many friends at all.
Interviewer: Do you know why Ali doesn't have so many friends at all?
Peter: He tries to act tough, so we beat him up all the time.

This is something the interviewer wanted to learn more about, and Peter willingly discussed it. The narrative follows the classic pattern of how an instance of bullying is carried out. If the interviewer's minimal encouragement and questions about when and how things happened are removed, this was how Peter described the course of events:

Nah, he wants to fight and all, so I say to Goran ... he was supposed to fight with Goran, right... We couldn't fight at school. Then we wouldn't have been able to fight long enough, you know? At that point, I had already beat him up once before. So I said to him that he shouldn't fight with Goran and stuff. Since Goran, he, he is pretty good at fighting. So he broke Ali's nose and all... But first it was Ali who had the upper hand, then he hit Goran in the nose so that he began to bleed. I came over, then kicked Ali in the stomach, so that he began to cough and stuff. Then Goran kicked him two times in the nose, and then he broke his nose.

This happened 'a good while ago'. It began as a dispute and turned into an agreement to fight. The boys fought a bit 'such that both of them were somewhat injured'. Then something happened that should not have happened, according to Peter and the other bystanders. Peter repeated the same set of events over again to bring attention to the two significant elements: at a certain point in the fight, Ali was on top, and towards the end, Goran would not stop. Peter said:

Then Ali managed to push Goran down. So I hit him in the nose too... several times, kicked him in the stomach, so that he began coughing and stuff. Then Goran came and kicked him two times in the nose, and then I pushed Goran away. Since Goran wouldn't stop.

Peter explained that he was scared that it was going to go too far:

In any case, Goran would not stop, I have seen him fight hundreds of times. He will not stop. He has to, at least when...at least when blood is running all over the place and stuff. And he is screaming like crazy and stuff. I pushed Goran so that he fell on his face.

When Peter got involved, Goran just stood up and stopped. The interviewer wanted to know if anyone else could have stopped Goran, but Peter would not say that for sure. Peter was able to stop him because they were real buddies and stuck together. Peter, Goran and the other boys in their little social circle were the ones who had control of and defined what course of events were necessary. First, it seemed like Goran and Ali were going to fight to settle a disagreement between them. Yet Ali was warned that he could not win. If that was about to happen, then everyone would come to Goran's aid, and they would not have any pity for Ali. Goran could continue to fight but, at that point, it was just a way for them all to hurt Ali enough for him to be humiliated. In Peter's narrative, he was the one who left the 'hard work' to Goran, but he was actually in control: he decided what was needed and to what extent. When he finally entered and stopped the attacks on Ali, it was not out of sympathy, but rather, because 'enough was enough' to prove humiliation. At the same time, he was diminishing the risk that Goran would subsequently be punished. Peter wanted to protect Goran since he was his friend: 'So if Goran had done any more damage, it might have gotten risky for him.' Peter did not describe this fight as an event that had spun out of control. He determined that, from the amount of bleeding and screaming, Ali had been taught his lesson: specifically, that he must not think that he could belong to their community of boys who dared to be tough.

The interviewer had several follow-up questions: how did things go with Ali afterwards; were there many children there watching the fight whilst it happened; were there any adults who noticed it? Peter's interest in what happened to Ali was limited, and that was surely part of the story's logic: 'Oh, it was fine. He only broke half his nose. On this side, since Goran kicked him from the side, so that he hit him in the nose.' He then explained:

There were a lot of people standing there watching. But no-one wanted to stop it, you know, it's just kind of like that...see blood, you know. That's the kind of thing they think is cool.

An adult teacher had seen the fight from a distance. He came over after it happened, but he said that he had seen it all from the beginning. Peter doubted that, saying: 'But it's probably not true since no teacher would have just watched it from the very beginning.' Still, in the aftermath, the discovery led to sanctions but this did not really bother Peter:

What that teacher said was just 'blah, blah, blah, blah, blah', then he took Ali with him and then...then Goran just...he just didn't give a shit...hap, nothing happened. Goran just got a note to take home, and then it was over.

We knew from other interviews with Peter that he and his friends practised not feeling anything when adults scolded them. Before, he might have had a guilty conscience, but not anymore. The interviewer also wanted to know how things went with Goran at home after the fight – whether he got scolded or anything. Peter knew that Goran did not usually get scolded much at home, and he thought that Goran was someone who could endure quite a bit:

Then he hits pretty hard. He's been boxing since he was a little kid. There is both Goran and his older brothers. So yes, he has learnt to hit others.

Ali's mistake, for which he suffered, was that he hoped and believed that he could become one of them. He strove to attain the masculine aura with which the toughest guys seemed to surround themselves, and he tried to utilise the tools that he thought were valid currency amongst Peter and his friends; namely, to be able to fight and take a hit. He did not follow the same path as Sharif by keeping to himself or finding a friend who also did not belong anywhere.

Although I suggest here that children who are subjected to bullying as a form of social exclusion by a defined social circle may themselves influence its occurrence, I do not mean to justify the actions of those who subject them to abuse and humiliation. However, this is meant to demonstrate that incidents of bullying are part of – and derive their power from – a social game between positions, groupings and ties of friendship in a social landscape that exists at and around school. There are negotiations between both boys and girls that revolve around who one can be, and with whom one can be that person. A lack of empathy was not something these boys were born with, but it was something they trained themselves to practise when they were working on getting older.

To turn to yourself and find 'the person you are' is an impossible task for a 12-year-old as well as for most others. It is a prerequisite to grow by your age – regardless of gender, but in a gendered way. Age must simply be utilised to demonstrate something about oneself and one's possibilities. Certain meaning must be attached, and such meaning must be gathered from cultural discourses that are available, applicable and recognisable. Moreover, a child who is attempting to become a youth must in some way also appropriate gendered forms and make them into a unique expression of self. This has to do with finding an expression that one is comfortable with, before someone else makes the decision about who one is about to become. For some of the children who were marked as 'foreigners', it seemed to be more difficult to find signs of becoming older that Norwegian children considered acceptable. That is why it is so important to have allies who are also trying to figure out the same thing. But many children also simultaneously experience that certain people who were previously their allies are no longer of use.

Discussion: how does bullying arise?

Bullying is an interpersonal phenomenon that is closely linked to the desire to belong and the fear of exclusion (Hanish et al. 2005; Hansen 2011b; Jimerson et al. 2009; Rigby 2004; Søndergaard 2009). It is a way for children to exercise and demonstrate exclusion among themselves. Intense engagement in one's own and others' friendships follows from the fact that, for children and youths, a necessary condition of personal development is creating a sense of belonging with other children. It is simply the way they do it. Growing older in a physical way – which is something actualised in the transition between ages 12 and 14 – must be linked to the existential task of changing oneself according to one's age. This task is conveyed and distributed as alliances and friendships between children (Crick and Ladd 1993; Faircloth and Hamm 2011).

Children recognise each other as companions mostly through markers that confirm their similarity and potential reciprocity. This means that hanging out in the same places and being of the same age and gender serve as tools of communication. Yet this is refined to a code in which activities, skills, preferences and properties convey messages about the person one is trying to become. Bullying exists as a possibility – a sort of side-effect of how children pick up on and utilise perceptions about how they can grow older here in this place, at this school, in this class, amongst these girls and these boys. The task – to grow older in a way one can account for – is emotionally linked to the expectation of and hope for recognition and community. Such hope is directly linked to the fear of being excluded, as well as to the grief of actually being so (Rigby and Griffiths 2011; Søndergaard 2009).

A child's vulnerability becomes connected to the idea that someone else may question who the child can be within a social field to which that child potentially has access and entry. Life at and around school constitutes such a place for everyone, and each and every child must find a way to be at school in relation to the distinctions and rankings that matter there. It is fairly obvious that participation in the social field offered by school is central to a child's development. It delineates a landscape for children as allies and supporters of each other, but also as distinct from each other.

If I were to judge – based on my experiences with interviewing a selection of children from the same social landscape over a certain period of time, during which both the formation and dissolution of friendships were under intense negotiation – then I would say that the polar opposite of alliances and community is not necessarily hate and aggression. Rather, it is disregard. For most of the children interviewed, it was as though the other children were simply there, doing their own thing. There were a few social circles that many children followed from a distance, even children who were not really part of them. As mentioned earlier, it was the girls who were referred to as 'popular' and, to a certain extent, the group of tough guys to which Peter and Goran belonged. These boys referred to themselves as people who had the guts to violate the rules of conduct (Haavind 2003). Thus, the majority of children at school did not matter very much to anyone else, other than those who were perhaps their closest friends and allies. Power structures and majority assessments were created with regard to what a child could be like and with whom they could hang out, and most of the children were familiar with and largely adhered to these tacit rules (Mouttapa et al. 2004). There was a certain security in subordination. If one stayed on the outside or one pulled away in time, then they could avoid the more dramatic forms of exclusion. It may seem like too much of an effort to question a child who keeps to himself.

In many ways, the examples given here are typical of similar episodes that many others described. Norah understood that the popular girls questioned who she was, and she adapted to that and suffered from insecurity. Ellen turned elsewhere when Gwen abandoned her. When Ellen displayed her devotion to her new girlfriend, they were both protected, but then also fell outside the sphere of interest delineated by the girls in Gwen's group. The emotional mismatch that later arose between Gwen and Diana did not escalate to open conflict. Gwen did not use her annoyance to attack Diana directly, but she used it to gain sympathy and strengthen her affiliations with the other girls. They stuck together as a powerful majority and refrained from maintaining any emotional resonance with Diana. For Diana, the lack of emotional resonance with the other girls began a sort of reorientation of who she could be, and thereby also with whom she could hang out. Sharif had never personally participated in the school community much beyond activities that were open to everyone. Further, since his only companion in class was Chen, a boy with whom he only hung out at school, he could not achieve a valid definition of friendship between boys turning 14 in this particular place. Sharif and Chen shared this lack of definition, which was what brought them together and put them outside of the others' sphere of interest.

Peter is separate from the other children who have been mentioned because he had to deal with Ali – the boy who kept trying. Ali's desire to fight Goran was a recurrent need to belong amongst certain other boys. Yet he should not have expected that he would be someone with whom they wanted to hang out. I am not able to conclude why Peter and the others would not even consider having Ali in their group. Even though they did not directly refer to the fact that he was a 'foreigner', the inclusion criterion for accepting someone with immigrant parents – like Goran – was that he never made them think about the fact that he is a foreigner. It was clear that whenever Ali made them see him as a Muslim from the Middle East, they put all the responsibility for their sentiments on him. They also wanted to show the other children that he was not allowed to hang out with them, and these others became somewhat complicit in allowing it to happen. At the same time, Peter and all of the others tried to conceal what was happening from the adults who might try to stop them. All the boys knew that, as soon as the fighting started, they would keep the same tack. They warned Ali that he did not stand a chance and, in that moment, the course of action escalated to Ali being bullied. The boys succeeded in emptying the space of empathy. Ali could not avoid realising that the bystanders were participants. He would not be harmed more than was necessary for them to succeed in shifting the blame onto him. The adults could scold and punish them, but it did not really make a difference. It was as though he brought it upon himself. As previously mentioned, Ali learnt his lesson, and afterwards Peter was certain that he would not try again. The bystanders also learnt this lesson. By protesting and turning against Peter, Goran and the others in their social circle might help them deal with their own social anxiety about being excluded, but instead they did this by putting the blame on Ali, who allowed himself to become a victim.

After what happened, Ali – along with all the bystanders and everyone else who heard about the fight – knew that making another attempt to belong would result in the same outcome. 'Who does he think he is?' was the question implied. When Ali stopped imagining things, peace would be restored. And everyone else learnt something about the risk of imagining things that were not supported by the others. The possibility, but also the danger, attached to all personal development is the power of imagination itself: in order to move and transform oneself, everyone must draw on a capacity to go beyond what is given and imagine who one is going to be and how one can get there. At the same time, it is necessary to recognise one's own limitations and the constraints that are attached to one's social position.

I began by saying that something could be learnt by linking bullying to how friendships form between children. Whilst it is appropriate to refer to these two phenomena as opposites of each other – and the fact that bullying is a deviation from all of the assumptions about what character-ises friendship – there remains the task of understanding how these two phenomena can precondition each other. Instead of pointing out that bullying happens because some children are ruthless, I have sought to present the idea that bullying can emerge somewhat unplanned because the formation of friendships and the social communities created by the children themselves are so valuable to them. The lines of connection from friendship to bullying are dynamic.

Firstly, children's renegotiations of friendship are intensified by social transitions and changes. I have studied the transition from childhood to youth, especially the way that children – and later, youths – execute and manifest this transition. Thus, to a degree, I have been able to see how different types of friendships are put to the test, and whether or not they pass. In addition, there are meanings connected to gender in these transitions, which are central to this negotiation; this means that it is not merely about how each child can prove that they are in the process of growing up, but also how they do so specifically as boys and girls. Even though the relationships between boys and girls intensify at this age – and there is a cultural expectation that this is precisely what is meant to happen – a general point is that same-sex communities are the sustaining element when friendships become transformed. The social landscape into which I have been allowed through the children's narratives included children who were marked by their ethnic affiliation and skin colour as well as children who, even though they did not belong to the majority, could draw upon the majority's taken-for-granted hegemony with regard to what could help a boy or girl become a youth. Many, but not all, of those who were marked as 'immigrants' came from families in which other conceptions prevail with regard to how children are supposed to become older and what significance references to hete-rosexuality should have. At school, there was relatively frequent inter-action across ethnic divides, but friendship and the children's own companionships were still affected by the fact that these divisions would receive greater – and not less – importance as they grow older. For most of the youths who are forming friendships, one or another type of similarity is often used as a short cut to reciprocity.

Secondly, the significance of belonging and being able to make oneself older alongside others is inextricably linked to the fear of being rejected and excluded. For better or worse, it makes for a dynamic social life. At the same time, it is necessary to emphasise again and again that the social transition in which children become youths cannot be made without a personal effort from each child. The personal process of developing cannot take place without a social foundation, nor without personal investment. Everyone gets to know their own abilities and possibilities, which are there because they created them and had others hold them up. Thus, inclusion and exclusion are not located in a static landscape, but in a dynamic combination of the participants' social and personal changes. What I have attempted to demonstrate is that the children often made adjustments themselves and pulled away in time; in that way, they prevented any potential violent rejection. It is possible to turn the causal relation on its head by saying that most children and youths reorient themselves and direct their developmental efforts in different ways so that bullying does not happen. Yet I have also demonstrated that, paradoxically enough for some, this can make bullying necessary in a subjective sense – that is, it can lead to a sort of justification when an instance of bullying develops. In this quasi-justification, those who passively see, know and/or hear about it play an important role. They are all participants in closing off empathy and reducing other opportunities. In this, there is also an assumption that bullying does not occur primarily because some children are weak and cannot defend themselves, other children are ruthless, and the majority are passive and unfeeling. Rather, there is an assumption that bullying is driven by the consequences of its occurrence, and these occurrences affect those who get involved. Bullying can create weakness through humiliation, it can lead to a feeling of arrogance in those who bully, and it can represent an exercise in indifference for those who bear witness to it.

7   Non-simultaneity in cyberbullying

Jette Kofoed

A girl from another school threatened Emma with assault and death in a text message via a popular social-networking site. During my interview with her, Emma said: 'Of course I'm really, really scared that she'll actually come to my home, because she knows where I live, that she'll turn up at my house with a group of friends and beat me up, or that I'll meet her in the street because she's also said, "Just wait 'til I meet you in the street." That time she was over at the school, when the others told me she was there, I just started to shake and my head spun and I cried all the way home.'

The story that Emma told me is one of several accounts of one particular incident that I utilise in my analysis. I draw upon the entangled understandings of this particular cyberbullying incident in order to think about *acts of recognition* of cyberbullying, and how these acts of recognition become a part of the entangled events themselves. The stories describe how (mobile) telephones and social-networking sites are an integral part of Emma's life and the lives of most children in contemporary Danish schools. Their mobile phones are rarely further away than their pockets or school bags, and they visit social-networking sites on a daily basis. Their hands reach for these devices that enable them to engage in and extend their connections with others.[1] Social-networking sites like MySpace, Facebook, Habbo, Speek and Arto[2] plus mobile phones have become significant players in Emma's life with her peers: text-messaging and cyber-life in general have infiltrated the

---

[1] See Laursen (2006); Priøtz (2007); and Winther (2007, 2009) for other investigations of the use of mobile phones by children and young people in a Scandinavian context.

[2] Arto is a popular social-networking site for children and young people in Denmark; in 2009, it had about 900,000 profiles. Since then, Facebook has taken over as the most popular social-networking site among young people in Denmark. Not all children and young people set up a profile on Arto; some would not dream of using the site. However, it was not unusual (in 2009) for up to half of the students in a specific class to have profiles on Arto, with user names like 'sugarbaby', 'i-love-holly' (reciprocated by Holly with 'i-love-kate'), 'wannabexo3' or 'barbieH5'. In Denmark, many children and young people who use Arto also have profiles on Habbo, MySpace, Speek and Facebook. Arto, Speek and Habbo are Danish social-networking sites for youths. See Larsen (2005, 2007) for studies of arto.dk.

relationships between Emma and her peers, shaping what is possible. They couldn't imagine life without them. Social-networking sites are thus used to create, maintain and dismantle social relations and are defined as 'web-based services that allow individuals to: 1) construct a public or semi-public profile within a bounded system; 2) articulate a list of other users with whom they share a connection; and 3) view and traverse their list of connections and those made by others within the system' (boyd and Ellison 2007).

In this chapter, I propose new ways to think about the many forces at work when text-messages and updates circulate amongst schoolchildren within and beyond the schoolroom, specifically when they are not just reciprocal declarations of affection like 'i-love-holly' and 'i-love-kate'. I demonstrate how the very nature of this material–temporal–discursive space makes 'knowing what is going on' impossible in any definitive sense.[3]

The accounts that inform my analysis in this chapter are part of the corpus of data collected in a larger research project that deals with cyber-bullying. In the larger project, the dataset consists of thirty-one individual interviews, four focus-group interviews and multiple classroom observations conducted during three months of fieldwork, as well as twenty-five drawings and seventy essays produced by the students; they were between 10 and 15 years of age, and attended one of four schools near large cities in Denmark. Because I have found that 'the field' transcends a school's physical boundaries, it also became necessary to move out of the school-room and into parks, streets and cyberspace. Thus, I followed the children and technologies across a number of sites and conducted fieldwork at several locations – both real and virtual.

The analysis presented in this chapter is based upon a case that emerged as part of this fieldwork, and one school in particular was selected based on reports of cyberbullying incidents. This specific part of my project included one month of participant observations, virtual fieldwork on social-networking sites and ten individual interviews; the excerpts ana-lysed here are taken from interviews with students between 13 and 14 years of age. These interviews were processed through mapping exercises (Clarke 2005), with a particular focus on positional and affective maps.

The rhizome as a basic theoretical concept

It could be said that all accounts of cyberbullying tell the same story. But putting it like this implies that there is one course of events with identifi-able causal relations; with one point of origin, one perpetrator and one

---

[3] Analyses based on empirical data from this study have previously been published in Kofoed (2009); Kofoed and Ringrose (2012); and Spears et al. (2012).

victim. A linear story. However, the data suggests another way of thinking. In this chapter, as mentioned, I develop a different way of thinking by drawing upon Gilles Deleuze's concept of the rhizome.[4]

A *rhizome* is the rootstock of certain plants; its branching in the earth functions as the plant's reproductive structure. Rhizomes are not roots but systems of tubers that connect the plants, usually underground. Many types of grass are rhizomatic, as are anemones, ginger, mint and irises (Deleuze and Guattari 1980/2005; Sutton and Martin-Jones 2008). Deleuze and Félix Guattari explain their image of the rhizome as a philosophical concept as follows:

> ...unlike trees or their roots, the rhizome connects any point to any other point, and its traits are not necessarily linked to traits of the same nature. [...] It is composed not of units but of dimensions, or rather directions in motion. It has neither beginning nor end, but always a middle (milieu) from which it grows and which it overspills. [... It] operates by variation, expansion, conquest, capture, offshoot...it has multiple entryways and its own lines of flight. (Deleuze and Guattari 1886/2004: 23)

The concept of the rhizome makes it possible to grasp how the social–discursive–temporal–technological formations involved in cyberbullying are entangled with each other and enter into a constantly displaced circulation; the concept presents a thinking technology that enables a reconsideration of how we think, and a theoretical–analytical shift in how we take difference and movement into account. Positions in social space are continually dispersed and distributed in unpredictable ways. The instability of positions itself is not new. What I propose in this chapter is to extend the analysis of displaced positions into contexts that involve cyberbullying, drawing upon my earlier work (2004, 2007, 2008a) as well as Phoenix et al. (2003), Staunæs (2004), Søndergaard (1996/2000) and Wetherell and Maybin (1996). Furthermore, by drawing upon the writings of Brennan (2004), Gregg and Seighworth (2010) and Massumi (2002), I show how affect as intensity and affects appropriated as envy, fear, distrust, embarrassment, joy and anger travel amongst peers, and how those affects emerge in more bodies than those who may immediately appear to be involved. Further, as affects travel amongst the entangled subjects, one affect – for example, envy – merges into fear, into embarrassment, into relief and into other indefinite affects and intensities. Technologies are both detached from and attached to specific bodies, which rules out the possibility of definitively linking particular subjects to

---

[4] In applying Deleuze's concept of the rhizome in concrete empirical analyses, I draw upon a number of works: Deleuze (2001, 1886/2004, 1990/2006); Fuglsang and Sørensen (2006); Nigianni and Storr (2009); and Parr (2005), to name only the most important.

messages and to particular affects. Sara's mobile phone, for example, was associated with her when her name was displayed on the phone receiving her call, yet fingers belonging to other bodies quickly keyed messages in her name. Such detachment creates new possibilities for virtual subjectification, making it necessary to map both the specificity and the travelling of affects.[5] I suggest that the affective rush and drama of the altercations lie at the heart of cyberbullying.

The official story and the others: an analytical strategy

My purpose in presenting the following accounts of a case of cyberbullying is not to uncover an unambiguous story – complete and nuanced – nor is it to determine which account is correct and which is incorrect. Instead, I apply Deleuze's concepts in order to develop multivalent perspectives on what I term the Unambiguous Tale. I argue that we must abandon the certainty that the Unambiguous Tale both draws upon and establishes, and instead listen to many voices in order to carry out analyses through which we can develop a new way to read cyberbullying. My wish is to analyse the phenomenon in ways that children and young people can recognise as congruent with their experiences, and to develop a language for addressing these phenomena. This chapter thus presents a view of how the different voices and accounts do not combine to make up one complete act of cyberbullying, but instead present a picture of multiple flows of actions/times/spaces/voices that those involved recognise as cyberbullying. Thus, it has been necessary to abandon the certitude of a true story.

A belief in the Unambiguous Tale is evident in the empirical material; the officially accepted story is that such a tale does exist. Therefore, I begin with a 'story about what really happened', using it as a point of departure in my analytical strategy. By attending to one fixed point of view, it becomes possible to inquire about the differences between one account and another as well as the movement between them. I begin in the middle with 'what really happened' and allow my analysis to grow and overspill its point of departure.

When one works with accounts of cyberbullying, it becomes evident that the distribution of positions from which the Unambiguous Tale operates – i.e. the positions of 'bully', 'victim' and 'bystander' that are maintained by traditional research on bullying (Olweus 1992) – are by no means stable. Positions, meanings and affects slide, shift and become entangled in a confusion of times, technologies, places and subjects.

---

[5] These points are further developed in a paper co-written with Jessica Ringrose (Kofoed and Ringrose 2012).

The threads stretch out; they cannot be recounted as one story, but rather, as circulations of affects, rhizomatic positions, temporal shifts, forceful speaking and interactive technologies. I develop the concept of *non-simultaneity* in my analysis, closely connecting it to the empirical accounts. The proposed new reading of cyberbullying is then opened up by applying the concepts of rhizome and non-simultaneity, and it leans against other concepts such as 'popularity regime', 'relational distribution', 'distribution of weakness' and 'encryption'. I elaborate on each of these concepts as I take them up in the analysis of the stories.

Bitchfights

Emma's story, which was recounted at the beginning of this chapter, involved a number of people and different technologies – social-networking sites and mobile phones – across school contexts. The concrete event was that the girl by whom Emma felt threatened came to school and wanted to talk to Emma. Some of Emma's classmates met the girl, stopped her from coming into the school and managed to send Emma a text message, telling her that the girl was in the vicinity. Emma said that a conflict of this nature was known as a 'bitchfight'. A bitchfight might, for instance, be featured on Arto or Facebook in the space where site users comment on each other's evaluations. Bitchfights take place both in the schoolyard and on social-networking sites. When asked to explain 'bitchfight', Emma chose the phrase 'girl crisis'. When searching online for the term 'bitchfight', one is directed to a number of YouTube videos in which young girls are engaged in close physical fights that resemble wrestling, with what looks like a fairly large number of combatants. Their bodies are entangled, and it isn't always easy to tell which arm belongs to whom. In these arbitrarily chosen, short clips, we saw two-to-five girls' bodies in an intense, staged physical struggle. The fights are typically referred to by titles like 'Carrie v. Jackie'. Of course, it is a far cry from these clips to Emma's situation, and the point is not that the bitchfights in which Emma was involved are the same as these staged and visually presented physical fights. But it is worthwhile to consider whether, and in what ways, these physical fights can be considered images of what Emma was involved in and what she called bitchfights. And we might also consider the extent to which the tangled body parts and relations as well as the formulation 'Carrie v. Jackie' indicate something significant that we must notice in this conceptual–empirical analysis.

The rhizomatic conceptual–empirical analysis that follows includes the swarm of interactions that are discernible in bitchfights; it includes topics such as Laura's and Emma's experiences of fitting in, their anxieties about being excluded from the group to which they thought they belonged, their thoughts about gaining admittance to that group and about how others have to be pushed out. Not least of all, I attend to the high-status technologies that are definitive elements in the constitutive processes of daily life both in and out of school. Offline life is by no means isolated from online relations. On the contrary, they are entangled within youth life and in processes of subjectification in a number of different ways. This points to the need to re-address the distinction between 'virtual life' and 'real life' and theorise it in new ways.

The 'Unambiguous Tale'

I encountered the Unambiguous Tale at several of my fieldwork schools. The version that forms my point of departure here does not feature Emma as the central figure, but rather, Laura and Ellen. This Unambiguous Tale was first presented by a school principal who reported that the school had recently had a case of cyberbullying. Her account mentioned a number of events involving a group of girls from the same seventh-grade[6] class as well as police reports, teacher involvement, conflict management, weeping girls, frustrated teachers and dismayed parents. When I look through the empirical material, I can identify the sequence of events in the narrative that circulated amongst the parties involved – stories circulate and gain some fixity – and the school principal wasn't the only one who told it. Both adults and children narrate, and no dominant narrative voice can be discovered. The voices talk about a girl who picked on another girl on a social-networking site, and this situation developed into an aggressive and intense affective conflict between the girls. The story is structured around a traditional linear narrative with a beginning, an elaboration, a conflict, a point of no return, an escalation of the conflict and then the climax, followed by catharsis and resolution of the conflict. In this dramatic linear narrative, the plot can be mapped out with an unambiguous allocation of fixed positions (bully/victim/bystander). The Tale gives no doubt that Sara was the one who was bullying, Ellen was the one being bullied, and Victoria, Molly and Mia, in particular, were the bystanders.

Offensive comments about Ellen were written on the wall of her profile page on the social-networking site (using terms like 'hooker', 'bitch', 'you think you're really something but you ought to die'), and were further commented on by Victoria and Molly. The evaluations and comments escalated into threats, and Ellen retaliated. Some of these

---

[6] This corresponds to eighth grade/year in American or British schools.

messages were printed out and others erased. There was an attempt to sort out the story amongst the other students in their class, who became divided into sympathetic and aversive camps. Several teachers were drawn into the matter, and the sequence of events was eventually unravelled. After this class activity, Sara was given a warning. The school principal explained how the now Unambiguous Tale elicited a demand for a public apology:

Sara had to give Ellen an apology, she had to say 'sorry' to the whole class for lying to them, and then I made her apologise for having been so terribly cruel to Ellen, she absolutely had to tell her she was sorry, and she did.

In this version of the Tale, the main points and the distribution of positions were as such: Sara was bullying; Ellen was bullied; and the class watched. The educators acted responsibly, demanding acceptable behaviour at school. The school principal's account of the matter has a particular dramaturgical clarity, and both major and minor traces of story, plot and distribution of positions can be recognised in the interviews I conducted with the girls.

In these interviews, the girls touched upon parts of the Tale in different ways and to varying degrees. It is not my intention to represent the Unambiguous Tale as a caricature lacking solidarity. It is hardly surprising that its main features can be clearly identified in the school principal's narrative. The Tale is distinguished from the stories that follow because it has a conclusion; the other stories do not conclude in the same way with an apparently definite ending. In the Tale, the ending consists of conflict resolution at the point where an apology is demanded from one position (Sara's) to another (Ellen's). Here, the ending reflects the fact that, on the basis of an explanatory clarification, the school principal has passed judgment on the course of events. It is this possibility of clarification that characterises the Unambiguous Tale. In this Tale, as in a court of law, it is possible to clarify what happened and who did what. The school principal must take action, and in order to do so, she must be able to distribute positions – no matter how difficult this might be. So it isn't surprising that clarification, an ending and a conclusion to the story appear in the version where the school principal has a strong voice. When action and judgment are called for, the recourse is to have certain types of interpretation where the allocation of guilt and responsibility is a prominent feature. What was done? Who did it? Who was subjected to it? And who should be punished? The Unambiguous Tale thus raises problems that point to a fundamental supposition that guilt is allocated between a victim and a perpetrator, and that these cannot even momentarily be one and the same person.

To sum up, my point here is that the Unambiguous Tale appears most clearly in the school principal's account, but that does not mean that the principal is the only one to tell this story. The Tale has several authors and no authoritative owner; rather, it is passed on, elaborated on and cited by many people, ranging from the school principal to students.

Ambiguous tales

It is especially remarkable that this linear account of what happened did not provide an outline for any of the stories recounted by the girls in the interviews. Sections of the story can certainly be discerned, but the same story does not structure their various perspectives on what otherwise appears to be the same case. As further interviews brought new aspects of the events to light, it became increasingly difficult to find out what provoked the conflict in the first place, to find a thread connecting them or even to determine what the events were actually about, how they developed, how many parties were involved or how the positions were allocated.

In what follows, I further highlight aspects of the events in order to show how the Unambiguous Tale is interrupted and interfered with by ambiguous narratives, by complexity and by contradictions. I start with Ellen (the Unambiguous Tale's victim), who described what she thought about Sara (the Tale's bully who had to apologise):

Ellen: I'm scared I might do bad things to her sometimes, you know, I'm scared I might bully her in some way. Or not exactly bully her; just be a bit mean to her.
Interviewer: What might you do?
Ellen: I might say things to her, make remarks all the time and such. I could badmouth her to others or something.
Interviewer: Do you do that?
Ellen: Yes, I do . . .
Interviewer: Yes? Who do you talk about her to?
Ellen: Laura and Caitlin and Molly and Olivia, I talk to them all about it, nearly all the girls.
Interviewer: So you're actually already doing it?
Ellen: Yes.

Ellen's story here indicates an adoption of many different positions. Elsewhere, she maintained the story that she was bullied and felt abused. Some of her account can be recognised from the Tale. But she also circled around her own experience of harassing others, going into detail about the best way to hit people. With this, she demonstrated how she could adopt a plurality of positions.

Sara's story, on the other hand, began at a different place and, even though some of the same actors figured into it, they were allocated different positions:

Sara: And then suddenly, Molly managed to turn Ellen against me because they're best friends, so she got her against me too, and they started to bully me ... by, for instance, calling me a 'whore' and other things, 'bitch' and that, and they said it out loud in class and started to write hate texts and badmouthing me on Messenger and putting their names to it and that.

Interviewer: And writing your name?

Sara: No, writing it in their own names. For instance, Ellen wrote, 'Sara, you stinking whore, get back on the streets' or something like that, in her own name so everyone in, you know, everyone could see it.

It is not easy to keep track of the different names. But in this excerpt from a much longer discussion of the class's local history, the reader should especially take note of how the distribution of positions differs both from those in the Unambiguous Tale and from Ellen's account. Here, it is Sara who felt persecuted by Ellen, who had been positioned as the bullying victim in other versions of the story. The same students were involved, but they were assigned different positions. Sara, Ellen and the other girls all willingly agreed to be interviewed, which gave me the idea that there was some kind of agreement on what the story was about. What readers should particularly notice in the following pages is how the positions shift and are displaced in activities that are recognised as cyberbullying. My analysis focuses on these sliding positions. This does not mean that more stable positions are not found in other cyberbullying events. By focusing on the slips, shifts and breaks, I am making the point that it is sometimes different. Applying the concepts of the rhizome and displaced and dispersed positions, I pursue this observation in my analysis of how positions slide or become fixed. But first, I explain how bullying is conceptualised in this chapter.

Why talk about *acts of recognition* in cyberbullying?

Rather than focusing on 'cyberbullying', I am interested in activities that are recognised as cyberbullying. The intention is multiple: to allow the field itself to indicate that certain activities are labelled as cyberbullying; and I am studying these activities. Another intention is to suggest that the discourse on bullying may be one factor in the production of such bullying. Jessica Ringrose analyses the discourse on bullying in a British context and indicates how it functions as a co-producer in contexts where there is bullying (Ringrose 2008). A similar co-production is found in the particular situations I examine here. The phrase 'activities that are recognised as cyberbullying' makes it possible to establish analytical distance and wrench oneself free of the expectation of being able to judge whether a case really is bullying or just innocent teasing, or whether it is a case of serious violence.[7] My interest here is focused instead on the constitutive conditions that are manifested in the empirical material.

There is one further point concerning the use of this phrase: it associates the designation 'bullying' with activities and actions, rather than with specific children or young people. In what follows, I use the phrase 'activities that are recognised as cyberbullying' from time to time and refrain from referring to particular children as bullies, victims and/or bystanders. However, I must emphasise that, by writing and analysing in this way, I am not overlooking, denying or belittling the suffering of these children or the bullying experiences that have wreaked such serious havoc in their lives. Rather, my intention is to comprehend these experiences across different types of empirical material, using other reading strategies and concepts[8] than those that essentialise evil or the drive to exclude and then fasten them onto individuals.

What is cyberbullying?

Much of the research that deals with cyberbullying is quantitative, and thus it differs in theoretical and methodological approach. A number of international studies have investigated technologies and exclusion (Kowalski et al. 2008; Patchin and Hinduja 2006; Shariff 2008; Smith et al. 2008; Ybarra and Mitchell 2004). The analysis presented here seeks to bring into view those aspects that are close to the experiences that children and young people have with these technologies and the practices of exclusion.

Canadian researcher Shaheen Shariff, who has worked extensively with cyberbullying, writes:

One of the problems I have always had with definitions of 'bullying' is that they were too simplistic and therefore invited reactions, policy and programmatic responses that failed to recognise its nuances and complexities. In the case of cyberspace, because of the range of possibilities, the fluidity with which it is possible to move from one form of technology such as email, MSN, Facebook, MySpace, web-blogs, chat rooms and so on, and the capacity for millions of people

---

[7] See Søndergaard, page 47, for a discussion about the relation between teasing, bullying and conflict; also Frosh et al. (2002) for a similar discussion of these phenomena and their intra-relatedness.

[8] For reflections on this type of reading strategy, see Kofoed (2004) and Staunæs (2007).

to read and participate in various forms of communication, any definition of cyberbullying must be applied with a caveat. Cyberbullying must be understood in the specific paradigmatic context in which it is presented. More importantly, when we define a behaviour, it is important to remember it as an action that takes place in a particular context, at a particular time, with various influences operating on the individual(s) who take the action. (2008: 28)

Shariff thus regards definitions of bullying with caution,[9] giving weight to the local manifestations of cyberbullying, with an interest in tracking down the activities that are recognised as cyberbullying as well as discovering what generates them and with what consequences. I want to add a further aspect; namely, the expectation the participants have about participating in the life of the class. This expectation should be taken into account throughout my analysis, since a central thread in all the data is the experience of being excluded from a relational network to which they all have a legitimate expectation of belonging. It is possible that some school classes do not function as an all-encompassing or inclusive community, even though the school class is primarily conceived of as a community (Anderson 2000; Kofoed 2004). However, it is not my project here to point out possible discrepancies between intention and practice, but instead to show how potential exclusions are created in relation to a legitimate expectation of being part of the community that the class is presented as being. An important aspect of learning to be a student is to acquire and maintain expectations of community. The kinds of school communities in which cyberbullying takes place are those to which children have a legitimate expectation of belonging as part of the process of becoming appropriate and acceptable as a student.[10]

The narratives of children and youths that concern cyberbullying must be understood in relation to this expectation. Cyberbullying thus takes place in contexts in which children are not only obliged to participate, but in which participation is structured around the class's supposed community. All the participants become students from the knowledge that their expectation of participation is legitimate, whether or not it is fulfilled. The acts of recognition regarding bullying practices, which are presented in the following, must therefore be understood in relation to this particular

[9] Shariff is not alone in having reservations about definitions of bullying. This concern is shared by others; for instance, Meyer (2007b). Other researchers distinguish between cyberbullying and online harassment (Burgess-Proctor et al. 2009; Hinduja and Patchin 2009). One central discussion considers the extent to which cyberbullying differs from what comes to be called 'traditional' bullying. Is it 'an old problem in a new guise' (Campbell 2005) or 'a new bottle but old wine' (Li 2007)?

[10] For reflections on and analyses of appropriateness in different contexts (cf. Haraway 1991), see inter alia Juelskjær (2009); Kofoed (2004, 2008a); Kofoed and Staunæs (2007); Myong (2009); Staunæs (2004); Søndergaard (1996/2000, 2000, 2008).

structure of the expectation of community, inclusion and legitimate participation.

Frozen stories

Here, I wish to suggest that the Unambiguous Tale may be viewed as the freezing of entangled affects, temporality and positionings. Such a freezing emphasises that a dynamic *movement* can become a fixed and stable *entity*, in relation to which the readings of other movements (past and future) are determined; in this case, for example, the decisions that must be made by professional educational practitioners. But I also want to point out how this frozen entity gains hegemony by circulating amongst and being cited by the parties involved. It is important to note that 'fixed freezing' of this kind may also take place amongst teachers and principals, in which case the Unambiguous Tale derives legitimacy from the principal's office, from the staffroom and probably also from the theories of bullying that operate simplistically in everyday school life wherein the bully and victim have distinct and separate positions.[11] Ironically, the freezing of the Tale is repeated in this chapter, where it is unambiguously presented as the hegemonic narrative to which the other narratives in the empirical material all relate. Thus, it is not only the subjects and technologies in the field that are being studied, but also the researcher with her MP3 recorder, her transcriptions and her mobile phone as well as the technologies she uses to comprehend the phenomenon and offer her understanding of it in ways that can be recognised as understandable – all of these elements promote the freezing of the Unambiguous Tale.

In the following analysis, I apply the concept of the rhizome and also suggest other concepts that can help make visible the slippage and displacement within positions that are evident in the experiences described and evoked in the empirical accounts. As already mentioned, one of the central concepts that I develop in the analysis is *non-simultaneity*. It is important to emphasise that the introduction of the idea of non-simultaneity was made possible by analysing rhizomatic movements in the specific detailed accounts within the empirical material. The reading was then opened up by applying concepts like 'rhizome', 'non-simultaneity', 'popularity regime', 'distribution of weakness' and 'encryption'. And it is important to emphasise that this reading should not be seen as the only possible option, but rather, as one of several for attempting to comprehend the many apparently unreliable and incoherent voices. But

[11] See Ringrose (2008).

all of this unfolds in the following pages. While continuing, the reader must bear in mind the introductory section, with Ellen's and Sara's narratives about their experiences with volatile positions.

Experiences of non-simultaneity

As we have seen, the Unambiguous Tale made a convincing entry into the accounts, but at the same time, its absence from the interviews with Laura, Ellen and the others is noteworthy. Their accounts do not lend themselves to being understood as a single jigsaw puzzle because the different students do not seem to relate their perspectives as though they were part of the Unambiguous Tale, or to allocate positions (bully, victim, bystander) in such a way that agreement can be reached. So what is absent in these interviews? The young people seemed to be familiar with the Unambiguous Tale. Laura recounted what she considered to be the beginning of the Tale as such:

Laura: It started with . . . Sara and Ellen, they were staying together, and they had just met one of Ellen's friends there.
Interviewer: OK.
Laura: Sara really liked him, so in the night she took Ellen's mobile phone and got his number and started to write to him without Ellen knowing . . . and she knew that Ellen was crazy about him and that's how she started up with Simon who they had met and Ellen was really pissed off and unhappy about it and they fell out.

According to Laura's account, the conflict started when Sara took an attractive boy's phone number from Ellen's mobile phone. This is a completely different starting point than the one established in both the Unambiguous Tale and in the narratives of several of the girls; the Unambiguous Tale as a structuring principle has disappeared. There are, however, traces of the Tale's elements in the distribution of positions in the accounts of both Laura and the others (including Emma). In Laura's account of how the conflict arose after Sara took a number from Ellen's mobile phone, a preliminary division into 'perpetrator' and 'victim' is recognisable from the Unambiguous Tale. But later in the interview, Laura talked about how, on the social-networking site Arto, Molly wrote that Sara is 'a hooker with huge tits', and this degenerated into a long, drawn-out conflict between Sara and Molly, with Ellen involved as an onlooker; this distribution of positions cannot easily be found in the Tale.

The positions slid and changed places within each individual's account and between the different narratives. Each interview contained accounts of severe and painful experiences with cyberbullying, and each contained fragments of the Tale. However, new and different students figured into each interview (not only Ellen and Sara, who alternated between the positions of 'bully' and 'victim', but also Emma, Simon, Nick, Molly and Shannon) along with other accusations (not just 'hooker' and 'filthy pig' but 'love-thief', as well as threats), other schools (the school of which this seventh-grade class is a part as well as schools from which students have transferred and other schools in the neighbourhood) and other affects (not only fear that the threats would be acted on, but also agitation, guilt resulting from having written 'fuck you, you fat pig' and the joy of having a companion whilst doing it). The various accounts of a case recognised as bullying did not start from the same event but from numerous different affects, incidents and causes. In the Unambiguous Tale, Ellen was allocated the position of victim. Parts of the Tale were acknowledged by Sara and Victoria, but they asserted that Ellen actually bullied Sara, and they brought in Jennifer, who no longer attended their school. Parts of Sara's account contained features from the Unambiguous Tale, but she also talked about experiences of both being bullied and bullying someone else. Thus, the linear structure of the Unambiguous Tale is complicated by quite a number of accounts with a number of different starting points and just as many 'conclusions'. But in a rhizomatic reading of the narratives, what is particularly interesting is not that the linear story is intersected by other equally linear stories, but that non-linearity and narrative entanglements become visible. This opens up new possibilities for comprehending the phenomenon that is recognised as cyberbullying in ways other than the acceptable, unambiguous agreement; it enables an observation of how relations are distributed and become threatening.

Threatening distribution of relations

In several of the interviews, certain terms were used to characterise the events. 'Bitchfight' or 'girl crisis' are the terms used locally to explain the activities in which Laura v. Ellen alternated with Ellen v. Sara and Molly v. Victoria, and in which Arto and mobile phones were potential battle auxiliaries. Let us look at how Laura – who had experience with moving between v. Shannon v. Ellen v. Arto – perceived the shifting relations, and how instability in the distribution of relations was feared. This may help us achieve a fuller understanding of what bitchfights between 14-year-old girls can be about. This is what she said:

Laura: Once they'd become best friends, Shannon became pissed off . . .
            there was also something about Ellen and Olivia being best friends

and then falling out, and then Ellen got to be best friends with me and Alicia and so on, and she got to be pissed off or unhappy about it, or else when she's unhappy she gets pissed off and then she gets aggressive and violent and that . . . she makes threats but she doesn't do anything.

Interviewer: What does she threaten with?

Laura: 'I'll kill you', 'I'll beat you up so you can't stand on your own legs', things like that.

Here, Laura's narrative exemplifies how an entanglement of potential adversaries can originate, and also how friendships that have become embittered can result in threats sent by text message. It also demonstrates how the distribution of positions and relations can simultaneously be stable and potentially threatening, and how these relations can shift. Attention to what does not yet exist, to what may come to be and its relation to 'now' and 'previously' is especially nourished by the ideas inspired by Deleuze about becoming, time as non-linearity and potentiality, and also by Patti Lather's concept of 'the no longer, and the not yet' (2007). The term 'relational distribution' enables one to attain an understanding of relations as being constantly negotiated and constructed. In this sense, relations are not definitively distributed but are repositioned and redistributed within a community whose limits are never absolutely fixed. The observed entanglements indicate that it is never possible to state definitively how many persons are involved, or to simply distribute a finite number of relations. Quite the contrary: it is clear how the distribution of relations is constantly emerging, and how relations cannot be understood in isolation (bully/victim/bystander) but must be understood as being entangled with each other. The term 'relational distribution' gives the potential to comprehend this reciprocal tangling of relations. Laura had more experience to draw upon, and she described how she participated in bullying a girl in her class, and how she was threatened into sending her a text message and going to find her in the street:

They bullied Caitlin because she was fat and a lot of other things, and I didn't join in so they said 'OK, Laura, you can't be with us if you won't do the same things as us', and I thought, 'Oh, can't I? That's something new', because they'd been bullying her for a year or something like that and I hadn't done anything, and each time they did it and I didn't join in, they always said that I should also say something to her, and in the end I'd been with them so much that I began to say the same things to her, it got to be automatic. I said the same as them so as not to be kept out of things.

. . . And Caitlin got so upset each time and I had a bad conscience, but I still enjoyed it a bit because she was annoying. . . . There was also something about 'you fat cow' and such things, really over the top. When I got home my conscience was really bad and I actually couldn't think about anything else, and then I went to school again and it was the same, and that's how it went on and on and on. ... Sometimes, when they got mad over nothing, sometimes they started to bully me because I hadn't bullied that other one, that Caitlin.

This excerpt from the interviews makes it clear that the distribution of relations surrounding Caitlin can appear unstable and potentially threatening, in the sense that a relational distribution that appears stable can actually change and be especially threatening because a person can be struck by the assessment of who is wrong. The threat is felt to be ostracism by the legitimate community of the class. This was the experience that Laura described in her account of how she started to participate in the bullying of Caitlin, but also how she might be ejected from the group she was part of and become the one who was suddenly threatened with ostracism. Laura's actions can be regarded as attempts to escape the insecurity about her own position; that is, to safeguard herself from being singled out by the others as someone who doesn't belong. Laura's story is not isolated; many other students told similar stories about dealing with the threat of relational distribution.

The concept of non-simultaneity

These are stories about the experience of what may be called non-simultaneity. 'Non-simultaneity' is a term that expresses the presence of displaced positions and displaced time; their entanglements and interactions. It denotes incongruence between positions, temporality and forces of various kinds (such as different affects or the different wishes, wills and desires present in the interaction between several persons). Non-simultaneity can occur in many situations where connections and interactions actually function. I propose to refer to this lack of accord as non-simultaneity instead of using terms like 'asynchrony' in order to indicate how different temporalities play a significant role in the development of cyberbullying. But I also intend to show how temporalities interact with other forces, such as spatiality, values, technologies and affects. The point is that it is impossible to know in advance which values, affects, etc., might be in action; it is only possible to say that elements other than temporality can be out of joint. Time, and especially displaced time, is a central concept, but temporal displacement must always be understood in connection with displacements in position, technological admission, affects and the many other forces at work. I choose to use 'non-simultaneity' as a term that is less idiomatic than 'asynchrony' as well as to emphasise the applicability of the concept to both time and other interacting forces, and to establish necessary analytical distance.

At this point in the analysis, I no longer refer only to positions but also to these other interactive forces. I have already mentioned 'affects' several times. I draw upon Deleuze Patricia Clough, and Brian Massumi in conceptualising *affect*. The basic idea builds on Deleuze's assumption that 'affect is the change or variation that occurs when bodies collide, or come into contact. As a body, affect is the knowable product of an encounter, specific in its ethical and lived dimensions and yet it is also as indefinite as the experience of a sunset, transformation or ghost' (Colman in Parr 2005).

This allows me to address the sensations appropriated by certain affects – such as envy, fear or joy – as well as the intensities that are indefinite and not appropriated by a particular and recognisable affect. When adding Clough and Massumi's shared point about affects referring 'generally to bodily capacities to affect and be affected or the augmentation or diminution of a body's capacity to act, to engage, and to connect such that auto affection is linked to self-feeling of being alive – that is, aliveness or vitality' (Clough 2007: 2), it becomes analytically possible to address the affective tenor of cyberbullying in ways that allow for the multiplicity in both affecting and being affected. My assertion that the concept of non-simultaneity should also be applied to affects is based on the empirical analysis. The accounts of actions that are recognised as cyberbullying are imbued with many kinds of affects – fear, curiosity, joy, pleasure, uneasiness, disappointment, distrust – and with intensities not (yet) appropriated by particular affects. It would be difficult to ignore the ways in which affects occupy time and place, and how they appear to move and travel; and also how Sara, Ellen and the others both affected and were being affected. Affects appear to be an important aspect of school life; therefore, they are an analytical concern as one of the forces at work in activities that are recognised as cyberbullying.

If there is continuity between Laura's affective self-perception and her perception of how others position her, then her position is probably one of relative peace and contentment. If, on the other hand, there is (potential) non-continuity between Laura's self-perception and her perception of how others see her, then discontent and perhaps even weakness will enter her being. Affective non-continuity thus acts as an important ingredient in the subjective act of becoming a student. In a sentence borrowed from Lene Myong Petersen, it can be said that 'the discursive becoming of the subject presupposes a constructed continuity between "self" and manifestation' (2009: 13). Manifestation could also mean the Other's assessment of 'self'. Myong Petersen continues:

Doubt, or the possibility that this continuity is not present, exists as a premise for the subject's self-assessment. Synchrony between taken for granted continuity and potential discontinuity can clearly be perceived as the constitutive premise of subjective becoming. (ibid; author's translation)

Going further with this emphasis on the duality of continuity perceived as 'taken for granted' and the non-continuity that can potentially arise between self-perception and others' perception of who one is, it might be suggested that this duality has affective significance for the ways in which a student can participate in the apparently natural and legitimate community of the school class.

Laura experienced non-continuity between her own self-perception and the degrading evaluation voiced by the others, and this constitutes a collapse in affective continuity. Technologies add a temporal aspect of non-simultaneity, wherein the lack of affective intensity is postponed, fastened, slowed down or distorted by the interaction with the technology.

This displacement thus applies to both speed and positions as well as to affect-producing collapses that are felt to be violent, offensive and/or threatening (e.g. Emma is scared, Caitlin feels threatened, Ellen fears reprisals).

Popularity regime

The feeling of (or fear of) suddenly not belonging, of not knowing where the accusations and threats are coming from or might come from, of insecurity about the stability of one's position – was mentioned in several interviews as the reason why such collapses, or potential collapses, were experienced as threatening. What characterises these collapses is an uncertainty about whether the future distribution of relations will correspond to their distribution up to the present time. But there is more to this: here, the concept of non-simultaneity has a special applicability because it is the combination of non-simultaneity + the threat of exclusion + degradation + digital mediation; this cocktail figured repeatedly in the interviews. It appears that when the slippage between self-perception and others' perceptions, desires and will becomes too great, then the threat of exclusion joins non-simultaneity; and when the content is degrading and media are added, the result is an act that is recognised as cyberbullying. All these elements added together contribute to the entanglement. But it should not be assumed that if we calculate the sum correctly we will know what's going on; rather, these elements indicate the multiplicity of forces that interact, mingle with and displace each other in rhizomatic movement. It is precisely this uncertainty that intensifies the affects and the language involved. It is impossible to predict the point at which non-simultaneity and non-continuity will become too great, and this unpredictability colours the narratives. These uncertainties are labile, and sudden changes in who is or might be the 'dirty pig' can mean an abrupt exclusion for some and an equally abrupt inclusion for others.

These uncertainties are managed within what might be called a 'popularity regime' in which relations are determined by the degree of popularity. However, it is not only the distribution of relations that is determined within this regime, but also the negotiation of the distribution of weakness amongst the parties involved. I term this the 'distribution' of weakness to indicate that relations – and the meanings connected to these relations – are determined in synch with each other and are never absolutely fixed. This does not imply that there is a certain amount of weakness that must be distributed in any given class. Laura's account of how she moved from being the one who excludes to being the one excluded can be understood as a negotiation of power relations in the distribution of strength and weakness. Her bad conscience after sending nasty text-messages coexisted with her attempts to ensure that she herself was not struck by nasty messages; she strove to protect herself in relation to the distribution of weakness that she saw inflicted on Caitlin.

+ technologies

Thus far, I have discussed the Unambigious Tale and the way in which it becomes frozen or fixed, and also the non-simultaneity and non-continuity manifested in many of the narratives. However, I have not dealt explicitly with technologies, mobile-phone practices and social-networking site practices. This might imply that I am operating with a division between the virtual and the non-virtual – but this is by no means the case. These technologies seem to be a greater or lesser element in the activities reported by the youths. On the one hand, the technologies have a special function; and on the other, they cannot merely be regarded as a new ingredient added to the processes of inclusion and exclusion. Some accounts of actions that can be recognised as cyberbullying appear to resemble modes of exclusion that are sometimes termed 'face-to-face bullying' (Almeida et al. 2009; Steffgen 2009). Other accounts suggest that the virtual and non-virtual cannot be separated but must be understood as closely linked to each other. The empirical material thus indicates a need for two different types of approach. The theoretical–analytical ambition is to attain a deeper understanding of inclusion and exclusion when technologies are part of the process by *both* accepting a division between virtual and non-virtual whilst *simultaneously* transcending this division by tracing the movements created in the entangled distribution of relations (Kofoed 2008b).

Arto invites evaluations

The social-networking site Arto invites its users to announce their moods; for example, in its input field 'mood'. There is a form to fill out: How do I feel? Why? Today's upper; Today's downer; What I've done; What I have to do; What I'm listening to. The 'moods' of the different profiles on Arto manifest a wide spectrum of sentiments, from 'you&I for ever treasure girl I love you so much its incredible' to 'fuck you you bitch you should die'.

These updates thus contain declarations of love, death threats, invective and comments on body sizes and shapes as well as on accessories. Active users tend to update their 'mood' on a daily basis and check the moods of others. For those youths who regularly use sites like Arto and Facebook, a degree of familiarity with the latest updates appears to be an important condition for being able to navigate through life at school. It also seems to be important for a youth's participation to update their own mood and to know who has commented on others' moods, to know who has been 'on' and in general to follow the ongoing assessment of relations. A youth checks their own groups as well as those that are in proximity to them. Names are not always mentioned in these mood evaluations. Messages and comments are often encrypted in ways that usually render them incomprehensible except to the initiated. Despite these encryptions, being on display on the internet is considered to be extreme exposure. Encryption of messages also implies that if comments are printed out and shown to an educational professional in a complaint about receiving abuse on the internet, it can be difficult for the adult to determine what the comment actually says, and what or who is being evaluated.

My premise here is that these practices of evaluating others' affects in cyberspace are an important element in activities that can be recognised as cyberbullying, where assessments of well-known others are circulated and displayed for an unlimited number of observers. Social-networking sites are important players within many relations. With regard to the significance of cyber life, one of the young people said, 'If you're not on Arto, you don't exist.' Social-networking sites present a mobile structuring of positions, temporalities and moods, with an associated expectation of updates and follow-ups.

Circulation of assessments

With these mood evaluations and other online interactions, the non-simultaneity in intensity appears to be particularly visible. Perhaps this mobility and non-simultaneity of affects are what Sara experiences when she feels afraid of what she might read on Arto. She is especially scared of

Ellen's evaluation about what happened earlier in the day. Yesterday, it was Victoria who was scared; but today, she is full of trust, feeling secure and included with Ellen and Anna, and looking forward to the plans they have in the afternoon. For a short time, Victoria's sense of powerlessness in life is replaced by the satisfaction of being included. But Caitlin has become irritated and angry as Laura and Anna grow more sure of Victoria's preference for them. This is the kind of complication to which I refer when I call this a situation of displaced positions. And non-simultaneity of affective intensity explains what is added to the situation by cyber life. The girls are not engaged with the same affects at the same times. They are angry, happy, miserable, disturbed and elated at different points of time that are displaced in relation to one another. It is important here to point out that displacement does not imply that the girls feel precisely the same things, but rather, that their affective movements in relation to each other are meaningful in the way that they manifest recip-rocal responses and reactions. The exchange of mood evaluations is interrupted and continued, and it is uncertain who has read what. At the same time, these comments are accessible to an infinite audience.

The exchange of positions and affects takes place more rapidly than can be reproduced in the freezing of rhizomatic movement that I described earlier. It seems that no position can be guaranteed stability and perma-nence. When Ellen logs on to check Sara's interpretation of what hap-pened during the break today, and when the next day Sara can't be sure that Ellen has actually read her mood evaluation or whether she has been on Arto at all, there is a revelation of non-simultaneity in affective inten-sity. Ellen's reaction to Sara's mood evaluation might be mediated by her father reading the message and telling her his interpretation of it. This mediation might lead Ellen to think and react differently, in a way that Sara could not understand. Sara might not be completely sure whether Simon has read the same comments and thus whether his strange behav-iour in physics class had anything to do with her mood evaluation. All these uncertainties are not meant to be a caricature of an incomprehen-sible youth life; rather, they present a picture of the tumult that young people tell us leads them to the computer, their hands reaching for the mouse and logging on before they are fully aware of it. Here, I am offering a way to understand this tumult in terms of non-simultaneity of intensity.

The presence of social-networking sites, with their mood evaluations and status updates as a movement in youths' reciprocal relations, also makes it one of the locations from which affects are circulated. Affects do not merely circulate between subjects, but also between subjects and technologies. And the point is that when social-networking sites are involved, the non-simultaneity in the intensity of affects becomes particularly visible. Bodies partake in and are commented on in the mood evaluations, which have moved on to be actualised in new places, commented on, whispered about and scrutinised at different times by both tangible and intangible bodies. A mood evaluation displays rhizomatic movements that cannot be reduced to any one body or any one point. When social-networking sites are involved, affects seem to be pushed back and forth in barely recognisable relations whose content, order and ownership are displaced. It almost seems as if 'mood' is cut off from the students' relational practices, only to be reinstalled as 'mood' in cyberspace and to (over)expose the affects that are now activated and set in motion.

In Sara Ahmed's words: 'Emotions work to shape the surfaces of individual and collective bodies. Bodies take the shape of the very contact they have with objects and others' (2004: 1). Ahmed is not concerned with cyber life; but one might almost believe that this is a description of the circulation and displacement of affects in cyberbullying. If we suppose that a person does not exist merely in one present moment, as a 'now', then we might also claim that the 'no longer' and 'not yet' (of significance in mood evaluations) are simultaneously embedded in the moment and displaced. In this actual moment – one Tuesday morning, for instance – Sara is no longer filled with yesterday's anger and Ellen is not yet worried about the anger that Sara expressed yesterday evening. Ellen doesn't read about it until a little later when it is no longer evening and Sara's anger no longer exists to the same extent. Cyber life thus appears to delay and forestall messages and subjectification whilst it intensifies them at the same time. It looks as if displacements and affects organise relations, designate them and ascribe meaning to them. The organisation of relations takes place in rhizomatic movements in which there is no central point but rather branching relations, and where the popularity regime I discussed earlier is also in motion and being circulated in affective assessments. These assessments both intensify and dismantle relations; but both aspects are engaged in the rhizome. The dismantling of relations and the potentially new allocation of weakness are not ejected from the rhizome but constitute a part of it that is also in motion.

The art of being anonymous yet visible

Is there something special about actions that can be recognised as cyberbullying? It seems that there is an art to placing references that indicate which student is being targeted. Perhaps the person whose fingers are at work on the keyboard is both the same and different from the subject visible on the screen as 'sugarbaby22' or 'mehmet2400' (2400 is the postal code for a certain multicultural area of Copenhagen), and who evaluates other subjects whose subjectivity is constructed and announced in similar ways (Sundén 2002).

Cyber-subjectivity and encryption were significant to Mary, who had also been interviewed for the research project on cyberbullying. Mary was one of the young people who described themselves as 'cutters' (youths who cut themselves). The empirical material contains accounts of cutting from several young people who knew about it from others or from their own practice.[12] Here, Mary's account is inserted into the Unambiguous Tale as well as Ellen's and the others' interpretations of it.

In Mary's account, the words 'I hope you hit the right spot' referred to cutting. Amongst this group of young people, it was well known that Mary was a cutter, and they had no doubt that 'I hope you hit the right spot' referred to Mary using a razor blade to cut into her arms. The seriousness of the hope that Mary should hit the right spot – that is, cut into an artery – was displayed on the screen, and no-one doubted who was meant. The youths were unanimous and unhesitating in recognising that it must be Mary when the message was later recounted and discussed in the corridors, on the stairs and in the classroom. In the interview situation, it was related with certainty that this comment was about Mary. But her identity was never unambiguously revealed in the message. This raised a number of questions: to which student does the encrypted message refer? The Mary displayed on her profile on the social-networking site? The Mary in the schoolyard? The one who is interviewed? The one who cuts herself? Who and how many people know which one is meant?

There were still more questions. According to the students, none of the adults knew that cutting was practised amongst this group. This is the only case that had been reported to the school principal. The exchanges and comments on the social-networking site were printed out and used as evidence in a case where someone felt hurt, bullied and abused. The adults concerned were horrified: do young people really talk to each other like that? Are they so coarse? Is this how they interact? Is this what they get up to online? The printouts told their own story. As soon as the news spread amongst the students that certain comments had been printed out and given to the adults, the online exchanges were erased. The traces placed there disappeared. All parties involved were called into the principal's office, and they each told their version from their own perspectives, making it impossible for the professional educationalists to figure out what on earth had been going on. Because, although the

---

[12] Mary's account is taken from another part of the empirical material.

comments provided evidence in a case that was recognised as cyberbullying, the contours of the involved parties faded before the eyes of the adults who were supposed to intervene once the case was reported to the professional educationalists. Thus, the parties involved appeared to multiply.

On the one hand, the messages written online become evidence in ways that distinguish this kind of case from others in which writing is not involved; on the other, this evidence seems to crumble in the hands of the professional educationalists due to the encryption of identity and the subtle nature of the message as well as the presence of multiple students. It might be said that the mobility and instability of virtual existence could be utilised to erase traces of subjectification and positioning. Names are rarely mentioned, and hints are only understood by the initiated – those familiar enough with local details to recognise to whom the comments refer. The initiated are often quite numerous, making it possible for a large number of people to identify the person being commented on. Many of the children and young people expressed concern about this aspect of the situation, and they spoke of it as showing something embarrassing, difficult and private to an innumerable public. For the professional educationalists, the case was unmanageable: they were expected to exert control and enforce discipline but were confronted with traces of evidence that vanished and did not return. Perhaps the case was also unmanageable because they expected to recognise narratives and positions in some kind of fixed form: who is being referred to? Do they go to this school? How many are there? And what is meant by 'I hope you hit the right spot'?

Why listen to unreliable voices?

Where does the narrative start, where does it end and which events deserve a place in the circulating and cited stories? To whose stories should a school's professional educationalists listen? And how can they make sense of the many voices that do not seem to be referring to the same events? Of course, the researcher – without the same obligation to take action – is in a different situation. In contrast, my obligation is to try to understand processes that are both coherent and productive of meaning, and which simultaneously appear scattered and fragmented.

An analytical approach inspired by Deleuze has made it possible to show how these entangled cases cannot be recounted as if they were one case; rather, they should be seen as circulations of affects, of rhizomatic positions and as effective technologies. It thus becomes possible to show how these girls could give (in)consistent accounts of 'what happened', and how experiences of non-simultaneity can indicate activities that are recognised as cyberbullying. Therefore, I have suggested that, although these apparently inconsistent accounts appear to point in different directions and away from the Unambiguous Tale, they nevertheless indicate how activities that are recognised as cyberbullying are not structured by means of unchangeable positions. Instead, it appears that such activities are characterised by non-continuity between self-perception and the others' perception of a person, and by non-simultaneity.

The conceptual model presented in this chapter also contains an interest to sketch such rhizomatic movements in ways that do not reduce these emerging phenomena to either new Unambiguous Tales or unreliable voices. The task I set for myself was to show the chaotic organisational modes of the school's social life and its co-existence with frozen versions of the Unambiguous Tale. This chapter has thus presented a view of the different voices and accounts – not as they contribute to one overall narrative, but how they work together to comprise actions that are recognised as cyberbullying. Although I have attempted to portray a story with less consistency and more openings for different types of voices to make themselves heard, this has not been done to disallow the claims of a bullied child, the bully and the bystanders, or of a culture that enables bullying. The aim is to better understand the entire situation. I have endeavoured to accentuate the plurality of narratives in an attempt to create space for research into normative and politicised fields such as bullying without prejudging particular relations. This is important because the theoretical ambition is to produce research that raises questions without preconceptions about the meaning of particular phenomena, in a way that creates space for multiple meanings to be heard and permits the conversion of power relations and entrenched processes of meaning creation – however briefly they might last (Deleuze 1886/2004; Lather 2007; Law 2007). But it is not merely an academic exercise for me to attend to what Lather has called 'messy spaces' in order to focus on a minority perspective (Kofoed 2004; Staunæs 2005). My intent is also to draw attention to minority perspectives for those with authority in the life of a school. In this case, it was shown that the minority perspectives challenge the absolute power of the Unambiguous Tale, with many voices dispersing the story instead of making it possible to assemble it into one linear account. I traced the stories without preconceptions as to who was right or how many parties might be involved. The chapter can therefore be seen as an invitation to educational professionals to think in terms of this maelstrom of perspectives. It could be that the voices should not be regarded as unreliable simply because they cannot be combined into one story about what happened. This may be simply because what happened was not a single incident. Listening to the many voices may give access to other actions and ways of understanding.

What is clear is that professional educators' interventions will be limited in their effectiveness if they try to locate an individual perpetrator who carries the characteristics of 'bully' in his/her own body. What I have made clear in this analysis is that there are many players, including technology and the social-networking sites themselves. Trying to find a slice of time that can be fixed and positions that are stable enough to create an Unambiguous Tale may be a starting point, but it is within the rapid movement, the fluid affects, the multiple players and sites, and the collective vulnerability that any useful answers to 'what is going on' may be found.

8   The life and death of bullying

Robin May Schott

Introduction: bullying and violence

Although earlier generations of teachers and parents often viewed bullying as a banality – an ordinary part of growing up in which 'children will be children' – bullying has come to be understood as a complex relational dynamic that can take place within schools, workplaces, prisons or other institutions. In this chapter, I explore strategies for understanding the relationship between bullying and violence. Sometimes, bullying is a matter of life and death. I am not claiming that all bullying is an issue of extreme violence, although some cases of bullying are indeed linked to extreme violence. But a review of the literature on bullying indicates how deeply interconnected the concepts of violence and bullying are with each other. One could even argue that the connection between bullying and violence is the condition for the possibility of the research field on bullying to emerge.

Scandinavian research in this area began in the early 1970s with the publication of work by Peter-Paul Heinemann (1972) and Dan Olweus (1973). But intense public attention to bullying began in response to bullying-related youth suicides: in Norway in 1982, newspaper reports on the suicides of three boys between the ages of 10 and 14 described the suicides as probably caused by severe bullying (Olweus 1993a: 1–2). This aroused considerable concern among the general public and in the mass media, which resulted in the Norwegian Ministry of Education launching a nationwide campaign against bullying in 1983. Similarly, public shock was generated in Japan in 1986 when a 13-year-old schoolboy committed suicide in Tokyo. His classmates had treated him as if he were dead and staged a mock funeral for him in their classroom. Even some of the teachers wrote messages of condolence that said, 'Goodbye and have a peaceful sleep.' In 1994, the Tokyo High Court recognised that mental *'Ijime'* (the Japanese counterpart of 'bullying') was the cause of the victim's suicide, and the parents of two of his classmates were ordered to pay damages (Morita et al. 1999: 311–12).[1]

---

[1] See also my discussion in Chapter 2.

Decades later, the connection between bullying and youth suicide is still strong in the public consciousness. In the United States, similar incidents include the death of 18-year-old Tyler Clementi, who jumped off the George Washington Bridge near New York City on 22 September 2010, two days after his roommate and another student at Rutgers University in New Jersey broadcast Clementi's sexual encounter with another man on the internet, in what could be viewed as cyberbullying and hate-related use of the internet. In 2006, 13-year-old Megan Meier from Missouri committed suicide after she was cyberbullied by the mother of one her former friends.[2] These cases also raise legal questions, such as whether new legislation should be introduced regarding cyberbullying.[3] Other bullying-related suicides in the United States include the death of 15-year-old Phoebe Prince, who hanged herself at her home in South Hadley, Massachusetts, on 14 January 2010, only months after having moved from Ireland with her family; she had been vilified by other students both to her face and via the internet.[4] And 17-year-old Erik Mohat shot himself on 29 March 2007 at his home in Ohio in what his parents called a 'bullicide' – after prolonged bullying, he killed himself after a classmate's public comment in class: 'Why don't you go home and shoot yourself; no one will miss you'.[5] Three other youths in his class had also killed themselves in bullying-related suicides that year.

It is not only youth suicides that have been linked to school bullying, but also school shootings. Since the shootings at Columbine High School in Colorado on 20 April 1999 (the 110th birthday of Adolf Hitler) in which two high-school seniors killed twelve students and one teacher, debates have raged about whether bullying played a part in causing this massacre. Brooks Brown, a childhood friend of the shooters Eric Harris and Dylan Klebold, wrote in his book, *No Easy Answers*, 'Eric and Dylan are the ones responsible for creating this tragedy...However, Columbine is responsible for creating Eric and Dylan' (Brown and Merritt 2002: 163). He also wrote about bullies who constantly shoved and harassed other children, knowing that the teachers would turn a blind eye to the brutalisation of

---

[2] http://topics.nytimes.com/topics/reference/timestopics/people/m/megan_meier/index.html; last accessed 22 November 2010.

[3] www.govtrack.us/congress/bill.xpd?bill=h111-1966; last accessed 22 November 2010. The site provides information about the Megan Meier Cyberbullying Prevention Act introduced in 2009.

[4] www.nytimes.com/2010/03/30/us/30bully.html; last accessed 22 November 2010.

[5] http://abcnews.go.com/Health/MindMoodNews/story?id=7228335; last accessed 22 November 2010.

students who were not their favourites.[6] Subsequent school shootings have also been seen as a possible response to bullying, including the massacre at Virginia Tech in Blacksburg, Virginia, where a university senior killed thirty-two people on 16 April 2007. And the 18-year-old man who killed eight people and himself at Jokela High School in Finland on 7 November 2007 had also been a victim of bullying for years.[7]

Bullying has thus been linked to life-or-death issues of violence – both as suicides and school shootings – in the public consciousness. Anti-bullying movements have contributed to the narrative that these forms of lethal violence are caused by bullying. In various ways, researchers who have turned to this field in the last twenty years have taken for granted the intimate connection between bullying and violence. In Peter K. Smith's edited anthology, *Violence in Schools: The Response in Europe* (2003), European and Scandinavian researchers predominantly define school violence in terms of bullying, and the research on school programmes to prevent school violence largely focuses on bullying. As the Finnish contributors to Smith's volume noted, 'It appears to be incorrect to make a strict distinction between bullying and violence in schools...' (Björkqvist and Jannson 2003: 191). Many reported cases of violence in schools were actually cases of bullying or of revenge for bullying. And these authors describe severe violence in schools as the 'tip of the iceberg of bullying-related problems' (ibid.). The authors of the report from Ireland about school violence also note that 'most empirical studies of aggressive behaviour in schools in Ireland have focused on bullying rather than violence...' (O'Moore and Minton 2003: 283).[8]

In the reports from Europe and Scandinavia, 'bullying trumps violence' but amongst US researchers, one finds the opposite tendency and

[6] Other authors refute the charge of bullying as a factor in the Columbine shootings and claim that the 'bullying' idea took on a force of its own because of the anti-bullying movement in the US. Dave Cullen writes that, although there was considerable evidence that bullying was a problem at Columbine High School, there is no evidence that bullying led to the murders (Cullen 2009: 158). Cullen instead draws upon the psychopathic theory of personality disorder, writing of Eric Harris, 'His brain was never scanned, but it probably would have shown activity unrecognizable as human to most neurologists' (ibid.: 242).
[7] 'Jokela School Shooting on November 7, 2007; Report of Investigation Commission', Ministry of Justice, Finland; Publication 2009: 1, 49–50.
[8] However, in their discussion about violence by teachers towards students, these authors also note instances of extreme physical violence being used under the guise of classroom 'discipline' and mention cases of sexual abuse of students at the institutional schools that are run by religious orders. A four-part television series, *States of Fear* (1999), featured harrowing accounts of abuse, which led to 145 cases of legal proceedings that involved allegations about the sexual or physical abuse of children (O'Moore and Minton 2003: 286).

'violence trumps bullying' (Devine and Lawson 2003: 335). In an American context, 'fear is a close companion of insecurity' (ibid.: 337) and, on the internet, discussions about violence are literally linked to advertisements for security systems and metal detectors in schools. The focus of American research on violence is connected to an understanding of school bullying in relation to broader forms of social violence and, with this background, researchers are attuned to the racial, ethnic and socio-economic composition of both youths and their families. From their corner of the world, American researchers criticise the Europeans' 'walled in' theories of bullying and intervention that are school-specific and which 'wall out' other alternatives that focus on school, family, peer groups and community ecologies (ibid.).

Hence, there is a broad consensus – in the public consciousness, in governmental initiatives and amongst researchers – *that* there is an important connection between violence and bullying. But *how* to understand the nature of this connection is more difficult. The approach proposed by Dan Olweus has become dominant; it focuses on single acts that are carried out by one individual against another. It is descriptively close to a commonsense understanding of the 'facts' of a situation.[9] But as I try to indicate, it is less adept at understanding the 'human facts' or the human meaning of the incidents (Nussbaum 1995: 105). For that – and, in particular, to understand how bullying and violence appear from the perspective of the one who is bullied – we need to turn to other resources.

Paradigm one: the intersection of violence and bullying

After the youth suicides in Norway in 1982, the country's Ministry of Education launched a nationwide campaign against bully/victim problems in 1983. As a member of a small committee appointed by the Ministry, Dan Olweus was able to persuade the political leadership to fund research connected to the campaign, and he was given responsibility for the nationwide survey (Olweus 1999b: 30).[10] Olweus is the pioneer in this field of research, and he proposed a definition of bullying that has

---

[9] It is often the case that studies are so rooted in commonsense views of individual behaviour that the conclusions of the reports are too obvious to generate change. As obvious conclusions, the authors note 'more boys than girls indicated that they had been bullied or victimized, there are higher rates of bullying in vocational schools, younger students have been found to be victims more frequently than older pupils, and so forth' (Devine and Lawson 2003: 348).

[10] Dan Olweus's research does not specifically address the issue of bullying-related suicide. However, other sources indicate strong connections between increased suicidal thoughts amongst both victims and bullies, although these studies made it impossible conclusively to determine whether bullying leads to suicide (Yale University 2008).

been broadly accepted (I discuss this definition in detail in Chapter 2). He defines school bullying in the following terms: 'A student is being bullied or victimized when he or she is exposed, repeatedly and over time, to negative actions on the part of one or more other students' (Olweus 1999a: 10). The three essential components in Olweus's view are that bullying is: (1) aggressive or intentional harm-doing; (2) carried out repeatedly and over time; and (3) carried out in a relationship character-ised by an imbalance of power (ibid.: 11). There is nothing in his defi-nition that specifically addresses the issue of violence – nothing that makes violence an internal condition or a component in the definition of bully-ing. However, his definition does imply that there are aspects of the bullying dynamic that have the potential to carry violence with them – e.g. aggressive behaviour, harm-doing, imbalance of power – suggesting that those with more power might use violence against those with less power.

Olweus emphasises that although all bullying is a subcategory of aggres-sion, not all aggressive behaviour is violent. Violence is defined as 'aggres-sive behaviour where the actor or perpetrator uses his or her own body or an object (including a weapon) to inflict (relatively serious) injury or discomfort upon another individual' (ibid.: 12). Thus, violent bullying is bullying by physical means. In other words, bullying and violent behav-iour are both subsets of aggression. Violent bullying is found where these two subsets intersect, as in a Venn diagram, when a bully uses his/her own body or an object to inflict injury upon another individual.

Olweus's discussion of the relationship between bullying and violence is closely linked to an everyday understanding of these terms. As he notes, many forms of violence have nothing to do with bullying – for example, conflicts between strangers in a restaurant line or aggression between persons of equal physical or mental strength. And much bullying has nothing to do with violence, as in bullying through words, gestures or intentional exclusion from a group. He defines violence as a discrete, individual act that is carried out by one individual, and it is violent because (and only because) the aggressor uses his/her body or a physical object as an instrument to inflict harm.

In this approach, which I subsequently refer to as *paradigm one*,[11] violence and bullying intersect during a specific episode and moment in time when an aggressor uses his/her body or an object to inflict injury on

---

[11] I do so in order to stress how widely Olweus's work has been accepted in the field; my interest is not primarily to criticise him as an individual author but rather, to focus attention on how these concepts map the field. I thank my eXbus colleague Inge Henningsen for urging me to keep this more general focus.

another person. An indisputable majority of researchers in Europe and Scandinavia who study bullying adopt *paradigm one*. This definition has many advantages. Its focus on aggressive individuals who intentionally inflict harm on weaker individuals is close to ordinary views of human relations. And in providing a relatively simple definition that is easily operationalised, *paradigm one* is suitable for quantitative scientific approaches that focus on counting and recording the number of incidents (Devine and Lawson 2003: 347). Moreover, this approach makes a clear distinction between physical violence and other forms of violence, such as symbolic violence embodied in language or the systemic violence within economic and political systems, which appears as part of the normal state of affairs and is thereby invisible (Žižek 2008: 1–2). These latter forms of violence are much less amenable to an approach that utilises counting and recording.

But even though researchers widely adopt this definition of bullying, they also tend to identify bullying and violence; in this way, they overlook Olweus's proposal that bullying and violence should be treated as intersecting subsets. On the one hand, it is possible to criticise these researchers for their lack of conceptual clarity in shifting the discourse from violence to bullying. On the other hand, this conceptual slippage may contain a latent challenge to the view of violence as the use of a body or physical instrument to inflict injury on another person. Violence may also involve something quite different, such as when structures of authority permit and thereby sanction long-standing practices of violence – for example, the aforementioned situation in Ireland or when the repetition of harm-doing habituates victims to these practices, as I discuss below.

The life-or-death issues of bullying have provided the historical backdrop, public interest, political will and governmental funding for research on bullying, but the ordinary understanding of the relationship between bullying and violence that is systematised in *paradigm one* does little to address these issues. Researchers may need to find inspiration in other arenas to think about the dynamic relations between bullying and violence by which they become life-or-death issues.

Literature as a sideways approach to violence and bullying

Whereas *paradigm one* provides a plausible description of bullying that is close to our ordinary understanding of the facts of a situation, it does little to examine the subjective meaning of these facts. It does posit a certain structure of intent in the perpetrator, which I suggest is problematic (see Chapter 2). But it does not begin to convey how these events might be perceived or experienced by those who are victims of bullying. In this sense, *paradigm one* leans up against an objectivist – as opposed to a subjectivist – approach, thereby buttressing its scientific stance.

In what follows, I look to John Ajvide Lindqvist's vampire novel *Let the Right One In* (2009; published first in Swedish in 2004) as a way to take a 'sideways' approach to violence and bullying. Slavoj Žižek argues that sometimes one needs to take a sideways approach and look awry at problems of violence since there is something tremendously difficult about confronting them directly (Žižek 2008: 3).[12] If we focus on the testimonies of those who have suffered, it is easy to be overwhelmed by feelings of horror. One cannot read about youths committing suicides or 'bullicides' or about school massacres without affective engagement. From a researchers' perspective, these accounts may create moralising attitudes towards 'perpetrators' and 'victims' that block understandings of the processes and events, which, in relation to individual cases, can become bound up with judgments about psychopathology, depression, etc. And yet a cold analysis of violence seems to participate in the horrors (ibid.). There needs to be a strategy that allows us to look askew at the life-or-death issues of bullying and violence – to jar us from a naïve understanding of the events without being either overwhelmed or indifferent to victims' experiences.

Turning to artistic description may provide such a resource because it is a way to extract the 'inner form' from a confused reality (ibid.: 5). There is a long tradition of thinkers who reflect on the kind of truths revealed through literature and their effect on readers – the pleasure one takes in the company of others, the birth of fancy and its impact on moral life, the cast of mind that the novel generates and which one takes in approaching one's own world (Nussbaum 1995: 35–44). Literature reveals a truth about the world of actions, emotions and sentiments in all their complexity and ambiguity (de Beauvoir 2007: 72–3). Simone de Beauvoir suggests that literature provides an opening to a truth that is not available to other genres; a truth about the singular, temporal 'gush' of existence (ibid.: 81).

One effect of literature is that it creates an empathic response in readers. Historian Lynn Hunt, in writing about the birth of the idea of human rights in the late eighteenth century, argues that 'new sensations about the inner self' were induced by the novels of this period that created an 'imagined empathy', an imagining that 'someone else is like you' (Hunt 2007: 32). Philosopher Martha Nussbaum focuses on realistic novels and

---

[12] During a seminar discussing an earlier version of this chapter, my eXbus colleague Jette Kofoed quite appropriately suggested that I take a 'sideways' approach to this problem. This strategy avoids dealing with issues from a top-down approach that moves from theory to empirical example, or from a bottom-up approach that moves from empirical example to theory; otherwise, these seemed to be my only two options.

'the ability to imagine what it is like to live the life of another person who might, given changes in circumstance, be oneself or one of one's loved ones' (Nussbaum 1995: 5). The claim that fiction produces this strong form of empathy – imagining that someone else is like you – may be overstating the case, especially when one leaves the genre of realistic fiction as I propose to do here. But even though a character may be strange and unlike oneself or anybody one might love, the character's humiliation, hate and need for friendship become meaningful to a reader whose experience of these same emotions becomes activated by the narrative. In this way, the reader is invited into the minds and bodies of the characters and gains insight into the effect of certain circumstances on their emotions and inner lives (ibid.). Readers may then take these insights with them in addressing their own worlds. This is true for judges, as was seen when, at his nomination hearing, US Supreme Court Justice Stephen G. Breyer spoke about the role of novels: 'Each of these stories involves something about human passion. Each of these stories involves a man, a woman, children, families, work, lives. ... And so sometimes I've found literature very helpful as a way out of the tower' (ibid.: 79). And it is also true for philosophers and social scientists who are struggling to come to terms with the violence of bullying and with the dominant model for understanding in this field.

Let the Right One In is a text about bullying and violence that is very far away from ordinary understandings. It is placed in the gothic genre – a horror novel that describes a fallen world where the protagonist is isolated, meets a villain who epitomises evil and becomes saved through union with a loved one.[13] The novel explores the world of bullying in relation to the underside of scientific rationality – through a meeting with the supernatural in the figure of the vampire Eli. The novel connects two characters who suffer from two parallel worlds of exclusion. Thirteen-year-old Oskar is tormented and humiliated by a group of boys at school who repeatedly pull down his pants, knee him in the groin, pursue him into the bathroom and make him squeal like a pig. Oskar feels like he has been killed a hundred times and says repeatedly, 'I don't exist.' One day in the courtyard of his apartment building, he plays a game where he pretends to be a mass murderer, and he meets Eli – a 200-year-old vampire in the body of an 11-year-old child with an ambiguous gender identity – whose need for human blood is the driving force behind the 'real' murders in the novel. Oskar is later horrified when he discovers that his new friend is a vampire. But when Eli rescues him from being drowned by his tormenters, Oskar

---

[13] http://cai.ucdavis.edu/waters-sites/gothicnovel/155breport.html; last accessed 19 January 2011. For a more scholarly discussion of gothic literature, see Sedgwick (1986).

leaves his life behind to become Eli's companion and helper. The novel provides an opportunity to get a glimpse into a world where bullying becomes a life-or-death issue (and where some of the most horrific episodes are based on the author's reconstruction of his own biographical experience); further, it avoids the limits of the dominant scientific discourse on bullying as well as the ethical and moral issues of directly engaging in victims' testimonies.

It is a risky business to explore the relationship between bullying and violence through a work of popular culture that weaves together a narrative about school bullying and vampires.[14] But in my view, this is a revealing portrayal of the lived experience of bullying, where 'lived experience' is the phenomenological term for the meanings in everyday existence that are uncovered via a first-person point of view. In the context of this novel, one may ask: what are the lived experiences of youths who are in situations of being bullied or being bullies? How does the novel help us 'look awry' (Žižek 1995: vii) at theories of bullying and violence? What concepts are missing or inadequately developed in the dominant approach? What aspects of this lived experience, which are usually left unexamined, come into view as they are re-fashioned into fiction? Working with fiction may be seen as an arena for fieldwork that is not restricted by the methodologies of quantitative studies or qualitative interviews. In fact, one of the implications of a novel about bullying that is set in the genre of vampire fiction is that it implicitly challenges the idea that scientific explanations can adequately capture some of the essential features of bullying and violence. We need to suspend our ordinary expectations since there is nothing reasonable or sensible in this world of vampires: where a vampire may live for two hundred years without aging as Eli does; where a vampire can only survive by feeding on the blood of living human beings whose bodies must then be immediately shut off to prevent them from contamination and becoming undead; and where vampires can only cross a threshold if they are invited in. Approaching this fieldwork, one is in a position similar to the anthropologist who studies something radically 'other'. In doing so, anthropologists note that the goal is not so much to learn what others are like, but to use this knowledge to confront one's own most basic presuppositions about how to think about human existence.[15]

---

[14] After viewing the film version of *Let the Right One In* (2008) with me, my then 17-year-old daughter said sceptically: 'Well, you can't exactly write a handbook about bullying that advises kids who are bullied to make friends with a vampire.'

[15] Ghassan Hage, in his keynote speech 'The Politics of Purposelessness?', made this argument at the conference, 'Futures in the making – youth, conflict and potentiality' at the University of Copenhagen, 20 January 2011.

Human facts and the limits of *paradigm one*

Let the Right One In provides an opportunity to explore issues of bullying and violence from the perspective of the one who is being bullied; therefore, it is a useful lens to reflect on the contributions and limits of *paradigm one*. As *paradigm one* stresses, bullying takes place when actions are repeated over time. But when an act of violence is repeated over time, such as one child kneeing another in the groin every day, then one must ask: is it an example of violent bullying each time this act is performed against a child? What happens when a child like Oskar has been hurt so many times that, when everyone else in the class runs outside for recess, he thinks: what is the best way to avoid getting hurt? By staying in the hallway or going outside? As in the novel, a child in this situation might want to join the rest of the class in the schoolyard, yet he thinks, 'but there was no point...someone would knee him, another pull his underpants up in a wedgie' (Lindqvist 2009: 8).[16] Thinking about this example, we may wonder whether it makes sense to split up the process of violence into discrete moments where only the moments that involve the use of a body part or physical object are violent. When a child feels so terrorised that it does not matter whether he is actually kneed in the groin by another child – is that moment *not* part of the process of violence? In other words, the definition of the intersection of violence and bullying in *paradigm one* focuses on the bully as a subject who commits a specific act at a specific moment, thereby treating both violence and bullying in terms of sporadic episodes.

In contrast to this approach, it is crucial to understand that violence and bullying are not episodes that erupt in a single moment, with no connection to the past or present. As Bruce Lawrence and Aisha Karim argue in writing about violence:

Whether individual or group-specific, whether erupting in the private or in the public domain, violence is always and everywhere process. As process, violence is cumulative and boundless. It always spills over. It creates and recreates new norms of collective self-understanding. Violence as process is often not recorded because it is internalized; it becomes part of the expectation of the living, whether framed as revenge or as fear, but most important, its creation must remain transparent... (Lawrence and Karim 2007: 11–12)

As in the example above, the violence in a bullying incident cannot be isolated in the specific moment when one child pushes his knee into the

---

[16] This scene is described in the opening chapter of *Let the Right One In*, which I discuss later.

groin of another child. But the violence is an event, and its occurrence and re-occurrence becomes part of the expectations of the child who is bullied. In this case, a child's fear of going out to the schoolyard is a crucial moment in understanding the relationship between violence and bullying.

Another problem with treating the relationship between bullying and violence as a single act instead of as a process is that it creates a sharp division between physical and affective aspects of this experience. In the example above, Oskar did not go out to the schoolyard, and he was glad that he was off the hook for this recess. He went to the bathroom, realising that he had pissed his pants again. Hearing steps in the hallway, he hid in one of the stalls and locked the door, just as the outer door opened. His pursuers hit and kicked the door to the bathroom stall, calling him 'Piggy'.[17] Oskar knew that there were certain rules for this game. He couldn't simply have unlocked the stall door and been done with it: 'Theirs was the intoxication of the hunter, his the terror of the prey. Once they had actually captured him the fun was over and the punishment more of a duty that had to be carried out' (Lindqvist 2009: 10). The other boys insisted that he squeal like a pig, which he did with all of his might, not even noticing when the others had gone. The only blood spilled was his own, from a nosebleed he got while he was squealing.

In this isolated incident, no physical violence was used and, in fact, the only physical harm was self-inflicted by Oskar: wetting his pants, digging his fingernails into the palms of his hands while he was squealing and getting a nosebleed. This illustrates that some physical harm can be the result of the body's own reaction to the process of terrorisation and not simply the result of being assaulted. Viewing bullying and violence as process, instead of as single isolated episodes, implies that we must keep our focus on the temporal process; that is, what preceded a specific incident and what a child's expectations are about future incidents. And it also implies that we must view the physicality of the harm not just in terms of the instrumental use of a body part or object, but as a bodily experience of harm where a child's own body assumes a role in the repeated process of harm-doing. In one sense, it doesn't matter whether the nosebleed resulted from a punch in the nose or was a spontaneous reaction to fear. In both cases, it may be a sign that 'someone had been killed here. And for the hundredth time' (ibid.: 11). Recognising the

---

[17] *Lord of the Flies* (1954) is a novel about a group of schoolboys who are stranded on a desert island after their aeroplane crashes. Piggy is the name of the boy who argues for rules, agreement and for 'law and rescue' as better than 'hunting and breaking things up'; he is killed by Roger in the book's penultimate chapter (Golding 1958: 201). The final chapter is entitled 'The Cry of the Hunters'.

body's own role in spontaneous or self-inflicted harm, such as incontinence, spontaneous nosebleeds, headaches and stomach-aches, suggests that it is artificial to create a sharp divide between physical and psychic experiences of bullying and violence.[18] Physical harm does result from the use of a body part or object to inflict force on another individual, but it also results from a repeated pattern of harm-doing by which the body – through habit and fear – learns its role so well that the use of force is no longer necessary to achieve the same effects. In other words, *paradigm one* treats the recipient of violent bullying in strictly passive terms, without recognising the embodied subjectivity of the one who is bullied as part of this interrelation between individuals. In the novel, Oskar zealously plays the game of squealing like a pig in order to protect himself from greater injury as well as to keep the dirty secret that he wet his pants.

One of the key insights in *paradigm one* is the importance of repetition in bullying. But when actions take place repeatedly over time, they also have an impact on the habits of mind of those involved in the interaction. Psychologist Ervin Staub, whose research ranges from the Nazi Holocaust to bullying in schools, argues that one of the central insights he has learned from studies of children is 'learning by doing'. Staub writes:

Learning by doing is a basis for developing values, motives, the self concept, and behavioral tendencies...People begin to see their engagement in the activity as part of themselves...People come to see themselves as agents and begin to consider and elaborate on the reasons for their actions. If there are benefits to others, even imagined ones, they begin to find the activity worthwhile and its beneficiaries more deserving. If there is harm to others, progressively the victims' well-being and even lives will lose value in their eyes. (Staub 1989: 80)

Learning by doing plays an important role along the continuum of destruction, which Staub sees as a central process in both large- and small-scale harms (ibid.: 238). In other words, repetition – which is so central to the approach to bullying and violence in *paradigm one* – is not just repetition of the same. Even when the same actions are repeated, they

---

[18] On its anti-bullying website, the US Department of Health and Human Services lists warning signs of bullying; these include headaches, stomach-aches and other physical ailments; http://stopbullyingnow.hrsa.gov/hhs_psa/pdfs/sbn_tip_7.pdf; last accessed 17 January 2011. And Australian researchers have argued that the stress of being bullied triggers the body to create more cortisol and adrenaline, which leads to an increased heart rate, digestive problems and tight muscles. For children, this often means constant headaches, stomach-aches, sore throats and respiratory infections. www.qualityhealth.com/childrens-health-and-parenting-articles/effects-bullying-childrens-health; last accessed 17 January 2011.

become part of a process by which individuals *redefine* their values and identities.

This insight that repetition is a process of change makes it difficult to accept the use of the term 'intersection' to describe the relationship between bullying and violence as if it were logical and static.[19] Instead, the relationship between bullying and violence should be understood as a dynamic relationship that has implications both for those who repeatedly carry out acts of harm and for those who are repeatedly harmed by them. In asking how violence becomes part of the frame of bullying, we should ask how it is 'witnessed, internalized, and reproduced by individuals'.[20] As with violence (Lawrence and Karim 2007: 12), one of the most significant effects of violent bullying is the creation of new norms for self-understanding.

Hence, *Let the Right One In* challenges some of the most basic assumptions about bullying that are expressed in *paradigm one*. Instead of seeing the relationship between bullying and violence as a relationship of intersection, bullying is presented in the novel as a matter of life or death; existence or non-existence. To be more precise, bullying as a life-or-death issue is also an everyday occurrence. One kernel of truth in *paradigm one* is the insight that repetition is a crucial dimension of bullying. Through repetition, the 'killing of the self' becomes normalised and appears as an inescapable aspect of a child's lived experience.

Social death and friendship

Not only does this novel provide a critical look at some of the assumptions in *paradigm one*, but through exploring the subjective experience of being bullied, it also directs attention towards different issues and concepts. In focusing on bullying as a life-or-death experience, the book captures something that was central to the emergence of study in the field of bullying research. The fundamental theme of existence or non-existence

---

[19] The term 'intersection' in *paradigm one* should not be confused with the notion of 'intersectionality' that has become widely used in feminist and post-colonial theory. *Paradigm one* uses the notion of intersection as in Venn diagrams, and it is a formal representation of members of different subsets. It focuses on the logical relationship between members of two different subsets: the subset of violent actions and the subset of bullying actions. Intersectionality refers to membership in multiple social categories, such as gender, race, class or disability. The relevant categories in theories of intersectionality are identity categories defined by systems of subordination. The central insight of intersectionality is that there is an interaction between systems of subordination, such as patriarchy and racism (Crenshaw 1994: 110).

[20] In writing about youth violence, Colette Daiute and Michelle Fine note that it is also necessary to understand how youths witness violence at their schools, homes, on their streets, in the media and how they avoid it, as well as 'how they reproduce the very violence imposed on them; and how they organize for change' (Daiute and Fine 2003: 5).

is announced at the beginning of the book, in the scene in the school bathroom that I described earlier, where Oskar thinks, 'Someone *had* been killed here. And for the hundredth time' (Lindqvist 2009: 11). And Oskar's phrase, 'I don't exist anymore' is a refrain that occurs at significant moments; for example, after he realised that nothing about his new friend Eli was normal (ibid.: 340) and after he started a fire in his school classroom, knowing that his tormentors were going 'to start training him again' to squeal like a pig when he returned to school (ibid.: 493, 497). And to the reader of *Lord of the Flies* who is familiar with the fate of Piggy in this classic story about the dynamics of group violence amongst youths, it is clear that existential killing may lead to physical killing, as we see with the two attempts on Oskar's life towards the end of the book.

What does it mean to live even though one has been killed; even though one does not exist anymore? The logical disjunction that one is either alive or dead is not much help in understanding this lived experience, but one needs another way to think about being a kind of 'living dead'. The notion of the living dead is not just a concept drawn from religious spheres or from the supernatural (where the terms 'living dead' or 'undead' are used in the vampire genre), but is also rooted in historical studies of slavery. American sociologist Orlando Patterson developed the concept of 'social death' to describe some of the central features of historical slavery, and the term has subsequently been used in a wide range of contexts – from Zygmunt Bauman's reference to people who are not connected to cyber-life (Bauman 2007) to feminist philosophers in discussions about war rape (Card 2007: 71–86; Schott 2009b: 83–8) and sociologists of health care in discussions about AIDS and dementia. Patterson focuses on the structural patterns of slavery by which certain individuals become non-persons; that is, they are socially negated. Patterson notes that the Egyptian word for 'captive' meant 'living dead' (Patterson 1982: 42). In his view, two forms of social death are apparent: it happens to those who do not belong to a community because they are outsiders, and to those who become outsiders because they do not belong. The latter refers to those who have experienced 'overwhelmingly downward' social mobility – those who are internal exiles and have been deprived of all claims to community (ibid.: 42, 44). Social death, however, does not merely point to the marginality of individuals in relation to a community, such as when one is deprived of all civil rights.[21] There is also the opposite movement, where those who are

---

[21] In Imperial China, criminals who were sentenced to a lifetime of labour were public slaves, in the sense that they were deprived of their civil rights. These men were legal non-persons; their wives could remarry and their property was distributed to their heirs (Patterson 1982: 43).

marginalised are also integrated into the community. They exist in a kind of limbo, in what anthropologists refer to as a 'liminal state', neither fully alien nor fully entitled to be part of the community. In this liminal state, the slave's life as a quasi-person was fully dependent on their masters' authority, and it was he who mediated between the socially dead and the socially alive (ibid.: 46).

Although the concept of social death has been criticised for not being an accurate description of historical slavery,[22] its most productive meaning is to describe 'a compelling metaphysical threat', where the fear of social death is not just an incapacity but also a 'generative force' by which slaves needed acts of imagination in their existential struggle for survival (Brown 2009: 1244–6). In this latter sense, the concept of social death is also useful for addressing issues of bullying and violence. It can be understood as a metaphysical *threat* that a person will become an internal exile, suffering overwhelmingly downward mobility and becoming wholly dependent on another's authority.

Although the response to this metaphysical threat may be to choose death (as in cases of suicide), more often the response is to find practices of survival where the imagination can provide important resources to create social vitality.[23] Here, a sideways approach has certain advantages. In *paradigm one*, the experience of the individual who is persecuted in violent bullying disappears entirely from the definitional frame. And in focusing on testimonies of those who have been persecuted, it is difficult not to morally side with their survival strategies. For example, in discussions about historical slavery, the role of imagination in survival strategies is described as one of the 'oppositional activities' that are meaning-making (ibid.: 1235). It may be tempting to moralise the strategies of those who struggle against the threat of social death. But during the journey into the strange world of bullying and vampirism presented in *Let the Right One In*, moral 'gut reactions' can be temporarily put to rest. Here, we can see that the persecuted boy Oskar does indeed draw upon his imaginative resources for survival. And imagination allows him to assume the standpoint of another, which is one of the important criteria in Hannah Arendt's discussion about the role of imagination in creating enlarged thinking (Arendt 1982: 42–3). But Oskar's imagination does

[22] Vincent Brown argues that one of the weaknesses of this concept is that it appears as a stand-in for a description of historical slavery. As such, this concept tends to focus on universal patterns, as opposed to specific descriptions, and on oppression rather than how the enslaved respond to oppressive conditions. Hence, he argues that scholars of slave resistance have very little use for the concept (Brown 2009: 1242).

[23] Claudia Card uses the term 'social vitality' in reference to what can be lost through genocide.

not follow the normative direction of universality that Arendt has in mind, wherein the imagination 'goes visiting' to take on the standpoints of all others; his imagination does not go visiting in every possible direction in order to develop an enlarged empathic thought. For example, Oskar does not try to assume the standpoint of Jonny, who is persecuting him and who lost contact with his own father whom he misses deeply; nor of his mother, who is a single parent trying to hold onto her son through his favourite foods and their television-watching rituals; nor of his father, who could never handle adult responsibility and turns to alcohol, costing him his marriage and perhaps his relationship with his son. The standpoint Oskar does adopt, however, is that of a murderer: 'He saw the world through the eyes of a murderer, or so much of a murderer's eyes as his thirteen-year-old's imagination could muster. A beautiful world. A world he controlled, a world that trembled in the face of his actions' (Lindqvist 2009: 25). When Oskar plays the game in which he is a mass murderer who can make Jonny squeal like a pig before Oskar hacks him to death, he is creating an 'oppositional' activity, but his fantasy of survival is striated with lethal thoughts. Living in a situation where bullying is a question of existence or non-existence does not create morally upright thoughts in Oskar, but rather, opens an imaginative space where questions of moral right or wrong can be safely put aside.

Or so he thinks. It is when Oskar repeats this game in the courtyard, stabbing a tree with his knife, whispering 'Go on, squeal like a pig' (ibid.: 39) that he meets Eli. Although Oskar is horrified when he later discovers that his new friend is a vampire, Eli insists that he/she is just like Oskar, repeating the incident in the courtyard (ibid.: 387). For Oskar, the difference is that he does not really kill people. For Eli, the difference is that he/she kills for survival, not for revenge and enjoyment. This is a form of an imaginary that is 'beyond good and evil', to use the phrase that Friedrich Nietzsche introduced to challenge philosophers to put aside their customary value-feelings and false judgments (Nietzsche 1886/1955: 4).[24] It is in this world beyond good and evil that Jonny and his older brother try to drown Oskar in a swimming pool, after offering him the choice of having his eye poked out or of drowning (he preferred the latter), and where Eli, an 'angel' (Lindqvist 2009: 518), rescues Oskar, leaving the heads of his two tormenters at the bottom of the swimming pool.

What are the implications for human relations if we live in an anti-moral universe, beyond good and evil? Typically, philosophers and sociologists

---

[24] Håkan, the man who loved Eli, murdered for him and was willing to give his life for him, admitted that he had never wondered 'whether Eli was "evil" or "good" or anything else. Eli was beautiful and Eli had given him back his dignity' (Lindqvist 2009: 237).

treat morality as the basis for the existence of human relations. By virtue of sharing a common world that is based on some shared norms, it is possible to build both intimate, private relationships and public relations. Sociologist Helen Fein calls this the shared 'universe of obligation', 'towards whom obligations are owed, to whom rules apply, and whose injuries call for amends' (Fein 1979: 4). But in a universe of violent bullying, where the notion of a universe of obligation has no say, morality does not provide the basis for human relationships. Rather, it is strategies for survival and the need for friendship that do. In this context, philosophical arguments that friendship 'promotes the general good' and debates about whether 'our obligations to our friends sometimes trump our moral duties' (Helm 2009: 15–16) miss the point that morality and friendship may have nothing whatsoever in common. The intensity of the bonds of friendship, which are formed in this world beyond good and evil, in turn can have violent consequences – such as the beheading of Oskar's tormenters or real-life school massacres such as the one at Columbine.[25]

Hate and bullying

This foray into the strange world of bullying and vampirism challenges many ordinary presuppositions: it challenges the view that one is either living or dead (and not living dead), and that strategies for survival and friendship should be understood in moral terms (and not beyond good and evil). It also challenges another common assumption: that negative emotions such as hate have no role in understanding violent bullying dynamics.[26] In the 'intersection' of bullying and violence in *paradigm one*, the bully uses his/her physical body or an object with the intention to inflict harm on another individual. This objective description can cover many kinds of intentionality. But the primary intention is to strengthen the bully's position of power. There is no explanatory role for negative emotions on the part of the bully, and there is no focus on consequent negative emotions on the part of the one who is bullied. Looking at the case of this novel, there is a sense in which *paradigm one* fits the situation of bullying. At the beginning of the book, the boys who torment Oskar do not hate him;

[25] The friendship between Eric Harris and Dylan Klebold created a 'dyad phenomenon', which was an important element in their 'performance violence' (Cullen 2009: 244, 247). In situations where single shooters carried out school massacres, such as at Virginia Tech, the internet became a medium for them to identify with the Columbine shooters.
[26] One could also discuss the role of disgust, closely related to the notion of abjection (see Schott's and Søndergaard's chapters on pages 21 and 47, respectively). In *Let the Right One In*, the primary form of disgust is Oskar's disgust with himself rather than him being an object of disgust to others.

they just enjoy tormenting him. Their feelings towards Oskar are better characterised by indifference than by any negative emotion. But Oskar hates them in response to his being killed a hundred times (Lindqvist 2009: 388). His persecutors only develop hate after Oskar fights back, injuring Jonny's ear. Then they were determined to get payback in the swimming pool, and when Oskar looked up from the pool into Jonny's brothers' eyes, 'they looked completely crazed. So filled with hate' (ibid.: 513).

This case raises the general question of what role hate plays in bullying dynamics. So far, the issue of hate has primarily been raised by researchers in relation to the question: should bullying itself be classified as a hate crime? Elizabeth Englander makes this claim, arguing that bullying should be considered a 'junior hate crime'[27] (Englander 2007: 206). Hate crimes target individuals because of their membership of a specific group. In Englander's view, bullying is usually directed towards children with 'perceived differences'. Although these differences may be obvious – such as race, class, religion or sexual identification – in her classification of difference, Englander includes qualities like excelling academically, having divorced parents or belonging to an unpopular group or club (ibid.: 206, 210). It is important to stress that sometimes bullying is in fact a hate crime, such as when individuals are targeted because of their sexual orientation (as in the case of Tyler Clementi mentioned at the beginning of this chapter) and, in these cases, legal measures with regard to hate crimes should apply. But Englander's approach is problematic for two reasons: first, it stretches the concept of 'group membership' so thin that it becomes virtually meaningless. In her account, group membership becomes defined as any form of perceived difference that could apply to any individual characteristic (hair or eye colour, musical taste, etc.). Second, she overlooks the way in which differences are produced as significant by the bullying dynamics themselves. Therefore, it is misguided to view qualities such as excelling academically, for example, as potential causes of bullying.

The discussion about whether bullying is a hate crime assumes that it is the bullies who do the hating.[28] As such, this debate follows the dominant

---

[27] I thank Thomas Brudholm for this reference.
[28] One can make a similar observation about shame and bullying. Research on these subjects focuses primarily on how bullies discharge shame. Eliza Ahmed and John Braithwaite write, 'Shame acknowledgement means discharging shame through accepting responsibility and seeking to put things right. In contrast to this, bullies tended to displace shame through externalizing blame and anger. Victims tended to internalize shame – others' rejection of them was not discharged but internalized' (Ahmed and Braithwaite 2005: 303). Hence, the authors focus on parents' use of different shaming techniques, and they study the value of reintegrative shaming theory (see also Ttofi and Farrington 2008). As elsewhere in bullying research, the focus on the perpetrator and the role of the home environment imply that there is no discussion about shame as an affect experienced by

interest in group-focused hate discourses – such as racism, homophobia and xenophobia – that articulate a form of projective, collective hate. But as evidenced in the novel, hate may develop not amongst the bullies, but in the one who is bullied. Hence, in understanding the role of hate in bullying, it is useful to focus on what Thomas Brudholm calls 'retributive reactive hatred – the hatred felt by victims and witnesses of *actual* atrocities or evildoing – [which] is a response to actual events or actions and the attitudes displayed in them' (Brudholm 2010: 306–7). This is a hate that is based on the experience of harm, in contrast with a projective hate that is based on prejudice or irrational beliefs. There are many moral issues raised in relation to hate: is hatred pathological, or can it be considered morally justifiable in some cases (ibid.: 290)? But here, instead I want to look at how hate is produced in the context of bullying as a life-or-death issue. It is important to stress that an individual in this situation does not hate because of his/her personality. In the novel, Oskar had friends earlier in his school life: 'It was only in fifth grade that he started being picked on seriously. At the end of that year he had become a full-fledged target and even friends outside his class had sensed it' (Lindqvist 2009: 16). Nor does Oskar hate his persecutors because of social prejudices based on class or family status (in this case, there is more similarity than difference). He hates them because he is in a situation of having been 'killed' a hundred times. His hate is a response to the threat of social death. One would be hard-pressed to imagine how a child could not hate his/her tormentors as long as they continue to pose a threat to the child's existence. We might even say that hate is central to the production of the identity of being bullied.

In this sense, the hate found in bullying situations illustrates what Sara Ahmed calls the 'sociality of emotion' (Ahmed 2004: 8). Ahmed challenges the ordinary understanding of emotion as a subjective property that belongs to the interior being of a self and becomes expressed to the outside world (the 'inside out' approach to emotion) (ibid.: 9). But she also challenges the notion that is present in some social theories of emotion, which suggests that emotions originate in social and cultural practices and penetrate individual subjectivity (the 'outside in' approach to emotion) (ibid.). Both approaches are problematic because they assume that there is a pre-existing and fixed distinction between inside and outside – between individual and social – rather than looking at processes where the 'me' and the 'we' are constructed in relation to each other. Instead, we should look at how 'emotions create the very effect of the surfaces and boundaries that

those who are bullied. For this, bullying researchers could glean much from discussions about shame in phenomenology and in post-Holocaust studies (e.g. Agamben 1999b: 87–136; Levi 1989/2008: 52–67).

allow us to distinguish an inside and outside in the first place. So emotions are not simply something 'I' or 'we' have. Rather, it is through emotions or how we respond to objects and others that surfaces or boundaries are made: the 'I' and the 'we' are shaped by, and even take the shape of, contact with others' (ibid.: 10). From this perspective, hate is not an unfortunate side-effect of being bullied. Nor is hate just a morally appropriate response to wrongdoing. Hate is central to the dynamics of bullying, and it helps demarcate the differences in position between bullied and bully. But hate, like any other affect, is dynamic rather than static, and it shifts in relation to situational dynamics. When Oskar seriously hurts his tormentor, then the bully who had previously been indifferent becomes overwhelmed by hate. The concepts of 'circulation',[29] proposed by Ahmed, and 'traveling affect', proposed by Kofoed and Ringrose (2012: 9), address how affect changes within relational processes, how it defines subject positions as it travels between them and how it varies in intensity.

New directions for research on bullying

I have argued that *paradigm one*, although close to ordinary assumptions, is both a limited and misleading approach to understanding the relationship between bullying and violence. First, in treating this relationship as a form of intersection – where the violent dimension of bullying consists of using a body part or instrument to inflict harm during a single action – *paradigm one* undermines its own central insight into the role of repetition in this process. As the notion of repetition indicates, violent bullying is a process and not a series of isolated acts. And it is through the process of repetition that attitudes and norms of understanding become reshaped, both on the part of the bullies and the bullied. The reshaping of attitudes and expectations towards the future may be the main effect of violent bullying. Second, in defining the relationship between bullying and violence solely in terms of the bully's actions, *paradigm one* discounts the role of the bullied's subjectivity. In this way, the paradigm overlooks the ways in which the individual who is bullied also participates in the process of

---

[29] In Sara Ahmed's view, emotions are social – not because they are passed from one individual to another, as in a model of contagion (Ahmed 2004: 11), but because affect 'circulates between signifiers in relationships of difference and displacement' (ibid.: 45). By this, she means that when hate is found in a narrative or a discourse, it does not reside in a specific object, but travels between different figures, aligning them as objects of hate. Hate does not reside, for example, in the black body as the object of hate for the racist, nor does it reside in the white body as the subject of hate. Rather, hate accumulates as it travels between black bodies and homosexual bodies and foreign bodies, all of which may appear to pose a threat to the white subject.

violence, particularly in relation to self-inflicted violence via spontaneous physical reactions and sometimes by choice (as in self-harming behaviours like cutting).

I have tried to find an alternative way to understand the relationship between violence and bullying through this sideways venture into the world of gothic fiction. Through the novel *Let the Right One In*, readers may gain some insight into the lived experience of bullying from the perspective of the bullied. From this viewpoint, bullying is a matter of life or death of the self. This sideways analysis introduces new concepts or 'episteme' into the discussion about the relationship between bullying and violence, and I have suggested adapting the term 'social death'. As this case suggests, friendship may be a crucial strategy for survival in the face of the threat of social death, even when friendship puts individuals beyond ordinary moral understandings of good and evil. And this analysis also opens up for the centrality of the negative affect of hate in the relationship between violence and bullying.[30] In the context of bullying, the issue of hate is not just whether it can be understood as having moral merit, but also how it is a survival strategy that is part of a circulating web of interactions and affects. Trying to understand the relationship between violence and bullying from the lived experience of the bullied brings violence into the frame of bullying, rather than treating violence as instrumental and episodic. Here, I have focused on the threat of social death in bullying, taking seriously the role of violence as the founding condition for the field of research on bullying.

Although I have focused on how the subjectivity of the bullied recasts the way in which bullying and violence are understood in *paradigm one*, I am not arguing for a victim-based approach as an exclusive perspective in this debate. There are other perspectives as well, including analyses of situational processes. For example, sociologist Randall Collins, who adopts many of the same assumptions as *paradigm one*, would nevertheless understand the role of violence in bullying in terms of the situational dynamics of tension and fear within interactions.[31]

---

[30] There is ample room in this field to explore other affects in bullying relationships, including shame (see note 28 above) and abjection (Søndergaard 2010).

[31] Randall Collins discusses the emotional rhythm in a conflict situation, introducing terms such as 'confrontational tension' and 'forward panic' (in which one rushes towards confrontation rather than escaping from it) (Collins 2008: 85). I am not arguing in support of his theory of violence, which Darius Rejali has called a 'one size fits all approach' (private communication). But I do want to acknowledge that, in bullying, there may also be room for an analysis of situational dynamics that is independent of the subject positions involved.

What implications do these episteme – highlighting the roles of social death and social vitality, friendship and hate – have for future research on bullying? Quantitative studies of bullying often begin by presenting the definition of bullying in *paradigm one* before asking children to respond to questions about bullying; for example, whether and how frequently they have experienced bullying, over how long a period and at what age. Perhaps one implication of these new episteme is that different questions should be posed: have you felt like you have been killed? Do you feel like killing the person(s) who killed you? Are you overwhelmed with hate? Clearly, there are ethical concerns with such questions, which could be understood as an incitement to commit violence. And yet, for those of us living with children and adolescents who experience situations of bullying, such questions may be very close to sentiments expressed over the dinner table. I mention this to remind us that the researcher's role in this field may also be one of containment. Therefore, it is important to bear in mind the limits of the knowledge we produce in this field.

In my view, the sideways approach to studying bullying and violence contributes an opening up – as opposed to an isolating – of the field of bullying research. This field has been extraordinarily homogenous in its research paradigm with relatively little cross-fertilisation from other fields. Although we may not be able to ask youths, 'Have you been killed?' or 'Do you want to kill?', we can study the concept of social death as it appears in a wide range of other fields – from studies of extreme violence to psychological studies of illness and health – in order to ask what we can learn about this concept in these different contexts, and how it can shed light on the phenomenon of bullying. We can study social vitality and the role of friendship in survival strategies, as well as the ways in which hate and other negative affects like disgust function. We can study the dynamics of situations that escalate violently or disperse in intensity. In other words, we can situate bullying in the complex field of human interaction instead of isolating it or 'walling it in' in the field of research on bullying.

Part III

School talk

9 New solutions for bullying and harassment: a post-structural, feminist approach

Elizabeth J. Meyer

Introduction

Scholarship that investigates aggression between peers at school has been growing steadily since Dan Olweus published his early work on bullying, *Aggression in the Schools: Bullies and Whipping Boys* (1978). In the late 1980s and 1990s, several studies replicated Olweus's work and established his terminology and methodology as the most influential and dominant in this field. As a result, a central body of research has been instituted; it is highly valid and reliable in certain areas but perpetuates important omissions and silences in others. This chapter presents an overview of the knowledge presented in bullying and harassment studies of secondary schools through a post-structural, feminist lens in order to identify the gaps in existing research and propose alternative frameworks for more inclusive research and intervention programmes. With an aim to improve our understanding and future approaches, this chapter also discusses how the gendered hierarchies that exist in secondary schools and related aspects of social power have been mostly unaddressed by researchers and anti-bullying intervention programmes. In particular, we need to better understand the relationships between bullying, sexual harassment, hetero-normativity, homophobic and transphobic behaviours, and the challenges related to making schools safer and more inclusive for all students.

In order to situate this analysis of bullying and harassment studies in the context of existing knowledge, it is important to investigate three related but distinct areas of educational research: (a) bullying; (b) harassment; and (c) sexism, homophobia and transphobia in schools. These fields were chosen due to their clear links to issues of gender and bullying. Questions relating to gender and sexual orientation are central to this critique because I am interested in exploring the under-researched relationships between gender and sexual orientation, as well as bullying and harassment in schools. Until quite recently, there has been a dearth of academic research and educational programmes connecting these areas. Although the issue of homophobia may appear to be linked solely to issues of sexual orientation, I argue that homophobic behaviours are often closely tied to the policing of gender-role performance as constructed within a heterosexual matrix (Butler 1990) in schools (Meyer 2006, 2008a). This is an important level of analysis that is often ignored when studying bullying and harassment within the school environment.

The chapter begins with an overview of bullying research focusing on secondary schools. The field of bullying research has the longest tradition and farthest-reaching influence on investigations and interventions addressing aggression and its related physical and psychological harm to individuals in schools. Bullying is recognised as a problem worldwide, and research into the phenomenon has been strongly influenced by Dan Olweus's work in Norway. This research is essential to understand; it has an enduring impact on current practices as evidenced by the proliferation of certain kinds of anti-bullying policies and programmes in schools today.

The second section of the chapter focuses on harassment studies and how they relate to bullying research. This is a more recently defined phenomenon, and almost all empirical articles on this subject have been situated in the context of secondary schools. The most prevalent theme of these studies, with few exceptions, is that of (hetero)sexual harassment by young men towards women. The third section presents relevant reports and studies related to the question of homophobia and transphobia in schools. This topic is the least often addressed in academic research and school-based interventions. The impact of this omission on academic research is discussed, and suggestions are given for how to adapt further research and interventions to be more inclusive of the gendered dynamics of bullying and harassment in schools. The fourth section introduces the most recent developments in research on bullying, harassment, homophobia and transphobia; this work started to emerge around 2007. The final section presents recommendations for bullying researchers and intervention programmes, with a view to helping them address key issues related to gender and sexual orientation, which would ensure more effective and lasting changes to school cultures.

This chapter is based on an earlier literature review that included data from over one hundred peer-reviewed journal articles and published reports; it was designed to demonstrate how current research and the resulting policies and practices in the field of bullying and harassment have largely ignored the influence of certain forms of social power, such as race, ethnicity, disability, gender and sexual orientation; these are important to understand in order to reduce bullying and harassment in schools (Meyer 2007a[1]).

---

[1] For readers interested in the methods used to identify and include articles, refer to Meyer (2007a).

Bullying research

In 1977, Dan Olweus published his first study on the problem of bullying in Norway in an English-language journal. Since then, he has consistently set the agenda for research in this field: from defining bullying to structuring how researchers study the problem using student surveys and quantitative methods, as well as creating interventions and evaluations of programmes to reduce bullying in schools. The impact of his work on the direction taken in this field of study is evidenced by how regularly his studies are cited in other research. In an analysis of fifty-five bullying articles published in peer-reviewed journals between 1997 and 2007, his work was cited in forty-four (80 per cent). The eleven articles that did not refer to his work approached various aspects of the bullying question from new positions, including issues related to truancy, victimisation, sexuality, law, social work and peer-counselling frameworks. The perspectives offered in the articles that do not cite Olweus are important to consider, as they offer an alternative point of view to understanding certain nuances of bullying in schools that have not been structured by Olweus's specific constructions and definitions of bullying and how to investigate it. The following section provides an overview of bullying studies, and offers questions to consider in order to re-think the research done on bullying in schools.

Bullying: Olweus's influence

The forty-four studies that cite Olweus's work embrace his definition of bullying and, to varying degrees, apply his approach to quantifying the problem in specific contexts. In most of these studies, the approach was a paper-and-pencil survey instrument completed by students that addressed issues such as:

- Prevalence of bullying and victimisation (Adair, Dixon et al. 2000; Borg 1999; Byrne 1994; Olweus 1977, 1978; Rigby, Cox and Black 1997)
- Links between bullying, mental health, depression and suicide (Bond, Carlin et al. 2001; Coggan, Bennett et al. 2003; Rigby and Slee 1999)
- Links between bullying and physical health (Slee 1995c; Sharp 1995)
- Links between bullying and delinquency (Rigby and Cox 1996)
- Measuring the effectiveness of bullying-intervention programmes (Arora 1994; Naylor and Cowie 1999; Olweus 1996)
- Student perceptions of and attitudes towards bullying (Boulton, Bucci and Hawker 1999; Boulton, Trueman and Flemington 2002; Hazler, Hoover and Oliver 1991; Land 2003)
- Coping strategies of students who have been bullied (Naylor, Cowie and del Rey 2001)

- Who gets bullied (Siann, Callaghan et al. 1994)
- Special-needs students impacted by bullying (Whitney, Nabuzoka and Smith 1992)
- Bullying in the transition from primary to secondary school (Pelligrini and Long 2002).

Three studies were aimed at understanding bullying in schools from the educators' perspective: one with teachers in Malta (Borg 1998); and two with teachers in the United Kingdom (Boulton 1997; Sharp and Thompson 1992). With the exception of studies authored by Olweus in Norway, and due to his significant impact in influencing this field of study, the sample of articles was limited to English-speaking countries. Of the remaining ten studies that cited Olweus, six evaluated intervention programmes and employed mixed methods (Boulton 2005; Boulton and Flemington 1996; Cartwright 1995; Cowie 1998; O'Toole and Burton 2005; Sharp and Smith 1991), and only two (Hepburn 1997b, 2000) used a qualitative form of inquiry to access deeper levels of understanding about how bullying and power dynamics play out at school. Hepburn's articles offer some important insights and are discussed later in this section. The remaining two studies presented surveys of existing literature and made recommendations for schools trying to reduce bullying (Batsche and Knoff 1994; Hoover and Juul 1993).

These quantitative studies consistently rely on the following definition of bullying introduced by Olweus:

A student is being bullied or victimized when he or she is exposed, repeatedly and over time, to negative actions on the part of one or more other students ... it is a negative action when someone intentionally inflicts, or attempts to inflict, injury or discomfort on another.... Negative actions can be carried out by words (verbally), for instance, by threatening, taunting, teasing, and calling names. It is a negative action when somebody hits, pushes, kicks, pinches or restrains another – by physical contact. It is also possible to carry out negative actions without the use of words or physical contact, such as by making faces or dirty gestures, intentionally excluding someone from a group, or refusing to comply with another person's wishes. (1993a: 9)

As Schott points out (see Chapter 2), this definition and approach to understanding bullying is individualistic and relies heavily on behavioural psychology to explain bullying as a problem grounded in conflicting personality types and patterns of individual aggression. Further, this paradigm does not examine or account for the socio-political context in which these interpersonal dynamics and individuals are situated.

The one significant variation on this definition was offered in an Australian study by Phillip Slee: 'Bullying behavior may be considered to represent the oppression of one individual by another individual or group of persons, where the behavior (psychological or physical) is typically repetitive and deliberate' (1995c: 216). His use of the word *oppression* is unique, as it implies that there are broader social forces at work that are reinforcing the power imbalance between bully and victim. Although the ramifications of using this word are not fully explored in his study, Slee does acknowledge how the external influence of Australian 'macho' values might impact addressing bullying in schools: 'In the Australian context it is possible that the emphasis on male stereotypic values of "toughing it out" and not "dobbing" on your "mates" accounts for educators [*sic.*] reluctance to address the issue' (ibid.: 223).

Slee's article, along with four other quantitative studies, are the only ones that offer a broader understanding of social contexts, identities and gender, and how they shape and reinforce certain power dynamics within schools. Many studies reported variations by gender in their findings, but did not include a critical analysis of how gender – and, as a result, sexuality – might shape and impact the way in which bullying is played out at secondary schools. The other studies that considered these social influences include a study of students with disabilities who were targeted by bullies (Whitney, Nabuzoka and Smith 1992); an analysis of how ethnicity impacts experiences with bullying (Siann, Callaghan et al. 1994); and an examination of the intersection between bullying and sexual harassment (Land 2003). Irene Whitney, Dabie Nabuzoka and Peter K. Smith's article was the first study that noted, 'At its most insidious, bullying focuses on vulnerable young people who are regarded as being different because of their ethnic origin, class, sexual inclinations, or physical or learning difficulties' (1992: 3). This study also recognised the shortcomings of the Olweus-designed questionnaire; instead, it used individual interviews with 179 children to explore victimisation patterns and found that children with special needs were more likely to be selected as victims (33 per cent) than those without any special needs (8 per cent) (ibid.: 5).

A second project in the United Kingdom explicitly addressed ethnicity in its examination of bullying at London and Glasgow schools (Siann, Callaghan et al. 1994). The quantitative study concluded that, in the experience or perceptions of bullying, there were no statistically significant differences between ethnic groups. However, the researchers did report that more ethnic-minority students believed that ethnic-minority students were more likely than majority students to experience bullying (ibid.: 123). This may indicate that the researchers' survey instrument was not designed to identify subtler or more covert forms of bullying that involve bias. Deborah Land's research on teasing, bullying and sexual harassment is the only Olweus-related study that offers a feminist critique of these behaviours; it is discussed more fully below.

The main weakness in the bullying studies that build upon Olweus' research is that they fail to explore and acknowledge the influence of larger social forces, such as racism, ableism, sexism and homophobia, and they lack an understanding of power relations and dominance in peer groups. Canadian researcher Gerald Walton also noted this trend in his analysis of bullying research and public discourse (2005). Bullying studies that apply the Olweus paradigm recognise various forms of verbal aggression but, with few exceptions, never explore the relationship they have with social biases and cultural norms. They address the issue of 'name-calling' but never explore what names are being used to hurt and insult students. As the harassment studies show, many of the insults used by bullies reinforce dominant concepts of white, masculine, heterosexual, able-bodied superiority. In the aforementioned articles, several referred to gender and the ways in which certain aspects of masculinity and femininity might alter how bullying is performed and experienced by each gender (Cowie 1998; Naylor, Cowie and del Rey 2001; Pelligrini and Long 2002; Slee 1995c). But only the article by Land looked specifically at issues of sexual harassment and its relation to bullying.

Bullying: critical voices in the crowd

In her US-based study, 'Teasing apart secondary students' conceptualizations of peer teasing, bullying and sexual harassment' (2003), Land highlights the lack of connection between gender and harassment in most bullying research. Her findings are interesting in that they indicate that students consider teasing to be mainly non-physical, and verbal sexual behaviour is not viewed as harassment (ibid.: 158). These are important findings to consider, as students play a central role in defining what behaviours are tolerated and acceptable within a school culture. If their experiences lead them to believe that verbal sexual behaviour should be tolerated, then they will silently endure and fail to report incidents of verbal harassment; sometimes, they will even begin to engage in this behaviour because it is viewed as acceptable at their school. This silencing of and ignoring verbal harassment perpetuates the invisibility of this behaviour and its negative impact on students. This theme of silencing and ignoring certain types of aggression in schools re-emerges in harassment and homophobia research.

Finally, the two qualitative studies that cited Olweus – both conducted by Alexa Hepburn in the UK (1997b, 2000) – are important for several reasons. First, they are the only studies that acknowledge the importance of Olweus's work in influencing this area of research. They also introduce a new way of conceptualising and approaching the problem. This is not said to diminish the importance of the previous quantitative studies: these early works were important because they legitimated the investigation of bullying as a problem at schools. Each of these studies were able to replicate central aspects of Olweus's work in Norway to demonstrate that bullying was also a problem in their countries and at their schools. However, as mentioned earlier, these familiar frameworks also allowed certain omissions and silences to be reproduced. But Hepburn takes the issue of bullying and moves beyond numbers, definitions, individualising bullies and victims to evaluate isolated interventions. Her articles 'Teachers and secondary school bullying: a postmodern discourse analysis' (1997) and 'Power lines: Derrida, discursive psychology and the management of accusations of teacher bullying' (2000) use discourse analysis to understand how teachers construct their understandings of bullying in schools. These articles offer an in-depth analysis of language and power, and how they can be used to understand facets of bullying in schools. Although Hepburn does not explicitly use gender as a tool of analysis, she presents a rich and detailed perspective on how to understand the use of language in exercising power within the normalising discourses of a school.

Bullying: research not citing Olweus

Of the eleven bullying studies that did not cite Olweus's work, three are of interest here as they focus specifically on issues relating to gender and sexuality. The first is a study by Vivien Ray and Robin Gregory (2001) on the experiences of children of gay and lesbian parents in Australia, the second is by Neil Duncan (2004) about popularity and sexual competition amongst girls in secondary schools in the UK, and the third is by Ian Wilson, Christine Griffin and Bernadette Wren (2005) on the experiences of youth with 'atypical gender identity organization'. The other eight studies included:

- An examination of truancy (Irving and Parker-Jenkins 1995)
- A legal analysis of administrator liability in addressing bullying (McGrath 2003)
- Four bullying-prevention programme evaluations (Bagley and Pritchard 1998; Naylor and Cowie 1999; Peterson and Rigby 1999; Price and Jones 2001)
- A survey of student victimisation in US public schools (Nolin, Davies and Chandler 1996)
- The experiences of Chinese students in schools in the UK (Chan 1997).

Only one of these included any discussion or analysis of behaviour related to ethnicity (Chan 1997), and none addressed race, gender, disability or sexual orientation. The three studies that did incorporate some of this analysis are discussed below.

Ray and Gregory (2001) examined important aspects of homophobia in the school culture, and how it impacted the lives of students with gay or lesbian parents. Their findings indicate that almost half of the children in their study were targeted for bullying as a result of their parents' sexual orientation (45 per cent). The abuse included verbal teasing and joking, as well as physical and sexual violence. It was also clear that schools often inadequately responded to homophobic language or bullying and, in some cases, teachers joined their students in making homophobic remarks. Many of these students reported feeling unsafe at school, and that they did not feel confident in teachers' abilities to deal with the issues (ibid.: 34).

Duncan (2004) explored an important dimension of bullying amongst girls in his article 'It's important to be nice, but it's nicer to be important: girls, popularity and sexual competition'. This project investigated the sexualised element of much of the bullying that goes on between girls in secondary schools, including accusations of being a lesbian or heterosexual promiscuity. The related power dynamic is that, in every case, the harassers were described as 'popular girls' (ibid.: 137). What is interesting about Duncan's use of the term 'popular' is that his participants defined it in a q-sort activity, and the items that were most strongly associated with 'popular' were: 'is very loud', 'is very popular with boys' and 'is very fashionable'. These were all associated with high social status at the school and heterosexual attractiveness. Duncan describes the girls' definition of popularity as 'an ability to gather other girls around them and to manipulate and coerce social relations in their favour' (ibid.: 144). The factor 'is a lesbian' was also defined as the one 'least likely to be associated with being a popular girl' (ibid.: 146). This exploration of power and popularity amongst girls in secondary schools reinforces the notion of the centrality of male heterosexuality in determining social hierarchies in school. The girls' internal hierarchies appeared to be built upon 'boy-centred' ideals, and they never questioned or challenged the dominance of these patriarchal, hetero-normative values in their social groups.

The third study examined the experiences of eight children between the ages of 14 to 17 with 'atypical gender identity organization' and their interactions with peers in school (Wilson, Griffin and Wren 2005). Seven of the eight participants had experienced homophobic bullying by their peers that was a result of their 'cross-gender behavior' (ibid.: 309). The authors addressed the problems these youths experienced due to others confusing their gender identity and sexual orientation; they acknowledged that these experiences appeared to result from transphobia, which they defined as, 'an underlying fear of those who appear different from the traditional norms of masculinity and femininity' (ibid.: 310). The students in this study experienced great amounts of stress and minimal amounts of peer support in connection to their gender identities, and the authors concluded that this distress was caused by the reaction of others 'not allowing the child to engage in their desired behaviors' (ibid.: 313). This study is important, as it is the only one of the pre-2007 bullying studies that specifically addressed issues of transgender youths, gender non-conformity, and how gender identity and sexual orientation are commonly conflated.

As the analysis of the above studies has shown, bullying research has generally failed adequately to address larger social issues related to heteronormativity, gender identity and expression, sexual orientation and other related forms of social oppression. Alternatively, a more critical feminist approach to understanding social power and student behaviours in secondary schools has been attended to in several studies examining the phenomenon of harassment.

Harassment research

Although bullying and harassment are intimately linked (Duncan 2004; Renold 2000; Stein 1995), very few scholars, educators and curriculum specialists have simultaneously addressed these issues. By not integrating each other's work, a barrier exists between these fields of inquiry that limits the resources and approaches available to scholars, educators and activists attempting to understand and transform student behaviours at school.

Current harassment studies have focused primarily on the narrowly defined issue of (hetero)sexual harassment of females by males. Seven of these articles were presented from a legal perspective – mostly establishing the duty of school administrators and teachers to defend and protect students from harassment (McFarland 2001; Roth 1994; Sorenson 1994; Wolohan 1995). Other legal or policy analyses have discussed issues related to school-board liability (Howard 2001), the limitations of harassment policies (Reed 1996) and human-rights issues (Mock 1996). The twenty others were empirical studies; of these, eleven focused on various forms of (hetero)sexual harassment in schools (Bagley, Bolitho and Bertrand 1997; Corbett, Gentry and Pearson 1993; Lahelma 2002; Larkin 1994; Lee, Croninger et al. 1996; Miller 1997; Roscoe 1994; Timmerman 2003, 2005; Uggen and Blackstone 2004; Whitelaw, Hills and De Rosa 1999). They examined multiple gender and power dynamics in schools, including:

- teacher–student (Corbett, Gentry and Pearson 1993; Timmerman 2003);
- student–teacher (Ferfolja 1998; Miller 1997); and

- student–student (Lahelma 2002, 2004; Larkin 1994; Lee, Croninger et al. 1996; Nishina and Juvonen 2005; Nishina, Juvonen and Witkow 2005; Roscoe 1994; Timmerman 2003, 2005; Uggen and Blackstone 2004; Whitelaw, Hills and De Rosa 1999).

Four articles addressed issues of race, ethnicity and racism (Lahelma 2004; Lee, Croninger et al. 1996; Phan 2003; Ryan 2003), and two articles addressed the general concept of bullying. Of these twenty empirical studies, only four linked the issues of sexual harassment and homophobia (Ferfolja 1998; Lahelma 2002; Timmerman 2003; Williams, Connolly et al. 2005); these are discussed in more detail at the end of this section. Only two studies emerged in both of the searches on bullying and harassment (Naylor and Cowie 1999; Rusby, Forrester et al. 2005). These overlapping articles did not explicitly address the differences in these terms and seemed to use them interchangeably. This can lead to confusion and misunderstanding, particularly in conducting research. These terms must be clearly defined and their differences made explicit in order to better understand and respond to different categories of behaviours.

Since anti-bullying programmes have become so common in North American schools, many educators confuse any type of aggression, fighting or conflict with bullying. As a result, certain racist, sexist, homophobic and transphobic behaviours are ignored or simply punished with no attention to the underlying harmful messages. The sad truth is that research indicates that youths (particularly girls and students of colour) experience more long-term negative harms from such biased insults (Gruber and Fineran 2007, 2008; Poteat and Espelage 2007), even though these groups are most likely to be ignored by teachers. In Canada and the US, there are different legal and policy frameworks that affect how we track and respond to incidents that violate constitutionally protected classes of people; as a result, it is essential that we are able to distinguish between bullying and harassing behaviours.

Harassment defined

The definition for bullying was established by Olweus and has been widely agreed upon by scholars in the field. The definition of harassment is more fluid; depending on the discipline of the researcher, it can vary from narrow legal and policy definitions to broader theoretical constructions. I offer the following definition of harassment as adapted from Land (2003): any biased behaviour that 'negatively impacts the target or the environment'. It differs from bullying in that bullying, by definition, is directed at a specific individual and can include any kind of insult or harmful behaviour. Harassment, by definition, is biased in nature and

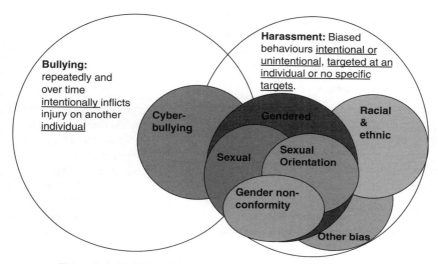

Figure 9.1. Bullying, harassment and gendered harassment

can include behaviours or comments that insult or demean a social group, can be directed at an individual or have no specific targets. The result of this behaviour is to create a hostile environment that impedes the ability of individuals to work or study effectively.

Some forms of bullying can also meet the definition for harassment if they are intentional and directed at an individual. However, other forms of harassment are not bullying; e.g. the prevalent use of expressions such as 'no homo' or 'that's so gay'. Although these terms may not be directed at an individual with the intention to harm or to bully, they create a hostile climate for people who are bisexual, gay, lesbian or questioning their sexual orientation. These comments communicate a tolerance for homophobic attitudes and behaviours and, when they permeate the culture of a school, they send a message that it is not okay to be gay. Another example would be a group of male students loudly talking about certain aspects of female bodies and/or comparing their female classmates' body parts. Although these sexist comments are not directed towards the young women, hurtful comments that are loud enough to be overheard create a hostile environment. The overlaps between bullying and harassment are illustrated in Figure 9.1.

This definition of harassment can be accurately applied to all the studies found in this search, with the exception of three studies that used the term *peer harassment* but did not investigate any form of biased behaviours (Nishina and Juvonen 2005; Nishina, Juvonen and Witkow 2005;

Rusby, Forrester et al. 2005). These scholars appear to be more situated in the bullying framework, citing Olweus and other bullying researchers as key influences in their arguments and analysis.

Sexual harassment

The earliest article that explored female students' experiences with sexual harassment was Kelly Corbett, Cynthia S. Gentry and Willie Pearson Jr.'s study, 'Sexual harassment in high school' (1993), which presented the findings of a survey that asked university students to report their recollections of sexual harassment by secondary-school teachers. The article marked the emergence of this field of scholarship and was followed by June Larkin's groundbreaking research, 'Walking through walls: the sexual harassment of high school girls' (1994), in which the main goal was to understand young women's experiences of sexual harassment in schools, and how it interferes with their education. In addition to exploring verbal and physical harassment, Larkin introduced the concept of *visual harassment*, which included leering or 'invasive watching' as well as sexual gesturing. These categories are important to add to investigations, as they expand how we construct our understanding of behaviours that create hostile environments for students in schools. Larkin's study also confirmed the pervasiveness of such behaviour and how it had been normalised due to the frequency of incidents, responses by male peers and the silence around it in schools.

In 1996, Valerie E. Lee, Robert G. Croninger, Eleanor Linn and Xianglei Chen's study provided the first quantitative data presented in an academic journal on the frequency, severity and consequences of sexual harassment in American secondary schools. Lee and her team used survey data of a nationally representative sample of 1,208 students in grades 8–11;[2] the data were collected by Harris Interactive for the American Association of University Women (AAUW). The researchers concluded that harassment was disruptive for all students but had a more severe impact on girls and black students due to the context of the school. They also concluded that students who are harassed – particularly those severely harassed – experience academic and psychological problems.

Christopher Bagley, Floyd Bolitho and Lorne Bertrand's 1997 study surveyed 1,025 adolescent Canadian girls in grades 7–12.[3] They defined sexual assault as either: 'indecent exposure; physical (unwanted sexual touching through to rape); and other (mostly verbal harassment)' (ibid.:

[2] This corresponds to years 8–11 in British schools.
[3] This corresponds to years 7–12 in British schools.

362). The researchers concluded that girls who reported being assaulted 'often' were more likely to report emotional distress and were more than five times as likely to have exhibited suicidal behaviours as students who were assaulted less frequently or not at all. They determined that males are also subjected to sexual harassment, but rates are 'much lower and the connection with mental health problems is much weaker' (ibid.: 365); this established links between some types of long-term harm caused to students when they experience harassment at school. The issue of racism is also related to such deeply embedded sexism in schools; both are consistently silenced and ignored despite the documented negative impact they have on students. Two studies bring these effects to light.

Racial harassment

In Tan Phan's study 'Life in school: narratives of resiliency among Vietnamese–Canadian youths' (2003), issues of ethnicity and racism were central in the experiences of his participants. Phan conducted a qualitative study of eleven academically successful youths who had been born in Vietnam but later immigrated to Canada; each of his participants grew up in low-income neighbourhoods in Vancouver. The students in this study all perceived racism as a common problem in the classroom and had witnessed racist acts against their Vietnamese classmates. They had felt 'silenced, marginalized, or even criminalized, while others received privileged treatment' (ibid.: 560). These resilient youths consistently refused to be defeated by racism, developing a 'resistance stance' in order to succeed (ibid.: 565). Much of the racism they experienced came in the form of persistent stereotyping and negative assumptions on the part of their classmates and teachers. Many white Canadians would not recognise such acts as blatantly racist, which is a complicating problem that James Ryan investigated in his 2003 study of school administrators.

In his introduction, Ryan explains that racism in education is often most evident at the school level. He clarifies by saying, 'It is here that the various and complex forms of racism emerge in their obvious and not so obvious guises, in the name-calling, harassment and the interpersonal conflict, in the subtle stereotyping and taken-for granted understandings and practices, and in curricular and organizational patterns' (ibid.: 145). The results of this survey indicated that 'many principals were reluctant to acknowledge that racism occurred in their schools...and do not see racism as systemic' (ibid.: 149–50). They tended to minimise or justify students' uses of racist language by indicating that they did not believe it was racially motivated. He also contends that 'most administrators are conservative in their practice. They tend to orient their actions toward supporting and conserving the system in which they work and have difficulty when it comes to challenging or changing integral parts of it' (ibid.: 159). These findings are important, as they relate directly to how many administrators respond to incidents of gendered harassment. Just as Ryan believes that principals can have a positive impact on racist and anti-racist practices in their schools, I argue that they can have a similar impact on how sexist, hetero-normative and homophobic practices are repeated or challenged – and potentially transformed.

Overlaps in sexual and homophobic harassment

In the studies of harassment at secondary schools, only four made any specific mention of the potential links and impact of homophobia and sexual harassment (Ferfolja 1998; Lahelma 2002; Timmerman 2003; Williams et al. 2005). Most of the articles offered a feminist critique of power and gender roles in schools, but very few pushed this line of thinking to its logical next step: to understand heterosexism, and how it connects sexual harassment and homophobic harassment.

The first harassment study to address homophobia was conducted by Tanja Ferfolja in Australia (1998). Her study of six lesbian teachers at government secondary schools in Sydney included examples of the neg-ative impact of the schools' heterosexist structures, and the role hegem-onic masculinity plays in teaching male students to disrespect gay men, women and lesbians in particular. Ferfolja explains: '...harassment is based on the need to maintain power through the maintenance of socially constructed gender roles...anti-lesbian harassment encompasses both [misogyny and homophobia], doubly oppressing women through its maintenance of heterosexist discourses and simultaneously assuring male power' (ibid.: 403). The teachers talked about their challenges in confronting 'underhand harassment', which Ferfolja explains includes whispers, jokes or comments about lesbianism in the teacher's presence without directing it at her. Even when students were disciplined for their behaviour, it was not defined as homophobic harassment in any of the cases. The teachers spoke about taking stress leave and feeling sick, depressed and 'under siege' as a result of their students' behaviour. This research shows how teachers and students alike can be harmed when a school allows such harassment to continue.

The second study that included a discussion of homophobia in schools was Elina Lahelma's article 'Gendered conflicts in secondary school: fun or enactment of power?' (2002). In her discussion about the forms of sexual harassment observed in a Finnish school, she discussed *sex-based harassment* that is enacted through terms derogatory to females, such as 'sissy' for boys and 'slut' for girls. She goes on to explain that boys are vulnerable to being called 'homo' 'because they are the *wrong* sort of boys' (ibid.: 302).

Greetje Timmerman's 2003 study from the Netherlands, 'Sexual harassment of adolescents perpetrated by teachers and by peers: an exploration of the dynamics of power, culture, and gender in secondary schools', offers a unique theoretical framework for understanding this problem. She examined student-on-student harassment using a Culture Model, which assumed that sexual harassment reflects school culture, due to the fact that it is a public phenomenon and occurs on a daily basis. In her findings, she reported that the Culture Model was relevant in describing both student-on-student harassment as well as teacher-on-student harassment. This means that the culture of a school accepts the public and persistent sexual harassment of female students by their teachers and peers – and male students and teachers comprised an overwhelming majority of the perpetrators. Although both male and female students were targeted, girls were subjected to more persistent and severe harassment. Timmerman added that sexual harassment of boys 'tends to be more verbal and homophobic in nature' (ibid.: 242).

The fourth article examined the link between sexual orientation and psycho-social adjustment in a sample of ninety-seven sexual-minority adolescents in Canada (Williams et al. 2005). The researchers concluded that sexual-minority youths reported more sexual harassment, more bullying, less closeness with their mothers and less companionship with their best friends (ibid.: 471). These findings indicate that social support and peer victimisation are important factors that contribute to emotional and behavioural difficulties, and also that schools and families need to work proactively to reduce these harms for the health of all youths in schools. Although this article does not provide any critical analysis of gender or sexual orientation, it is the only bullying or harassment study that used Olweus's bullying questionnaire to quantify the incidence and impact of homophobic harassment at secondary schools. The next section presents information from studies that explicitly explored the prevalence and impact of homophobia in schools.

Homophobia research

Before 2007, few articles were published in peer-reviewed journals on the subject of homophobia and bullying at secondary schools – and even fewer addressed the issue of transphobia. However, several empirical studies were conducted in K–12[4] schools by US-based advocacy groups such as the Gay, Lesbian and Straight Education Network (GLSEN), the AAUW and Human Rights Watch. The eighteen articles published in peer-reviewed journals mostly described the problem of homophobic harassment in schools and its impact on targeted students. These studies addressed the following questions:

- Victimisation and the mental-health impact for sexual minority youth (D'Augelli, Pilkington and Hershberger 2002).
- Relationships between hegemonic masculinity, bullying and harassment (Klein 2006; Phoenix, Frosh and Pattman 2003; Renold 2003, 2007; Stoudt 2006).
- The experiences of 'same-gender loving' youths of colour in schools (Parks 2001).
- The relationship between educators' personal beliefs and professional behaviour regarding homosexuality (Sears 1991).
- How issues of homophobic bullying are addressed through policies and curriculum (Adams, Cox and Dunstan 2004).
- Peer regulation of hetero-normativity (Chambers, Tincknell and Van Loon 2004; Chambers, Van Loon and Tincknell 2004).
- Hetero-normativity, homophobia and bullying in primary schools (Renold 2000, 2002, 2006).
- The prevalence of anti-gay discourse in secondary schools (Smith and Smith 1998).

The remaining five articles addressed: intervention programmes (Peters 2003; Szlacha 2003); legal and policy issues in the US (Faulkner and Lindsey 2004; Fineran 2002); a review of the literature (Thompson and Johnson 2003); and youth violence in Europe (Junger-Tas 1996). The common thread in these studies was the recognition that hetero-normativity and homophobia are prevalent in schools, and that they impact students in a variety of negative ways. Related to this is the lack of clear policies that address homophobia or consistent intervention by school personnel to stop homophobic behaviour. I now examine in greater detail the five studies (Phoenix, Frosh and Pattman 2003; Renold 2000, 2002; Smith and Smith 1998; Stoudt 2006) that explore the multiple dimensions of gender and sexual orientation, and how they influence students' experiences in school.

---

[4] This designation refers to schools, usually in the US, that accommodate students from kindergarten to twelfth grade (which corresponds to year 12 in British schools).

Scholarly articles

The earliest published study was George Smith's article, 'The ideology of "fag": the school experience of gay students' (1998). Using institutional ethnography, Smith explored how speech (e.g. graffiti, verbal abuse, anti-gay activities, etc.) informs the experience of gay teenagers at school. He concludes, 'The social relations of heterosexuality and patriarchy dominate public space, being gay is never spoken of positively (in these informants' experiences)' (ibid.: 309). He describes how the institution of the school 'often gives tacit approval' (ibid.: 321) for anti-gay activities, as well as how gender relations are experienced within the hetero-normative context of the school. This study offers a detailed description of how homophobia is used as a tool of aggression, and how schools consistently ignore and allow the persistence of this form of harassment.

Emma Renold's research into primary schools in the UK discusses concepts similar to those outlined by Smith. In her two articles, '"Coming out": gender, (hetero)sexuality and the primary school' (2000) and 'Presumed innocence: (hetero)sexual, heterosexist and homophobic harassment among primary school girls and boys' (2002), she explores similar practices and the impact they have on students in their final year of primary school. Her studies were the first to explicitly link homophobia and (hetero)sexual harassment in primary schools, and to explore how they influence young students' construction of their gender and sexual identities. Renold writes that her participants revealed 'how homophobic performances are more about gender than sexual practices and are a means of regulating and policing the boundaries of hegemonic heterosexual masculinities' (2000: 322). In her later article, she explains that these practices 'provide ways of resecuring gender dichotomies, creating and maintaining dominant masculinities and passive subordinate femininities, and policing heterosexual hierarchies' (2002: 429). She also discovered variations in how this policing differed for boys and girls: 'Girls who transgressed dominant femininities were not homosexualized. Derogatory terms such as "dyke" and "lesbo" had not entered the verbal repertoires of pupils from the two research schools. They were, however, masculinized and called "boys" and were routinely labeled "weird"' (2004: 431).

The fourth study to examine the intersections of homophobia and gender issues was Ann Phoenix, Stephen Frosh and Rob Pattman's 'Producing contradictory masculine subject positions: narratives of threat, homophobia and bullying in 11–14 year old boys' (2003). The authors concluded that their participants constructed masculinity as 'synonymous with "toughness," physical aggression and homophobia and antithetical to femininity and compliance with teachers' (ibid.: 184–5).

They also found that their participants constructed different versions of themselves in the group interviews as compared to the individual ones – they tended to be more 'stereotypically boyish' when surrounded by their peers (ibid.: 187). The authors also point at the connection between homophobia and misogyny, which is important to understand, as this link lies at the heart of the concept of gendered harassment – or any behaviour that acts to police traditional gender norms. They explain that 'boys labeled as gay were seen as possessing the same characteristics that were denigrated in girls. Hence, homophobia was intertwined with misogyny' (ibid.: 188).

This study is also interesting because it explicitly examined the links between racialised identities and gender and sexuality. Asian boys, who were constructed as 'not powerful or sexually attractive', and Turkish boys, who 'work hard and spend all their time together', were targets for homophobic name-calling. In contrast, black boys were less likely to be called 'gay' and were seen as 'strongly heterosexual' and 'super masculine' (ibid.: 190, 191). Finally, the conclusion of this article offers an insight that can inform future examinations of bullying and harassment in schools: the authors write that 'boys in this study reported that teachers in the schools in which we worked did not define homophobic name calling as bullying and so did not impose sanctions on those who engaged in it' (ibid.: 193). This analysis of how boys position themselves and experience their identities in schools provides useful insight into research on how educators see and respond to gendered harassment in schools.

The fifth and final study provided a similar analysis of hegemonic masculinity in an American secondary school. Brett Stoudt's article 'You're either in or you're out: school violence, peer discipline, and the (re)production of hegemonic masculinity' (2006) examined practices of hazing, teasing and bullying at Rockport, an all-boys private school. Stoudt reported on the prevalence of misogynistic and homophobic discourses, which were meant to reproduce and affirm the dominance of hegemonic masculinity: 'It becomes so embedded in the daily school experience that many students no longer make the connection between calling someone a "pussy" or "homo" and insulting a particular group of people' (ibid.: 280). Stoudt's mixed-method study of 148 mostly white, upper middle-class students led him to conclude that 'the teaching and reinforcing of hegemonic masculine values are part of Rockport's (not so) hidden curriculum, a form of symbolic violence that helps to perpetuate patriarchal dominance' (ibid.: 285). It is important to note the role that masculinity plays in these examinations of school-based homophobia. Without a deeper understanding of how gendered behaviours shape students' experiences in schools, attempts to reduce homophobia at school will likely achieve minimal success.

In 2003, Laura Szlacha published the first article to evaluate the effectiveness of the only state-wide (Massachusetts) initiative in the US to address homophobia in schools. Her study identified key factors that improve the 'sexual diversity climate' in schools for all students. Although a state-wide programme was initiated in 1993, only 21 per cent of the schools had implemented all three recommendations by 1998 (2003: 64). This indicates that, even when there is strong policy support and institutional resources allocated for anti-homophobia programmes, the educators who are responsible for implementing it display great resistance. In the next section, I discuss fourteen non-peer-reviewed empirical studies and explore how their findings are important to consider when constructing our understanding of bullying and harassment.

Research reports

'Hostile hallways' (Harris and Associates 1993) was the earliest published report to document incidents of homophobic harassment in schools and their impact on the students targeted. Harris and Associates conducted this groundbreaking study for the AAUW, and it aimed to understand the prevalence of sexual harassment in schools; it included a question that asked if participants had ever been called 'gay' or 'lesbian' at school, and became the first quantitative data available on the prevalence of this problem. What is interesting about this study is that it was followed up eight years later (Harris Interactive 2001); the researchers found that the one form of harassment that had increased since the previous study was calling another student 'gay' or 'lesbian'. Boys reported that this happened twice as often and girls three times as often as a decade earlier, whereas most other forms of harassment had remained constant or decreased (ibid.: 21). This study also showed that harassment was occurring in public spaces in the presence of adults. The three most common sites where harassment was reported were: the hallway (64 per cent), classroom (56 per cent), and gym or playing field or pool area (43 per cent); these figures contradict many bullying studies, which indicate that bullying happens where there is minimal adult supervision. The study also shows that forms of sexual harassment may be more public and widely accepted at schools.

In 1995, the Safe Schools Coalition of Washington, USA (Reis 1995) published the first study in which the issue of homophobia in schools was central. This was important work, as it provided data for advocates who were working to improve the learning environment for gay, lesbian, bisexual and transgender youths. In this study, Beth Reis documented fifty different incidents of anti-gay harassment, ranging from name-calling to beatings and rape (ibid.: 15). Her work also confirmed several of the findings from the AAUW study, including: harassment is usually a public event; most harassers are fellow students; most harassers are male; and in most cases, adults do not take appropriate action against the offender(s) (ibid.: 20). These studies show that the adults responsible for ensuring that students have a safe learning environment consistently fall far short of their duties, and we need to better understand why this happens.

Following Reis's groundbreaking study, several similar reports were issued four years later: GLSEN's first National School Climate Survey (1999) as well as two more studies from the Safe Schools Coalition of Washington: a meta-analysis of eight population-based studies representing the experiences of 83,000 youths (Reis and Saewyc 1999); and a follow-up study on incidents at Washington schools (Reis 1999). These three studies added to the understanding of the negative impact of homophobic harassment in schools. The meta-analysis of several large-scale, population-based studies highlighted the fact that gay, lesbian and bisexual (GLB) students were at higher risk for several forms of dangerous behaviour compared to their heterosexual peers. GLB youths were over four times more likely to have attempted suicide, were three times more likely to have been injured or threatened with a weapon at school, and were three times more likely to miss school because of feeling unsafe (Reis and Saewyc 1999: 9). Reis's follow-up study (1999) provided greater detail by conducting in-depth interviews and including a larger number of participants than the original study. Her report explored how adults' inaction impacted targeted students. She explains:

These cases of apparent neglect by adults were very troubling to respondents. They spoke about months of verbal violence and public humiliation by peers that preceded a young person's resorting to fists or dropping out of school, or, in one instance, committing suicide. In each instance, adults had multiple opportunities to put a stop to the very public abuse of a child or teen and failed to do so. (ibid.: 20)

GLSEN's first study also highlighted the problem of adults failing to intervene effectively. The organisation has conducted follow-up studies every two years (GLSEN 2001; Kosciw 2004; Kosciw and Diaz 2006; Kosciw, Diaz and Gretytak 2008), and the most recent report showed that 84 per cent of GLBT students report being verbally harassed at school, and 52 per cent were cyberbullied (Kosciw, Greytak, Diaz and Bartkiewicz 2010). Sadly, 62.4 per cent of students who were harassed or assaulted at school did not report the incident to school staff, believing that little or no action would be taken, or that the situation would become worse if reported. This lack of intervention by educators in incidents of verbal harassment is a recurring theme in the studies on sexual and homophobic harassment. In order to reduce the incidence of bullying and harassment at school, the problem of ignoring – and therefore, accepting – certain forms of aggression needs to be addressed.

Human Rights Watch published a study, 'Hatred in the hallways: violence and discrimination against lesbian, gay, bisexual, and transgender students in U.S. schools' (Bochenek and Brown 2001), which critiqued American schools and the Federal government for violating its obligations to provide protection from discrimination according to international law. This national, qualitative study exposed the prevalence of the problem in American schools, and it was the first to explicitly address the related issue of students targeted for gender non-conforming behaviour. The authors assert that:

It quickly became obvious from our research that the abuse of lesbian, gay, bisexual, and transgender youth is predicated on the belief that girls and boys must strictly adhere to rigid rules of conduct, dress, and appearances based on their sex. For boys, that means they must be athletic, strong, sexist, and hide their emotions. For girls, that means they must be attentive to and flirtatious with boys and must accept a subordinate status to boys. Regardless of their sexual orientation or gender identity, youth who violate these rules are punished by their peers and too often by adults. (ibid.: 49)

This report also noted the repetitive 'official inaction' by teachers and administrators (ibid.: 81). Participants repeatedly told stories about teachers and administrators ignoring their reports of harassment and being blamed for bringing it on themselves. Students also reported harassment and anti-gay jokes from the same adults (ibid.: 83).

With the exception of the AAUW studies (Harris and Associates 1993; Harris Interactive 2001) and the Oregon Safe Schools Meta-Analysis of youth studies (Reis and Saewyc 1999), many of these early studies focused primarily on youths who identified as gay, lesbian or bisexual, and thus missed the experiences of students who did not identify as such; this includes youths who were 'closeted', those questioning their sexual orientation, and transgender and heterosexual youths. In the past few years, studies with a more diverse pool of participants have emerged. In 2002, the National Mental Health Association of the US conducted a phone survey with 760 randomly selected youths between the ages of 12–17 to determine their experience with and opinions about anti-gay bullying in their schools. The organisation found that if a student was identified as 'gay', he/she was perceived to be twice as vulnerable to bullying as students who were 'fat' or 'dress differently', and were more than three times more likely to be targeted than students with disabilities or for one's racial identity (NMHA 2002: 2).

Another study conducted by the California Safe Schools Coalition (2004) had a large random sample of students (n=230,000); it was innovative because of its attention to issues of homophobia and gender nonconformity, as well as its exploration of how teacher responses affect students' experiences at school. This report supported the findings of earlier studies about the prevalence and negative impact of sexual and homophobic harassment in schools, and it added to them by exploring the related pervasiveness and impact on students who are targeted for being 'not as masculine as other boys' or 'not as feminine as other girls'. With regard to teacher response, students reported that teachers or staff were 'unlikely to intervene' to stop bias-motivated comments, particularly those related to sexual orientation and gender presentation (ibid.: 14). The most encouraging finding from this study is the fact that, when students see teachers putting a stop to negative comments and slurs related to sexual orientation, the students report less name-calling and stronger feelings of school safety (ibid.: 19). These findings are important, as they demonstrate the impact that effective intervention can have on the experiences of students at school.

In 2005, Harris Interactive conducted a study for GLSEN, 'From teasing to torment: school climate in America', which used a nationally representative sample of students and teachers to explore their experiences with and attitudes towards school harassment. This study found that LGBT students are three times as likely as non-LGBT students to not feel safe at school (22 per cent versus 7 per cent), and that public-school students were less likely to feel very safe at their schools than private- or parochial-school students (44 per cent versus 81 per cent) (GLSEN 2006: 8). This was also the first study to ask teachers about the reasons they do not intervene. The top three reasons were: unable to reach/ identify student(s) (14 per cent); remarks made in joking manner/no intention to hurt (9 per cent); and another teacher/administrator had already intervened (9 per cent) (ibid.: 39).

This study also examined the intersecting variables of race/ethnicity, gender, sexual orientation and class, and how these factors impacted students' perceptions and experiences at school. Based on students' response to the question, 'How often are students bullied, called names, or harassed for the following reasons?', the frequency of such harassment was ranked in the following order: (1) the way they look or body size (39 per cent); (2) people think they are gay, lesbian or bisexual (33 per cent); (3) how masculine or feminine they are (28 per cent); (4) their ability at school (16 per cent); (5) their race/ethnicity (14 per cent); (6) their family does not have a lot of money (13 per cent); and (7) their religion (8 per cent). When broken down by race/ethnicity, the data show that black and Latino students were more likely to report that harassment occurs 'very often/often' on all measures except religion. When broken down by sexual orientation, GLBT-identified students were more likely to report that harassment occurs 'very often/often' in each category (ibid.: 28). These data are important, as they indicate that members of marginalised groups are more likely to report experiencing multiple forms of harassment – and at higher levels than other students.

Cyberbullying

A newer area of investigation is online aggression. Michele L. Ybarra and Kimberly J. Mitchell published one of the earliest studies on this issue in 2004; their work reported the outcomes of the first Youth Internet Safety Survey (YISS), which was conducted in 1999–2000. In this study, only 19 per cent of 1,500 adolescents surveyed were regular Internet users. Of these, only 12 per cent were aggressors, and 3 per cent–4 per cent had been targeted for some form of online aggression. More studies that examined this phenomenon began to emerge in 2006. In the GLSEN National School Climate Survey, researchers used the now-recognisable term *cyberbullying*, which they defined as 'using an electronic medium, such as emails or text messages, to threaten or harm others' (Kosciw and Diaz 2006: 27). According to their research, 41 per cent of LGBT students had experienced this type of harassment over the previous year. This was four times higher than the national average of 9 per cent, as reported in the second YISS conducted in 2005 (Wolak, Mitchell and Finkelhor 2006: 10). This second YISS report placed a strong emphasis on the sexualised element of much online behaviour including: solicitations; unwanted exposure to sexual material; posting of personal information; and pictures. The researchers found that girls were targeted twice as often as boys for sexual solicitations, but more boys were exposed to unwanted sexual material than girls. They also found that girls experienced higher rates of online harassment (58 per cent versus 42 per cent), and reported much higher rates of 'distressing incidents' online (68 per cent versus 32 per cent). This area of bullying research is highly relevant to issues of gendered harassment; Shaheen Shariff and Rachel Gouin (2006) argue that cyberspace is becoming an increasingly hostile environment – particularly for young women, who tend to be targets for sexual harassment online.

Other studies have paid no attention to issues of sexual and homophobic harassment online or merely broke down their data by gender. For example, Qing Li's study (2006) on cyberbullying at lower-secondary schools (grades 7–9[5]) reported that one in four students had been cyber-bullied; in terms of gender differences, males were more likely to be cyberbullies than females, and female targets were more likely to notify adults. Several other studies on cyberbullying began to establish data on the prevalence and characteristics of this behaviour, but repeated many of the same silences and omissions noted with regard to research on tradi-tional bullying (Hinduja and Patchin 2008; Kowalski and Limber 2007; Patchin and Hinduja 2006; Williams and Guerra 2007; Wolak, Mitchell and Finkelhor 2007; Ybarra, Diener-West and Leaf 2007). However, as with traditional bullying, the studies by GLSEN (2006) and others (Ybarra, Espelage and Mitchell 2007) have shown that many forms of cyberbullying are also cyber-harassment: they are biased and create a hostile environment for anyone exposed to the racist, sexist, homophobic or transphobic content of the posts. This related field of study is an important one for educators and researchers to consider as youths' inter-actions spill out of the schoolyard and into cyberspace.

The new wave: 2007 to now

There has been a significant shift in bullying and harassment research since 2007. It is difficult to determine what influenced this shift, but several articles published in peer-reviewed academic journals at that time began to explicitly and more consistently discuss bullying, sexual harassment, homo-phobia and even transphobia. This new wave of research includes many studies by Dorothy Espelage and V. Paul Poteat, which have helped to provide much-needed data about the intersections of bullying, sexual harass-ment, homophobia and transphobia; the new research also includes studies that have examined the phenomena using quantitative, qualitative and mixed methods. The studies can be generally categorised into three groups: youth studies, professionals' perspectives and transgender experiences.

Youth studies

Many of the youth studies have examined in closer detail the harms related to various forms of bullying, sexual harassment and homophobia. These researchers examined issues such as the association between bullying, sexual harassment, homophobia and other harms, including: negative peer-group climate (Poteat 2008); dating violence (Espelage and Holt 2007); and psychological and social distress amongst lower- and upper-secondary

---

[5] This corresponds to years 7–9 in British schools.

school students (Poteat and Espelage 2007). Joseph G. Kosciw, Emily A. Greytak and Elizabeth M. Diaz (2009) described the demographic and ecological factors that can contribute to a hostile climate for LGBT youths, and they reported that LGBT youths in rural communities and communities with adults who are less well-educated may face particularly hostile school climates. A study by V. Paul Poteat and Ian Rivers (2010) explored the use of homophobic language in bullying, and found that the use of anti-gay epithets was significantly associated with students in the primary bully role as well as the 'reinforcer' and 'assisting' roles.

In addition to the negative impact associated with homophobia at school, researchers also began exploring some of the protective factors that may provide a buffer from these hostile environments. They also focused more attention on some under-researched groups, including bisexual youths and youths questioning their sexual orientation. For example, Dorothy Espelage, Steven Aragon, Michelle Birkett and Brian W. Koenig (2008) reported that youths questioning their sexual orientation were at greater risk than LGB youths in several categories, including: teasing, drug use, depression and suicidal thoughts. However, the researchers also indicated that parental support and an inclusive school climate tend to act as protective factors against depression and drug abuse. Similarly, in a 2011 study published in the American journal *Pediatrics*, Mark L. Hatzenbuehler reported that LGB youths had been significantly more likely to attempt suicide over the previous twelve months compared with heterosexuals (21.5 per cent versus 4.2 per cent); however, amongst LGB youths, the risk of attempting suicide was 20 per cent greater in unsupportive environments. Therefore, youths who were in a more supportive[6] social environment also had a lower risk of attempting suicide. Joseph P. Robinson and Dorothy Espelage also reported on the particular risks to students at lower-secondary schools (2011), especially bisexual youths. They asserted that the majority of LGBTQ-identified youths are *not* at risk for suicide, peer victimisation and school absences; however, compared with straight-identified youth, 'an unusually large per centage of LGBTQ-identified youth are at elevated risk' (ibid.: 326).

To address the gaps and silences that were pointed out in the earlier sections of this chapter, several studies began to integrate the divergent fields of research. For example, James E. Gruber and Susan Fineran published two articles that examined bullying and sexual harassment

[6] Supportive factors included: having a gay–straight alliance; school policies that protect LGB students; and a higher presence of LGB couples in their county (Hatzenbuehler 2011).

together. Their studies were able to carefully examine the incidence and impact of bullying and sexual harassment (including sexual-orientation harassment) on girls' health (2007) and on both boys and girls (2008). What they found was that secondary-school girls experienced more bullying and sexual harassment as well as poorer health outcomes than their counterparts at lower-secondary school, but the impact of these experiences was less severe amongst secondary-school students. Gruber and Fineran theorise that the difference in outcomes may be the result of better support systems and coping mechanisms amongst secondary-school girls, or it could be due to some of the challenging developmental changes that occur during the lower-secondary school years (2007). In their second study, the authors reported that girls were bullied or harassed just as frequently as boys, and that sexual minorities experienced higher levels of both. They found that sexual harassment had more adverse effects on more health outcomes than bullying, and these effects were more prevalent amongst girls and sexual minorities (2008).

My theoretical article, 'A feminist reframing of bullying and harassment: transforming schools through critical pedagogy' (2008a), was intended to challenge the current dominant bullying discourses; it advocated for a more integrated and critical approach to the problem, which allowed issues of gender, sexual orientation, race, ethnicity and disability to be brought into the foreground with regard to how schools approach the issue. It also introduced the term *gendered harassment* to show how many forms of bullying – as well as sexual, homophobic and transphobic harassment – are often linked to the public performance and policing of heteronormative expectations for gender roles. In 2008, Rosalyn Shute, Larry Owens and Phillip Slee also set out to address some of the gaps between bullying and harassment studies. They built upon Neil Duncan's concept of *sexual bullying* (1999) to frame their study, 'Everyday victimization of adolescent girls by boys: sexual harassment, bullying or aggression?' In their research, they found that boys report less boy–girl aggression than girls and teachers, and that the boys often said they were 'only joking' and believed that the girls took their behaviour too seriously. Duncan also published a study with Owens in 2011 that validated his aforementioned work (Duncan 2004) on popularity in girls' friendships and the primacy of heterosexual desirability in peer hierarchies.

Another indicator of the increased attention to explicitly including issues of sexual harassment and homophobia in bullying research was the publication of a comprehensive literature review of bullying research and interventions in the journal *Educational Researcher*; this explicitly included a section on LGBT-related bullying and harassment (Swearer, Espelage et al. 2010). The social–ecological framework discussed in this article presents a more holistic approach to understanding the related problems of bullying, peer victimisation and various forms of harassment, which in turn has the potential to lead to more integrated and effective solutions. The next group of studies to integrate these issues placed greater focus on teachers' and professionals' response to problems.

Professionals' perspectives

There is a limited amount of research on how teachers perceive and respond to bullying and harassment, and even less that addresses issues of gender and sexuality in particular. The first article on this topic explored teachers' perceptions of and responses to bullying and gendered harassment[7] at secondary schools (Meyer 2008b). In this study, which was based on in-depth interviews with secondary-school teachers, I found that a complex interaction of internal and external influences created a context that prevented teachers from consistently and effectively intervening in most forms of gendered harassment. A second study conducted by GLSEN reported the results of the first year of a professional-development programme on LGBT issues with teachers at New York City schools (Greytak and Kosciw 2010). In this article, the authors report that the training programme was 'an effective means for developing the competency of educators to address bias-based bullying and harassment, and to create safer school environments for LGBTQ students' (ibid.: v). In order for this training to have maximum influence, they recommend that more educators participate in the training, and that ongoing support and reinforcement of the ideas and messages presented in the programme are provided. The third area of research that emerged post-2007 includes studies that specifically address the topic of transphobia by exploring the challenges and needs of transgender students in schools in relation to bullying and harassment.

Transgender experiences

Two reports by advocacy organisations in the US (GLSEN) and Canada (Egale) specifically addressed the phenomenon of transphobia and its relation to sexual harassment, bullying and homophobia in schools. Both of these studies reported that transgender students experienced even higher rates of victimisation and more severe forms of harassment than straight, gay, lesbian or bisexual students (Greytak, Kosciw and Diaz

[7] This term includes sexual harassment, homophobic harassment and harassment for gender non-conformity.

2009; Taylor et al. 2011). Jennifer K. McGuire, Charles R. Anderson, Russell B. Toomey and Stephen T. Russell (2010) also published a study, 'School climate for transgender youth: a mixed method investigation of student experiences and school response'. In this article, the researchers report that the harassment of transgender students was pervasive, which had a negative impact on these students' feelings of safety at school. However, they noted that when schools took clear action to reduce harassment, these students reported having stronger connections to school staff, which in turn improved their feelings of school safety. Utilising data collected from one primary school that was in the process of supporting a student in her social transition from male to female (Luecke 2011), a fourth study published in *The Journal of LGBT Youth* specifically addressed how best to support transgender youths. Although this was not explicitly a bullying or harassment study, it contains a focused discussion about safety issues, educating peers about bullying and other ways to create safe and inclusive school contexts. This body of newer research offers important social analyses of these behaviours, and it can be instructive as more inclusive anti-bullying and school-violence prevention research, policies and programmes emerge. It is encouraging to see greater inclusiveness with regard to gender and sexual orientation in these recent studies, but there is still a significant gap in research on the experiences of and ways to better support transgender and gender nonconforming youths; this omission needs to be addressed.

Conclusion

There has been a significant amount of research done in relation to the issue of bullying, but less with regard to gendered, sexual, homophobic and transphobic bullying and harassment in schools. The bulk of bullying and harassment studies have been informed by the psychological tradition of looking at and measuring individual behaviours and experiences; thus, they do not attend to the social contexts in which they occur. The failure to consider work done by scholars in parallel fields has resulted in studies that do not fully apply or build upon the findings of earlier research. The majority of bullying and harassment studies have focused on either quantifying or qualifying the problem from students' perspectives, which has been an important first step in bringing attention to this problem in schools. However, these studies miss an important aspect of life at school when they fail to consider the impact that race, ethnicity, disability, class, gender identity and expression, sex and sexual orientation have on the power dynamics present in relationships. Although a few of these studies explore how boys and girls bully differently, these studies overwhelmingly ignore the larger influence of hetero-normativity, gender identity and expression and sexuality on students' lives, as well as how students exercise social power within their school communities and peer relationships.

On the other hand, although many of these harassment studies are framed with a feminist lens and focus on power dynamics organised along gender lines, most are constructed along the male–female binary of the heterosexual matrix. The inability of these studies to acknowledge or even mention acts of homophobic and transphobic harassment or the influence of race and ethnicity on these behaviours is disheartening. It also highlights what could and could not be discussed in research circles during the 1990s when much of this work was being done. This points to the importance of addressing blind spots in the knowledge generated by research in general – and bullying research in particular – as well as the value gained from combining results from various modes of inquiry and schools of thought.

The third wave of research related to gendered hierarchies and harassment in schools – i.e. studies on homophobia – did not emerge in academic journals until quite recently. The studies that clearly explore issues of gender, sexuality and power in schools have primarily been conducted by independent advocacy groups, such as Human Rights Watch, the AAUW, the California Safe Schools Coalition and GLSEN – all of which strive to make their findings widely accessible in a timely manner. Their reports have documented the problem over time and have provided a foundation for more recent studies on bullying and harassment in schools. The post-2007 wave of research has begun to synthesise these three related fields of study, and it offers valuable data and recommendations for schools that are working to create comprehensive policies and educational programmes to reduce all forms of bullying and harassment.

New directions

There needs to be additional research that explores how teachers and administrators perceive and respond to acts of homophobia, sexism and transphobia. Media coverage of these issues has surged in North America since autumn 2010, when there was a peak in publicised suicides by young men who had been subjected to homophobic harassment. The Canadian province of Quebec launched a campaign against homophobia and is providing 7 million dollars[8] of funding to community groups to work with schools and groups against homophobia; the province of Ontario launched a sex-education curriculum and mandate to allow Gay–Straight Alliances in

---

[8] At the time of writing, this is equivalent to 5.33 million Euro.

all public schools to address issues of student safety and inclusion. The US state of California tightened its anti-bullying laws to require an update of policies and procedures to ensure a proper response to all forms of bullying, particularly forms of biased harassment; it also requires inclusion of LGBT people in the social-sciences curriculum. These initiatives are exciting, encouraging and important; however, more research is needed to understand what is effective about these initiatives, and how they may impact the actual experience of students in schools.

Researchers should more actively include the voices of students when framing their questions and designing their methodologies in order to be able to understand the language, peer culture and social dynamics of which adults are often unaware. This is a field of study that is ripe for Participant/Social Action Research that could examine how to shift the culture of a school, and empower its current community members to be a part of a lasting process of change. We also need to work more across disciplines – such as social work, counselling, psychology, education, sociology, law, gender and sexuality studies and political science – to create a more holistic view of what happens in K–12 schools, teacher-education programmes and communities so that education and intervention programmes are more nuanced and linked to the specific social contexts of each region and school community.

The fields of teacher education, school counselling and school leadership also need more attention. There has been limited investigation into how teachers, counsellors and administrators are trained to understand and address cases of bullying and harassment. We need more information to understand how education professionals are currently being prepared to handle these realities in the classroom, and to what extent they are learning how to:

(1) become leaders and advocates for social justice in their school communities;
(2) address bullying and harassment in systemic and culturally relevant ways;
(3) effectively discuss issues of gender and sexual diversity in inclusive and age-appropriate ways.

As noted earlier, more attention should be paid to research on gender non-conforming and transgender youths,[9] a population that is currently very vulnerable and under-served in schools. We need to expand our understandings of gender and how – in the case of these students – the institution is often as responsible as the peer group for a great deal of

---

[9] Other terms used to describe this population include gender atypical, gender creative, gender fluid, gender independent and genderqueer.

hostility and safety concerns. Families need more data from the research community to leverage support for their children, and to make schools more accessible and supportive of gender diversity – starting in kindergarten. Research is needed on best practices, professional-development models, case studies and ethnographies of families and institutions that have navigated this process in healthy and inclusive ways.

In addition, further studies are needed to investigate overlapping forms of oppression – including racism, sexism, ableism, homophobia and transphobia – and to provide information and support for educators working to eradicate all forms of violence and harassment in schools. It is important to understand the genealogy of the fields of bullying and harassment; the deep roots of these research areas – combined with the significant gaps between what we know from new research, and what is actually happening at schools – work to perpetuate the silences and omissions that have been sustained through three decades of research. Many parents and teachers ask me why their current school policies and intervention programmes are not working or do not explicitly address issues of sexual harassment, homophobia and transphobia. With this chapter, I hope to help explain the reason for this problem. By recognising how this field has developed and then working to share new knowledge with education professionals, we can more effectively fill these gaps and revise programmes to improve the experiences for all students in schools. I am encouraged by the new directions that bullying and harassment research is taking, and optimistic that the results of these studies will build upon the work of previous researchers with a view to challenge and contribute to the ongoing conversation about how to make schools safer and more equitable for all students.

10 Sanctions against bullying and disruptions at school

Helle Rabøl Hansen

A young couple breaks up. They are both around 15 years of age, but in different classes at the same school. After their break-up, the boy texts a photo of his half-naked, now ex-girlfriend to a group of friends at school. It triggers a huge disruption. The photographed girl is very unhappy; her father is furious and complains to the school. Schoolmates participate indirectly in different ways. School officials immediately step in. Two girls, who were particularly active in texting the photo, are banned from spending time together. Certain students are sent home to contemplate their actions, and all parties involved are called to a meeting in the principal's office, where the police are also present. The intervening teachers believe their efforts have been productive: the turmoil quickly subsides, the students resume normal school activities and daily life continues as it was before the incident.

A narrative about how this incident with the texted photo was subsequently handled circulates around the teachers' staff room as a successful 'war story' (Orr 1996). As an example of consequences, the case is brought up in the staff's group debates and discussions about interventions against bullying. But was this incident actually a case of bullying? The teachers who were directly involved are in doubt. Nevertheless, the story continues to be used as an example of a bullying intervention that succeeded.

The incident with a texted photo of a girl's bare breasts illustrates a recognisable course of events. The pattern is that sanctions that were originally intended as punishment for bullying are being used by teachers to handle a variety of disruptions that threaten the school's demand for peace and order. This chapter discusses, from a teacher's perspective, why this extension of sanction strategies occurs, and how perceptions of bullying are connected with punishment and disruptions within school culture. My starting point is school life and teacher life at a regular primary and secondary public school[1] in a Danish suburb. The Oat School is where the incident with the texted photo occurred. I pursued two empirical paths into the school: firstly, I conducted a document analysis of the school's action plan to curb bullying; secondly, I followed 8 teachers during some

---

[1] In Denmark, nearly 85 per cent of all schoolchildren attend public schools.

of their work at the school. My underlying premise is not that the action plan and practice are intertwined in a direct cause-and-effect relationship, but rather, that they constitute a versatile text–context relationship. Consequently, I analysed the action plan and the existing practice separately, but with attention to both the divergence and connections between the two types of data.[2]

Bullying, disruptions and noise

To enforce sanctions against acts of bullying is not an uncommon strategy in schools. In 2008, the Danish Parliament discussed legislation that would have expanded the powers of school administrators to give detentions or suspensions, expel students or organise emergency classes for students who bully other students (Antorini 2008). In the media debate about the issue, there has regularly been a call for consequences in the form of various types of sanctions. Sometimes the discussion was prompted by cases where targets of bullying had left a school or workplace. One could say that parts of the debate were characterised by the notion 'punish the bully – not the victim'.

However, there is more at stake than student-related bullying in the case of the girl's bare breasts at the Oat School. Here, an extra dimension was added; specifically, disorder and noise during teaching. Although the sanction rationale comes from perceptions about how to handle bullying, bullying as an action has in fact become less central. This chapter looks at each stage in the process of mixed issues, where different factors cross and merge into each other. Such factors are, for instance, when acts of bullying are perceived to be a problem inherent in a child; when teaching is challenged; and when teachers' perceptions of bullying clash with students' experiences of bullying.

The Oat School is apparently not a unique example of how sanction strategies are used to achieve order. This juxtaposition of various problems is also reflected in the following quotation from an article on the website of the Danish Ministry of Children and Education. The article is one of several with specific advice to schools about bullying intervention:

We discovered that acts of bullying are not a problem in our sixth-grade class.[3] However, it was very problematic for teaching if certain students made a lot of noise. We therefore decided to make use of a so-called 'shadow timetable', which means we always have the ninth-grade[4] timetables nearby, and if someone is noisy

---

[2] Analyses based on this empirical material were also published in Hansen (2009, 2010, 2011a and b).
[3] This corresponds to seventh grade/year in American or British schools.
[4] This corresponds to tenth grade/year in American or British schools.

during class, we put them in one of the ninth-grade classes. No one thinks it is funny to be 'on display' among older students, and this type of sanction has only been used a few times. There is already less noise in [one of the sixth-grade classes], and the students' well-being has improved. (Danish Ministry of Children and Education 2007)

'Shadow timetable'[5] is the name of a sanction originally designed to punish a bully who does not listen to reproach. But in this case, a student is punished by being sent out of class to sit in another class. In the above example, the sanction is not used to punish acts of bullying but rather, noisy and disruptive actions. The positive result of using the sanction is emphasised by the teachers, as they subsequently notice less noise and disorder in the class and also that 'the student's well-being has improved'. The effect of the punishment is the discomfort of sitting in a strange class with older students. This article excerpt figures into a context in which teachers are advised about interventions that target bullying, despite the lack of an actual bullying problem in the above example.

Action plans with a bullying ontology

Legislation about the educational environment was passed in Denmark in 2001, which increased schools' focus on the 'psychological teaching environment'. In the legislation's notes, emphasis was placed on an obligation to 'try to prevent acts of bullying and effectively intervene if bullying does occur' (Danish Ministry of Children and Education 2000/1; note to legislation LSF 40). Some municipalities followed up by implementing a local provision that obliges schools to implement action plans. In 2002, the Oat School prepared an action plan about bullying; it was being revised during the time I conducted fieldwork at the school, and it is thus the focus of my analysis.

To study action plans about bullying – understood as a set representation of decisions to discourage bullying amongst students – is important for several reasons: firstly, current action plans about bullying are local, political documents that, at the level of practice, represent and reflect the greater political attention given to bullying in recent years. In other words, most schools have decided to comply with legislators and organisations concerned with children's legal rights (e.g. the National Council for Children in Denmark) to develop local bullying policies. Many schools have uploaded their action plans to their websites, and the documents are part of a 'labelling' of schools to the surrounding world.

---

[5] This sanction is described in Olweus (2000), for instance.

Secondly – and as a consequence of the first reason – schools in Denmark are increasingly implementing action plans about bullying or for students' well-being and contentment (Danish Ministry of Children and Education 2008). Thus, to have a written policy about bullying is common in many schools today. The political focal point for children's rights organisations has primarily been to ensure that there is a written bullying policy at the schools, so the task today focuses on which content to include.

Thirdly, action plans are typically documents with an implicit bullying ontology. Whether they adhere to a certain view of the nature of bullying is not necessarily reflected in the text, nor is it expected from the writer. Nevertheless, the action plans do often adhere to a specific understanding of the nature of bullying. The question is whether this understanding is also reflected in practice, and whether it affects the type of intervention strategies teachers select and use.

'We', 'everybody' and 'well-being'

The opening sentence and the following manifesto establish the only 'we' in the action plan at the Oat School. It is not a trivial 'we', as it represents communicatively the authors of the document. This 'we' signals some sort of community behind the document. Yet since the author and 'we' may not always be convergent, let us take a closer look at the cast of characters in the opening remark of the action plan:

Excerpt from action plan:
We do not accept bullying at the Oat School.
The parties of the school, parents, teachers and students commit to taking bullying seriously. Everybody must work towards the social well-being of the class.
The aim is to achieve a school free from bullying where everybody's sense of security in everyday life is cherished.

'We' could be the administrators or the school as such. Those being addressed in the document do not constitute a 'we', but rather, an 'everybody' that is comprised of the parties of the school, students, teachers and parents. 'Everybody' denotes those who take on certain tasks (which I elaborate on later) by using phrases such as 'teachers must protect victims of bullying', 'parents must pass on information' and 'students on the student council must comment on the action plan'.

In addition to the 'we' and 'everybody', there also seems to be a 'self' indirectly represented in the text, since 'everybody' must personally commit to undertaking the task. The political and legal obligations are not enough. The individual participants must take this matter 'seriously', which qualifies the task in the sense that this is an area where everyone is expected and required to relate reflectively to the task. In combination, 'we' and 'everybody' can also be understood as an 'us'; that is, all of us who take this 'seriously'. 'Us' can thus constitute the writers of the action plan as well as those being addressed in it, and this then raises the question as to whether some parties are *not* included in this 'us'.

Aside from the presentation of 'we' and 'everybody', it is interesting to note that this part of the text also introduces a certain positive term: 'well-being'. Well-being is constructed as the opposite of bullying, because it is understood as a condition that ensures security. In academic literature about bullying and anti-bullying political-campaign texts, a state of well-being is commonly presented as something that should exist instead of bullying. Well-being, in the form of security, constitutes a target towards which 'everybody' must work. I return to this point later in the chapter.

Individual features or group dynamics?

Within the anti-bullying movement in recent years, there have been discussions about where to place the emphasis in understanding the reasons for bullying. Are causal explanations for bullying found primarily within an individual or within group culture? Can this gap between an individual and the group be detected in the action plan's text? My first point of departure is the definition in the glossary of the document.

Excerpt from action plan:
Definition of bullying
Dan Olweus's definition is:
'A person is being bullied when he or she repeatedly, and over time, is subject to negative actions from one or more people.' (author's translation)
The word 'mobning' [the Danish word for bullying] originates from the English word 'mob', which means a large and disorderly crowd. The point here is that it refers to a group harassing an individual person. Bullying is thus not a conflict between equal parties.

Both the action plan's definition of bullying and the etymological definition of the Danish word for bullying, '*mobning*', make use of pluralities. From the definition in the action plan, it appears that acts of bullying are done by 'one or more people'. A plurality of individuals also emerges in the remaining text, such as the following quotes: 'The classes lack unity and a group feeling', 'friendship class agreements' and 'class rules'. These formulations suggest that bullying is considered a phenomenon that, to a certain degree, affects not only individuals but also groups. The rest of the document identifies two persons as the central actors in a bullying situation: the bullying victim and the bully.

The bullying victim is described in the section 'Signs of bullying'.

Excerpt from action plan:
Signs of bullying
Short-term reactions:
1. Truancy. Losing interest in going to school.
2. Aggression with no apparent reason.
3. Sadness.
4. Introversion.
5. Clinging to an adult. Refuses to go out during break time.
6. Poor school performance.
7. Nightmares and bedwetting.
8. Lacking desire to tell parents about school life.
9. A general lack of self-confidence.
10. Concentration problems.
11. Complaints of stomach-ache.
Long-term reactions:
1. Lack of or poor social integration.
2. Failing self-confidence and self-worth.
3. Difficulties bonding with others.
4. Blames oneself.
5. Depression.
6. Self-effacing behaviour.
7. Suicidal.

The signs of being bullied are listed as short-term and long-term reactions. The victim is portrayed as someone who demonstrates a number of negative psychological and physical reactions; for example, the child who clings to an adult during break time, performs poorly at school and may eventually exhibit suicidal behaviour. The two lists of reactions above are materialised as objective facts and, at first sight, they resemble the lists of symptoms we know from diagnostic discourses.

The profile of the bully is outlined in the section 'Preconditions for bullying'.

Excerpt from action plan:
Preconditions for bullying
1. A person must signal that he or she is an easy target for bullying.
2. Someone in class must have the background and aggressive nature that characterises a bully.
3. The bully must have allies; opportunists who encourage and support the bullying. (Although very strong and experienced bullies can act without support.)
4. The school has too few or unclear rules, has no clear profile or has not taken a stand on negative behaviour.
5. The efforts of the school are not preventive.
6. The social environment is not welcoming, either in class or at the school as such.
7. The class lacks unity or a group feeling.

8. The teachers overlook or ignore acts of bullying.
9. The parents are uncommitted.

Here, the bully is described as a person with an aggressive 'nature' and a 'background' that promotes this characteristic. Moreover, it is noted that a bully has allies, but can also act alone if he or she is 'strong and experienced'.

The first two points in the list of preconditions concern characteristics of bullies and victims of bullying. The text is formulated in the imperative: 'A person must signal that he or she is an easy target for bullying' and 'Someone in class must have the background and aggressive nature that characterises a bully.' The imperative mood continues throughout the list and gives an impression that the factual information expresses a social standard that will gain acceptance in classes with bullying problems.

The list of preconditions contains a duality into which bullying is simultaneously contextualised; e.g. 'the class lacks unity or a group feeling', and decontextualised as well as individualised; e.g. 'someone in class'. The text indicates that some moods are perceived as common whilst the important characteristics and reasons are ascribed to an individual. A school's cultural aspects – such as the class's solidarity, teachers' inaction and/or an unwelcoming social climate in the class – are not elaborated upon in detail throughout the document in the same way as the individual relations. Thus, as the action plan takes shape, the emphasis is gradually moved to the side of the individual. The overall presentation of the core of bullying underscores that it concerns a problematic relationship between two actors: a victim and a perpetrator.

The prevailing paradigm

A section about 'Preconditions for bullying' can also be found in other local action plans (Hansen 2011a; Henriksen and Hansen 2006). Clear parallels to corresponding outlines may be drawn in the book *Bullying – Prevention and Solutions* by Gunnar Höistad (1999), which belongs to the category of individualised understandings of bullying where the reason for bullying is described as a negative interaction between children with different qualities – either strong or weak. Dan Olweus, whose name is attached to the definition of bullying in the Oat School's action plan, is a central thinker in this perception of bullying. Olweus calls acts of bullying 'malicious behaviour' (Olweus 2004), and he explains the central role of the individuals involved in bullying as follows:

There is no doubt that the individual perspective is crucial when it comes to understanding the issue and mechanisms of bullying. To justify this thesis, I can briefly mention, for instance, that bullies and their victims basically represent very different personality types and behavioural patterns. (ibid.: 67; author's translation)

Olweus describes the bully as a person with positive self-confidence, aggressive behaviour and who is often very articulate: 'The class teacher must be aware that bullies come across as tough and confident. Moreover, they are clever at talking themselves out of difficult situations' (Olweus 2000: 79). This precise, defining and declaratory information about the phenomenon of bullying in the Oat School's action plan is taken from these personality-focused approaches.

Sanctions as interventions

When the reasons for bullying are linked to personality, this invites interventions that primarily target specific, designated individuals. The notion of 'readiness' has been given a specific section in the Oat School's action plan; it deals with interventions targeting the bully:

Excerpt from action plan:
Possible actions against the bully:
1) Talk to the bully and call attention to the school action plan and possible consequences:
   – The bully is isolated during certain breaks
   – The bully is called to a serious conversation with the school administrators
   – The bully must stay within eyesight of the teacher on playground duty for a certain number of breaks
   – The bully is deprived of a privilege of some kind
2) Parents are informed and called to a meeting.
3) BCW[6] is contacted. An action plan is produced; e.g., shadow timetable or daily contact.
4) Pedagogical and psychological counselling / social services department is contacted. The bullying may become a case for a psychologist/social worker.
5) Notification given to the police (the school, social services and police collaboration). The bully may have violated criminal law.
6) Transfer to the Child and Youth Psychiatry Center.

It should be noted that the list of possible actions against a bully focus solely on regulating his/her actions, rather than encouraging all parties to regain composure and reflect on their own participation, which was suggested in the opening manifesto of the action plan. This indicates an assumption that the bully is not included amongst the people who vow to adhere to the action plan. The student who bullies is thus not included in

---

[6] This is an abbreviation for the 'Behaviour, Contact and Well-being' team at the school.

the 'we' and 'everybody' established by the text, but instead he/she is excluded from the community that is expected to relate reflectively to its own participation in school life. Thus, the conception of the bully seems to be characterised by an assumption that he/she is different than the other actors at the school, in the sense that a bully's actions should be regulated. Moreover, the bully is not assumed to take bullying 'seriously' in the same way as those being addressed in the action plan.

If the bully is a person who, as the aforementioned quote by Olweus suggests, will behave 'confidently', 'aggressively' and be able to talk his/her way out of trouble, then the action plan appropriately suggests a range of counter-reactions in the section 'Possible actions against the bully'. In other words, the list of consequences may be seen as a step-wise increase in the use of sanctions; an acceleration of punishments where a subsequent and more radical step is taken if the previous step is ineffective. The descriptions in the bully profile and the list of gradually intensifying sanctions could be considered potential adversaries in a battle of power struggles. The school, armed with sanctions, appears as one opponent; and the bully, armed with confidence, appears as the other. In this interpretation, the intensifying punishment may be an attempt to re-establish a lost order, which implies that acts of bullying interfere with the school's objective to ensure well-being and security.

The escalating punishment in the list of sanctions begins with a reprimand ('conversation') and increases by various regulating measures, ending with being reported to social services and/or the police or being referred for psychiatric treatment. In the last stages, bullying has become a case for authorities other than the school, which indicates that the situation is being taken seriously, and that the 'we' from the opening text of the action plan has now expanded to include more parties. The proposed sanctions that the school may implement are those specified in the list; i.e. 'the bully is isolated during certain breaks' and 'the bully must stay within eyesight of the teacher on playground duty for a certain number of breaks'. In a 'conversation' with the bully, the school must inform him/her of the possible consequences. Thus, a conversation is the first step on the escalating list of sanctions.

The criminal and legal character of the action plan

The sanctions listed include measures that restrict the bully's freedom of movement; in that respect, the sanctions resemble the type of punishments used in adult criminal convictions, which also employ restrictions on personal freedom. Another element that resembles criminal law is the focus on guilt (*culpa*), and here the bully is seen as the party who inflicts guilt. The individualised perception of the bully that is implicit in the action plan helps to produce a notion of guilt-punishment that is directed towards the bully.

Here, bullying patterns amongst students are presented as a problem of criminalised deviation and, in this conception, the bully is positioned as someone who has, at a minimum, violated the rules (is regulated in 'conversation'), is semi-criminal (is regulated through restrictions on personal freedom), is fully criminal ('notification given to the police') or possibly ill ('transfer to the Child and Youth Psychiatry Centre').

The interest in presenting acts of bullying as a criminal problem and the bully as a criminal or sick person may be to win support for the escalation of sanctions and consequences. This logic of correlations in the action plan's argument structure may also reflect the expected logical progression of interventions, which run in almost consecutive steps.

But the law is at play at more levels in the action plan than in aspects of criminal justice. We also see a particular and not insignificant use of warrant, which strengthens the argument for punishment as a solution to bullying problems. Here, warrant signifies validity or legality. To understand how the warrant comes into play in the argument, I examine what the argument seeks to justify by asking what is deemed valid. For that purpose, I utilise philosopher Stephen Toulmin's basic model of argumentation. The starting point is that almost any argument consists of three elements: claim, grounds and warrant (Toulmin 1974/1994), even though each of the elements is not always explicitly expressed. The *claim* is the conclusion or position for which the sender seeks support, and which is argued for by means of the two other elements of the basic model. *Grounds*, or data, is the information the sender presents to bolster the claim. *Warrant* connects the evidence to the claim and authorises that the claim is accepted on the grounds of the evidence. In practical reasoning, the warrant typically constitutes a general viewpoint, and thus in principle it is not fully comparable with legal provision, which refers to, e.g. a specific written section of legislation. In Toulmin's argumentation model, however, warrant is understood in an everyday sense as something that is deemed valid and thereby correct, which is also called *doxa* by rhetoricians (Andersen 1995). In a sense, the bullying action plan contains a warrant with both legal content and an everyday practical meaning. In order to interpret the impact of the warrant on the argument within the action plan, it is necessary to examine more closely how the warrant connects to the claim and evidence.

My starting point is the claim that introduces the document and for which support is sought; i.e. 'a school free from bullying is achieved if all parties of the school commit to taking bullying seriously'. The focal point of the support is a commitment and an expectation that this commitment will be taken seriously. Another consistent and central claim in the action plan is that the bully is identified as the key figure in the problem.

The third element in Toulmin's basic model of argumentation, the warrant, is comprehensively developed and explicitly emphasised in the action plan. As a result, the warrant appears not only indirectly, which is often the case in everyday, practical argumentation.

Based on Toulmin's basic model, the warrant can be identified at two different levels in the action plan. The implicit warrant lies in the undertone and *doxa* of the entire text, which is represented by the assumption that bullying equals dissatisfaction for the victim (who suffers) and the bully (who is criminal). Because psychological and physical abuse is damaging to the victim, we must take bullying seriously. Here, the warrant functions as the link between information about the content of bullying, and the claim that the parties of the school must undertake anti-bullying tasks. At the explicit level, the legal provision is represented in the action plan through quotations from the preamble of the legislation regarding primary and secondary education. Here, the core phrase is: 'School efforts must therefore be characterised by intellectual liberty, equality and democracy':

Excerpt from action plan:
Danish Act on Primary and Secondary Education:
§1, item 2. The Danish primary and secondary schools must develop working methods and provide a framework for experience, concentration and enterprise, so students develop cognition, imagination and confidence in their own ability and background to take a stand and act.

Item 3, points 2 and 3. The Danish primary and secondary schools must prepare students for participation, co-responsibility, rights and duties in a society of freedom and democracy. The schools' efforts must therefore be characterised by intellectual liberty, equality and democracy.

The quotations from the Act stand without comment in the Oat School's action plan, although we must assume that bullying is considered incompatible with the spirit of the Danish Act on Primary and Secondary Education. It is also stressed that we are dealing with an area of authority where the law prevails, due to phrases in the action plan such as: 'Bullying may become a case for a psychologist/counsellor' and 'Notification to the police'.

The two levels of warrant in the document – the implicit and the explicit – make the warrant of the argumentation more significant. The weight of the warrant is combined with the emphasis on regulatory authorities, which gives the action plan a legislative character. The Oat School's action plan is a document with a high degree of legal and regulatory weight. The rules thus seem to be in balance. Support may not only be won through conviction but also through obligation. As a result, the legal content reinforces the expectation that those addressed in the document will do their tasks in earnest.

Various authority strategies at play

The action plan gains authority in various ways. It draws upon what might be called a lexical and diagnostic authority and, as a whole, it gives the impression of a text that includes research and non-fiction qualities by virtue of its quotations that contain definitions of bullying, lists of bullying reactions and preconditions of bullying. Moreover, it draws on legal authorities – partially by means of the direct legal provisions, and partially by imitating the model of a criminal case.

Both the research-like and legislation-based sections in the action plan as such draw upon the law and legality. The existence of bullies at a school is constructed as a social regularity (i.e. as a social rule that applies), and the anti-bullying effort is disseminated as a legal entitlement (i.e. as rules implemented by law). The two types of law, as rules in force, intertwine and imbue the action plan with a certain rationality that is not open for discussion amongst the people who comprise the 'we'.

Pro-punishment and contra-punishment

The Oat School's action plan has characteristics of being a case study of bullying, where bullying and bullying positions are described in a particularly recognisable manner. The descriptions lay the groundwork for a range of gradually stricter sanctioning measures that target the bully. One can deduce that punishment is seen as the answer to the problem. The question of more or less sanctioning was precisely the main focus of the school's annual educational council meeting in 2007, where the action plan was going to be reviewed and confirmed. Teachers and educators from the after-school centre as well as the school's principal and vice principal[7] participated in the meeting.

Howard from the BCW team presented the action plan section by section. During the presentation, minor amendments were suggested, particularly regarding language or organisation. An actual debate began about the section on 'Possible actions against the bully', which suggested an escalation of sanctions. Kate, a younger teacher, began:

---

[7] In Danish, the *skolerektor* and *vicerektor*.

Kate (teacher):	I would suggest a re-write to 'bully is deprived of one or more privileges' because it is too vague as it is now: 'the bully is deprived some kind of privilege'.
Edward (educator):	I do not believe in punishment. I suggest a completely different sentence that centres on helping the children to stop bullying. It is a matter of responsibility for everyone in the actual situation.
Dorothy (teacher):	I totally disagree; [in a loud voice] there must be consequences, otherwise it has no effect.
Irene (educator):	I agree with Edward, punishment is not the solution to problems of bullying.
Gregory (teacher):	We have just included it as an option that may be used.
Edward:	There must be a direct correlation between what the student does and the punishment, otherwise they will not understand it. They do not necessarily see their actions as anything other than everyday life.
Dorothy:	Edward, not all children are 6 years old. Some of them are 15, you know.
Gayle (teacher):	It doesn't say that this will happen, but that there is a possibility for it to happen.
Brian (school manager):	I think we lack something about dialogue and relation between the involved parties…I am not too keen on this list of points, there are one, two, three…
Dorothy:	If we skip all the negative consequences – can we do that? Then we have no response options.
Brian:	Then I would prefer if it said that it would be determined from case to case.
Gregory:	Well, it depends how you define bullying, but now where we've had a serious text message incident, it was actually helpful to have point number one. (Pause in conversation. Silence.)
Howard (teacher):	OK, we'll write the corrections to this part here, the one with 'one or more privileges…'
Dorothy:	It's good to have possible and tangible consequences at hand, because the student can relate to that instead of 'Oh well, what should I do?' Now it's clear.

At the meeting, the decision was made to change the phrase 'some kind of privilege' to 'one or more privileges'. The progress of the discussion covered a range of positions from sanctions as a clear indication of consequences to sanctions as an inappropriate measure against bullying – a stance that was primarily put forth by the educational after-school staff. In between these two positions, there is what we, with some exaggeration, might call 'the middle position' – exaggeration, because the viewpoints as such may be interpreted as pro-punishment and contra-punishment, although on the condition that the list of sanctions represents intervention *possibilities* rather than intervention *demands*.

The contra-punishment quotations have four areas of attention: firstly, we see resistance to punishment based on belief ('I do not believe in. . .'); secondly, 'help' replaces punishment in some statements; thirdly, it is stressed that punishment does not solve 'bullying problems'; and fourthly, the educators note that a student may not understand the connection between action and sanction. The sanction supporters, however, emphasise the notion of 'consequence', being 'effective' and having 'clear' response options. It is also noted that the older students are generally aware of their actions ('some of them are 15'), and that sanctions have already been helpful in a serious situation.

As a result, two oppositions materialise during the meeting: the *firm wing* that advocates for more consequences and visibility in the choice of sanctions; and a *laissez-faire wing* that does not believe in punishment as a solution to bullying. The teacher Gregory's comment that having possible sanctions was 'helpful' in the 'text message incident'[8] functions as a positive validation of the effect; his comment gives extra weight to the sanction supporters. After Gregory's comment, there was a pause in the conversation and the decision was confirmed; the rationale for stricter punishment was given tacit support, although on the condition that the measures *could* be used, but *must not necessarily* be used. This opening towards a middle position becomes the compromise between the pro- and contra-punishment positions, even though the wording of the final decision increased the criminal tone because it introduced a higher degree of linguistic firmness by saying 'one or more' instead of 'some kind of'.

As an outsider, I interpret the discussion as movements between either a 'yes' or 'no' position with regard to using punishment as a tool in intervention. Yet the opposition between pro- and contra-punishment only reveals a little about the various aspects, and does not reveal anything about what 'consequence', 'firmness' and 'visible reactions' might otherwise mean to the teachers and students at the Oat School.

To learn more about this aspect, I introduce the teacher Christopher's experiences with how the school environment and local environment affect the sense of security and safety amongst the group of teachers. I also take a closer look at Christopher and his colleagues' response to possible incidents of bullying at the school.

---

[8] Gregory is referring to the incident described in the opening of this chapter about a photo of a female student's bare breasts that was texted around the school.

Preventing powerlessness

Christopher is 38 years old and has worked at the Oat School for nearly eight years. He teaches mostly maths, science and technology, and is the class teacher for one of the sixth-grade classes.[9] He explained:

> There is a neighbourhood down by the main road and ring road. It is a housing estate. And there is a huge area of social housing where it is cheap to live, but it is also an area where the municipality houses someone, like a single mom with children and so on, you know. So we really have two types of clientele, and on top of that we have 40 per cent bilingual. Naturally, all of the groups have some problems, but it's also clear that if we were in an area with 98 per cent Danish students, who lived in a housing estate with their mom and dad, then we might have problems with some parents demanding a high academic level. Well, here we have a lot of parents who do not care much about the school.

In this quotation, Christopher draws a picture of the school environment, and his view is shared by many of his colleagues. The picture is part of a recognisable description of the common perception of local conditions that is discussed in the teachers' staff room. The children from the housing estate no longer constitute the majority of students, as was the case when the school opened twenty-five years ago. It is especially the older teachers who consider children from the housing estate to be the most *well-adjusted* for school. In recent years, the school has accepted children from adjacent areas with social housing. Christopher finds that it is in these areas where many parents show no interest in the school. A 'before' and 'now' image of the local environment and working conditions exists in the teachers' staffroom. The present conditions are considered to be more distressing than earlier; for instance, there has been an increase of so-called 'difficult cases' that entail more work of a social nature. The description of the local environment is thus not only a portrait of the environment itself, but it also serves as a narrative that emerges from the negotiation of opinions and from the teachers' shared repertoire (Lave and Wenger 1991). For some of the teachers, the narrative ties together meaningful correlations between the social conditions of the surrounding neighbourhood and the teachers' concrete working conditions at the school.

Sometimes the teachers feel that the social tension culminates in fierce confrontations between teachers, students and/or parents. Christopher said:

> Well, it could be someone [a colleague] who is threatened by a parent. And yesterday, a student threw something at the head of a teacher and she went out like a candle. I don't know if it was a coincidence, but it was 'coincidentally' a student with whom she has a difficult relationship. [. . .] One year, we had a student

---

[9] This corresponds to seventh grade/year in American or British schools.

who brought in a baseball bat, and he actually said it was to beat me. He also called my colleague a 'cunt', and I was called 'fat Christopher, you're gonna die'.

Here, Christopher discusses an episode between himself and a student from the seventh grade.[10] The boy brought a baseball bat to school, and on several occasions he told his classmates that he was going to beat Christopher. In fact, the baseball bat was raised behind Christopher's back several times to indicate that the boy was ready to give a blow. Rumours spread about the plan, and the boy was immediately expelled from school. Christopher was very affected by the situation immediately after the incident. His colleagues supported him and, as a precaution, he talked to a psychologist once. But otherwise, Christopher does not believe the incident 'affected' him as much as other, more severe, incidents have other colleagues – possibly because the attack was never realised. He said:

I think what makes some people break down is the direct confrontation, and that you cannot – well, the fact that you cannot win, so to speak. It's not only about maybe being knocked down. It can also be what you bring as a teacher. If you are up against too much, then it has happened that colleagues have said: 'I'm going home for three months now, right!'

Christopher explains that, amongst the group of staff at school, on average two teachers per year take long-term sick leave due to pressure, stress and being 'up against too much':

HRH: Is it some kind of 'breakdown'?
Christopher: Yes, and a sense of powerlessness: 'Now I'm no longer in control, now it's the student who maybe controls the class.' It's such a shame.

In my analysis of the action plan, I stressed that the intervention strategy described could be interpreted as an escalation of sanctions to be used against 'opponents'. Christopher's words about 'control' and 'winning' also come from a vocabulary of so-called power struggles. The words echo being in a battle arena, and to the staff it seems difficult and like a struggle to do their professional work – i.e. to teach. The narrative about the sense of powerlessness felt by his colleagues on long-term sick leave can be seen as the lost order that Christopher believes can be re-conquered through being consistent and direct, as I present shortly. Let us first take a closer look at the story about what preceded the threats to beat Christopher:

Christopher: Well, we had this boy [the student with the baseball bat], who was actually quite good at school, but he started to not really care. It

---

[10] This corresponds to eighth grade/year in American or British schools; approximately age 13 or 14.

may be that he thought we were out to get him, and maybe we were with things like 'Come on, get started and take out your things.'

HRH: But why did he take it out on you?

Christopher: Well, it was probably because I was the teacher who gave him boundaries. I was the one who dragged him to the office when it was really bad, right! He and the others managed, at the end, to trash a lot of furniture and commit theft in the gym. We may have had such cases earlier too, but recently there have been more.

Christopher believes he became the target of the boy's threats because he was '*the* teacher who gave him boundaries'. The implication here is that some teachers do not. According to Christopher, his consistent behaviour and use of consequences resulted in the student's violent anger. In other situations, however, Christopher finds that enforcing consequences can be effective. He said:

We probably have a special workplace relationship, me and Dorothy. We've had classes together before, and we are sort of very, how can I put it – teacher-wise, we are much more straightforward. There are types of teachers that I will never become. It's sort of navel-gazing. Any little thing, then we'll have to spend hours talking, and it often ends with more stuff than what constituted the problem. It builds up.

Consequence as a strategy seems to indicate that more contradictory results come into play. The consequence strategy entails opposition to being reproved and dragged to the office. Meanwhile, the struggle between power versus powerlessness – and between the student's opposition forces and the teacher's forces – is strengthened, which leads to more consequences and a further aggravation of the tense relationship. Nevertheless, Christopher finds that being consistent and direct is the best way to stop problems.

Christopher often mentions his partnership over many years with his colleague Dorothy; a relationship that is periodically extended to their colleague Stephen. Christopher finds that their triad functions well; they do many activities together across their classes, and they do things 'exactly as we like it'. When Christopher uses 'we' in his descriptions of everyday life at the school, it often refers to Dorothy, Stephen and himself. He also mentions teacher types who are not part of the 'we'. They are teachers who Christopher thinks add to the problems by talking too much without acting. Christopher said:

We agreed that we will not accept children in the hallway and stuff like that. But some teachers allow them to hang out there anyway. That way, things start to slip, and it's kind of just pissing people off, right! Some overlook something, and others strike.

The 'we' Christopher creates here refers to another 'we'; i.e. the school's group of staff, which has made a joint decision. Christopher finds that some colleagues disrespect the 'agreed'. He sees himself as part of the group who will 'strike'; Christopher has not been on long-term sick leave due to stress and pressure, and he may feel that enforcing consequences is part of a strategy to prevent a sense of powerlessness.

Participating in the teacher community

A recurring theme in this part of Christopher's narrative is how the social history of the local environment seems to influence daily work; e.g. more social tasks that are added to the regular teaching. Another theme is Christopher's experience with how being direct and enforcing consequences can reduce problems, just as his sense of 'we' in his group of close colleagues is a theme about understanding each other and being consistent. Thus, ensuring that consequences make sense to students who are violent and disruptive is more than an individual and personal activity; the sense-making and action process also includes other colleagues' experiences of tension in teacher–student relationships, and shared experiences of being direct and consistent as a problem-solving strategy.

Inspired by social practice theory, which is a collective term for theories that focus on the correlation between people's actions, practice and communities (Lave and Wenger 1991), the 'more direct' approach toward disruptive students may be understood as a way to participate in the teacher practice, and the triad's teacher community co-creates the teacher practice. The shared understandings in Christopher's group regarding how disruptions should be handled, their shared experiences and their shared stories are woven into the practice movement and, by participating in this process, the consequence strategy becomes meaningful to Christopher. He is part of a 'we', and his triad has created closeness within their work community and a deep knowledge of the other triad members' actions and skills. As a result, a 'practice cluster' has emerged within the larger community in the teachers' staff room, with shared understandings of how to act.

We have now seen how some teachers establish and maintain a meaningful use of consequence in a working life where they attempt to prevent a sense of powerlessness. What does this correlation look like when teachers write and talk about bullying, and also when they are faced with possible bullying situations between a student and the lived school life?

Bullying or fleeting incidents?

Christopher finds it difficult to identify specific situations or processes of bullying. He said:

Today, for instance, we had a fourth-grade[11] class where someone freaked out; I mean, they are constantly fighting. Then they convince others to join them; they just want to chase someone as a group. But the victim is rarely the same person. Well, I really have no idea. I think it's been a long time since I've had a class where I thought, 'This is truly a bullying victim.'

Jeremy from the BCW team and editor of the action plan on bullying is also doubtful whether he has seen any clear cases of bullying. He said:

When I try to recall whether I have seen any bullying cases myself, and no, I don't think I have. No, we have not had cases that we have defined as bullying cases. There has been a lot of teasing. And there have been many fleeting incidents, but I don't think we have had sort of an actual bullying case.

Christopher and Jeremy seem to be looking for something specific, such as events that are not 'fleeting' and situations in which 'the victim is the same person'. The two teacher colleagues cannot recall any course of events that have had the form and repetition expected in bullying cases.

It does happen, however, that a few children at the Oat School complain about being ostracised by their peers. In such cases, the teachers may doubt whether the described situation is in fact a case of bullying; for instance, Stephen, Christopher's colleague from the triad, talked about a student called Lewis:

I don't actually think that I have any examples where I can point at one and say: 'This is really someone who is being bullied.' We had Lewis, who moved to another school, and he was very sad. You might say he was a student who thought he was being bullied. Again, I think he is one of those who keeps to themselves. He was liked. At one point, we made sort of a survey of who the students wanted to spend time with and so on. In that survey, he was actually chosen by others, but one sees oneself differently, and that's why he started skipping school and things like that.

Stephen does not think Lewis was 'truly' a victim of bullying. That statement implies an expectation of bullying positions that are more real, and thus reflective of an actual and real bullying situation. 'Real' rather than the idea of being a victim of others' bullying (like Lewis). Lewis may not be recognised as someone who is being shunned because he, amongst other things, had been named in a class survey where students were asked to write the names of others they would like to spend time with.

Doubt and controversy about whether someone is being bullied is a recurring theme, both in the aforementioned teachers' observations of various events, and in individual students' statements about their experiences. This also applies in the case of Michelle.

---

[11] This corresponds to fifth grade/year in American or British schools.

Victim and matrices of bullying

Michelle is 13 years old and attends one of the seventh-grade[12] classes at the Oat School. She has friends in the ninth-grade[13] classes whom she meets during breaks to smoke cigarettes, but she feels lonely in class. Michelle mentions that, amongst other things, she is never invited to join common class activities in their free periods and during breaks. Her mother has contacted the school several times because she thinks Michelle is being bullied:

Stephen: Then Michelle's mom comes to us and says that Michelle is being bullied. She is the type who keeps to herself. I don't know if that is bullying. She contributes with nothing.

HRH: What does Michelle say to you?

Stephen: Well, she hardly says anything to us. She is really at that age where she would rather do the opposite of everyone else. So, if we would like to talk, she doesn't.

HRH: But she keeps to herself?

Stephen: Not always, she joined Sophie and Andrew [students in her own class]. They are no longer at the school. Then she picks someone else and kind of threatens them by saying, 'If you don't join me, I'll tell that you have stolen something in the shop.' She is not really interested in bigger groups because she has nothing in common with them. She is rather far-out in everything she does. She has lots of personal problems. She has some anxiety, lies awake at night and so on. Many things come into the picture.

The teachers see Michelle as a student who does not want to 'talk' to them. There is no 'clinging to an adult' or 'refusing to go out during break time', which are some of the characteristics of a bullying victim that the action plan described. Instead, Michelle avoids talking to teachers and does not mind going outside during breaks. Michelle is hardly considered to be a weak victim, but rather, is seen as an active student who threatens other students and acts in opposition to the teachers. Michelle's situation cannot be explained by saying the school community is shunning her, but rather, the opposite; she herself de-selected the community because she has nothing 'in common' with them.

A shared characteristic in the cases of Lewis and Michelle are narratives about how they keep to themselves. Some of the teachers interpret the ways in which Lewis and Michelle are not part of the community as deliberate solitariness and not as bullying. In this conception, being solitary is in opposition to being bullied. Yet the same narratives may

---

[12] This corresponds to eighth grade/year in American or British schools.
[13] This corresponds to tenth grade/year in American or British schools.

also be read in other ways, and thus a vague outline of a matrix begins to emerge for what a 'real' bullying victim looks like to the teachers: isolated (and not with friends during break time, *like Michelle*), seeking adults (and not rejecting teachers, *like Michelle*) and a person nobody ever chooses (and not someone chosen by others, *like Lewis*).

Another reason why the teachers do not see Lewis and Michelle as victims of bullying may be that their classmates do not match the prevailing paradigmatic view on active profiles of bullying. Within this paradigm, the bully is an aggressive person and the act of bullying is a criminal action. Based on this account, the teachers find the students' disregard of Michelle too minor to be an aggressive criminal assault, and they may even find it understandable because they think Michelle is 'far-out'.

Children who feel bullied are here met with a disqualification of their complaints, and a clash thereby occurs between student experiences and adult understandings. For both Michelle and Lewis, the conflict resulted in changing schools.

'War stories' in the teachers' staffroom

The doubt and uncertainty about whether specific situations at the Oat School constitute bullying or not, or whether students are 'true' victims of bullying are interesting because, in practice, the doubt is in contrast to the certainty and clarity of the emphasis put on sanctions as an appropriate intervention against bullying. The clarity is expressed in the school's action plan, but also in some of the comments made at the educational council meeting, where the description of sanctions in the action plan was enhanced. The contrast lies in the fact that the punitive sanctions rest on a very simplified identification of a phenomenon that is not simple, but very complicated in the lived school life. The teachers' perceptions of the positive effects of sanctions thus stem from specific situations (other than bullying cases), where punishment proved successful in settling unrest and chaos; for instance, when teachers were addressed in certain ways. Christopher said:

At one point, we had some issues with use of language. You should not, as a teacher, accept being called a 'big fat pig' or something like that. There are some limits where we've said, 'This is not OK.' Last year, when the seventh graders were in sixth grade,[14] we really had to intervene and say, 'You know what, if you do not talk properly to each other, you should not be here.' Two or three were sent home, and it had a preventive effect. It helped tremendously.

---

[14] This corresponds to eighth grade/year and seventh grade/year, respectively, in American or British schools.

The Oat School has given suspensions on several occasions if a student shouted 'cunt', 'faggot' or 'fat bastard' at teachers or other students. Suspension has also occurred in cases of 'break-time ravaging', as Christopher calls it. According to the teachers involved, suspension had an immediate and positive effect in these cases. Even though the exact term 'suspension' is not explicitly mentioned in the action plan on bullying, the aforementioned cases of suspension are given as examples of how sanctions can have a generally positive effect. Being expelled from school for a shorter or longer period of time is in line with 'losing one or more privileges', which is one of the consequences mentioned in the action plan on bullying. Suspension is a lost privilege in the form of a student being denied access to the school's social and educational environment.

One particular incident at the school is often mentioned at meetings in the teachers' staffroom: the case of the text message with the photo of a girl's bare breasts that circulated around the school and caused a great deal of disruption. Like the stories about the school's social environment, the story about the text message also forms part of the teachers' shared repertoire. The elements of conflict, drama and swift elimination of the problem make it a suitable 'war story', according to anthropologist Julian Orr (1996). War stories are stories about winning or losing battles that circulate around a community; they are used to confirm and/or maintain certain opinions and choices of strategy. The 'war story' about the text message with the bare breasts plays a role in the negotiation of opinions about the positive effects of sanctions. The incident was referred to at the educational council meeting where the action plan's section on sanctions was discussed, and the example came up regularly in my interviews with teachers at the school. The story of the texted photo legitimates the sanction strategy in situations of disruption, chaos and disorder, but at the same time, Jeremy and other teachers at the Oat School questioned whether the incident was in fact a case of bullying. Jeremy said:

The question is whether that case can actually be defined as bullying because it's a one-off incident, and there hasn't been anything previous, so it's not like the culmination of something that had been going on. I mean, like something that has been accumulating and then suddenly the trump card is played. It wasn't accidental, but it was a sudden situation, and it is not our impression that there has been any sequel. But it naturally gives reason to discuss again and again the question of mobile phones and the entire media world.

The reactions to the text message with the bare breasts illustrate what seems both certain and uncertain to the teachers involved. It is certain that the sanction had a positive effect on the disruption, but it is uncertain whether the incident was actually a case of bullying. This certainty/uncertainty runs through the intersection of bullying, sanctions and other themes, such as disorder and chaos at the school. There is certainty that sanctions (including the sanctions mentioned in the action plan) have had an effect on the use of bad language, break-time ravaging and the text-message incident. It is uncertain whether situations such as one fight or one conflict in a fourth-grade class were cases of bullying, and whether children (and their families) who complain about bullying are in fact victims. When I drew Christopher's attention to this observation about certainty and uncertainty, he responded:

I think those things [the sanctions] were put in the action plan because of all the other things that happen when the students behave in a way that we do not accept.

By saying 'all the other things that happen', Christopher seems to refer to situations that are not considered bullying but rather, actions with a negative character, such as destroying school property or calling a class-mate or teacher a 'cunt'. Although the stringent description of bullying in the action plan cannot be recognised in practice by, for instance, Christopher, Jeremy and Stephen, the designated anti-bullying strategy is still accepted. Could it be that the sanctions, rather than the bullying, have become the pivotal point of the action plan? The reason may be that some teachers at the Oat School believe it is necessary to use sanctions when school rules are violated; e.g. if teaching is disrupted, when colleagues are 'up against too much' or if someone, such as Christopher, wants to avoid dealing with too much. As a result, sanctions become not only a means to restore order, but also a strategy of self-retention, and the punitive measures in the school's action plan on bullying then entrench the practice through such acts of teacher self-retention.

In combination, the action plan and teacher practice can be seen as local student-regulating systems within what Michel Foucault calls 'micro criminal law', meaning that the mechanics of punishment are established locally where 'macro criminal law' does not apply (Foucault 2008: 194).

In support of more order

I have now examined two aspects of Christopher's narrative. The first described the relation between the working conditions he experienced, and his need to be consistent and enforce consequences. The second aspect was how Christopher and his colleagues perceived bullying at school. The two aspects seem to merge, in the sense that the effective use of sanctions against disorder and disruption in everyday life at school influence teachers' attitudes towards sanctions as a possible intervention strategy against bullying. The production of meaning in and around one context (the attitude about having consequences for disruptions) is exported as decision logic to another context (students bullying each other). In this process, the action plan's section on sanctions gains local, meaningful footing when there seems to be consensus amongst the teachers. The process can also be read in the opposite direction; namely, that the decision logic applied in the perception of how to combat bullying seems to inform the use of sanctions in cases of disruption. We are thus dealing with a chain of events that can be understood in the following way. The action plan describes an expected process in which bullying is first identified, and subsequently the school intervenes with a sanction:

$$\boxed{\text{Bullying}} \rightarrow \boxed{\text{Sanction}}$$

Based on the analyses of various actions and incidents at the Oat School, we have seen that, in practice, the sanctions that are intended to combat bullying are also used to punish other types of actions that are *not* identified as bullying, such as 'break time ravaging', 'foul language' and text-message disruptions. But bullying has not been entirely discarded from this process; partly because the sanctions are taken from strategies designed to combat bullying, and partly because there seems to be a general agreement amongst the teachers that peace and quiet are important elements for well-being; therefore, peace and quiet are incompatible with bullying. 'Peace and quiet' almost seems to represent a shield against bullying and a guarantee of well-being. This generates a correlation that is not represented by concrete and experienced processes, but rather, is an argumentation structure that supports more discipline. Bullying now functions as an argumentation qualifier, but not as a directly experienced phenomenon:

$$\boxed{\text{Noise, disruption, chaos}} \rightarrow \boxed{\text{Sanction against bullying is used}} = \boxed{\text{Order}}$$

The warrant to use sanctions against bullying also becomes a warrant to use sanctions to achieve more order in school, which, from the teachers' perspectives, is sometimes overly challenging. This movement may be reinforced by the portrayal of bullying as a criminal problem, which underlines the fact that we are dealing with significant issues that require sanctioning powers to solve them.

Well-being as a warrant for sanctions

Achieving a state of 'well-being' seems to be the goal, and thus bullying, disruptions and sanctions come to function as replaceable arguments for achieving the same; i.e. a state of well-being. An explanation is found in the conception that well-being is the absolute opposite of bullying. Disguised as an intention to create more well-being, it thus becomes possible to employ anti-bullying tools in situations of disorder and various types of disruptions, even if those disturbances are not recognised as bullying. The conception seems to be that ensuring well-being must be put ahead of bullying. Meanwhile, some of the teachers find it hard to identify bullying when it is based on an individualised, figurative perception of bullying. The contradiction is transcended by the demand for more peace and quiet, which then constitutes the overall aim of an intervention.

We can now return to the beginning of this chapter and the question of why punishments meant to combat acts of bullying are used in other situations. The chaos and disruption that occurred at the Oat School after the circulation of an intimate text message were, in the eyes of the teachers, handled quickly with effective reactions involving the police, and appropriate sanctions were used against the students involved. In the example from the online article on the website for the Danish Ministry of Children and Education, also in the eyes of the adults, noise and disorder were successfully handled by using sanctions – i.e. the so-called 'shadow timetable'. The use of anti-bullying sanctions in these situations was legitimated by introducing an extra element to the anticipated progression from bullying to sanction. As illustrated above, the extra element is disturbances to order at the school. Therefore, it makes sense to the teacher that, when students from sixth grade are too noisy in class, they should sit in a ninth-grade class – even if they have not bullied anyone. Here, the sense of well-being authorises a general use of anti-bullying sanctions to ensure more peace, order and discipline. It is also interesting that, in this process of achieving more order, it appears less relevant for the teachers involved to investigate whether bullying incidents have actually been reduced.

Well-being as a warrant for this movement generates a new claim, which is the claim of a shift in effect: peace and quiet during teaching generates peaceful student relationships, which are understood as an absence of bullying. From the teachers' perspective, it is not an absolute necessity to identify bullies and victims of bullying in practice, or to make sure a given situation is in fact a case of bullying. From their perspective, it is 'sufficient' to simply identify the noisy and disruptive students.

The question now is whether the efforts to achieve more order also entail a shift in meaning if the teacher–student relationship is allowed to overshadow the understanding of the student–student relationship. The question is also whether interventions against bullying fade into the background for the benefit of needs that the teachers believe are more critical; i.e. being able to teach without being called a 'cunt' or 'fat bastard', and being met with an openness to learning. In this context, we may interpret the situation as one where actors who are under pressure encounter other actors who are also under pressure. The students Lewis and Michelle asked for understanding of their situation from a group of teachers who discovered that, from time to time, they or their colleagues had to fight to conduct their professional work with dignity.

11   When classroom culture tips into bullying

Helle Rabøl Hansen, Inge Henningsen and Jette Kofoed

Classroom culture is comprised of several factors that influence the level of bullying that occurs within a school class. Students' negative evaluations of classroom culture correlate to a higher amount of bullying incidents; this finding was revealed in analyses of the statistics from a study conducted with primary-school students in the greater Copenhagen area about bullying amongst children. Classroom culture differs across classes, of course, but more bullying is often reported once the assessments have been negative.

This chapter is based on analyses of quantitative material[1] from a survey in which 1,052 students in eighth and ninth grades[2] in Denmark answered questions about their everyday school lives as well as their experiences with bullying. As such, this chapter is about bullying and how the class itself influences whether or not students report bullying incidents. We include the different individuals *as well as* the community that the students constitute as a whole. We discuss a variety of experiences in school life that involve students who report that they do well within the student community but do not get along with their teachers, and students who report that they get along with their teachers but not with their fellow students. We talk about the complexity of school life, which is impossible to categorise simply as 'those who thrive' and 'those who do not thrive', and we focus on factors that appear decisive in terms of whether or not students are subjected to bullying.

The results we present here are based on a study with multiple foci; namely, how the students interact with each other, their parents, their schools (including their teachers) and their classes, and we also look at anxiety amongst the students. This investigation allowed us to acquire knowledge in a number of interrelated areas. We present statistics that tell

---

[1] Analyses based on the same quantitative material were also published in Henningsen (2011); and Hansen, Henningsen and Kofoed (2012).

[2] This corresponds to ninth and tenth grade/year, respectively, in American or British schools.

us about what the children reported regarding their school lives. However, first and foremost, we present the associations between bullying and other relationships in the students' lives, which shed light on the nature of bullying. In all, sixty classes participated in the study, and almost all of them had experiences with students being bullied, students bullying others, or both. This does *not* mean that all of the classes continually experienced bullying. What it does mean, however, is that bullying is not a peripheral phenomenon only experienced by a few. Therefore, on the following pages, we qualify *how* bullying affects students as well as *how many* it affects. We then relate the incidence of bullying to certain factors of which students reported being afraid. But to begin, we present the major findings of this study, after which we explain methods and analytics and, finally, we differentiate our findings.

Data

The study was based on questionnaires answered by 1,052 students in eighth and ninth grades.[3] All of the schools located in three municipalities (Ballerup, Albertslund and Brøndby) west of Copenhagen, Denmark, were invited to participate in the study; thirteen out of twenty schools accepted. The students who answered the questionnaire were spread across sixty different classes. A research assistant from our project distributed the questionnaire amongst the classes, and this assistant was also present whilst the students filled out the questionnaire in order to answer any clarifying questions that might arise. The data was collected between November 2009 and January 2010.

The questionnaire was designed to be compatible with other Danish and international investigations; e.g. DAPHNE (Smith 2010), Københavnhavnerbarometeret (2009) and Obermann (2011). The items concerning classroom culture expanded upon questions that Marie-Louise Obermann used in her study, and a design based on classroom interviews ensured a negligible drop-out rate. In the questionnaire, the students answered a number of questions about themselves, relationships with their schools, their class and their parents as well as their experiences with bullying. The primary ambition of the study was not to determine levels of bullying, but to investigate the relationship between classroom culture and bullying. This relationship can most likely be generalised, even though the students were recruited from a limited geographical area.

---

[3] This corresponds to ninth and tenth grade/year, respectively, in American or British schools.

Main results

The data showed that 13 per cent of the students reported experiences with being bullied over the previous school year; this is equivalent to every ninth student, or two-to-three students in each class. We work from the hypothesis that if one student reports active bullying, then there are probably more students in the class who are not thriving. This does not necessarily mean that we presume that additional students are being bullied. But it does mean that we assume that the mere occurrence of somebody being bullied within a community – in this case, the class – will affect how other individuals within that community function as well as how the class itself functions. Or, to look at it from another perspective, we assume that the way the class constructs its community will affect whether and how bullying occurs.

The absolutely central finding in this part of the study is that there is a significant association between the occurrence of bullying and how classroom culture functions. In addition, we found an association between bullying and being afraid.

'Classroom culture' is a term we use based on the students' answers to a number of questions (see Appendix Table 11.1); hence, it is an analytical term. When classroom culture is malfunctioning, the risk of bullying increases; however, there is no unequivocal association between these two conditions. There are classes where most of the students thrive, but where bullying nevertheless occurs. And there are classes with a malfunctioning classroom culture that finds expression in ways other than bullying. However, we found that an arrow pointing to life in the class is significant as to whether classroom culture evolves into bullying; this is what we want to pursue, so a significant part of this chapter showcases this point and its necessary elaborations. Here, we want to emphasise that we present associations and not causal relationships.

We also asked about other aspects of school life, including the students' views of themselves, their general feelings about school attendance and their relationships with their parents. And here we noticed an interesting difference in the response patterns between self-reported bullies and their victims. Students who reported experiences of being a bully had a rather more negative attitude towards school attendance than other students, but they had good relationships with their peers. It was quite the opposite for students who reported experiences of being bullied. Attention should be given to the fact that, for them, there is a connection between bullying and being afraid of something during school hours; students who reported being bullied were more fearful in a number of ways than those who were not bullied. But there was one thing the students all had in common: regardless of their bullying experiences, many of them were afraid of not performing well enough academically. We return to these findings later in the chapter. But firstly, we clarify how we conducted our investigation and describe the acute challenges presented to our systematic and methodological approach.

The class as an analytical unit: methods and analytical strategy

In the questionnaire, we used the prevalent terminology when asking children about having been bullied and having participated in the bullying of others. On a technical level in our questions, we reproduced a general distinction in the bullying research that addresses the fact that the numbers to which we refer as 'occurrences of bullying' are produced by counting these two positions (bully and victim). The qualitative-orientated contributions to the eXbus research have, in different ways, challenged this thinking (particularly Kofoed 2009; Schott 2009b; Schott, Chapter 2; and Søndergaard 2009) through the understanding that it can be problematic to maintain these two simplified positions (bully and victim) in situations involving bullying. Despite these objections, we nonetheless conducted our study on the basis of this differentiation since it allows us to contribute to the international research-based debate associated with the prevalent quantitative studies of bullying – all of which are based on exactly this differentiation. In our analysis, we let this distinction become entangled with other themes, enabling us to divide the varied social life within the children's classes into meaningful components. However, our results must be viewed in light of the nuances apparent in other parts of the eXbus material, where we found these positions (bully and victim) to be both reproduced and challenged (Kofoed 2009; Kofoed and Ringrose 2012). Also, in some classes, it might be more natural to adopt the position of 'bully' or 'victim' in relation to the other answers one chooses to give.

Thus we have decided to use the established categories from international studies (Cross et al. 2008; Hinduja and Patchin 2008; Kowalski and Limber 2007; Smith 2010) whilst still posing questions directed at the aspects of bullying with which we are particularly engaged; as already mentioned, this concerns 'class as a community' and 'being afraid'. Specifically, our emphasis on the fact that school life can contain aspects of being afraid was inspired by *Københavnerbarometeret* (the *Copenhagen Barometer*), an ongoing annual study of well-being in primary-school life in the municipality of Copenhagen.

From the outset of this chapter, it is imperative that we establish a central premise for making sense of the statistics. This concerns the manner in which we engage with the phenomenon 'class'. In the early work done by eXbus, it became apparent that it was not only the individual her- or himself, but also the group of which an individual is a part that is important in determining whether students experience bullying (Kofoed and Søndergaard 2009). This is why we have attempted to address 'the class' as an entity in a quantitative context as well. We have done this by constructing a numerical score for classroom culture, after synthesising the individual students' assessments of how they experience life in their classes. We are particularly interested in investigating how bullying manifests itself, so we collected answers at the class level. Of course, we take an interest in individual subjects. But we are *also* interested in the groups of which individuals are co-creators. Hence, a 'double' analytical move is needed in which we focus on both individuals and groups. We do this to prevent ourselves from referring only to individuals, and to ensure that our analysis genuinely takes both individuals and groups into consideration.

How do we find such groups? When we do qualitative studies, we ask individuals; they are given a voice. In quantitative studies, we combine these individual voices into groups – for example, groups by gender (all the boys or all the girls) or perhaps those who were born in the same year (all the 14-year-olds). In this analysis, we combined all the individual voices into another group – namely, 'the class' – and then we subjected this collection of voices, the class, to further analysis by exploring how it connects to the presence of bullying as well as numerous other factors.

With this method and analytical strategy, we drew upon a theoretically informed interest in the relationship between the individual and the group (Hansen 2011b; Khawaja 2010; Kofoed 2004; Nissen 2012) as well as on being able to develop knowledge specifically about the relationship between classroom culture and the presence of bullying. Whilst designing the questionnaire and establishing adequate strategies of analysis to handle a substantial data-source, we also drew upon (in the broadest sense) the socio-cultural understanding that many different aspects join forces in the production of phenomena. We know this from gender studies (Staunæs 2004; Søndergaard 1996), from studies of school life (Bjerg 2011; Juelskjær 2009; Kofoed 2004, 2010; Staunæs 2004) and from studies of management (Amhøj 2007; Staunæs and Søndergaard 2006). In our analysis, we drew upon these theories, which are informed by a perspective of intersectionality that highlights how the entanglement of many forces join together in the production of social phenomena (Kofoed 2008a; Phoenix 2006; Staunæs and Søndergaard 2011).

This way of establishing a class-index does not locate conditions that solely characterise bullies/victims of bullying. Instead, we found what affects more students. We can also say that we found probable factors within these tables; factors that were observed by a plurality of students in the classes. This picture of the class creates a record of the dominant understandings within a given unit. This means that, throughout this chapter, we move between individuals and communities. We cannot take out the classes, nor is it possible to reduce the numbers to individuals alone. This means that in this chapter 'the class' refers not only to a social unit of individuals, but also constitutes an analytical category.

Asking about the phenomenon of bullying

In our questionnaire,[4] we emphasised that we were interested in the individual student's experiences with bullying. We also included a suggested definition of bullying; we explicitly asked the students to only refer to this if they had some doubt about how they themselves understand the phenomenon of bullying.

In bullying research, there is a recurring discussion amongst researchers and practitioners about whether to include definitions in the questionnaires students are given (for an overview of this discussion, see Hansen 2011a). There are benefits and drawbacks to either providing or omitting definitions. The advantage of not including a definition of bullying could be that the question then prompts a student's self-assessment. The disadvantage could be that we end up with a very broad and undefined category with regard to the study's aim to investigate the coherence between bullying and general classroom culture. Conversely, including a definition in the questionnaire could result in it becoming the scholarly categorisation that defines the study. In this particular survey, we chose the middle road. *Firstly*, we specifically asked the students to answer based on their own experience(s) of bullying at school; and *secondly*, we offered a possible definition of bullying as we see it from the perspective of a school class (Hansen 2005). Since then, a focus group consisting of students in the seventh and eighth grades[5] helped us rewrite our questions in a language and manner that resonates

---

[4] We would like to thank Nina Hein, Marie-Louise Obermann, Jo Niclasen and Ditte Dalum Christoffersen, all of whom contributed to the development of the questionnaire. We also want to express our gratitude to Jo Niclasen and Ditte Dalum Christoffersen for collecting and coding the data. Finally, we would like to thank the schools that participated as well as the many students who answered our questions.

[5] This corresponds to eighth and ninth grade/year, respectively, in American or British schools.

with 13-to-15-year-olds. The text about bullying from the question-naire is shown below.

Bullying

The next questions we ask concern bullying in your class as well as in your school.

They refer both to being bullied and to being a bully. We would like you to answer the questions from *your* experiences of what bullying is.

If you are in doubt about the meaning of the word 'bullying', perhaps you can find help in the way we have explained bullying, which goes something like this:

- Bullying at school is when a student is persecuted or excluded by her or his schoolmates – or some of the schoolmates – for a longer period
- Bullying can take place in many different ways: face-to-face, over the phone, the internet or an online chat. Bullying can be direct and visible, or indirect and hidden.

There are also other ways to explain bullying. The most important thing, however, is that you answer in a manner that feels right to you.

In lieu of this, the students were asked about experiences with bullying at their schools.

Have you been bullied by anyone from school since the summer holidays?

and

Have you yourself been involved in the bullying of anyone from school since the summer holidays?

Both questions offered these possible answers: 'yes, a lot'; 'yes, a little'; and 'no'.

By using this approach to ask about the students' experiences with bullying, we suffer from no illusion that we can 'map' all the bullying that may potentially happen in any particular class. There will most likely be periods of time and episodes that some would classify as bullying, but where the students involved do not experience what takes place as bullying; conversely, there will be occurrences that some may consider to be more innocent than bullying, but which those involved experience as bullying. We return to this issue and similar problems later in the section about 'hidden positions'. We do not expect to reveal any absolute truths about bullying within school classes; rather, we wish to investigate a number of patterns in the students' answers that relate to the phenom-enon. These patterns constitute the analytical unit that we study.

Occurrences of bullying

We want to emphasise that we count something specific when we process quantitative material. This 'something', however, is not 'bullying' as such, but something we have chosen to label the 'occurrences of bullying'. This is not a word game, but a central point – we wish to point to the fact that *bullying per se* cannot be counted just like that. It is always something specific about bullying that we count. In this chapter, this 'something' consists of the students' self-reported specifications about episodes of bullying. In other words, when we emphasise this self-reporting, it stresses that all of our counting is based on the students' own reports of active bullying. It also implies that we operate with the knowledge that it is possible to count, yet the way in which we analyse the data challenges an unspecified assumption that all bullying is then quantified. School life consists of both active and latent bullying. What we can count is active bullying as the students understand it. The ways in which we include this consideration lie within the double movement: precision in terms of *what* we are counting, and precision in terms of the analyses of *how* active bullying can be integrated with potential bullying.

We take a closer look at the answers to these questions in the following section; specifically, by examining how these occurrences of bullying appear. Firstly, we look at how bullying is distributed in terms of individuals.[6]

In terms of those who have been bullied or participated in bullying others, we distinguished between two categories of answers: 'yes, a lot' and 'yes, a little'. The preliminary focus groups that participated in the pilot-test of the questionnaire made us aware of the limitations of only presenting answer categories for 'yes' and 'no'. The 14-to-15-year-olds' resistance to the answers available in the pilot-test made us change the design and include their suggestions about how to differentiate the answer categories. This undoubtedly means that we have received more positive answers than we would have if we had only presented one answer category for 'yes'.

Of the students responding, 12.9 per cent reported that they had been bullied and 17 per cent reported that they had participated in the bullying of others. As shown in Table 11.1 and Table 11.2, the numbers are quite high compared with other Danish studies (Due et al. 1999; Due and Holstein 2003; Due and Rasmussen 2007, 2011), which are based on different designs as well as different methods of estimation. The ratio between those who bully and those who are bullied is on a par with several international studies. In this survey, we saw no significant difference between boys and girls in terms of the number of students who indicated that they have been bullied (13.3 per cent of the girls and 12.9 per cent of the boys). However, there were relatively more boys than girls who

---

[6] All tables are based on data from Henningsen (2011).

Table 11.1 *Have you been bullied by anyone from school since the summer holidays?*

Have been bullied	Percentage of all	Number of respondents
Yes, a lot	2.1	21
Yes, a little	10.8	107
No	87.1	866
Total	100.0	994

(58 students did not answer this question.)

Table 11.2 *Have you participated in bullying someone from school since the summer holidays?*

Have bullied others	Percentage of all	Number of respondents
Yes, a lot	2.0	20
Yes, a little	15.0	147
No	83.0	814
Total	100.0	981

(71 students did not answer this question.)

indicated that they have participated in the bullying of others (12.9 per cent of the girls and 20.2 per cent of the boys). This result is also on a par with other international studies. Many of these studies report a sizeable number of double-aggressors; i.e. children who are both bullies and victims of bullying. In the present study, we had 34 students who reported that they had both been bullied and bullied others. Thus, 28 per cent of the self-reported victims were also self-reported bullies. Amongst the students who reported that they were not bullied, only 16 per cent reported having bullied others. This means that the incidence of bullying others is almost twice as high for victims as for non-victims.[7] However, the number of double-aggressors was so limited that we can safely assume that they do not significantly influence the following analysis.

Because we are interested in the level of bullying within a class, we calculated the number of self-reported bullies and victims of bullying for each of the participating classes. These are compared in Figure 11.1[8]. In

[7] The association is statistically significant ($p=0.011$).
[8] In both Figure 11.1 and Figure 11.3, we omitted three unrepresentative classes with very few students.

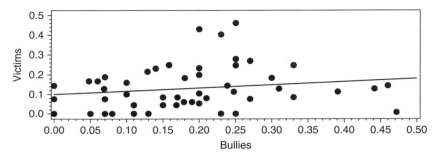

Figure 11.1. The proportion of self-reported victims of bullying in relation to the proportion of self-reported bullies within classes
Note: Each dot signifies one class. Along the X-axis, we have the proportion of self-reported bullies; along the Y-axis, the proportion of self-reported victims of bullying in the class. The position of each dot signifies the interrelationship between the two.

most of the classes we examined, there were students who answered that they consider themselves bullies and others (or the same) who answered that they consider themselves victims of bullying. There is a tendency towards a logic of 'the more victims of bullying, the more bullies'. But this correlation is not strong, which means that there may be more bullies than victims in some classes and vice versa. So how can we understand that the relation between bullies and victims is inconsistent in these types of self-reporting studies? To begin with, we rarely come across just one student bullying another single student. More often, we see that several students join forces to bully another student or one student bullies several other students. And we even see bullying across different school classes. Finally, we cannot exclude the fact that an opposition to assuming the role of both bully and victim influences how the final picture is presented (Hansen 2005; Søndergaard 2008). A related phenomenon is found in a number of international intervention studies, where a decrease in the number of bullies was not accompanied by a decrease in victims and vice versa (Farrington and Ttofi 2009).

What is significant for bullying?

As already mentioned, the class itself and classroom culture have been central to our work. Therefore, we are particularly interested in investigating what bullying looks like when we compare the answers to our questionnaire on a class level; we want to be able to handle 'the class' as a unit within a quantitative context. We have worked from the hypothesis

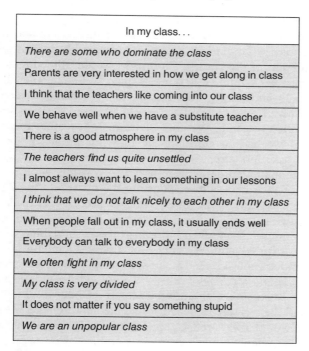

In my class...
There are some who dominate the class
Parents are very interested in how we get along in class
I think that the teachers like coming into our class
We behave well when we have a substitute teacher
There is a good atmosphere in my class
The teachers find us quite unsettled
I almost always want to learn something in our lessons
I think that we do not talk nicely to each other in my class
When people fall out in my class, it usually ends well
Everybody can talk to everybody in my class
We often fight in my class
My class is very divided
It does not matter if you say something stupid
We are an unpopular class

Figure 11.2. Statements about classroom culture

that the class matters in terms of whether or not bullying occurs as well as in terms of the amount of bullying that occurs. In the following, we show that there *is* an association between high levels of contentment within the class and low occurrences of bullying. The questionnaire included a group of questions composed with the intention to construct a score – termed 'self-reported class culture' in the following – that would be a measure of the contentment within the class. The questions ranged from asking about hierarchies in the class, friendships and hostilities to relationships with professional adults and parents, and the relationships between students. These can be seen in Figure 11.2.

The justification that this selection of statements provides an adequate description of life in a school class is partially based on results from the qualitative sub-projects in eXbus that point to the relevance of several of these statements (e.g. parents' impact on bullying and teachers' perceptions that some classes are unpopular are both meaningful). In addition, the selection is based on other studies (*Københavnerbarometeret* 2009; Obermann 2011), which inspired us to include statements like 'We do not talk nicely to each other in my class'. Otherwise, studies on how life in the class influences bullying are rare; therefore, we further enhanced these statements during a series of focus-group interviews with students prior to the implementation of the survey. From this, we developed statements such as 'Teachers like coming into our class' and 'When people fall out in my class, it usually ends well'. The students themselves made us aware of dimensions that we would have missed if we had based the questionnaire solely on published research. We could have included other meaningful statements, but we had to consider the time limitations imposed by completing the questionnaire.

In the questionnaire, students were asked to consider several general statements about their classes in response to the question: 'How do you experience your class most of the time?' The attached statements lie within a positive–negative field of tension that contains statements such as 'The atmosphere in our class is good' and 'It is okay to say something stupid' or 'My class is very divided' and 'We fight a lot' (these statements are reproduced in Appendix Table 11.1). The answer-categories were: *I completely disagree, I disagree, I do not disagree or agree, I agree* and *I completely agree*. In the subsequent calculations, these were scored as -2, -1, 0, 1 and 2, respectively, and the answers to negative statements were reversed so that a positive score would always reflect a positive attitude. For each class, we were then able to calculate a score for class culture by averaging all the answers from all of the students in the class. Thus, a positive score corresponds to a class with a positive opinion of its classroom culture.

In Figure 11.1, we looked at each class's number of self-reported victims of bullying and self-reported bullies. Figure 11.3 shows scatter plots of these numbers drawn against classroom culture. It appears that low scores for classroom culture correspond to a high level of bullying, but not in a 1:1 ratio. Rather, we see a statistical association, and we do not suggest that all classes fit into this pattern. This is one of the central findings of the study: in general, when the self-reported classroom culture is positive, there is also a low level of self-reported bullying. Conversely, a negative classroom culture tends to be associated with a high level of bullying.[9] This is interesting,

---

[9] One could imagine that when self-reported contentment within the class correlates with a high number of students who report that they have been involved in bullying, it is because the students involved in bullying evaluate classroom culture negatively whilst the other students do not concur. To investigate this, we conducted two new regression analyses in which classroom-culture scores were computed only on the basis of the students in the class who had *not* been involved in bullying – either as a victim or a bully. We still found a negative gradient for the regression line; however, it was less pronounced. So even if we view the experience of the class via students who were not involved in bullying, we find that there is an association between bullying and classroom culture, just to a lesser degree.

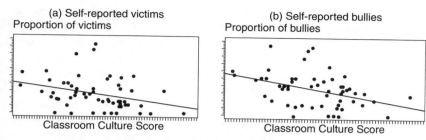

Figure 11.3. Proportion of victims of bullying (a) and bullies (b) within the individual classes in relation to self-reported classroom culture
Note: The lines in the graphs represent lines of regression (calculated in SAS with class size as weights). The negative gradient in both figures is significantly different from 0. The figures should be read as such: each dot represents a class; the X-axis indicates class culture, the Y-axis indicates the occurrence of bullying. (a) indicates victims of bullying, and (b) indicates bullies; and the position of each dot signifies the interrelationship between the two. We find the slope of the line to be most interesting because it indicates the relation between the incidence of bullying and classroom culture. When the lines (as shown here) have a negative gradient, there is a connection between high values of classroom culture score and a low level of bullying; the statistical analysis shows that with a high degree of certainty this association is not due to coincidences.

because this finding challenges prevalent international theories that emphasise the individual characteristics of bullies and victims as well as simpler and causal explanatory models (Olweus 2000). This is discussed later in the chapter.

Dimensions of the students' perceptions of school life

Naturally, we asked the students about issues other than just their opinions of the class. We asked about students' self-image, relationships with their families and their own relation to the class[10] as well as the school. These subjects cover a number of statements. For example, there are statements about what we have chosen to term 'self-image' (e.g. 'I get along well with other people' and ' I think that I have more problems than other students my age'), statements about students' relationships with their parents (e.g. 'In my family, we do many things together' and 'I

---

[10] Here, we would like our readers to notice that we differentiate between both the students' self-evaluated relation to their classes ('me and my class') and the students' characterisation of their classes.

find it difficult to talk to my parents about my problems'), statements
about attending school (e.g. 'I feel happy about my grades' and 'I don't
like going to school') and statements about the students' relation to their
class (e.g. 'I have no real friends in my class' and 'I think that I fit in quite
well with my class'). All sixty individual statements are presented in
Appendix Table 11.1[11]. In the questionnaire, students were asked to
reveal their position on each statement. Again, their answers were scored
as -2, -1, 0, 1, 2 and negatively framed answers were reversed. Score
averages for each statement, as classified by the self-reported bullying
status, are also reported in Appendix Table 11.1. These averages are
shown in Figure 11.4, where the black dots correspond to the answer
'no', light-grey dots to the answer 'yes, a little' and dark-grey dots to the

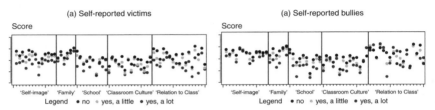

Figure 11.4. Average score for 60 statements. Victims of bullying and
bullies are classified according to bullying status
Note: Figure 11.4 is based on the average scores in Appendix Table 11.1.
The specifications 'Self-image', 'Family', etc., correspond to the divisions
in the table. Figure 11.4 (a) describes the victims of bullying. The dots
specify the average score for each statement from students who answered
that they had not been bullied (black dots), from students who answered
'yes, a little' (light-grey dots) or students who answered 'yes, a lot' (dark-
grey dots arrows) to questions about being bullied. Figure 11.4 (b) shows
the same averages when students were classified by answers to questions
about having bullied others. Only a few students (21 and 20, respectively)
answered 'yes, a lot'; therefore, these averages (dark-grey dots) have a high
degree of uncertainty. It is the relative position of groups with different
bullying status that is of primary interest in this study.

---

[11] Class-based scores were computed for these other groups of statements, and regression
analyses were performed with the proportion of self-reported bullies and victims, respectively, as response variables. For victims of bullying, only 'my own relation to the class'
had any predictive value, whilst 'self-image', 'relations to family' and 'relations to school'
turned out to be unimportant. For bullies, 'my own relation to the class' had some
predictive value, whilst 'relation to school' had a major influence. Again, 'self-image'
and 'relations to family' did not show any influence. Inclusion of other class-based scores
in the regressions in Figure 11.3 did not cause substantial changes.

answer 'yes, a lot'. Bearing in mind that a positive score always reflects a positive attitude, we can see a systematic trend for self-reported victims of bullying: here, non-victims (black dots) have the highest score whilst the score for students who reported extensive bullying (dark-grey dots) is somewhat lower. Students who reported a limited amount of bullying (light-grey dots) tend to fall in between these scores, but the differences are small in many instances. The picture is less unequivocal for self-reported bullies, especially when it comes to statements about students' relations to their class.

In order to gain an overview and be able to delve further into the material, we classified all sixty statements by statistical tests, investigating for each statement whether score averages – as classified by the self-reported bullying status – were significantly different. The results are summarised in Figure 11.5. A 'yes' answer in the category of 'victims of bullying' indicates that a self-reported victim of bullying agreed with a given statement to a greater extent than others; a 'no' answer indicates that there was no significant difference between the answers given by a victim of bullying and others. We did the same for bullies. The point of departure for the following analysis is not whether students agreed or disagreed with a given statement, but whether students involved in bullying as self-reported victims or bullies agreed to a greater extent than their peers. The classification was carried out by separate Kruskal-Wallis tests.[12] More detailed results are presented in Appendix Table 11.1 along with specifics of the statistical analysis.

What do self-reported bullies and victims of bullying have in common?

To a greater extent than others, both bullies and victims of bullying attend classes in which they fight, communicate using rude language and where the general atmosphere is bad. This is not surprising because, in the preceding section, we have already shown the association between bullying and a general low level of positive classroom culture. In both groups, we found a predominance of students who were fed up with school and who believed that they have more problems than others. Furthermore, to a greater extent than others, both bullies and victims of bullying reported that they do not get along with others. But here, the two groups separate: the bullies specified that they get along with other students (i.e. are popular in class), but do not get along with adults (e.g. parents and teachers); it was the reverse for victims of bullying.

[12] To avoid the problem of mass-significance, we used a Bonferroni-correction in the statistical tests even if this might lead to not recognising substantial correlations.

Statement	Victims of bullying agree more with statement	Bullies agree more with statement
Experiencing that there is fighting in the class/communication is rude/bad atmosphere	Yes	Yes
Do not get along with others/more problems than others	Yes	Yes
Fed up with school	Yes	Yes
Experiencing the class as divided/intolerant/hierarchical	Yes	No
Experiencing her-/himself as a loner/left out/unpopular[1]	Yes	No
Feeling lonely/of no use	Yes	No
Is afraid	Yes	No
Does not get along with her or his family	No	Yes
Is bored/bad relationship with teachers No inclination to learn/unhappy about grades	No No	Yes Yes
Does not experience interest from the adults at school/has no faith in adults	No	Yes
Gets into trouble/fights/laughs at others	No	Yes

[1] *Self-reported bullies considered themselves to be significantly more popular than other pupils.*

Figure 11.5. Relationships between bullying and positions on self and school life

Note: A 'yes' answer in the category of 'victims of bullying' indicates that victims agreed with a given statement to a greater extent than others; a 'no' answer indicates that there was no significant difference in the answers given by victims of bullying and others. The same explanation corresponds for bullies. The classification was based on separate Kruskal-Wallis tests (with a Bonferroni-correction). More detailed results as well as the statistical analysis are presented in Appendix Table 11.1.

Specifics for self-reported victims of bullying

If we look at what separates victims of bullying from other students, but examine the areas where there is no difference between bullies and other students, then to a greater extent than other students, victims of bullying experience their classes as hierarchical, divided and intolerant. At the same time, they experience themselves as being alone, outside the class community, unpopular and useless more often than other students.[13] They also specified that they are more afraid, an issue to which we return later. However, victims of bullying do not differ from other students in terms of relationships with their families. The same applies when they were asked about a number of concrete relations in connection with their schools. They were no more bored than other students, they were no less happy about their grades, they did not experience any substantial degree of desertion or lack of adult interest at school, and they did not get into trouble more frequently than other students.

Specifics for self-reported bullies

The results on all counts were exactly the opposite with bullies: they considered themselves to be popular, they were not afraid or lonely and they did not experience their class as intolerant and divided. They did, however, have more problematic relationships with their parents than other students, and they could be characterised as bored and lacking an inclination to learn, as well as being dissatisfied with their grades. They also reported more negative relationships with the adults at their schools, they got into trouble more often and they laughed at fellow students to a greater extent than other students.

It is worth noting three factors here: the first concerns academia, specifically teaching, readiness to learn and relationships with teachers; the second concerns students' relationships with their classmates and the status of the students' experiences in their classes; and the third concerns the students' relationships with adults, both at school and at home. With these three factors as points of attention, we can sum up the tendencies as such: students who reported that they have bullied others have a negative relation in terms of school attendance, but they have good relationships with their schoolmates. Conversely, students who reported that they have been bullied have a positive relation in terms of school attendance, but they have problematic relationships with their peers. The third factor concerns relationships with adults, where bullies reported more negative relationships with both parents and teachers, whilst victims of bullying have relationships with adults that are no worse than any other students.

---

[13] We emphasise that the analysis does not answer whether students agree or disagree with a given statement, but whether students involved in bullying agree or disagree to a greater extent than the other students in their classes.

Hidden positions

These contentment-variables are based on answers from students who answered 'yes' to the question about whether they have experienced being bullied or have participated in the bullying of others in comparison to those who answered 'no'. Thus, the presentations of school attendance and school life are based on answers from students who seem to readily accept their positions. However, qualitative studies in the eXbus research point towards the fact that other kinds of positioning are also at play when a class develops patterns of bullying. We present four examples. *Firstly,* there are students who fellow classmates claim are victims of bullying, but the student involved experiences a loss of pride and believes that naming her- or himself a 'victim of bullying' is an invitation to shame and low status (see, for example, Søndergaard 2008). *Secondly,* there may be students who do not perceive themselves to be bullies, nor do their teachers recognise them as such, but a victim of bullying may nonetheless point to them as a bully (see, for example, Hansen 2011a). *Thirdly,* it is possible that positions of bullying amongst the students are constructed in ways that are consistent with an opposition strategy towards the school and adults in general. This strategy may signify that it is more correct to answer 'no' to the question about whether one is afraid of anything, despite the fact that a student might actually be afraid of some of the things to which the question refers. If such a 'no fear' position is extrapolated, it is also possible to imagine that some students would be quite willing to answer 'yes' to the question about being a bully and 'no' to the question about being a victim of bullying. *Fourthly,* qualitative studies point towards the fact that the positions of 'bully' and 'victim' are not always fixed but can be interchangeable, transposed, transformed and adapted over time (Kofoed 2009), which means that there are likely to be other respondents who could have conveyed other stories if we had asked in different ways.

The hidden and silent positions indicate that the stories that stand out in our analyses constitute particular components of a picture rather than producing an intact, finished portrait. The material cannot enlighten us about how students whom the other students consider to be a bully or victim – but who do not agree with this position themselves – relate to school, the class, themselves and their families, or if the student who accepts a bullying position is recognised as such by other students. Thus, there is also silent or hidden knowledge within our material.

Hard core victims and hard core bullies

We have already shown that students who answered 'yes, a lot' to the question about whether they had experienced bullying were generally more negative in their answers than students who had not been bullied or only bullied a little. This is a small group, so their answers have not carried much weight in the statistical tests; however, it would be fair to modify this description. From what we have seen, the differences amongst those students who have been bullied and other students – in almost all instances – are more explicit when we look at the frequent victims of bullying. We found that victims of bullying did not differ from other students in terms of relationships with their families. To a great extent, this is also true for frequent victims of bullying. They did not experience any larger degree of desertion and lack of interest from adults in their schools, nor did they get into trouble more often than other students. Their relationships with teachers were much like those of the other students, as was their inclination to learn. On the other hand, they expressed boredom and dissatisfaction with their grades, and they were considerably more afraid than other students.

In terms of bullies, the students who answered 'yes, a lot' to the question about whether they have participated in bullying others considered themselves to be popular. They have worse relationships with their parents than other students, and they have considerably worse relationships with teachers and their schools. They are bored and have much less inclination to learn than other students, including other bullies. In this sense and to an extreme degree, they construct themselves as students who are afraid of nothing and act in opposition to the school, the teachers and learning in general.

Classes with students who are afraid

The survey included a number of questions about what students fear in their school lives. This focus on being afraid of something in school life was primarily informed by the methodology implemented by the *Copenhagen Barometer* and their findings, in which it became quite obvious that students are afraid of different aspects of school life (*Københavnerbarometeret* 2009). Combined, these findings have focused attention on what students report being afraid of and how this intersects with the prevalence of bullying.

Table 11.3 should be read as: 11.1 per cent of the students answered 'yes', they are afraid of being bullied; 26.7 per cent were afraid of being left out; and 25.6 per cent were afraid of being ridiculed. If we look at all three questions together, we see that 37.4 per cent of the students stated that they are afraid of being either bullied, left out or ridiculed. These three aspects can be described as relationally orientated because all three

Table 11.3 *Answers to the question 'Are you afraid of...' (The numbers in the table indicate the percentage of students who answered 'yes' or 'no' to each item.)*

Are you afraid of...?	Yes (%)	No (%)
Being bullied	11.1	88.9
Being left out	26.7	73.3
Being ridiculed	25.6	74.4
At least one of the above*	37.4	62.6
Not performing well academically	33.3	66.7
Total number of respondents	1,044	

*This proportion of 'yes' answers indicates the proportion of students who were either afraid of being bullied, left out or ridiculed.

Table 11.4 *Answers to the question 'Are you afraid of...' classified by positions of bullying. (The numbers indicate the percentage of students who answered 'yes' to the question.)*

Are you afraid of...?	Percentage of 'yes' answers						All
	Victims of bullying			Bullies			
	Yes, a lot	Yes, a little	No	Yes, a lot	Yes, a little	No	
Being bullied	76.2	37.7	5.2*	0.0	8.2	12.0	11.1
Being left out/alone	76.2	50.0	22.2*	20.0	27.9	26.3	26.7
Being ridiculed	71.4	49.1	21.2*	5.0	25.2	26.5	25.8
At least one of the above	90.5	71.7	31.5*	25.0	40.1	38.8	37.4
Not performing well academically	38.1	45.8	31.0	30.0	32.7	33.2	33.3
Total number of respondents	21	107	966	20	147	814	1,044

*= the difference between groups is significant.

questions concern acceptance, recognition and respect from the other students in one's class.

Victims of bullying are more afraid than other students

If we divide the students into groups based on their self-reported bullying positions, we come up with Table 11.4.

Students who stated that they have been bullied are also more afraid of being bullied, left out/alone and ridiculed than students who have not been bullied. Thus, students who reported that they have been bullied are the most afraid of these relationally orientated factors. And students who indicated that they have been bullied a lot are more afraid than students who reported that they have only been bullied a little. For instance, more than 90 per cent of students who indicated that they have been bullied a lot are afraid of at least one of the relationally orientated factors. In terms of these, there is a correlation between being subjected to bullying and being more afraid than other students. It is perhaps not surprising that, within the group of victims of bullying, many report that they are afraid – but it is remarkable that the level is so high.

Are bullies also afraid?

A student indicating that he/she is a bully does not seem to make any difference in terms of whether or not they were afraid. In other words, students who reported that they have participated in bullying others are no more and no less afraid than other students. Only students who stated that they have bullied a lot stand out in the results by being *less* afraid than other students.

Students who reported that they have bullied a lot stand out because, to a very large degree, they expressed that they are not afraid of the factors that relate to the other students in their classes. However, they are on par with other students in terms of being afraid of not doing well academically.

Experiences of being bullied produce an increased fear of being bullied

If we differentiate between relationally orientated factors, it becomes possible to investigate the connection between being afraid of being bullied and the actual incidence of bullying within the previously elapsed school year.

More than half of the students who were afraid of being bullied had already been bullied within the previously elapsed school year (57 out of 107). This means that there is a correlation between being afraid of being

Table 11.5 *Connection between being afraid of being bullied and actually being bullied within the previously elapsed school year*

Have been bullied	Afraid of being bullied		
	Yes	No	Total
Yes	56	71	127
No	51	809	860
Total	107	880	987

bullied and experiences of being bullied, in the sense that experiences of being bullied probably make students more afraid of being bullied again in the future. Bullying thus creates a trail of fear. Conversely, only 6 per cent (51 out of 860) of students who had not been bullied were afraid of being bullied.

Not performing well academically

We noticed this result: the more a student experiences being bullied, the more afraid the student will be. In addition, when students reported having a lot of experience as a bully, they also reported that they were less afraid of being ostracised, bullied or excluded than other students (all other students; i.e. also students who reported that they had not been involved in bullying). However, there was one thing of which many students (across different positions of bullying) were afraid, and that was not performing well academically. One-third of all students stated that they were afraid of this.

The difference we wish to highlight here is that we see two contrasting trends in the answers: the first, being afraid of not performing well academically, is a matter that concerns the curriculum; and the second more directly involves a student's relationships with peers. We describe later how bullying interacts with these two dynamics in different ways.

Furthermore, we saw that there is no connection between having been subjected to bullying and being afraid of not performing well academically.[14] This is interesting because, in much of the literature on bullying, there is a presupposition that learning challenges are linked to being a victim of bullying. We cannot exclude that this may be the case; however, the surprising aspect in our study is the finding that being afraid of not performing well was not solely experienced by victims of bullying, but was actually connected to the entire group of students, including the bullies. This could indicate that we are dealing with a fear that is related more to school attendance on a general level than to the issue of bullying. In other words, being afraid of not performing well academically was a common experience for all students.

Even if there is no statistical association between being afraid of not performing well and the level of bullying within a class, we could still ask whether there is a connection between this and bullies distancing themselves from school. When we view the results in light of other findings of the study which indicate that bullies in particular have a negative opinion

---

[14] The difference is not statistically significant.

of attending school, then it begs the question: what is the connection between being an active bully and school readiness? This indicates that an interest in the consequences of bullying – in terms of the victims – should be expanded to include an interest in what bullies achieve in class. Here, it becomes relevant to mention the discussion that Helle Rabøl Hansen raises in her article '(Be)longing – an understanding of bullying as a longing to belong' (2011b). She points to the fact that the purpose of attending school can become misplaced for students who develop bullying communities because participation in the bullying 'we' begins to make more sense than adjusting to school life.

Summary and discussion

As described earlier, on average, two-to-three students in each of the classes that participated in the survey self-reported that they had been bullied within the previously elapsed school year. The quantitative analyses have shown that classroom culture is a significant factor in terms of the incidence of bullying in a school class as compared to other factors, such as relationships with parents, the student's self-image and their general relation to school.

The more negatively students in a class describe the classroom culture, the higher the rate of reported bullying. As mentioned, we operate with an analytic about classroom culture that makes it possible to identify how self-reported occurrences of bullying intersect with other aspects of school life. The quantitative analyses point to interesting differences in the patterns of answers given by bullies and victims of bullying. Students who reported that they have participated in bullying others have a more negative attitude towards school attendance than other students, but they report having satisfactory relationships with their peers. Conversely, students who reported that they have had experiences of being bullied did not have a particularly negative attitude towards school attendance, but they reported having problematic relationships with their peers. Finally, students who reported that they have participated in bullying others had a more negative relationship with their parents and teachers than other students, whilst those who have experienced being bullied had relationships with adults that were no worse than those of other students. If we divide the students according to how much they reported being bullied in the quantitative material, we find that students who have been bullied are more afraid of 'all sorts' of things than students who have not been bullied. Students who have experienced being bullied a lot reported that they were more afraid than students who have been bullied only a little. Conversely, those who reported having been bullied were no more afraid than other students. The small group of students who participated in bullying a lot reported that they were not afraid of any of the listed factors. This means that, if we ask a student who has not been bullied whether he/she is afraid of being bullied, 5 per cent would answer 'yes', and if we ask someone who has been bullied a lot, three out of four would answer that they are afraid of being bullied. But these students are not only afraid of being bullied; they are also afraid of many other things.

The class as an analytical unit

The analytical unit 'the class' has made it possible for us to observe how the prevalence of bullying is differentiated, and how occurrences of bullying are related to other parts of school life of which we were not aware when we started this study. We have drawn upon a theoretically informed interest in the relationship between the individual and society, which has made it possible to generate new knowledge about classroom culture and the prevalence of bullying. This point of departure facilitated a certain direction for our analytical work, which has had to move between counting and multiple analytical readings, whilst focusing on both active bullying and latent bullying within a complex school life.

In quantitative surveys, attention is often paid to social categories like gender, social class, ethnicity, nationality and race. 'Classroom culture' is a way to address an entanglement of forces: not just single forces, but their inter- and intra-actions (see Søndergaard 2009). The analysis we have presented here cannot be read as a measurement of single forces – be it teachers' influence, the importance of technologies, the impact of parents or similar. Instead, the analysis must be read as a measurement of the entanglements of various forces and their inter- and intra-actions. We label this entanglement of forces 'classroom culture'.

Classroom culture can be lived in a number of ways. It can be characterised by a dynamic shared life gathered around teaching. Or the specific culture of a class can be divided by gender, or it can have developed strong patterns of exclusion. Patterns of exclusion are what we have addressed in this chapter, and patterns of extreme exclusion are labelled 'bullying'.

We have focused on classroom cultures that develop such extreme exclusions by looking at the indicators that seem to be influential when school life tips over into bullying. What we find is that the life that students and teachers jointly create at school seems to constitute a particularly important parameter that needs to be considered if we intend more fully to understand the prevalence of bullying. Obviously, any given culture of a school class is always living – regardless of the nature of this culture, it is always there. What we are saying is that *how* the particular culture of a class is formed is centrally important to whether or not there is fertile ground for bullying.

(Cap)ability, learning and bullying

In the survey, we found a differentiation between how students' social life at school is related to their academic life. With this understanding, there appears to be a variety of ways in which experiences of bullying influence a student's interest in learning. Thus, bullying does not necessitate an undifferentiated reduction in all students' inclination to learn.

Most of the students who were subjected to bullying reported just as much interest in learning as other students, and they were equally happy with their academic grades. This does not correlate with students who reported that they have experienced being bullied a lot. Students who participated in bullying other students generally expressed less interest in academic learning at school, and at the same time, they were unhappier about their grades than other students. In our analysis, we found that one-third of the students were afraid of not performing well academically. Even though this has no statistical relevance to the incidence of bullying within a class, we consider it an interesting finding because it suggests that the conditions under which bullying emerge are important. In other words, a more general component of school life is pointed at here as being important.

We could say that a school's core task is to provide structured academic learning, and the fact that a great number of students reported being afraid of not performing well academically is linked to this core task. If we include other parts of school research here, we may speculate about just how – in a slightly polemic sense – (cap)ability should be promoted within schools, and how it becomes an important aspect of school life to students (Bjerg 2011; Gilliam 2009; Kofoed 2004; Staunæs 2004). To a certain extent, we could say that no matter which social position a student holds in the class, a condition they all share is the fear of not performing well academically. Even if a student might be immediately recognisable to other students as one of the 'troublemakers' or as one of the students who opposes the school (Gilliam 2009; Hansen 2011b; Willis 1977), they still may report being afraid of not performing well. We could also regard this as a matter of discipline, where students at school develop contextualised knowledge about becoming a proper student (Kofoed 2004). A proper student is also one who recognises the school's demand for (cap)ability. This does not indicate that appropriate 'studentness' equals (cap)ability, but rather that the sense of what it means to become an appropriate student becomes modified in relation to the school's contextualised demands and expectations. In other words, being afraid of not performing well academically can be included as a condition of being a student at school and, indirectly, it is also a condition of being a student in a culture where bullying occurs.

Being afraid

Throughout the analysis, it has become clear how being afraid seems to be significant in relation to the classes included in this survey. This finding invites a reflection about how school life is also an affective event, and how bullying is embedded in an affective school life (see also Kofoed, page 159). In this survey, we investigated a particular emotion; namely, what is labelled as 'being afraid of' something. In order to pursue this further, we turn to the work of Sara Ahmed, who focuses on fear in particular and on how emotions travel and stick, so to speak, in general (Ahmed 2004; Kofoed and Ringrose 2012). Ahmed argues that being afraid is related to 'that which is not yet in the present, in either the spatial or temporal sense of the here and the now. Fear responds to that which is approaching, rather than already there' (Ahmed 2004).

This Ahmed-inspired attention to fear allows us to point out how bullying is presumably not only a matter of what has already happened, but also a matter of what can possibly happen in the future. Via this quantitative data, new questions may be qualified: for example, perhaps what the students reported being afraid of is not only actions that took place yesterday, but a fear of what might possibly strike tomorrow? Perhaps such ways of being afraid can also be understood as an effect of being afraid? Perhaps emotions of fear travel regardless of whether a student fears school life in general or fears bullying in particular?

In this way of conceptualising emotions, these feelings are not assumed to be private or owned by the subject. On the contrary, subject and emotions are dissociated analytically. Thus, it becomes possible to identify how emotions participate in the maintenance and undermining of relations and social systems (ibid.: 117). The intersection of this kind of theory with the quantitative data allows for new questions, such as: could it be that being afraid at school is not exclusively an issue for those who report being afraid in specific ways? Could it be that this is also a valuable insight into how classes become woven together, and how classes that experience bullying are perhaps constituted in particular affective ways –

also through fear? Perhaps fear travels in particular amongst those students who experience uncertainty in classes with bullying.

When classroom culture tips into bullying

The overall finding in these analyses is that the ways in which classroom culture develops is important to whether or not there is fertile ground for bullying. The phenomenon we address here as being particularly important is the tipping point – where classroom culture spills over into extreme exclusion. Based on these quantitative analyses, we find that the prevalence of bullying is high when students consider a classroom's culture to be negative along the parameters discussed in this chapter. The presence of a number of these parameters (and possibly more and others that we have not scrutinised here) may indicate that the culture of a class is developing patterns of exclusion that may lead to bullying.

Appendix: Dimensions of school life and bullying

In the study, students were asked to respond to a number of statements with 'I completely agree', 'neither agree nor disagree', 'disagree' or 'completely disagree'. In the following, the scores have been allotted the values 2, 1, 0, −1, −2. In Appendix Table 11.1, we state the average score for the students as classified by their bullying status.

For every statement, the three-score averages for victims of bullying and bullies, respectively, were compared to a Kruskal-Wallis test. The p-value for these tests is indicated in columns 4 and 8. To avoid problems of mass-significance, we used a Bonferroni-correction in the statistical tests, where a level of significance of 5 per cent became equivalent to a p-value in the separate tests of 0.0008. The symbol * or ** indicates significance with the Bonferroni-correction; + indicates that separate tests would not give significance on a 1 per cent level, and ++ means it is not significant on the 5 per cent level.

A Bonferroni-correction implies that it is safe to trust the significant differences. However, we must expect that the differences not found to be significant may still turn out to be real if examined within a more purposive design. However, it is clear that many of the insignificant results have the p-value in a separate test setting of more than 5 per cent (equivalent to ++). The averages for the answer 'yes, a lot' often differ from the other two averages, but because they are based on very few students, these differences are not reflected in the statistical tests.

Appendix Table 11.1. *The average score from statements about school life as classified by students' bullying status.*

Statement	Have been bullied				Have bullied others			
	Yes, a lot (1)	Yes, a little (2)	No (3)	p-value (4)	Yes, a lot (5)	Yes, a little (6)	No (7)	p-value (8)
Self-image								
I get along with other people	−0.26	0.46	0.81	**	0.25	0.56	0.78	**
I am happy with my body	−0.21	0.17	0.40	+	0.35	0.23	0.37	++
I have a good life at present	−0.07	0.49	0.76	**	0.72	0.54	0.72	+
I think that I have more problems than other children my age	−0.73	−0.15	0.30	**	−0.27	−0.05	0.28	*
I am often lonely	0.08	0.49	0.88	**	0.90	0.85	0.80	++
I often feel completely useless	−0.34	0.40	0.75	**	0.65	0.73	0.68	++
There are many things I am really good at	0.07	0.58	0.50	++	0.52	0.47	0.50	++
I am one of the popular students in class	−1.34	−0.57	−0.23	**	0.45	−0.04	−0.39	**
I prefer being on my own	−0.30	0.02	0.16	++	−0.16	0.12	0.13	++
I like myself	0.02	0.48	0.55	+	0.60	0.47	0.53	++
I often think that I am no good at all	−0.09	0.28	0.63	**	0.15	0.44	0.59	++
I can do things just as well as most other people	−0.02	0.37	0.49	+	0.25	0.33	0.48	++
I do not think I have much to be proud of	−0.17	0.36	0.58	*	0.50	0.44	0.56	++
Relationship with family								
I find it difficult to talk to my parents about my problems	−0.05	0.08	0.23	++	−0.30	0.01	0.27	**
I can always count on my parents	0.45	0.76	0.77	++	−0.10	0.48	0.83	**
In my family we do many things together	−0.35	0.04	0.23	+	−0.72	−0.02	0.27	*

There are many problems in my family	0.17	0.41	0.59	+	−0.35	0.21	0.64	**
My parents take an interest in what I do at school	0.64	0.86	0.87	++	0.85	0.72	0.91	–
I get along fine with my family	0.79	1.01	1.02	++	0.30	0.85	1.06	**
Relation to school								
I like school	−0.55	0.42	0.80	**	0.50	0.55	0.75	+
I do not get along with my teachers	0.21	0.24	0.33	++	−0.60	−0.02	0.40	**
I am bored at school	−0.93	−0.26	−0.38	+	−1.50	−0.58	−0.31	**
The school takes an interest in its students and supports them if they have problems	−0.08	0.03	−0.08	++	−0.60	−0.26	0.00	–
I like going to school right now	−0.59	0.14	0.26	–	−0.55	0.06	0.28	*
I trust the adults at my school	−0.03	−0.01	0.01	++	−0.50	−0.23	0.07	*
The most important things in my life take place outside of school	−1.21	−1.25	−1.33	++	−1.60	−1.45	−1.27	+
There are adults at my school who I can talk to if I have problems	−0.23	0.09	−0.16	+	−0.70	−0.33	−0.07	–
I do not like going to school	−0.59	0.24	0.23	+	−0.85	0.00	0.29	**
I am happy with my academic grades	−0.83	0.01	0.07	–	−0.05	−0.30	0.11	*
Classroom culture								
There are some who dominate the class	−1.07	−0.87	−0.55	*	−1.03	−0.79	−0.56	+
Parents are very interested in how we get along in class	0.31	0.09	0.20	++	−0.13	0.08	0.23	++
I think that the teachers like coming into our class	−0.07	−0.17	0.05	++	−0.18	−0.20	0.05	–
We behave well when we have a substitute teacher	−0.40	−0.49	−0.35	++	−0.66	−0.72	−0.30	**
There is a good atmosphere in my class	−0.58	−0.18	0.31	**	0.05	0.09	0.26	**
The teachers find us quite unsettled	−1.28	−1.13	−0.90	+	−1.35	−1.20	−0.91	–

Appendix Table 11.1. (cont.)

Statement	Have been bullied				Have bullied others			
	Yes, a lot (1)	Yes, a little (2)	No (3)	p-value (4)	Yes, a lot (5)	Yes, a little (6)	No (7)	p-value (8)
I almost always want to learn something in our lessons	0.08	0.09	0.04	++	-0.96	-0.17	0.12	**
I think that we do not talk nicely to each other in my class	-1.03	-0.88	-0.34	**	-1.04	-0.65	-0.37	*
When people fall out in my class, it usually ends well	-0.44	0.12	0.27	–	-0.22	0.11	0.25	+
Everybody can talk to everybody in my class	-0.49	-0.40	0.09	**	-0.54	-0.11	0.05	+
We often fight in my class	-0.83	-0.33	0.05	**	-0.60	-0.40	0.06	**
My class is very divided	-1.10	-0.98	-0.69	–	-1.21	-0.92	-0.71	+
It does not matter if you say something stupid	-1.12	-0.57	-0.17	**	-0.19	-0.27	-0.24	++
We are an unpopular class	-0.15	0.31	0.25	++	0.89	0.20	0.23	–
Relation to class								
I do not have any real friends in my class	0.01	0.65	0.99	**	0.72	1.05	0.90	++
I sometimes feel left out by my class	-0.45	0.15	0.83	**	1.11	0.74	0.70	++
I see a lot of my classmates after school	-0.55	-0.23	0.11	–	0.02	0.03	0.06	++
I feel alone in my class	0.00	0.62	1.02	**	1.21	1.03	0.91	++
I like having fun	0.25	0.59	0.69	++	0.86	0.81	0.64	+
I am one of the students who is often told off	0.35	0.26	0.30	++	-1.56	-0.43	0.46	**
My best friends are in my class	-0.65	-0.19	0.06	+	-0.44	-0.23	0.07	+
I do not dare say anything in our lessons	-0.30	0.43	0.47	++	0.89	0.52	0.41	++
Sometimes I laugh at other students	-0.39	-0.39	-0.30	++	0.61	0.17	-0.45	**

	-0.70	0.18	0.53 **	-0.56	-0.02	0.58 **
I often get into a fight with someone from my class	-0.70	0.18	0.53 **	-0.56	-0.02	0.58 **
I miss my classmates when I am on summer holiday	-0.95	-0.47	-0.21 –	-0.72	-0.40	-0.24 ++
I would rather not participate in class parties and trips away	-0.15	0.60	0.73 –	0.33	0.68	0.70 ++
I often come up with things we can do in class	-1.48	-0.77	-0.63 *	-0.78	-0.70	-0.67 ++
I am often afraid of going to school	0.20	0.88	1.21 **	1.00	1.03	1.17 ++
I feel that I fit into my class quite well	-1.15	0.02	0.52 **	0.33	0.31	0.42 ++
I often get into physical fights at school	0.60	1.00	1.01 ++	0.00	0.65	1.09 **
In my class, it is important to keep track of what the other students think	-0.80	-0.70	-0.38 –	0.06	-0.39	-0.43 ++
Total number of respondents	21	107	866	20	147	814

Key to p-values:
**$p < 0.0001$
*$0.0001 < p < 0.0008$
–$0.0008 < p < 0.01$
+$0.01 < p < 0.05$
++$0.05 < p$

Part IV

Adult perspectives

12   Parental positions in school bullying: the production of powerlessness in home–school cooperation*

Nina Hein

Not long before starting his first year of school, Mark falls off his bicycle and his broken leg is put in a cast. For the first two months at school, he is unable to join his classmates on the playground during breaks, and he does not become part of any of the groups that are quickly established amongst the boys in the class. Mark's parents sense that he is having an awkward start, but he doesn't tell them much, and they trust the teachers to keep things under control. Besides, they expect Mark to cope; he thrived socially earlier at kindergarten. Nevertheless, Mark's parents are a little concerned about the instability caused by some teachers going on maternity leave, a succession of substitute teachers, etc. When Mark increasingly begins to complain to his parents that three of the boys in his class keep calling him names like 'fatty', 'blubber' and 'hippo', help is not forthcoming from his substitute teacher, who does not feel she can do anything.

Mark's parents contact the parents of some of the boys involved; however, despite productive conversations, the boys don't stop teasing Mark. His parents hesitate to take up the matter with the principal; they are worried that their complaint might be seen as a critique of the school with possible negative consequences for Mark. It is not until Mark is in second grade,[1] now convinced that he is being bullied, that his parents turn to the principal. 'Going to school shouldn't be like that,' states the principal sympathetically, and Mark's parents leave his office happy and relieved. They feel that the principal acknowledged Mark's problems and they expect that, as the head of a Danish *folkeskole*,[2] where bullying is treated as a serious matter, he will now come to Mark's rescue: that he'll *do something*.

---

* A slightly different version of this article was also published in Kofoed and Søndergaard 2009.
[1] This corresponds to third grade/year in American or British schools.
[2] A municipal primary and lower-secondary school.

By approaching the school regarding their son's social problems within his class, Mark's parents expect their initiative to establish further co-operation on the matter between home and school. This expectation is shared by many Danish parents whose children encounter bullying situations.

In Denmark, the concept of home–school cooperation is a given on both sides of the school gates. Parents and teachers are expected to communicate and cooperate together, not least of all when a child experiences problems at school. It is made clear in the preamble to the Danish Act on Primary and Lower Secondary Education[3] that a school must cooperate with parents regarding a student's academic and personal development. However, what exactly the various parties can expect from this cooperation – and how the responsibility is divided between them – is frequently less clear.[4]

In connection with a research project entitled 'Parental positions in student bullying', I interviewed a number of parents whose children had previously found themselves bullied at school. Many of these interviews include stories about how both parents and children initially expected that, by working together, the adults – parents, teachers, the principal – would be able to help the child being bullied. However, these expectations were not met. On the contrary, the child's situation at school worsened; the parents grew increasingly frustrated, powerless and desperate, and the relationship between home and school became one of conflict rather than cooperation. Why? How should the course of events as outlined by the parents in the interviews be interpreted? How can it be that parents, despite all their efforts, are unable to assist their children in bullying situations when working with school staff?

The experiences and perspectives of parents regarding bullying amongst children is a relatively uncharted field of research, both in Denmark and other countries.[5] To the extent that research has dealt with the position of parents in relation to children's bullying practices, the focus has been on establishing a correlation between, on the one hand, the amount of love, structure or setting of boundaries within the home and, on the other hand, children's aggression and involvement in bullying at school.[6] This perspective on the role of parents in children's bullying reflects a widespread belief that children's behaviour – both within and

---

[3] *Folkeskoleloven.*   [4] See Nielsen (2001).
[5] Exceptions include Fors (1995); Mishna (2004); Mishna et al. (2006); Sawyer et al. (2011); and Solberg (2004).
[6] For reviews of the literature within this area, see Nickerson et al. (2010) or Smith and Myron-Wilson (1998), for example.

outside of school – is directly contingent on their upbringing and circumstances at home.

My intention in this analysis is not to apportion blame and responsibility between home and school: indeed, I assume that all parties have the well-being of the child at heart. Instead, I hope to provide insights on the sequence of events that the parents have divulged to me, as seen from their perspectives.[7] Therefore, I point to a number of dynamics that generate powerlessness within the sequence of experiences that these parents have in common, despite their highly divergent situations and backgrounds,[8] and I seek to understand how these dynamics and sequences develop.

The empirical data

The analysis here is based upon interviews from a qualitative dataset compiled amongst parents whose children have experienced being bullied at school. I established contact with these parents through a broad appeal for 'parents whose child has experienced bullying at school'. I circulated an e-mail to every staff member at the university where I work, asking colleagues to urge friends, family and acquaintances with such experiences to contact me. This was how I made contact with the majority of the parents I interviewed, whilst a few parents contacted me themselves after reading about the eXbus project in the press. I also established contact with some parents through an advisory body within the National Association of Schoolparents.[9]

As such, contact was made with twelve parents who felt they had relevant experiences that they wanted to share. Employing this recruitment procedure, I did not make contact with parents whose children had been unequivocally identified as 'bullies' at school, but only with those whose children were the targets of bullying. I spoke to single parents and parents in nuclear families; I interviewed parents individually and, in some cases, couples together. It is these interviews that form the basis of my analysis, and it is important to note that, within the dataset, my focus was not directed towards the interviewees as individuals. Rather, I concentrated on the *experiences* of these parents and their possibilities for

[7] My focus has entirely been on parents' perspectives and experiences, and I have sought insights into what it is like to be in their situation. Therefore, the analysis reflects that, e.g. teachers' experiences of and perspectives on the same issues have not been taken into account.

[8] The parents interviewed vary considerably in terms of their level of education, marital status, level of income and geographical location: their children attend large schools in large towns, smaller, provincial schools or little village schools.

[9] *Skole og Forældre*: www.skole-foraeldre.dk.

understanding and constituting themselves as subjects in this particular situation.[10]

In terms of structure, I started the interviews by asking the parents to tell me their stories from the point where they thought the bullying began. In line with Susan Chase (1995), I deliberately urged the parents to narrate their lived experiences and how they understood having a child who was being bullied at school, rather than to make suggestions about the social and psychological dynamics at play. During the interviews, which were primarily conducted in the respondents' homes, I encouraged a chronological presentation of events, and inquired about the parents' experiences, understandings, feelings, actions and thoughts as well as about how they perceived the understandings and actions of the other parties concerned. The parents I interviewed had children between the ages of 7 and 15 at the time of the events outlined and, in all cases, the sequence of events was spread over several years; typically, two-to-four years.

Shared interpretive spaces and parallel chains of events

The parents' stories are, of course, different. At the same time, they also contain a number of interesting similarities. The narratives seem to illustrate variations on a common sequence of events and certain dynamics common to these parents, all of whom made an active effort to help their child when he/she felt bullied at school. The point is not that this sequence of events and the dynamics behind it constitute an inevitable process for all parents whose children are bullied at school; however, in studying the empirical data, the contours of certain patterns become apparent. These patterns indicate, amongst other things, the ways in which the parents attempted to gain an overview of their child's actual situation at school. At first, they had no idea what was going on – not until their child told them something. If they contacted the school, the teachers also told them something, but these two accounts often diverged considerably. Sometimes, the parents of classmates provided a third source of information. On the basis of these sources and their own interpretations of the situation, the parents tried to piece together an understanding of their child's experiences at school.

The parents' compound understandings of their child's experiences at school were usually produced in a process of ongoing dialogue with both the child and the school. The parents I interviewed typically contacted the

---

[10] See St Pierre (2009) for a critique of the use of 'voice' and human experience in qualitative research as an 'authorization of the lived', rather than as that which we should seek to explain.

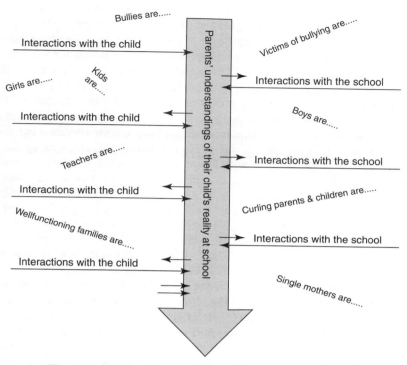

Figure 12.1 Parents' composite understanding of their child's reality at school.

child's teacher and/or principal first and, to varying degrees, utilised the school's representations of the child's situation at school in their subsequent interactions with the child. For example, Mark's parents, as described later, adopted the principal's view that Mark was being 'too sensitive', and thus attempted to 'toughen him up' at home. In the same way, the parents drew upon interactions with their child in their ongoing interpretations of the child's experiences at school as well as in meetings with teachers, the principal, etc. (see Figure 12.1). Parents tried to take action and find their bearings within an interpretive space comprised of the school's understandings and views of the child's experiences at school on one side, and of the child's own understandings and views of his/her experiences on the other.

The parents' shared interpretive spaces regarding their children's lives in school were also comprised of understandings about teachers, parents, home–school cooperation, children, bullying, etc., which were widely culturally accessible and which were implicit in many of the exchanges and discussions that took place between parents, children and the schools. In the cooperation between home and school, these cultural understandings[11] were evident in the explanations the school provided for why the child (re)acted a certain way. The child's sense of being a victim of bullying or exclusion was thereby interpreted and explained by the school, drawing upon familiar cultural understandings concerning what are considered to be normal ways of reacting; these are based on the child's age, gender, personality or family circumstances. Due to their common legitimacy as tools of explanation, these interpretations contributed to the parents, who otherwise had a different understanding of their child's situation at school, experiencing a conflict of interests: what should they believe? And how should they strike a balance between being a caring parent – acknowledging the child's feelings and taking responsibility for his/her well-being – and being the type of parent who is considered a sensible and legitimate partner in home–school cooperation? In some cases, the parents wavered and began to have doubts, both with regard to their child's experiences and their own judgement.

As part of this balancing act between being a caring parent and a legitimate partner in cooperation with the school, there was an ongoing process of (self-) assessment and appraisal: am I doing a good enough job in relation to my child? In relation to the school? The parents' accounts demonstrate how they constantly reflected upon their ability as a parent, whilst also undergoing appraisal by teachers and principals. The analysis suggests that, in the cooperation between home and school, it is not only the child's reactions and attitudes that are interpreted and explained on the basis of widespread cultural understandings regarding the individual, but also the reactions and attitudes of their parents. Certain aspects – such as an individual parent's perceived personality, gender and social class – are employed as explanations for their reactions and behaviour. In terms of the parents' suffering and their efforts to ensure their child's well-being, these interpretations work as part of the apparatus that invalidates and disempowers the parents.

In the following, I have selected the narratives of three parents based on both shared characteristics and variations in the assembled dataset. Cutting across these narratives, I offer a chronologically ordered analysis that seeks to illustrate how the parents were gradually forced to concede their growing powerlessness. This powerlessness occurs through a process in which they – by attempting to act as responsible and caring parents and by participating in home–school cooperation – contributed to an

---

[11] The term 'cultural understandings' is elaborated on later in this chapter.

escalation of the conflict and the exclusion that they originally sought to help their children escape.

It is a basic condition of modern, western parenthood that a parent must consider and look after a child's overall well-being in contexts where the parent is frequently absent. In other words, a parent must consider the well-being of a child in places where he/she cannot personally assess the situation, but is instead limited to representations mediated by others. This condition of parenthood is especially pronounced in relation to children's school lives. School constitutes a crucial element of children's lives: a structured parallel universe alongside their lives at home that has its own separate reality, its own set of codes and logic, and which simultaneously affects and is affected by the home and family. Nevertheless, when assuming parental responsibility for their child, parents are limited to relying on the accounts provided by the child him/herself or by others within the school to determine the situation.

In this study, each of the parents I interviewed stated that he/she lacked information from the school, and each requested greater transparency regarding the social environment within the class and their child's position and attitudes at school. However, according to the parents' accounts, the teachers met this request with a more-or-less explicit response – that there is no reason for parents to involve themselves in matters that the teachers can take care of themselves in the classroom. Alternatively, an argument was put forth that there were insufficient resources available to provide parents with regular updates regarding an individual student's social life at school. Consequently, when parents were faced with a child who said that he/she felt uncomfortable in class, was being teased, beaten up, bullied, ostracised, etc., then they were initially left with nothing to go on other than what their child told them. If they then contacted the school and encountered teachers and/or a principal who appeared to possess other knowledge about their child's situation at school, this was often the beginning of a long and disempowering process marked by conflict.

Gut feelings and faltering strategies

Let's now return to the story of Mark and his parents. The parents held an initial meeting with the principal, who seemed to acknowledge that Mark's situation was a problem that needed to be addressed. He voiced the opinion that 'going to school shouldn't be like that', leaving Mark's parents feeling relieved and hopeful. However, the principal has not actually *done* anything as far as they can tell. They don't *know* whether he has held meetings with the parents of Jason, Tom and Nick, and they don't *know* whether he has taken any action in relation to the class – if so, they certainly haven't heard about it. They stated later that they were left wanting information and transparency. Meanwhile, Mark continues to grow increasingly unhappy and tells his parents more and more about his bad experiences at school.

When Mark's parents again contact the principal to find a solution, he proffers a more clear-cut interpretation of the situation: obviously, he says, the other boys shouldn't call Mark 'fatty', but the problem might be more that Mark is *too sensitive*. With this, the principal provides an interpretation related to Mark's personality. He points to how Mark *is*, an explanation that is detached from the actual situation at school. In their attempt to understand their son's situation, this new input seems to make sense to Mark's parents. Like the principal, they draw upon the culturally embedded notion about an individual's innate personality that is stable across both time and space. Mark's parents bring this understanding into their home and connect it to their own belief that Mark *is* a sensitive boy, just like his father who was also bullied at school. In that sense, they try to go along with the principal's interpretation of the situation and his positioning of Mark as not strong enough to cope with what they, for the time being, choose to understand as run-of-the-mill teasing. Subsequently, Mark's parents make a concerted effort to change him:

Mother: And we worked a lot with that at home. I mean, you know . . . I mean all the way down to that, let's say I bought him some clothes – he couldn't be bothered buying clothes and stuff like that. So I bought him some clothes and I'm like: 'I've bought you some clothes'. Then he says: 'They're ugly', he says – you know what they're like! 'Yeah', I say. 'Then they'll match your face', stuff like that. Kind of to try and . . . I mean, he knows I don't mean it. And we've worked a lot with that at home, because Paul [Mark's father] is really sensitive about that kind of thing, but there's no reason why Mark should go through life like that, because it just makes things harder, doesn't it. (. . .)
Father: Yeah, but we've also – or rather you've also used a special tactic on him with that stuff. I mean, that we've actually also bullied him a bit with various things – affectionately, but . . . And then he's been allowed to answer back.

Tine K. Jensen (2002) points to the ways in which adults often interpret children's behaviour by applying available cultural understandings; for example, with regard to what constitutes typical age- and gender-related behaviour. At the same time, certain types of behaviour are generally attributed to a child's (stable and context-independent) personality.[12]

[12] Jensen (2002) refers to Norwegian psychologist Hanne Haavind who, as early as 1987, highlighted this way to apply available cultural understandings when interpreting children's behaviour (Haavind 1987).

She also calls attention to the way our understanding of a child's 'personality' is typically associated with both certain expectations regarding behaviour and a sense of what such a child needs from adults. In Mark's case, his parents try to do the right thing. They initially accept the principal's identification of Mark's personality as the root of the problem. Their subsequent reasoning seems to be that, in order to cope at school, a sensitive child like Mark should not be safeguarded; on the contrary, such children need toughening up so that their innate personalities can be challenged and, if possible, realigned to produce more appropriate emotional responses.

Mark's parents also attempt to change how Mark reacts by using rational argumentation: 'They're not teasing you because you're fat. They're teasing you because they think it's funny that you get so angry when they call you "fatty",' they explain. As such, they inadvertently tell their son that the reason he is bullied on a daily basis is not because he is overweight, but because he gets *too* angry, he's *too* sensitive, *too* thin-skinned.

Before continuing with the narrative by Mark's parents, I introduce a couple of other narratives from the data to illustrate how the parents – despite differences in their children's situations and variations in their own strategies for navigating these situations – seem to follow parallel pathways.

Peter's mother suddenly realises that her son is having serious problems at school during a parents' evening, where Peter's teacher discloses to both her and the rest of the assembled parents that Peter is a victim of bullying. As with Mark, Peter suffers daily jibes, such as 'fat bastard'. He has occasionally complained to his mother and told her a little about what takes place, but she has interpreted the situation as being typical of conflicts amongst boys of his age (cf. Jensen's point above) and shrugged it off. However, the discussion at the parents' evening alters her view of Peter's situation in class. In addition, just a few months later, she is forced to consider a different representation of Peter's situation – a situation in which she is given a more active role:

Mother: But then, it couldn't have been more than a couple of months, then there's one-on-one meetings with the teacher. And, plain and simple, everything had been turned upside down. Now, it was actually Peter causing all the trouble. It was him who was to blame for all the conflicts and for turmoil in the classroom. He was incapable of sitting still and if it wasn't one thing, it was another. And if they tried taking him out of the classroom to talk about things, he broke down in tears and got upset. So they had to try and figure out what was wrong with the boy, because something was definitely not right. (...) When she [the teacher] said that she couldn't understand what was wrong with Peter, she basically intimated that the problem must be here. Something must be wrong at home.

NH: Did she say that directly?

Mother: Well, she said directly that there must be something at home: 'Can you think of anything at home that might cause him to get so upset?' So I said: 'No, nothing. The only thing out of the ordinary in our household is there's no dad living there. Apart from that, there's nothing unusual.' We also have our daily routine – get up in the morning and come home and cook dinner, have a bath, do homework and...I mean, there's no difference there... Of course, I get tired always being 'on duty', but it's not much of a difference. But she really wanted there to be something causing it at home.

Peter's teacher says that she thinks there is something wrong with Peter. She seems to operate with two possible models of interpretation: either there is something wrong *inside* Peter – and she will later send him to the school psychologist to find out – or Peter's problems are contingent upon something *at home*.

Jensen (ibid.) highlights how interpretations that link children's difficulties to the shortcomings of the primary caregiver (usually the mother) are both well known and widely used amongst parents today. The above account demonstrates that such interpretations are also applied beyond the parent–child relationship, as Peter's teacher interprets his problems at school as a reflection of problems at home. Peter's mother is thereby given the impression at an early stage that she herself is under scrutiny when it comes to Peter's problems at school. The teacher's relatively discreet inquiry about whether an issue at home might explain Peter's behaviour at school prompts his mother to link this to her general impression that there exist certain shared cultural understandings regarding single mothers and children from *that* kind of home. These understandings have yet to be directly articulated in the dialogue between Peter's teacher and his mother, but as she explained to me, she could already sense which way the wind was blowing.

Next, the school initiates and organises a series of meetings between Peter's mother, the principal and the teacher to try and solve Peter's problems/the problems with Peter. Peter's mother never discovers how the school defines *its own* responsibility in tackling his problems. But her responsibilities are quite clear:

The way it was is that we were supposed to discuss what had happened and what was to be done. One of the things was, for example, that when Peter came home from school, I wasn't supposed to ask whether anything bad had happened and if he'd been involved in any conflicts, and I can understand that because of course it would make him dwell on it. But then I was supposed to try and ask him if anything good had happened, because then he'd focus on all the good things, because he was supposed to have some positive experiences at school. But he never came home and said that something good had happened.

Peter's mother can understand why she is not supposed to ask Peter directly about his negative experiences at school. She is well aware of the popular psychological perspective the school incorporates into the plan of action. This view, with roots in cognitive psychology, suggests that problems can be sustained or even exacerbated by talking about them, whilst focusing on good experiences can bury problems in positive thoughts. In this way, Peter's mother is given responsibility for the extent of and the manner in which Peter is affected by his negative experiences of being bullied at school. However, from Peter's mother's perspective, the problem is that Peter does not have any positive school experiences on which they can focus.

Peter tells his mother that he still gets called 'fat bastard' at school every day. That he is unhappy. The school informs her that Peter is involved in conflicts, and he causes trouble and turmoil in the classroom. That he is unhappy. And that there must be something wrong with the boy. Initially, Peter's mother did not question how the school articulated the problems. She now voices her surprise that the situation has changed so radically in a matter of months, and she informs the school that both she and the rest of her family have an entirely different impression of Peter outside of school. However, she otherwise allows herself to be identified as the mother responsible for a child with whom there is something wrong.

Based on her understanding of the dynamics of bullying, and with her desire to take responsibility and help her son, Peter's mother then decides that one way to stop the bullying is for Peter to lose weight. She sends him to a health resort for overweight children with the hope that he will become a little less plump, a little less obvious a target for bullying and thereby also a little less vulnerable in relation to classroom conflicts. I return to Peter's story later.

Parental figures and streams of subjectification

Caitlin's parents become concerned for their daughter's well-being at school when she voices how she increasingly feels insecure and isolated in her class. This development runs parallel to Caitlin's growing academic difficulties and that she must spend more and more time away from the class receiving special-needs teaching. Caitlin's mother ponders long and hard about how to tackle the situation. She is well aware of the discourse within Danish education, as presented in the media, concerning pushy modern parents: the ones who continually bother their child's teacher at all hours of the day with first one thing then another. She does not want to be *that kind* of parent. For a long time, she is unsure whether or not to share her concerns with the school. She recounted:

As a parent, I feel like it's a real balancing act between taking care of things yourself and knowing when you have to say, like, that this is the school's responsibility, you know? Such a delicate balance. And when are you supposed to ask for help, when are you meant to say, 'We'll take care of that at home', you know?

It is a delicate balance, as Caitlin's mother puts it. She does not want to ask the school for help if her daughter's problems should in fact be dealt with at home. She does not want to seem like 'one of those parents' who blame the school for no apparent reason. Nevertheless, as Caitlin's academic and social situation gradually worsens, her mother contacts Caitlin's teacher for help several times. The teacher refers Caitlin to the school psychologist:

Mother: There was a period where she was really upset. At the time, she was seeing the school psychologist to help her get less upset about some of that stuff. And it was like, according to Caitlin, the psychologist gave her some advice to put on rose-tinted glasses and see things in a positive light, that kind of thing. But I've never heard from an adult what was said. So, to put it bluntly, it was bloody hard for me to offer my support, you know? I mean...

NH: You had no idea what was going on?

Mother: Not a clue, and no-one would tell us anything either. She [the psychologist] quit too.

NH: Could you tell me whose idea it was? Was it the school that thought Caitlin should see a psychologist, or was it your idea?

Mother: Well, I reckon it was the teacher. I think it was the teacher because I think she was annoyed, plain and simple, that it didn't go away, that we felt there were problems all the time, you know?

Caitlin comes home and informs her mother that the school psychologist advised her to 'put on her rose-tinted glasses' in order to develop a more positive view of her social situation in the class. The same psychological understanding would also seem to exist at Peter's school: if children learn to focus on positive things instead of getting hung up on negative school experiences, then a lot of problems will just sort themselves out. However, Caitlin's mother is not presented with this interpretation of her daughter's problems by the school psychologist herself; she says later that she could never reach her, and then one day, the psychologist quit.

A lack of transparency seems to be something that all the parents had to deal with: partially being unable to ascertain for themselves what was happening to their child at school and forming their own opinion; partially the schools' frequent neglect in informing parents about conflicts between students, unless the school itself was unable to find a solution; and partially in cases like this, where Caitlin's mother could not get into contact with the school psychologist her daughter has been seeing, despite making persistent efforts. The question arises: given this lack of transparency with regard to the social aspects of their children's school lives, which conditions do parents need to act responsibly in terms of their children's behaviour at school?

As outlined above, Peter's mother felt she had been singled out and made a scapegoat after being assigned the position of 'disadvantaged single mother of a son with problems at school': a position generally associated with the type of parent who gets *insufficiently* involved. At first, she is *called in* for numerous meetings in the principal's office so she can assume responsibility for Peter's problematic behaviour. Later, after becoming aware that Peter is being bullied and is unhappy at school – and being strongly committed to doing something about it – it is Peter's mother who must request meetings to discuss matters. Most of the other parents I interviewed were not called in for any meetings at all: they contacted the school themselves and requested a meeting. This is because the children in question did not exhibit noticeably inappropriate, aggressive or disruptive behaviour; they were merely being bullied or excluded. For these parents, they felt they had to actively distance themselves from another parental stereotype in the dialogue between school and home: the vivid notion of 'the modern parent'; 'the doting, over-protective parent'; the type of parent who gets *too* involved.

The parents' accounts suggest that they positioned themselves in relation to a type of 'abstract parental figure'[13] concealed in terms such as 'curling parents',[14] 'project parents' and 'modern parents'. This abstract parent is comprised of a number of familiar attitudes and behaviours, all of which indicate *over-involvement* in their child's life. Parents are over-protective and at the child's beck and call, carefully removing all obstacles from their path at the expense of any regard for solidarity, as well as the needs and interests of others. It is more or less this view of the modern parent that was found in the results of a survey conducted amongst 806 teachers working at Danish *folkeskoler*.[15] Of the teachers surveyed, 85 per cent believed that parents today are more narrowly focused on their own child than parents were fifteen years ago. Similarly, in the corresponding qualitative study, the teachers expressed the opinion that children today are more spoilt and self-centred than previous generations; they are 'curling children' who are adversely affected by their parents treating them as a 'project':

[13] See Søndergaard (1994) for an examination of the concept of 'abstract figures'.
[14] The term 'curling parents' is a Danish concept that corresponds to the British 'lawn-mower parents', which refers to parents who figuratively walk in front of their children and try to clear the way for them, removing any obstacles they might encounter.
[15] Panel study for the professional journal *Folkeskolen*, October 2006, conducted by Scharling Research for the professional journal *Folkeskolen* and the business newsletter *A4 Weekly*; accessed 8 September 2008; www.folkeskolen.dk.

In their eagerness to take care of their children, parents limit their opportunities for autonomous development. As a result, some [children] get used to other people solving their problems for them. The curling children are not used to having to work at things. (Panel study for the professional journal *Folkeskolen*, October 2006: 7; translated from the original Danish)

The abstract 'modern parent' becomes an active participant in home–school cooperation, partly because parents – especially middle-class parents – are familiar with the concept and the prejudices that surround it, and they find that being invested in their child's welfare at school can all too easily be interpreted as a sign that they are one of *those* parents. As a result, they reflexively attempt to relate their own self-realisation as parents to – and particularly in opposition to – this abstract figure.

Soul-searching and doubts

The deliberations that Caitlin's mother undergoes are characteristic for the situation in which many parents find themselves: 'My child tells me that he/she is having a bad time at school. What's that all about? Should I contact the school? Or is there something I can do about it at home? It's probably best if I discuss it with the school. After all, they know what's going on, and I'll be better equipped to help if we work together.'

In the case of Caitlin's mother, the teachers choose to interpret Caitlin's academic and social difficulties in class as entirely separate phenomena. Her mother later recounted that, when Caitlin was 10 years of age and experiencing more academic difficulties, the school decided to ask the school psychologist's trainee to conduct a type of test on Caitlin. At a subsequent meeting with the psychologist and his trainee, the class teacher, the maths teacher and the principal of the school, Caitlin's parents receive the conclusion: Caitlin's problems may be the result of minor brain damage. Her parents are stunned. They do not recognise their daughter in the way she is described at the meeting. Nevertheless, once home, they discuss whether as parents they have a blind spot regarding their daughter. As time goes by, Caitlin becomes ever more distressed about attending school and increasingly struggles academically.

The school psychologist, who counselled Caitlin so that she could learn to become less upset by situations at school, now sends her home with a message: 'Tell your parents to stop worrying so much.' So Caitlin's mother mulls it over and begins to wonder: is that what it is? Is it just us creating non-existent problems? The psychologist's message hits home with Caitlin's mother because it utilises a common cultural understanding in its interpretation of her as a mother who worries too much. This interpretation is used to explain her attitudes; e.g. 'she reacts like this to her daughter's problems *because* she is an over-anxious mother', which is thereby implicit because there isn't anything that warrants a concerned reaction. Caitlin's mother becomes unsure of herself. Maybe the school psychologist and teacher are right? She continued:

It all ended with the school psychologist saying that she [Caitlin] didn't have any problems. And, to be honest, I think that's a strange thing to conclude when I have a daughter who comes home in tears – maybe not every day, but certainly several times a week. (. . .) That's the role you have as a parent, that it's not me that's the expert, it's the teacher, and it's the school psychologist, and it's the school's staff who are the experts in all this. So, up to a point – then you have to trust that they're right.

This mother has a daughter who comes home from school in tears several times a week. Yet she has the school psychologist implicitly telling her that her daughter's biggest problem is her over-anxious parents. Caitlin's mother is in doubt. She feels that her authority and her right of definition are secondary to that of the experts. Moreover, she does not want to be perceived as being difficult. Therefore, despite her actual experiences and a firm gut feeling that tells her otherwise, she incorporates the psychologist's words and the teacher's innuendo into her own mental image of what is wrong with Caitlin, and she uses this in her ongoing attempts to take suitable care of her daughter. She said:

The thing that's really difficult is seeing the role you play yourself, you know? And, I would expect, both as teacher and as parent, then you're going to be the carrier of something or other, you know? And when is that a good thing, when is it a bad thing? And that's why I think, like I told you earlier, that for certain periods, we kind of tried to ignore it a bit, whilst at other times, we tried to get more involved when she told us stuff. Ask more detailed questions, and why do you think this and that, and analyse, analyse, you know? But somehow or other, well, we didn't really feel like there was much we could do.

Just like Mark's parents and Peter's mother, Caitlin's parents try to follow the school's suggestions and look inward at the child and/or themselves as parents: if we can just toughen Mark up a bit, then things will probably get better; if Peter loses weight and I refrain from discussing his negative experiences at school with him, then his problems will probably go away; if we examine our role as parents and try out different strategies regarding our degree of involvement in Caitlin's welfare at school, then what we've been doing wrong will probably become clear.

Caitlin's mother visits a psychologist with a private practice in order to discover whether it is, in fact, she as a mother who is doing everything wrong:

I mean, sometimes I've felt, like, really upset on my child's behalf about the way things were. And that's also why, at some point, I thought to myself: 'Well, is it me that's doing something completely wrong here?' And I myself sought out help in order to get, how should I put it, some tools to deal with that properly, you know?

During her first three or four years at school, Caitlin expresses her growing unhappiness to her parents. She is upset about always being the last one picked when students are asked to form groups or to choose a partner; upset about always watching the popular girls leave the game when she asks to join in; upset that on several occasions, she has been one of only two girls in the class not invited to a birthday party. Nevertheless, as a result of her contact with the school, Caitlin's mother starts to wonder whether she as a mother has conjured up her daughter's problems out of thin air. Therefore, she visits a psychologist herself to get help in dealing with the situation *properly*, something she has been led to believe she has yet to master.

Divisions intensify and standpoints take root

Despite Caitlin's mother's attempts to scrutinise her own role in her daughter's unhappiness at school and, even though Caitlin's parents try to brush aside their daughter's attempts to talk about her problems, Caitlin *still* voices her growing unhappiness at school. Her parents develop a stronger sense that their perspective on their daughter's situation is in conflict with the school's perspective.

Likewise, Peter's mother has to acknowledge that, despite her efforts, Peter's situation at school remains the same. After spending five weeks at the health resort for overweight children, Peter returned in otherwise good spirits, having enjoyed his stay and lost a lot of weight:

Mother: He'd lost almost, well, actually he'd lost more than 10 kilos. And he was over the moon. And he had high expectations now he was going back and he'd lost weight, so now he wasn't the fat kid anymore, you know? But it stuck to him. And then all the meetings started up again. Because I guess I feel that the teachers could keep more of an eye on things. But they said they were doing everything they could to ensure the other kids didn't say this and that. But the conflicts were often during breaks. So they [the children] were either in the classroom by themselves, or they were down playing table tennis by themselves, and then things happened. And then I say it might be an idea if there was someone there to keep an eye on them. But they [the teachers] didn't have time for that.
NH: There was no supervision, or there was no...?
Mother: No, and 'At their age, they should know how to behave themselves.' And then I said: 'Well, apparently, they don't.'

Peter's mother starts to change her perspective. Peter is still being bullied at school, and she finds the school's response unsatisfactory. She becomes increasingly aware that her understanding of the situation places her in opposition to the school.

Mark's parents are also forced to acknowledge that their efforts to 'train' Mark to cope with bullying are not really helping. Mark frequently becomes distressed at bedtime when he tells his parents about the indignities he has suffered that day. In addition, he starts having nightmares on school nights; at weekends and during school holidays, he sleeps soundly. Mark's parents once again turn to the school for help, but there seem to be a number of obstacles. Amongst these is an understanding – apparently shared by some of the staff at Mark's school, just like at Peter's school – that you cannot react to events that you have not *witnessed* yourself. To them, the presence of an adult when the bullying takes place is necessary to assess the situation and judge what *really* happened.[16] Within the data, there are numerous examples of teachers legitimating their failure to intervene in bullying by claiming that they 'didn't see it with their own eyes'.

Meanwhile, for Mark's parents, the experience of being powerless to help their child becomes more and more pronounced. Mark's mother recalled:

By now, we had reached the point where we thought, 'Is it us who are crazy, is it really our child that's the problem? Is it us that expect too much from the school, is it us?' Each time we went there, they just said. . .sometimes, when we phoned the maths teacher. . .someone had kicked over Mark's desk during a maths lesson. She hadn't seen a thing: 'I can't help you, I didn't see it,' she said. I mean, we just felt utterly powerless [she cries].

Like Caitlin's parents, Mark's parents start to doubt their own judgement: have we got it all wrong? They experience an almost surreal failure of the school staff to recognise their observations and viewpoints as meaningful. They feel, as Mark's mother put it, utterly powerless, completely unable to do anything to improve Mark's situation.

As illustrated by these two last-quoted passages, the staff at schools sometimes justified their reluctance to act against bullying by explaining that they can't act on something they have not personally witnessed. According to the parent interviews, on other occasions, this reluctance to act was due to the teachers/principals not acknowledging the child as a 'proper' victim of bullying. The reasons why the schools did not recognise

---

[16] This is also found by Mishna et al. (2006).

the child as such seem manifold. One common characteristic, however, is that a child's position as a victim of bullying is far from straightforward or stable; e.g. as the position has been outlined in the various offshoots of Dan Olweus's definition of bullying, bullies and victims (see Schott, Chapter 2). This definition has had tremendous influence on Danish schools' action plans to address bullying (see Hansen 2009). Mark provides a clear example of a bullying target whose position may appear ambiguous from perspectives that only acknowledge the victim of bullying in a stable and unequivocal victim position:

Mother: I mean, for Mark, whenever there was anybody who actually wanted to play with him, he was game. Even if it was one of the kids calling him 'fatty' again the next day.
Father: There was Jason, and then there was Tom too.
NH: OK, as if they all of a sudden thought he was good enough?
Father: Yeah.
Mother: Then they had this kind of twisted thing where they were supposed to vote for 'friend of the week' or something every week at school. And Mark actually voted for Jason sometimes, if he hadn't called him 'fatty' for a week.

In Peter's case, the teacher sees him as a boy who used to get bullied, but who now just creates problems for himself and those around him with his poor behaviour in the classroom. However, when Peter's mother combines the teacher's accounts with Peter's and with her own observations, she sees a boy who can no longer figure out how else to make contact with others because he has been bullied and ostracised for such a long time:

NH: Did she [Peter's teacher] say that he caused trouble? She didn't say that he bullied others, or...?
Mother: No, but he couldn't behave himself.
NH: Behave...?
Mother: And he couldn't be around the other kids without pushing them, or taking a swipe at them, or taking their things, or... And at some point, well, maybe it's because he actually wants to be part of the group, but he doesn't get the chance because there's always someone hounding him. So, in order to get a bit of attention, maybe that's why he acts like he does, because he craves a bit of attention, and he has to belong somewhere, right?
NH: Yes, and that's what you said?
Mother: Yes.
NH: How did she respond?
Mother: Well, she said, 'Apparently not, seeing as how he behaved the way he did.'

Due to Peter's behaviour, his class teacher does not believe that Peter wants to be part of the group. Nor does she acknowledge him as a victim of bullying any longer; Peter does not fit the position of a bullying victim as she understands it, based on the prevailing definitions of bullying.[17]

All of the parents in this study have their own personal and unique stories: different children, different schools, different parenting strategies. Nevertheless, a shared characteristic of the various narratives seems to be that, to begin with, the parents tried to stay in line with the schools' interpretations and to follow their action plans. Subsequently, the parents found that their attempts to toughen up, ignore, explain or manipulate their children failed to stop the bullying and/or exclusion. At this point, after focusing on their child's situation at school for an extended period – and having been involved in ongoing interactions with both the child and school staff – parents usually start to develop their own interpretations of the situation. These interpretations often result in parents opposing the school's perspective, and giving primacy instead to the child's expression of unhappiness. They then draw upon this representation of the situation in subsequent meetings with the school. At this point in the process, parents typically become more frustrated with the whole situation. Some find themselves regarded as troublemakers, and they sense that they are in the process of being annexed to a category of understanding that they had otherwise sought to avoid. All of them experience becoming increasingly powerless in terms of being able to help their child escape his/her predicament. Caitlin's parents start to approach her teachers more frequently, but there seems to be continuing disagreement over the severity of Caitlin's problems. Her mother said:

When we were sitting there at all those meetings, and there had been a lot of them over the years, then it was kind of a bit – ugh – weren't we being a bit pedantic or awkward or...

Mark's parents also repeatedly contact the principal but begin to sense that he is not taking them seriously; that he is stringing them along:

Mother: And we've sat in that principal's office a hundred times, and nothing happens. There haven't been...actually, I don't even think any of the other kids' parents have been called in... (...)
Father: And I feel as though our name – with a lot of people – has a ring of 'Oh no!' around the school.
Mother: It was us who were difficult.
Father: It was us who...
Mother: And I still can't shake that off.

---

[17] Mishna et al. (2006) also point to how teachers' and parents' expectations regarding the personality and behaviour of a victimised child influence their perception of whether a certain incident should be understood as bullying or as a normal conflict between peers.

Here, the parents feel aggrieved at how the school strips them of their legitimacy by positioning them as troublemakers. They cannot understand why their numerous appeals to the principal have not led to consequences for the bullies; they are familiar with other schools' action plans against bullying where expulsion is the ultimate punishment. Mark's parents are well aware that this is how bullying is handled at modern Danish schools, and by now they want to be well rid of Mark's tormentors. But they experience that the principal fails to impose any consequences on the boys who have been humiliating their son on a daily basis, and also that the principal increasingly regards their appeals as whinging and grumbling rather than as legitimate and meaningful concern about the well-being of their son. Therefore, it becomes crucial to Mark's parents that the school recognise their son's position as a victim of bullying, thereby acknowledging them as parents legitimately looking out for their child's welfare. And this is where a shift occurs. At this point, Mark's parents become fully conscious of the incompatibility between their own perspective and the school's perspective of the situation.

As a result of this new understanding of an actual opposition, the parents in my study began to make more explicit demands of the school than before. They framed their demands in their own understanding of the situation, and were no longer hesitant and unsure of themselves with regard to striking a balance between their child's descriptions and the school's interpretations. If they had previously doubted whether it was a case of what they would consider 'proper' bullying or ostracism from the class community, they were now convinced. For the most part, the parents became more explicit in assigning responsibility to the school and demanding that staff make a genuine and appreciable effort to end the bullying.

Powerless parents, fortified figures

At this point, the home–school cooperation has developed into a more-or-less explicit battle to define the child's situation at school: is the child a victim of bullying, and does he/she thereby have a right to the help that the parents – in alignment with the prevailing Danish view of how to address school bullying – expect this position to trigger? Or rather, are the problems of the child's own making and attributable to his/her personality, age, gender, home life or family background? Parents seem to face a challenge on two fronts: firstly, the schools do not seem to acknowledge the children as victims of actual, 'proper' bullying; secondly, the accounts indicate that the parents lose their right to be taken seriously by the school once they reject the school's perspective and no longer regard their child's or their own attitudes as the root of the problem. Part of the issue seems to be that these parents now openly declare that they believe what their child tells them about his/her experiences at school. By challenging the school's perspective, they intimate that they trust what their child is telling them *more* than the accounts and interpretations of the school staff. In doing so, the parents unknowingly take a big step. This step leads them to a classificatory position that, from that moment on, will colour how the parents are received by teachers and principals, and how the school understands and reacts to them: they have become 'those kind of parents'. They have become an easily recognisable example of a particular parental figure given various designations, all of which refer to a parent who is *too involved* in their child's welfare at school.

In an extended contribution to the discussion in a Danish national newspaper,[18] the principal at a school in Copenhagen divides parents into two groups: 'destructive' and 'constructive' parents. Under the head-line 'Twelve pointers for "terrorist parents" in Danish public schools. How to ruin your child's schooling – and how to be a constructive parent', he takes an ironic look at the attitudes of destructive versus constructive parents towards their child's school. Markers along the destructive route include: 'Always believe what your child comes home and tells you about what has happened.' ... And: 'If your child is involved in a serious matter at school, assume your child is in the right. ... Fight for your child.' In other words, according to this principal, amongst the most destructive things a parent can do are to trust their child and to engage in his/her experiences of life at school. This understanding fits with a view about parents' interpretations of their children's accounts, which Jon K. Lange wrote about in *The New Responsibility – Tools for Conflict Management and Cooperation Between Teachers and Parents*.[19] Lange explains why it is inex-pedient for modern parents to trust and apply their adult interpretations to what their children tell them about their experiences:

Children have yet to fully develop their brain functions and structures for recog-nition, understanding and the storage of things and events from their everyday lives. Therefore, there is usually considerable variation in a story about, e.g., a birthday party as told by a child and an adult, respectively. ... A child will typically comment on the number of fizzy drinks or pieces of cake he/she had at the party. The adult, meanwhile, will better remember whether or not it was a pleasant and cosy day. ... All adults have a tendency to apply their own interpretations to a child's experiences and to what the child says about his/her everyday life, but this

---

[18] '12 gode råd til 'terroristforældre' i folkeskolen. Sådan smadrer du dine børns skolegang – og sådan handler de konstruktive forældre'; in the daily newspaper *Politiken*, 7 June 2008.
[19] Currently only available in Danish. Lange (2007): *Det nye ansvar – værktøjer til konflikthåndtering og samarbejde mellem lærere og forældre*.

tendency is especially pronounced amongst adults who do not work professionally with children. (Lange 2007: 21; translated from the original Danish)

The understanding seems to be that one neither can nor should trust what a child says about his/her experiences. Children's brains are simply insufficiently developed to be capable of understanding what *actually* happened in a given situation. And Lange argues that problems arise because adults – especially parents who do not work professionally with children – tend to apply their own adult interpretations to their child's primitive understanding of what happened.

As part of her fieldwork at a primary school in Copenhagen, Ph.D. fellow Hanne Knudsen (2008b) attended a training session for teachers in which they – working alongside an actor and using role-playing exercises – were to practice 'the difficult parent consultation'. Based on a categorisation of the parents established beforehand by the school's management team, it was apparent that it was not the consultation itself that was difficult, but rather, the parent as an individual. According to Knudsen, this categorisation seemed familiar to the assembled teachers. The five categories of 'difficult parents' were: (1) the extremely well-prepared parent; (2) the self-seeking parent; (3) the parent who says 'yes', but does not follow through and instead lets things slide; (4) the angry/ aggressive and reproachful parent; and (5) the parents who disagree with each other.

According to Knudsen, a common characteristic of these five categories was that the parents were not 'cooperative'. They did not accept the teacher's descriptions and assessments of their child, nor the responsibility conferred on them as parents to shape their child as befits his/her position as a school student. For example, the so-called angry/ aggressive and reproachful parent was characterised as pointing a finger at the school as being responsible for the child's social and/or academic problems. In such cases, the teachers in the exercise had a clear strategy: either 'evasion' by pretending to listen and expressing partial agreement with the parent; or returning the locus of responsibility to the child. In the training exercises, the two primary objectives of the parent consultations became: *firstly*, to get the parent to accept the teachers' descriptions of the child and their allocation of responsibility (to the parents); and *secondly*, to avoid the parent flying off the handle. Knudsen concluded: 'The school's relationship with the parents is trained – but only as a counter to resistance. There is a risk that the result will be that the only thing common to a group of teachers is the image of the phantom parents and a shared experience of distaste' (2008a: 20; translated from the original Danish).

This categorisation of parents is not a local invention. Bette Prakke et al. (2007) address the relationship between difficult parents and stress, depression and physical illness amongst schoolteachers in the Netherlands. The goal of this research is to help teachers develop appropriate attitudes and coping strategies for dealing with challenging parents, and it divides such parents into the following seven categories: 'Excessively worried parent, Unsatisfied parent, Uncooperative parent, Neglectful parent, Overprotective parent, Involved-uninvolved parent, and Fighting parent' (ibid.).

These excerpts from research, newspapers and popular literature provide examples of how certain ideas about parents seem quite widespread within the teaching profession. In many cases, the general understanding of parents seems to suggest that teachers need to be on guard and develop coping strategies to deal with them in order to take care of themselves and their health. As outlined in Knudsen's description, one such strategy is to 'evade' the angry/aggressive and reproachful parent, and to escape their fury by pretending to listen and expressing partial agreement. Another strategy is to place responsibility squarely back on the child and his/her parent(s). This can be considered in relation to the parents' narratives within my empirical data, where the parents of Mark, Caitlin, Peter and all the other children were unable to understand why the school did not take them seriously. Why did the principal often agree with them, yet still not take any action? Why was the finger pointed back at their child or at themselves as parents, both in terms of the cause of the problems and the responsibility for solving them?

The parents experience powerlessness, but they seem unaware that their powerlessness is partially generated by their persistent attempts to do the right thing: the more they react and the more they apply various strategies to help their child, the more they add substance to the stereotypical figure that now constitutes the framework within which their behaviour is interpreted – and the more invisible and invalid they become as individual parents with genuine reactions to their child's experiences at school.

Mark's parents' experiences with the school's principal provide an illustrative example of how parents who involve themselves in their child's problems at school – especially in ways that the school staff find challenging – can end up in an invalidated position within the home–school cooperation, falling outside the realm of 'empathic relevance' (Søndergaard 2009). At the age of 10, Mark starts mentioning to his parents that he has contemplated suicide. Again, they contact the principal and experience that he now seems to regard them as irrelevant to receive empathy and understanding:

Mother: So, when he started [that year], then he actually started to talk about. . .
            about committing suicide. I don't know how serious he was, but it was
            something he, like, mentioned. . .
NH: What did he say?
Mother: Yeah, but I actually can't really remember – in fact, I reckon I've blocked it
            out because I really can't remember exactly. But I do remember that we, at
            that point, talked about that now it really had to, I mean, now it really had
            to stop, all of this. And so I wrote a long, long mail to Patrick [the
            principal]. . . . And so we wrote to Patrick that now. . .we wrote it like it
            was, that now they had to make a decision, or else we'd basically have to
            take him out of school because we actually considered it tantamount to
            parental neglect to keep on sending him to school, and we couldn't keep
            on. . . And we wanted them to find some kind of solution, but, at the same
            time, when it came to the suicide stuff, we – because we had no idea how
            the local authorities. . . . . . In a way, we didn't feel like it should be Mark
            who was a case for the local authorities. . . So, I wrote to [Patrick] that if
            there were going to be meetings with other people than him attending,
            then we wanted to know who had been told what. That's to say, we wanted
            to be asked for permission first before they started talking about, like, how
            about Mark and suicide. . . Then we got a reply of like a line or two,
            something like that, where he wrote that 'a piece of confidential informa-
            tion was of no use' to him.
NH: That a piece of confidential information was of no. . .?
Mother: Was of no use to him.
NH: Seriously? That was his response to being told that your son had talked
            about suicide?
Mother: Yes, a child in fourth grade.[20]

During a long, drawn-out process, Mark's parents have been pushed so
deep into a box labelled 'whinging, awkward parents' that the principal is no
longer capable of seeing them and encountering them as parents who are
crying out to get help for their seriously unhappy child – which they clearly
are, regardless of their attitudes and regardless of any questions about guilt,
truth and responsibility. Their experience is one of being entirely invalidated as meaningful subjects, and in the context of the school, they now
encounter rejection and bowed heads no matter where they turn.

The inevitable rupture

After a series of events lasting several years, all of the parents I interviewed
finally reached the conclusion that the only way to change the situation
was to escape the present context in which they had abandoned any hope
of becoming worthy and legitimate participants. The parents found it
necessary to extend beyond the home–school cooperation and to

---

[20] This corresponds to fifth grade/year in American or British schools.

withdraw from the community of parents and, in some cases, from the local area entirely to generate the possibility of being listened to and recognised as parents with legitimate attitudes and valid feelings, and to be able to give their child a new chance.

Following Mark's parents' realisation that they are completely powerless within the framework of the relationship between home and school, they try to reach out to an authority who is capable of trumping the principal's position of power: thus, they contact their town's mayor. As luck would have it, he recognises them as 'good citizens', listens to their story and decides to take concrete action. He writes to the principal at Mark's school and demands an ongoing effort to improve Mark's situation. Subsequently, and in connection with a planned division of Mark's class, Mark is put into another class away from Jason, Tom and Nick, and the bullying gradually subsides. For Mark's parents, intervention by the mayor provides some redress and changes Mark's situation at school.

Peter's mother also contacts the mayor of her town, but she never receives a response. Following yet another violent incident on the school playground, she takes Peter out of school and promises him that he'll never have to go back. However, the principal believes she is overreacting and refuses to provide the necessary disenrollment papers that would allow her to enrol Peter in another school. Peter's mother tries to contact the other local municipal schools, but is kept at arm's length: she is told that the municipality's principals will meet and discuss the case. Whilst Peter is stuck at home, hoping his mother will soon find him a new school, she receives a letter from the school administrators at his former school. The letter states that the school will report the case to the public authorities if she does not ensure Peter's attendance. Peter's mother later described her doubts; she felt vulnerable in her already-designated position as a culpable, single mother. Could they do that? Can they take Peter away from her?

At a meeting two months later, the principals from the local municipal schools reach an agreement that Peter should return to his former school, where it is believed they are best equipped to accommodate what are now referred to as 'Peter's needs'. Peter's mother refuses and finally manages to find a new school for him. Nevertheless, his former school continues to put up a struggle and impose conditions for releasing Peter: his mother must agree to subject herself and her home to a so-called 'Paragraph 50' assessment[21] before Peter is allowed to change schools. Peter's mother sees no other alternative than to consent: 'Because otherwise, they think

---

[21] § 50: '(1) Where it must be assumed that a child or a young person is in need of special support (...), the municipal council shall ensure that the conditions of the child or the young person are investigated. Any decision to do so shall be made with the consent of the

you have something to hide, don't they, and I really want my son to go to school,' she said later.

Peter starts at his new school and settles in well. He makes friends, and the teachers there define him as 'a completely normal teenager'. His mother awaits the Paragraph 50 assessment of their home, but never hears anything more about it. In the small town where they live, both Peter's mother and the teachers and parents from Peter's former class continue to look away when they encounter each other on the street.

Similarly, Caitlin's parents come to the conclusion that it is necessary to break away from the current setting if their daughter is going to have a better school life. At the age of 12, Caitlin is finally moved to another school within the local authority and, in her parents' view, she is transformed. She quickly becomes socially well-integrated in her new class, and most of her academic difficulties evaporate over the course of the first six months. She leaves secondary school with good grades and continues her studies at college.

Summary

My intention in this chapter is to shed light on the experiences of parents who are trying to help their child manage a situation where he/she feels excluded or bullied at school. I have demonstrated that home–school cooperation does not always meet parents' expectations of being a joint effort to support the bullied child; in many cases, instead it reinforces an experience of inadequacy and exclusion for both the child and his/her parent(s). In my analysis, I highlighted the disempowerment of parents that is produced in home–school cooperation and which leaves them feeling that they have little opportunity to contribute to improving their child's situation at school.

I contend that the disempowerment of parents takes place through a number of related conditions and dynamics. Firstly, the lack of transparency that parents often experience when seeking insight into their child's life at school; this places the parents at a disadvantage if the child is having social problems there. In many cases, the children tell them about incidents that school staff either do not recognise as bullying or do not acknowledge as such because they did not themselves witness the episode(s) in question. Secondly, the way in which teachers and/or principals interpret children's reactions to what the children perceive as bullying

custodial parent or other person having custody and a young person over the age of 15, but see subsection (9) hereof and section 51 below. (2) In the course of its investigations, cf. subsection (1) hereof, the municipal council shall make an overall evaluation of the following factors relating to the child's or young person's (i) development and behaviour; (ii) family; (iii) school; (iv) health; (v) leisure time activities and friendships; and (vi) other relevant factors.' Source: Consolidation Act on Social Services. Found at: http://english.sm.dk/MinistryOfSocialWelfare/legislation/social_affairs/social_service_act/Sider/Start.aspx or exclusion processes at school – that is, as a reflection of their age, gender, personality or home life, rather than of their experiences at school – contributes to undermining parents' trust in their own judgement. The parents are usually already familiar with the cultural understandings that underlie the school's interpretations, and they begin to doubt whether there is actually something wrong with their child or whether their child's experiences are merely part and parcel of childhood and adolescence. They themselves experience being placed within certain widespread categories of cultural understanding, which are then used to explain their reactions in the home–school cooperation: Caitlin's mother reacts the way she does *because* she is an over-anxious mother, a sub-species of the modern 'curling parent', rather than a mother displaying rational reactions to her daughter's actual situation at school; Mark's parents keep contacting the principal *because* they're difficult, rather than parents who have legitimate and understandable reasons to establish a dialogue, etc.

Thus, and in terms of identifying the cause of their child's social problems within the school context, parents find that the finger is pointed back at their child or towards them as parents. As a result, they become uncertain of both their own abilities as parents and the accuracy of their child's accounts. At times, the parents attempt to align themselves with the school's interpretations and action plans. They try to take an analytical and critical stance in relation to their child's accounts and also how they tackle the child's problems. But when, despite their best efforts, they witness their child's situation worsening, powerlessness begins to take hold. With regard to the problems that surround their child's well-being at school, the parents' reactions and understandings are de-legitimated by the school staff using their gender, social class, marital status, parental type, etc., as an explanatory framework. One consequence is that the more parents employ the coping strategies available to them – and the more they try to do what seems to them to be the right thing – the more they confirm the de-legitimated position that they have been assigned. With this, they risk escalating, expanding and becoming part of the conflicts as well as the violating, exclusionary dynamics from which they originally sought to rescue their child.

Moving forward

In this analysis, I have sought to broaden and qualify insights into parents' perspectives of their experiences with the cooperation between home and school in connection with bullying amongst children. I realise that a qualitative investigation into teachers' and principals' perspectives on the same problems could bring forth an entirely different perception of positions and the sequence of events, and undoubtedly also point to experiences of inadequacy and powerlessness. Nevertheless, with regard to their child's unhappiness at school, it is clear that the problems encountered by parents in home–school cooperation constitute reality from their perspective; these problems are deeply frustrating and disempowering for the parents. Is it possible to envisage other approaches to the cooperation between school and home – approaches where parents, teachers and principals are better able to work together to ensure that a child is thriving at school? In conclusion, I suggest some possible paths to follow.

When children voice their unhappiness about school, there is good reason to take them seriously. The analysis here indicates that schools frequently discount children who experience bullying because teachers have a different experience of a child's situation in relation to his/her classmates. Written definitions of bullying seem to be employed as a tool to sort out who can and who cannot be recognised and acknowledged as a 'proper' victim of bullying. The anti-bullying action plans, which are now a requirement for Danish *folkeskoler*,[22] oblige schools to implement a number of measures once they have acknowledged a case of bullying. It can be vital for a vulnerable child, and his/her parents, to be acknowledged as a victim of bullying because this acknowledgement triggers an expectation of diligence and concrete initiatives by the school to solve the problem. Meanwhile, the schools commit considerable resources to acknowledge a child as a victim of bullying, and they are understandably eager to establish clear boundaries regarding what qualifies as bullying. But what about the child who is still having difficulty no matter how we decide to designate the situation? Is it an appropriate strategy for parents and the school to try to establish the 'truth' about a child and his/her situation at school? Would it be more productive – for both the home–school cooperation and the well-being of the child – to acknowledge and show interest in the *differing perspectives* of both the children and adults, instead of fighting over the 'truth'? For a child, the 'truth' is reality as he/she experiences it. Other children in the class most likely have other experiences of the same situation, and both parents and school staff can have their own perspectives and interpretations. Events look different from different perspectives and with different expectations, so there is every reason to acknowledge a child's pain when he/she experiences bullying or ostracism from the class community – regardless of whether others take a different view of the situation. Parents and teachers encounter a child in entirely different situations, and each have particular

---

[22] Since August 2009, Danish *folkeskoler* have been required to compile an anti-bullying strategy as part of a set of value guidelines.

knowledge about the child in relational contexts; both parties need to draw upon this knowledge in order to work appropriately for the child's well-being and development (see Højholt 1996/2005 and Larsen 2005). Therefore, instead of discussing who is *right* in the description of a child and his/her situation at school, it would be more constructive to listen to, take an interest in and respect the other party's knowledge of a child's behaviour in both domestic and school contexts, respectively.

In *Parental Cooperation – Research in Communities* (1996/2005),[23] Charlotte Højholt argues that we should abandon discussions about what children 'are like', and instead discuss what children do and under what *conditions* they do what they do. She demonstrates how adults' perceptions of what a child 'is like' are tied to the context in which they spend time with the child, as well as their intentions and areas of responsibility in relation to the child. As such, different adults can experience the same child as either alert or restless, creative or disruptive, entertaining or annoying (ibid.: 35). Instead of describing what a child 'is like', Højholt writes, descriptions of children's situations – what the others did; e.g. how a child was rebuffed by classmates, reprimanded by adults, taken away from what she was doing, etc. – can provide opportunities for under-standing an action within a specific context and with certain particular factors at stake (ibid.).

In relation to bullying, it seems key to attempt to understand a child's behaviour and experiences within a relational and historical context: what is going on between the children in the class, and what relational problems pre-date the current situation? Is Peter's aggressive way of responding to even the slightest teasing perhaps engendered by a history of bullying that has affected his expectations about others' behaviour towards him and thereby his patterns of (re-)action? Are Caitlin's sizable academic and social problems within her class due to the fact that she *is* a quiet girl, perhaps suffering from minor brain damage? Or can her problems be partially understood because she has considered herself to be excluded from both the academic and the social community within the class for a number of years?

With this analysis, I hope I have illustrated what it can be like to belong to the sub-species 'the awkward parent', who has a child who feels bullied at school. And I hope it is clear how a failure in cooperation between parents and teachers/principals infects the families of vulnerable children and how, as a result, children run the risk of becoming enshrined in powerlessness, guilt and desperation both at home and at school.

---

[23] Only available in Danish: Højholt (1996/2005): *Forældresamarbejde – forskning i fællesskab.*

13   Traces of being bullied: 'dynamic effectuality'

Charlotte Mathiassen

Introduction

In this chapter, I address how remembered experiences of being bullied as a child may affect a person differently at different times and places as well as across times and places.[1] I have chosen to refer to this emotionally and socially challenging phenomenon as 'dynamic effectuality'.[2] The analysis in this chapter is based on a qualitative interview study about memories of being bullied as a child, which I describe in further detail below.

Time is often considered to be one-dimensional and linear, but the data from this study about adults' remembered experiences of being bullied suggests that the participants move easily between notions of the past, present and future, both in their descriptions of memories of being bullied as children and in their descriptions of the subjective meaning of these experiences today. For this reason, I found the concept of 'traces' particularly helpful. It moves beyond the idea – perhaps simplified – that negative experiences from childhood leave a static 'mark' and only have a negative influence on adult life. The trace concept embraces the notion that an experience may exist as a memory whilst no longer existing within the present subjective practice. Furthermore, the trace concept encompasses an understanding that socially and emotionally challenging episodes and their implications are not necessarily static in their emotional

---

[1] It should be noted that other life events that occur during the bullying phase obviously affect how bullying influences the present and the future. In this chapter, I focus on bullying. The complex effectuality between non-bullying life events and bullying are outside the scope of my analysis here.

[2] 'Dynamic effectuality' is my translation of the Danish concept *virkningsforhold*, which means literally 'effect relations'. Effect relations could indicate a (mono-)causal approach to the relation between remembered experiences of being bullied and the present adult life, which is contrary to the ambition in this chapter; thus, 'dynamic effectuality'. This term is intended to encompass the dialectical, and thereby dynamic, relations between past, present and future. Furthermore, it is intended to include the analytic ambition to record the narratives as they change across time and contexts; i.e. situations, other people and other experiences. The definition of 'dynamic effectuality' is further developed and specified within this chapter.

quality and influence; the way these episodes are remembered *and* influence a person's lived life may vary according to the situation and context, and therefore also over time. The prospects for the future, the influence of recollected bullying and the current situation all appear to be mutually dependent. Therefore, we must include the present and the future in our understanding of how childhood bullying influences our adult lives, and we should recognise that the three factors influence each other in an endlessly iterative helix.

My analysis in this chapter illustrates which traces are important in my efforts to understand the dynamic effectuality between being bullied as a child and an individual's shaping of his/her present adulthood. I focus on how being bullied draws and leaves traces, as well as on how the past, present and future are intertwined in a variety of ways; this point is central to an analysis of dynamic effectuality.

In the following, I present the reader with different traces[3] and with examples of dynamic effectuality based on five selected narratives from my research. Of particular interest are the traces that are connected to events in the past, which also appear to play an influential role in the present lives of the study participants. The way in which events in the past have a dynamic effectuality in and with the present is subject to a number of different influences. In addition to how a bullying event actually unfolded in the past, the cultural circumstances, the location and the other actors surrounding and participating in the event play a role in how being bullied becomes significant, makes sense and how it influences a person, both in the past and the present. Furthermore, whether and how a person perceives his/her future – as set against the background of his/her present description of memories of being bullied as a child – is also influential. By employing the concept of 'traces', my analysis takes the reader through different times, locations and ways in which being bullied gains significance, makes sense and influences adulthood. To a certain extent, one could say that a number of traces are always drawn throughout

[3] The trace concept is also used in an historical (Assmann in Bjerg 2011) and literary–philosophical narrative context (Ricoeur 2004). The historian Reinhardt Kosselck distinguishes between memory as a trace – which includes the sensory memory and memory as a trajectory – and memory as embedded in language. Researcher Aleida Assmann (Bjerg 2011) addresses this distinction in her work on memory. I do not employ an historical or philosophical approach, but rather, a psychological one. My use of the trace concept is informed by the qualitative empirical material and, consequently, I do not distinguish between direct sensory memory and memory conveyed through language, both of which are exemplified in the primary material. Although it seems useful to include the perspectives of Assmann and Ricoeur, a more detailed discussion of their perspectives is outside the scope of this chapter.

a lifetime, but not all of them are relevant to how *being bullied* affects an individual in adulthood.

The study and its theoretical and methodological approaches

Qualitative empirical method

This chapter offers an analysis of the traces of recollections from adults' emotionally and socially challenging experiences of being bullied as a child. It is based on interviews and research I conducted in collaboration with my colleague Eva Silberschmidt Viala during 2008–9 in which thirty-six adults between 20 and 65 years of age were asked about their child-hood memories of bullying.[4] Our qualitative interview study was designed to investigate: how adults make sense of their childhood experiences of bullying; and how adults handle their childhood experiences of bullying once they have become adults (Mathiassen and Viala 2009). The initial theoretical point of departure was a cultural–psychological approach in the broadest sense. In our interviews, we drew upon phenomenological inspiration: we emphasised the participants' own experiences and local-ised perspectives on their childhood experiences, and examined the impli-cations of these experiences in adulthood.

All of the interview participants were recruited from two large compa-nies or two adult colleges (*højskoler*) located in Denmark; this represented twelve men and twenty-four women, each of whom described his/her experiences of bullying during childhood.[5] At the adult colleges, we conducted another four mixed (men and women) group interviews as well as participant observation; the interviews with the companies' employees were all individual. In general, our informants fell into differ-ent levels with regard to education, social–economic hierarchy and career position: of those from the companies, some were employed as service workers, some as researchers and yet others as office staff or managers. Furthermore, all of the interview participants had assumed different

---

[4] Although our research is comprised of the same qualitative empirical data, Viala's analysis and chapter in this anthology incorporate interviews with different informants; the iden-tities of all of our informants have been made anonymous. We also do not employ the same analytical strategies or concepts. See Viala's chapter, page 361, for a different analysis of other elements from our interview material.

[5] Qualitative studies in this field are particularly rare. One example is Malaby (2009), who interviewed adult men about their childhood recollections of hegemonic displays of violence and being bullied, and examined the sense they make of these experiences as adults. Malaby refers to Ortner (2005), who concludes that experiences from school days maintain a constant influence on the adult psyche (Malaby 2009: 872).

positions in the bullying process: there were some who had bullied, some who had been bullied and some who had mostly been observers. The informants I include in my analysis were in their mid-thirties to mid-forties at the time of our study and, in this chapter, I focus on personal memories recounted by five individuals from the companies, each of whom attended school in the 1970s and 1980s. This is significant because, currently, all schools in Denmark must define a strategy to deal with bullying (Mathiassen and Viala 2009). But when these participants were children, bullying was not on the school agenda to the extent it is today; in fact, several schools did not focus on bullying at all in any way (ibid.).

The material that informs this chapter was generated through qualitative interviews. During the individual interviews with the company employees, we encouraged each participant to describe his/her own experience with bullying. In terms of the dataset, this means that the accounts have a high degree of personal depth and details, both with regard to concrete events as well as the emotional shifts associated with these events. The central premise of my investigation is that any exploration of the implications of having been bullied in the lives of adults must start with the idea that 'knowledge always arises from the social life of participants' (see Schott, Chapter 2). Because the participants described episodes from their own lives, I chose an explorative, 'bottom-up' approach and my analysis is based upon their narratives.

The interview material consists of the informants' 'remembered experiences' of being bullied as well as their descriptions of the 'experienced significance' of their memories. Their exploration of their present lives and existence as well as their past lives and experience of being bullied were contextualised. This means that the informants were encouraged to describe specific events and the contexts in which their remembered incidences of bullying took place; that is, where it occurred, who was there and what reasons might have led to the bullying. Their descriptions focused on the meaning (Bruner 1990) of the events and the concrete contexts in which these meanings appeared to them. For example, participants were asked questions such as, 'How did the other children handle what happened?' and 'How did the adults, teachers and parents handle what happened?' We also asked each participant about the function of bullying – in relation to the class community as a whole and to the individuals who were actively engaged in the bullying.

Additionally, we tried to determine how each participant's social network was structured, so we asked about his/her family relationships. In this sense, we focused on how and to what extent understanding, experiencing and managing occurrences of bullying can vary in and across contexts (see, for example, Dreier 2008) and in different time periods. It was central to our research to understand how being bullied was addressed by the informants, if at all. Were the children subjected to a dominant discourse that defined being bullied as simply something to be endured as a normal part of childhood? Did they have to deal with being bullied on their own?

As a point of departure, the participants' perceptions of what counts as bullying are manifold. Therefore, my analysis is not based on a pre-defined understanding of what it means to be bullied; the complexity of life influences how phenomena are experienced and how they acquire subjective sense. Thus, because the topic of these discussions had to be relevant to them (cf. Holzkamp 2005; Jensen 2006), the participants decided which themes in their present and past lives should be included in the interviews. In this way, the interviews adopt a first-person perspective as explored and described in Schraube (2013) and Schraube and Osterkamp (2012), and my analysis takes the participants' perspectives and understandings into account. This means that the localised experiences, meanings and perspectives of the individuals involved are what matter rather than a third-person researcher's perspective, defined beforehand and 'from above'. Furthermore, because the participants shared their experiences of being bullied as well as their personal sense of these experiences in their lives today, they are in a position to help scholars understand how such experiences draw and leave traces in their lives.

Understanding memory

The object of this chapter, *traces of memories from emotionally and socially challenging childhood episodes*, calls for a brief explanation of how the concept of memory is used. Memories are not direct replicas of the past. Inspired by memory researchers (see, for example, Levine and Pizarro 2004: 537), emotionally powerful episodes or occurrences are remembered with more detail than episodes or occurrences experienced as less powerful. More recent research suggests that memory is dynamic and processual (Thomsen and Brinkmann 2009), a point that Frederic Charles Bartlett argued in the 1930s (Bartlett 1932/1997; Wagoner 2011). The events that inform this analysis have been reinterpreted by the storyteller in dialogue with the interviewer,[6] but it is important to

---

[6] Middleton and Brown (2005) argue that memory is a social process. Based on this understanding, I suggest that individuals recall memories both in interviews and because they are being interviewed. Thus, interviews dealing with memory could be described as a kind of memory praxis.

remember that these re-interpretations originate from real episodes; they are not merely constructions. Understanding memory in this way is an approach that has been used by many scholars whose research focuses on school-life memories (e.g. Bjerg 2011). Consequently, I understand memory as a social process in which the 'rememberer' draws upon concrete, real episodes. At the same time, a person remembers episodes in collaboration with whomever he/she is conversing, and thereby also interprets these episodes. Memory functions as a process, which is furthermore influenced by the past, the present and the imagined future. As in storytelling (Bruner 1990), memories include a cultural level of meaning. They are persistent as well as fluid and negotiable. The version recounted verbally in interviews is the personalised and mediated version of the significance given to the remembered experience.

Theoretical inspirations and analytical tools

Adults' memories of being bullied as children become part of the multifaceted interplay that informs interests and experiences in their present lives. In other words, the analysis of dynamic effectuality between the remembrance of being bullied and the shaping of a later life must include: occurrences in childhood; the manner in which those experiences become significant and make sense to the now-adult individual; and additional experiences that the adult has had and perceives as being important and central to his/her life.

In an effort to anchor the traces of being bullied within this analysis, the concept of the 'life-project' is helpful (Bertelsen 1994). My use of the concept here is part of a field of study that addresses the psychological aspects of an individual's perceptions of agency in his/her life (Bertelsen 2010). The focus is centred on how people are themselves engaged in their own life-projects. In other words, the analytical premise of this approach is that, in one way or another, everyone engages in the process of shaping his/her own personal life. The term 'life-project' was inspired by phenomenological psychology and existentialist psychology (Bertelsen 1994). By looking at life-projects as they were revealed in my interviews, it becomes possible to investigate how the participants' recollections of being bullied as children play a part in shaping their personal lives as adults. A premise in all people's lives is that *some but not all* possibilities are available. All lives are tied to the conditions of possibilities. At the same time, a person has some degree of freedom in terms of actively shaping his/her life in different ways (e.g. Bertelsen 1994; Dreier 2008). By using the concept 'life-project', the central analytical questions in the following analysis are: What role does being bullied play in the shaping of 'life-projects' for the people who participated in this study? What role do people's 'life-projects' play in the way that being bullying 'works' within the life in question? My suggestion is that memories of the past contribute to the shaping of life-projects in the present, just as perceptions of the future contribute to how present life-projects are shaped.

This analysis is anchored in socio-cultural theory, meaning that the aforementioned theoretical approach is built on actual, lived lives. Thus, socio-material, socio-cultural and interpersonal circumstances and relationships – including material and contextual aspects – are relevant. As an extension of the argumentation that some but not all possibilities are available in a person's life, we must note that processes of personal development cannot take any course and direction.[7] My intention is to maintain the concrete connection between the individual, his/her recollections, the actual context in which the person found and finds him/herself and, finally, the actual contexts that he/she moved and moves across (Dreier 2008).

As mentioned, the perspectives of the participants in this study were central in defining whether or not their experiences could be categorised as being bullied. For my analysis, I chose the relationships and occurrences that the participants defined as having affected them on a social and emotional level in their adult lives. The exploration of traces thus incorporates the participants' subjectivity, as well as their own interpretations and the significance of their memories of being bullied. Some of Jerome Bruner's (1990) arguments about the ways in which people make sense of their experiences have inspired this chapter's socio-cultural and cultural–psychological foundation. In his later works, Bruner stresses that he considers psychology to be a culturally orientated discipline.[8] He emphasises that the way an individual makes sense of his/her experiences and the cultural signifiers and context that pervade the individual's life are mutually dependent on one another. In other words, how we make sense of our experiences and how that sense is developed is not exclusively a private and individual matter. Inspired by Bruner's cultural–psychological perspective, the exploration of traces in this chapter may thus shed light on how individuals make sense of their personal experiences by drawing on cultural meanings – assuming that the person has chosen to share this knowledge with the interviewer.[9] By investigating whether a person

---

[7] This point is emphasised in several other publications; e.g. Dreier (2008) and Valsiner and Lawrence (1997).

[8] See, e.g. Bruner (1990: 19).

[9] Inspired by an activity theory (Leontjev 1983), this chapter distinguishes between *sense* (personal) and *meaning* (social). As such, this analysis offers a close study of how individuals make sense of culturally informed meanings.

describes being bullied as an experience that continues to have relevance in his/her adult life, it is possible to discern whether traces of these experiences have been drawn from the past into the future – and if so, how these traces manifest themselves. In particular, I was interested in exploring: whether an individual reflected upon his/her experiences of being bullied as a child; whether he/she intentionally focused on these memories and their significance; and finally, whether the individual acted and made decisions based on these reflections.

Potentiality and dynamic effectuality

This analysis has been inspired by several terms that have been developed through and shaped by the qualitative, empirical material. In my analysis of traces, various kinds of dynamic effectuality emerge, such as the ways in which being bullied as a child influence an individual both as a child and later in adult life. I have chosen to refer to these implications as 'the potentiality of being bullied' and 'the potentiality of the experience of being bullied'. My use of *potentiality* in this chapter underlines the possibility, and not the definitiveness, of an event. Here, the potential is in focus. This understanding of potentiality shares similarities with Aristotle's discussions of potentiality (*dynamis*) as something that possesses the possibility of being put into practice in the real world (*energia*) (Jensen 2006: 142). According to U. H. Jensen's interpretation of Aristotle (ibid.), potentiality implies a possible realisation of the imagined event. However, Giorgio Agamben (1999a), who also uses the concept of potentiality, elaborates on Aristotle's approach but does not see the possibility of actualisation as a definitive part of the potentiality concept (ibid.: 186). Agamben describes this as the subject's sense of 'I can' (ibid.: 177–8). His understanding of 'I can' stems from the Italian verb *potere*, meaning 'to be able to'. Thus, although 'I can' embraces potentiality, the outcome thereof is not definitive. In this way, it might be helpful to think of 'I can' as 'I might': potentiality becomes a potentiality itself.

Building on this dialectically informed analytical structure, 'I can' – the subjective sense of potentiality – cannot be understood without taking into account the individual who experiences it. In other words, a person's material, social and interpersonal circumstances are both dependent and definitive of one another, and they influence how potentiality is experienced. Throughout this chapter, I employ this understanding of potentiality in my analysis of how being bullied influenced the study participants. I share Agamben's understanding of the concept of potentiality, with regard to the term's mercurial character. Experiences *can* be significant, but exactly what that significance may be is not clear at the time the experiences occur. In addition, the potentiality of such experiences may also entail *a lack* of significance. Thus, it is possible to have a sense of potentiality as such. Part of an event's potentiality thereby encompasses the possibility that it may or may not signify something with particular meaning. We can experience something that has potentiality without it ever having to materialise into something real – yet, despite this fact, it may still have a strong impact on a person.

The 'potentiality of *experiences* of being bullied' refers to how actual experiences of being bullied as a child *can* become influential during a person's lifetime. Here, the *actual experiences* of being bullied are central. This concept embraces an infinite amount of varying meanings and influences that being bullied can have in adulthood. Employing the concept of potentiality in this context emphasises the experiences of potentiality, but not causality (i.e. causing a specific effect in adult life). It is possible that an adult *can* experience certain emotions or participate in specific kinds of social acts that he/she understands as being influenced by childhood experiences of being bullied. But it is also possible that he/she will not. Thus, the 'potentiality of *experiences* of being bullied' refers to the series of various meanings and influences that being bullied as a child can have on adult life. Regardless of whether the potentiality of being bullied is actually realised in a specific influence, the individual is aware that these experiences *can* have an influence on how he/she perceives him/herself and his/her behaviour as an adult. This form of potentiality in and of itself has an influence on the individual.

In contrast, the 'potentiality of *being* bullied' refers to a situation in which a person *could* become the object of bullying. In other words, it refers to situations in which the phenomenon of bullying *could* occur. Here, the 'potentiality of being bullied' pertains to a child who observes how other children are bullied and who thus chooses to navigate according to the possibility that he/she might be the next target. This concept focuses on the act of bullying as it is observed in lived life and its potentiality to unfold into actual events of bullying. It is important to note that the act of bullying does not necessarily have to be directed towards a child who attempts to navigate according to the act of bullying. A child acts in this manner because he/she believes that bullying might become part of his/her own reality. In this way, bullying has an influence when there is a perception that the subject *could* be bullied and also when the subject *is* actually bullied. Temporally, 'the potentiality of being bullied' is played out in real time, whereas the 'potentiality of *experiences* of being bullied' refers to the influence of something that happened to a child in the past, which is then transferred and given meaning and influence in the adult's present; this is a process that has a degree of transformation to it.

These two concepts are connected whilst also pointing in different directions. In the following, I illustrate this dynamic effectuality through some of the descriptions offered by the study participants.

The potentiality of being bullied

With Russell's story, I wish to describe the potentiality of being bullied as a child as something that *could* influence a child's life. Here, my focus is on bullying played out in real time, not the influence that previous experiences of being bullied *could* have in adulthood. The child's knowledge of this potentiality – with all its inconclusiveness and expressed as something that does not yet exist – could nevertheless turn into something, according to how he/she has navigated. The children tried to find ways of acting in the classroom, as well as in less formal children's environments that were influenced by an idea of how the social environment *could* develop in exclusionary ways, such as in the case of bullying. Russell described his school years as defined by insecurity. *Insecurity* was his central and spontaneous focus in our interview: 'When I think back on my school days, I think of them as being socially insecure.' Russell was referring to a time during his early school years when both the teachers and students participated in bullying. He witnessed how some children were tied up and spat on, how some had their belongings ruined and how others were bullied by the teachers in front of their schoolmates. Russell explained:

I didn't, you know, feel bullied as such, but it was worse than [being bullied] would have been, because it was the same atmosphere, and it actually got worse, I'd say [...]. There was such a sense of insecurity. I never actually felt afraid, but it was not a, you know, good feeling. It was more like ... it is difficult to describe, but it was sort of like a ... [pause]. How to explain ... [long pause]. I was afraid, you know, I was afraid that – it was really rare that it happened – but it was always there, at the back of your mind, that you could be called something or other.

Here, Russell described how the potentiality of being bullied became a driving force in his school years: 'It was always at the back of your mind,' he explained. In this way, he was constantly aware, perhaps even on guard, not knowing *if* he might be the next target. This insecurity was nourished by the fact that there were no adults in whom he could confide.[10] According to Russell, the school was structured in such a way that it was possible for the students to interact with one another quite violently, including bullying of a particularly extreme physical nature, without any

---

[10]   In this study, it was often the case that the adults either did not know, did not interfere, or both. This is something that is also in Malaby's (2009) study of boys' experiences of being bullied and the significance of bullying in their adulthoods.

adult interference. For Russell, the insecurity and fear to which he was subjected during his school years functioned as warning signs. These signs told him about the conditions that could position him in the centre of bullying processes. For example, it could entail a situation in which a child who bullies focused on him and not on others. He feared this! He feared being singled out in this way, which could mean that he was the next bullying target. For Russell, the potentiality of being bullied materialised in the bullying scenarios that he imagined could occur in the immediate future. As a result, he chose to act in ways that allowed him to predict and strategically avoid the realisation of such potential scenarios.

In Russell's narrative, he referred to bullying as something that is primarily physical. However, in his last years of primary school, Russell was also ridiculed and teased. This teasing was of a different character than the physical bullying he described above, and it was not until later in the interview that he mentioned being subjected to this. He described an episode in which he approached a girl on whom he had a 'crush' and asked her if she wanted to go out on a date with him. He did this because another boy told him that the girl was 'crazy about him'. This boy had been Russell's best friend for several years, but by this time, their friendship had faded. Russell told us that the girl 'just stared at me as if I was an idiot'. Afterwards, he found out that the other boy made up the whole story about the girl's supposed feelings for Russell in order to humiliate him.

So firstly, Russell had already lost a long-standing friendship because he and the other boy did not have much in common anymore, which contributed to his feeling lonely and insecure. And secondly, this episode with the girl occurred, which only exacerbated the humiliation and sense of loneliness he already felt: 'This was one of the reasons why I withdrew completely from everything [the parties and girlfriends] in eighth and ninth grade,[11] because I just felt like they had made such a fool of me; I was really insecure and stuff.'

Russell described how specific, humiliating experiences had a pronounced influence on his personal life as a young person. Russell stressed that it was the loneliness and insecurity – caused by the teachers' public intimidation of students plus the physical and verbal abuse amongst the children – that caused his problematic and sometimes emotionally painful school years. In my use of the analytical category 'the potentiality of being bullied', it is possible to see the traces drawn by bullying, despite the fact that someone like Russell *does not* refer to himself as an object of bullying. He is nevertheless affected by the bullying he experienced, even though he

---

[11] At the age of 15; *8.* and *9. klasse* in Denmark correspond to ninth and tenth grade/year, respectively, in American or British schools.

did not describe himself as the target. In other words, even when an individual does not define him/herself as an object of bullying, it is still possible that acts of bullying towards other children will influence him/her. Moreover, these experiences can continue to affect the person in question into adulthood.

Another aspect of the concept 'the potentiality of the experiences of being bullied' addresses how being bullied as a child can also have a long-term influence on an individual into adulthood. This notion may also be understood through the concept of potentiality, which is my focus for the remainder of this chapter. Let us stay with Russell for now and explore how his childhood experiences of bullying and insecurity became influential in his present adult life. Thereafter, I elaborate upon the concept of 'the potentiality of the experiences of being bullied' by incorporating perspectives expressed by some of the other participants in my research study.

Interpersonal distance as dynamic effectuality

Russell was influenced by the negative emotional climate at school and by the processes of bullying there, despite the fact that he did not primarily consider himself a target of bullying. In the third grade,[12] it was already common for children in Russell's class to taunt one another, a practice that was inspired by the arrival of a new boy who acted this way.[13] In the interviews, Russell told us that in primary and secondary school, he was the 'class clown', a tactic he used to get attention. He explained that his role as the clown was necessary for him to feel relevant and attractive to the others within the social community at school. Teasing was a spontaneous way of interacting, and Russell was designated as the one who told dirty jokes: 'It sort of became my way of getting attention,' Russell explained, 'but deep down [I] felt really uncomfortable [. . .] having to play the part of someone who is sort of a clown.' Inspired by Preben Bertelsen's (1994) theory of life-projects – and within the context of insecurity and teasing, and the sense that Russell could at any moment become the next object of bullying – it seems as though Russell's 'project' during those difficult school years entailed playing the class clown in order to attract his schoolmates' attention. Within the narrow social space afforded to Russell at this time in his childhood, I suggest that he was trying to negotiate his position and manage his school life around the sub-project of being 'the clown'. Because of the 'potentiality of being bullied', Russell developed a strategy – being the clown – that allowed him to avoid and handle dangers both

[12] This corresponds to fourth grade/year in American or British schools.
[13] This was the same boy as in the above example with the girl on whom Russell had a crush.

emotionally, in terms of taking action, and in the way he positioned himself in the class.

But what about later in life? What traces were drawn? What did Russell's childhood experiences of being bullied influence? When asked directly, Russell said that he is 'rather tentative when it comes to letting people in'. He also often establishes a 'slightly ironic distance' to other people and believes that, because of these tendencies, he does not dare to 'be [him]self'. In the social interaction with his childhood peers, he had been assigned a 'role to play', and his peers 'mirror' him in this role. From Russell's perspective, it seems that playing the clown has left traces of a need to try to hide who he really is, giving the 'clown' the job of outwardly representing him. In his present work life, Russell often finds himself 'recreating [this] taunting manner' whilst, at the same time, he 'do[es] not feel very comfortable doing so'. The taunting manner is something that Russell believes he has taken from his school years and brought into his adult life. In his professional life, the experiences of being bullied as a child seem to *influence* his current social interaction, which, amongst other things, consists of 'playing roles' rather than 'being yourself' – a pattern with which Russell is dissatisfied.

However, this pattern is not consistent; it does not reappear at any given place or time. Instead, it is particularly in present situations that Russell utilises the 'taunting tone': 'Well, there is a lot of irony, you know, half-irony, meant to signal that 'Oh, we're such good friends, and that's why we talk to each other like this'.' Here, Russell adds that he employs this manner in situations where it is important to demonstrate that he and the person to whom he is speaking are good friends. In other words, when a present situation calls for consensus about friendship and openness with which he does not feel comfortable, Russell's 'taunting manner' reappears. The point is that, for Russell, such present situations seem to encourage this 'taunting manner', and it makes sense for him to reach back to his school years' repertoire. At first, there seemed to be no direct connection between Russell's experiences of being bullied as a child and his use of the taunting manner as an adult. However, there is an indirect connection because this form of communication was his way of creating a social role for himself during his school years when bullying was an ever-present possibility. Russell told us that he felt insecure as a child, primarily as a consequence of what he observed happening to others, and also what he feared could happen – and to some extent, did happen – to him. In turn, these experiences have come to play a role in his adult life as well. In the following, I take a closer look at which specific situations seem to encourage certain dynamic effectuality in present adult lives after being bullied as a child.

Emotionality as dynamic effectuality

This chapter is based on people's descriptions of their memories. In retelling emotionally difficult experiences, many of the study participants became emotionally distressed, and the past seemed to 'come alive' during our interviews. Fiona is a woman in her mid-forties who was interested in how experiences later in life are connected to having been bullied as a child. She spoke about herself in general terms: 'One can sort of see later what kind of influence it had, or what happens to children who have been bullied . . . also because, I think that sometimes one forgets, to a certain extent, how much it actually leaves its mark on children. . .'[14]

In the middle of telling her story, Fiona interrupted herself because she became sad and started to cry. We had barely begun the interview, and it became clear that she was emotionally distressed by talking about how being bullied as a child had influenced her later in life. She emphasised that she did not expect to react this way. During the interview, Fiona seemed to relive her remembered experiences, and the significance of being bullied as a child was so troubling that she reacted with spontaneous tears, which surprised her.[15]

There are different ways to understand the connection between the interview situation, how Fiona shapes her present adult life and the way that past events affect her emotionally. One way of understanding could be to think of the interview as a condensed context. The researcher was focused on understanding Fiona's memories of bullying experiences and, prior to the interview, Fiona prepared for this situation by purposefully re-engaging with her memories of these experiences. *This* condensed context heightens the emotional experience of her remembering. It was the concrete interview situation that activated her strong emotions. But there are other conditions in Fiona's present life that might be relevant to gaining insight into the strong reaction she experienced during our interview. Fiona had recently quit her job because she was unhappy at the company. When we spoke, she was in the process of evaluating her life, and so she was perhaps particularly focused on the question of whether or not she was happy with how her life was unfolding: she seemed doubtful.

Based on a review of memory research, Linda J. Levine and David A. Pizarro (2004) conclude that we must assume that people's current

---

[14] In Danish, Fiona used the word *spor*, which has been translated here as 'mark'. However, the word *spor* may also be translated as 'trace' or 'track', placing Fiona's comments directly into the analytical language used in this chapter.

[15] Ethical concerns and precautions against unethical interviewing are described and discussed in Mathiassen (2011).

evaluations of what happened in their past will influence their present reconstruction of emotional experiences and reactions in the past. Actual psychological problems or simply being in a bad mood can play a particularly negative role in how we make sense of past experiences (Mineka et al. 2003; Nørby 2007). Based on her present life situation, is it possible that Fiona has remembered and reinterpreted her childhood experiences of being bullied as having been especially difficult and painful? In addition, could it be that the specific interview context – which can encourage 'confidential conversations' (Fog 2004) – brought the emotional influence of being bullied as a child to the foreground? It is not my intention to suggest that such experiences were not painful or were not recalled as such, but it may mean that the interview context makes a person's emotions especially intense and prominent. This emotional influence may prompt a person to take seriously both the past and present meanings of these remembered experiences. And at times, fundamental existential considerations may occur that, in a dialectic interplay with the remembered experiences of having been bullied, can clarify which forms of dynamic effectuality and traces are active in a person's adult life. Thus, let us look at how Melissa described her memories, and explore how her reflections can contribute to our understanding of how being bullied as a child may influence adult lives.

Extensive dynamic effectuality

Melissa is in her late thirties and employed as a scientist at a university. She described the relationship between being bullied as a child and her present day well-being as follows:

There was a time in my childhood when I felt quite bad, and I did not get along with my schoolmates or anyone else at the school I attended. So those are the things that I feel are still with me today, even though it might be twenty-five or thirty years ago. There are still things – I can almost picture some of the . . . . I can remember some of the things people said and did to me. You know, I remember exactly how it was . . . . And maybe it is some of those . . . . You have pictures and you think, you know, 'Well, that's the way it well was . . .; it must have done something or other [to me].'

Melissa continued:

For example, this is about – in this case, having been bullied. . .I think . . . . I come from a really tiny village, where the 'who-do-you-think-you-are' attitude[16] is quite

---

[16] The 'who-do-you-think-you-are' attitude referred to here is a loose translation of a cultural phenomenon in Scandinavia called *janteloven*, or 'Jante's law'. This is not actual

pervasive. I don't think my parents were quite provincial enough, let's put it that way. I mean, they were proud and happy that we had a lot of opportunities to try different activities if we wanted to. They didn't want us to miss out just because we had moved to the middle of nowhere and stuff like that. But this meant that there were perhaps other parents in the community that didn't respect that. And this showed up in how they reacted if their children started whining about something that I was allowed to do. [Then they'd say], 'It's completely ridiculous that Melissa is allowed to do that. She should just do what everybody else does.'

Melissa had been 'allowed to go to more than one horse-riding school' and, at one point, her father decided that she should be allowed to go to a riding school in the neighbouring village, where the horses were better and the teachers more competent. Thus, she took riding classes in the village where she lived as well as in the bigger village nearby. According to Melissa, the other parents thought it was 'silly' because they 'presumably' thought it was excessive. For Melissa, experiences of being bullied and excluded as a child play central roles in her present sense of well-being and how she shapes her adult life: 'So that is where it all started . . . and, I mean, that it is where it all began.' Let us take a closer look at the traces that seem to move in dynamic effectuality between the past and the present.

Transactual (dialectical) effectuality

When Melissa graduated from university, her family wanted to celebrate in her home town, where her parents still live. Melissa rejected the idea, arguing that she did not want to be singled out again like she had been as a child when the other children said she probably thought that she was 'better than everybody else'. The way that Melissa reacted to the possibility of being celebrated in her home town as an adult is indicative of how her childhood experiences of exclusion might continue to have a hold on her, giving those experiences a definitive role in the present. It seems that Melissa cannot stand the thought of being subjected to a re-enactment of the humiliation she suffered as a child. She knew that her parents had been encouraged by neighbours to hold a local celebration marking their daughter's achievement, but Melissa insisted that people still might say nasty things behind her back, which was something she wanted to avoid at all costs:

> juridical law; rather, it is a form of social discipline that keeps individuals from feeling a sense of entitlement and from gaining more influence, opportunities, etc., than their peers (see also Viala's chapter on page 361). In my understanding of Sandemose's argument (Sandemose 1994/1999), *janteloven* is reflected in local 'community ideas' about what 'you' can do and 'who' can do what; in other words, a locally based (i.e. in his city by Jante) rule meant to retain the existing norms; it can also be described as a small town's demand for social 'leveling' (*nivellering*).

My parents only hear about the people that come over and say, 'That's good and congratulations and all that . . . .' People are not going to walk up to them and say, 'Why on earth are you making such a big deal, celebrating Melissa?' Of course, they wouldn't. They just think or talk about it at home, maybe.

In rejecting her parent's suggestion to celebrate in her home town, Melissa referred to episodes that happened twenty years ago: '[I] could tell it's really deep-seated, this thing, you know. [Drawing attention to myself is] just not worth it [because the celebration] would only reconfirm to them that I think I'm better than everybody else.' For Melissa, the memory of having been humiliated as a child is still so vivid that she insists on down-playing her achievements today; she does not want to step into the 'spot-light' and show off her achievements and abilities. Her early experiences appear to follow her into her current life, leaving clear traces. Meanwhile, there are other aspects of how she has shaped her present life that are connected to how her childhood experiences were influential in the ways described above.

For Melissa, there was a lot at stake in her choice to become a scientific researcher. She was sometimes unsure that this was the right decision – and she still is. Nevertheless, she has continued working in this field because 'It's probably in me somehow; if you start something, you have to . . . you want to do it well . . .' There seems to be a dialectical connection between how Melissa's sense of self has developed and the way she relates to her professional life today. During her university years, she considered changing her professional path. However, positioning herself as someone who wanted something different than the people she left behind in her home town functioned as a driving force in her decision to stick with her original choice: 'There might be something in me that. . .I have, once and for all, told them that I'm different. And that I want something different than what they [her classmates] want. So, therefore, it would have been like a failure to stop.' In other words, if Melissa had not followed through with her professional plans, thus positioning herself as someone who was different (and better) than her classmates, then she would have suffered a defeat.

Melissa is unhappy with the way her life has been and continues to unfold: 'My career has been the centre of attention for many years now, but I haven't done brilliantly, if you know what I mean.' As with Fiona, Melissa was in the process of assessing her life, and she wondered whether choosing to focus on being a researcher was the right professional choice. She explained, 'I think that maybe concentrating my efforts [on research] over the past ten years has been wrong.' She wonders why she has not yet had children, despite the fact that she believes having children is a central part of life. It seems that Melissa's focus on being a researcher – which had been her dominant life-project up to the present – is becoming less important, whilst another project is moving into the foreground; namely, starting a family. The course of Melissa's life seems to be shifting and new needs are emerging, coincident with the fact that her career ambitions have not been realised.

It is possible that one of the reasons that Melissa has trouble distancing herself from memories of being bullied as a child is because she does not feel comfortable with her current adult life and the future perspectives it holds. She set a professional goal for herself (an academic career) that is in contrast with the way of life prevalent amongst her childhood peers, who have chosen to stay in their home town and live by its norms. However, she is dissatisfied with her current life-project and the potential future this path indicates. Thus, one could argue that distancing herself from the way of life chosen by her childhood peers has not brought Melissa the satisfaction she expected. Do the experiences in her present life interact with the negative definitions and experiences that she has maintained from her childhood? And in fact, do they reinforce one another?

We sense the emotional traces from Melissa's childhood past; we can observe how these are nourished in the present and projected into her imagined future. The concept of traces allows us to see the connection between Melissa's memories of being bullied as child, the way she has dealt with those experiences in the interim and the way in which she has made use of these experiences as motivating factors for staying in a professional setting where she is not thriving. It is as if the bullying schoolmates of her past – to whom she continues to feel somehow accountable – are present in her current professional decisions. In other words, Melissa's professional decisions seem to be influenced by her childhood experiences, and also by how she has reinterpreted those experiences. For this reason, we might say that there is quite a distinct connection between Melissa's past and present. In addition, clear traces also appear to be drawn between the challenges that she is facing in her present life, and the ways in which she imagines her future will be influenced by the choices she makes in the present.

Emotional (re-)becoming and dynamic effectuality

In the following, I illustrate two forms of dynamic effectuality: firstly, we see how returning to the physical location where childhood bullying experiences occurred can intensify their influence in the present; and secondly, I address how imagined future scenarios can make emotions 'work' in ways that are similar to an individual's previous emotional responses in actual past experiences.

Melissa's story illustrates that the experience of being bullied draws traces in a (singular and) rather clear manner when she finds herself at the location where the bullying occurred – namely, her home town. The influence of being bullied continues to be relevant in her present life; it is apparent, for example, in her choice to refrain from speaking to a particular individual she passes in her home town, a person who bullied her when they were children: 'He hurt me so completely back then that I have nothing to contribute there.' Within the context of her home town, her rejection of the former bully is reawakened and reinforced. Here, Melissa experiences emotions similar to those she experienced as a child. As an adult in the present, Melissa's reaction is based on her emotional state as a child and, as a consequence, she rejects the person who previously bullied her and who, of course, has also grown up. As such, her home town – the specific setting of Melissa's childhood experiences – functions as a kind of intersection where her past and present subjectivities meet. From Melissa's point of view, the ways in which she and the person who previously bullied her were positioned as children became re-established in the present, including the emotional repertoire that accompanied these positions. Within this intersection, the dynamic effectuality between past experiences and the present is apparent through a re-experienced emotional quality. To some extent, this emotionality is transferred into the present and thus continues to function as a negative force in Melissa's adult life, as illustrated by her present rejection of the person who previously bullied her in her home town. I refer to this dynamic effectuality as 'situation-specific, emotional (re-)becoming'. This means that parts of an individual's former responses within the intersection between past and present seem to re-emerge in their original forms and take on new meanings in the present. I elaborate on this in due course.

Melissa's way of dealing with this intersection is reminiscent of what other study participants recounted from their experiences of attending class reunions. They explained that being bullied as children did not play a dominant role in their adult lives, *but* when they attended class reunions, they experienced a similar atmosphere, emotions and positioning as when they were schoolchildren. Henry explained:

It was strange, because it wasn't long before I felt like the old atmosphere was re-established. And I actually felt quite bad afterwards. Suddenly I felt ... I mean, I felt like I had moved on. I must have been about 30 at the time, a student at graduate school, and I had three children. And then to come back and suddenly feel, wow, afterwards. It went so fast. Especially that guy ... who had been my best friend, who sort of ditched me in primary school. In no time at all, he managed to put me in a place that left me feeling like I was right back in the middle of it, without any sense of self . . . And I felt myself jumping right in, you know? I mean I just felt that, wow, these roles just sit so deeply in us and in no time at all, they are re-established, just like that.

Several of the study participants referred to experiences where they felt like they were repositioned as schoolchildren again, and all of them found this unpleasant and surprising. I suggest that in specific recollection praxes, such as a class reunion, the past seems to cover the present adult context like a blanket and, for a short while, things return to how they used to be. The same thing appears to have happened to Melissa when she returned to her home town, and even when she merely thought about returning. Also, by taking the *context* of certain phenomena into account, it becomes clear that traces from past experiences are not exclusively permanent and static.

We may continue this line of thinking and move across contexts, such as those between everyday life and extraordinary occurrences – which is the case with a class reunion or returning to one's home town for a visit. With these events, we can see examples of what I categorise as 'situation-specific, emotional re-becomings'. This means that past emotions become prevalent and influential again when an individual in the present day is put into a situation with a group of people he/she knew from school. We might even say that, when past emotions are put into a context along with present emotions, then positionings and self-perceptions gain a particular power. The participants who attended class reunions had to manoeuvre between memories and emotional responses from their pasts and their positionings in the present whilst, at the same time, they had to manage an actual interface with now-adult individuals with whom they share a troubled past. Participants who attended such reunions found them emotionally challenging, as if they had been transported back to 'how things used to be'. The kind of repositioning that seems necessary to avoid experiencing such 'situation-specific, emotional re-becoming' must take place *in* the actual situation, taking into account everybody's contribution. But it is apparent from the narratives that this is a challenging task, which might explain why people who attend such reunions often experience them as emotionally distressing – and as if they 'become as they were' in the past.

Identifying with pain as dynamic effectuality

In Melissa's story, resentment is apparent. She described, for example, how a classmate made fun of her after giving a presentation in class, which 'knocked [her] out'. She continued, 'The happiness you just felt . . . is completely smashed (...). It is episodes like that that I still remember to this very day, and then I think, "Why did she have to do that?" Melissa found it easy in the present to gain access to these painful emotions of her past. At the same time, the pain that she so readily accessed contributes to her continued and current emotional pain over the past. Recounting a story of pain and harassment is indicative of the 'emotional trace' that past events have left in Melissa's life. This dialectic relationship between the past and the present may be Melissa's way of making sense of her experiences, and how her memories of these experiences influence her present life.

Let us stay with the psychological aspect for a moment: Melissa considers the connection between her experiences of being bullied as a child and her present social context. She reasons, 'I think it still might be with me ... this thing of feeling bad about being excluded, you know? ... Even though I might [in adult life] realise that, 'Well, you're never going to be part of the inner circle because, well, that's just hopeless'; I'm so far outside of that circle that they can't even ... I guess I just still dreamt about being included ...' It seems that Melissa was positioned as an outsider as a child, and it is possible that she even accepted that position because she continued to participate in activities that were rejected by the childhood cultural codes of her home town. Melissa explained that her childhood dream of belonging to the inner circle became intertwined with her present and general unease about being excluded in her adult life. At the same time, she was also re-evaluating her life-project; a process that, amongst other things, was dominated by specific doubts about her professional life and, in general, whether she 'actually chose the wrong path'. These are major existential concerns with which Melissa appeared to be struggling in her present life as well as during the interview. As discussed, some of the elements of humiliation and rejection that she remembered from her childhood were actively accessible to her in the present, and these emotions might enhance her more-or-less intentional urge to be different from her former classmates.

One way of understanding Melissa's choice to continue down a particular professional path is to look through the lens of her life-project as an 'outsider'. For example, she describes herself as different from her family because she has not had children. To her, the consequences of not having an optimal career include not having children, something she believed her family would hold in high regard. Her childlessness also marks her as being different; different on all counts and compared to everyone else. I suggest that Melissa's experience of being different may be understood as a sense of identity that appears to be defined by and through pain. This 'sense of identity defined by and through pain' may be one kind of trace that is linked to the experience of being bullied as a child.

Although Russell was affected in a different way, his experience of having to play roles and the experience of being bullied as a child were also influential. In the following, Wendy's story helps to plot other existential influences of having been bullied as a child.

Debilitating *and* inspirational dynamic effectuality

Wendy explained:

... precisely because I was subjected to [bullying] as a child, I constantly have that little nagging voice: 'Am I good enough, am I pretty enough and can I live up to people's expectations' and all that.

This is painful for Wendy. Her self-denigration is quite pervasive, and she connects her experiences of being bullied as a child to her view of herself today. She was negatively criticised as a child, and these experiences seem to play a role in her feelings of insecurity and her inconsistent sense of self in relation to other people's expectations of her in the present. With regard to self-esteem, Wendy explained that being bullied as a child had drawn 'negative traces'.[17] Wendy had tried to work through these negative feelings with a psychologist and in coaching sessions. She emphasised that her negative self-esteem is a strong force in her life, and she wishes to be free of it – but so far, she has not had much success. Having been bullied appears to have an *undermining* influence in Wendy's life because, to some extent, she has grown doubtful of her own value.

Wendy does not experience her low self-esteem as consistent over time and place, however. Depending on the situation in her life, Wendy describes herself in different ways. At some times and in certain situations, Wendy experiences herself as unable to act whilst at other times, her will to act is almost *fervent* and she challenges herself. For example, Wendy practises martial arts. In her training sessions, she is constantly challenged, and she likes to push herself even further. When she is successful, she sees this as a way to strengthen her self-esteem. The multiplicity of meanings becomes apparent and thereby the ways in which the traces may be varied, both in terms of content and intensity. Wendy described how she is generally preoccupied with achieving in order to gain recognition. But there are several nuances in how her preoccupation with achieving works. She explained: 'To a great extent, I think that I'm trying to prove something to myself, rather than to the outside world.' Inspired by G. H. Mead's symbolic interactionism (1934) and Lev Vygotsky's socio-genetic thinking (Valsiner and van der Veer 2000), I suggest that the way in which

[17] These are Wendy's own words.

Wendy internalises the meanings and evaluations she has encountered have become inner verbal tools. These tools enable her to negotiate with herself; e.g. whether or not she is 'good enough'. Thus, the ways in which she achieves become meaningful in how she interprets her personal value, and Wendy is focused on achieving well.

As we have seen in the analysis, the present is also influential in how an individual interprets his/her past.[18] How is this relevant for the analysis of Wendy's remembered experiences, and their significance to her now? Because of her present adult experiences, does Wendy reinterpret her experiences of being bullied as a child as something that has led to her present low self-esteem? She described, for example, how a former boss was able to 'start up those mechanisms in me that make me think that I'm not good enough'.

Wendy spoke about a long period when she became increasingly unsure of herself; this accompanied her boss's humiliating acts. Because she was bullied as a child, she believes that she is 'predisposed' to low self-esteem. In her view, her experiences with a demeaning boss illustrate that, because she was bullied as a child, she finds it difficult 'to stand up for [her]self' today. Despite the fact that she is quite capable of 'standing up for others', Wendy believes that her childhood experiences contribute to her 'put[ting] up with being "stepped on" for too long'. She argues that other 'normal' people would protest much earlier. In Wendy's sense-making, being bullied as a child has caused her to not take her own interests seriously enough, and this has led to feeling humiliated by her boss as an adult.

Wendy's reflections about herself and her self-esteem add significance to her experiences. Being bullied is an *undermining experience*, but Wendy's descriptions are also ambiguous. In other areas of her life, she actually attributes positive significance to her experiences of being bullied as a child. For example, she couples her own experiences of being bullied with her attention to other people's well-being, a tendency that I noted amongst some of our other interview participants. Wendy referred to this as her 'guideline': that a person should 'treat others the way that you would like to be treated'. Wendy told me with satisfaction that, in her work, she makes an effort to be a positive influence on and for others, and that she also helps people who are less fortunate than herself. Specifically, she has sought out humanitarian jobs, and this has been her general

---

[18] Wendy also describes other contributions to her present sense of well-being. The point is that, according to Wendy, it is not only her experience of being bullied as a child that has had an influence on her current sense of well-being; other experiences also come into play. Traces from these experiences may also be influential and worth investigating.

guideline for how to define her professional profile. In our conversations about her work, it became apparent that her childhood experiences with bullying were also a positive driving force in her life because she now chooses to use these negative experiences positively to benefit others. It is neither obvious nor predictable how the potentiality of being bullied as a child will be played out as an adult.

Social sensitivity as dynamic effectuality

We could say that Wendy has described herself both as a *victim* and as a *humanitarian*. How can we understand the tension between these two positions in Wendy's story? Is it possible that she feels and felt humiliated whilst she simultaneously – and consequently – chose to shape her adult life around an ethical professional project, which has been reflected in her choice of employment? It seems as though, based on her experiences of being bullied as a child, Wendy prefers to position herself as a morally aware individual instead of as a victim. The latter position confirms her negative experiences, but the former allows her to ascribe meaningful and positive significance to her negative past experiences. The influence of her experiences could be characterised as a trace of distrust and insecurity that has not manifested itself as restrictive bitterness or blockage – as it did for Melissa, to some extent. Wendy explained that she is aware that her experiences have formed her social and compassionate attitude. I suggest that her experiences of being bullied as a child have drawn a humanitarian and moral trace into her adult life. Wendy exemplified this when she said: 'Well, I just think that it has made me a lot more aware of how important it is to treat other people nicely and to be proud of who you are; to not waste a lot of time on this "Am I good enough?" stuff.'

With the project concept in mind, it seems that Wendy's life-project is to be particularly interested in the welfare of others, thus defining herself as someone who interacts with people in an inclusive and accepting manner. In this project, acknowledgement from others is definitive. This is neither obvious nor does it develop in a linear fashion: there are movements back and forth, and different themes are central at different times, places and positions. Nevertheless, the combination and complexity seem to function as a particular driving force that is anchored by a sense of decency and a need to be acknowledged for good deeds.

Research on the effects of being bullied

Thus far, I have identified several types of dynamic effectuality. I have touched on concrete ways in which the potentiality of being bullied as a child has significance on adult life. Specifically, I have discussed how these types of dynamic effectuality function in a dialectic fashion, are context-bound and, in some cases, coexist across contexts. I have suggested that the influences and implications of being bullied as a child are not static, nor can they be described as leaving a clear, irrefutable mark.

To conclude this chapter, I shift my focus to some of the existing research on bullying. Much of the research that investigates the correlation between being bullied as a child and what this may mean later uses quantitative methods. In addition, this research does not usually address what happens after formal schooling and into young adulthood (Mebane 2010).[19] As a result, the research presented in this chapter contributes to the existing research on the influence of being bullied as a child in three significant ways: firstly, it focuses on the influence on adults of being bullied as a child; secondly, it is based on qualitative methodology; and thirdly, it investigates complex types of dynamic effectuality.

The quantitative methods and data about the negative effects of bullying, which are already so plentifully represented in academic literature, operate with a combination of predetermined variables that 'weigh' the negative consequences of being bullied as a child. The significance of being bullied as a child is commonly represented in this way through statistical research, and reference is often made to *statistical contexts*. The research produced from such quantitative methods and statistics show that children who were continuously subjected to bullying may suffer negative physical and emotional – as well as cognitive and socio–emotional – consequences for both children and adolescents (Hawker and Boulton 2000; Salmon et al. 2000; Sourander et al. 2000). Further, there is thorough quantitative documentation of the harmful effects of bullying on children and young adults[20] (e.g. Due et al. 2005; Kumpulainen 2008; Vreeman and Carroll 2007). Examples of these negative effects given by the research include suicidal thoughts, insomnia and feelings of helplessness and trauma. The research also mentions depressive symptoms and damaged self-esteem amongst adults as a result of having been bullied as children (ibid.; see also note 20 below).

---

[19] For exceptions, see, e.g., Schäfer et al. (2004).

[20] David Hawker and Michael Boulton (2000) conducted a meta-analytical review of a cross-section of studies published between 1978 and 1997. According to the authors, the research emphasises that being bullied has significant negative consequences for the children and young adults represented in the research they reviewed. Such consequences include generalised anxiety, social anxiety, depression and loneliness. As several studies describe (Due et al. 2005; Henningsen 2009; Lindberg 2007; Rigby 2002b; Sourander et al. 2000), being bullied can have long-term negative repercussions on an individual's health, development and learning.

Research is limited on the correlation between experiences of being bullied as a child and adult life, a point that has been raised in different studies (e.g. Lund et al. 2008[21] and Mebane 2010). The existing quantitative research on the consequences of being bullied suggests that both non-physical and physical bullying in childhood can have negative consequences for an individual later in life (Kokko and Pörhölä 2009; Mebane 2010), such as psychological and psycho-pathological difficulties in adulthood (Kumpulainen 2008; Lund et al. 2008; Mebane 2010). As an example, Kristiina Kumpulainen (2008) writes: 'Rarely does any single behaviour predict future problems as bullying does' (ibid.: 121). In her conclusion, Kumpulainen draws upon different quantitative studies on the negative effects of being bullied, having bullied others or having adopted both positions in bullying events. One may argue that these analyses present a more simplified notion of causality – that is, the 'if this...then that' kind of thinking that comes from a focus on testing the negative effects of bullying on an individual in a more mono-causal manner, which might have consequences that are too simplistic: after all, not every individual who has been bullied as a child describes the difficulties that these various quantitative studies present. The point here is that knowledge about why this is the case must also be developed, and specifically within the field of bullying.[22] Through the concepts of traces and potentiality, I have made an effort to illustrate the variability of influences that being bullied as a child can have on adult life, and thereby offer another kind of contribution to the exploration of how childhood bullying might influence adult life as well as how adults handle their experiences differently.

Paying analytical attention to traces, potentiality and dynamic effectuality

This chapter has shown that being bullied as a child may have a variety of influences on an individual's adult life. For some, the negative feelings connected to having been bullied as a child may become a positive driving force later in adult life, whilst others believe their childhood experiences have had a negative influence up to the present day. By adopting an analytical angle that focuses on dynamic effectuality, we are able to

---

[21] They argue that prospective, longitudinal studies are needed if we wish to substantiate the claim that there are significant negative effects that stem from being bullied as a child, such as adult depression.

[22] One could also adopt a resilience perspective (see, e.g. Sommer (2012) and Unger (2012).

consider the potentiality of being bullied and the potentiality of the experiences of having been bullied. In other words, these experiences will always hold a potential power, but with this analytical tool, it need not be interpreted as having an inherent and distinct direction. Thus, the way in which traces are formed – if they are formed – remains an open analytical question. In my use of the trace concept, openness and indecisiveness are central characteristics. The potentiality of the experience of being bullied *could* (in Agamben's sense) be experienced purely as potentiality, which in itself can have a significant influence on a person's life. The adult individual who was bullied as a child may be influenced in many ways, but he/she navigates according to how these potential influences are understood. Thus, by acting upon potentialities, actual new and present experiences are made, regardless of whether or not the imagined and potential influence of past events materialises.

The other form of potentiality that I have presented in this chapter – the potentiality of being bullied – functions in a similar way as described above, but it is also different. With this, a child experiences being bullied as a potentiality, and the bullying does not necessarily ever actually occur. Nevertheless, or perhaps even in spite of this, the potentiality of being bullied can still prompt a particular pattern of navigation amongst a group of children. This aspect of potentiality may accommodate the possible realisation of the phenomenon, but equally important, it may also shed light on how children navigate according to something that *could* happen. Thus, bullying is not just an event, but also a not-yet-realised phenomenon. As we have seen, this kind of potentiality can also have a decisive influence on an individual, both in the short term and later in life. This has been analysed here as the potentiality of being bullied.

My claim is that it is productive to view bullying experiences in this manner. It influences our understanding and curbs reductionist explanations of how experiences of being bullied as a child can influence adult life. This seems to be a useful contribution and offers a necessary nuance to the aforementioned academic literature that exists on the topic. Through a situated and cross-context-based analysis, this chapter adds to our understanding of how the past, the present and the future are linked, and how various everyday-life contexts play a role in the influence that bullying *can* have. Here, the concept of traces is particularly useful. Many childhood experiences can contribute to the traces that become apparent in adulthood, and the dynamic effectuality may also vary. To an individual, traces can signify something positive, something negative and even something neutral. Furthermore, it is productive to look at traces as something that does not only move from the past to the present. It is useful to include the current situations and relationships in an individual's life when evaluating how the past makes sense in the present, and how it is projected into the future.

In addition, perceptions of the future influence how traces manifest themselves, how they move and even how they change their course. The concept of traces has been utilised to help us understand the connections between the past, present and future. One could criticise the concept of traces in the same way as the concept of 'trajectory'; i.e. as being built on a presumption that the progression of an individual's development has a specific, determined course.[23] The concept of 'trajectories of participation' (see, e.g. Dreier 1999 or Mørck 2006) has deterministic undertones due to its etymological relationship with a bullet's trajectory, which refers to the bullet's determined route after being fired (discussed in Mathiassen 2012). However, the 'trajectory of participation' concept can help to clarify how individuals are spun into socio–material conditions and significant relationships from which they have difficulty freeing themselves. How, then, is the concept of traces helpful? This concept was used to illustrate the movements I observed in the research participants' descriptions of their experiences during and after being bullied, and in their descriptions of possible future projects. In a broader sense, all of these projects could be referred to as 'potentialities'. Various traces become intertwined and weave in and out of each other. As a result, the concept of traces embraces dynamic effectuality, processes and approaches to life and its challenges rather than inert *effects* and *causations*. What do I mean by this?

As shown above, a great deal of research has focused on the suffering and psychological wounds connected to bullying. The negative influences of having been bullied are well documented whilst, at the same time, a closer look at the 'life-quality' of the participants in this study revealed that it is impossible to reach a conclusive verdict about bullying and its influence on adults (see also Henningsen 2009; Mebane 2010). Some studies indicate that negative experiences of being bullied can be converted into a kind of social skill if an individual comes to terms with the experiences (Kokko and Pöhölä 2009).[24] Together with the concept of dynamic effectuality, the purpose of this chapter has been to move past the mono-causal and one-dimensional syllogisms that are inappropriate and reductionist in this context. In my analysis of individuals' experiences with

---

[23] It is a criticism that can also be directed at theories that focus on phases in an individual's development; phases that have to be passed through in a particular order to avoid the risk of developing in the 'wrong' direction.

[24] This is an exception that I have come across within the research material (Mathiassen 2011).

different bullying events, I have drawn upon socio-cultural approaches, anthropological psychology and a critical psychological approach. This framework has inspired me to include the many influences and multiple contexts that are integral to any understanding of how people's experiences with bullying evolve and affect them over time. Here, the work presented in Jette Kofoed and Dorte Marie Søndergaard's edited volume (2009) and Søndergaard's chapter in this anthology (see page 47) has also been inspirational. The traces and types of dynamic effectuality that I have investigated can be seen as the result of canalisation and life-projects that move with and against each other whilst still conforming to and challenging one another. Traces may offer a way to describe experiences in a lived life and, at the same time, the concept is an analytical tool for understanding such experiences. An individual may retrospectively consider traces, and traces may also function as a kind of guide that leads a person through life. Through the insights I gained from this study's interview material, traces offer one way to understand the empirical material – and life. The potentiality of bullying experiences produces variable traces that move back and forth across time and place.

14 'Is something wrong with me?': a context-sensitive analysis of school bullying

Eva Silberschmidt Viala

A memory of being bullied

When Linda's father got a new job, the whole family moved from a small city to a small farm on the other side of the country. At the time, Linda was 9 years old and was just about to start third grade.[1] Together with her family, Linda was looking forward to the move and, although she liked her school, she thought it would be exciting to start at a new school. Her first experiences were positive. The school was small with only sixty students, and the teachers seemed nice. But it did not take long before Linda got a different impression. To begin with, the girls made unpleasant and demeaning comments about her hair, clothes and mannerisms. When they chose teams, she was always picked last, and sometimes the girls would refuse to continue playing if Linda wanted to join in. Nobody wanted to be with her when they did group work during class, and she was often not invited to her classmates' birthday parties.

In the beginning, Linda told her teachers about these experiences; they would then appeal to the class, saying that the children should be 'nice' to Linda. As it became clear that this made no impact, she gradually stopped saying anything. The episodes continued and became more intense. When Linda got on the bus in the morning, she was particularly afraid of the boys sitting in the back. They seemed threatening. They would call her nasty things or push her. What was most hurtful was when the girls formed a circle around Linda on the school's playground and took turns pushing her from side to side while they called her mean names. For this reason, Linda started running to the school library when the recess-bell rang: a teacher was there, so she was safe. At other times, she would try to hide in the bathrooms because she could lock herself in there. The girls would sometimes throw a glass of cold water over the locked door and onto her head, but it was still better than having to stand completely alone and vulnerable in the school playground.

Linda told her story during an interview about her memories of being bullied as a child in the 1960s. She started by saying that it was hard to remember specific episodes, but in her re-telling, the memories were conjured up again. She was surprised that they could still bring back so many feelings, and she

---

[1] This corresponds to fourth grade/year in American or British schools.

described how she could recall the frustration, the loneliness and the knot in her stomach from when she was a child. She perceived these assaults as acts of bullying, and she has since tried to understand why she became a target. She wondered if maybe something was wrong with her.

The interview with Linda did not offer any conclusive answers. However, my point of departure in this chapter is that Linda perceived these acts to be bullying and that, in her attempt to understand these experiences, she focused on her personal characteristics and the circumstances of her upbringing in relation to her experiences of being bullied as a child. Of course, this is not how Linda referred to it – instead, it is an apt description of how I have chosen to 'translate' her attempt to find fault with herself – that 'something was wrong' with her. At the same time, Linda insisted that 'a combination of things' contributed to the bullying and its intensification. In my analysis, it is this 'combination of things' that suggests that there are many elements to consider when we try to understand bullying, and the reasons cannot be reduced to children's personal characteristics and/or upbringing. Linda's personal characteristics and upbringing may seem to play a role, but the social hierarchy both in and outside of school and the socio-cultural relations in the local community are also relevant in understanding how Linda became a target of bullying. This raises some basic questions about the nature of bullying: why was Linda a target? What role did she play in these acts, and how does this relate to other aspects of her life from that time? Is it possible to draw any conclusions about what role her personal characteristics and upbringing might have played in her being chosen as a target of bullying?

From a cause–effect perception to context-sensitive analyses

As discussed by Schott (2009b), the dominant approach amongst researchers studying the causes of bullying has been to assign a particular meaning to victims' personal characteristics and upbringing (see also Ellwood and Davies 2010). Many Danish and international researchers have tried to pinpoint particular factors that play a central role in whether a child will become a bully or be singled out as a target. Thus, investigating the phenomenon of bullying entails finding causation and/or correlation between bullying and certain factors, such as a child's personality, diagnoses or the psycho-social and socio-economic conditions within the family. These initiatives typically employ quantitative research methods and design (see, for example, Due et al. 2009; Jablonska and Lindberg 2007) or qualitative case studies that involve children and/or families in various forms of treatment (see, for example, Wai-Yung et al. 2010).

The notion that the causes of bullying may be found in a child's personality, personal characteristics or upbringing has also become a common belief amongst school principals, teachers and parents, and this is seen as a meaningful analytical framework. In her study about the position of parents in cases of bullying, Nina Hein (see page 301) finds that teachers and school principals commonly ascribe the causes of bullying to problems in a child's home (such as parents' divorce), despite the fact that such events may have occurred in the child's distant past. In Danish schools, these tendencies are also discernible in official strategy plans and teachers' guidelines that address bullying at school. In one research project about teachers' attitudes towards bullying, Helle Rabøl Hansen and Inge Henningsen (2010) discovered that, although teachers seem to be interested in the social dynamics of the class, they claim that a child's upbringing is still more influential with regard to bullying at school. Consequently, when teachers were asked for concrete suggestions to address the problem, they tended to recommend options that concentrated on individual schoolchildren (ibid.).

However, the idea that there is a clear cause-and-effect relationship between children's personal characteristics, their upbringing and bullying is being met with increased criticism from social scientists and researchers who suggest instead that bullying should be understood as a complex social and cultural phenomenon (see Ellwood and Davies 2010; Eriksson et al. 2002; Galloway and Roland 2004; Kofoed and Søndergaard 2009). Their argument is that, amongst other things, an intense focus on children's personal characteristics and upbringing diverts attention away from the contextual conditions that contribute to generalised and de-contextualised analyses, and also leads to individualised and personalised understandings of bullying. This can happen when problems at school are attributed to the family, because bullying is typically understood as the result of problematic family relationships and/or a child's lack of social skills and not, for example, as a product of the interactions and dynamics within the classroom.

The goal and focus of this chapter

My goal here is to take a context-sensitive look at the relations between children's personal characteristics, their upbringing and bullying at school. This is not to reject the possible significance that children's personal characteristics and upbringing may have on the bullying phenomenon, but rather, to understand how – in different ways – children's personal characteristics and upbringing influence the bullying practices that emerge in a classroom; for example, in conjunction with the social and cultural conditions and opportunities that characterise the school as well as the other social contexts in which children find themselves and within which they must act. At the same time, the goal of this chapter is to contribute an analysis of how adults' memories of bullying are shaped by specific dominant ideological and socio-cultural forms of understanding that are meaningful in how bullying can be comprehended, managed and remembered.

My understanding of bullying as a complex phenomenon – one that is enacted through several open-ended social, discursive, material, technological and subjective forces – has been developed by eXbus (Kofoed and Søndergaard 2009) and refers to the idea that conditions both inside and outside of the school are significant to how bullying practices develop. This may refer to the school as an institution, classroom norms and values for social interaction amongst the schoolchildren and/or their use of technological media, such as mobile phones or social-networking websites. But other elements must also be taken into account, such as the teachers', school principals' and parents' way of dealing with bullying as it relates to problem-solving and conflict resolution between the children. Thus, a child's personal characteristics and upbringing are only *one* of many forces that may influence whether he/she will be subjected to bullying. Therefore, if we are to gain deeper insights into the complex dynamics that inform bullying practices, it is inadequate to focus solely on the individual child.

As an analytical framework, the notion that several interrelated forces are at play in the phenomenon of bullying makes it possible to gain deeper insights into the complex dynamics that inform bullying. However, this approach also raises some troublesome questions about how to understand the interactive entanglements between these different forces. I am particularly concerned about the role or the 'status' of what could be termed the 'subjective' forces if they do *not* serve as an analytical point of departure for why some children become targets of bullying. If we are to approach the practice of bullying as a social and cultural phenomenon that is defined by several interrelated forces – such as social dynamics, processes and norms inside and outside of school – then what role does a child's personal characteristics and upbringing play? If these factors are only to be understood as *one* of many interrelated forces, then how should we understand the impact of these subjective forces? For example, how should we address the significance of a child's physical appearance or family background? At the other extreme, it also seems problematic to over-accentuate the meaning of social relations at school and the mechanisms of inclusion/exclusion that are prevalent in this environment, thus sacrificing an analysis that considers an individual's context and personal history.

In this chapter, I present an analysis that adopts a socio-psychological approach to child development (see, for example, Haavind 2007a; Hedegaard and Fleer 2008; Kousholt 2011). From this point of view, children's development is theorised in relation to their participation and engagement in various significant contexts of their lives. As such, psychological processes and personal characteristics are not analytically separated, but are analysed in relation to the circumstances of which the children are a part. This implies an analytical focus that systematically asks how a child may develop and act within the different social contexts of which he/she is a part and by which he/she is influenced. Consequently, my approach here addresses a child's position and agency at school as being formed by many different contexts. This means that my analysis focuses on *how* a child's personal characteristics and upbringing become meaningful, *how* they are negotiated and *how* they become important and significant within the social context of school. This creation of meaning may occur across contexts and within children's relationships to one another, where norms regulate their interactions, their reciprocal positionings[2] and, in the end, their ability to socially navigate through their school years. Thus, I wish to achieve a more nuanced and sensitive view of how social processes and contextual factors may contribute to shaping the conditions and opportunities within which children are able to act.

Empirical data

In this chapter, I examine two women's memories of being bullied as children. These interviews were part of a larger research project that I conducted in collaboration with Charlotte Mathiassen during 2008–9, in which thirty-six adults between 20 and 65 years of age were asked about their childhood memories of bullying.[3] All of the interview participants were recruited from two large companies or two adult colleges (*højskoler*) located in Denmark; this represented twelve men and twenty-four

[2] Here, I draw upon Bronwyn Davies and Rom Harré's term 'positioning' (1990), which underlines the double movement of being positioned and taking a position as constitutive for an understanding of who we are and who we can be. This may be understood as a process that is played out within specific social and cultural norms. The point is developed and sharpened by Dorte Marie Søndergaard (2000), who stresses that social and cultural norms can encompass *possibilities* whilst also creating *limits*. Thus, it becomes clear that we need to understand contextual conditions as conditions that may include limits as well as possibilities for a child's participation.

[3] Although our research is comprised of the same qualitative empirical data, Mathiassen's chapter in this anthology has another objective and incorporates interviews with different informants; the identities of all our informants have been made anonymous. We also do not employ the same analytical strategies or concepts. See Mathiassen, Chapter 13, page 331, for an analysis of different elements from our interview material.

women, each of whom described his/her experiences of bullying during childhood. At the adult colleges, we conducted another four mixed (men and women) group interviews as well as participant observation; the interviews with the companies' employees were all individual. In general, our informants fell into different levels with regard to education, social–economic hierarchy and career position: of those from the companies, some were employed as service workers, some as researchers and yet others as office staff or managers. Furthermore, all of the interview participants had assumed different positions in the bullying process: there were some who had bullied, some who had been bullied and some who had mostly been observers.

Our qualitative interview study was designed to investigate: how adults make sense of their childhood experiences of bullying; and how adults handle their childhood experiences of bullying once they have become adults (Mathiassen and Viala 2009). The initial theoretical point of departure was a cultural–psychological approach in the broadest sense. In our interviews, we drew upon phenomenological inspiration: we emphasised the participants' own experiences and localised perspectives on their childhood experiences – that is, we focused on how each participant experienced the context in which the bullying took place: where it occurred, who was there and what reasons might have led to the bullying – and examined the implications of these experiences in adulthood.

During the individual interviews with the company employees, we encouraged each participant to describe his/her own experience of bullying. In terms of the dataset, this means that the accounts have a high degree of personal depth and details, both with regard to concrete events as well as the emotional shifts associated with these events. We also asked each participant about the function of bullying when they were children – in relation to the class community as a whole and to the individuals who were actively engaged in the bullying. Additionally, we tried to determine how each participant's social network was structured, including asking about his/her family relationships. In this sense, we focused on how and to what extent understanding, experiencing and managing occurrences of bullying can vary in and across contexts (see, e.g. Dreier 2008) and in different time periods.

The first case that I explore in this chapter is based on Linda's memories of being bullied as a child, and the second on Susan's memories. Both women see themselves as victims of bullying. However, in contrast to Linda's experience, the bullying at Susan's school developed slowly over time. In the beginning, she was a thriving child who loved going to school, but she gradually became rejected and, eventually, she was completely excluded socially. Before I continue with Susan's and Linda's narratives, let me first discuss the methodological challenges presented by using memory in my analysis.

Memory as a methodological tool: when adults speak from the perspective of children

Linda's and Susan's narratives about bullying are based on their memories of events that happened many years ago; Susan was at school in the 1970s and Linda in the 1980s. Their memories may be understood as reconstructions of certain events from their childhoods, which are based on their specific *present* perceptions of bullying. According to cultural psychologist Jerome Bruner (1990, 1994), the typical form for framing experiences (and our memories of them) is a narrative form that, in turn, contributes to how we make sense of our lives.[4] One of Bruner's central arguments is that our way of life depends on shared meanings and shared concepts, and that the function of our narratives is to find an 'intentional state that mitigates or at least makes comprehensible deviations from a canonical cultural pattern' (1990: 49–50). Thus, these memories may be understood as ways to create meaning; that is, negotiating differences in meaning and interpretation, particularly when something extraordinary or problematic is experienced (ibid.). For this reason, memory may be understood as a socio-cultural process and not only as an individual process for storing information. This means that an analysis of Linda's and Susan's memories must pay attention to socio–cultural and historical circumstances – both those they were in when the memories were created and those in which they find themselves today.

Another important point with regard to addressing memory as a methodological tool is that memories can change depending on 'where' the narrator is in his or her life when the story is told. Amongst others, Marianne Horsdal (1999) has suggested that a narrator chooses, hierarchises and places life events in a specific order based on how meaningful the event is in the person's current perspective. This perspective is the point from which and context wherein the event or story is re-told, and therefore it may be decisive in how a memory is demarcated or presented (ibid.: 39).

Finally, it is important to note that Linda's and Susan's memories are characterised by their adult perspectives on what happened in their childhoods; in the interim, they have gathered experiences that contribute to reframing their childhood experiences in different ways. Thus, Linda's and Susan's memories hold particular analytical potential because the

---

[4] See also Polkinghorne (1988), Atkinson (2001), Middleton and Brown (2005) and Riessman (2008) for elaboration on this point.

child's perspective is mediated through the now-adult's interpretation and understanding of what happened when they were children. As we try to obtain a deeper understanding of what was at stake in the contexts of which they were a part as children, we could say that their memories of bullying are based on complex and ambiguous interpretations of specific events and sequences of events that are associated with bullying, and that these interpretations have been continuously developed, nuanced and/or modified since the events originally occurred.

For this reason, Linda's and Susan's recollections do not represent any absolute truth. Instead, their memories tell us something about what seems to be meaningful to each of them when their stories are retold and about how the socio-cultural hegemonic discourses upon which they draw may influence the interpretations that are achieved. Therefore, in the following analysis, I direct my attention towards listening to and following how the child's perspective is mediated through the adult's perceptions and interpretations, and how and why (cor-)relations are made between certain events in their narratives. My main analytical questions are thus: which elements and dynamics are spoken about as conditions for the emergence and development of bullying? How are other elements associated with bullying in the women's efforts to understand and explain what happened to them? In what ways are their personal characteristics and upbringing presented as being influential in how they were able to act at school? What other conditions contributed to how they were able to participate in the social context of school?

The continuing struggle to belong

Susan's story is about a challenging school life. Her first memories of being bullied are from the age of 10, when she was taunted about her thin legs and excluded from social activities at school. The teasing got worse, and Susan was made fun of, humiliated and excluded. This continued until obligatory schooling ended in the tenth grade[5] when she was 16 years old.

During these years, Susan's parents got divorced and her father subsequently committed suicide. But in Susan's memories of being bullied as a child, she did not directly connect these personal events to being bullied because, as she explained, her father's suicide 'overshadowed' the bullying; her primary focus at school became hiding the details of his death from her schoolmates. She also underwent therapy as a young adult, during which the pain and guilt she felt about her father's suicide was the central focus – and not her experiences of having been bullied and

[5] This corresponds to eleventh grade/year in American or British schools.

what role bullying may have played during this difficult time in her childhood.

The dilemmas and possibilities connected to individual-based psychology

When Susan spoke about her childhood, she described a particularly loving and harmonious home-life. She spoke about growing up in a nuclear family in the Danish city of Aarhus at the end of the 1960s. Her mother did not work outside the home, and she was dedicated to 'being there' for Susan and her brother, who is older by two years. When Susan started school in the neighbourhood, she could already read and write. She described herself as a trusting child who was active in class and who had lots of friends. 'I was always raising my hand [in class],' she explained and continued:

I remember that there was this boy who I thought was really cute and so when we were supposed to get new seat assignments – that's how it worked in third grade[6] – I raised my hand and said 'I want to sit next to Thomas' [she starts to laugh]. I mean, that was something I could do then...

That Susan 'could' do such things is not just a matter of being active in class; rather, it addresses the ability to be herself. This stands in sharp contrast to the school experiences that began to develop just a year later in the fourth grade.[7] Susan's role and position in the class began to change, and she went from being a thriving child who looked forward to going to school every day to becoming – over the next six years – a lonely and insecure girl.

Reflecting on the possible reasons for why she became a target of bullying, Susan seemed to be particularly focused on the circumstances that formed her as a person. For Susan, the connection between her upbringing (i.e. her experiences within her family) and feeling 'right' emerged as central in her ability to feel and act self-confident at school. She explained:

It's all those experiences from your childhood that make you feel 'right'. It's weird because I tend to see the first ten years of my life as the best years a child could have. There was so much love and care. ... So, I think I got that core. But I also think that it was picked apart or broken into pieces from all those experiences at school. I was left feeling like I was a total loser at school.

A framework from individual-based psychology appears to be significant in Susan's memories. Her explanation, for example, that everything from

---

[6] This corresponds to fourth grade/year in American or British schools.
[7] This corresponds to fifth grade/year in American or British schools.

a person's childhood 'makes you feel right' presents the understanding that the family is *the* developmental arena for a child. For this reason, it makes sense (to Susan) to look within this arena for the causes of bullying. In addition, the notion of a 'core' appears to be a powerful concept that frames her experiences of bullying in specific ways. Following Bruner's line of thinking, I suggest that Susan's method of meaning-making is based on interweaving her childhood upbringing with specific (and dominant) socio-cultural discourses on bullying that contribute to her framing what she – as an adult – considers to be relevant. Thus, the fact that Susan sees a connection here is not surprising. However, as clarified in the following section, these kinds of interpretations can generate quite a bit of frustration. Again and again, Susan asked herself why she was not able to stick up for herself and stop the bullying. Despite the fact that the most central and meaningful aspect of her childhood memory is that she had a strong core (which was later 'picked apart' and 'broken into pieces'), it seems as though the connections between bullying and her personal characteristics and upbringing no longer made sense to her. If her core was so strong, she wondered, why was she not able to stand up for herself as a child?

Susan's story does not offer a clear answer to this question. However, as the interview progressed, she also offered other kinds of interpretations that may contribute to a new understanding of the relationship between her personal characteristics and upbringing and bullying. For instance, there is a contradiction in Susan's narrative of herself as a thriving child with a strong core and her memory of herself as a shy, dependent child who avoided conflicts. The latter is particularly associated with her older brother. Comparing herself to him, Susan described experiences from her childhood and youth where she felt less independent and less socially competent than he. This led to the following description of herself:

> I was such a quiet child. There was no 'fight' in me. . . . I didn't know how to react to things. I felt like I just didn't have the know-how.

Remembering Bruner's argument that memory functions as a tool that enables us to negotiate meaning with ourselves and with others, it appears that Susan frames her memories in such a way that she is able to see new connections between bullying and her personal characteristics and upbringing. Through her memories of herself as a quiet child who did not have a fighting spirit and did not know how she would react to things, it becomes possible for Susan to understand bullying as closely linked to her lack of personal competences. This type of interpretation seems to allow Susan to gain a better understanding of *why* she became a victim of bullying – but conversely, this interpretation also contributes to a percep-tion of bullying as a phenomenon that is individualised and thus fixed in

Susan. Bullying appears (to some degree) to be something that is self-inflicted and, in the interview, it seemed to be both painful and difficult for Susan to handle. She started to cry and explained that she feels fundamentally unsure of whether she is 'good enough'; a feeling that has accompanied her since she was a child. The pervasiveness of this insecurity is expressed in a recurring dream that seems to be a manifestation of Susan's loneliness and low self-confidence: she is lying in a coffin in an empty church because no-one has come to her funeral. In her dream, she is not a person who is worthy of respect.

From examining Susan's narrative of her childhood experiences, it becomes clear that she feels she is at fault and somehow responsible for the bullying she experienced as a child. At the same time, though, it is also possible to locate other circumstances beyond this personal sphere that contributed to her exclusion at school. When Susan talked about the 'girl cliques' at her school, it is possible to understand how the girls in these cliques – with their ongoing negotiations and mutual positionings – regulated and controlled group membership. But also how the criteria for the mechanisms of inclusion/exclusion that Susan encountered were closely linked to the school context in general. In other words, Susan's ability to deal with her life at school was, to a great extent, formed by the positioning possibilities and limits allowed by the social framework at school.

Conditions for inclusion and exclusion at school

According to Susan, she began to be bullied sometime during the fourth grade.[8] It did not start suddenly, from one day to the next, but developed gradually. She had two girlfriends at school who were also excluded from the 'popular' clique, and she no longer played with the girls in that clique as she had done earlier. She was not invited to social events anymore, and she felt like they made fun of her all the time. Slowly, she was completely excluded. She felt like she was at the absolute bottom of the social hierarchy – a feeling that was confirmed when she discovered that she was the only one who was not invited to a sleepover. Sometimes, she explained, these feelings were replaced by a burning desire to belong, but that wish was never realised.

The following is an excerpt from the interview in which Susan remembered her school years:

Susan: And then came puberty [and with it] cliques. It was also because when I was ten or eleven, we got a new girl in the class and she dominated everything. She was the one who ran the whole show . . .

[8] This corresponds to fifth grade/year in American or British schools.

Interviewer:	What happened? Can you describe it in more detail?
Susan:	Those cliques with the popular girls? They didn't let others in, and I think I just gave up. I thought, 'I'm not even going to try to get in their group'. Also, because it was the powerful girls that were in that group, and I was always much more insecure. I guess I just recognised that I didn't belong there.
Interviewer:	Thinking back, what was it that made them so powerful?
Susan:	They were cool. They were the cool girls, and I was this tomboy. I played soccer, and plus there's the whole age question. Some matured really fast, and I definitely did not. I was still lanky and skinny.
Interviewer:	So it was the girls whose breasts developed first?
Susan:	Yeah, the mature girls. They were interested in boys, and I just wanted to play soccer with them. There were a couple of us – at least three – that were like that. So we had our own little group, and it worked well at the beginning. But you know, at school everything can change fast and, all the sudden, I only had one girlfriend left. And then when *she* was accepted by the cool girls, I was left all alone.

By describing herself as someone who 'gave up' and who was 'insecure', Susan creates a connection between her personal characteristics and bullying. But in these descriptions of what happened, it is also possible to draw more connections between bullying and the social life of the class. In her narrative, Susan saw a close connection between bullying and the new girl at school. She remembered this girl as a dominant and controlling personality who was a central catalyst for the establishment of cliques at school. But puberty also emerges as an important dynamic with regard to how the girls positioned themselves within the social hierarchy as well as the framework within which they and Susan were able to position themselves and negotiate social legitimacy. 'And then came puberty', Susan said, thereby making another connection between puberty and bullying. This connection draws attention to that fact that the criteria for participation in the popular-girl cliques were volatile. But, again, it also suggests a close relationship between Susan's personal characteristics (especially her physical development) and bullying. Using puberty as a yardstick, the girls' biological development was measured and if they were developed 'enough', access was granted to certain social groups. This had an influence on how Susan was able to participate and position herself in relation to these groups. At Susan's school, breasts were seen as a sign of maturity, and thus they became a symbol of power. For this reason, Susan's physical appearance was problematic with regard to her position at school. Her body had not yet taken on a womanly shape – she was 'lanky and skinny' – and this barred her entrance into the popular-girls' clique. This kind of 'gendering' is both ambiguous and unavoidable (Søndergaard 2008). It is difficult to change one's outer appearance and, specifically, the size of one's breasts. In addition, Susan's mention of puberty points to a new relationship between boys and girls; one that is based on flirting and heterosexual perceptions of romance and love. From this perspective, Susan's continued desire to play soccer with the boys at recess could be interpreted as a sign of her *imm*aturity. Thus, her opportunities for participation were even more limited because she did not meet the new social criteria and expectations for how boys and girls should interact with each other.

In Susan's narrative, the volatile nature of the social hierarchy at school and the dynamics of how the girls positioned themselves also became apparent. A case in point is that one of her girlfriends was accepted into the popular-girls' clique. Susan did not recall how this came about, but she described how her other girlfriend attempted to gain access to the popular-girls' clique by inviting all of the girls in their class to a slumber party, excluding only Susan:

I think with her – the one who had the slumber party – it was a way to get connected to the other girls. I don't think she wanted to be mean to anyone, but I think it was a way. . .that she thought, 'Maybe they'll accept me now.' I think acceptance is the key word. That's what it's about. You just want to be accepted, especially by the popular girls, the leaders. Because then it rubs off on you. If they accept you, then you must be OK . . . . There were times when they were really awful to her. You know, with comments. They were really mean to her. And I didn't do anything about it. You know, again, I just didn't dare take up the fight.

Not only does this quote offer insight into the social rules guiding the clique, it also gives us an idea of what counts as legitimate and acceptable behaviour amongst the girls. It is interesting, for example, that her friend's attempt to gain access and belong to the popular girls' clique is described as legitimate. Although this had painful consequences for Susan (she was the only girl not invited to the slumber party), it was accepted as an understandable tactic that made sense. In this continuing struggle to belong, the girls constantly manoeuvred to ensure a good position for themselves within the hierarchy and, as such, any tactic was legitimate. The same is true for Susan's lack of support for her friend who, at times, was also a target of bullying. Although Susan felt ashamed that she did not help her friend, her inaction is also understandable within the interpretational framework that is the point of departure for her narrative. She was only trying to protect herself, the reasoning goes, and so it was acceptable to stand by and do nothing, even though 'they were really mean to [the other girl]'.

This episode exemplifies a central point within classic social psychology: human beings have a fundamental and existential need to belong to a social group (see, for example, Tajfel and Turner 1986). Therefore, Susan and her friend's need for acceptance and their struggle to belong to the popular-girls' clique must be seen as an expression of their existential need to belong. Here, 'social exclusion anxiety' (Søndergaard 2009) is a helpful concept in understanding the struggle Susan mentioned in the quote above. According to Søndergaard, this social exclusion anxiety is one of the major driving forces in bullying. With regard to Susan and her friend's attempts to belong, it is important to take into account their vulnerability as well as the contradictory forces that are at play: in Susan's case, her inability to stand up for herself and her friend is indicative of the powerful need to belong, but also of the anxiety connected to being excluded.

Susan's outsider position at school may thus be understood as the result of several interrelated forces: her upbringing, her relationship with her older brother, the formation of cliques at school, the girls' biological development, her struggle to belong and her anxiety about being excluded. All of these elements had variegated influences that formed her ability to participate in the social context of school. In the following, I address Susan's father's suicide and the pedagogical practices that characterised the school; these conditions also appear to have played an important role in Susan's ability to handle her life at school.

Constraints in pedagogical practice

Susan did not make a direct connection between her father's suicide and being bullied, but as mentioned earlier, she felt that her father's death 'overshadowed' the bullying she experienced. In listening to how Susan spoke about being bullied, however, it seems as though her mother's way of dealing with the suicide played a central role. Susan explained that, as a result of her parents' divorce, her mother went from being a 'stay-at-home mom' to a full-time student and later to working full-time. After the divorce, the children stayed with their mother, who subsequently became the primary caregiver and breadwinner. In this connection, Susan remembered her mother as distant and unapproachable. Two years after the divorce, Susan's father committed suicide and, according to Susan, her mother reacted by becoming even more remote. She did not want to talk to the children about what had happened. This meant that Susan became eager to obscure her father's suicide and hide this information from her schoolmates. It appears that – due to her mother's distance – her father's suicide became a taboo topic, which thereby came to function as a barrier to Susan's participation in the social context of school. 'If only it had been cancer or an accident, then my classmates would have felt sorry for me,' Susan remembered thinking. Instead, she made an effort to hide the facts about her father's death. This may be why Susan described her experiences of being bullied as 'overshadowed' by her father's suicide. The details surrounding his death certainly seem significant in how Susan was able to understand and deal with the social challenges that she encountered at school. It is as though these challenges faded into the background as she tried to uphold a façade that hid the details about her father's tragic demise. In other words, Susan's narrative suggests that it made sense for her to distance herself socially from the other children at school because it served her goal of obscuring the facts about her father's death from them. In addition, Susan's own perception of guilt and responsibility in connection with her father's suicide may also have contributed to her belief that she was to blame for the bullying she experienced.

It is also relevant to address Susan's attempts to cover up her father's suicide in relation to the pedagogical constraints at school and her abilities to act within them. In the fourth grade,[9] the children got a new teacher who did not get on well with the class's maths teacher. Susan remembered how the tension between the two teachers meant that they were less engaged with the children and, as a result, the atmosphere in class began to deteriorate. The situation was exacerbated because the new teacher tended to favour certain students over others; in this context, Susan remembered feeling overlooked. At the same time, the school hired a new principal who implemented a series of pedagogical methods for teaching at the school. Susan described these new plans as 'circle talk' pedagogy, explaining that the goal was for social problems to be discussed democratically amongst the students in class and then solved within this context. But this raises the question: what forms of agency did this kind of method offer the children?

Inspired by British sociologist Nikolas Rose (1999), we may see 'circle talk' pedagogy as a controlling technology or a particular form of power that is meant to shape, regulate and steer children towards specific ideals and behaviour. According to Susan's description, 'circle talk' pedagogy seemed to be based on an ideology wherein the children were expected to solve problems in the class through group dialogue (assisted by the teacher). This kind of problem-solving is based on democratic principles, the right to self-determination and joint responsibility for social cohesiveness within the class. Such pedagogical practices are certainly reminiscent of the principles that pervaded the Danish school system in the 1970s, and which focused on children's ability to listen, debate and solve problems together (Knudsen 2010). Bolstered by Rose's arguments, I suggest that a child's consciousness and agency are disciplined and controlled in direct and indirect ways through this kind of practice. In 'circle talk' pedagogy, there appears to be a certain correlation between power, a perception of problems and subjectivity. What role did this practice assign to Susan?

[9] This corresponds to fifth grade/year in American or British schools.

Susan explained that she did not want to 'subject herself' to these discussions, so she stayed home on the days when circle talks were planned. The notion of 'subjecting' oneself to something may be understood in several ways. In my view, Susan may have felt as though she was expected to offer something about herself. This expectation is based on the idea that class members could only solve problems together through group dialogue if personal disclosures were made. The assumption is that, within the group, individual students respect each other. But what happens if this is not the case? Who is then responsible for addressing problems? And who is responsible for finding solutions?

Susan's choice to stay home on circle-talk days bears witness to the fact that the 'opportunity' to share her social challenges – and even divulge the details surrounding her father's suicide – with the group whose rejections she experienced every day was problematic and troubling. It may even have seemed like a threatening proposition to engage in a circle talk with the same children who hurled humiliating comments at her or rejected her outside of the circle. For this reason, within the only pedagogical framework that the school offered, it became nearly impossible for Susan to deal with her father's suicide and the exclusion she was experiencing. In fact, the circle-talk practice seems to have exacerbated her sense of exclusion because she was unable to participate in the (pseudo-)accepting forum it was meant to represent. Further, because no-one felt responsible for speaking to her or to the class about what had happened in her family, this forum also contributed to Susan's belief that her father's suicide was shameful.

Thus, Susan's vulnerable position within the class cannot merely be reduced to a problematic upbringing or insufficient social skills. Although her father's suicide appears to have functioned as a barrier to her social participation at school, and despite the fact that Susan herself attributed her struggles to social incompetence, her difficult position at school was also connected to other elements. The school's pedagogical policy on problem-solving and the socio–cultural norms amongst the students – particularly their rules for inclusion and exclusion – were influential and contributed to her (in)ability to act within this framework at school.

I now turn my attention to Linda's memories of bullying and the circumstances that framed her ability to participate in the social context of school. Linda's memories are also characterised by multifarious and complex narratives about bullying, in addition to her own interest in how her personal characteristics influenced events in her childhood. But her story also offers insight into how the social processes and norms *outside* of school play a role in how bullying begins and develops. Thus, we are able to gain a new understanding of how a child's personal characteristics and upbringing may become meaningful within the context of bullying and its role in life outside of school.

Being boiled alive: the wish to be accepted and sticking up for yourself

As mentioned at the beginning of this chapter, when Linda told us about her memories of being bullied, she was preoccupied with her own guilt and responsibility in relation to what had happened. She was concerned about whether something was wrong with her and, in this connection, she also drew upon the framework of individual psychology – just as Susan did. However, it is significant that Linda perceived the possible means for interpretation provided by this framework to be inadequate; therefore, in her efforts to understand and explain what happened to her as a child, she continually pulled in other elements. In the following analysis, I focus on how Linda's opportunities to participate within the social context of school became a series of movements; in these, her family's geographical move from city to country and the class's internal social dynamics and interactions in particular contributed to shaping her ability to act and manoeuvre within the school context – especially in interaction with the socio-cultural possibilities and constraints of the local community.

The meaning ascribed to Linda's personal characteristics and upbringing cannot be isolated from the other contexts of which she was a part. Instead, they become meaningful through the analytical lens of social dynamics and processes. Linda's observations are particularly interesting because, after three years of being subjected to bullying, she was suddenly able to reject the bullying and stand up for herself. Thus, in order to examine how her personal characteristics and upbringing were created, negotiated and changed in the context of school as well as across contexts, my analysis also focuses on what contributed to her being able to make these movements.

'The good childhood' frame: opportunities and dilemmas

Linda's memories were closely linked to her perceptions of 'the good childhood'. This means that she was preoccupied with the possible correlations between her upbringing and life at school; in turn, this influenced how she chose to frame her memories. Her ideas about 'the good childhood' were exemplified in the following excerpt from the beginning of our interview:

I grew up in a totally normal, good and solid Danish nuclear family. It was the world's best childhood; nice siblings and a mom and dad that were supportive, helped us with homework and were attentive. It was all that a privileged child like me could dream of. My very first year at school, kindergarten, and the first grade were really great. Nobody bullied me. I didn't have any problems.

As described in this quote, Linda sees a close connection between her first years at school and having grown up in 'a good and solid Danish nuclear family'. Her description of her childhood as 'the world's best childhood' may be interpreted in many ways. Just like Susan, Linda's perception seems to be that loving and caring parents create happy and independent children. This echoes the dominant discourse about child development that is presented by individual-based psychology, in which certain cause–effect rationalities appear more meaningful than other approaches. Inspired by Horsdal (1999), we may also understand Linda's focus on her 'good childhood' as a narrative tool: here, she utilises the contrast that was established between a romanticised past (her upbringing) and the difficulties that followed (her school years), which were later overcome. Alternatively, her approach could also be an attempt to present herself as a 'normal' child who was worthy of respect. In other words, because she had a 'good and solid' childhood and did not have difficulties in her early school years, she herself is able to suggest that she may not have constituted the root of the bullying problem after all.

Regardless of how we interpret her narrative approach, the central point in Linda's story (and her perception of herself) is that she had previously been happy and functioned well at school. This may be the reason why, throughout our interview, she continued to return to the question of why she became a target of bullying. Something was troubling her, and she struggled to understand her challenging position: why did a well-supported child like her become a target of bullying?

In a related story, she mentioned her younger brother, who seemed to thrive in the new school, and this appears important in relation to Linda's pronounced introspection and fault-finding within herself: why wasn't he bullied as well? Even if her brother's social success at school was due to the fact that he had been placed in a '*better*' class, it seems to be a reminder and confirmation to Linda that their shared upbringing could not be blamed. From this, Linda seems to conclude that her troubles at school could only be her own fault – because she lacked social skills or personal competences. But was it her fault? Had she been too sure of herself or had she been arrogant? Or was she bullied because she had red hair, wore the wrong clothes and started wearing glasses during that time?

No matter how closely linked the idea was that she could be at fault or be held responsible for the bullying she experienced, other relevant circumstances and elements in Linda's narrative must also be taken into account. When describing problems in a recent romantic relationship where she also struggled to stand up for herself, she introduced the following metaphor, which is useful in understanding how subtle the processes and social dynamics of bullying can be:

If you put a frog into a pot with cold water and then slowly turn up the heat, the frog will not notice that it's getting warmer and warmer. In the end, it will die, of course. If you throw a frog into a pot with boiling water, it will feel the heat right away and get out. You know, metaphorically. I've thought about that a lot lately. Remembering to stand up for yourself. That I am aware of when the water starts to get too hot. Because I don't think I notice it if I don't make an effort to be attentive all the time.

This story about a metaphorical frog that is boiled alive because it does not notice that the water is gradually becoming dangerously hot is not just an unpleasant tale. One can almost sense how destructive practices like bullying can become so comprehensive and strenuous that they could be compared to being boiled alive. The metaphor also solidifies the point about what it is like to stand up for oneself against bullying: from the image of a frog that does not sense the growing heat in the pot before it is boiled alive, we get a glimpse of how difficult it can be to deal with daily insults and rejections at school. In addition, the metaphor illuminates how this daily experience of humiliation, exclusion and harsh insults can begin to feel like an unavoidable part of everyday life, despite the fact that these things are generally upsetting and unbearable. Following this line of thinking, Linda's story about the frog may be interpreted as an analogy for how the aberration of bullying slowly becomes normalised.

However, it also points to the strategies that Linda was able to consider, such as seeing it as her responsibility to notice when the metaphorical water is getting too hot; to be attentive that a situation is becoming uncomfortable; and to save herself in time. Still, Linda insisted that it was probably 'a combination of things' that contributed to her being bullied as a child. In the following, I take a closer look at the various interrelated forces that contributed to Linda's inability to participate in the social context of school. Here, I would argue that socio-cultural limitations, the pervasive norms of the local community and the internal social dynamics at school influenced how Linda's personal characteristics and upbringing were framed and thus became meaningful for her positioning at school.

Power and norms within the socio-cultural context

In trying to explain what happened at school and why she was singled out, Linda said there was a girl in her class who apparently felt threatened by her. This girl thought that Linda was competing with her because she was from the city and had a different background from the other children at the school. Linda explained:

So my parents chose to move to the other end of the country ... and I ended up in a little class of, all together including me, nine kids. ... I had come from a private school with 'upper-class girls and boys' in a town close to Copenhagen [the capital of Denmark]. And you know, we lived a totally different life. And so suddenly I went to school with the bus driver's daughter and people like that, and I think I just tried to continue [my life like it had been]. I actually really liked my new school, and I had some great teachers. But there was this girl [in the new school], she really thought that I was competing with her. It dawned on me ten years later. You just can't see that kind of thing when you've just arrived, you're new and it's the first time you've ever changed schools and all that. She really thought I was competing with her.

Returning to Søndergaard's concept of 'social exclusion anxiety', it is possible that Linda's arrival upset the existing social order within the class (Søndergaard 2009), and that this perceived threat was then harshly punished with social exclusion. The daily insults and rejections that were directed at Linda – particularly with regard to how she looked – may in fact have been part of such a social dynamic. In any case, this is the type of social dynamic to which Linda was referring when she mentioned competition in the above quote.

The taunting and bullying about Linda's physical appearance intensified after the school photographer came to take the students' portraits. Linda remembered that no-one in her class wanted to exchange pictures with her (an otherwise common practice amongst the children) because, they explained, she looked 'too ugly' in her portrait. The photographs seemed to provide particularly powerful fodder for the children's production of contempt, which served to hold Linda in a specific social position. In contrast to the humiliating yet fleeting comments hurled at Linda in her everyday school life, the pictures could be displayed again and again, day in and day out. Thus, over time, the school portraits became a constant reminder that Linda was 'too ugly' to participate in the social context of school.

However, Linda's story also provides other insights that can enhance our understanding of bullying and contribute to new interpretations. Linda's reflections about her family's move from the city to the countryside and the challenges that her parents encountered in the local community especially shed light on the importance of the social processes and norms outside of school with regard to the bullying she experienced. Here, the children's interaction and mutual positioning seems closely linked to the social stratification and processes that characterised the community. Therefore, in the following, I concentrate on how certain circumstances *outside* of school may also become significant to how social order is upheld and negotiated *inside* of school.

Linda's family's move from the city to the countryside was not merely a geographical change, but also a change from one environment to another. Thus, their relocation implies a move to different socio-cultural and economic norms and values. In this light, bullying may be seen as a form of power that serves to embed and regulate the social context of school in accordance with the pervasive norms and values outside of school – for example, that 'Copenhageners' had better not believe they are anything special. We can thus understand the children's behaviour and mutual positionings within the school context as being shaped by the structural organisation linked to cultural norms and values in the local community (see also Mathiassen and Viala 2009), and it is within this framework that Linda's opportunities for participation were negotiated. One could also say that the children's interactions and mutual positionings were based on negotiations about what Linda could do and be under the prevailing socio-cultural conditions. This means that Linda's upbringing (her middle-class background from a town close to Copenhagen) and her personal characteristics (talkative and self-confident) cannot stand alone in our efforts to understand the social phenomenon of bullying. Rather, the definitive norms and values of the wider community and the social hierarchy within the school seem to play an intrinsic role in forming the socio-cultural possibilities and limitations within which Linda and her schoolmates could think, negotiate and act.

Linda's position within the class and her opportunities to participate in the activities and social life of both her class and the school are thus closely linked to the material, cultural and socio-economic possibilities that her family had. But at the same time, the analysis points to the significance of Linda's personal characteristics and upbringing as elements that were being continuously negotiated and thus also changed within the school context in which she found herself. For example, Linda was seen as a threat to the ruling social hierarchy at school, which indicates that her personal presentation (i.e. behaviour, appearance) and upbringing were inscribed with a specific meaning vis-á-vis the socio-cultural norms that structured the local community. For this reason, the children may have considered it appropriate to punish Linda with harsh insults and rejection or to typecast her as 'the Copenhagener', despite the fact that she did not actually come from Copenhagen. This became a problem for Linda because it attenuated her ability to legitimately negotiate her position. She was denied access to the local social-negotiating conditions for inclusion because she was led to believe that she was not 'anything special'. Therefore, Linda's position cannot be understood solely on the basis of her personal characteristics and/or upbringing. Instead I would suggest that, *together* with the dynamics of interaction amongst the children at school and the socio-cultural norms of the local community, these subjective forces played a central role in forming and framing her opportunities to participate in the social context of school and in her ability to act as a subject.

Movements across contexts

As already alluded to, after several years of being bullied, Linda was suddenly able to stand up for herself. In our interview, she explained that she just 'exploded' one day. She berated her schoolmates, she remembered, and yelled, 'That's ENOUGH!' It happened during gym class; a teacher was standing nearby and heard what was going on but did not intervene. Afterwards, Linda decided to leave school and began walking home through the fields. It was November, and she was still wearing her gym clothes. It was cold outside and she was ten kilometres from home. One might ask: after so many years of putting up with being bullied, what was it that caused Linda to suddenly stand up for herself? Perhaps she was reminded of her positive early school experiences, to which she repeatedly referred in the interview, in the sense that she *had been* able to function well at school. Perhaps her parents' struggles to become integrated into the local community made her think that it was not (only) she who had a problem. In Linda's memories, her activities with Girl Scouts seem to have played a predominant role in her gaining self-confidence. Returning to a point I touched upon in this chapter's introduction – i.e. that children move between various contexts – I am intrigued by Linda's movement between the two contexts of school and Girl Scouts. How should we understand this movement, and what does it mean? Regarding her Girl Scouts experiences, Linda explained:

One way or another, somebody there believed in [me]. 'You're really good at that. You can do this.' It really helped me to have that kind of haven, where there were people who believed in me.

In this quote, Linda gives an important signal by referring to Girl Scouts as a 'haven'. This was a space where she felt safe and where she was not subjected to bullying. But it was also a space where she was acknowledged and encouraged. At Girl Scouts, Linda discovered that she was good at things and people there believed in her. One of the dominant claims amongst developmental psychologists has been that a child's primary and most important developmental arena is within the family, where fundamental norms, values and experiences are made (see Burman 1996 and Haavind 1987 for a critical analysis of this claim). Other researchers have suggested that a child's development is not as private or as closely linked to the family as this claim suggests because children move in, out and across a *variety* of formative contexts (i.e. developmental arenas). These contexts could be the family, school, after-school clubs or other recreational activities (see, for example, Dreier 2008; Hedegaard and Fleer 2008; Højholt 1996/2005; Kousholt 2011). For this reason, I believe it is important to address a child's upbringing in the family home as well as to include analyses of the conditions and possibilities linked to different contexts (i.e. other than family and school) in which children are active.

By looking at Linda's opportunities to participate in the social context of school and by adopting an inquisitive approach to how mechanisms of inclusion and exclusion work, we discover that she was presented with radically different opportunities in each social context. Through her participation in Girl Scouts, Linda described feeling acceptance and recognition, and this provided her with new kinds of experiences that may have allowed her to change her subjectivity within the school context. In Girl Scouts, Linda was also included in a different group of children her own age, which granted her access to another sense of 'we'. I suggest that her experiences with Girl Scouts significantly contributed to her ability to interpret her bullying experiences at school as unacceptable. In other words, from feeling accepted in another context, she was able to recognise that the metaphorical water had become too hot. Through her experiences with Girl Scouts, Linda developed self-confidence and a sense of belonging amongst other peers, and this played a definitive role in her ability to stand up for herself vis-á-vis the bullies at school.

When children's personal characteristics and upbringing cannot stand alone

Both Susan and Linda were the targets of destructive behaviour during their school years. They referred to this behaviour as acts of bullying, and they were eager to understand why it transpired and how they might have been responsible for it. They both asked, 'Was something wrong with me?'

Research on bullying has long been dominated and influenced by an approach grounded in individual-based psychology where, in an effort to localise the causes of bullying, a child's personal characteristics and upbringing are assigned central significance. In this chapter, I addressed how this approach may be problematic and suggest that it may overlook the myriad dynamics that comprise the various parts of a child's everyday life. Further, I questioned what status should be given to the subjective forces (here, understood as a child's personal characteristics and upbringing) when other forces (such as social, discursive and material elements) are considered in an analysis of why some children become targets of bullying.

This chapter has focused on two women, Linda and Susan, and their memories of being bullied as children. My analytical point of departure was their attempts to understand why they became targets of bullying. In particular, I was interested in the notion that there was 'something wrong' with them. I explored the level of importance that their personal characteristics and upbringing might have played in forming and framing their opportunities to participate in the social context of school. This was examined through an analytical lens that was sensitive to the interplay of social dynamics and processes both inside and outside of the school context; these included the mechanisms of inclusion and exclusion at school, their schools' pedagogical practices and policies, and the other conditions and possibilities that defined the women's childhoods. My goal has been to contribute to the ongoing academic debate with a context-sensitive analysis of how Susan's and Linda's vulnerable social positions as schoolchildren were formed. But I was also eager to offer a new understanding of how the individual dimension could be described when juxtaposed with the phenomenon of bullying. Thus, I focused on two aspects: firstly, that bullying may emerge as a social practice due to many forces that interact with one another; and secondly, that a child's ability to participate in the social context of school develops and is formed by – and across – all of the social contexts in which he/she is involved. In other words, I tracked how events and different series of events connected to bullying are remembered, focusing on the ways in which a child's personal characteristics become significant in his/her opportunities to participate within the social context of school and, in particular, how these subjective forces interact with the various constraints and possibilities that are prevalent in the contexts of which the children are a part.

Linda's and Susan's attention on their own roles in and responsibility for the bullying to which they were subjected seems to confirm the notion that a child's personal characteristics and upbringing are meaningful when seen in relation to the social practice of bullying. In fact, the two may go hand in hand. However, their focal point could also be analysed as an expression of specific dominant socio-cultural discourses about contemporary bullying. These discourses probably had an impact on how Linda and Susan were able to frame their memories and determine which connections were meaningful to them.

Another central conclusion that emerges from the analysis is that a child's social position and opportunities to participate in the social context of school are formed by many interrelated and open-ended forces, both inside and outside of the school context. The cause of Susan's vulnerable position at school cannot merely be reduced to her father's suicide. Instead, her father's suicide had an influence on her ability to participate in the social context of school, just as her mother's way of dealing with his death, the mechanisms of inclusion and exclusion within the girls' cliques, and the norms informing the school's pedagogical practices had an influence on Susan's ability to act within and manage her school life. In other words, the *interaction* of all these dynamics were at the core of her childhood difficulties at school: Susan's ability to engage in the social context of school was regulated and controlled by the other girls' negotiations and reciprocal positioning – the rules of which continued to change over time; puberty in particular also appeared as a central factor in how the girls strived to position one another and, within this framework, Susan continually attempted to negotiate her social position and legitimacy; and finally, her wish to belong and her fear of being excluded contributed in meaningful ways to how the girls' social interactions and mutual positionings were formed.

Similarly, Linda's memories of having been bullied as a child cannot be traced back only to her lack of personal skills or her upbringing. Despite the fact that Linda emphasised her own responsibility for being bullied, I suggest that social interactions and mutual positionings at her school were closely connected to the social stratification and processes that were representative of the local community. Thus, Linda's ability to participate in the social context of school was shaped by a variety of social dynamics outside of the school. For example, her upbringing (e.g. the material, cultural and socio–economic possibilities her family had) became a central factor in how she was positioned at school vis-à-vis the socio-cultural opportunities and limitations that informed the local community. Thus, bullying may be seen as a form of power that controls and regulates social interaction at school, and which mirrors the norms and values that define the social context outside of school: the 'Copenhagener' should not think that she is anything special in a small country town. With the term 'social exclusion anxiety', I further claim that the mechanisms of inclusion and exclusion at Linda's school were connected to a perception that she challenged the social order that had already been established before she arrived. This kind of social dynamic led to Linda being subjected to daily insults and rejection; these comments were mostly about her physical appearance. Amongst other things, school portraits were used as a tool in the children's production of contempt. However, through Linda's positive acceptance and participation in Girl Scouts, she was able to benefit from other experiences that contributed to her ability to stand up for herself.

In conclusion – and through Linda's and Susan's memories – my analysis has shown that children's psychological processes and personal characteristics cannot be isolated from the various contexts in which they participate. For this reason, it is necessary to challenge the individual-based psychology approach to bullying and to give the individual dimension new content and meaning. One solution might be to focus on *how* children's personal characteristics are negotiated and changed within and outside of the social context of school and how, through these processes, these subjective forces become meaningful and regulate the children's interactions and mutual positionings at school. This requires us to turn our analytical focus *away* from the notion that personal characteristics and/or upbringing can be isolated from the surrounding social context and thus claimed to be the root of children's behaviour in the classroom. Instead, we must go beyond personal and behavioural characteristics and investigate the particularities of children's everyday lives, in order to explore the conditions for inclusion and exclusion that inform the social context of school. Within this context, we may *then* focus on how a child's personal characteristics and upbringing become significant and regulate children's mutual positionings.

Part V

Moving forward

15 From technically standardised interventions to analytically informed, multi-perspective intervention strategies

Dorte Marie Søndergaard

Bullying and a lack of contentment are serious problems in the lives of many schoolchildren. In a survey conducted in 2009 by the Danish research group eXbus, 13 per cent of the 1,052 students surveyed from across sixty school classes (Danish *8. and 9. klasse*[1]) reported having been bullied within the previously elapsed school year, and 17 per cent of the students responding reported having been active in bullying others during the same time frame (see Hansen, Henningsen and Kofoed, Chapter 11, page 267). The World Health Organisation (WHO) publishes the international Health Behaviour in School-aged Children (HBSC) reports, which contain the results of surveys conducted in forty-one countries every four years; these reports indicate a rather varied prevalence of bullying[2] (Currie et al. 2004, 2008). For example, in the UK in 2006, 20 per cent of the students surveyed reported having been bullied and 6 per cent had bullied others; in the US, the corresponding numbers were 19 per cent bullied and 33 per cent bullying, whilst 20 per cent of the Danish students had been bullied and 9 per cent had bullied others. In Norway, 8 per cent of the students reported having been bullied and 4 per cent had bullied others. Although this is a small representative selection, it shows the variance of the statistics; nevertheless, bullying seems to exist across national borders and across historical periods of time. Not surprisingly, parents, teachers, students and politicians are all demanding answers as to how this problem can be diminished and perhaps even eliminated.

---

[1] These classes correspond to ninth and tenth grade/year, respectively, in American or British schools.

[2] The surveys employ the following definition: 'a student is being bullied when another student, or a group of students, say or do nasty and unpleasant things to him or her. It is also bullying when a student is teased repeatedly in a way he or she does not like or when he or she is deliberately left out of things. But it is **not** bullying when two students of about the same strength or power argue or fight. It is also *not* bullying when a student is teased in a friendly and playful way' (Currie et al. 2008: 159, emphasis in original; Currie et al. 2004: 133).

In this chapter, I argue that a multi-perspective intervention strategy can be an important part of answering these demands because bullying is a complex social phenomenon that is inadequately addressed by one-size-fits-all interventions (Casebeer 2012; Cross and Barnes, Chapter 16). The ability to operate flexibly within shifting contexts is important to an intervention strategy in relation to complex social phenomena. It is important to bear in mind that the contexts in which bullying takes place are characterised by ever-changing social conditions, shifting actors and continuously emerging dilemmas and social manoeuvrings. All of these shifting conditions impact the intervention in and/or prevention of destructive social practices – and I argue that a multi-perspective intervention capable of flexible implementation will prove to be more effective and helpful than standardised techniques and fixed sets of behavioural rules. Thus, the reader will not find any behavioural rules or suggestions about standardised intervention techniques in this chapter. Instead, I draw some overall lines along which it is possible to reflect upon the implications of the intervention and/or prevention strategies and initiatives that practitioners may plan or try to develop; these lines were inspired by the analyses and results included in this anthology as well as in some of the contributing authors' other published work on bullying. Following the development of thinking technologies implied in this body of work, I outline here a set of strategies for reflection that are directed at practice.

First, however, I take a very brief look at the most common way to approach practitioners' need for inspiration with regard to interventions and/or intervention models.

Experimental intervention studies and measurement

Most of the typical attempts to produce answers about how to minimise the problem of bullying come from researchers across countries in the form of experimental intervention studies. One of the most prominent authorities on such intervention studies, the Campbell Collaboration, performed an international review of intervention programmes on bullying (Farrington and Ttofi 2009). They found a total of 622 reports that deal with the prevention of bullying. Of these reports, forty-four referred to studies of programmes that met Campbell's meta-analytic standards, which include specific selection criteria. The Campbell Collaboration selected only those studies that base their work on the following four research designs: (1) randomised experiments; (2) experimental-control comparisons with 'before' and 'after' measures of bullying; (3) other experimental-control comparisons; and (4) quasi-experimental, age-cohort designs (ibid.). The forty-four programmes included a wide range of programme elements, such as parental training, playground supervision, disciplinary methods, classroom management, teacher training, classroom rules, working with peers, etc. A number of elements were found to have a positive impact, but further investigations (Henningsen, Hansen and Søndergaard 2010), pointed to intensity and longevity of the efforts as the only stable, positive elements in terms of effectiveness. However, the Campbell Collaboration's review found very mixed results with regard to the effects of these intervention programmes.[3]

In Scandinavia, a report from Skolverket[4] (2011) provided an overview of the effects of several anti-bullying programmes in thirty-nine Swedish schools. Here, too, very mixed results were observed. The conclusion of Skolverket's report indicates that peer-education (i.e. student-to-student) measures, teacher training and more rigorous playground monitoring are some of the elements that have had a positive effect. On the other hand, elements such as, for example, providing parental information, relationship-building efforts between teachers and students, and educational materials were assessed as being ineffective. Counter-effective measures included elements based on educating students to be observers and monitors within their schools, just as separate lessons for children about bullying and mediation proved to have direct negative effects (ibid.: 187–8).

Many questions can be raised about such reviews, particularly about the very rigid versions like the meta-analyses done by the Campbell Collaboration (Farrington and Ttofi 2009). Henningsen, Hansen and Søndergaard (2010) discuss the Campbell review in detail, but I remind readers here of a few significant reservations that emerged from this discussion. The Campbell report ends up excluding 578 out of the 622 reports and articles about anti-bullying programmes that the researchers identified in the databases, and this exclusion was based on selection criteria that, as previously mentioned, grant privilege to very specific research designs. Only forty-four articles and reports remained that could be included in their review, and the criteria for inclusion were the result of strictly internal paradigmatic preferences. Overall, this practice caused a rather comprehensive loss of knowledge concerning the field.

[3] On average, the number of bullies decreased by 20–23 per cent following the implementation of the programmes, and the number of bullying victims decreased by 17–20 per cent. However, the most successful programmes were comprised of only a few students or were based on a less effective research design. Furthermore, it appears that the average positive effects were strongly influenced by a number of major Norwegian programmes, but the good results were not reproduced in other countries (Farrington and Ttofi 2009; Henningsen, Hansen and Søndergaard 2010; see also Cross and Barnes, Chapter 16).
[4] Skolverket, the Swedish National Agency for Education, is the central administrative authority for the public-school system, publicly organised preschools, school-aged childcare and for adult education: www.skolverket.se/2.3894/in_english/2.1141/the-swedish-national-agency-for-education-1.61968 (last accessed 28 April 2012).

The definition of bullying upon which the review bases its meta-analyses comes from the first paradigm[5] of bullying research: 'The definition of school bullying includes several key elements: physical, verbal, or psychological attack or intimidation that is intended to cause fear, distress, or harm to the victim; an imbalance of power (psychological or physical), with a more powerful child (or children) oppressing less powerful ones; and repeated incidents between the same children over a prolonged period (Farrington 1993; Olweus 1993a; Roland 1989). School bullying can occur in school or on the way to or from school. It is not bullying when two persons of the same strength (physical, psychological, or verbal) victimise each other. Bullying primarily involves imbalance of power and repeated acts' (Farrington and Ttofi 2009: 9).

Within the first paradigm, the positions are usually understood as relatively stable (i.e. those who bully, bullying victims, bystanders) and are considered to be determined mainly by an individual's inherent characteristics and personality – which are supposedly generated from his/her childhood experiences and primary caregivers (i.e. mother) (for a critical discussion, see Schott, page 21. This rather static and individualising understanding of the bullying problem connects much more easily with the experimental designs that are given priority in the Campbell Collaboration's preferred review practices and the programmes that were chosen for review. But an understanding of bullying as a phenomenon that emphasises complex dynamics involved in the enactment of bullying practices necessitates research designs that generate 'evidence' via methods and measurements that are attuned to encountering and representing social complexity, situated movements and changes, complicated interactions and displaced positionings.[6]

To many practitioners, particularly politicians, evidence-based approaches such as these may seem seductive with their promises of truth and efficacy: the studies promise definitive knowledge about 'what works' and the 'truth' about 'effective' bullying-intervention practices. But this seduction calls for discussion – both in terms of methodology vis-à-vis very complex phenomena like marginalisation and bullying in social groups, and in terms of the conceptual presumptions that underlie these approaches. The evidence-based methodological approach is modelled after the paradigmatic clinical experiments conducted in the field of medicine; in this approach, the central premise is that the phenomenon one wishes to study and/or change remains the same, even within different

---

[5] For more on the first and the second paradigms, see the Introduction, and Schott on page 21.

[6] For more on the concept of 'positioning', see Davies (2000); Davies and Harré (1990).

groups and settings. Thus, it is supposed that physical phenomena – like pneumonia or cardiac arrest – remain sufficiently similar across groups of patients except for variations in incidence.

In terms of bullying positions, an approach based on such a notion of evidence presumes that the characteristics of bullying as well as bullies and victims remain sufficiently comparable across school classes and between different groups of children to allow for intervening experiments in a positivist sense. Accordingly, it is thus presumed that an intervention (just like a medical treatment) could be standardised and 'dosed' across these varying contexts – allowing 'evidence' about its efficacy to be produced via measuring and observing the changes that are expected to result from the standardised intervention (i.e. 'medicine') given in the experiment. But as the chapters in this anthology have shown, social reality does not operate with the same standard mechanisms that the biology and chemistry found in the human body – and with which medical science operates – are presumed to do; yet this science fostered the evidence-based methodologies that have been adopted in social–scientific, educational and other areas of research.

Another intriguing aspect of the Campbell Collaboration's review practices is their separation of programme elements in order to measure the impact of each element of intervention disregarding the co-variations amongst them. In the review, potential synergies and the effects of interaction between specific sets of elements are not addressed. Perhaps, however, it is precisely the combination of particular sets of elements that allow certain interventions to work – or prevent them from working. Perhaps the reason why some elements work is because they work *together* – or as Karen Barad would say, because they intra-act in particular ways (Barad 2007). Following the eXbus point that bullying is a consequence of many intra-acting forces (see, e.g. my earlier chapter on page 47), it might be relevant to suggest that the simultaneous enactment and entanglements of many intervening practices – that is, encountering the problematic on many levels, from many perspectives and angles, and by means of many actors' engagement and increased understanding of the phenomenon – enacts an effect, rather than intervention techniques taken one by one and measured separately. Thus, instead of studying the effect of single elements and measuring them as isolated phenomena that are added as single elements on top of each other, we might consider methods of evaluation that are capable of focusing on the intra-activity amongst a more comprehensive range of changing practices: multi-perspective intervention strategies. That is, if we are to embrace some of the premises of the experimental studies within this field.

In other words, when it comes to bullying, we should question how effective it actually is to generate knowledge with a notion of evidence based on an approach to 'what works' as framed by positivist thinking. It seems as though a great deal of knowledge is lost through this approach since the rigid standards of research designs – which are ill-suited to evaluate complex phenomena like bullying and social marginalisation – prevent even more knowledge from being generated. As already mentioned, a phenomenon enacted by complex dynamics necessitates research designs that generate knowledge via methods that are suited to encountering this complexity, which includes situated movements and changes, complicated interactions and displaced positionings.

Social reality, relational praxes and meaning-making processes amongst children, teachers, parents and school administrators are enacted in different ways and follow less predictable routes. Some researchers might even assert that this applies in physics and biology as well – that what we take to be physical, biological, chemical phenomena belonging to the natural sciences are also the effects of open-ended, material–discursive enactments (Barad 2007). I do not address that discussion here, but rather, point to the fact that marginalisation and bullying are part of intricate social patterns; they are practices of open-ended enactments, and their character calls for less of a technically standardised approach and more of an analytically informed, flexibly implemented and socially sensitive way to meet these intricate, entangling and complicated social processes in all of their continuous becomings, transformations and volatile reiterations.

In order to maintain some kind of direction and cooperation within a multi-perspective intervention strategy, it is important to keep in mind the extensive range of relevant actors involved in the enactment of children's everyday lives. Obviously, it is necessary to include the students themselves, parents, teachers and school administrators. But teacher-training educators, politicians, researchers, university professors who teach pedagogy, psychology, the social sciences, etc., are all relevant in this context because of their ability to set agendas for the conditions of school practices, school materialisations and the development and/or reiteration of discourses. All of these actors are – in varying ways and at different levels – active forces involved in the enactment of children's everyday lives, in their social relating and in the potential bullying that occurs between them. Effective anti-bullying interventions would address as many of these actors as possible to develop analytically informed knowledge and ongoing practices to reduce bullying.

This ambition – this multi-perspective intervention and prevention strategy – cannot be realised at the level of everyday life in schools by means of standardised techniques; rather, it calls for points of focus and analytical attention that can guide flexibly implemented praxes. These analytical attentions should be flexibly put to use via praxes within specific school classes and in the whole school – depending on the specific social patterns and problematics found in various contexts – and via praxes in educational politics and teacher training. As a fundamental premise, this strategy calls for analytical knowledge about the character of these complicated social–relational becomings. And for the adults who are directly involved with schoolchildren's everyday lives, all of this requires the ability to interact and work with the social practices that are continuously emerging between them.

Points of focus and analytical attention in a multi-perspective intervention strategy

In the following, I list a set of key foci and analytical points of attention, which can be used as a point of reflection – or a 'test', one could say – in relation to the intervention and prevention practices as they are developed and implemented by teachers, principals and/or others across settings and groups of involved actors vis-à-vis bullying as a phenomenon between children at school. This list is generated from the work of the authors in this anthology and, in that regard, the rationale and basis for each of the points can be found within the chapters included here (or in the other texts to which the contributors refer); these should be consulted for more comprehensive, analytical knowledge about the points.

Each analytical point of attention includes a 'litmus test' to help focus the point, and a brief outline of the analytical and theoretical points upon which this focus is built; in some instances, there are examples to help readers remember. Whenever policies, procedures, initiatives, strategies, etc., are developed and included in school action plans and teachers' guidelines to address bullying, this list may be helpful as a way to remember the points of the thinking technologies. The idea is to encourage educational practitioners, politicians and parents to reflect upon their initiatives by means of these analytical points of attention.

(1) Consider the *understanding of individuals and communities*, which is embedded within the overall thinking technology that is implied in the intervention and/or prevention strategy or policy you are about to implement in relation to bullying practices at school.

Litmus test: Ask yourself if you are about to get caught in the trap of individualisation: are you laying the groundwork for practices that will point to and/or position individuals as guilty, weak, hopeless, evil, naïve or any other unequivocal, fixed category? Or are the practices you are about to develop – the initiatives you are about to implement – designed to keep a focus on the social dynamics of the school class; for example, by replacing emphasis on the individual ('whose fault is this?') with alternative questions such as: What makes it necessary, obvious or attractive for a certain child or group of children to act in ways that are destructive to other children? What feeds the anxieties, hopes and fears that are enacted in their practices (i.e. what makes the child(ren) hit, despise, exclude, persecute, etc.)? Does the intervention and/or prevention strategy contribute to repairing the social dynamics and relational praxes in ways that diminish that need and these anxieties?

Background: This point is based on the alternative definitions of bullying provided by Schott (see page 21), Søndergaard (see page 47) and in the Introduction to this anthology (see page 1) as well as the analyses of the complex mechanisms and dynamics embedded in the social interactions between children (see all the chapters in this anthology; also, Søndergaard 2008, 2011, 2013a and b). These conceptualisations of the relational praxes between children take a critical stance towards the exclusive focus on an individual, which merely generates engagement with individual responsibility, guilt, powerlessness, etc. This is often done in ways that overlook social dynamics and encourage adults to consider punishing and excluding individual children instead of initiating reparative efforts within the entire social community of children.

(2) Consider *the level and focus* of intervention and/or prevention as described and initiated in your anti-bullying strategy or policy.

Litmus test: Ask yourself which level of 'social negotiation' your strategy addresses and moves towards. There may be work to do at all levels, but remaining at one of the first two levels described below will trap you in individualising strategies.

Level 1 – the individual level: When initiatives against bullying work at this first level, the activities, discussions and interventions address which children to include/exclude; e.g. teachers tell particular children that they should or should not exclude certain other children, or the teachers demand that particular children include a particular (marginalised) child when they play. Discussions revolve around individual children and their access to the social community.

Level 2 – the level of concrete terms for participation: When initiatives against bullying work at this second level, the activities, discussions and interventions address which terms or conditions may or may not be legitimate in relation to inclusion/exclusion; e.g. teachers discuss with particular children what kind of music, sports, bikes or clothes are legitimate targets for contempt or praise. Codes are negotiated for what is appropriate or inappropriate – and with these codes, there are implications for the individual children who may be associated with whatever has been pointed out as being either despicable or acceptable.

Level 3 – the level of cultural standards: When initiatives against bullying work at this third level, activities, discussions and interventions address the cultural codes and standards that saturate the relational praxes between the children. In other words, the initiatives address how narrowly or broadly to constitute the norms and the access to participation within the children's community – and how narrow these norms and the access to appropriateness must be. Negotiations should revolve around: how do we expand diversity, how do we elicit inspiration for diversity amongst ourselves and how do we appreciate differences and disagreements whilst still being a community?

Background: This analytical focus is based on the definition of bullying – and the processes and mechanisms it involves – that was also referred to in the first point of attention about understanding individuals and communities (i.e. seek inspiration from all the chapters in this anthology). In particular, the conceptualisations about social exclusion anxiety, the closing down of empathy – and the potential emergence of empathetic irrelevance – as well as the production of contempt versus dignity described in my other work are important in relation to this point of attention. Helle Rabøl Hansen's conceptualisation of 'longing for belonging' (2011a) is also significant.

(3) Consider whether your intervention and/or prevention strategy or policy promotes the *production of dignity or the production of contempt*.

Litmus test: Ask yourself if the discourses, the processes, the materialisations and the forms of social encouragement that are embedded in the practices you are cultivating to prevent or intervene with regard to bullying promote dignity for all members of the community (i.e. the group of children, the school class). If you cannot determine whether or not they produce dignity, you may want to ask the opposite: is there any danger that this intervention and/or prevention initiative encourages the production of contempt for some children or as a process distributed within a group of children?

Background: The production of contempt or dignity works as a key mechanism that enacts inclusions/exclusions and ultimately bullying practices (see Chapter 3, page 47). The production of contempt may alleviate social exclusion anxiety and, therefore, it may be appealing as a relational praxis for children in need of relief. At the same time, the potential that contempt production will increase within a group may intensify social exclusion anxiety, thereby creating a mutual reinforcement of destructive effects like anxiety and contempt. Thus, intervention and/or prevention initiatives must work to minimise social exclusion anxiety in order to simultaneously reduce contempt production. When working on this dignity-enhancing strategy, it is important to avoid any temptation to selectively produce contempt towards particular children as a means of punishment or as part of a strategy to (potentially) restore social balance or compensate for imbalances ('to give them a taste of their own medicine'). Contempt is poisonous within any social community. Any further contempt production will lead to processes of circulating affects that merely serve to propagate anxiety and distress instead of dissolving the tension within the children's community.

(4) Consider whether your intervention and/or prevention strategy or policy is built upon *understanding the social, the affective and the learning aspects* of school life as entangled and entangling amongst the children. *Litmus test*: Does your anti-bullying initiative take for granted any exclusions amongst these aspects? For example, does it consider learning processes to be demarcated and merely instrumental and/or that the social and affective aspects of a child's life are irrelevant to teaching and learning? Is the initiative sufficiently sensitive to enhancing community-building elements as an integrated part of didactic tools and processes? And is the strategy or policy sufficiently sensitive to the social and cultural learning that entangles children's participation in classroom work, group work, discussions during class, etc., as well as the children's relational praxes, play and other activities in their spare time, breaks and recess?

Background: In terms of the analytical attention points, these questions are based on the entanglement community-building didactics of the social, the affective and the learning aspects of school life as described by Haavind, Hansen, Hein, Kofoed and Søndergaard (all in this anthology). Studies about community-building didactics are particularly relevant, especially those developed by Helle Plauborg, who defines these pedagogical practices as teaching initiatives (which aim to enhance the progression of learning in teaching environments) and meaningful learning activities as entangled in the simultaneous and mutual development of sociality. She understands sociality here as building communities and participating with dignity in the education and life of the school class. Community-building didactics seek to co-think learning aspects with social aspects and to avoid any dichotomy between them – and thereby, these didactics challenge the tendency to prioritise learning processes over 'the social' and, alternatively, to consider 'the social' as a prerequisite that must be established before learning. Community-building didactics, Plauborg argues, merge both learning and social practices (2011; see also Hansen 2011a; Osterman 2000).

(5) Consider whether the intervention and/or prevention practices in the anti-bullying initiative, strategy or policy are sufficiently *sensitive to various forms of bullying* – and check which potential new forms of exclusion may be affected by the intervention and/or prevention strategy.

Litmus test: Does the anti-bullying initiative, strategy or policy that you are developing or about to implement address the fact that bullying can take many forms and move across many different levels? Will the initiative be able to recognise and encounter bullying in all of its displaced versions, where different children are acquisitioned by bullying practices[7] and marginalised positionings along with – and perhaps even simultaneously with – the enacted, fixed positionings of 'the bully', 'the bullying victim' and 'the bystander' categories? And is the strategy sensitive to the fact that every form of inclusion creates a risk of new exclusions that will have to be addressed? Is the strategy sensitive to the mergers that occur in practices of bullying and other forms of marginalisation, such as those related to sexism, homophobia, racism, etc.?

Background: The empirical analyses by Kofoed as well as Søndergaard (see pages 159 and 47, respectively) show that the bullying positionings vary. In some children's communities, and during some periods of time, bullying may create fixed positionings amongst children. In other communities and during other periods of time, bullying may take the form of shifting and displaced positionings. In the same or yet other children's communities, sudden bursts of bullying events may occur. In other words, bullying and marginalisation practices may be realised by means of a diversity of relational patterns and positionings, and fixed as well as shifting positions. And they may merge with sexist, racist, homophobic actions or other forms of marginalisation that are connected to minoritising processes in the children's communities (see Meyer, page 209).

(6) Consider the ability of your intervention and/or prevention strategy or policy to anticipate the particular *positioning of the bullying target(s)* and the dilemmas they may encounter with regard to seeking help and understanding outside their peer community or from adults.

Litmus test: Does this anti-bullying strategy or policy presume that marginalised and/or bullied child(ren) should step forward and claim their position as victims? Does this anti-bullying initiative expect and presume that bullying targets should point out particular persecutor(s) to claim justice and enforce retribution? Does the strategy presume that designated or chosen victims are endowed with respect and confirmation when, for

---

[7] For more on the concept of categories acquisitioning certain children, see McDermott (1993).

instance, they are crying or confessing their feelings of vulnerability and loneliness? Or does the strategy take into account the difficult situation of which victims may be a part – with all the intricate dilemmas, fears and paradoxical ties of loyalty that may characterise the relationship with their persecutor(s)? Does it take into account the difficult situation where children in the shifting marginalised and marginalising positionings may be caught up in blurred loyalties as well as circulating and changing affects; for example, revenge and gratefulness, arrogance and humiliation? Has the strategy been sufficiently thought through with regard to the markers and tools that may allow the (for now) 'victim' to move with dignity and prestige back to participating within the community?

Background: When a child is positioned as despised and marginalised or even abjected, he/she becomes irrelevant as a participant in the community. Thus, the child's ability to influence the always emergent social order and the conditions for inclusion/exclusion within the social groups to which they 'belong' becomes dramatically reduced, even counteracted (see Hein, Mathiassen, Viala and Søndergaard in this anthology; also Søndergaard 2008, 2011). A bullied child has a very limited access to negotiate the conditions for inclusion with any legitimacy. In groups that are characterised by displaced and shifting positionings between the marginalised and marginalising, bullied and bullying, the potential to change places may encourage a child to remain in the vulnerable positioning and avoid external involvement. In other words, an insistence on remaining part of the community may seem like a more promising strategy than reinforcing one's own marginalisation by declaring victimhood and calling for help.

A bullied child may consequently choose to 'deny' his/her position as marginalised or bullied; he/she may choose to laugh along with the bullies in an attempt to manifest belonging and participation in the group – and thus hope for a better chance at legitimacy and influence later. This strategy may be expensive (in terms of ongoing exposure to relational harm), but the child may see no alternative. He/she may not trust the ability of adults to help; may not believe there is the possibility to be reintegrated into the group if considered a betrayer; may not be able to let go of the desire to be an insider within this particular group of children; may not realise that this treatment and these norms are not necessary or 'natural' conditions within children's communities, etc. Thus, intervention strategies cannot be based exclusively on the 'confessions' of bullied children and their demands for 'justice'.

(7) Consider whether your intervention and/or prevention strategy or policy is sufficiently sensitive to the always emergent means of communication and relating at work amongst the children – such as their movements between *real and virtual practices of relating*.

Litmus test: Does the intervention and/or prevention strategy co-think the communication and relational dilemmas and possibilities that all contemporary children access by means of SMS and MMS devices on their mobile telephones along with the chat forums and profiles on social-networking websites, and thereby the access they have to comment on each other's profiles and messages on these websites? Does the initiative co-think the interactions and relational patterns that are built through real–virtual gaming practices?

Background: When technology entangles children's relational praxes, then the processes recognised from real life and the patterns of relating both continue and transform. As demonstrated by Jette Kofoed's analyses (see Chapter 7), technology affects non-simultaneity in terms of the intensity of the affects and emotions that are part of the communication patterns amongst children. Along with the infinite audience and unlimited accessibility, another particular characteristic of virtually mediated interaction is the potential anonymity of senders that technology enables (e.g. via mobile telephones and social-networking websites). Real–virtual gaming practices also sustain existing patterns as well as produce new patterns of relating, and thereby feed the intra-activities that enact children's communities, and sometimes bullying, with particular horizons of imageries and experiences. Thus, it is necessary to co-think these factors in any prevention and/or intervention strategy (Højgaard, Juelskjær and Søndergaard 2012; see Kofoed, page 159; Kofoed and Ringrose 2012; Spears et al. 2012; Søndergaard 2013a and b).

(8) Consider whether your intervention and/or prevention strategy or policy fuels or encourages the *demonisation of parents*, either intentionally or unintentionally.

Litmus test: Does the intervention and/or prevention strategy allow sufficient space for parents' perspectives, understandings and dignified positionings with regard to the relational trouble in which their child(ren) may be involved? Considering the discourses on parent positioning that circulate in public debates and which may be used by teachers and principals – e.g. in letters, emails and/or during meetings between school professionals and parents – then it becomes important to question the subject positionings that parents are invited to assume. And as a result, how are parents invited to participate in processes of the school's work that involve their child(ren)? Which strategies of communication and cooperation do the initiatives promote in order to prevent and/or overcome struggles about 'the only and pure truth' between those involved? And which alternative strategies could be expanded to invite multiple perspectives into these processes and thus seek development and mutual understanding?

Background: In many countries, we experience a common discourse that says parents are demanding, irresponsible, overbearing and difficult. These parental configurations are widespread – not only amongst school professionals, but also in the media and the general public. Parents are typically categorised as either too worried and over-indulgent, too angry and aggressive, too engaged or too underprivileged. In cases of bullying or marginalisation, these discourses easily create disrespect for parents as legitimate resources for important knowledge about their child(ren)'s well-being as well as their experiences with and perspectives on the conditions of everyday life at school. Nina Hein's analyses (see Chapter 12) demonstrate how such parental discourses – combined with the widespread, individualising discourses about 'those who bully', 'bullying victims' and 'bystanders' – tend to encourage school professionals to ascribe the trouble and distress a child is having at school to the child's home: the problems at school are attributed to an individual child's personality characteristics, which in their turn are believed to have developed at home and outside of school; thus, the assumed and appointed characteristics are considered to be the consequence of having parents who are too aggressive, too indulgent, too preoccupied with their careers or too engaged with their child(ren). When parents seek help from the school with regard to the bullying problem in which their child(ren) are involved, school professionals may employ such parental discourses and individualising thinking technologies, more or less directly meeting parents with suspicion, ridicule and perhaps even rejection.

(9) Consider whether your intervention and/or prevention strategy or policy fuels or encourages the *demonisation of teachers*, either intentionally or unintentionally.

Litmus test: Does the intervention strategy take into account the possibilities and impossibilities that are embedded in the teachers' positionings; that is, their working conditions and everyday reality in terms of work pressure, their need for and varying degrees of access to education for themselves, support from school administrators, their access to help in relation to dilemmas and trouble in the classroom, etc.?

Background: As pointed out by Helle Rabøl Hansen (see Chapter 10 and 2011a), discourses about bullying and about the character of 'contemporary' children vary amongst teachers, and these discourses obviously entangle their understanding of bullying and marginalisation practices amongst the children in their school classes. But if teachers are supposed to commit to the use of intervention and/or prevention initiatives, then their experiences with work conditions, dilemmas and the pressures of everyday life as a schoolteacher must be taken into account and given the same type of respect that should be shown for the dilemmas and pressures at work amongst the children. In other words, being able to encourage dignity-producing processes and relational praxes amongst children requires that dignity-producing processes and relational praxes are also realised amongst teachers, parents, school administrators and educational professionals.

(10) Consider how sensitive your intervention and/or prevention strategy or policy is with regard to how *the conceptualisations of inclusion and diversity* are managed.

Litmus test: Does the intervention and/or prevention strategy or policy presume overly static ideals of children's communities as being free from conflicts? Is it characterised by ideals of close friendship between all the children, and thereby imply a condemnation of any kind of distance amongst the children and/or exclusion from activities and social groups? Or does it help children navigate the common processes of inclusion/ exclusion that are at work in all social communities? Does it help build their ability to read the codes and to manoeuvre in ways that allow the community to maintain cohesiveness and solidarity whilst simultaneously allowing for varieties in and the emergence of differences, preferences and shifting patterns of closeness and distance?

Background: Bullying may be seen as an extension and distorted version of children's social practices wherein they build communities and establish social order via shifting inclusions/exclusions. When practices of exclusion intensify and become more extreme whilst effecting genuine expulsion and/ or an effort to produce it – either physically, socially, psychologically and/or symbolically – it becomes relevant to engage the concept of bullying (see the Introduction, page 1; see also Schott, page 21; Søndergaard 2011 and page 47). With this approach to bullying, it becomes unnecessary to understand all inclusions/exclusions as destructive processes within a social group – they may simply be a part of the ordinary conditions for building communities and social order; as such, they are merely challenges for the children to handle, but also a kind of process that needs acknowledgement, support and a certain amount of facilitation from teachers and other relevant adults. In these efforts to facilitate, it is important to acknowledge diversity as a source of inspiration, but also to respect its potential when seeking some close friendships as well as not seeking close friendships with everyone. Adults need a sensitive approach to the various kinds of sameness and difference that may work within a children's community: not all kinds of sameness should require or oblige children to connect in close friendships, and not all differences need to be problematic or a reason not to seek friendships. Obvious types of sameness may overshadow and hide similarities and differences at other levels and in other aspects. The same goes for differences: obvious differences may overshadow and hide similarities and differences at other levels and in other aspects (Myong and Søndergaard 2013). Realising the complex nature of such patterns and shifting processes will make understandings of and approaches to destructive versions of exclusion, marginalisation and bullying more precise and effective, and it will provide adults with more flexible and nuanced tools to manoeuvre through these shifting processes whilst helping facilitate the children's relational praxes.

Conclusion

These points of analytical attention – which are outlined here as a list of key foci and questions to be continuously raised as a way to reflect on and evaluate one's practices – are meant to be a tool that can be used to maintain the direction and cooperation within a multi-perspective intervention and/or prevention strategy or policy vis-à-vis bullying and extreme marginalisation at school.

In a multi-perspective intervention strategy, the ability to operate flexibly within shifting contexts is crucial. It is important to bear in mind that these contexts are characterised by ever-changing social conditions, shifting actors and continuously emerging dilemmas, social manoeuvrings, affects, hopes, fears and experiences of success and failure amongst the children involved. All of these fluctuating and shifting conditions impact the intervention in and/or prevention of destructive social practices – and the navigation strategies, with their analytical foci and points of attention, will prove to be more effective and helpful than technically standardised, one-size-fits-all techniques and fixed sets of behavioural rules. Standardised techniques presuppose equally standardised behavioural patterns amongst both children and adults at school. Techniques and socio-technical recipes will always fall short vis-à-vis the complexity described here and in the other chapters in this anthology.

Although the analytical points of attention allow for a flexible implementation of embedded principles and knowledge – and this flexibility obviously comprises the only advice that can be given in relation to navigating complex social, cultural and subjective dynamics, such as those addressed in this anthology – even these points of attention need to be continuously developed, refined and expanded. Only the mutual sharing of experiences and the continuous conceptual development of this complicated field of research and practice can provide the groundwork for this type of expansion – and thereby also for a professional contribution to improving the well-being and contentment of children at schools that are haunted by bullying and extreme practices of marginalisation.

16 One size doesn't fit all: re-thinking implementation research for bullying prevention

Donna Cross and Amy Barnes

The push for evidence to inform school-based strategies to reduce bullying has led to a multitude of intervention research projects that aim to determine how best to prevent and/or reduce these behaviours. Although government and non-government organisations, practitioners and researchers have emphasised the importance of evidence-based research to prevent harmful behaviours (American Psychological Association 2005; Bero et al. 1998; Eccles et al. 2005; Fixsen and Blase 2009; Glasgow et al. 2006), this emphasis rests on the assumption that those who implement interventions can or should be able to apply evidence-based strategies within their own unique contexts, in a manner as close as possible to that intended by the programme developers (Bero et al. 1998; Campbell et al. 2000; Durlak and DuPre 2008; Fixsen and Blase 2009; Glasgow et al. 2006; Wandersman et al. 2008). Accordingly, evaluation studies of bullying-prevention interventions may assess implementation fidelity by including measurements of the extent to which teachers and schools adopt and implement strategies. In addition, given that a lack of implementation fidelity may contribute to a reduction in the likelihood of positive outcomes, implementation research assesses the variables that influence the adoption, implementation and maintenance of intervention components (Durlak and DuPre 2008). Resulting insights may prompt modifications to intervention strategies or garner extra support for those who are expected to implement them.

However, the implementation of interventions may be affected by countless individual, social and cultural factors that impact school communities. The challenge of evaluating the influence of such factors is aptly described in a quote sometimes attributed to Albert Einstein (date unknown): '. . .not everything that counts can be counted, and not everything that can be counted counts'. This perspective highlights the important nexus between qualitative/inductive and quantitative/deductive research methodologies and – in this context – suggests that quantitative approaches alone may be necessary but insufficient to truly understand complex phenomena like school-based intervention implementation. This nexus is supported philosophically by pluralism and methodologically by triangulation, suggesting that a combination of methodologies could be utilised to focus on different but equally important dimensions of the same phenomenon.

This chapter suggests that utilising a purely quantitative approach to implementation research limits understanding of the complex social contexts in which implementation takes place, and thus limits efforts to support those who implement bullying-prevention programmes. Just as bullying behaviour itself emerges from a complex interplay of influencing variables, we contend that researchers investigating and attempting to address this phenomenon require both qualitative and quantitative methodologies to conduct research that is relevant to the target audience(s), and especially to address implementation-related questions such as:

- How can the elements of an intervention programme be developed to ensure they meet the strengths and needs of the target audience(s) as well as those individuals who will disseminate and implement the programme components?
- To what extent can programme elements be modified to suit the target audience(s) during implementation whilst maintaining programme fidelity?
- How can the programme's implementation with the target audience(s) be monitored/measured?
- What do the implementers like/dislike about the intervention, and what would they implement again and why?
- What else is required to support effective and ongoing programme implementation?

We argue that utilising a mixed methods approach and ensuring engagement with the perspectives of all stakeholders provides essential understandings that allow us to *examine* our approach to and methods for conducting intervention research. This approach minimises Type III errors (i.e. when the presence or lack of an intervention effect is incorrectly attributed to a particular cause, such as flawed programme implementation), and also allows 'implementers' to modify programme elements to meet the strengths and needs of their target audience whilst continuing to work towards intended health and well-being outcomes.

Bullying-prevention programmes: does one size fit all?

Given that bullying is a complex systemic problem with multiple factors associated with its manifestation, the programmes most likely to be effective in producing positive outcomes are multi-dimensional, whole-school programmes that incorporate prevention and intervention strategies to target all levels of the school community (Cross et al. 2012; Rigby and Slee 2008; Vreeman and Carroll 2007). However, it appears that bullying-prevention programmes do not consistently translate into positive outcomes when implemented in schools. Some whole-school interventions appear to be only modestly successful at reducing bullying and aggression amongst young people (Rigby and Slee 2008). Rachel C. Vreeman and Aaron E. Carroll (2007) and Anna C. Baldry and David P. Farrington (2007) assessed twenty-six and sixteen school-based bullying prevention programmes, respectively, reporting that only around 50 per cent demonstrated positive outcomes for student behaviour. The remaining interventions resulted in inconsistent, small or undesirable effects. Further, few studies have investigated the long-term sustainability of these programmes in schools and/or the sustainability of the programme results.

When further considering this issue, evidence that the effectiveness of bullying-prevention programmes varies according to group and location may indicate the influence of differing social contexts on programme outcomes. For example, the Olweus Bullying Prevention Programme achieved a 50–70 per cent reduction in bullying behaviour amongst 11–14-year-old students in Norway following eight or twenty months of the intervention, respectively. There was also a reduction in other anti-social behaviours (e.g. vandalism, drunkenness and truancy), improved social climate (e.g. discipline, positive social relationships and positive attitudes towards school) and enhanced student satisfaction with school (Olweus 1997). However, implementation of the same programme in other regions and countries has yielded inconsistent outcomes (Smith et al. 2004).

Similarly, the KiVa Antibullying Program in Finland (Kärnä et al. 2011a, b) incorporates universal strategies (e.g. school curriculum, an anti-bullying computer game, high-visibility vests for recess supervisors, guides for parents); indicated strategies (e.g. individual and small-group discussions with those involved in bullying situations, follow-up meetings, recruiting pro-social and high-status peers to support targets of bullying); and training days and school-network meetings to support the programme's implementation by teachers and schools. Evaluative research suggests that, after widespread dissemination and implementation in Finnish schools, KiVa can reduce the prevalence of bullying victimisation, enhance empathy for victimised students and anti-bullying attitudes, and decrease bystander reinforcement of bullying behaviour (Kärnä et al. 2011a, b). However, the extent of positive outcomes varies according to classroom and school, and KiVa's effectiveness has been more strongly demonstrated amongst primary-school students (aged 6–12 years) than secondary-school students (aged 13–17 years), particularly in comparison to those in early secondary school (aged 13–14 years; Kärnä et al. 2011b). This variance may suggest the impact of differential implementation (Kärnä et al. 2011a) and indeed, the number of fully implemented KiVa lessons varies between teachers and schools (Kärnä et al. 2011b).

Thus, a limitation of the evidence-based approach is the difficulty associated with achieving positive outcomes when strategies are implemented in real-world settings, perhaps in part due to varying implementation of these strategies. The degree to which evidence-based strategies (once their effectiveness has been established in controlled trials) are successfully adopted, implemented and sustained by school communities is influenced by a multitude of variables unique to different school environments. As such, the inconsistent effectiveness of interventions as outlined above may suggest that 'one size *doesn't* fit all' when intervening to prevent and manage bullying.

The impact of contextual factors on school implementation

A successful approach to bullying prevention at one school may be unsuccessful at another, as the context within which schools must implement policies and practices is often very different. Contextual factors may challenge schools' 'intervention fidelity', or the extent to which they implement the core components as intended by the intervention developers (Gearing et al. 2011). The various barriers to implementation of the core components of bullying-prevention programmes typically presented by individuals, schools and/or the community include competing demands on teachers' time and energy; a lack of funding, staff, time support and training for staff who will implement the programme; and a perception that social and emotional outcomes are less credible in schools compared to academic outcomes.

The nature and extent of such barriers to implementation are likely to be further influenced by factors such as school size, children's socio-economic status, cultural and religious background, and staff willingness and/or capacity to implement and sustain intervention strategies (Beets et al. 2008; Durlak and DuPre 2008; Fixsen and Blase 2009). Consequently, the intended effects of a programme may not be consistently demonstrated across different age groups, schools, locations, cultures and social and economic contexts. This is highlighted by a review of eighty-one studies that measured the implementation of health-promotion programmes and identified six levels of factors that influence the extent and fidelity of implementation (Durlak and DuPre 2008):

(1) Community-level factors (politics; funding; policy).
(2) Provider characteristics (perceived need for and benefits of innovation; self-efficacy; skill proficiency).
(3) Characteristics of the innovation (compatibility or fit with priorities, values and culture; degree to which the programme can be adapted to fit).
(4) Organisational factors and capacity (positive work climate; openness to change; shared vision and commitment).
(5) Specific processes and practices (shared decision-making; input and involvement of community members; coordination with other agencies; communication; strategy planning; clear roles and responsibilities; leadership and programme advocates; administrative support).
(6) Factors relating to the Prevention Support System (training; technical assistance).

The potential range, complexity and interaction of such factors highlights the difficulties researchers may face when attempting to assess barriers to school-based implementation. This indicates the importance of implementation research to better understand the nature of such barriers and how best to overcome them.

How is implementation evaluated?

Implementation research involves evaluating the extent to which research-based strategies are translated into practice, and identifying the activities and factors that positively or negatively influence the likelihood and extent to which this occurs (Eccles et al. 2005; Fixsen et al. 2005). The extent and 'success' of intervention implementation is often measured according to one or more of the following criteria (Durlak and DuPre 2008):

- Fidelity to the intended intervention protocols, practices and procedures.
- Dosage; i.e. the quantity and strength of the delivered intervention.
- The quality of the delivery of intervention components.
- Programme reach; i.e. the proportion of the targeted group involved in the intervention.
- Participant responsiveness, or the extent to which students are engaged and interested in the intervention as it is being delivered.
- Monitoring other services the participants have received, which may influence outcomes.
- Adaptation or the degree to which unexpected changes are made during the process of implementation.

Data relating to these criteria is typically evaluated categorically (i.e. comparison of outcomes of groups differing in level of implementation) or continuously (i.e. level of dosage or fidelity correlated with outcomes) (ibid.). By analysing the relationship between these variables and intervention outcomes, researchers attempt to identify the elements of programme implementation that best promote or limit effectiveness and sustainability.

However, given the six levels of contextual factors identified by Joseph A. Durlak and Emily P. DuPre (2008), it may be difficult to assess accurately the presence and influence of such variables using quantitative research methodology alone. Although quantitative measures can indicate that teachers and schools have not implemented strategies as instructed, they may be unable to explain *why* this was so. This limits our ability to adjust strategies or provide additional support to assist teachers and schools in overcoming implementation barriers. Analysis of qualitative data, guided by systematic frameworks for implementation research (Campbell et al. 2000; Fixsen et al. 2005; Medical Research Council 2000; Wandersman et al. 2008), would benefit the identification and exploration of characteristics associated with successful implementation and thus guide efforts to implement bullying-prevention programmes. Durlak and DuPre's contextual factors should be kept in mind as variables that may influence implementation when utilising these frameworks.

Implementation as a process

For example, Dean L. Fixsen et al. (2005) suggest that implementation should be conceptualised as a process rather than a single, discrete event. The stages of the implementation process are as follows:

(1) **Exploration and adoption:** become aware of the need for an innovation; acquire information about innovations; assess fit between the intervention and needs; make a decision; mobilise information, resources and support.

(2) **Programme installation:** put structural supports into place – e.g. ensure funding and human-resources strategies; develop policy; secure additional resources and staff.

(3) **Initial implementation:** evaluate initial changes in skill levels, capacity, and culture, etc.

(4) **Full operation:** the programme is fully operational when new learning is integrated into policies, practices and procedures. The innovation gradually becomes the accepted new practice. If fidelity is high, effectiveness should approximate the original evidence base.

(5) **Innovation:** dealing with challenges in difficult contexts presents the opportunity to refine and expand practices and programmes. This may be desirable (innovation) or undesirable (drift).

(6) **Sustainability:** when the intervention is sustained over subsequent years, skilled staff must be replaced by other skilled staff; the community must adjust to changes without losing components of the programme.

Researchers who require a clear understanding of intervention implementation should investigate the impact of contextual factors at each point of this process, and qualitative research would enhance their ability to fully identify and explore these factors. It should also be noted that timing is important in implementation research – evaluation that occurs too early in the process of implementation (e.g. during the stage of 'initial implementation') may indicate poor outcomes simply because the programme is not yet fully operational (ibid.). Qualitative research would again help to clarify where schools are situated on the continuum of implementation.

Should implementation fidelity be expected?

Given the impact of social, economic and organisational contexts on when and how well the implementation of a programme will occur, as well as the likelihood of core components being implemented (ibid.; McCormick et al. 1995), a focus on enhancing schools' fidelity (Gearing et al. 2011) to an established programme is likely to be problematic. In addition to having limited capacity to capture the complexity of the implementation process, quantitative measures of intervention fidelity may erroneously assume that departure from intervention guidelines represents inaccuracy or flawed implementation. Durlak and DuPre's (2008) list indicates the almost insurmountable challenge faced by programme developers in addressing all factors and subsequently designing 'one' bullying-prevention programme with components that, if implemented with fidelity, would suit the needs and strengths of the many conditions influenced by these six levels of factors within school communities. This approach does not take into account the possibility that implementers may *need* to adjust evidence-based strategies in order to make them fit their needs and contexts. This raises the question of whether school-programme developers should expect that innovations can or should be implemented with as little as possible modification. Is it possible that implementation fidelity could be evaluated by adherence to intended student outcomes instead of, or in addition to, adherence to programme components?

Before attempting to implement evidence-based strategies to prevent bullying, the implementer(s) should have an understanding of and be reassured that these strategies are a good 'fit' for the needs, strengths and challenges of their schools and communities (Fixsen et al. 2005). This may require the collection of both quantitative and qualitative information from teachers and school staff, students themselves, parents and the broader community, as well as consideration of the cultural, social and economic context of a school. This requires input from stakeholders and the target audience(s) at all stages of the implementation process. Scales that measure communities' readiness for change may be useful (e.g. Community Readiness Model), although their predictive validity is currently unclear.

Everett Rogers' Diffusion of Innovations model (Rogers 2002), however, provides a useful tool to examine the factors that may influence the extent to which preventative and intervention strategies are accepted and acted upon by staff, teachers and students. 'Diffusion' describes the process by which new ideas/practices ('innovations') are communicated and spread amongst individuals, organisations and communities over time. The rate of adoption is influenced by the innovation's/ programme's:

- **Relative advantage** compared to what it replaces. Evidence of advantage tends to be less influential than others; e.g. colleagues' *perception* of its advantage.
- **Compatibility** with pre-existing values, experiences and needs.
- **Complexity**; i.e. how difficult it is to understand and use the programme.
- **Trialability**; i.e. the degree to which the programme can be experimented with before commitment.
- **Observability**; i.e. the extent to which the results of the programme are clearly visible to others.

Diffusion is often a social process – individuals evaluate an innovation according to the perception of other peers who have adopted it. However, it can be particularly difficult to diffuse *preventative innovations* because the rewards are delayed, somewhat intangible and uncertain (i.e. low in relative advantage) (ibid.). Thus, although the Diffusion of Innovations model highlights the need for prevention and intervention strategies that are carefully tailored to the targeted communities and offers a means for understanding the process by which these strategies are adopted, more substantial engagement with the needs of specific communities is required.

Instead of 'one-model' interventions, strategies may need to be disseminated such that they can be modified or *selected* according to the contextual characteristics of a school, its staff and students as well as their parents. Such individual tailoring requires a framework to both qualitatively and quantitatively assess the needs, strengths and challenges of school communities, and to involve members of the school community in the selection and implementation of appropriate strategies.

A 'Common Elements Approach' to implementation research

The Common Elements Approach (Chorpita et al. 2007) involves coding and identifying core elements that are commonly shared in evidence-based programmes for application to particular community/client characteristics and needs, which results in 'sample aggregate profiles' to address a health problem; for example, bullying. Although limitations may be associated with this approach, it may also help to simplify and enhance the process of intervention implementation.

Using a similar approach, researchers at Edith Cowan University in Perth, Australia, have developed an evidence-based assessment that can be used by members of the school community to evaluate the needs and strengths of their schools, and thus guide the selection of intervention strategies. In 2004, a set of guidelines for the prevention and management of bullying was compiled, organised and qualitatively validated according to the Health Promoting Schools domains (Pearce et al. 2011). These guidelines were quantitatively tested in 2000, 2002 and 2005 as part of three large-scale (n=2,000+) longitudinal randomised-control trials with both primary- and secondary-school students (Friendly Schools studies: Cross et al. 2003, 2004, 2011). In 2010, the guidelines were reviewed and updated according to current empirical evidence, with a particular aim to provide more guidance in relation to covert and cyberbullying behaviours (Pearce et al. 2011). The guidelines have been categorised into six broad, *whole-school indicators (common elements)*, and each provides a statement of evidence and key areas for action:

(1) Building capacity for action.
(2) Supportive school culture.
(3) Proactive policies, procedures and practices.
(4) School community key understandings and competencies.
(5) Protective school environment.
(6) School–family–community partnerships.

As seen in Table 16.1,[1] these indicators have been used *to develop a screening tool* for schools in order to assess the extent to which they have implemented the recommended whole-school strategies to prevent and manage bullying, and thereby to identify areas for further action. The strength of this approach is the provision of a framework that draws upon evidence-based research but is also guided by quantitative and qualitative

[1] Table 16.1 was first published in Pearce, N., D. Cross, H. Monks, S. Waters and S. Falconer 2011. 'Current evidence of best practice in whole-school bullying intervention and its potential to inform cyberbullying interventions', in *Australian Journal of Guidance and Counselling* 21(1): 1–21.

Table 16.1 *Whole-school indicators to reduce bullying*

Evidence to Practice – Whole-School Indicators to Reduce Bullying	
✓ Indicator One: Building Capacity for Action Schools that assess and improve capacity for implementation of strategies to prevent and manage bullying behaviours will help to ensure school action is effective, sustainable and system-wide. To optimise the impact of school action, sufficient leadership, resources, organisational support and compatibility with school needs and context are crucial (Baldry and Farrigton 2007; Bosworth, Ginggiss, Potthoff and Roberts-Gray and DuPre 2008; Rigby and Slee 2008; Roberts-Gray et al. 2007; Smith et al. 2003; Stevens et al. 2001 Ttofi and Farrington, 2011; Vreeman and Carroll 2007).	Key action areas: • Valuing committed leadership • Planning for system support • Mobilising resources • Compatibility with school community needs
✓ Indictor Two: Supportive School Culture A positive school climate or culture that is created and maintained, provides safety, encourages open communication, supports a sense of connectedness to the school, and protect students from the risks of bullying. The quality of relationships between and among staff, students and families is vital in fostering a safe, supportive and engaging learning school environment (Bacchini et al. 2009: Baldry and Farrington 2007: Bradshaw et al. 2008: Glew et al. 2005; Luiselli et al. 2005; Smith, Boulton and Cowie 1993: Smith and Sharp 1994; Ttofi and Farrington 2011).	Key action areas: • Positive school ethos • Classroom practice and environment • Peer group influence
✓ Indicator Three: Proactive Policies, Procedures and Practices Schools with clear and consistent policy, procedures and practices send a strong message to the whole-school community about the school's beliefs and actions to provide a safe and supportive school environment. It provides the school with a framework to guide school expectations and reporting for the prevention, early response and case management of bullying behaviours. School policies should be promoted to the whole-school community particularly at times of higher risk such as orientation and transition. Positive behaviour should be encouraged and rewarded at the whole-school level among studenrs (Cross et al. 2009; Luiselli et al. 2005; Rigby 1997; Baldry and Farrington 2007; Smith and Sharp 1994; Ttofi and Farrington 2011).	Key action areas: • Policy development and implementation • Behaviour expectation approaches • Orientation and transition • Targeted student and family support

✓ Indicator Four: School Community Key Understandings and Competencies

Schools that provide mechanisms to improve staff, student and family understandings and competencies are more likely to effectively prevent, identify and respond to bullying incidents. Key understandings about bullying include the nature, prevalence and types of bullying, as well as information about bystander roles. These understandings are supported with competencies needed to prevent, identify and deal with bullying incidents effectively consistently (Baldry and Farrington 2007; Ttofi and Farrington 2011).

Key action areas:
• Staff professional learning
• Student learning through the curriculum
• Key understandings and skills for families

✓ Indicator Five: Protective School Environment

A well-designed maintained and supervised school environment will help to promote learning and positive social interactions among students and staff. The building design, location, provision of space, facilities and activities for recreation and learning (including through technology) can positively influence student behaviours (Gould League 2010; Learning Through Landscapes 2003; Smith and Sharp 1994; Ttofi and Farrington 2011).

Key action areas:
• Physical school attributes
• Supervision
• Supportive facilities and activities

✓ Indicator Six: School–Family–Community Partnerships

Schools that build partnerships between the school and Students' families and local organisations, through consultation and participation, foster vital support to reduce bullying behaviours recognising that it is the responsibility of the whole-school and wider community. Linkages should be made with local health, educational and community. Linkages should be made with local health, educational and community agencies that provides services to students and their families (Atlas and Pepler 1998; Baldry and Farrington 2007; Cairns and Cairns 1991; Duncan 1999a, 1999b; Espelage and Swearer 2003; Farrington 1993; Hemphill, Toumbourou and Catalano 2005; Olweus 1999a; Olweus and Limber 2010; Roland 2000).

Key action areas:
• Engaging families
• Working with the wider community and services providers

understandings of the needs and difficulties experienced by school communities, and which offers school communities some flexibility in tailoring bullying-prevention strategies to allow them to ensure these strategies are best suited to their unique contexts. The screening tool was operationalised in 2010–12 as part of a randomised controlled trial – called the Cyber Friendly Schools cyberbullying prevention project – and in 2011–15 as part of the 'Strong Schools, Safe Kids' Project, which aims to build school and system capacity to more effectively implement whole-school indicators to reduce bullying. The findings of these studies will allow us to evaluate the effectiveness of this approach.

Involving student voices: 'Nothing about us without us'

When using an approach such as that described above, the need to involve members of the school community in the development of intervention programmes is emphasised. In particular, the possibility of achieving effective and sustainable implementation is likely to be enhanced when strategies are relevant to and engaging for young people, and if students are given responsibility for and ownership of strategy selection and implementation. Therefore, students should be involved in the process of developing, implementing and evaluating interventions, as highlighted by models of student involvement in the development of policy and practice; e.g. Harry Shier's 'Pathways to Participation' (Shier 2001).

The Australian Cyber Friendly Schools Project (PEET) was a formative research project conducted at secondary schools throughout Western Australia during 2008–9 (Cross et al. 2010). The project aimed to actively engage schools, students, parents and the community to develop cost-effective, feasible and effective evidence-based policies, practices and strategies to reduce cyberbullying. In addition to reviewing the literature and collecting qualitative data (via focus groups and face-to-face interviews) as well as quantitative survey data about the prevalence and harms of cyberbullying, the project researchers committed to ensuring that students were involved in the development and implementation of strategies and resources to help parents, teachers and students prevent and/or manage cyberbullying.

A major part of this commitment was via the *Cyber Friendly Student Summit* in which students were involved in the strategic planning and development of policies and practices, including advocacy for future action to reduce young people's harm from the use of information communication technology. The summit was attended by 195 students (123 girls and 72 boys between 14 and 15 years of age) who were encouraged and supported to express their beliefs about what young people, adults, schools, governments and industries should do to improve cyber-safety and reduce cyberbullying. Electronic voting technology, table discussions and other activities were used to elicit students' thoughts about the results of recent research and prompt them to share their knowledge and develop ideas about solutions to cyberbullying. At the end, students were encouraged to discuss and develop actions to take when they returned to their schools. Focus-group interviews were conducted six months later to follow-up, with a goal to identify the enabling and disabling factors amongst students who attempted to implement cyberbullying-prevention activities at their schools.

A major result of the Summit was the formation of the Cyber Friendly Student Reference Group, a group of more than 120 young people between the ages of 14 and 16 from twenty-six different schools. On a regular basis, these students provide ideas and strategies to enhance the implementation and sustainability of cyberbullying prevention and intervention strategies. Referring to the contextual needs they identified, these young people have guided decisions related to the selection of components for the Cyber Friendly Schools study's programme; in turn, this has helped to enhance implementation and sustainability of the programme.

Conclusion

When developing bullying-prevention programmes and other school-based interventions, it is essential to engage student voices and ensure that schools have the capacity and willingness to translate policies and recommendations into effective and sustainable strategies. This is because programme implementation is an ongoing and challenging process, and the likelihood of a positive impact on student behaviour may be influenced by numerous contextual factors at each level. Implementation research is a useful way to better understand how interventions are implemented as well as the barriers that may be encountered; however, the body of research appears limited by its focus on measuring the 'fidelity' to one-size-fits-all programmes. A focus on quantitative measures of implementation fidelity may limit the detection and clear understanding of influential contextual factors as well as strategies to overcome them. A more flexible approach to ensuring that interventions are a good 'fit' for the school communities they target is to provide an outcome-based framework (informed by both quantitative and qualitative methodology) that allows school communities – including staff, students and families – to assess their specific strengths and needs in relation to bullying prevention, and to subsequently select relevant and appropriate bullying prevention strategies. This would allow school communities to 'tailor' interventions to their own requirements and thus enhance the process of effective and sustainable implementation to ensure positive outcomes.

Bibliography

Abrams, D., M. A. Hogg and J. M. Marques (eds.) 2005. *The Social Psychology of Inclusion and Exclusion*. Philadelphia: Psychology Press.

Adair, V., R. S. Dixon, D. W. Moore and C. M. Sutherland 2000. 'Ask your mother not to make yummy sandwiches: bullying in New Zealand secondary schools', in *New Zealand Journal of Educational Studies* 35(2): 207–21.

Adams, N., T. Cox and L. Dunstan 2004. 'I am the hate that dare not speak its name: dealing with homophobia in secondary schools', in *Educational Psychology in Practice* 20(3): 259–69.

Adorno, T. 2001. *Problems of Moral Philosophy*, translated by R. Livingstone. Palo Alto, Calif.: Stanford University Press.

Agamben, G. 1998. *Homo Sacer: Sovereign Power and Bare Life*, translated by D. Heller-Roazen. Palo Alto, Calif.: Stanford University Press.

1999a. *Potentialities: Collected Essays in Philosophy*. Palo Alto, Calif.: Stanford University Press.

1999b. *Remnants of Auschwitz: The Witness and the Archive*, translated by D. Heller-Roazen. New York: Zone Books.

2009. *What is an Apparatus? And Other Essays*, trans. David Kishik and Stefan Pedatella. Palo Alto, Calif.: Stanford University Press.

Agevall, O. 2008. 'The career of bullying: emergence, transformation, and utilisation of a new concept', in Rapport No. 29, School of Social Sciences, Växjö University, Sweden: 1–71.

Ahmed, E. and J. Braithwaite 2005. 'Forgiveness, shaming, shame and bullying', in *The Australian and New Zealand Journal of Criminology* 38(3): 298–323.

Ahmed, S. 2004. *The Cultural Politics of Emotion*. Edinburgh University Press.

Almeida, A. 2009. 'Are moral disengagement and empathy related to cyberbullying practices?', presented at the conference *The Good, the Bad, the Challenging: the user and the future of information and communication technologies*: Copenhagen.

Althusser, L. 1971. 'Ideology and Ideological State Apparatuses (Notes towards an Investigation)' in *Lenin and Philosophy, and Other Essays*, trans. Ben Brewster. London: NLB: 121–73.

American Psychological Association (APA) 2005. 'Policy statement on evidence-based practice in psychology' (online), APA Council of Representatives; www.apa.org/practice/resources/evidence/evidence-based-statement.pdf (last accessed 10 October 2013).

Amhøj, C. B. 2007. 'Det selvskabte medlemskab, managementstate, dens styringsteknologier og indbyggere' [The self-constructed membership, management state, its technologies of governance and residents]. Ph.D. thesis, Graduate School of Management Technology, Copenhagen Business School.

419

Andenæs, A. 1991. 'Fra undersøkelsesobjekt til medforsker? Livsformsintervju med 4–5-åringer' [From research object to co-researcher? Life mode interviews with 4–5-year-olds], in *Nordisk Psykologi [Nordic Psychology]* 43(4): 274–92.

Andersen, P. Ø. 1995. *I Retorikkens Hage [In Rhetoric's Garden]*. Oslo: Universitetsforlaget.

Anderson, S. 2000. *I en Klasse for Sig [In a Class of His Own]*. Copenhagen: Gyldendal Press.

Antorini, C. 2008. 'Flertal for S forslag om styrket anti-mobning i skolerne' [Majority of Social Democrats propose to strengthen anti-bullying measures in schools]; www.antorini.dk/index.php?id=506 (last accessed 20 May 2009).

1982. *Lectures on Kant's Political Philosophy*. University of Chicago Press.

Arora, C. M. J. 1994. 'Is there any point in trying to reduce bullying in secondary schools? A two-year follow-up of a whole-school anti-bullying policy in one school', in *Educational Psychology in Practice* 10(3): 155–62.

1996. 'Defining bullying: towards a clearer general understanding and more effective intervention strategies', in *School Psychology International* 17: 317–29.

Asher, S. R., J. T. Parkhurst, S. Hymel and G. A. Williams 1990. 'Peer rejection and loneliness in childhood', in S. R. Asher and J. D. Coie (eds.) *Peer Rejection in Childhood*. New York: Cambridge University Press: 253–73.

Atkinson, R. 2001. 'The life story interview', in J. F. Gubrium and J. A. Holstein (eds.) *Handbook of Interview Research: Context and Method*. Thousand Oaks, Calif.: SAGE Publications Ltd: 121–40.

Atlas, R. S. and D. J. Pepler 1998. 'Observations of bullying in the classroom', in *The Journal of Educational Research* 92(2): 86–99.

Atwood, M. 1988. *Cat's Eye*. New York: Doubleday.

Bacchi, C. L. 1999. *Women, Policy and Politics*. London: SAGE Publications Ltd.

Bacchini, D., G. Esposito and G. Affuso 2009. 'Social experience and school bullying', in *Journal of Community & Applied Social Psychology* 19: 17–32.

Bagley, C., F. Bolitho and L. Bertrand 1997. 'Sexual assault in school, mental health and suicidal behaviors in adolescent women in Canada', in *Adolescence* 32(126): 361–6.

Bagley, C. and C. Pritchard 1998. 'The reduction of problem behaviours and school exclusion in at-risk youth: an experimental study of school social work with cost-benefit analyses', in *Child & Family Social Work* 3: 219–26.

Bagwell, C. L. and M. E. Schmidt 2011. *Friendships in Childhood and Adolescence*. New York: Guilford Press.

Baldry, A. C. and D. P. Farrington 2007. 'Effectiveness of programs to prevent school bullying', in *Victims & Offenders* 2(2): 183–204.

Bansel, P., B. Davies, C. Laws and S. Linnell 2009. 'Bullies, bullying and power in the contexts of schooling', in *British Journal of Sociology of Education* 30(1): 59–69.

Barad, K. 2003. 'Posthumanist performativity: toward an understanding of how matter comes to matter', in *Signs: Journal of Women in Culture and Society* 28 (3): 801–31.

2007. *Meeting the Universe Halfway: Quantum Physics and the Entanglement of Matter and Meaning*. Durham, NC: Duke University Press.

Bartlett, F. C. 1932/1997. *Remembering: A Study in Experimental and Social Psychology*. Cambridge University Press.

Batsche, G. and H. Knoff 1994. 'Bullies and their victims: understanding a pervasive problem in the schools', in *School Psychology Review* 23(2): 165–74.

Bauman, Z. 2000. *Liquid Modernity*. Cambridge: Polity Press.

2007. *Consuming Life*. Cambridge: Polity Press.

Beets, M. W., B. R. Flay, S. Vuchinich, A. C. Acock, K. K. Li and C. Allred 2008. 'School climate and teachers' beliefs and attitudes associated with implementation of the Positive Action Program: a diffusion of innovations model', in *Prevention Science* 9(4): 264–75.

Benjamin, S., M. Nind, K. Hall, J. Collins and K. Sheehy 2003. 'Moments of inclusion and exclusion: pupils negotiating classroom contexts', in *British Journal of Sociology of Education* 24(5): 547–58.

Beran, T. N. 2006. 'A construct validity study of bullying', in *The Alberta Journal of Educational Research* 52(4): 241–50.

Berne, S. 1999. *Bullying: an Effective Anti-bullying Program for Secondary Schools*. Cheltenham, Victoria: Hawker Brownlow Education.

Bero, L. A., R. Grilli, J. M. Grimshaw, E. Harvey, A. D. Oxman and M. A. Thomson 1998. 'Closing the gap between research and practice: an overview of systematic reviews of interventions to promote the implementation of research findings', in *British Medical Journal* 317(7156): 465–8.

Bertelsen, P. 1994. *Tilværelsesprojektet: Det Menneskeliges Niveauer Belyst i den Terapeutiske Proces [Life Project: the Levels of Humanity Illuminated in the Therapeutic Process]*. Copenhagen: Dansk Psykologisk Forlag.

(ed.) 2010. *Aktør i Eget Liv: om at Hjælpe Mennesker på Kanten af Tilværelsen [Actor in his Own Life: About Helping People on the Edge of Existence]*. Copenhagen: Frydenlund.

Bjerg, H. 2011. 'Skoling af lyst: fantasier og fornemmelser i tre elevgenerations erindringer om livet i skolen, 1950–2000' [Schooling of desire: fantasies and feelings in three generations of students' memories of life at school, 1950–2000]. PhD thesis, Department of Learning and Education, Aarhus University, Denmark.

Björkqvist, K. and V. Jannson 2003. 'Tackling violence in schools: a report from Finland', in P. K. Smith (ed.) *Violence in Schools: The Response in Europe*. London: Routledge Falmer.

Bochenek, M. and A. W. Brown 2001. 'Hatred in the hallways: violence and discrimination against lesbian, gay, bisexual, and transgender students in U.S. schools'. New York: Human Rights Watch; www.hrw.org/reports/2001/uslgbt/ (last accessed 17 May 2012).

Bollmer, J. M., R. Milich, M. J. Harris and M. A. Maras 2006. 'A friend in need: the role of friendship quality as a protective factor in peer victimization and bullying', in *Journal of Interpersonal Violence* 20(6): 701–12.

Bond, L., J. B. Carlin, L. Thomas, K. Rubin and G. Patton 2001. 'Does bullying cause emotional problems? A prospective study of young teenagers', in *British Medical Journal* 323(7311): 480–4.

Bonds, M. and S. Stocker 2000. *Bully-Proofing Your School: a Comprehensive Approach for Middle Schools*, 2nd edn. Longmont, Colo.: Sopris West.

Borg, M. 1998. 'Secondary school teachers' perception of pupils' undesirable behaviours', in *British Journal of Educational Psychology* 68(1): 67–79.

1999. 'The extent and nature of bullying among primary and secondary schoolchildren', in *Educational Research* 41(2): 137–53.

Boulton, M. J. 1997. 'Teachers' views on bullying: definitions, attitudes and ability to cope', in *British Journal of Educational Psychology* 67(2): 223–33.

2005. 'School peer counselling for bullying services as a source of social support: a study with secondary school pupils', in *British Journal of Guidance and Counselling* 33(4): 486–94.

Boulton, M. J. and I. Flemington 1996. 'The effects of a short video intervention on secondary school pupils' involvement in definitions of and attitudes towards bullying', in *School Psychology International* 17: 331–45.

Boulton, M. J., E. Bucci and D. D. Hawker 1999. 'Swedish and English secondary school pupils' attitudes towards, and conceptions of, bullying: concurrent links with bully/victim involvement', in *Scandinavian Journal of Psychology* 40: 277–84.

Boulton, M. J., M. Trueman and I. Flemington 2002. 'Associations between secondary school pupils' definitions of bullying, attitudes towards bullying, and tendencies to engage in bullying: age and sex differences', in *Educational Studies* 23(4): 353–70.

Bourdieu, P. 1979. *Distinction*. New York: Routledge.

boyd, d.m. and N. B. Ellison 2007. 'Social network sites: definition, history, and scholarship', in *Journal of Computer-Mediated Communication* 13(1): 210–30.

Bradshaw, C. P., L. M. O'Brennan and A. L. Sawyer 2008. 'Examining variation in attitudes toward aggressive retaliation and perceptions of safety among bullies, victims, and bully/victims', in *Professional School Counseling* 12(1): 10–21.

Brennan, T. 2004. *The Transmission of Affect*. Ithaca, NY: Cornell University Press.

Brown, B. and R. Merritt 2002. *No Easy Answers: The Truth Behind Death at Columbine*. New York: Lantern Books.

Brown, V. 2009. 'Social death and political life in the study of slavery', in *American Historical Review*, December: 1231–49.

Brudholm, T. 2010. 'Hatred as an attitude', in *Philosophical Papers* 39(3): 289–313.

Bruner, J. 1990. *Acts of Meaning*. Cambridge, Mass.: Harvard University Press: chapter IV.

Bruner, J. 1994 'The "remembered" self' in U. Neisser and R. Fivush (eds.) *The Remembering Self: Construction and Accuracy in the Self-Narrative*. Cambridge University Press.

Burgess-Proctor, A., J. Patchin and S. Hinduja 2009. 'Cyberbullying and online harassment: reconceptualizing the victimization of adolescent girls', in V. Garcia and J. Clifford (eds.) *Female Crime Victims: Reality Reconsidered*. Upper Saddle River, NJ: Prentice Hall.

Burman, E. 1996. 'Deconstructing developmental psychology: a feminist approach', in *Nordiske Udkast [Nordic Draft]* 2: 3–17.

Butler, J. 1990. *Gender Trouble*. New York: Routledge Falmer.

1995. 'For a careful reading' in S. Benhabib, J. Butler, D. Cornell and N. Fraser (eds.) *Feminist Contentions: A Philosophical Exchange*. New York: Routledge: 127–43.

1999. *Gender Trouble*. New York: Routledge.

2004. *Precarious Life*. London: Verso.

2005. *Giving an Account of Oneself*. New York: Fordham University Press.

Byrne, B. J. 1994. 'Bullies and victims in a school setting with reference to some Dublin schools', in *The Irish Journal of Psychology* 15(4): 574–86.

Cairns, R. B. and B. D. Cairns 1991. 'Social cognition and social networks: a developmental perspective', in D. J. Pepler and K. H. Rubin (eds.) *The Development and Treatment of Childhood Aggression*. Hillsdale, N.J.: Lawrence Erlbaum Associates: 248–78.

California Safe Schools Coalition 2004. 'Consequences of harassment based on actual or perceived sexual orientation and gender non-conformity and steps for making schools safer'; University of California (Davis).

Callaghan, S. and S. Joseph 1995. 'Self-concept and peer victimization among school children', in *Personality and Individual Differences* 18: 161–3.

Campbell, M. 2005. 'Cyber bullying: an old problem in a new guise?', in *Australian Journal of Guidance and Counselling* 15(1): 68–76.

R. Fitzpatrick, A. Haines, A. L. Kinmonth, P. Sandercock, D. Spiegelhalter and P. Tyrer 2000. 'Framework for design and evaluation of complex interventions to improve health', in *British Medical Journal* 321(7262): 694–6.

Card, C. 2007. 'Genocide and social death', in R. M. Schott (ed.) *Feminist Philosophy and the Problem of Evil*. Bloomington: Indiana University Press.

(ed.) 1999. *On Feminist Ethics and Politics*. Lawrence: University Press of Kansas.

(ed.) 2003. *The Cambridge Companion to Simone de Beauvoir*. Cambridge and New York: Cambridge University Press.

Cartwright, N. 1995. 'Combating bullying in a secondary school in the United Kingdom', in *Journal for a Just and Caring Education* 1(3): 345–53.

Casebeer, C. M. 2012. 'School bullying: why quick fixes do not prevent school failure', in *Preventing School Failure: Alternative Education for Children and Youth* 56(3): 165–71.

Cawood Højgaard, S. 2007. 'Velkommen til pussyland: unge positionerer sig i et seksualiseret medielandskab' [Welcome to pussyland: youth positions in a sexualised media landscape]. Ph.D. thesis, Department of Learning and Education, Aarhus University, Denmark.

Chambers, D., E. Tincknell and J. van Loon 2004. 'Peer regulation of teenage sexual identities', in *Gender and Education* 16(3): 397.

Chambers, D., J. van Loon and E. Tincknell 2004. 'Teachers' views of teenage sexual morality', in *British Journal of Sociology of Education* 25(5): 563–76.

Chan, Y. M. 1997. 'Educational experiences of Chinese pupils in Manchester', in *Multicultural Teaching* 15(3): 37–42.

Chase, S. 1995. 'Taking narrative seriously: consequences for method and theory in interview studies', in Y. S. Lincoln and N. K. Denzin (eds.) *Turning Points in Qualitative Research: Tying Knots in a Handkerchief*. New York: Alta Mira Press: 273–96.

Chorpita, B. F., K. D. Becker and E. L. Daleiden 2007. 'Understanding the common elements of evidence-based practice: misconceptions and clinical examples', in *Journal of the American Academy of Child and Adolescent Psychiatry* 46(5): 647–52.

Clarke, A. E. 2005. *Situational Analysis: Grounded Theory after the Postmodern Turn.* London: Sage Publications.

Clough, P. 2007. *The Affective Turn: Theorizing the Social.* Durham, NC and London: Duke University Press.

Coggan, C., S. Bennett, R. Hooper and P. Dickinson 2003. 'Association between bullying and mental health status in New Zealand adolescents', in *International Journal of Mental Health Promotion* 5(1): 16–22.

Collins, R. 2008. *Violence: A Micro-Sociological Theory.* Princeton University Press.

Colman, F. J. 2005. 'Affect', in A. Parr (ed.) *The Deleuze Dictionary.* Edinburgh University Press: 11–13.

Cook, C. R., K. R. Williams, N. G. Guerra, T. E. Kim and S. Sadek 2010. 'Predictors of bullying and victimization in childhood and adolescence: a meta-analytic investigation', in *School Psychology Quarterly* 25(2): 65–83.

Corbett, K., C. A. Gentry and W. J. Pearson 1993. 'Sexual harassment in high school', in *Youth & Society* 25(1): 93–103.

Cowie, H. 1998. 'Perspectives of teachers and pupils on the experience of peer support against bullying', in *Educational Research and Evaluation* 4(2): 108–25.

Crenshaw, K. 1994. 'Mapping the margins: intersectionality, identity politics, and violence against women of color', in M. A. Fineman and R. Mykitiuk (eds.) *The Public Nature of Private Violence.* New York: Routledge: 93–118.

Crick, N. R. and G. W. Ladd 1993. 'Children's perceptions of their peer experiences: attributions, loneliness, social anxiety, and social avoidance', in *Developmental Psychology* 29(2): 244–54.

Cross, D., M. Hall, E. Erceg, Y. Pintabona, G. Hamilton and C. Roberts 2003. 'The Friendly Schools Project: an empirically grounded school bullying prevention program', in *Australian Journal of Guidance and Counselling* 13(1): 36–46.

Cross, D., M. Hall, G. Hamilton, Y. Pintabona and E. Erceg 2004. 'Australia: the Friendly Schools Project', in P. K. Smith, D. Pepler and K. Rigby (eds.) *Bullying in Schools: How Successful Can Interventions Be?* New York: Cambridge University Press: 187–210.

Cross, D., T. Shaw, N. Pearce, E. Erceg, S. Waters, Y. Pintabona and M. Hall 2008. 'School-based intervention research to reduce bullying in Australia 1999–2007: what works, what doesn't, and what's promising?', in D. Peplar and W. Craig (eds.) *Understanding and Addressing Bullying: An International Perspective.* PREVNet Series, vol. I. Bloomington, Ind.: Authorhouse.

Cross, D., T. Shaw, L. Hearn, M. Epstein, H. Monks, L. Lester and L. Thomas 2009. *Australian covert bullying prevalence study* (ACBPS). Retrieved from www. deewr.gov.au/Schooling/NationalSafeSchools/Pages/research.aspx

Cross, D., D. Brown, M. Epstein and T. Shaw 2010. 'Final report to the Public Education Endowment Trust (PEET): strengthening school and families' capacity to reduce the academic, social and emotional harms secondary students experience from cyber bullying', in *Cyber Friendly Schools Project (PEET)*: Child Health Promotion Research Centre, Edith Cowan University, Perth, Australia.

Cross, D., Q. Li, P. K. Smith and H. Monks 2012. 'Understanding and preventing cyberbullying: where have we been and where should we be going?', in Q. Li, D. Cross and P. K. Smith (eds.) *Cyberbullying in the Global Playground: Research from International Perspectives.* Chichester, West Sussex, UK: Wiley-Blackwell: 287–305.

Cullen, D. 2009. *Columbine.* London: Old Street Publishing.

Currie, C., S. N. Gabhainn, E. Godeau, C. Roberts, R. Smith, D. Currie, W. Picket, M. Richter, A. Morgan and V. Barnekow (eds.) 2008. 'Inequalities in young people's health: health behaviour in school-aged children. International report from the 2005/2006 survey', in *Health Policy for Children and Adolescents* No. 5; WHO Regional Office for Europe: Copenhagen.

Currie, C., S. N. Gabhainn, T. Torsheim, R. Välimaa, M. Danielson, E. Godeau and G. Rahav (eds.) 2004. 'Young people's health in context: international report from the HBSC 2001/02 survey', in *Health Policy for Children and Adolescents* No. 4; WHO Regional Office for Europe: Copenhagen.

D'Augelli, A. R., N. W. Pilkington and S. L. Hershberger 2002. 'Incidence and mental health impact of sexual orientation victimization of lesbian, gay, and bisexual youths in high school', in *School Psychology Quarterly* 17(2): 148–67.

Daiute, C. and M. Fine 2003. 'Youth perspectives on violence and injustice', in *Journal of Social Issues* 59(1): 1–14.

Daiute, C., Z. Beykont, C. Higson-Smith, L. Nucci (eds.) 2006. *International Perspectives on Youth Conflict and Development.* New York and Oxford: Oxford University Press.

Danish Ministry of Children and Education / Undervisningsministeriet 2000/1. 'Bemærkn. til lovforslag 2000/1 LSF 40; forslag til lov om elevers ogstuderendes undervisningsmiljø' [Note to legislation 2000/1 LSF 40;proposal to law on students' teaching environment]; www.retsinformation.dk/Forms/R0710.aspx?id=90951 (last accessed 20 May 2009).

2001. 'Lovnr. 166 af 14/03/2001 Gældende; lov om elever og studerendes undervisningsmiljø' [Law nr. 166 of 14/03/2001 Applicable: lawon students' teaching environment]; retsinformation.w0.dk/Forms/R0710.aspx?id=23705 (last accessed 20 May 2009).

2007. 'Antimobbeforløb på Krogårdsskolen' [Anti-bullying process at the Krogård school]; http://www.uvm.dk/Uddannelse/Tvaergaaende%20omraader/Temaer/Mobning/Mobning/Udd/Folke/2007/Jan/070111%20Antimobbeforloeb.aspx (last accessed 20 May 2009).

2008. 'Fakta fra skolelederundersøgelsen' [Facts from the survey of school principals]; www.sammenmodmobning.dk/neobuilder.200804071518183 5000043069.htm (last accessed 20 May 2009).

Davies, B. 1982. *Life in the Classroom and Playground: The Accounts of Primary School Children.* London: Routledge and Kegan Paul.

1989/2003. *Frogs and Snails and Feminist Tales: Preschool Children and Gender.* Sydney: Allen and Unwin.

1996. *Power/Knowledge/Desire. Changing School Organisation and Management Practices*. Canberra: Department of Employment, Education and Youth Affairs.

2000. *A Body of Writing 1990–1999*. New York: Alta Mira Press.

2004. 'Identity, abjection and otherness: creating the self, creating difference', in *International Journal for Equity and Innovation in Early Childhood* 2(1): 58–80.

2008. 'Re-thinking "behaviour" in terms of positioning and the ethics of responsibility', in A. M. Phelan and J. Sumsion (eds.) *Critical Readings in Teacher Education: Provoking Absences*. The Netherlands: Sense Publishers: 173–86.

2011. 'Bullies as guardians of the moral order or an ethic of truths?', in *Children and Society* 25: 278–86.

Davies, B. and S. Gannon 2009. *Pedagogical Encounters*. New York: Peter Lang.

Davies, B. and R. Harré 1990. 'Positioning: the discursive production of selves', in *Journal for the Theory of Social Behaviour* 20: 43–63.

Davies, B. and R. Hunt 1994. 'Classroom competencies and marginal positionings', in *British Journal of Sociology of Education* 15(2): 389–408.

Davies, B., S. Gannon, C. Laws and J. Edwards 2007. 'Neoliberal subjectivities and the limits of social change in university–community partnerships Asia-Pacific', in *Journal of Teacher Education* 35(1): 27–39.

de Beauvoir, S. 1949/1974. *The Second Sex*, translated by H. M. Parshley. New York: Vintage Books.

2007. *L'existentialisme et la Sagesse des Nations [Existentialism and the Wisdom of Nations]*. Paris: Gallimard.

Deleuze, G. 1886/2004. *Foucault*. Frederiksberg, Denmark: Det Lille Forlag.

1980. 'Cours Vincennes 12/21/1980'; www.webdeleuze.com/php/texte.php?cle=190andgroupe=Spinozaandlangue=2 (last accessed 10 February 2010).

1990/2006. *Forhandlinger: 1972–1990 [Negotiations: 1972–1990]*. Frederiksberg, Denmark: Det Lille Forlag.

1995. *Negotiations 1972–1990*, translated by M. Joughin. New York: Columbia University Press.

2001. *Two Regimes of Madness: Texts and Interviews 1975–1995*. Paris: Semiotext(e).

and F. Guattari 1980/2005. 'Tusind plateuaer' [Thousand plateaus], in *Kapitalisme og Skizofreni [Capitalism and Schizophrenia]*. Copenhagen: Det Kongelige Danske Kunstakademis Billedkunstskoler.

Devine, J. and H. A. Lawson 2003. 'The complexity of school violence: commentary from the US', in P. K. Smith (ed.). *Violence in Schools: The Response in Europe*. London: Routledge Falmer.

Diken, B. and C. Bagge Laustsen 2005a. 'Becoming abject: rape as a weapon of war', in *Body & Society* 11(1): 111–28.

2005b. *The Culture of Exception: Sociology Facing the Camp*. London: Routledge.

Douglas, M. 1966. *Purity and Danger: An Analysis of the Concepts of Pollution and Taboo*. London, New York and Boston: Routledge & Kegan Paul.

Dreier, O. 1999. 'Personal trajectories of participation across contexts of social practice', in *Outlines: Critical Social Studies* 1: 5–32.

2008. *Psychotherapy in Everyday Life: Learning in Doing; Social, Cognitive and Computational Perspectives*. New York: Cambridge University Press.

Dreyfus, H. L. and P. Rabinow 1982. *Michel Foucault: Beyond Structuralism and Hermeneutics*. University of Chicago Press.

Due, P., M. T. Damsgaard, R. Lund and B. E. Holstein 2009. 'Is bullying equally harmful for rich and poor children? A study of bullying and depression from age 15 to 27', in *European Journal of Public Health* 19(5): 464–9.

Due P., B. E. Holstein and P. S. Jørgensen 1999. 'Mobning som sundhedstrussel blandt store skoleelever' [Bullying as a health threat amongst large schoolchildren], in *Ugeskrift for Læger* [*Weekly Newsletter for Physicians*] 161: 2201–6.

Due, P. and B. E. Holstein 2003. *Skolebørnsundersøgelsen 2002* [*Schoolchildren Survey 2002*]; Department of Public Health, University of Copenhagen.

Due, P., B. E. Holstein, J. Lynch, F. Didrichsen, N. G. Saoirse, P. Scheidt, C. Currie and the Health Behaviour in School-Aged Children Bullying Working Group 2005. 'Bullying and symptoms among school-aged children: international comparative cross sectional study in 28 countries', in *European Journal of Public Health* 15(2): 128–32.

Due, P. and M. Rasmussen 2007. *Skolebørnsundersøgelsen 2006* [*Schoolchildren Survey 2006*]; Department of Public Health, University of Copenhagen.

and 2011. *Skolebørnsundersøgelsen 2010* [*Schoolchildren Survey 2010*]; National Institute of Public Health, Southern Denmark University.

Duncan, R. D. 1999a. 'Maltreatment by parents and peers: the relationship between child abuse, bully victimization, and psychological distress', in *Child Maltreatment* 4: 45–55.

1999b. 'Peer and sibling aggression: an investigation of intra- and extra-familial bullying', in *Journal of Interpersonal Violence* 14: 871–86.

Duncan, N. 1999c. *Sexual Bullying: Gender Conflict and Pupil Culture in Secondary Schools*. London and New York: Routledge.

2004. 'It's important to be nice, but it's nicer to be important: girls, popularity and sexual competition', in *Sex Education* 4(2): 137–52.

Dunn, J. 2004. *Children's Friendships: The Beginnings of Intimacy*. Oxford: Blackwell Publishers.

Durlak, J. and E. DuPre 2008. 'Implementation matters: a review of research on the influence of implementation on program outcomes and the factors affecting implementation', in *American Journal of Community Psychology* 41(3): 327–50.

Eccles, M., J. Grimshaw, A. Walker, M. Johnston and N. Pitts 2005. 'Changing the behavior of healthcare professionals: the use of theory in promoting the uptake of research findings', in *Journal of Clinical Epidemiology* 58(2): 107–12.

Elliott, M. 2001. *Kidscape Primary Child Protection Programme: Good Sense Defence*. London: Kidscape.

Ellwood, C. 2007. 'Transformations: report of a pilot study into transformative strategies in schooling'; Centre for Educational Research, University of Western Sydney.

and B. Davies 2010. 'Violence and the moral order in contemporary schooling: a discursive analysis', in *Qualitative Research in Psychology* 7: 85–98.

Englander, E. 2007. 'Is bullying a junior hate crime? Implications for interventions', in *American Behavioral Scientist* 51: 205–12.

Eriksson, B., O. Lindberg, E. Flygare and K. Daneback 2002. *Skolan – en Arena för Mobbning [The School – an Arena for Bullying]*. Stockholm: Skolverket: 98.

Espelage, D. L. and S. Swearer 2003. 'Research on school bullying and victimization: what have we learned and where do we go from here?', in *School Psychology Review* 32(3): 365–83.

and (eds.) 2004. *Bullying in American Schools: A Social–Ecological Perspective on Prevention and Intervention*. Mahwah, NJ: Lawrence Erlbaum Associates/ Routledge.

Espelage, D. L. and M. K. Holt 2007. 'Dating violence and sexual harassment across the bully–victim continuum among middle and high school students' in *Journal of Youth and Adolescence* 36(6): 799–811.

Espelage, D. L., S. R. Aragon, M. Birkett and B. W. Koenig 2008. 'Homophobic teasing, psychological outcomes, and sexual orientation among high school students: what influence do parents and schools have?', in *School Psychology Review* 37(2): 202–16.

Faircloth, B. S. and J. V. Hamm 2011. 'The dynamic reality of adolescent peer networks and sense of belonging', in *Merrill-Palmer Quarterly* 57(1): 48–72.

Farrington, D. P. 1993. 'Understanding and preventing bullying', in M. Tonry (ed.) *Crime and Justice*, vol. 17. University of Chicago Press: 381–458.

and M. M. Ttofi 2009. 'School-based programs to reduce bullying and victimization', in *Campbell Systematic Reviews 2009*: 6. Open-access article: www. campbellcollaboration.org.

Faulkner, A. O. and A. Lindsey 2004. 'Grassroots meet homophobia: a Rocky Mountain success story', in *Journal of Gay and Lesbian Social Services: Issues in Practice, Policy, & Research* 16 (3–4).

Fein, H. 1979. *Accounting for Genocide*. New York: Free Press.

Ferfolja, T. 1998. 'Australian lesbian teachers – a reflection of homophobic harassment of high school teachers in New South Wales government schools', in *Gender and Education* 10(4): 401–15.

Fineran, S. 2002. 'Sexual harassment between same-sex peers: intersection of mental health, homophobia, and sexual violence in schools', in *Social Work* 47(1): 65–74.

Fixsen, D. L. and K. A. Blase 2009. 'Implementation: the missing link between research and practice', in *NIRN Implementation Brief No. 1*; Frank Porter Graham Child Development Institute, National Implementation Research Network, University of North Carolina (Chapel Hill).

Fixsen, D. L., S. F. Naoom, K. A. Blase, R. M. Friedman and F. Wallace 2005. 'Implementation research: a synthesis of the literature'; Louis de la Parte Florida Mental Health Institute, National Implementation Research Network; University of South Florida (Tampa).

Fog, J. 2004. *Med Samtalen som Udgangspunk [With the Conversation as a Starting Point]*. Copenhagen: Akademisk Forlag.

Fors, Z. 1995. *Makt, Maktlöshet och Mobbning [Power, Powerlessness and Bullying]*. Stockholm: Liber.

Foucault, M. 1977. *Discipline and Punish: The Birth of the Prison*. London: Penguin.

1978. *The History of Sexuality: Vol. I*, translated by R. Hurley. New York: Pantheon: 94; cited in Horton, P. 2011. 'School bullying and social and moral orders', in *Children and Society* 25: 268–77.

1980. 'The confession of the flesh', in *Power/Knowledge: Selected Interviews and Other Writings*. New York: Harvester Wheatsheaf.

1985. *The Use of Pleasure: The History of Sexuality: Vol. II*. New York: Random House.

2000a. 'Interview with Michel Foucault', in J. D. Faubion (ed.) *Michel Foucault: Power. Essential Works of Foucault 1954–1984, Vol. III*. New York: The New Press: 239–97.

2000b. 'So is it important to think?', in Faubion (ed.) *Michel Foucault: Power. Essential Works of Foucault 1954–1984, Vol. III*. New York: The New Press: 454–8.

2000c. 'Truth and juridical forms', in Faubion (ed.) *Michel Foucault: Power. Essential Works of Foucault 1954–1984, Vol. III*. New York: The New Press: 1–89.

2001. 'Socialmedicinens fødsel' *[The birth of social medicine]*, in *Distinktion* 3: 11–24.

2007. *Security, Territory, Population: Lectures at the Collège de France*. Houndsmills, UK: Palgrave-Macmillan.

2008. *Overvågning og Straf: Fængslets Fødsel [Discipline and Punish: The Birth of the Prison]*. Frederiksberg, Denmark: Det Lille Forlag.

Frosh, S., A. Phoenix and R. Pattman 2002. *Young Masculinities: Understanding Boys in Contemporary Society*. New York: Palgrave Macmillan.

Frønes, I. 1998. *De Likeverdige [On Equal Terms]*. Oslo: Universitetsforlaget.

1999. 'Kameraterne og moderniteten' [Pals and modernity], in L. Dencik and P. S. Jørgensen (eds.) *Børn og Familie i det Postmoderne Samfunnet [Children and Families in Post-modern Society]*. Copenhagen: Hans Reitzel Publishers: 273–87.

Fuglsang, M. S. and M. Sørensen (eds.) 2006. *Deleuze and the Social*. Edinburgh University Press.

Galloway, D. and E. Roland, 2004. 'Is the direct approach to reducing bullying always the best?', in P. K. Smith, D. Pepler and K. Rigby (eds.) *Bullying in Schools: How Successful Can Interventions Be?* Cambridge University Press: 37–53.

Gay, Lesbian and Straight Education Network (GLSEN) 1999. *National School Climate Survey*. New York: GLSEN.

2001. *National School Climate Survey: Lesbian, Gay, Bisexual and Transgender Youth and Their Experiences in Schools*. New York: GLSEN.

and Harris Interactive 2005. *From Teasing to Torment: School Climate in America, a Survey of Students and Teachers*. New York: GLSEN.

Gearing, R. E., N. El-Bassel, A. Ghesquiere, S. Baldwin, J. Gillies and E. Ngeow 2011. 'Major ingredients of fidelity: a review and scientific guide to improving quality of intervention research implementation', in *Clinical Psychology Review* 31(1): 79–88.

Gilliam, L. 2009. *De Umulige Børn og det Ordentlige Menneske: Identitet, Ballade og Muslimske Fællesskaber blandt Etniske Minoritetsbørn [The Impossible Children and the Decent Man: Identity, Trouble and Muslim Communities amongst Ethnic-Minority Children]*. Århus Universitetsforlag.

Girard, R. 1979. *Violence and the Sacred*. Baltimore, Md.: Johns Hopkins University Press.

1986. *The Scapegoat*. Baltimore, Md.: Johns Hopkins University Press.

Glasgow, R. E., L. W. Green, L. M. Klesges, D. B. Abrams, E. B. Fisher, M. G. Goldstein, L. L. Hayman, J. K. Ockene and C. Tracy Orleans 2006. 'External validity: we need to do more', in *Annals of Behavioral Medicine* 31(2): 105–8.

Glew, G., M. Fan, W. Katon, F. Rivara and M. Kernic 2005. 'Bullying, psycho-social adjustment and academic performance in elementary school', in *Archives of Pediatric and Adolescent Medicine* 159(11): 1026–31.

Golding, W. 1958. *Lord of the Flies*. London: Faber and Faber.

Gould League 2010. *Schoolgrounds for living and learning – 2005 case studies*. Retrieved from www.gould.org.au/html/documents/2005CaseStudies_000.pdf

Gregg, M. and G. J. Seigworth 2010. *The Affect Theory Reader*. Durham, NC: Duke University Press.

Greytak, E., J. Kosciw and E. Diaz 2009. *Harsh Realities: The Experiences of Transgender Youth in Our Nation's Schools*. New York: GLSEN.

Greytak, E. and J. Kosciw 2010. *Year One Evaluation of the New York City Department of Education Respect for All Training Program*. New York: GLSEN.

Gruber, J. E. and S. Fineran 2007. 'The impact of bullying and sexual harass-ment on middle and high school girls', in *Violence Against Women* 13(6): 627–43.

2008. 'Comparing the impact of bullying and sexual harassment victimization on the mental and physical health of adolescents', in *Sex Roles* 59, 1–13.

Gubrium, J. F. and J. A. Holstein 2003. 'Postmodern sensibilities', in J. F. Gubrium and J. A. Holstein (eds.) *Postmodern Interviewing*. London: SAGE Publications Ltd: 3–18.

Guerin, S. and E. Hennessy 2002. 'Pupils' definitions of bullying', in *European Journal of Psychology of Education* 17(3): 249–61.

Gulbrandsen, L. M. 1998. *I Barns Dagligliv: en Kulturpsykologisk Studie av Jenter og Gutters Utvikling [In Children's Everyday Lives: A Cultural–Psychological Study of Boys' and Girls' Development]*. Oslo: Universitetsforlaget.

2002. 'Storbyjenter' [Girls in the big city], in K. Thorsen and R. Toverud (eds.) *Kulturpsykologi: Bevegelser i Livsløp [Cultural Psychology: Life Course Transformations]*. Oslo: Universitetsforlaget: 103–27.

2008. 'Utforskende samtaler med unge mennesker og foreldrene deres' [Exploring conversations between young people and their parents], in B. P. Bøe and B. R. Olsen (eds.) *Utfordrende Foreldreskap [Challenges in Parenting]*. Oslo: Gyldendal Akademisk: 243–67.

2003. 'Peer relations as arenas for gender constructions among young teen-agers', in *Pedagogy, Culture and Society* 11(1): 113–32.

2006. 'Fra småjenter til ungjenter: heteroseksualitet som normativ utviklings-retning' [From little girls to teenage girls: heterosexuality as a normative directive for development], in *Tidsskrift for Kjønnsforskning [Journal for Gender Research]* 30(4): 5–20.

Haavind, H. 1987. *Liten og Stor: Mødres Omsorg og Barns Utviklingsmuligheter [The Big One and the Little One: Maternal Care and Children's Developmental Possibilities]*. Oslo: Universitetsforlaget.

2000. 'Den lille og den store utviklingen i psykoterapi med barn' [The small and the large development in psychotherapy with children], in A. Holte, M. H. Rønnestad and G. H. Nielsen (eds.) *Psykoterapi og Psykoterapiveiledning [Psychotherapy and Psychotherapy Supervison]*. Oslo: Gyldendal Akademisk: 112–45.

2007a. 'Accountability in persons: what is in the telling to others about yourself?', in J. Kofoed and D. Staunæs (eds.) *Magtballader: 14 Fortællinger om Magt, Modstand og Menneskers Tilblivelse Power Troubles: 14 Narratives of Power, Resistance and Human Becoming]*. Copenhagen: Danmarks Pædagogiske Universitetsforlag: 159–78.

2007b. 'Involvering og representasjon i den utviklingsrettede samtalen' [Involvement and representation in conversations directed at developmental changes], in H. Haavind and H. Øvreeide (eds.) *Barn og Unge i Psykoterapi, Bind II: Terapeutiske Fremgangsmåter og Forandring [Children and Youth in Psychotherapy, Vol. II: Therapeutic Approaches and Change]*. Oslo: Gyldendal Akademisk: 21–45.

2003. 'Masculinity by rule-breaking: cultural contestations in the transitional move from being a child to being a young male', in *NORA, Nordic Journal of Women's Studies* 11(21): 89–100.

2005. 'Towards a multifaceted understanding of children as social participants', in *Childhood* 11(1): 139–53.

2006. 'Den nye Norah' [The new Norah], in *Samtiden Tidsskrift for Politikk, Litteratur og Samfunnsspørsmål [The Contemporary Journal of Politics, Literature and Social Issues]* 115(4): 52–64.

2011. 'Livsformsintervju med barneklienter' [Lifemode interviews with child clients], in M. H. Rønnestad and A. von der Lippe (eds.) *Det Kliniske Intervjuet, Bind II: Møte med Barn, Ungdom og Eldre [The Clinical Interview, Vol II: Encountering Children, Youths and the Elderly]*. Oslo: Gyldendal Akademisk: 133–50.

Hanish, L. D., P. Ryan, C. L. Martin and R. A. Fabes 2005. 'The social context of young children's peer victimization', in *Social Development* 14(1): 2–19.

Hansen, H. R. 2005. *Grundbog mod Mobning [Textbook against Bullying]*. Copenhagen: Gyldendals Lærerbibliotek.

2009. 'Straf mod mobning og skoleuro' [Punishment against bullying and disruptions at school], in J. Kofoed and D. M. Søndergaard (eds.) *Mobning: Sociale Processer på Afveje [Bullying: Social Processes Gone Awry]*. Copenhagen: Hans Reitzel Publishers: 133–66.

2011a. 'Lærerliv og elevmobning' [Teachers' life and bullying amongst students]. Ph.D. thesis, Department of Learning and Education, Aarhus University, Denmark.

2011b. '(Be)longing: mobning forstået som længsel efter at høre til' [(Be)longing: bullying understood as a longing to belong], in *Psyke and Logos [Psyche and Logos]* 2(32): 480–95.

and I. Henningsen 2010. 'Lærerforståelser om elevmobning: en lærersurvey' [Teacher understandings of student bullying: a teacher survey], in *Pædagogisk Psykologisk Tidsskrift [Journal of Educational Psychology]* 47(1): 3–21.

Hansen, R. H., I. Henningsen and J. Kofoed 2013 (forthcoming). *Pædagogisk Psykologisk Tidsskrift [Journal of Educational Psychology]*. Copenhagen: Psykologisk Forlag.

Haraway, D. 1991. *Simians, Cyborgs, and Women: The Reinvention of Nature.* London: Free Association Books.

  1992. 'The promises of monsters: a regenerative politics for inappropriate/d others', in L. Grossberg, C. Nelson and P. A. Treichler (eds.) *Cultural Studies.* New York: Routledge: 295–337.

Harris and Associates 1993. *Hostile Hallways: The AAUW Survey on Sexual Harassment in America's Schools.* Washington DC: American Association of University Women.

Harris Interactive 2001. *Hostile Hallways: Bullying, Teasing, and Sexual Harassment in School.* Washington DC: American Association of University Women Educational Foundation.

Hastrup, K. 1992. *Det Antropologiske Projekt: om Forbløffelse [The Anthropological Project: on Amazement].* Copenhagen: Gyldendal Press.

Hauge, M.-I. 2009. 'Bodily practices and discourses of hetero-femininity: girls' constitution of subjectivities in their social transition between childhood and adolescence', in *Gender and Education* 21(3): 293–307.

  and H. Haavind 2011. 'Boys' bodies and the constitution of adolescent masculinities', in *Sport, Education and Society* 16(1): 1–17.

Hawker, D. S. J. and M. Boulton 2000. 'Twenty years' research on peer victimization and psychosocial maladjustment: a meta-analytic review of cross-sectional studies', in *Journal of Child Psychology and Psychiatry* 41(4): 441–55.

Hazler, R. J., J. J. Hoover and R. Oliver 1991. 'Student perception of victimization by bullies in school', in *Journal of Humanistic Education and Development* 29: 143–50.

Hedegaard, M. and M. Fleer 2008. *Studying Children: A Cultural – and Historical – Approach.* Glasgow: Open University Press.

Hegel, G. W. F. 1808/1991. 'Hvem tænker abstrakt?' [Who thinks abstractly?], in G. W. F. Hegel, *De Store Tænkere [The Big Thinkers].* Copenhagen: Munksgaard: 66–71.

Heinemann, P.-P. 1972. *Mobbning: gruppvåld bland barn och vuxna [Bullying: Group violence amongst children and adults].* Stockholm: Natur och Kunst.

Heintz, M. 2004. 'Mobbning: ett groupthink-fenomen? En gruppsykologisk fördjupning av mobbning' [Bullying: a groupthink phenomenon? A group-psychological deepening of bullying]. Master's thesis, School of Social Work, Lund University, Sweden.

Helm, B. 2009. 'Friendship', in *Stanford Encyclopedia of Philosophy*; plato.stanford. edu/entries/friendship (last accessed 2 February 2011).

Hemphill, S. A., J. W. Toumbourou and R. Catalano 2005. *Predictors of Violence, Anti-social Behaviour and Relational Aggression in Australian Adolescents: A Longitudinal Study.* Melbourne, Australia: Centre for Adolescent Health.

Henningsen, I. 2009. 'Sammenhænge mellem mobning, barndomserfaringer og senere livskvalitet' [Correlation between bullying, childhood experiences and later life quality], in J. Kofoed and D. M. Søndergaard (eds.) *Mobning: Sociale Processer på Afveje [Bullying: Social Processes Gone Awry]*. Copenhagen: Hans Reitzel Publishers: 191–225.

2011. 'Resultater fra Vestegnsundersøgelsen 2009–10' [Results from the Vestegn survey 2009–10]; eXbus working paper: www.exbus.dk.

H. R. Hansen and D. M. Søndergaard 2010. 'Hvad måler Campbell Collaboration? En kritisk kommentar til rapporten: 'School-Based Programs to Reduce Bullying and Victimization'' [What does the Campbell Collaboration measure? A critical commentary on the report: 'School-Based Programs to Reduce Bullying and Victimization']; open-access paper: www. exbus.dk

Henriksen, K. and H. R. Hansen 2006. 'Skolernes handleplaner mod mobning er ikke gode nok' [The schools' action plans against bullying are not good enough]; www.amoktrix.dk/front.htm (last accessed 20 May 2009).

Hepburn, A. 1997a. 'Discursive strategies in bullying talk', in *Education and Society* 15(1): 13–31.

1997b. 'Teachers and secondary school bullying: a postmodern discourse analysis', in *Discourse & Society* 8(1): 27–48.

2000. 'Power lines: Derrida, discursive psychology and the managment of accusations of teacher bullying', in *British Journal of Social Psychology* 39(4): 605–28.

Hinduja, S. and J. W. Patchin 2008. 'Cyberbullying: an exploratory analysis of factors related to offending and victimization', in *Deviant Behavior* 29: 129–56.

2009. *Bullying Beyond the Schoolyard: Preventing and Responding to Cyberbullying*. Thousand Oaks, Calif.: Corwin Press.

Hodges, E. V., M. E. Boivin, F. Vitaro and W. M. Bukowski 1999. 'The power of friendship: protection against an escalating cycle of peer victimization', in *Developmental Psychology* 35(1): 94–101.

Höistad, G. 1999. *Mobning: Forebyggelse og Løsninger [Bullying: Prevention and Solutions]*. Værløse, Denmark: Billesø & Baltzer.

Holzkamp, K. 2005. 'Mennesket som subjekt for videnskabelig metodik' [The human as a subject of scientific method], in *Nordiske Udkast [Nordic Draft]* 33 (2): 5–33.

Hoover, J. H. and K. Juul 1993. 'Bullying in Europe and the United States', in *Journal of Emotional and Behavioral Problems* 2(1): 25–9.

Horsdal, M. 1999/2005. *Livets Fortællinger: en Bog om Livshistorier og Identitet [Life Narratives: a Book about Life Stories and Identity]*. Copenhagen: Borgens Forlag.

Horton P. 2011. 'School bullying and social and moral orders', in *Children and Society* 25: 268–77.

Howard, J. P. 2001. 'School board liability for student–peer harassment and discrimination: 'deliberate indifference' and beyond?', in *Education Canada* 42(1): 32–3.

Hughes, T. 1857. *Tom Brown's Schooldays*. London: Macmillan.

Hunt, L. 2007. *Inventing Human Rights: A History.* New York: W. W. Norton & Co.

Højgaard, L. and D. M. Søndergaard 2011. 'Theorizing the complexities of discursive and material subjectivity: agential realism and poststructural analyses', in *Theory & Psychology* 21(3): 338–54.

Højgaard, L., M. Juelskjær and D. M. Søndergaard 2012. 'The 'WHAT OF' and the 'WHAT IF' of agential realism: in search of the gendered subject', in *Kvinder, Køn og Forskning [Women, Gender and Research]* (21)1: 67–80.

Højholt, C. (ed.) 1996/2005. *Forældresamarbejde: Forskning i Fællesskab [Parental Cooperation: Research in Collaboration].* Copenhagen: Dansk Psykologisk Forlag.

Indiana Department of Education 2003. 'White paper on bullying prevention and education'; www.doe.state.in.us/legwatch/docs/Bullyingpaper2004session.doc (last accessed 22 June 2007).

Irving, B. A. and M. Parker-Jenkins 1995. 'Tackling truancy: an examination of persistent non-attendance amongst disaffected school pupils and positive support strategies', in *Cambridge Journal of Education* 25(2): 225–35.

Jablonska, B. and L. Lindberg 2007. 'Risk behavior, victimization and mental distress among adolescents in different family structures', in *Social Psychiatry and Psychiatric Epidemiology* 42: 656–63.

Jacobson, R. 2010. 'Narrating characters: the making of a school bully', in *Interchange* 41(3): 255–83.

Jensen, T. B. 2006. 'Praksisportrættet: om at indsamle og anvende skriftlige kvalitative data i en forskningsproces' [The portrait of practice: about collecting and applying written qualitative data in a research process], in T.B. Jensen and G. Christensen (eds.) *Psykologiske og Pædagogiske Metoder: Kvalitative og Kvantitative Forskningsmetoder i Praksis [Psychological and Pedagogic Methods: Qualitative and Quantitative Research Methods in Practice].* Roskilde Universitetsforlag: Frederiksberg, Denmark: 95–122.

Jensen, T. K. 2002. 'Mistanke om seksuelle overgrep: foreldres fortolkning som kulturell praksis' [Suspicion of sexual abuse: parents' interpretation as cultural practice', in K. Thorsen and R. Toverud (eds.) *Kulturpsykologi: Bevegelser i Livsløp [Cultural Psychology: Movements in the Life Cycle].* Oslo: Universitetsforlaget: 76–102.

Jimerson, S. R., S. M. Swearer and D. L. Espelage (eds.) 2009. *Handbook of Bullying in Schools: An International Perspective.* New York and Oxon, UK: Routledge.

Juelskjær, M. 2009. 'En ny start: en undersøgelse af bevægelser og relationer i/ gennem tid, rum, krop, sociale kategorier via begivenheden skoleskift' [A new start: an investigation of movements and relations in/through time, space, bodies and social categories via the event of changing schools]. Ph.D. thesis, Department of Learning and Education, Aarhus University, Denmark.

Junger-Tas, J. 1996. 'Youth and violence in Europe', in *Studies on Crime and Crime Prevention* 5(1): 31–58.

Kärnä, A., M. Voeten, T. D. Little, E. Poskiparta, A. Kaljonen and C. Salmivalli 2011a. 'A large-scale evaluation of the KiVa antibullying program: grades 4–6', in *Child Development* 82(1): 311–30.

2011b. 'Going to scale: a nonrandomized nationwide trial of the KiVa antibullying program for grades 1–9', in *Journal of Consulting and Clinical Psychology* 79(6): 796–805.

Khawaja, I. 2010. 'To belong everywhere and nowhere: tales of Muslimhood, collectivity and belonging'. Ph.D. thesis, Roskilde Universitetscenter, Denmark.

Klein, J. 2006. 'Cultural capital and high school bullies: how social inequality impacts school violence', in *Men and Masculinities* 9(1): 53–75.

Knudsen, H. 2008a. 'Forældreledelse [Parent leadership]: Let's be careful out there!', in C. Sløk and K. Villadsen (eds.) *Velfærdsledelse [Welfare Leadership]*. Copenhagen: Hans Reitzel Publishers: 69–97.

2008b. 'Har vi en aftale? (U)mulighedsbetingelser for mødet mellem folkeskole og familie' [Do we have an agreement? (Im)possible conditions for the meeting between public school and family]. Ph.D. thesis, Department of Learning and Education, Aarhus University, Denmark.

2010. *Har Vi en Aftale? (U)mulighedsbetingelser for Mødet mellem Folkeskole og Familie [Do We Have an Agreement? (Im)possible Conditions for the Meeting between Public School and Family]*. Copenhagen: Nyt fra Samfundsvidenskaberne.

Kofoed, J. 2004. 'Elevpli: inklusion-eksklusionsprocesser blandt børn i skolen' [Concerning pupils: processes of exclusion and inclusion amongst children at school]. Ph.D. thesis, Department of Educational Psychology, Aarhus University, Denmark.

2008a. 'Appropriate pupilness: social categories intersecting in school', in *Childhood* 15(3): 415–30.

2008b. 'Muted transitions', in *European Journal of Psychology of Education* 23(2): 199–212.

2009. 'Genkendelse af digital mobning [Recognising digital bullying]: Freja vs. Ronja vs. Arto vs. Sara vs. Emma', in J. Kofoed and D. M. Søndergaard (eds.) *Mobning: Sociale Processer på Afveje [Bullying: Social Processes Gone Awry]*. Copenhagen: Hans Reitzel Publishers: 99–132.

2010. 'Et liv med teknologier, VERA' [A life with technologies, VERA], in *Tidsskrift for Pædagoger [Journal for Pedagogues]* 51: 12–18.

Kofoed, J. and J. Ringrose 2012. 'Travelling and sticky affects: exploring teens and sexualized cyberbullying through a Butlerian–Deleuzian–Guattarian lens', in *Discourse: Studies in the Cultural Politics of Education* 33(1): 5–20.

Kofoed, J. and D. Staunæs (eds.) 2007. *Magtballader: 14 Fortællinger om Magt, Modstand og Menneskers Tilblivelse [Power Troubles: 14 Narratives of Power, Resistance and Human Becoming]*. Copenhagen: Danmarks Pædagogiske Universitetsforlag.

Kofoed, J. and D. M. Søndergaard (eds.) 2009. *Mobning: Sociale Processer på Afveje [Bullying: Social Processes Gone Awry]*. Copenhagen: Hans Reitzel Publishers.

2013. *Mobning Gentænkt [Bullying Reconsidered]*. Copenhagen: Hans Reitzel Publishers.

Kokko, T. H. J. and M. Pörhölä 2009. 'Tackling bullying: victimized by peers as a pupil, an effective intervener as a teacher?', in *Teaching & Teacher Education* 25: 1000–8.

Kosciw, J. 2004. *The 2003 National School Climate Survey: The School-Related Experiences of Our Nation's Lesbian, Gay, Bisexual and Transgender Youth.* New York: GLSEN.

and E. Diaz 2006. *The 2005 National School Climate Survey: The Experiences of Lesbian, Gay, Bisexual and Transgender Youth in Our Nation's Schools.* New York: GLSEN.

and E. Gretytak 2008. *The 2007 National School Climate Survey: The Experiences of Lesbian, Gay, Bisexual and Transgender Youth in Our Nation's Schools.* New York: GLSEN.

Kosciw, J., E. Greytak, E. Diaz and M. J. Bartkiewicz 2010. *The 2009 National School Climate Survey: The Experiences of Lesbian, Gay, Bisexual and Transgender Youth in Our Nation's Schools.* New York: GLSEN.

Kousholt, D. 2011. 'Researching family through the everyday lives of children across home and day care in Denmark', in *Ethos* 39(1): 98–114.

Kowalski, R. M. and S. P. Limber 2007. 'Electronic bullying among middle school students', in *Journal of Adolescent Health* 41: 22–30.

and P.W. Agatston 2008. *Cyberbullying: Bullying in the Digital Age.* Oxford: Blackwell Publishing Ltd.

Kristeva, J. 1982. *Powers of Horror: An Essay on Abjection*, translated by L. S. Roudiez. New York: Columbia University Press.

Kumpulainen, K. 2008. 'Psychiatric conditions associated with bullying', in *International Journal of Adolescent Mental Health* 20(2): 121–32.

Københavnerbarometer [*Copenhagenen Barometer*] 2009. Københavns Kommunes Børne- og Ungdomsforvaltning [Copenhagen Municipality's Child and Youth Management] www.bufnet.kk.dk/Skole/EvalueringOgProever/Koebenhavnerbarometer.aspx (last accessed 21 April 2012).

Ladd, G. W. 2005. *Children's Peer Relations and Social Competence: A Century of Progress.* New Haven, Conn.: Yale University Press.

Lahelma, E. 2002. 'Gendered conflicts in secondary school: fun or enactment of power?', in *Gender and Education* 14(3): 295–306.

2004. 'Tolerance and understanding? Students and teachers reflect on differences at school', in *Educational Research and Evaluation* 10(1): 3–19.

Land, D. 2003. 'Teasing apart secondary students' conceptualizations of peer teasing, bullying and sexual harassment', in *School Psychology International* 24 (2): 147–65.

Lange, J. K. 2007. *Det Nye Ansvar: Værktøjer til Konflikthåndtering mellem Lærere og Forældre* [*The New Responsibility: Tools for Conflict Resolution between Teachers and Parents*]. Frederikshavn, Denmark: Dafolo.

Larkin, J. 1994. 'Walking through walls: the sexual harassment of high school girls', in *Gender and Education* 6(3): 263–80.

Larsen, M. C. 2005. 'Ungdom, venskab og identitet: en etnografisk undersøgelse af unges brug af hjemmesiden Arto' [Youth, friendship and identity: an ethnographic study of youths' use of the website Arto]. Master's thesis, Aalborg University, Denmark.

2007. 'Kærlighed og venskab på Arto.dk' [Love and friendship on Arto.dk], in *Ungdomsforskning [Youth Research]* 6(1).

Lather, P. 2007. *Getting Lost: Feminist Efforts Toward a Double(d) Science*. Albany: State University of New York Press.

Laursen, D. 2006. 'Det mobile samtalerum: om unges kommunikations- og samværsformer via mobiltelefonen' [The mobile-conversation space: on youths' forms of communication and interaction via mobile telephone]. Ph.D. thesis, Syddansk Universitet, Denmark.

Laustsen, C. B. 2007. 'Med kameraet som våben: om billederne fra Abu Ghraib' [With the camera as a weapon: about photographs from Abu Ghraib], in *Politika* 38(2): 187–209.

Lave, J. and E. Wenger 1991. *Situated Learning: Legitimate Peripheral Participation*. Cambridge University Press.

Law, J. 2007. *After Method: Mess in Social Science Research*. London and New York: Routledge.

Lawrence, B. B. and A. Karim (eds.) 2007. *On Violence*. Durham, NC and London: Duke University Press.

Learning Through Landscapes 2003. *National School Grounds Survey*. Retrieved from www.ltl.org.uk/pdf/LTL-Survey-20031288585139.pdf

Lee, C. 2006. 'Exploring teachers' definitions of bullying', in *Emotional and Behavioral Difficulties* 11(1): 61–75.

Lee, V. E., R. G. Croninger, E. Linn and Z. Chen 1996. 'The culture of sexual harassment in secondary schools', in *American Educational Research Journal* 33(2): 383–417.

Leontjev, A. N. 1983. *Virksomhed, Bevidsthed, Personlighed* [*Company, Awareness, Personality*]. USSR: Sputnik/Progres.

Levi, P. 1989/2008. *The Drowned and the Saved*, translated by R. Rosenthal. London: Abacus: 52–67.

Levine, J. and D. Pizarro 2004. 'Emotion and memory research: a grumpy overview', in *Social Cognition* 22: 538–64.

Leymann, H. 1986. *Vuxenmobbning: om Psykiskt Våld i Arbetslivet [Adult Bullying: on Psychological Violence at Work]*. Lund, Sweden: Studenterlitteratur.
   and D. Zapf 1996. *Mobbing and Victimization at Work*. Letchworth: Psychology Press.

Li, Q. 2006. 'Cyberbullying in schools: a research of gender differences', in *School Psychology International* 27(2): 157–70.
   2007. 'New bottle but old wine: a research of cyberbullying in schools', in *Computers in Human Behaviour* 23(4): 1777–91.

Limber, S. and M. Small 2003. 'State laws and policies to address bullying in schools', in *School Psychology Review* 32: 445–55.

Lindberg, O. 2007. 'Skammen är det värsta' [The shame is the worst], in C. Thors (ed.) *Utstött: en Bok om Mobbning [Outcast: A Book about Bullying]*. Stockholm: Lärarförbundets Förlag.

Lindqvist, J. A. 2009. *Let the Right One In*, translated by E. Segerberg. London: Quercus.

Lorenz, K. 1966. *On Aggression*. New York: Harcourt, Brace & World.

Luecke, J. C. 2011. 'Working with transgender children and their classmates in pre-adolescence: just be supportive', in *Journal of LGBT Youth* 8(2): 116–56.

Luiselli, J. K., Putnam, R. F., Handler, M. W. and Feinberg, A. B. 2005. 'Whole-school positive behaviour support: effects on student discipline problems and academic performance', in *Educational Psychology* 25(2): 183–98.

Lund, R., K. K. Nielsen, D. H. Hansen, M. Kriegbaum, D. Molbo, P. Due and U. Christensen 2008. 'Exposure to bullying at school and depression in adulthood: a study of Danish men born in 1953', in *European Journal of Public Health* 19(1): 111–16.

Malaby, M. 2009. 'Public and secret agents: personal power and reflective agency in male memories of childhood violence and bullying', in *Gender and Education* 21: 371–86.

Marx, K. 1845. *Theses on Feuerbach*, translated by W. Lough; www.marxists.org/archive/marx/works/1845/theses/theses.htm (last accessed 1 April 2009).

Massumi, B. 2002. *Parables for the Virtual: Movement, Affect, Sensation*. Durham, NC: Duke University Press.

Mathiassen, C. 2011. 'Mobning i barndommen – brændstof i organisering af voksenlivet?' [Bullying in childhood – fuel for the organisation of adult life?], in *Psykologisk Set [Psychologically Seen]* 83: 5–17.

2012. 'Between freedom and captivity: life-projects of male ex-prisoners', in J. Valsiner and A. U. Branco (eds.) *Cultural Psychology of Human Values*. Charlotte, NC: Information Age Publishing.

and E. S. Viala 2009. 'Erindringer om mobning og det levede liv' [Memories of bullying and the lived life], in J. Kofoed and D. M. Søndergaard (eds.) *Mobning: Sociale Processer på Afveje [Bullying: Social Processes Gone Awry]*. Copenhagen: Hans Reitzel Publishers: 167–91.

McCormick, L. K., A. B. Steckler and K. R. McLeroy 1995. 'Diffusion of innovations in schools: a study of adoption and implementation of school-based tobacco prevention curricula', in *American Journal of Health Promotion* 9(3): 210–19.

McDermott, R. P. 1993. 'The acquisition of a child by a learning disability', in S. Chaiklin and J. Lave (eds.) *Understanding Practice: Perspectives on Activity and Context*. New York: Cambridge University Press.

McFarland, W. 2001. 'The legal duty to protect gay and lesbian students from violence in school', in *Professional School Counseling* 4(3): 171–9.

McGrath, M. J. 2003. 'Capping the heavy price for bullying', in *School Administrator* 60(4): 30.

McGuire, J. K., C. R. Anderson, R. B. Toomey and S. T. Russell 2010. 'School climate for transgender youth: a mixed method investigation of student experiences and school responses', in *Journal of Youth and Adolescence* 39 (10): 1175–88.

Mead, G. H. 1934. *Mind, Self, Society from the Standpoint of a Social Behaviorist*. London: University of Chicago Press, Ltd.

Mebane, S. 2010. '*Adult survivors of adolescent bullying: an exploration of long-term effects*'. Ph.D. thesis, Department of Educational Psychology, University of Illinois (Urbana-Champaign), USA.

Medical Research Council 2000. *A Framework for Development and Evaluation of RCTs for Complex Interventions to Improve Health*. London: Medical Research Council.

Meyer, E. J. 2006. 'Gendered harassment in North America: school-based interventions for reducing homophobia and heterosexism', in C. Mitchell and

F. Leach (eds.) *Combating Gender Violence In and Around Schools*. Stoke-on-Trent, UK: Trentham Books: 43–50.

2007a. 'Bullying and harassment in secondary schools: a critical analysis of the gaps, overlaps, and implications from a decade of research'; paper presented at the annual meeting of the American Educational Research Association: Chicago, Ill.; www.eric.ed.gov (ERIC #ED519662).

2007b. 'Gendered harassment in high school: understanding teachers' (non) interventions'; paper presented at the annual meeting of the American Educational Research Association: Chicago, Ill.

2008a. 'A feminist reframing of bullying and harassment: transforming schools through critical pedagogy', in *McGill Journal of Education* 43(1): 33–48.

2008b. 'Gendered harassment in secondary schools: understanding teachers' (non)interventions', in *Gender & Education* 20(6): 555–72.

Middleton, D. and S. Brown 2005. *The Social Psychology of Experience: Studies in Remembering and Forgetting*. London: SAGE Publications Ltd.

Miller, J. H. 1997. 'Gender issues embedded in the experience of student teaching', in *Journal of Teacher Education* 48(1): 19–28.

Mineka, S., E. Rafaeli and I. Yovel 2003. 'Cognitive biases in emotional disorders: information processing and social–cognitive perspectives', in R. J. Davidson, K. R. Scherer and H. H. Goldsmith (eds.) *Handbook of Affective Sciences: Series in Affective Science*. New York: Oxford University Press: 976–1009.

Mishna, F. 2004. 'A qualitative study of bullying from multiple perspectives', in *Children & Schools* 26(4): 234–47.

Mishna, F., D. Pepler and J. Wiener 2006. 'Factors associated with perceptions and responses to bullying situations by children, parents, teachers, and principals', in *Victims & Offenders* 1(3): 255–88.

Mishna, F., J. Wiener and D. Pepler 2008. '"Some of my best friends": experiences of bullying within friendship', in *School Psychology International* 29(5): 549–73.

Mock, K. 1996. 'Amending and defending our codes and commisions: focus on human rights', in *Canadian Social Studies* 31(1): 12–13.

Monks, C. P. and P. K. Smith 2006. 'Definitions of bullying: age differences in understanding of the term, and the role of experience', in *British Journal of Developmental Psychology* 24: 801–21.

Morita, Y., H. Soeda, K. Soeda and M. Taki 1999. 'Japan', in P. K. Smith, Y. Morita, J. Junger-Tas, D. Olweus, R. Catalano and P. Slee (eds.) *The Nature of School Bullying: A Cross-National Perspective*. London and New York: Routledge.

Mortimore, P., P. Sammons, L. Stoll, D. Lewis and R. Ecob 1988. *School Matters*. Wells, UK: Open Books.

Mouttapa, M., T. Valente, P. Gallaher, L. A. Rohrbach and J. B. Unger 2004. 'Social network predictors of bullying and victimization', in *Adolescence* 39 (154): 315–35.

Myong Petersen, L. 2009. 'Adopteret: fortællinger om transnational og racialiseret tilblivelse' [*Adopted: narratives about transnational and racialised origins*]. Ph.D. thesis, Department of Learning and Education, Aarhus University, Denmark.

Myong, L. and D. M. Søndergaard 2013. 'Om mobningens vandringer mellem enshed og forskellighed' [About bullying's wanderings between sameness and difference], in J. Kofoed and D. M. Søndergaard (eds.) *Mobning Gentænkt [Bullying Reconsidered]*. Copenhagen: Hans Reitzel Publishers.

Nansel, T., M. Overpeck, R. Pilla, W. J. Ruan, B. Simons-Morton and P. Scheidt 2001. 'Bullying behaviors among US youth: prevalence and association with psychosocial adjustment', in *Journal of the American Medical Association* 285: 2094–100.

National Mental Health Association (NMHA) 2002. 'What does gay mean? Teen survey executive summary'. Alexandria, Va.: NMHA.

Naylor, P. and H. Cowie 1999. 'The effectiveness of peer support systems in challenging school bullying: the perspectives and experiences of teachers and pupils', in *Journal of Adolescence* 22: 467–79.

and R. del Rey 2001. 'Coping strategies of secondary school children in response to being bullied', in *Child Psychology and Psychiatry Review* 6(3): 114–20.

Naylor, P., H. Cowie, F. Cossin, R. de Bettencourt and F. Lemme 2006. 'Teachers' and pupils' definitions of bullying', in *British Journal of Educational Psychology* 76: 553–76.

Nebraska School Safety Centre 2007. 'Anti-bullying and positive student behaviour'; www.nde.state.ne.us/safety/Anti-Bullying.html (last accessed 7 June 2007).

Nielsen, L. T. 2001. 'Evaluering af DISKO: dialog i skolen. Udvikling af samarbejdsformer mellem forældre og skole' [Evaluation of DISKO: dialogue in schools. Development of forms of collaboration between parents and schools]; the National Association of Teachers, the National Association of School Parents and the Danish Ministry of Education: Copenhagen.

Nietzsche, F. 1886/1955. *Beyond Good and Evil*, translated by M. Cowan. Chicago: Henry Regnery Company.

Nigianni, C. and M. Storr (eds.) 2009. *Deleuze and Queer Theory*. Edinburgh University Press.

Nishina, A. and J. Juvonen 2005. 'Daily reports of witnessing and experiencing peer harassment in middle school', in *Child Development* 76(2): 435–50.

and M. Witkow 2005. 'Sticks and stones may break my bones, but names will make me feel sick: the psychosocial, somatic, and scholastic consequences of peer harassment', in *Journal of Clinical Child and Adolescent Psychology* 34(1): 37–48.

Nissen, M. 2012. 'The subjectivity of participation', in *Mind, Culture and Activity* 10:4 332–49.

Noble, T. 2005. *Bullying Solutions: Evidence-based Approaches to Bullying in Australian Schools*. Frenchs Forest: Pearson Education Australia.

Nolin, M. J., E. Davies and K. Chandler 1996. 'Student victimization at school', in *Journal of School Health* 66(6): 216–26.

Nussbaum, M. 1995. *Poetic Justice: The Literary Imagination and Public Life*. Boston: Beacon Press.

Nørby, S. 2007. 'Emotioner og læring' [Emotions and learning], in Schilhab, T. and B. Steffensen (eds.) *Nervepirrende Pædagogik [Nerve-wracking Pedagogy]*. Copenhagen: Akademisk Forlag: 93–119.

O'Moore, M. and S. Minton 2003. 'Tackling violence in schools: a report from Ireland', in P. K. Smith (ed.) *Violence in Schools: The Response in Europe*. London: Routledge Falmer.

O'Toole, J. and B. Burton 2005. 'Acting against conflict and bullying. The Brisbane Dracon Project 1996–2004 – emergent findings and outcomes', in *Research in Drama Education* 10(3): 269–83.

Obermann, M. L. 2011. 'Moral disengagement in self-reported and peer-nominated school bullying', in *Aggressive Behavior* 37(2): 133–44.

Olssen, M. 2006. *Michel Foucault: Materialism and Education*. Boulder, Colo.: Paradigm Publishers.

Olweus, D. 1969. *Prediction of Aggression: On the Basis of a Projective Test*. Stockholm: Scandinavian Test Corporation: 11.

  1973. *Hackkycklingar och Översittare: Forskning om Skolmobbning [Whipping Boys and Bullying: Research on School Bullying]*. Stockholm: Almisphere Press.

  1977. 'Aggression and peer acceptance in adolescent boys: two short-term longitudinal studies of ratings', in *Child Development* 48: 1301–13.

  1978. *Aggression in the Schools: Bullies and Whipping Boys*. Washington DC: Hemisphere/John Wiley & Sons.

  1986. 'Mobbning: vad vi vet och vad vi kan göra' [Bullying: what we know and what we can do]. Stockholm: Liber 8: 34; cited in Agevall, O. 2008. 'The career of bullying: emergence, transformation, and utilisation of a new concept', in Rapport No. 29, School of Social Sciences, Växjö University, Sweden: 1–71.

  1992. *Mobbing i Skolen: Hva Vi Vet og Hva Vi Kan Gjøre [Bullying at School: What We Know and What We Can Do]*. Oslo: Universitetsforlaget.

  1993a. *Bullying at School: What We Know and What We Can Do*. Malden and Oxford, UK: Blackwell Publishing.

  1993b. 'Bully/victim problems among schoolchildren: long-term consequences and an effective intervention program', in S. Hodgins (ed.) *Mental Disorder and Crime*. Thousand Oaks, Calif.: SAGE Publications Ltd: 317–49.

  1997. 'Bully/victim problems in school: facts and intervention', in *European Journal of Psychology of Education* 12(4): 495–510.

  and S. P. Limber 2010. 'Bullying in school: evaluation and dissemination of the Olweus bullying prevention program', in *American Journal of Orthopsychiatry* 80(1): 124–34.

  1996. 'Bullying at school: knowledge base and an effective intervention program', in *Understanding Aggressive Behavior in Children: Annals of the New York Academy of Sciences* 794: 265–76.

  1999a. 'Sweden', in P. K. Smith, Y. Morita, J. Junger-Tas, D. Olweus, R. Catalano and P. Slee (eds.) *The Nature of School Bullying: A Cross-National Perspective*. London and New York: Routledge.

1999b. 'Norway', in Smith, Morita, Junger-Tas, Olweus, Catalano and Slee (eds.) *The Nature of School Bullying: a Cross-National Perspective*. London and New York: Routledge.

2000. *Mobning i Skolen: Hvad Vi Ved og Hvad Vi Kan Gøre [Bullying at School: What We Know and What We Can Do]*. Copenhagen: Hans Reitzel Publishers.

2004. 'Mobbning i skolan: några utvalda problemställningar och en kritisk efterskrift' [Bullying at school: some selected issues and a critical postscript]; *Nya Forskningsperspektiv på Mobbning [New Research Perspectives on Bullying]*. Stockholm and Copenhagen: Nordisk Ministerråd [Nordic Council of Ministers].

Orr, J. 1996. *Talking about Machines: An Ethnography of a Modern Job*. New York: Cornell University Press.

Ortner, S. 2005. *New Jersey Dreaming: Capital, Culture and the Class of '58*. Durham, NC: Duke University Press.

Osler, A. 2006. 'Excluded girls: interpersonal, institutional and structural violence in schooling', in *Gender and Education* 18(6): 571–89.

Osterman, K. F. 2000. 'Students' need for belonging in the school community', in *Review of Educational Research* 70(3): 323–67.

Palmen, H., M. M. Vermande, M. Deković and M. A. G. van Aken 2011. 'Competence, problem behavior, and the effects of having no friends, aggressive friends, or nonaggressive friends: a four-year longitudinal study', in *Merrill-Palmer Quarterly* 57(2): 186–213.

Parker, J. G. and J. Seal 1996. 'Forming, losing, renewing, and replacing friendships: applying temporal parameters to the assessment of children's friendship experiences', in *Child Development* 67(5): 2248–68.

Parkhurst, J. T. and S. R. Asher 1992. 'Peer rejection in middle school: subgroup differences in behavior, loneliness and interpersonal concerns', in *Developmental Psychology* 28(2): 231–42.

Parks, C. W. 2001. 'African–American same-gender-loving youths and families in urban schools', in *Journal of Gay and Lesbian Social Services* 13(2): 41–56.

Parr, A. (ed.) 2005. *The Deleuze Dictionary*. Edinburgh University Press.

Patchin, J. W. and S. Hinduja 2006. 'Bullies move beyond the schoolyard: a preliminary look at cyberbullying', in *Youth Violence and Juvenile Justice* 4 (2): 148–69.

Patterson, O. 1982. *Slavery and Social Death: A Comparative Study*. Cambridge, Mass.: Harvard University Press.

Pearce, N., D. Cross, H. Monks, S. Waters and S. Falconer 2011. 'Current evidence of best practice in whole-school bullying intervention and its potential to inform cyberbullying interventions', in *Australian Journal of Guidance and Counselling* 21(1): 1–21.

Pedersen, A.-J. B. 2008. *Mobning 2008 [Bullying 2008]*. Copenhagen: Børnerådet [the National Council for Children].

Pelligrini, A. D. and J. D. Long 2002. 'A longitudinal study of bullying, dominance, and victimization during the transition from primary school through secondary school', in *British Journal of Developmental Psychology* 20(2): 259–80.

Peters, A. J. 2003. 'Isolation or inclusion: creating safe spaces for lesbian and gay youth', in *Families in Society* 84(3): 331–7.

Petersen, L. M. 2009. 'Adopteret: fortællinger om transnational og racialiseret tilblivelse' [Adopted: narratives about transnational and racialised origins]. Ph.D. thesis, Department of Learning and Education, Aarhus University, Denmark.

Peterson, L. and K. Rigby 1999. 'Countering bullying at an Australian secondary school with students as helpers', in *Journal of Adolescence* 22(4): 481–92.

Phan, T. 2003. 'Life in school: narratives of resiliency among Vietnamese–Canadian youths', in *Adolescence* 38: 555–66.

Phoenix, A., S. Frosh and R. Pattman 2003. 'Producing contradictory masculine subject positions: narratives of threat, homophobia and bullying in 11–14-year-old boys', in *Journal of Social Issues* 59(1): 179–95.

Phoenix, A. and P. Pattynama 2006. 'Intersectionality', in *European Journal of Women's Studies* 13(3): 187–92.

Pikas, A. 1975. 'Så stoppar vi mobbning! Rapport från en antimobbnings-grupps arbete' [Then we stop bullying! Report from an anti-bullying group's work]. Stockholm: Prisma 16: 35; cited in Agevall, O. 2008. 'The career of bullying: emergence, transformation, and utilisation of a new concept', in Rapport No. 29, School of Social Sciences, Växjö University, Sweden: 1–71.

Plauborg, H. 2011. 'Klasseledelse og fællesskabende didaktikker – om meningsfulde læringsmuligheder og værdig deltagelse i undervisningen' [Class management and community-creating didactics – about meaningful learning opportunities and worthwhile participation in education], in *KvaN: Tidsskrift for Læreruddannelse og Skole* [*KvaN: Journal of Teacher Education and School*] 90: 31.

Polkinghorne, D. E. 1988. *Narrative Knowing and the Human Sciences*. Albany: State University of New York Press.

Poteat, V. P. 2008. 'Contextual and moderating effects of the peer-group climate on use of homophobic epithets', in *School Psychology Review* 37(2): 188–201.

Poteat, V. P. and D. L. Espelage 2007. 'Predicting psychosocial consequences of homophobic victimization in middle-school students', in *Journal of Early Adolescence* 27(2): 175–91.

Poteat, V. P. and I. Rivers 2010. 'The use of homophobic language across bullying roles during adolescence', in *Journal of Applied Developmental Psychology* 31 (2): 166–72.

Prakke, B., A. van Peet and K. van der Wolf 2007. 'Challenging parents, teacher occupational stress and health in Dutch primary schools', in *International Journal about Parents in Education* 1(0): 36–44.

Price, S. and R. A. Jones 2001. 'Reflections on anti-bullying peer counselling in a comprehensive school', in *Educational Psychology in Practice* 17(1): 35–40.

Priøtz, L. 2007. 'The mobile-phone turn: a study of gender, sexuality and subjectivity in young people's mobile-phone practices'. Ph.D. thesis, University of Oslo, Norway.

Quigley, L. 1959. *The Blind Men and the Elephant*. New York: Charles Scribner's Sons; cited in Thayer-Bacon, B. J. 1996. 'An examination and redescription of epistemology'; www.eric.ed.gov/ERICWebPortal/search/detailmini.jsp?_nfpb=true&_&ERICExtSearch_SearchValue_0=ED401279&ERICExtSearch_SearchType_0=no&accno=ED401279 (last accessed 15 March 2012).

Raffnsøe, S. and M. Gudmund-Høyer 2005. 'Dispositivanalyse: en historisk socialanalytik hos Foucault' [Dispositif analysis: a historical social-analytic of Foucault], in A. Esmark, C. B. Laustsen and N. Å. Andersen (eds.) *Poststrukturalistiske Analysestrategier [Poststructuralistic Strategies of Analysis]*. Frederiksberg, Denmark: Roskilde Universitetsforlag.

Ray, V. and R. Gregory 2001. 'School experiences of the children of lesbian and gay parents', in *Family Matters* 59: 28–34.

Reed, C. A. 1996. 'Harassment policies: structural limitations and hidden connections', in *Initiatives* 58(1): 21–6.

Reis, B. 1995. *Safe Schools Anti-violence Documentation Project: Second Annual Report*. Seattle: Safe Schools Coalition of Washington.

1999. *They Don't Even Know Me: Understanding Anti-gay Harassment and Violence in Schools*. Seattle: Safe Schools Coalition of Washington.

and E. Saewyc 1999. *83,000 Youth: Selected Findings of Eight Population-based Studies*. Seattle: Safe Schools Coaltion of Washington.

Renold, E. 2000. '"Coming out": gender (hetero)sexuality and the primary school', in *Gender and Education* 12(3): 309–26.

2002. 'Presumed innocence: (hetero)sexual, heterosexist and homophobic harassment among primary school girls and boys', in *Childhood* 9(4): 415–34.

2003. '"If you don't kiss me, you're dumped": boys, boyfriends and heterosexualised masculinities in the primary school', in *Educational Review* 55(2): 179–94.

2006. '"They won't let us play...unless you're going out with one of them": girls, boys and Butler's "heterosexual matrix" in the primary years', in *British Journal of Sociology of Education* 27(4): 489–509.

2007. 'Primary school "studs": (de)constructing young boys' heterosexual masculinities', in *Men and Masculinities* 9(3): 275–97.

Reyes, H. 2007. 'The worst scars are in the mind: psychological torture', in *International Review of the Red Cross* 89(867): 591–616.

Ricoeur, P. 2004. *Memory, History, Forgetting*. University of Chicago Press.

Riessman, C. K. 2008. *Narrative Methods for the Human Sciences*. Thousand Oaks, Calif.: SAGE Publications Ltd.

Rigby, K. 1997. *Bullying in Schools and What to Do about It*. Melbourne: Australian Council for Educational Research.

2001. *Stop the Bullying: A Handbook for Schools*. Camberwell, Victoria: ACER Press.

2002a. *A Meta-Evaluation of Methods and Approaches to Reducing Bullying in Pre-schools and Early Primary Schools in Australia*. Canberra ACT: Attorney General's Department.

2002b. *New Perspectives on Bullying*. London: Jessica Kingsley Publishers.

2004. 'Addressing bullying in schools: theoretical perspectives and their implications', in *School Psychology International* 25(3): 287–300.

2007. 'Bullying in schools and what to do about it'; www.education.unisa.edu.au/bullying/ (last accessed 22 June 2007).

2008. *Children and Bullying: How Parents and Educators Can Reduce Bullying at School*. Malden, Oxford, Victoria: Blackwell Publishing.

and I. Cox 1996. 'The contribution of bullying at school and low self-esteem to acts of delinquency among Australian teenagers', in *Personality & Individual Differences* 21(4): 609–12.

and G. Black 1997. 'Cooperativeness and bully/victim problems among Australian schoolchildren', in *Journal of Social Psychology* 137(3): 357–68.

and C. Griffiths 2011. 'Addressing cases of bullying through the method of shared concern', in *School Psychology International* 32(3): 345–57.

and P. Slee 1999. 'Suicidal ideation among adolescent school children, involvement in bully–victim problems, and perceived social support', in *Suicide and Life-Threatening Behavior* 29(2): 119–30.

2008. 'Interventions to reduce bullying', in *International Journal of Adolescent Medicine and Health* 20(2): 165–83.

Ringrose, J. 2008. '"Just be friends": exposing the limits of educational bully discourses for understanding teen girls' heterosexualized frindships and conflicts', in *British Journal of Sociology of Education* 29(5): 509–22.

Roberts-Gray, C., Gingiss, P. M. and Boerm, M. 2007. 'Evaluating school capacity to implement new programs', in *Evaluation and Program Planning* 30: 247–57.

Robinson, J. and D. L. Espelage 2011. 'Inequities in educational and psychological outcomes between LGBTQ and straight students in middle and high school', in *Educational Researcher* 40(7): 315–30.

Rogers, E. M. 2002. 'Diffusion of preventive innovations', in *Addictive Behaviors* 27(6): 989–93.

Roland, E. 1989. 'Bullying: the Scandinavian tradition', in D. P. Tattum and D. A. Lane (eds.) *Bullying in Schools*. Stoke-on-Trent, UK: Trentham Books: 21–32.

Roland, E. 2000. 'Bullying in school: three national innovations in Norwegian schools in 15 years', in *Aggressive Behavior* 26: 135–43.

Roscoe, B. 1994. 'Sexual harassment: early adolescents' self-reports of experiences and acceptance', in *Adolescence* 29(115): 515–23.

Rose, N. 1999: *Powers of Freedom*. Cambridge University Press.

Roth, S. 1994. 'Sex Discrimination 101: developing a Title IX analysis for sexual harassment in education', in *Journal of Law & Education* 23(4): 459–521.

Rubin, K. H., W. M. Bukowski and B. P. Laursen (eds.) 2009. *Handbook of Peer Interactions, Relationships and Groups*. New York: Guilford Press.

Rusby, J. C., K. K. Forrester, A. Biglan and C. Metzler 2005. 'Relationships between peer harassment and adolescent problem behaviors', in *Journal of Early Adolescence* 25(4): 453–77.

Ryan, J. 2003. 'Educational administrators' perceptions of racism in diverse school contexts', in *Race, Ethnicity and Education* 6(2): 145–64.

Salmivalli, C., A. Kaukiainen, M. Voeten and M. Sinisammal 2004. 'Targeting the group as a whole: the Finnish anti-bullying intervention', in P. K. Smith, D. Pepler and K. Rigby (eds.) *Bullying in Schools: How Successful Can Interventions Be?* Cambridge University Press: 251–74.

Salmivalli, C., K. Lagerspetz, K. Bjorkqvist, K. Osterman and A. Kaukiainen 1996. 'Bullying as a group process: participant roles and their relations to social status within the group', in *Aggressive Behavior* 22: 1–15.

Salmon, G., A. James, E. L. Cassidy and M. A. Javaloyes 2000. 'Bullying: a review: presentations to an adolescent psychiatric service and within a school for emotionally and behaviourally disturbed children', in *Clinical Child Psychology & Psychiatry* 5: 563–79.

Sandemose, A. 1994/1999. *En Flygtning Krydser Sit Spor [A Refugee Crosses His Tracks]*. Copenhagen: Schønberg.

Sandstrom, M. J. and A. L. Zakriski 2004. 'Understanding the experience of peer rejection', in J. B. Kupersmidt, and K. A. Dodge (eds.) *Children's Peer Relations: From Development to Intervention, a Decade of Behavior.* Washington DC: American Psychological Association: 101–18.

Sawyer, J. L., F. Mishna, D. Pepler and J. Wiener 2011. 'The missing voice: parents' perspectives of bullying', in *Children and Youth Services Review* 33: 1795–803.

Schäfer, M., S. Korn, P. K. Smith, S. C. Hunter, J. A. Mora-Merchán, M. M. Singer and K. van der Meulen 2004. 'Lonely in the crowd: recollections of bullying', in *British Journal of Developmental Psychology* 22: 379–94.

Scharling Research 2006. 'Læreroplevelser af elever og deres forældre' [Teacher experiences of students and their parents]. Copenhagen: Fagbladet Folkeskolen.

Schott, R. M. 2003. *Discovering Feminist Philosophy: Knowledge, Ethics, Politics.* Lanham, Md.: Rowman & Littlefield Publishers Inc.

Schott, R. M. (ed.) 2007. *Feminist Philosophy and the Problem of Evil.* Bloomington: Indiana University Press.

Schott, R. M. 2009a. 'Extreme and ordinary harms: reflections on the tragic paradigm'; manuscript.

2009b. 'Mobning som socialt begreb: filosofiske refleksioner over definitioner' [Bullying as a social concept: philosophical reflections on actual definitons] in J. Kofoed and D. M. Søndergaard (eds.) *Mobning: Sociale Processer på Afveje [Bullying: Social Processes Gone Awry].* Copenhagen: Hans Reitzel Publishers: 225–58.

Schraube, E. 2013 (forthcoming). 'First-person perspective in the study of subjectivity and technology', in *Subjectivity* 6(1).

and U. Osterkamp (eds.) 2012. *Psychology from the Standpoint of the Subject: Selected Writings of Klaus Holzkamp.* Basingstoke, UK: Palgrave Macmillan.

Searle, J. R. 2003. 'Social ontology and political power'; www.law.berkeley.edu/centers/kadish/searle.pdf (last accessed 27 March 2009).

Sears, J. 1991. 'Educators, homosexuality, and homosexual students: are personal feelings related to professional beliefs?', in *Journal of Homosexuality* 22(3–4): 29–79.

Sedgwick, E. K. 1986. *The Coherence of Gothic Conventions.* New York: Methuen.

Shariff, S. 2008. *Cyberbullying: Issues and Solutions for the School, the Classroom and the Home.* New York: Routledge.

and R. Gouin 2006. 'Cyber-hierarchies: a new arsenal of weapons for gendered violence in schools', in C. Mitchell and F. Leach (eds.) *Combating Gender Violence in and Around Schools.* Stoke-on-Trent, UK: Trentham Books: 33–42.

Sharp, S. 1995. 'How much does bullying hurt? The effects of bullying on the personal well being and educational progress of secondary aged students', in *Educational & Child Psychology* 12(2): 81–8.

Sharp, S. and P. K. Smith 1991. 'Bullying in UK schools: the DES Sheffield Bullying Project', in *Early Child Development and Care* 77: 47–55.

Sharp, S. and D. Thompson 1992. 'Sources of stress: a contrast between pupil perspective and pastoral teachers' perceptions', in *School Psychology International* 13(3): 229–42.

Shier, H. 2001. 'Pathways to participation: openings, opportunities and obligations', in *Children & Society* 15(2): 107–17.

Siann, G., M. Callaghan, P. Glissove, R. Lockhart and L. Rawson 1994. 'Who gets bullied? The effect of school, gender, and ethnic group', in *Educational Research* 36(2): 123–34.

Skolverket 2011. 'Utvärdering af metoder mot mobbning' [Evaluation of methods to combat bullying], Rapport 353: Stockholm.

Slee, P. T. 1994a. 'Life at school used to be good', in *Youth Studies Australia* 1: 20–3.

  1994b. 'Situational and interpersonal correlates of anxiety associated with peer victimisation', in *Child Psychiatry and Human Development* 25(2): 97–107.

  1995a. 'Bullying in the playground: the impact of interpersonal violence on Australian children's perceptions of their play environment', in *Children's Environments* 12(3): 59–72.

  1995b. 'Peer victimisation and its relationship to depression among Australian primary school students', in *Personality and Individual Differences* 18: 57–62.

  1995c. 'Bullying: health concerns of Australian secondary school students', in *International Journal of Adolescence & Youth* 5(4): 215–24.

  and K. Rigby 1993a. 'Australian school children's self-appraisal of interpersonal relations: the bullying experience', in *Child Psychiatry and Human Development* 23(4): 273–82.

  and K.Rigby 1993b. 'The relationship of Eysenck's personality factors and self-esteem to bully–victim behaviour in Australian school boys', in *Personality and Individual Differences* 14: 371–3.

Slee, P. T. and J. Mohyla 2007. 'The PEACE Pack: an evaluation of interventions to reduce bullying in four Australian primary schools', in *Educational Research* 49: 103–15.

Smith, G. W. and D. Smith 1998. 'The ideology of "fag": the school experience of gay students', in *Sociological Quarterly* 39(2): 309–35.

Smith, J., B. Schneider, P. Smith and K. Ananiadou 2004. 'The effectiveness of whole-school antibullying programs: a synthesis of evaluation research', in *School Psychology Review* 33: 547–60.

Smith, P. K. (ed.) 2003. *Violence in Schools: the Response in Europe*. London: Routledge Falmer.

Smith, P. K. 2010. 'Cyber-bullying: learning from the past, looking to the future'; open-access presentation; www.freeppts.net/mini/cyber-bullying-learning-from-the-past-looking-to-the-future-10553.png (last accessed 3 April 2012).

  and K. C. Madsen 1999. 'What causes the age decline in reports of being bullied at schools? Towards a developmental analysis of risks of being bullied', in *Educational Research* 41(3): 267–85.

  and R. Myron-Wilson 1998. 'Parenting and school bullying', in *Clinical Child Psychology and Psychiatry* 3: 405–17.

and S. Sharp (eds.) 1994. *School Bullying: Insights and Perspectives*. London: Routledge.

Smith, P. K., M. J. Boulton and H. Cowie 1993. 'The impact of cooperative group work on ethnic relations in middle school', in *School Psychology International* 14: 21–42.

Smith, P. K., H. Cowie, R. F. Olafsson and A. P. D. Liefooghe 2002. 'Definitions of bullying: a comparison of terms used, and age and gender differences, in a fourteen-country international comparison', in *Child Development* 73(4): 1119–33.

Smith, P. K., D. Pepler and K. Rigby (eds.) 2004. *Bullying in Schools: How Successful Can Interventions Be?* Cambridge University Press.

Smith, P. K., Y. Morita, J. Junger-Tas, D. Olweus, R. Catalano and P. Slee (eds.) 1999. *The Nature of School Bullying: A Cross-National Perspective*. London and New York: Routledge.

Smith, P. K., J. Mahdavi, M. Carvalho, S. Fisher, S. Russell and N. Tippett 2008. 'Cyberbullying: its nature and impact in secondary school pupils', in *Journal of Child Psychology and Psychiatry* 49(4): 376–85.

Solberg, A.-E. B. 2004. 'Foreldre: mobbingens skjulte ansikt' [Parents: bullying's hidden face], in E. Roland, V. G. Sørensen, M. S. B. Straume and A.-E. B. Solberg (eds.) *Sannhet for Barn. Løgn for skolen? Fortvilelse for Foreldre [Truth for children. Lying to school? Despair for parents]*. Collection of articles, Centre for Behavioural Research, Stavanger University College, Norway.

Sommer, D. 2012. 'Resiliens – forskning – begreber – modeller' [Resilience – research –concepts – models], in *Psyke og Logos [Psyche and Logos]* 32(2): 372–95.

Sorenson, G. 1994. 'Peer sexual harassment: remedies and guidelines under federal law', in *West's Education Law Quarterly* 3(4): 621–38.

Sourander, A., L. Hestealä, H. Helenius and J. Piha 2000. 'Persistence of bullying from childhood to adolescence: a longitudinal 8-year follow-up study', in *Child Abuse and Neglect* 24(7): 873–81.

Spears, B. A., J. Kofoed, M. G. Bartolo, A. Palermiti and A. Costabile 2012. 'Positive uses of social networking sites: youth voice perspectives', in A. Costabile and B. A. Spears (eds.) *The Impact of Technology on Relationships in Educational Settings*. London: Routledge.

St Pierre, E. A. 2009. 'Afterword: decentering voice in qualitative inquiry', in A. Y. Jackson and L. A. Mazzei (eds.) *Voice in Qualitative Inquiry: Challenging Conventional, Interpretive, and Critical Conceptions in Qualitative Research*. New York: Routledge: 221–36.

Staub, E. 1989. *The Roots of Evil*. Cambridge and New York: Cambridge University Press.

Staunæs, D. 2004. *Køn, Etnicitet og Skoleliv [Gender, Ethnicity and School Life]*. Frederiksberg, Denmark: Samfundslitteratur.

2005. 'From culturally avant garde to sexually promiscuous: troubling subjectivities and intersections in the social transition from childhood into youth', in *Feminism&Psychology* 15(2): 149–67.

2007. 'Subversive analysestrategier – eller governmentality med kjole, fjærboa og sari' [Subversive strategies of analysis – or governmentality of dress, feather boa and sari], in J. Kofoed and D. Staunæs (eds.) *Magtballader: 14 Fortællinger om Magt, Modstand og Menneskers Tilblivelse [Power Troubles: 14 Narratives of Power, Resistance and Human Becoming].* Copenhagen: Danmarks Pædagogiske Universitetsforlag.

2009. '"I am right behind him"': managing fear and boys in the time of the Danish cartoon crisis', in J. Hearn (ed.) *Intersectionalities, Power, and Identities.* London: Routledge.

and D. M. Søndergaard 2006. 'Corporate fictions', in *Norsk Tidsskrift for Kjønnsforskning [Norwegian Journal of Gender Studies]* 3: 69–93.

and D. M. Søndergaard 2011. 'Intersectionality: a theoretical adjustment', in R. G. Buikema, G. Griffin and N. Lykke (eds.) *Theories and Methodologies in Postgraduate Feminist Research: Researching Differently.* New York: Routledge.

Steffgen, G. 2009. 'Cyber bullying – the role of traditional bullying and empathy'; presented at the conference *The Good, the Bad, the Challenging: The User and the Future of Information and Communication Technologies*: Copenhagen.

Stein, N. 1995. 'Sexual harassment in school: the public performance of gendered violence', in *Harvard Educational Review* 65(2): 145–62.

Stevens, V., I. D. Bourdeaudhuij and P. Van Oost 2001. 'Anti-bullying interventions at school aspects of programme adaptation and critical issues for further programme development', in *Health Promotion International* 16(2): 155–167.

Stoudt, B. G. 2006. '"You're either in or you're out": school violence, peer discipline, and the (re)production of hegemonic masculinity', in *Men and Masculinities* 8(3): 273–87.

Sullivan, K. 2000. *The Anti-bullying Handbook.* Melbourne: Oxford University Press.

Sundén, J. 2002. 'Material virtualities: approaching online textual embodiment'. Ph.D. thesis, the Tema Institute, Department of Communication Studies, Linköping University, Sweden.

Sunstein, C. R. 2000. 'Deliberative trouble? Why groups go to extremes', in *The Yale Law Journal* 10(4): 71–119.

Sutton, D. and D. Martin-Jones 2008. *Deleuze Reframed: A Guide for the Arts Student.* London: I. B. Tauris & Co.

Sutton, J., P. Smith and J. Swettenham 1999. 'Social cognition and bullying: social inadequacy or skilled manipulation?', in *British Journal of Developmental Psychology* 17: 435–50.

Swearer, S. M., D. Espelage, T. Vaillancourt and S. Hymel 2010. 'What can be done about school bullying? Linking research to educational practice', in *Educational Researcher* 39(1): 38–47.

Sylvester, R. 2011. 'Teacher as bully: knowingly or unintentionally harming students', in *The Delta Kappa Gamma Bulletin* 77(2): 42–5.

Szlacha, L. 2003. 'Safer sexual diversity climates: lessons learned from an evaluation of Massachusetts safe schools program for gay and lesbian students', in *American Journal of Education* 110(1): 58–88.

Søndergaard, D. M. 1994. 'Køn i formidlingsproces mellem kultur og individ: nogle analytiske greb' [Gender in the communication process between culture and individual: some analytical approaches], in *Psyke og Logos* [*Psyche and Logos*] 15: 47–68.

1996/2000/2006. *Tegnet på Kroppen. Køn: Koder og Konstruktioner blandt Unge Voksne i Akademia* [*The Mark on the Body. Gender: Codes and Constructions amongst Young Adults in Academia*]. Copenhagen: Museum Tusculanums Forlag.

2000. 'Sandheden er en alvorlig og magtfuld konstruktion' [The truth is a serious and powerful construction], in *Norsk Medietidsskrift* [*Norwegian Media Journal*] 2: 50–60.

2002. 'Poststructuralist approaches to empirical analysis', in *International Journal of Qualitative Studies in Education* 15(2): 187–204.

2005a. 'Academic desire trajectories: retooling the concepts of subject, desire and biography', in *European Journal of Women's Studies* 12(3): 297–313.

2005b. 'At forske i komplekse tilblivelser' [Researching complex genesis], in T. Bechmann Jensen and G. Christensen (eds.) *Psykologiske og Pædagogiske Metoder* [*Psychological and Pedagogical Methods*]. Copenhagen: Roskilde University Press.

2008. 'Offerpositionens dilemmaer: om undvigelse af offerpositionering i forbindelse med mobning og anden relationel aggression' [Dilemmas of the victim position: avoiding victimisation related to bullying and other forms of relational aggression], in K. Lützen and A. K. Nielsen (eds.) *På Kant med Historien* [*On the Edge of History*]. Copenhagen: Museum Tusculanums Forlag: 160–95.

2009. 'Mobning og social eksklusionsangst' [Bullying and social exclusion anxiety], in Kofoed, J. and D. M. Søndergaard (eds.) *Mobning: Sociale Processer på Afveje* [*Bullying: Social Processes Gone Awry*]. Copenhagen: Hans Reitzel Publishers: 21–58.

2011. 'Mobning, mobbefryd, humor og fællesskab' [Bullying, enjoyment, humour and community], in Jensen, E. and S. Brinkmann (eds.) *Fællesskab i Skolen: Udfordringer og Muligheder* [*Communities at School: Challenges and Possibilities*]. Copenhagen: Akademisk Forlag: 45–78.

2012. 'Bullying and social exclusion anxiety in schools', in *British Journal of Sociology of Education* 33(3): 355–72.

2013a. 'Den distribuerede vold: om computerspil, mobning og relationel aggression' [Distributed violence: computer games, bullying and relational aggression], in J. Kofoed and D. M. Søndergaard (eds.) *Mobning Gentænkt* [*Bullying Reconsidered*]. Copenhagen: Hans Reitzel Publishers.

2013b. 'Virtual materiality, potentiality and subjectivity: how do we conceptualize real–virtual interaction embodied and enacted in computer gaming, imagination and night dreams?', in *Subjectivity* 6(1): 55–78.

Tajfel, H. and J. C. Turner 1986. 'The social identity theory of inter-group behavior', in Worchel, S. and L. W. Austin (eds.) *Psychology of Intergroup Relations*. Chicago: Nelson-Hall.

Taylor, A. 2008. 'Taking account of childhood excess: "bringing the elsewhere home"', in B. Davies (ed.) *Judith Butler in Conversation: Analysing the Texts and Talk of Everyday Life*. New York: Routledge: 195–216.

Terry, A. A. 1998. 'Teachers as targets of bullying by their pupils: a study to investigate incidence', in *British Journal of Educational Psychology* 68: 255–68.

Thayer-Bacon, B. J. 1996. 'An examination and redescription of epistemology'; www.eric.ed.gov/?q=redescription+of+epistemology&id=ED401279 (last accessed 15 March 2012).

Thompson, S. and L. Johnson 2003. 'Risk factors of gay, lesbian, and bisexual adolescents: review of empirical literature and practice implications', in *Journal of Human Behavior in the Social Environment* 8(2–3): 111–28.

Thomsen, D. K. and S. Brinkmann 2009. 'An interviewer's guide to autobiographical memory: ways to elicit concrete experiences and to avoid pitfalls in interpreting them', in *Qualitative Research in Psychology* 6(4): 294–312.

Thornberg, R. 2011. "She's weird!" – the social construction of bullying in school: a review of qualitative research', in *Children and Society* 25: 258–67.

Thorne, B. 1993. *Gender Play*. Buckingham, UK: Open University Press.

Timmerman, G. 2003. 'Sexual harassment of adolescents perpetrated by teachers and peers: an exploration of the dynamics of power, culture, and gender in secondary schools', in *Sex Roles* 48(5–6): 231–44.

Totten, M. and P. Quigley 2003. 'Bullying, school exclusion and literacy'; Discussion Paper for the Canadian Public Health Association.

Toulmin, S. 1974/1994. *The Uses of Argument*. Cambridge University Press.

Ttofi, M. M. and D. P. Farrington 2008. 'Reintegrative shaming theory, moral emotions and bullying', in *Aggressive Behavior* 34: 352–68.

    and D. P. Farrington 2011. 'Effectiveness of school-based programs to reduce bullying: a systematic and meta-analytic review', in *Journal of Experimental Criminology* 7: 27–56.

Uggen, C. and A. Blackstone 2004. 'Sexual harassment as a gendered expression of power', in *American Sociological Review* 69(1): 64–92.

Ulvik, O. S. 2005. 'Fosterfamilie som seinmoderne omsorgsarrangement: en kulturpsykologisk studie av fosterbarn og fosterforeldres fortellinger' [The foster family as a late-modern care arrangement: a cultural–psychological study of foster children's and foster parents' narratives]. Ph.D. thesis, Department of Psychology, University of Oslo, Norway.

Unger, M. 2012. 'Social ecologies and their contribution to resilience', in M. Unger (ed.) *The Social Ecology of Resilience: A Handbook of Theory and Practice*. London: Springer.

Valsiner, J. and R. van der Veer 2000. *The Social Mind: Construction of the Idea*. Cambridge University Press.

Valsiner, J. and J. A. Lawrence 1997. 'Human development in culture across the life span', in J. W. Berry, P. R. Dasen and T. S. Saraswathi (eds.) *Handbook of Cross-Cultural Psychology, Vol. 2: Basic Processes and Human Development*, 2nd edn.: Boston: Allyn & Bacon: 69–106.

Victoria Department of Education 2007. 'Safe Schools are Effective Schools'; www.sofweb.vic.edu.au/wellbeing/safeschools/bullying/defbullying.htm (last accessed 19 June 2007).

Vreeman, R. C. and A. E. Carroll 2007. 'A systematic review of school-based interventions to prevent bullying', in *Archives of Pediatric and Adolescent Medicine* 161(1): 78–88.

Wai-Yung, L., N. G. Man-Lun, B. K. L. Cheung and J. Wayung 2010. 'Capturing children's response to parental conflict and making use of it', in *Family Process* 49: 43–58.

Wagoner, B. 2011. 'Meaning construction in remembering: a synthesis of Bartlett and Vygotsky', in P. Stenner, J. Cromby, J. Motzkau, J. Yen and Y. Haosheng (eds.) *Theoretical Psychology: Global Transformations and Challenges*. Toronto: Captus Press: 105–14.

Walton, G. 2005. 'Bullying widespread: a critical analysis of research and public discourse on bullying', in *Journal of School Violence* 4(1), 91–118.

Wandersman, A., J. Duffy, P. Flaspohler, R. Noonan, K. Lubell, L. Stillman, M. Blachman, R. Dunville and J. Saul 2008. 'Bridging the gap between prevention research and practice: the interactive systems framework for dissemination and implementation', in *American Journal of Community Psychology* 41(3): 171–81.

Weber, M. 1905/1991. *The Protestant Ethic and the Spirit of Capitalism*. London: Harper Collins.

Wetherell, M. and J. Maybin 1996. 'The distributed self: a social constructionist perspective', in R. Stevens (ed.) *Understanding the Self*. London: Open University Press: 219–65.

Whitehead, S. M. 2002. *Men and Masculinities*. Cambridge: Polity Press; cited in Horton P. 2011. 'School bullying and social and moral orders', in *Children and Society* 25: 268–77.

Whitelaw, S., L. Hills and J. De Rosa 1999. 'Sexually aggressive and abusive behaviors in schools', in *Women's Studies Quarterly*, 27(1–2): 203–11.

Whitney, I., D. Nabuzoka and P. K. Smith 1992. 'Bullying in schools: mainstream and special needs', in *Support for Learning* 7(1): 3–7.

Wikipedia contributors 2007. 'Bullying'; http://en.wikipedia.org/w/index.php?title=Bullying&oldid=139596053 [last accessed 22 June 2007].

Williams, K. R. and N. G. Guerra 2007. 'Prevalence and predictors of internet bullying', in *Journal of Adolescent Health* 41(6, supplement): S14–21.

Williams, T., J. Connolly, D. Pepler and W. Craig 2005. 'Peer victimization, social support, and psychosocial adjustment of sexual minority adolescents', in *Journal of Youth and Adolescence* 34(5): 471–82.

Willis, P. 1977: *Learning to Labour*. New York: Columbia University Press.

Wilson, I., C. Griffin and B. Wren 2005. 'The interaction between young people with atypical gender identity organization and their peers', in *Journal of Health Psychology* 10(3): 307–15.

Winther, I. W. 2007. 'Tilgængelig, nærværende og potentielt fraværende: om unges mobiltelefoni' [Available, present and potentially absent: on youths' mobile-phone use], in *Dansk Sociologi [Danish Sociology]* 2.
    2009. 'Mobiltelefon – som fantomvæg' [Mobile telephone – as phantom wall], in Jerslev A. and C. L. Christensen (eds.) *Hvor Går Grænsen? Brudflader i en Moderne Mediekultur [Where Are the Limits? Fractured Structures in a Modern Media Culture]*. Copenhagen: Tiderne Skifter.

Wolak, J., K. Mitchell and D. Finkelhor 2006. 'Online victimization of youth: five years later'; the Crimes Against Children Research Center, University of New Hampshire (Durham).

2007. 'Does online harassment constitute bullying? An exploration of online harassment by known peers and online-only contacts', in *Journal of Adolescent Health* 41(6, supplement): S51–8.

Wolohan, J. 1995. 'Title IX and sexual harassment of student athletes', in *Journal of Physical Education, Recreation and Dance* 66(3q): 52–5.

Yale University 2008. 'Bullying and being bullied linked to suicide in children, review of studies suggest', in *ScienceDaily*; www.sciencedaily.com/releases/ 2008/07/080717170428.htm [last accessed 13 January 2011].

Ybarra, M. L. and K. J. Mitchell 2004. 'Online aggressor/targets, aggressors and targets: a comparison of associated youth characteristics', in *Journal of Child Psychology and Psychiatry* 45(7): 1308–16.

Ybarra, M. L., M. Diener-West and P. J. Leaf 2007. 'Examining the overlap in internet harassment and school bullying: implications for school intervention', in *Journal of Adolescent Health* 41(6, supplement): S42–50.

Ybarra, M. L., D. L. Espelage and K. J. Mitchell 2007. 'The co-occurrence of internet harassment and unwanted sexual solicitation victimization and perpetration: associations with psychosocial indicators', in *Journal of Adolescent Health* 41(6, supplement): S31–41.

Youth Education Service, New Zealand Police 2007. 'No bully'; www.police.govt. nz/service/yes/nobully/bully_info.html – eight (last accessed 12 March 2007).

Zabrodska, K., S. Linnell, C. Laws and B. Davies 2011. 'Bullying as intra-active process in neoliberal universities', in *Qualitative Inquiry* 17(9): 1–11.

Žižek, S. 1995. *Looking Awry: An Introduction to Jacques Lacan through Popular Culture*. Cambridge, Mass.: MIT Press.

2008. *Violence: Six Sideways Reflections*. London: Profile Books.

Index